AN AIR THAT STILL KILLS

HOW A MONTANA TOWN'S ASBESTOS TRAGEDY
IS SPREADING NATIONWIDE

Andrew Schneider
David McCumber

Previously published by G.P. Putnam's Sons in a hardcover edition as An Air That Kills © 2004 and in paperback by Berkley © 2005. All rights returned to authors in June 2008. This updated edition published in 2016. Images in this book are either public domain, or used with the permission of the creators or the owners, or supplied by the subjects.

Printed in the United States of America

Andrew Schneider
An Air That Still Kills
Cold Truth LLC
Seattle, Washington
authors@anairthatstillkills.com

1. Current affairs, Corporate corruption, Government ineptitude. 2. Libby, Montana, W.R. Grace, Asbestos, Vermiculite, Toxic poisoning. 3. New dangers discovered in Libby asbestos, Medical research. 4. Environmental Protection Agency, White House meddling. 5. Public Health Emergency.

Cover photo and dedication page photo by Andrew Schneider.
Design production by Denise Clifton, Tandemvines Publishing.
Editing by Joann Byrd, Kris Higginson and Kathleen Best.

ISBN 978-0-9851851-2-1

Contents

Pray for the dead and fight like hell for the living.

– Mother Jones, the miners' angel

This book is dedicated to Gayla Benefield, Les Skramstad, Paul Peronard, Chris Weis, Aubrey Miller, Keven McDermott, Matt Cohn, Alan Whitehouse, James Lockey, Brad Black and the other heroes who live those words every day.

Les Skramstad and Gayla Benefield carry crosses of those who have died.

Into my heart an air that kills from yon far country blows.

— A.E. Housman, A Shropshire Lad

PREFACE TO THE 2016 EDITION

WHEN WE PUBLISHED *An Air That Kills* in 2004, we told the story of the worst environmental disaster in U.S. history, and the toll it took on Libby, Montana, as well as potentially millions of unsuspecting Americans exposed to the asbestos-laced vermiculite mined there.

But the tragedy of Libby didn't end with the story David McCumber and I wrote. In ways both maddening and frightening, the calamity has continued to unfold and grow into an alarming threat.

Scientists and physicians have discovered that the asbestos fibers contaminating Libby vermiculite are thousands of times more dangerous than anyone suspected, inspiring the new title for this updated edition: *An Air That Still Kills.*

Government regulators have turned a blind eye, placing millions of people at risk in homes insulated with Libby vermiculite in North America – and beyond.

W.R. Grace, which owned the mine and ignored warnings that the vermiculite ore was killing miners and their families, walked away from criminal liability after a trial that became a showcase for a political feud between a judge and a Justice Department operative, possibly overshadowing science and the law.

Meanwhile, despite the U.S. Environmental Protection Agency declaring in 2014 that its work in Libby was mostly done, the illness and dying there and elsewhere have continued and could reach tens of thousands nationwide. But because no one is counting the bodies, policymakers aren't paying attention.

1

In an era of breathless, 24/7 "breaking news" updates, Libby has become yesterday's news. By expanding and updating our original book, I want to show that the tragedy of Libby has not only continued, it has grown more dire for millions of people who unknowingly live with the unique, life-stealing fiber.

– Andrew Schneider

PART 1: DISCOVERY

Grace's mine and vermiculite processing plant spewed 5,000 pounds
of asbestos fibers each day over Libby and the surrounding countryside.
(Courtesy McGarvey, Heberling, Sullivan & McGarvey)

The Cabinet Mountains rise high above Libby, Montana, and the Kootenai Valley, with Grace's Zonolite mine site in the foreground.
(Gilbert Arias, *Seattle Post-Intelligencer*)

A SINGLE LODGEPOLE PINE from what's left of Zonolite Mountain would be plenty. Fell it — watch out for the cloud of dust – skid it out, peel it, rip it into one-by-fours and sell it to a survivor of the plague on this place. It doesn't take much lumber to knock together two hundred simple crosses.

Take them to the body shop, prime them, spray them white.

Paint a name in black on each one.

That's probably enough for this year, if you don't look too hard into the past for more names. After all, for six decades, not one doctor put the actual words on a death certificate in Libby, Montana: asbestos-related disease. But now you're at it, don't stop making crosses. The little town of Libby will be needing two or three thousand more.

The federal government came in and did the biggest public health survey in its history.[1] A third of the town got what Gayla Benefield accurately calls "the death sentence." Mincing words is not her style.

The town already knows many of the names that will need to be painted. Miners, sure, some of them, men who actually dug the death out of the mountain — hauled it, milled it, swept it, sacked it, breathed it for two or three bucks an hour and glad to do it. Then wore it home on their clothes.

Men like Les Skramstad.

But here is the hard thing: Many of the miners are already gone, and most of the names still to be painted are those of their wives and children and grandchildren. Still others on the list have no family connection — no way to know exactly where or when they inhaled enough of the dust that covers Libby to lodge tiny fibers of tremolite asbestos into their lungs, to start the inexorable process of inflammation, pleural thickening, loss of lung function, fluid buildup and slow suffocation.

Some who might in some obscene way be considered lucky will go more quickly, from lung cancer or mesothelioma, a fancy name for another kind of death sentence, a cancer of the lining of the lung.

Death followed the vermiculite ore from Zonolite Mountain as closely as the asbestos fibers that contaminated it — followed it far from Libby, all across the country to more than 300 ore-processing plants, and farther yet. Today, in millions of homes, the hazardous material still rests, in attics and walls, to be sent into air, and lungs, with any disturbance. Asbestos from Libby was released into the air in New York City when the World Trade Center buildings collapsed.

Nobody knows how many people have died from it, or where, or how many more will die. Hundreds of thousands more people will be exposed to asbestos from other sources in this country — from brakes, from contaminated talc, from contaminated iron ore. From all the products containing asbestos that are still being legally manufactured and sold because of the power of an industry, here and in Canada, that has lied and covered up for a deadly century — and because of a government that has not protected us, its workers and consumers.

In Libby, even as the Environmental Protection Agency struggles to clean up the toxic mess, some unknown number of the kids who show no sign of illness now, as they ride their bikes down quiet streets or crowd boisterously into the Pizza Hut after a ballgame, will die the same way. That's what breaks Les Skramstad's heart, and what makes Gayla Benefield madder than a stepped-on snake.

Strong is a good word to describe Gayla. Picture Nordic blond hair fighting the gray in an attractive, functional cut, and an expressive mouth equally comfortable with a smile, a kiss or a swearword ("I can say 'Fuck you' without moving my lips," she says sweetly, pushing her glasses up with an extended middle finger). Her blue eyes betray a quickness of thought, and twinkle as a natural state of affairs, but go cold as Libby in February when the subject turns to asbestos. For good reason.

She lost her mother and father to Libby's curse. Now she and her husband David are diagnosed with the disease. Sixty-two members of their family have either died of the disease, have been diagnosed or remain at high risk. Gayla was one of the first to fight in court to get the W.R. Grace Company, owner of the vermiculite mine with asbestos in the ore, to be found responsible for the dying. After achieving that, she has never stopped fighting for the victims and their families, not for an instant.

At 67, Les Skramstad is still trim-waisted and muscular, and he still plays country music around town, as he has for forty years. After he was diagnosed with asbestosis in 1996, he became the first former miner to take Grace to trial and win, but that won't keep him alive. Since his trial, he has learned that his wife, Norita, and two of their children have the same disease that will kill him.

"I loved my job at Zonolite," he says quietly. Each of his shortening breaths is a gold coin to be spent wisely, and so he is very soft-spoken, even when his jaw sets and you can see the pain in his eyes. "I loved it so much that even if they had told me that I was endangering my life, I would probably have stayed.

"But if they'd told me it was killing my wife and my family too, I would have run like hell."

ON THIS DAY, MEMORIAL DAY 2001, Gayla and Les put aside their anger and concentrated on honoring the victims.[2]

As it is in so many small towns across America, Memorial Day is a big holiday in Libby, and perhaps the most meaningful. To most townspeople, family is the most important thing, and a natural part of that is to remember those who have gone before.

This year, for the first time, there was to be a public remembering, an acknowledgment of the many who have died from asbestos. That alone was an enormous thing for a town that had suffered in silence for so long, a town literally left to die by every branch of every government charged with making sure something like this does not happen. A town that for so many years either did not know or did not acknowledge what was killing so many. But by now the story was out, the truth unavoidable; people around the world knew about the dying in Libby, and so it was only right. some of the survivors decided, that the dead should be honored.

Two men led this effort. Mike Switzer has been diagnosed with asbestosis. His was one of the first families to settle in Libby, more than a century ago. Jim Racicot has been diagnosed with asbestosis. So have two of his brothers and his sister. His effort is most ironic; his second cousin, Marc, was governor of Montana when the dying became public knowledge, in 1999. Marc Racicot made concerned noises and did nothing of substance, many of his former neighbors in Libby say bitterly.

Mike Switzer and Jim Racicot got the materials for the crosses donated. They were built in Libby High School's shop class. The painting was done at Gene's Body Shop, and Stephanie Barry volunteered to paint the names.

Some of the local real-estate outfits and others at the Chamber of Commerce were a little nervous about putting the crosses where they'd be visible to everybody. They talked about putting them behind the Chamber offices, out of the way. Mike Switzer even got a phone call or two: "What are you trying to do to our town?"

Gayla went to the City Council and suggested that it would be a good idea to put the crosses at the cemetery, where so many people from the town would be coming for Memorial Day. So a vacant plot of land near the cemetery's rose garden was chosen.

The cemetery rests in bottomland, not far off Highway 2, behind the Venture Inn. Look down and you'll see a serene sea of grass and marble, somehow uniquely Montanan: Allen Lewis Kendall (born August 3, 1936; died September 1, 1998) is laid to rest beneath the epitaph ONE HELL OF A MAN, illustrated by engravings of a piece of heavy earthmoving equipment and a cowboy on horseback. Look up and you'll see towering sentinels of jack pine and larch, and beyond, all along the horizon, the peaks of the Cabinet Mountains, a wild and spectacular range that dominates the landscape around Libby, but is only a fingernail on the huge outstretched hand of the northern Rockies.

The night before Memorial Day, Gayla, Les, Mike, Jim and others set the crosses out in rows, military fashion. The next morning, when the pastel early light struck the crosses, tight against each other in the little clearing, the effect was more dramatic than anyone could have imagined.

Many people came — to add flowers, to walk among the crosses, to read the names. Some were carting long green oxygen tanks by their sides, like Don Kaeding, who said cheerfully, "Well, my name might be here next year." It would be.

Pastor Cam Foote of the Troy Baptist Church, who played baseball with Gayla's son and at 35 has been diagnosed with asbestosis, conducted a short prayer service. Then Les read the list of asbestos dead.

Look at Libby. Look at the scar of mining against the landscape. Look at the workingmen's houses where to this very day tiny spears of asbestos hover in the air like a judge's sentence. Look at the people who walk to the post office with slow, shuffling steps, rolling what's left of their lives beside them in the green tanks. Look at this piece of ground filled with simple white crosses, and you can almost hear Maybelle Carter and Johnny Cash singing one of Les's favorite songs:

Undertaker
Undertaker
Undertaker please drive slow
For that lady
That you're hauling
Lord I hate to see her go[3]

CHAPTER 1

EPA emergency coordinator Paul Peronard was assigned to show
that the Libby health crisis the Seattle newspaper was writing about
was blown out of proportion. (Andrew Schneider)

A MAN WHO HAS FALLEN off a mountain shouldn't have to take a call from his boss, even if he does work for the government of the United States of America.[1]

Paul Peronard lay on the living-room floor of his suburban Denver home on the morning of Monday, November 22, 1999. He had not moved for hours. The ice packs between his back and the carpet hadn't done much to stop the pain, and neither had the little white pills. Every deep breath, every slight movement, hurt like hell.

The day before, Peronard had done a professional job of wrenching his back because he'd done an amateur job of climbing the northwest face of Bastille. The 700-foot cliff attracts skilled climbers to Eldorado Canyon State Park about 30 miles northwest of the Colorado capital.

Peronard had climbed it before with ease. But this time, two-thirds of the way up the sandstone face, a minuscule outcropping on which he had placed his 180 pounds had disintegrated as he reached to force another chock or stopper into a crack in the red-and-gold rock. The heavy wedge of metal with a strong loop of cable is used by climbers as a secure but removable fixture to which a safety line can be attached to arrest a climber's fall.

He was 30 feet above the last chock he had wedged in. The device held just the way it was supposed to as Peronard tumbled past it and then on another 30 feet, at which point his rope played out and jerked him to a stop. He swung hard, back first, into the jagged face. Several times.

He felt lucky. He was alive, and since it was Thanksgiving week, he thought he'd manage to get some time to recover. Just after noon, Peronard's wife Tracy grabbed the phone before it finished its first ring. Steve Hawthorn, chief of EPA's emergency response section for the region and Peronard's boss, was already apologizing, so Tracy knew she was not going to like this conversation.

She handed Peronard the phone. "It's Steve," she said, rolling her blue eyes and shaking her head with the universal sign known to spouses everywhere: "You're not going anywhere."

His boss issued the perfunctory "Sorry to bug you when you're down," and proceeded: "Something weird has come up and Yellowtail wants you to handle it."

The invocation of Bill Yellowtail's name was a bad sign. The administrator of EPA Region 8, a Crow Indian and a Montana cattle rancher, Yellowtail only got involved when things were crappy, or about to become so.

Peronard listened for a few moments, then handed the phone back to Tracy with a wince. So much for taking the week off.

"Some damned newspaper in Seattle is claiming that hundreds of people in some place called Libby, Montana, are dead or dying from exposure to asbestos," Peronard told his wife. "Apparently Yellowtail told Hawthorn, 'I don't know what the hell is going on up there, but if it's true, go help those people.'

"They want me to go up and check out what's happening."

It was not the first time, nor the tenth, nor the twentieth, that Tracy had seen her husband jerked back to work at the spur of the moment to respond to some unknown community in the middle of nowhere that was having some kind of an emergency. That's what EPA's on-scene coordinators do.

When she was going to the hospital to give birth to their daughter Tristan, Paul was at a train derailment in Sweetwater, Tennessee. He had been on the road for their first five anniversaries. While she understood perfectly, Tracy didn't have to like it, and Peronard knew his redheaded wife well enough to tell that this time she was already angry. Her parents were scheduled to arrive the next day, and the rest of their Thanksgiving guests a day later.

Peronard sighed, tossed the ice packs away and started shoving clothes into a bright-blue square duffel with HAZMAT printed on the side in large yellow letters.

"I don't know what this is all about. I've got to see those stories," he said. "I need to know what I'm getting into here."

Tracy cranked up the Gateway PC sitting in the corner of the bedroom, hunted up the website for the *Seattle Post-Intelligencer* and started printing out the stories, which carried the tagline "Uncivil Action: A Town Left to Die."

Peronard softly moaned and cursed, not so much from the pain in his back but from what he was reading:

> LIBBY, MONT. — First, it killed some miners. Then it killed wives and children, slipping into their homes on the dusty clothing of hard-working men. Now the mine is closed, but in Libby, the killing goes on.
>
> W.R. Grace & Co. knew, from the time it bought the Zonolite vermiculite mine in 1963, why the people in Libby were dying.
>
> But for the 30 years it owned the mine, the company did not stop it.
>
> Neither did the governments. Not the town of Libby, not Lincoln County. Not the state of Montana, not federal mining, health and environmental agencies, not anyone else charged with protecting the public health.
>
> . . . A *Post-Intelligencer* investigation has shown that at least 192 people have died from the asbestos in the mine's vermiculite ore, and doctors say the toll could be much higher. The doctors and Libby's long-suffering families say that at least another 375 people have been diagnosed with fatal (asbestos-related) disease.

"This is just pure bullshit," he told Tracy. "If something this bad had happened, we'd know about it. Hell, everybody would know about it. It's got to be bullshit." An hour later, forcing himself to be congenial and professional, Peronard called Andrew Schneider, the guy whose name was at the tops of the articles.

"Hey. Interesting stories," he said, swallowing hard. "I'd really like to know where you did your sampling for asbestos, and how, and who analyzed it for you."

WELL, THAT WAS A LONG STORY, and much more than Schneider was going to volunteer to some stranger on the telephone. Truth to tell, the *Seattle Post-Intelligencer's* effort to get to the bottom of what happened in Libby started with a fluke and almost ended before it began.

In the summer of 1999, Montana was the last of nine western states that *Post-Intelligencer* writers and photographers were examining as part of a yearlong investigation into the impact of the 1872 General Mining Act. The Act allows corporations to buy public lands from the United States for a few dollars an acre, then extract gold, silver and other precious metals, paying no royalties and often leaving toxic environmental messes behind. Three staffers from the *Post-Intelligencer* were in different corners of the state.

Environmental reporter Robert McClure was in Helena, meeting with Jim Jensen at the Montana Environmental Information Center.[2] The group had just prevailed on the state to outlaw the use of cyanide in mining precious metals, a key step in curtailing future damage from hardrock mining.

About 250 miles northeast, in Harlem, Montana, Andrew Schneider, the *Post-Intelligencer's* senior national correspondent, and photographer Gilbert Arias were wrapping up work that would document the way mining companies, with the help of the United States government, had for more than a century screwed the Gros Ventre and Assiniboine tribes as they ripped gold out of their sacred Spirit Mountain and poisoned some of the water that supplied the reservation.

The journalists, having just finished their final interviews with tribal leaders, were down the street, grabbing a burger at the only café in town. Schneider's cell phone, which hadn't rung in a week, began chirping.

It was McClure. He'd finished his interviews with the environmental group but said Jensen had passed on a weird tip about some town called

Libby that might be having health problems because of a now-closed vermiculite mine. Jensen came up with the name of some lawyer and a local activist raising hell with the state government, but said he knew nothing else.

"He's going to send one of his investigators up tomorrow, to check the mine out," McClure said. "Vermiculite has nothing to do with hard-rock mining, but I thought you should know about it before you head home."

Home sounded great. Schneider and Arias had been on the road — in fact, what seemed like every road in eastern Washington, Idaho and Montana — for three long weeks. The novelty of driving through some of the most beautiful country in the West had worn off, and the idea of making a 200-plus-mile detour to chase a story that — even if it existed — had nothing to do with the mining series didn't sound like much fun. But still, it sort of smelled like a story and it was between them and home.

David McCumber, the *Post-Intelligencer's* projects editor, was called and accepted the detour to Libby with about as much enthusiasm as any editor would show when a reporter — senior or otherwise — says, "I'm just going to take a look at something that has nothing to do with what you think I should be doing."

By morning, Schneider and Arias were in Kalispell. The little town is encircled by Glacier National Park, the Hungry Horse Reservoir and the Flathead National Forest.

THE LAW OFFICES of McGarvey, Heberling, Sullivan and McGarvey are down the street from the picturesque old red Flathead County Courthouse.[3] Roger Sullivan agreed to see Schneider with all the warmth of a man scheduling a root canal.

"Yeah. There is a major problem, but I can't tell you much about it," Sullivan said, setting the tone for a puzzling and unpleasant 30 minutes of mostly one-sided discussion.

"Yeah. We've got the medical proof. Good proof." But he refused to say who the doctors were. "Lots of people have died in Libby because of the contamination from the mine." But again, he declined a request for names. "Get them from the courthouse."

The young lawyer and his partners obviously knew their legal stuff. Lying, not so casually, around Sullivan's office were copies of a recent half-page *New York Times* story on how the firm battled to get a $100-million settlement on behalf of 1,000 workers at an aluminum smelter in nearby Columbia Falls.

"Yes, we've settled several cases against W.R. Grace on behalf of miners and their families in Libby," he said. And no, he wouldn't give Schneider copies.

Schneider has been known to have a short fuse, but not usually when it comes to dealing with sources. He came close to making an exception with Sullivan.

"Come on, Roger. What's going on? You obviously aren't averse to publicity," Schneider asked, pointing to the *Times* article.

"I've got a lot more Libby cases in the pipeline, and I'm not going to blow them by going public. The judge doesn't like publicity. Grace will demand a change of venue if our people get quoted," he finally admitted. Sullivan's stance became even more confused when he said he "sent a ton" of documents to *The New York Times,* the paper in Kalispell and others. "They weren't interested. I'm not sure what some paper in Seattle can do, anyhow. Call me in a few months and we'll see," he said, nudging Schneider toward the door.

Sullivan's reluctance to help hadn't made the 90-mile drive to Libby any more enjoyable. And the phone call to the activist Jensen had mentioned, Gayla Benefield, did nothing to diminish the chill in the Montana air.

A bit older than Erin Brockovich, but with the same smart mouth, Gayla wasted no time before establishing that she would answer few questions, if any, and only after Schneider went up to the old vermiculite mine with her.

Much of the six-mile drive from Libby to the mine runs along the Kootenai River, which was named after the Indians who first inhabited this valley, Gayla explained. But the history lesson ended as they turned up Rainy Creek Road, the winding path to the mine.

Around the second bend, a car coming down from the mine waved Schneider to a stop. It was the environmental investigator that Jensen had sent up from Helena. "It looks okay to me," he volunteered. "It's just a tailing pile, and I don't see much to worry about."

"Shit. Open your damned eyes," Gayla bellowed as the investigator drove off. "What the hell does he mean, 'nothing to worry about'?" Her rant continued as they pulled into a parking area on the side of the road overlooking what was Grace's operation.

She waved a document in Schneider's face — a report from the Montana Department of Environmental Quality on the status of the mine.[4] "It says Grace spread yellow sweet clover and grass seed and planted 150 pine seedlings on each acre of the mine it reclaimed. Do you see any of that?" she seethed.

Only a scant stubble covered the pinkish-tan surface of the towering tailing pile, where hundreds of thousands of tons of waste rock, soil and asbestos dust had been dumped after the vermiculite ore was removed. A web of eroded gullies snaked through the pile. It was very dusty.

"The state says it is confident that no asbestos is blowing off the hill. Bullshit," she spat.

A month earlier, Gayla had taken Roger Sullivan and a friend up to the mine. "I hadn't been up there for thirty years, so I drove them up. When I saw the tailing pile I said, 'Oh, my God.' It hadn't been cleaned up," she told Schneider. Gayla said she stewed for weeks about the dust blowing off the site. Then the state government touched off the fuse on her temper.

She saw a legal notice in *The Western News* saying that the Department of Environmental Quality was considering giving Grace back the remainder of a $467,000 reclamation bond the state was holding, to cover the costs of restoring the property to an environmentally safe level if Grace went belly-up.[5] "Grace had already gotten back four hundred thousand dollars of its money. Now they wanted to give back the rest — sixty-seven thousand dollars," Gayla explained. "The number kept flashing in my head, sixty-seven thousand dollars. Mom's settlement with Grace was one hundred thousand dollars. After the lawyer's fees and expenses she got a check for sixty-seven thousand dollars. Somebody was sending me a message. Sixty-seven thousand dollars. I had to do something about Grace."

She spent a week calling every agency of the Montana government that might have some jurisdiction over Grace and the mine, asking if they were aware that hundreds of people in Libby had been diagnosed with asbestos-related disease. She was shuffled from one office to the next. Finally, someone at the Department of Environmental Quality asked her if she would like to sign a complaint against the return of the remaining money.

"Hell, yes," she said. And the state found itself forced to have a public meeting on whether the mine site was safe or not.

Schneider listened, then asked: "The mine killed your mother?"

"And my father," she said, lowering her voice to a normal level for the first time in an hour.

"When? How?"

"I'm not going to talk about it. I can't," she said, and began reading aloud from the state cleanup report again.

Schneider grabbed some empty plastic film cans from the back of the truck. He walked along the road and scooped three samples of the dusty pink soil into the cans, zipped them in a plastic bag and tossed them into his briefcase.

"This is the story I want you to do," Gayla said, pointing to the tailing pile.

"I don't know," Schneider responded. "You're right. The state screwed up. This mine obviously hasn't been reclaimed. It's probably a good story for your local papers."

Wrong thing to say.

"They don't care. None of them," Gayla erupted. "I've kissed the ass of every reporter from here to Missoula and no one wants to do anything."

It was a silent ride back to town.

Schneider talked her into having a cup of coffee, figuring that being in a public place might keep her volume down. Wrong.

He tried again to get her to explain what happened to her parents.

"It's always tragic when big companies screw over the environment, but it happens all the time," he tried to explain. "If what they did up there harmed people in this town and no one has done anything about it, then that's an important story and we'll look into it. But I need to know where to start. I need to know what it's all about."

For what seemed like forever, she said nothing, just stared at a spot on the pale green wall behind him.

"Look," she said softly. "Lots of people here have died because of that mine. And a hell of a lot more are dying and no one cares." Slamming her open hand on the table hard enough to shake the coffee out of their cups, she cranked up the volume. "No one. Not one single government agency. Not here. Not in Helena. Not in Washington. None of them gives a shit about what's happened to the people here.

"So what are you going to do about it?" she said, glaring.

Schneider carries a full ration of the journalistic skepticism that's needed to survive as an investigative reporter. Something was happening in Libby, but he was not convinced it was something his readers 440 miles to the west should give a damn about.

"Give me something to work with and I promise I'll look into it," Schneider said.

"I won't," Gayla yelled, but dropped her voice to a whisper, "because I can't. The lawyers said we can't talk to you. Sullivan called me before you got here, telling me what I could and couldn't say."

She was not at all sure about this brash reporter with the well-worn work boots and big-city ways. She had been trying to get Montana media interested in the Libby story for years, to almost no effect, and she didn't want to be disappointed again. She found Schneider arrogant and skeptical of things she knew to be true, and she was irritated.

What could a paper in Seattle do about this anyhow? she asked herself.

Schneider broke the silence.

"Is there an Italian restaurant in town?"

"Pizza Hut," she snapped, and she got up, turned on her heel and walked out.

It was another 24 hours before Schneider made it back to Seattle. He sat in McCumber's office and leaned back in a chair with his feet on his editor's desk.

"Something weird is happening in that town. I'm sure of it, but I don't know what it is yet," he said.

He had checked with Centers for Disease Control, the EPA office in Denver that covers Montana, and Montana's health department. "Nobody knows anything about sick people in Libby," he said. "All the agencies said that if a bunch of miners had died, they'd know about it. Even the three docs in Libby that I called said it was news to them."

"So let me get this right," McCumber asked. "You say the Grace operation mined vermiculite that's not covered by 1872 law. It's not a hardrock mine and won't fit into the series that we want to get into the paper some damn day and, on top of that, every government bureaucrat you questioned says you're full of shit."

"I know that, damn it," Schneider said, really riled now. "But didn't you hear me? Something may be killing those people out there, and it may be asbestos. I can buy off on the asbestos being a killer, but not that no one knows about it.

"This Benefield woman has a mouth, but she's not lying. Something real has got her Scandinavian temper raging."

The way Schneider saw it, he needed to jump on the Libby story. The hard-rock story was important, full of serious implications — political, economic and environmental. But this Libby story, if it checked out, was a story of government indifference or worse. It was also a story of people needlessly endangered and forgotten by the system.

"Unless I'm very much mistaken, this is a much more important story," he told McCumber.

When he said "more important story," it behooved his editor to pay attention, McCumber knew. Schneider hadn't won two Pulitzers by accident.

"I'm going to take a couple of days and make some more calls. I grabbed some dirt up at the mine. Maybe I'll find someone to analyze it," Schneider said. "Then we'll talk again."

For the rest of the week Schneider called the alphabet soup of federal agencies that should know about Libby's Zonolite mine. EPA headquarters said there was nothing in its files on Libby, nor anything to indicate that vermiculite contained asbestos. OSHA and its research arm — the National

Institute of Occupational Safety and Health — shrugged their bureaucratic shoulders. The Mine Safety and Health Administration at least had heard of the Montana vermiculite mine, but "there's nothing in the files that shows it was ever a problem," the press spokeswoman reported.

What was really bothering Schneider was that the check by *Post-Intelligencer* researchers of every daily newspaper in Montana and Idaho going back five years had turned up zip.[6] It would turn out that only a handful of short news items buried deep in various small papers had ever been written. (It would be nearly four years before they would discover an op-ed piece the *P-I* itself had run in June 1998, by Libby resident Asta Bowen, that had mentioned 88 deaths, but had passed unnoticed by the paper's news side, and all other media.) For the tenth time, Schneider picked up the plastic bag with its three film cans of dirt and moved it from one side of the desk to the other.

"Ah, what the hell. It's only money," Schneider mused, and called Keven McDermott, a senior investigator at EPA's Seattle regional headquarters.[7]

Yeah, she'd meet for coffee, she said, but she warned him that she was bringing her sometimes partner, Armina Nolan, who had worked as Region 10's asbestos coordinator. With the tenacity of junkyard dogs and absolutely no regard for authority figures, both women have given their managers ulcers as they chased polluters and environmental criminals throughout the Pacific Northwest.

The bag containing the soil samples sat in the center of the table, surrounded by two lattes and a café Americano.

"Don't be stupid. Of course you have to analyze it," snorted Nolan. "That's what you do with samples."

Always the peacekeeper, McDermott interrupted. "Bob Fisher, up at Lab/Cor, knows asbestos and does a lot of work for EPA. Take it to him and have him do a TEM analysis."

"A what?" Schneider asked.

"You want Transmission Electron Microscopy. It costs more, but if there's asbestos in the dirt, TEM will identify what it is. The cheaper tests won't," said McDermott, who quickly added, "Call us when you get the results."

Schneider drove the two miles to Lab/Cor and dropped off the three samples. "Eighty-five dollars each? Results in two days? Sure," he said, and made up a purchase order number that the *Post-Intelligencer's* bean counters would grow to know well.

Schneider was working halfheartedly on the mining story two days later when the test results from Lab/Cor beeped into his computer's fax program. There were eleven columns of information for each of the three samples of dirt collected near the mine, and only the column "analysis date" meant anything to him.

Back to the coffee shop.

McDermott and Nolan had no problem interpreting the analysis, but they were taking their sweet time sharing their knowledge.

"Put the damn lattes down and tell me what it says," Schneider demanded, not too gently, which was the absolute wrong thing to do with these two women. Immediately they spewed out a stream of scientific gobbledygook composed of words they were probably making up as they went along and having a good time while doing it.

"Okay. Okay. You win. I'm sorry," Schneider relented. "But what does it mean? Please."

"There's asbestos in the soil samples," McDermott said.

"Why is it there? Is it harmful? The town is six miles away. Can it hurt the people in Libby?" Schneider blurted out the first of a hundred questions racing through his head.

"We can't answer those questions from the results of these three samples," Nolan explained. "All I can tell is that the asbestos is a fiber called tremolite and there's a lot of it in the dirt you grabbed. But you've got to do more sophisticated testing if you want answers to those questions."

McDermott added: "If it were in our region, we'd go out and run our own tests, but Libby is about fifty miles beyond the Idaho border, and that's where our region ends. It's Region Eight's problem. Montana falls under Denver's control."

McCumber got excited when Schneider informed him of the test results. But they both agreed that all they could prove was that Montana's DEQ is wrong. Asbestos was still blowing off the supposedly reclaimed vermiculite mine. Not really a story for the *Post-Intelligencer's* readers.

There had to be something else.

Physicians in Libby claimed no knowledge of people being harmed by asbestos, but Schneider knew from past investigations that in many company towns, local doctors sometimes buckle under pressure to keep corporate health problems under wraps.

He called a friend in Boston — a pulmonologist, or lung specialist — who for years had treated shipyard workers with asbestos-related disease. The ex-Navy physician told Schneider that people living in small towns who have these diseases often go to major medical centers in other towns or nearby states. He offered up a list of lung specialists in the states surrounding Libby.

"It's a long shot," Schneider admitted. But he needed some sign or it was back to the mining story.

A reporter trying to convince a physician who doesn't know him to discuss his or her patients, even in a general way, redefines *Mission: Impossible.*[8] Two days of calls to nine doctors in Denver, Salt Lake City, Spokane, Portland, Seattle and Boise uncovered nothing. Schneider's pleas that he didn't need patient names, just whether they came from Libby, Montana, fell on deaf ears. He couldn't even get past the nurses and receptionists to talk to the doctors. His Boston friend agreed to try to smooth the way and sent out a flurry of e-mails to his western colleagues. It worked.

A doctor in Denver returned his call. He had treated six people from Libby. One had died of mesothelioma. One had lung cancer. Two had advanced asbestosis. Two others had milder cases and he didn't know what had happened to them. Schneider got through to a specialist in Salt Lake City who had three patients from Libby and a man from a plant in Great Falls, Montana, who had somehow worked with the same vermiculite ore. All had asbestosis; one was dead.

In Portland, a doctor had treated a man from Libby and a man from Troy for asbestosis and a local guy who worked at a Portland vermiculite processing plant for mesothelioma. He died soon after the physician examined him.

In Seattle, a pulmonologist and his two partners said they had treated many Bremerton Shipyard workers for asbestos diseases. But they couldn't recall anyone from Montana. But after checking their files, his nurse called to say they had also treated nine men from Libby, Troy and Eureka. One had mesothelioma, two had lung cancer and six suffered from asbestosis. Of the nine, four had died from their diseases, the nurse said.

A doctor from Boise, Idaho, reluctantly admitted he had treated patients from that corner of Montana, but he refused to discuss any numbers or conditions and slammed the phone down. The physician in Spokane said he couldn't add anyone to Schneider's growing list, but said he thought another doctor in Spokane, Alan Whitehouse, was treating a lot of people from Montana. Over the next two days, Whitehouse's nurse politely took repeated messages from Schneider, but Whitehouse never returned the calls.

McCumber sat in Schneider's cramped office, leaned on the reporter's paper-strewn desk and watched him list on a white board attached to the wall what the doctors had told him:

Twenty-one men. Seven dead. Fifteen cases of asbestosis. Three asbestos-related lung cancers. Three cases of mesothelioma. All but three were miners. One was a logger, and the remaining two may have worked at plants that processed the ore from Libby.

Scanning the numbers, McCumber said, "There's no way we can ignore this story," and headed to the publisher's office to warn J. D. Alexander that Schneider had found another way to loot the paper's already-strained budget.[9]

Schneider was already on the phone trying to find out where he could rent vacuum air pumps. They were needed to collect samples for the more sophisticated testing that McDermott and Nolan had said was required to find out if there was still a health hazard in Libby. Asbestos in dirt is bad for anyone messing with the soil. Asbestos in the air is a far more serious indicator of danger, because inhalation — breathing the stuff in — is the prime route of exposure.

Schneider thought he still knew how to take air samples. Twenty years earlier, in grad school, he had worked with the equipment. But twenty years is a long time. The sample-collecting had to be carefully done, accurately logged and recorded, or the testing was meaningless.

Back at the coffee shop again, McDermott fingered one of the three vacuum pumps Schneider had acquired. She held up the yellow, cigar-box-sized pump and lectured the reporter on filter cartridges, collection time, pump volume — a litany of technical considerations that had to be correctly addressed if the tests would stand up to the scrutiny the stories would clearly generate.

McDermott watched as Schneider filled pages in his notebook with her instructions. She was obviously not impressed with her student's grasp of the technology.

"I'll go with you," she volunteered, her green eyes glinting. But, she quickly added, "I can't and won't do any testing. EPA would have a fit if it knew I went into some other region looking for hazardous stuff. I'll take a couple of days of leave and watch you take the samples.

"With any luck, I can keep you from screwing up."

Gayla was less than exuberant when Schneider called to say he was coming back to Libby. Her frosty demeanor melted instantly when he said that the lab had found asbestos in the samples he'd collected on his first trip.

"I told you. I told you. Didn't I? When are you putting it in the paper?" she demanded.

"When I do more testing."

"Shit. What are you waiting for?"

"Bye, Gayla. See you soon," Schneider said, wondering whether she'd ever lighten up.

ONCE YOU GET PAST THE FLATLANDS of eastern Washington and head north from Spokane, the ride to Libby changes from beautiful to spectacular.

U.S. Route 2 winds through the Idaho panhandle. Lakes and mountains on one side, the other, or both. At Bonners Ferry, just shy of the Canadian border, Schneider, in his Jeep, and McDermott, in her Volvo wagon, followed the two lanes of Route 2 due east into the still-rising sun. Sixty-five miles from Libby and not a cloud marred the bright-blue sky. The tamaracks, aspens and cottonwoods shone with the vivid gold of fall.

About ten miles from Libby, the sun disappeared and a heavy fog suddenly shrouded the road. The Kootenai River was barely visible through the mist. The fog over Libby is an almost everyday presence. Locals sometimes bet on what time midmorning the sun will finally burn through. The daily air inversions are caused by God and not pollution. Libby, at an elevation of 2,066 feet, is the lowest spot in Montana. It's in a valley carved by the glaciers and deepened by the Kootenai as it cuts south from Canada. The Cabinet Mountains, which surround the town, keep the fog from blowing away until the sun finally burns it off.

The static on the radio finally cleared just as they approached the town.

"KTNY Libby. The voice of the Kootenai Valley — one-oh-one point seven."[10] A familiar song blared from the Jeep's speakers. Something from the '70s. Some English group. The Hollies, maybe.

The lyrics finally sank in: *All I need is the air that I breathe ...*

If I write that, nobody is going to believe it, Schneider thought.

KTNY's weather forecast called for rain or snow by nightfall. Best to get the air samples while it was still dry. They stopped at the top of Rainy Creek Road. The two-lane winding road — partially paved, the rest dirt and stone — was once the main access route to the mine. Now it is used by elk hunters, huckleberry and mushroom pickers, and others seeking access to the Kootenai National Forest land surrounding the mine.

With McDermott hovering nearby, Schneider quickly set up the monitors at different sites along the road. He taped one to a tree beside the road to see what was kicked up by the hunters and berry pickers in their trucks that drove by every few minutes. Another was staked in a large, flat pull-off area where the town kids partied. The third was at the far end of the tailing pile.

"Write it down. Now," McDermott chided. Schneider recorded the times the pumps were started, the airflow, the number of the filter cartridge, the precise time the pumps ran and the exact location of each — "15 feet west of red gatepost" and "midpoint between the road and burnt double tree trunk."

By the time the samples were collected, snow had begun to fall.

A half hour later, sitting in Gayla's kitchen, Schneider introduced McDermott as "Annie" and made no mention of her EPA employment. He explained to Gayla what the earlier tests showed and why he had to do the air sampling.

"I guess you do give a damn," she said, smiling for the first time.

Three cups of really strong coffee later, Schneider finished telling Gayla what the doctors at the various medical centers had said. She said nothing for a moment, but her blue eyes welled with tears. Then: "Come take a drive."

The gravel road from Gayla's house crossed the tracks where Great Northern ore cars laden with vermiculite once rumbled by. A left turn onto Route 2 paralleled the Kootenai into Libby, where faded banners from the "Nordicfest" still hung from the light poles. It took ten minutes to reach the Libby Cemetery. The frost-covered brown grass crunched under Gayla's feet as she walked slowly through wisps of fog. She visits the graveyard every Wednesday, because it holds so many of her friends and family.

"There are my folks," she said, pointing to the markers engraved with the names Perley Vatland and Margaret Vatland. "Dad was sixty-two and Mom was seventy-six. The mine killed them both." She looked up from the graves and stared into the middle distance, remembering. "Dad came home covered in white dust and it was all over the place. Mom was a fanatic about keeping the house clean. She bought the newest Kirby vacuum, but it would just suck in the fibers and blow them right back into the air. The filters couldn't stop them. Not at all."

She pointed to the next row of markers.

"Butch and John worked up there and they both died of lung cancer. Gladys was a secretary at the mine. The dust got her, too." Behind her was another row of granite slabs, commemorating more workers at Zonolite Mountain. More lay in the next row, and the next.

"You need to meet some people," Gayla said, heading off toward a neat, white house near the center of town.

Carrie Detrick leaned on a shovel in her garden that had been freshly tilled by a friend.[11] The black soil sparkled with pieces of vermiculite. At 67, she looked a lot better than she felt. She told Schneider that she and her husband, Bob, both have asbestosis. "I never worked at the mine," Carrie explained. "I just got it by living around here. Vermiculite is all over the place.

"I don't want my kids to get it. I don't want them to die from that stuff. I can accept it if these deaths end with my generation, but what if it's ticking away in our children?" Carrie said. She'd not had much luck, she admitted, persuading her two sons, ages 42 and 48, to get tested. "They're afraid of finding out, but I think they have to know. Most of the town just doesn't want to know."

At night, she said, she sits up in a chair because it's almost impossible to breathe if she lies down.

"I hate to die. I really do," she said, her voice dropping to a whisper. "I have a great-grandchild and six grandchildren and I want to watch them grow up. But I won't."

Through the closed kitchen door, Gayla could be heard bellowing at someone on the phone. A moment later she slammed through the door, mumbling as she searched for her cigarettes. "I have no idea why God created lawyers. We already had enough snakes slithering around."

"You were talking to Roger?" Carrie guessed.

"That little SOB is having a nut-out because I brought Schneider over here. He doesn't want me talking, you talking or anyone else talking, because he's afraid it will piss the judge off and hurt the rest of the cases. Well, screw Roger. It's time people were told what happened to us."

Carrie shoved a mug of coffee into Gayla's hand and she shut up. For the moment.

Back at Gayla's, the kitchen table was covered with piles of documents gathered from the trials of her mother, her father and Les Skramstad. Some were Grace's internal memos, a couple were government reports, another pile had medical records.

At first the documents were hard to interpret. The mountain, the company and the product that came from both — Zonolite — all shared the same name. Schneider had to plot it out to keep it all straight. Zonolite Mountain was where the vermiculite ore was mined. The vermiculite was heavily contaminated with tremolite, which is a particularly lethal type of cancer-causing asbestos. The vermiculite, with its accompanying poison, is run through a revolving oven at about 2,000 degrees where it is expanded or "popped" into a feather-weight insulation, sold for decades under the name of Zonolite.

"This is just part of the proof," Gayla said. And with the fervor of a tent preacher, she held up one piece of paper after another, waving them high.

"This shows that Grace knew about tremolite when they bought the mine from Zonolite.

"This is proof that Grace tried to silence the doctors in town."

On and on.

Schneider's eyes got wide. Investigative reporters get very happy when they have paper, but Gayla only gave him a few of the documents. She ignored his pleas for more. "I've got to wait until Roger cools down and I'll see what else you can have," she explained.

But with the ease of a tenured professor, she ticked off, faster than Schneider could write, some of the history of the mine, Grace's involvement and a long list of neighbors diagnosed by Spokane pulmonologist Alan Whitehouse as having asbestos-related disease. All people that Sullivan didn't want Schneider to interview.

She stared out the large picture window at the Kootenai rapidly flowing 150 feet away, closed her eyes and, in a hoarse whisper, recited a long list of names of those who had died from the exposure to the tremolite.

McDermott sat there silently, listening to Gayla's litany of the dead.

Slowly shaking her head, Gayla asked, "Where was EPA? Where was everybody?"

MCDERMOTT HEADED BACK TO SEATTLE, agreeing to drop off at Lab/Cor the air samples and the dirt samples from Carrie's garden, the ball field and the old expansion plant.

Schneider headed to his room at the Venture Motel, grabbed Libby's tiny phone book and tried to find the sick people on Gayla's list, and the survivors of those who had died. He called McCumber, and late into the night they talked, argued and talked some more about what was known and what was needed to get Libby's story into the *Post-Intelligencer*.

For three days, Schneider wandered the small logging community, trying to find the victims and the ones they left behind. Art Bundrock worked at the Zonolite mine for 19 years.[12] He had died four months earlier on the lawn in front of his house, having left his oxygen bottle inside.

"He hated being tied to that green bottle. It let him live, but it took his freedom. He'd always sneak off without it," said his widow, Helen.

Bundrock suffered with asbestosis for more than two decades. But the pain he suffered from his disease was nothing compared to the pain of knowing that Helen and four of their five children had gotten the disease from the dust on his work clothing.

"I've got it," Helen said, "and so do Donna, Robin, Mary and Bill. Only the youngest, Cindy, hasn't been diagnosed with it, and we're all praying for her."

As one family member after another got sick, Art Bundrock's pain became unthinkable. "It was like tearing his heart out piece by piece," Helen remembered. "He never quit crying for two weeks when I found out that I had it. And with the children, he just couldn't be consoled." She repeated the accusations, made by many, that managers at the mine had told the workers that the dust was harmless.

"They lied, but they did worse than that," she said, talking about when her son went to work for Grace. "Bill had to get a chest X-ray before they hired him. That X-ray showed he had asbestosis, and they never told him. They just let him go to work up there with all that poison. They never told him for the ten years he worked there."

And then Schneider met Les Skramstad. He found immediately that Les's passion for holding Grace accountable was as strong as Gayla's. He was just quieter about it. Maybe because he was dying of asbestosis and his lungs couldn't suck in enough air to allow him to shout. Maybe because he was just a quiet kind of guy.

Part of his life ended, he said, the day Whitehouse told him that his wife, Norita, and one of his children had the disease. He said he can't talk about it without crying, so he doesn't, much. "But from the time I get up until I finally fall asleep, what I did to my wife and kids is one big lump here," he said, thumping his chest.

He took Schneider on a tour of what's left of Grace's operation and introduced him to men he used to work with. Men shackled to green oxygen bottles.

Back at the Venture, Schneider found that Lab/Cor had faxed the result of the air sampling. Schneider called Nolan for her assessment.

She wanted more information, but she conceded that if the levels found by Lab/Cor "were at a workplace, the workers picking huckleberries in that area would have to wear a respirator and a protective suit."

It was snowing outside. Schneider watched the snow fall from a pewter sky and swirl corkscrews around the light poles in front of the motel.

Post-it Notes — 70 or 80 of them, pale pink, green and yellow, an inch square — were stuck to the wall of his room.[13] The four notebooks he'd used in the last three days were crammed with the names of the dead and dying that family members and friends had supplied. They're on the small stickers. The names from Gayla — Whitehouse's patients — were listed on a long, yellow sheet. The numbers the out-of-state physicians supplied were printed on an index card.

He counted, re-counted, stopped and counted the bits of paper again, then called McCumber.

"Best guess from putting everything together is that we can show that at least one hundred and fifty people have died from the asbestos in the mine's vermiculite ore. Another three hundred–plus are sick and dying," Schneider said. "David, this may be the tip of a very large iceberg."

"I'm coming home. I've got a couple of hundred questions to answer before we write this thing."

For the next four weeks, Schneider collected thousands of pages of documents. Many were supplied by lawyers other than Sullivan who had sued Grace. A large pile came from a Boston repository of Grace documents that the court ordered the company to establish and maintain after being found guilty of concealing documents from the government in a case involving the poisoning of water in Woburn, Massachusetts. And a foot-high pile was government reports sought under the federal Freedom of Information Act.

Schneider and McCumber worried about whether they might be counting the same victims from two sources. Citing patient confidentiality, none of the physicians who had told Schneider they had treated men from Libby would share the names of their patients. All but one agreed to compare a list of Whitehouse's Libby patients who had died and a list of the names that family members had given Schneider with the list of their patients to check for duplicates. Only three duplicate names were found.

Retired mining inspectors and other government investigators were located. Doctors who had been chased from Libby for reporting asbestos illness were tracked down. Former Grace officials were contacted. Repeated calls to the company itself brought only denials that it had ever done anything wrong.

Schneider talked to government officials, trying to find out why nothing had ever been done. He found the evidence of the state and federal governments' knowledge of the problem, and no evidence of action taken to address it.

He was stunned when John Wardell, the longtime coordinator of the EPA's operations in Montana, frostily told him, "We are not responsible if the workers went home before being properly decontaminated and brought asbestos into their homes. That's a personal issue."[14] Bill Yellowtail would be stunned, as well, by Wardell's attitude.

Alerted that the *Post-Intelligencer* was working on the story, the Kalispell *Daily Interlake* rushed a four-page report into the paper on November 14. When they asked Gayla for copies of her documents, she told them, "Where were you for the past fifteen years that this has been a local story? Go to the courthouse if you want information." She had implored the *Interlake* and the *Great Falls Tribune* to do something, but she'd never gotten anywhere. Journalism students from the University of Montana did a quick, but high-quality, series on the issue, which was published in *The Missoulian* for three days beginning November 20.

The *Post-Intelligencer's* first stories ran on November 18 and 19, spanning some six pages of coverage. Enraging Yellowtail. And putting an aching Paul Peronard on the phone with a reporter who'd just ruined his vacation.

Peronard listened as Schneider described the details of the testing and thought, *Not bad for amateurs, but they still have to have it wrong. That much asbestos couldn't have been kept a secret.*

He hung up. "The guy's a smartass," he told Tracy. "He asked me, 'Where was EPA twenty years ago?' "

Tracy said something soothing, but not much. She is about as unflappable as her husband. And he's not the only one in the family with an emergency pager on his belt. Tracy works as a volunteer victims' advocate, working with teenagers and rape and assault victims for the Lakewood Police Department.

And do not call Tracy a soccer mom. Yes, eight-year-old Tristan and her brother, ten-year-old Ove, do play soccer. But not near as much as their mother, who plays on four teams, including one in a co-ed league.

She shook her head at the EPA's latest assault on their family life, threw a couple of pairs of socks into her husband's blue bag and went outside to play with the kids.

THAT AFTERNOON, about 800 miles to the northwest, two other federal investigators were in Helena, Montana's capital, meeting with state emergency management and health officials to discuss the potential for terrorist attack.

It was a scenario that, almost two years before 9/11, seemed almost ludicrously unlikely. But EPA toxicologist Chris Weis and U.S. Public Health Service epidemiologist Dr. Aubrey Miller were trying to spread the word anyway. It was all but impossible to get emergency types to pay attention to something they never thought they'd have to deal with, like bioterrorism. But federal dollars came with the program, so officials from four states had gathered to hear from Miller and Weis on the subject of terrorists and deadly bugs.

Miller's cell phone and Weis's pager went off at the same time.

"That's a bad sign," Weis said, only half joking.

The two scientists from the Region 8 emergency assessment team got orders to postpone the bioterrorism talks and scramble two blocks over to EPA's Montana office for a conference call.

Weis listened to Max Dodson, the assistant regional administrator, rant about Libby, then told him that they had read the *Post-Intelligencer* stories and that "nobody, not even Mike Spence, Montana's medical director, knows a damn thing about these deaths.

"Spence said the reporter called him weeks ago and he told him that nothing that bad was happening anywhere in his state."

Not knowing that Peronard was already tapped for the job, Weis added, "Whichever on-scene coordinator you guys assign to this, please make sure he understands public health, because if there is any truth to it at all, this is going to be a really complex bitch."

Miller agreed.

"Just because some reporter throws some science and medicine in his stories doesn't mean he's right. This guy probably screwed it up. You just don't get asbestosis or asbestos disease in nonworkers or family. It just doesn't happen. I've been trained in this area, damn it," Miller growled.

EARLY TUESDAY MORNING, Peronard caught a flight from Denver to Salt Lake City to Kalispell. Weis, Miller and Wendy Thomi, an expert in helping EPA and the public communicate with each other, flew from Helena.

On the flight, Peronard had time to go over a fistful of hastily grabbed background papers on asbestos and wonder what he'd gotten himself into.

In October he'd finished honchoing another emergency cleanup in Montana at Ten Mile Creek, southwest of Helena. For decades, the waterway had been a natural drainage ditch for runoff from 150 gold, copper, lead and zinc mines. The creek provides about 80 percent of the water used by Helena's residents. The rising level of heavy metals demanded an emergency response, and Peronard had been tapped. He thought how straightforward that had been, compared to this case.

Arsenic, cadmium, manganese, lead, iron, zinc, even PCBs and dioxin, I understand, but asbestos? What the hell do I know about asbestos? he asked himself. Asbestos was supposed to have been taken care of years before. Whatever it was, he could handle it, or so Bill Yellowtail and other top EPA brass believed.

At a trim, muscular 5' 10", with his head shaved and a diamond stud in his ear, wearing boots, blue jeans and Patagonia fleece, Peronard looked more like the ski bums crowding the Delta flight than a government official en route to put out a fire that common sense said couldn't be burning. But his 15 years with the EPA made him eminently qualified for the job.

Peronard took his chemical engineering degree from Georgia Tech in 1984 — and soon found himself loading UPS trucks for a living. That was not the career path he wanted to pursue, and when he heard EPA was hiring, he jumped at it, starting in the agency's southeastern region in September

1985. Five years later, he was promoted to this job, being an on-scene coordinator for emergency cleanups.

He ranged all across the South, digging up toxic chemicals, butting heads with polluters, and with headquarters when necessary. And the war stories abounded, although it takes some urging to get him to tell them.

At one time, he thought his biggest, best cleanup was going to be an abandoned chemical complex near Brunswick, Georgia. For more than a half century, it had served as an oil refinery, a paint factory and a power plant. But then he cleaned up 27,000 barrels of bad stuff in Memphis. He handled toxic emergencies in two major floods, including a memorable effort near Greenville, Mississippi.

"There was a five-thousand-gallon diesel tank floating down the river. I got this small Coast Guard boat to bring me alongside this big old tank. It was a sublime moment. I'm in the middle of the Mississippi, which is roaring like hell at flood stage, got a little life preserver on, and I'm riding the tank, trying to get a rope on it. The Coast Guard guy thought I was nuts, but we got that tank back to shore."

His tattoos say a lot about his personality and the way he looks at the world. A parrot on his right shoulder marks him for life as a follower of Jimmy Buffett. On his left arm is a Kokopelli. The humpbacked dancing flute player is a mythical Hopi symbol of replenishment, music, charitable deeds and mischief. Tracy also has a tattoo, a peach. Peronard has a photograph of it in his office, but he wouldn't tell Schneider where his wife hid the peach.

Peronard's shaved head is not an affectation. He earned it one day in Greer, South Carolina, supervising the cleanup of another field full of old drums of toxic chemicals. He was bored, so he started working on the drums with the contractors who were loading them for removal.

It was summertime in South Carolina, hot, very damned hot, and he was wearing heavy gloves, a protective apron, a respirator and an air line. He was using his sparkproof tools, the way he was supposed to, but this was not a laboratory environment, and things don't always go according to the agency manual when you're sweating and swearing in the middle of a stinking toxic dump, wrestling with a drum marked INERT SOLIDS.

"This was about the hundred and fiftieth drum I'd opened that morning, a flathead drum with a ring that goes around the edge to seal it down.

"I couldn't get the damn thing open. The brass tools would give. It was rusted solid. So I'm just jamming the socket wrench in there. I'm hammering away on it. The lid still doesn't give, but the drum is so corroded it rips open.

"I could hear it sucking air into the drum. *Whoosh.* I just stood there like the very green fool I was, listening. The other two guys, the ones I was supposed to be supervising, heard the noise and just bailed, moved out and hit the ground. I started to move, but I stopped. It was interesting. What was going on?

"Boom. It went off. The lid flew up and ripped off my respirator. Then a fireball, a small one but still impressive, shot up. I'm sort of on fire now. Not a lot, but it got my attention."

The men he was working with sprayed him down with a fire extinguisher. He was lucky — no really deep burns. His face was bright red, his eyebrows were gone, and so was half of his long hair.

He thinks that the material in the drum, far from inert, was a Grignard reagent, used in the production of synthetic hydrocarbons. Grignard reagents are notoriously unstable, and they react explosively with water, alcohol and sometimes air. Victor Grignard got a Nobel Prize for discovering the reagents in 1912, which was not much comfort to Paul when this one damned near took his head off.

He stopped at a barbershop in Greer to see what could be done with his half-head of hair. Predictably, nothing. The barber shaved his head, and it has been that way ever since.

BY TUESDAY EVENING, what would become known as the "Libby team" gathered in the bare-bones, one-room conference center — Room 211 — of the Super 8 Motel, the best of Libby's sparse lodgings.

Weis had worked with Peronard before. The scientist thought Peronard was a bit of a cowboy, but he was always impressed that he got things accomplished in spite of the ever-present constraints of regulations and politics.

After getting out of college with a degree in biology and a working knowledge of surveying, Weis spent five years bumming around Africa and throughout the Caribbean. When he ran out of money he would find work as a surveyor for a couple of weeks. After going to Michigan State for his master's and Ph.D.s in both medical physiology and toxicology, he wound up teaching and doing research at the University of Virginia in Charlottesville until he saw an ad in *Science* magazine for a job with EPA in Denver.

Every EPA region has one or two emergency risk assessors, people trained to calculate how dangerous a toxic release is to the public or environment, but most rarely doff their lab coats or leave their offices. Weis stunned his colleagues because he began showing up at the spewing rail cars and burning chemical sites. His idea of "taking the science to the emergency" caught on.

Weis had stumbled onto Miller almost three years earlier, in 1997, in the great floods in Grand Forks, North Dakota. More than 60,000 people were forced from their homes, and the town was flooded. EPA went in to watch for environmental and health problems, of which there were many.

"A couple of days into the flood, I get these calls from EPA's guy in charge up there," Weis recalled. "He says that 'there's this punk kid up here from the U.S. Public Health Service that's asking all kinds of questions. Would you come up here and straighten him out?' "

He flew up. Grand Forks was completely evacuated, and the icechoked Red River was out of control. EPA's guys were sleeping on the wet floor of the firehouse and "the health service dorks got to sleep in the hospital," Weis says.

Weis made it to the darkened medical facility and heard noise and laughter. He turned a corner near the emergency department and saw three guys dressed like doctors with stethoscopes and lights on their heads racing gurneys down the hall. Weis jumped quickly to avoid two gurneys about to collide.

"Hi. I'm Aubrey Miller. Help me up," one of the riders said.

In the next three days, working almost nonstop, Miller and Weis got clean water running into the hospital and made the operating rooms functional. A dangerously mischievous but effective bond was formed.

Working with Miller convinced Weis that having a medical doctor on the assessment teams was a great idea. Miller, who was working for the Centers for Disease Control in its Cincinnati laboratories, fit the bill perfectly. Through bureaucratic sleight of hand and magical arm-twisting by Weis, the EPA set up an interagency agreement with the health service, and Miller moved to Denver with his family in 1999.

So these three men, the core of "EPA's best emergency response team," as Yellowtail boasted in public statements announcing the dispatch of crews to Libby, sat around the conference room, wishing that Super 8 had room service and pondering the pages of the *Post-Intelligencer* spread out over several tabletops. Other documents that Weis and Miller had colleagues fax to the motel were separated into several neat piles. All three men had asked friends at EPA in Denver and the National Institute of Occupational Safety and Health to ship out all the background material on asbestos that they could quickly gather.

Going through the newspapers, they made a list of every local official, victim, survivor and observer named in the long stories. From the thin Libby phone book and a town map they got from the front desk, they plotted every place they had to check out the next day. For a while they talked about asbestos. What the fibers look like. Where it comes from. How people get exposed to it. The pathways through which people get exposed. How it kills.

"Okay. Asbestos was bad stuff in the old days when everyone was using it," said Peronard. "Sure, some miners here had been exposed. Some died. Sure. That always happens. But not in these numbers," he said, holding up a chart from the *Post-Intelligencer.* "I just don't believe what the stories say. No way. A hundred and ninety-eight deaths? Bullshit. This is all contrary to what we know happens in cases like these. Not in those numbers and not people who didn't work in the mine."

"We'll take some samples, piss all over the *P-I's* story, and leave," Weis said.

Miller added, "It's just another media screw-up. We'll talk to the people in charge up here and put this baby to rest."

They went to bed figuring they wouldn't be here long.

The fog clung to the ground the next morning as the trio from Denver walked up to the small town hall. Immediately they were surrounded by a gaggle of television crews and reporters that had hustled into town from Spokane, Missoula and Kalispell.

"Whatever is going on here, we will figure it out and get to the bottom of it. That's our marching orders and that's what we're going to do," Peronard told them, and sauntered into the town offices.

The city fathers were peeking out a small window as if the reporters and photographers were a new species that had appeared out of nowhere. Peronard's team immediately made a roomful of friends when they told the locals they'd keep the press off their backs for a while. One after another, the elected and appointed officials of Libby and Lincoln County expressed shock and amazement that anyone would think there was a serious health problem in Libby. Many repeated what they'd told Schneider.

"It's really much ado about nothing," Libby mayor Tony Berget said. "We've got vermiculite all over this town and always have. It sparkles when the sun shines. Everyone has it in the gardens, it's used as fill, about everybody has insulated their houses and businesses with it.

"If it was making anyone sick, we would have been told by the county or the state or W.R. Grace," said Berget, who had been the mayor since 1996.

The county environmental expert said her office hadn't tested for asbestos for years and asked the EPA team, "Why should I?" She quickly added, "We don't even have the equipment to do it."

Dr. Brad Black, the part-time county health officer, looked a bit stunned, but said that no one ever talked about being sick from asbestos. He allowed that there may have been a couple of old-timers but nothing serious like the newspaper says. After a moment he added, "But I'm a pediatrician."

For an hour or more, the protests and denials of any knowledge continued. The federal trio took lots of notes. Berget got in a closing shot about how all environmental laws have hurt Libby; that not only did Grace close the vermiculite mine, but the tree-huggers have forced most of Libby's logging and lumber industry out of business. "That cost us a lot of jobs, and unemployment is about fifteen percent. Now this. You've got to show that there's nothing wrong here."

As they walked out, the EPA team agreed that based on what they had just been told, they would probably do exactly that.

The Kootenai River borders a dirt play field where the kids in town chased balls and romped. Beyond the field is the site where vermiculite ore was loaded on trains. And inside the tin-roof sheds were huge piles of vermiculite where kids climbed, rolled and swung on rope swings. (Cold Truth)

N O LIFE REMAINED on Zonolite Mountain that late November day. A light snowfall dusted the terraced slopes of the old mine, and the thin gray afternoon light revealed almost nothing. The buildings were gone; the dry mill, the laboratory, the main office, all gone.

A few short stems of grass struggled to find a foothold in what was left of the ground, where decades of dynamiting and the huge 'dozers, front-end loaders and dump trucks had carved the valuable vermiculite ore from the mountain.

Peronard and his team marveled at the beauty of this corner of Montana as they drove along the Kootenai River for a few miles east of town, and then took the hard left turn up unpaved Rainy Creek Road and bumped their way to the mine.[1] As they walked around the pitted mountainside, they saw nothing to help them understand what had happened here, nothing to indicate that this place had been the economic lifeblood of this valley. Nothing was left to tell the story of the four generations of men who had worked here, three shifts around the clock, taking good wages and every penny earned, pulling the shiny ore from the rock.

They heard no sound, saw no sign to betray the killer that had done its work here for more than seven decades.

Alan Stringer, W.R. Grace's last boss here, retired to San Juan Capistrano after the mine closed in 1990. Now the company had summoned him back to do their work again, and it was Stringer and Mark Owens who showed the mine to Peronard, Miller and Weis. Grace had sold the mountain years before to a group of three local men, including Owens, who called themselves the Kootenai Development Company.

Peronard thought it didn't look that bad compared to other mine restorations he'd seen. Lots of shiny stuff on the ground. Miller thought it looked like a pink lunar landscape, quite benign. They drove off Zonolite Mountain, wondering, *Why vermiculite? Why here? What happened?*

IT WAS THE SUMMER OF 1916. Europe was in the throes of the Great War and materials to produce the machinery of battle were in great demand.[2] A perfect example was vanadium, used in the hardening of steel.

Edgar Alley understood both war and vanadium. He was a Spanish-American War veteran and a metals-mining man. A Nebraskan, he'd done what a lot of young flatlanders did just before the turn of the century — he'd headed west, to the mountains, to seek his fortune. Before his war service, he and his brother, Roy Alley, had operated their own mining and milling concern in Butte, Montana, which was then the mining capital of the country, if not the world. Upon his return to civilian life, he'd worked for the giant Anaconda Copper Mining Company for several years.

In the West at that time friendships counted for a great deal, which is how Alley found himself possessed of the mineral rights to much of a sprawling hogback mountain visible from the muddy streets of Libby.

Alley had befriended an ailing, retired traveling salesman from Chicago, one B. M. Thomas, who was sent west by a doctor unable to prescribe anything for him except fresh air. Thomas found his air in Libby, and being entrepreneurial by nature, soon fell to prospecting. He became acquainted with John Rennie, who prospected for gold all over northwestern Montana. Rennie had a large placer-mining claim on a tributary of the Kootenai River that soon became known as Rennie's Creek, and then, by common usage, "Rainy Creek." He followed some quartz veins, even sinking a few shafts, but gave up after finding only a few traces of copper and lead. He told Thomas of his abandoned claim in the area, and Thomas promptly claimed the mineral rights for himself.

Shortly thereafter, a government geologist found that the area certainly did contain mineral potential, reporting that he had found vanadium, among other metals, in some of the samples he took. He also noted the presence of a large quantity of unusual rock, which the U.S. Geological Survey decided was a form of mica. None of which did Thomas any good. He succumbed to his ailments, leaving the mineral rights to his friend, Edgar Alley.

That was how Alley found himself most of the way up the side of a mountain at the end of a summer evening, embarked on what was likely a fool's errand. He had searched for days and failed to find any trace of vanadium, or anything else valuable, on the chunk of dirt to which he possessed mining rights.

Bram Stoker could not have imagined a more melodramatic setting for Alley's discovery. Standing high on the wild, windblown slope, surrounded by a vast, dark swath of pines, he'd watched the sun set on yet another fruitless day. He nearly decided to return to town just then. He knew his wife, Maude, was cooking dinner in their rooms on the third floor of Libby's only three-story building — the Libby Hotel, which Alley owned.

But one more of Rennie's shafts near the top of the mountain remained to be explored, and so Alley lit his miner's candle and resolutely left the lowering dusk for the unknown blackness of the old mine. As the prospector moved slowly along the dusty shaft, the tip of his candle penetrated the soft surface on the roof of the tunnel. What Alley saw left him transfixed with fear.

Imagine it: You are alone after sundown, high on a remote Montana mountain, crouching in an abandoned tunnel that could well contain bears or other wild beasts. Your candle — the source of whatever meager understanding you have of your surroundings — jabs into the wall, and you see the earth suddenly alive with what looks like a hundred worms, seeming to writhe all around the invading light.

A lesser man would have fled, screaming. But Alley slowly realized that the worms were actually flaky pieces of some mineral that had reacted to the heat of the candle by expanding in a twisting way. He quickly took all the samples of the strange mineral that he could carry, hiked down the mountain and drove home to dinner.

To Maude's exasperation, he kept putting little pieces of the mineral on the surface of the hot stove, and sure enough, each piece squirmed and grew larger, looking alive even in the safe environs of the kitchen, puffing up to several times its original size.

Alley examined the expanded pieces in wonderment. They were feather-light, bronze-hued, unlike any material he had ever seen. Over the next few days, he experimented incessantly with the bits of mineral. He discovered that after expansion, the substance was not only fireproof but was such a poor conductor of heat as to be potentially useful as an insulator.

At last, he thought. *I didn't fight a war and move Maude out here to Montana just to rent out hotel rooms in a little logging town. It is here, here in these wormy little miracles, I can feel it. Here is my fortune.*

Although Edgar Alley had a vision of riches flowing from his little bits of roasted rock, he was also a realist. He knew his find wasn't like a gold strike, with a network of ready buyers lined up worldwide. He had to make a market for the curious substance. So, after a couple of years of failed attempts to attract interest in the mineral on a regional level, he headed to the East Coast in the spring of 1919 with trunks full of samples. There, he had better luck. "I was fortunate in interesting several large manufacturers in the possibilities of the mineral, among whom were the Johns-Manville Asbestos Co.," Alley wrote several years later.

On the same trip, he showed samples to several government agencies in Washington, and there, too, he was met with enthusiasm and predictions of great commercial success. Alley reported that Oliver Bowles, chief mineral technologist in the Bureau of Mines, said that the heat expansion of the mineral was the most remarkable phenomenon he had ever witnessed. Alley returned to Libby much encouraged, and set about enlarging the areas of his claim to include as much of the ore deposit as possible. "The raw material is but two feet under the cover of soil, and to a depth of at least a hundred and fifty feet," he told prospective customers. "We've got a mountain of it." He decided to christen his product Zonolite, although scientists had already come up with a more logical Latin derivative, vermiculite (from *vermiculus,* meaning "little worm").

Alley installed a small furnace on his ranch, to fill an order for two tons of expanded Zonolite from a building-materials business in New Jersey. The little kiln finally burned up, but he managed to complete the order, which was shipped east in 70 coffee sacks.

Alley hoped it was only the first of many orders, but it was obvious that he would need to build something much larger to treat quantities of the ore. And by the spring of 1924, Alley had done just that, by opening a modest treatment plant on the J. Neils Lumber Co. siding on the edge of town. He had spent yet another winter back east, scouting out more customers, and he felt it was only a matter of time before his mine was one of the largest industries in the Northwest.

The mining had so far been done with pick and shovel, but Alley was confident that production could soon start on a large scale. "It will only be necessary to remove the overburden, a comparatively inexpensive procedure, and mine the Zonolite from an open pit with steam shovels," he enthused in an interview that summer with Libby's leading newspaper, *The Western News.*

Still, everything he was doing to grow his business was expensive, from making sales calls, to building a decent road to the mine, to opening the new plant, and he was running through his capital fast. He sold his share in the Libby Hotel to his brother-in-law, and, one by one, liquidated his other properties until all he had left was his ranch — and he took out a sizable mortgage on that.

None of that seemed to bother Alley in the slightest, and why should it? More and more companies were showing interest in trying Zonolite as an ingredient in everything from roofing to printers' ink. In November of 1924, after more than a year of negotiation with Great Northern Railroad, he managed to secure a relatively favorable shipping rate of $17 per ton to the East Coast. And in March 1925, Alley shipped out the first full carload of Zonolite, to a company in Hillsboro, Ohio, for use as an insulator in manufacturing bank vaults and office safes. A hard winter and early thaw had left the road to the mine nearly impassable, so to fill his growing list of orders Alley was forced to employ wagons pulled by teams of draft horses to get the ore from the mine to the mouth of Rainy Creek.

By that summer, Alley was officially trolling for investors. He made a presentation to Libby's Commercial Club, which functioned both as Chamber of Commerce and men's social club for the town's merchants, bankers and other businessmen. (Occasionally it deigned to meet jointly with its counterpart, the Libby Women's Club, usually in the evening at the opera house.) Alley told them of the warm reception his product was getting, and the club gave him an enthusiastic endorsement, including a resolution praising the company's management and offering the club's help in securing any needed financing.

Alley made similar presentations in nearby Kalispell and in Spokane, where he attracted the interest of an energetic gold-mining expert named James Keith, who made a sizable investment. Keith became president of the Zonolite Company and Alley the vice president and general manager. Later in the year, a group of industrialists from the East tried to buy the growing company — an offer Keith and Alley rejected. Keith, meanwhile, opened a processing and manufacturing plant in Spokane, and plans for a much larger processing plant in Libby were announced.

By January 1926, the new plant was being operated around the clock, with a capacity of 110 tons of expanded Zonolite per day. Alley told stockholders the plant reduced the company's cost per ton of product from $13 to $4.50. The first carload of the product from the new plant was shipped to the General Electric Company, but Keith and Alley received a nasty shock that very month when a group of Libby men headed by grocer H. C. Bolyard announced that it had secured two large claims to vermiculite deposits near the base of what was now known as Zonolite Mountain, and incorporated a new mining concern.

Alley must have felt especially stung when he learned that one of the new company's organizers was the most powerful man in Libby, Walter Neils of the J. Neils Lumber Company. Neils, president of the Commercial Club, had allowed Alley to open his first primitive treatment plant on the sawmill's property. Now, suddenly, they were competitors.

While the new company surely wanted to exploit all of the potential markets for vermiculite, just as Alley did, it had another goal as well. According to a story announcing the formation of the Vermiculite & Asbestos Company in *The Western News* of January 20, 1926, "A large body of very high grade amphibole asbestos lies within the company's holdings and is to be developed and marketed with the vermiculite products."

By the next spring, *The Western News* reported that the company's explorations had opened up "a length of at least 650 feet of almost solid asbestos with a width of 16 feet and the hanging wall has not yet been reached. Just how much longer and wider the deposit is can be told only by further exploring, but it is known that it is one of the largest deposits of asbestos ever uncovered."

The article added, "In most mines the asbestos is found in narrow veins a few inches wide ... here it appears in an almost solid mass yards wide."

MONTANA, LIKE MOST OF THE WEST, is geologically complex.[3] Dozens of geologists have launched their careers against the folds, thrusts and faults of its confusing structure. And the area around Libby is no exception.

A U.S. Geological Survey diagram of what is known as the Libby Thrust Belt looks like a five-layer cake of sedimentary and volcanic rock cut into two dozen slices and stuck back together by a drunken pastry chef. No wonder, given the forces that have been at work on this land.

One and a half billion years ago, on the piece of the Earth's crust that would become North America, a rift began to open. The ocean spilled in, burying modern-day Montana and Idaho under ten miles of marine sediment and creating the great Belt Basin. The opening grew, and about 750 million years ago, a piece of the crust that had been west of the basin broke off and floated southward, eventually becoming part of Antarctica. Slowly, the remaining part began moving west. It collided with smaller chunks of crust moving east, building up the West Coast and, because of pressure from the collisions, folding the Belt Basin into the pealts and valleys known today as the Rocky Mountains.

Geologists say that the most active period of mountain-building in Montana occurred from 80 million to 50 million years ago, as the dinosaurs were giving way to mammals.

At that time, six miles east of what is now Libby, a plume of magma rose up from the mantle, pushed through the sedimentary Belt rocks and stopped about a mile beneath the surface. The molten magma was rich in magnesium — and in water. "The secret of the Libby deposit is that the magma that created it was very water-rich," says Art Montana, a renowned geologist who recently retired as professor and chairman of Earth and Space Sciences at UCLA and who has studied the Libby region — and Zonolite Mountain itself — for decades.

"Most high-magnesium magma of this type is not so water-rich. And that is why we have vermiculite and tremolite, because both those minerals have some form of water in their atomic structure," Montana says. That first plume of magma was joined by others, which formed a dike around it. "Then the whole mess began to cool." The initial plume formed biotite, a kind of mica, from a combination of potassium, magnesium, iron and aluminum silicate. "At Libby, there is this core of almost solid biotite right in the middle of the mine. It's beautiful stuff, with crystals about the size of big dining room tables, almost unique in the world," Montana says.

As the magma cooled even more, tremolite, a type of asbestos, took form. "It formed almost everywhere throughout that initial plug because there was water available there," Montana explains. "Also, there was a tremendous amount of tremolite that formed along secondary quartz veins and dikes of magma."

It would be tens of millions more years before Zonolite Mountain would get its vermiculite.

During that time, wind and rain eroded the crust above the biotite plug. Great sheets of ice flowed over the region from the north, scraping the earth as they moved. By the time the last of the ice receded about 12,000 years ago, the mile-deep crust above the biotite plug had disappeared, and the softer sedimentary rock around it began to erode, leaving the mountain. The erosion also allowed the elements to go to work on the biotite, which is not particularly stable in this weathering environment, Montana says, and is easily broken down. At Zonolite Mountain, it broke down into vermiculite.

THE FLEDGLING Vermiculite & Asbestos Co., the second company to form, certainly knew how to attract attention.

In 1927, Bolyard hired a Californian named Frank J. Buck, who was ostensibly a "chemist and metallurgical construction engineer," but whose greatest talent seemed to be mining stockholders, not vermiculite ore. He cultivated newspaper reporters, and was frequently quoted in Libby, Spokane and elsewhere about the company's great promise.

At the same time — and perhaps as a quid pro quo for the coverage — Buck wrote and placed a series of breezy, conversational newspaper advertisements. In one of them, he described his own bona fides: "After being expelled from a half dozen American mining schools, I decided to try that little school in Freiburg, Saxony, as I could handle the lingo before I could English." He added that on graduation, he went to work at a mine near Johannesburg, South Africa, "to hob nob with the black boys and see if I could get them to work." One of his ads, in May 1927, was headlined FOLKS: WATCH THIS BABY MAKE MINING HISTORY IN LIBBY, MONTANA.

"This baby" (the V&A stock issue) "is a dandy infant to slap your bet down on. I honestly believe that even $500 invested today ... will mean a meal ticket for life," he promised. "I'm a hardboiled engineer and take a pride in my profession and I'm not afraid to say she's a 24 carat investment at a dollar a share and going skyward right soon."

Meanwhile, Alley told stockholders that his own company continued to increase production and find new customers. Alley would not give Libby reporters any specifics, saying in a pointed reference to Buck and V&A that the publication of such information in the past "has been taken advantage of by others who are attempting to ride into public favor through Zonolite." In February 1928, Alley announced that the company's business had increased dramatically both in Montana and elsewhere, and specifically cited Grogan-Robinson Lumber in Great Falls, which had decided to offer Zonolite as a house insulation product. Later that year, he announced large orders shipped to Seattle, Los Angeles and Antwerp, Belgium.

In 1929, Keith and Alley won a contract to lay insulation in Spokane's federal building. Between 15 and 20 tons of Zonolite was sprinkled between rafters and joists above the ceiling of the fourth floor. And in Hollywood, film companies discovered Zonolite's sound-deadening qualities and began insulating sound stages with the material.

Despite Buck's bluster, he and the V&A Co. were not successful in finding a commercial market for the tremolite. Asbestos manufacturers were used to the chrysotile they got mostly from Canada, and they found the tremolite fibers harder to work with.

So, like the Zonolite Corporation higher up the mountain, the company quietly turned its full attention to the much easier and more fruitful task of marketing vermiculite.

Both companies were slowed by the Depression, but as it ended, both Alley and Bolyard realized that the market for vermiculite was expanding just as the mineral did when applied to heat. The heat they needed if they were to take advantage of the market was capital. The Zonolite Co. was mining by open pit and the Vermiculite & Asbestos Co. was still mining underground, but both operations were struggling to fill orders, still mining only by pick and shovel.

In 1934, control of both companies passed to groups of Midwestern businessmen.

In August, a group of Chicago industrialists headed by Phillip D. Armour and Lester Armour of the famed meatpacking business bought the Vermiculite and Asbestos Co., changed its name to the Universal Insulation Co. and announced aggressive expansion plans. They included conversion to open-pit mining, the building of a mill and the purchase of the first steam shovel to be used on Zonolite Mountain. Within two years the company had built a second, much larger mill.

A few months earlier, in May, a group headed by W. B. Mayo of Detroit, for many years chief engineer of the Ford Motor Company, took control of the Zonolite Co., keeping Alley in charge of production and announcing ambitious plans to increase production. The new owners announced that most of the ore would be shipped in raw form from Libby and expanded in plants elsewhere.

Alley's persistence had paid off. The future of his company was assured and his fortune made, but he did not get to enjoy it for long. He died in a Spokane hospital in March 1935 at age 56, the victim of diabetes, high blood pressure and septicemia from a strep throat.

His obituaries called him an "industrialist" and an "eminent business-man," but his death certificate did not. E. A. Alley passed from this world labeled simply "Miner."

The place Alley had named Zonolite Mountain would produce many more death certificates with the same designation.

THEY HAD THE SAME LIST of potential customers. They had the same product. And they were duplicating each other's efforts to get the product to market.

So it made a lot of sense when the Zonolite Co. and the Universal Insulation Co. decided to merge in March of 1939.

The new company was named The Universal Zonolite Company. Its board of directors included the Armours and one of their business partners, a retired U.S. Senator from Kentucky named R. N. Camden. The new president of the board was Charles T. Fisher, cofounder of the famed Detroit car-body manufacturing company. The only Libby man among all these glittering captains of industry was M. F. Gay, Alley's brother-in-law and still the proprietor of the Libby Hotel.

One thing the company had plenty of was customers. In 1940, vermiculite use set an all-time high across the country, mainly in house insulation, but also in concrete, wallboard and roofing. And the U.S. Bureau of Mines reported that more than 90 percent of the country's supply came from Libby, Montana.

World War II only increased demand. The Navy couldn't put up new buildings fast enough to meet its demand, and in many of them they used a mixture of Portland cement and Libby vermiculite to make solid-slab roof decking. It made for speedy, easy construction and well-insulated buildings, but the biggest reason the Navy chose Zonolite for its roofs was for fireproofing. John Myers, Zonolite's on-site superintendent, said Navy tests showed that an incendiary bomb hitting a Zonolite-and-cement roof deck simply burned itself out without spreading damage.

By 1942, the Navy orders meant the company had to improve its ability to ship expanded ore quickly. So it arranged with Great Northern to build a much larger plant on a railroad right-of-way just east of town. The big wood frame building, sided and roofed with shiny corrugated metal, held two furnaces that could expand up to 1,400 bags of Zonolite per day, running three shifts around the clock.

The old Universal Insulation mill was now processing all the ore mined on Zonolite Mountain, and in 1943, something happened to underscore just how much ore was being mined and milled. The pile of tailings, or waste rock, below the mill shifted and slid en masse down the mountain, demolishing the bins used for storage of ore concentrate. New, larger bins were constructed, and the pile began to grow again. No one was injured in the slide, though long before anyone thought about what the miners were breathing, everyone knew vermiculite mining was dirty, dangerous work. Unstable rock, heavy machinery and rough working conditions all contributed to a string of injuries on the mountain, but Montanans understood that work was like that — logging and sawmill work, ranching and metals mining were similarly hazardous.

The dust and the danger didn't keep the jobs from being in high demand as Libby's boys returned from the war, boys no longer, many with new families to provide for. And with an explosion of new construction across the country, the demand for Zonolite kept increasing as well.

Zonolite Mountain was like a heart now, pulsing with the roar of steam shovels, pushing its geological hellbroth of vermiculite and asbestos along the arterial rails, washing across the country in every direction, to hundreds of processing plants, warehouses, factories, suffusing the flesh and bone of a new society. It would be added into wallboard, into roofing, into garden products. And worst of all, it would be placed undiluted into sacks that carried no warnings, sold as insulation and dumped in dusty, deadly profusion inside millions of walls and acres of attics in houses across America.

Gayla and David Benefield's log home beside the Kootenai River is a peaceful getaway for the red-haired rabble-rouser, and the coffeepot is always hot in her much-visited kitchen. (Andrew Schneider)

NGER WAS A CONSTANT in Gayla Benefield's life — stoked steadily by years of suffering and death in her family, and by more years of bureaucratic indifference. Most of the time, it burned quiet, but occasionally events would bring it bubbling dangerously close to the surface. Which had just happened.

She had heard about the EPA team coming to town and being squired around by local officials and Grace's people. Gayla's grapevine worked well, and the more calls she got, the more she fumed. *We're being screwed again,* she thought. *Finally, the government comes to town, people who can do something, and they're spending their time with people who don't think there* is *a problem, or people who know the truth and will bullshit them.*

She was still seething when the phone rang yet again.[1] This time, she heard someone she didn't know introduce herself as Wendy Thomi, a community coordinator for EPA, whatever *that* was. She wanted to know if Gayla could come down to the Super 8 and "chat for a bit." *Well, I'll be damned,* thought Gayla Benefield.

Twenty minutes later, she sat in a folding chair at the motel's spartan "conference room." Les Skramstad and his wife, Norita, sat nearby and Wendy Thomi thanked them for coming.

She said she'd gotten their names from the *Post-Intelligencer* stories and said she was sorry for all the suffering they'd gone through. Then she told them why she was part of the EPA team.

Les listened.

"She didn't quite say 'I'm from the government and I'm here to help you,' but she came mighty close."

But then he listened harder and was impressed.

Thomi came from the Silver Valley in Idaho, a 20-mile-wide strip that cuts through Idaho from the Montana state line almost to Washington. Her grandfather was a miner — lead and silver — at the infamous Bunker Hill mine. Two of his brothers died in the Sunshine Mine fire. She knew the toll that mining could take. She also knew how a company could put profits before safety.

Silver Valley continues to be one of EPA's longest-running Superfund projects, because the smelters that dotted the valley spewed thousands of tons of dust laden with lead and other heavy metals, contaminating miles of the valley and the people who lived there.

"Maybe that's why I'm so shocked at what happened to Libby," she said.

It was enough to get Gayla, Les and Norita to tell their tales.

Thomi sat there for two hours with her mouth hanging open, stunned at what they said.

"Paul and the others have to talk to you. Now," Thomi said, and asked if they could meet again in the morning.

It was a little before 10 A.M. when three rental cars pulled up in Gayla's driveway and people started pouring out. *God, they're young,* Gayla thought, standing by the open door.

The state of Montana could make a tourism video at Gayla Benefield's larch log home, confirming every big-city stereotype of the Montana lifestyle. Trophies from critters of all kinds adorn the high log walls — a mountain lion, two elk racks, two deer heads, a bighorn sheep, a whole bobcat, a lynx, a big bass and a couple of football-sized trout. Three rifles and a century-old shotgun hang below, along with branding irons and old photographs and drawings of family members.

Coffee and water were passed around. All the dining room chairs were filled, and lawn furniture was hauled out of the garage so more could sit. Peronard, Weis, Miller, Thomi and Diana Hammer, another community coordinator from Denver, all crammed around the kitchen table. Les and Norita sat on the edge of the group.

Gayla listened to the introductions, eyed Peronard's shaved head, earring and tattoos and thought, *I asked for help, Lord, and the government sends us a hippie and two yuppies.* The one named Miller was a medical doctor? Weis was a toxicologist? Both looked a little nerdy, a little out-of-place, more like professors than down-and-dirty working-in-the-field-type guys. *This couldn't possibly be a scientific team,* she thought. *They don't look old enough to drink.*

She glanced at Les, who gave his head a little shake, smiled and shrugged.

Dressed in jeans and her favorite pink-and-gray-checked blouse, Gayla listened to Peronard describe his meeting with the town biggies, his tour of the mine and other Grace facilities. Totally out of character, Gayla kept her mouth shut and listened as Peronard told her that he and the rest of the team had literally hundreds of unanswered questions.

Oh, shit, she thought, *why not just tell them what was really happening? All they can do is go back to Denver and tell their bosses they met a crazy old woman.*

Speaking in a style much softer and far more sanitized than they would ever hear again from her, Gayla pulled out binders of Grace documents gleaned from years of buttonholing not only the Kalispell law firm but every other lawyer or expert witness she could find that had been involved with a suit against Grace. She shocked her EPA visitors with the irrefutable paper trail showing what Grace knew and when they knew it.

Gayla went back to her bedroom office for a moment and retrieved a copy of Grace's "alpha list."[2] She pointed out the workers' names and the company's estimates of each person's asbestos exposure by years.

As she brewed the third pot of far-too-strong coffee, she ticked off the names of those on the list who had died from asbestos-related disease.

Weis held the list with both hands and stared at the names and dates. It was obvious that Grace knew how much asbestos some 1,800 of their workers had sucked down. He couldn't believe it.

Pens flew across notebooks and Grace's confidential memos, reports and letters were passed around.

Les watched the government investigators' growing excitement at what they were hearing and reading, and he beamed. *About damned time,* he thought.

They strained to hear Les's answers to the technical questions they asked. He had spoken slowly and softly even before asbestos hardened his lungs, but he gave them the answers they needed. If he couldn't explain a document, Gayla could, and so it went, hour after hour.

Peronard watched Gayla, and was mightily impressed. *She's not the typical miner's daughter who's pissed at the company that killed her dad but doesn't know much about how it happened,* he thought. *She's knowledgeable and credible and she grasps exactly what Grace did.* As the team was beginning to do.

Gayla's words and the two green binders, each two inches thick, had done their work. They provided the team with solid evidence that either the officials they had talked to were amazingly ignorant, or they were lying. Here was solid evidence that Grace knew of the danger to its workers. And if they needed anything more palpable, more physical than words on paper, they had Les Skramstad in front of them, struggling for the breath to have a conversation he'd dreamt of for years.

So they were convinced that the vermiculite was contaminated with asbestos, that miners died because of it and that Grace knew it. But Peronard, Weis and Miller had nothing concrete to prove the newspaper's most frightening allegation: secondary exposure. That people other than the miners themselves, people who never even visited the mine, were dying. They didn't realize it that afternoon, but Norita Skramstad and Gayla Benefield were both living proof.

Gayla said she couldn't go into those details today. "It could harm people who are in court with Grace," she said, showing them the door and shoving the binders into Peronard's arms. "Maybe when you get back, we'll talk some more."

It was Thanksgiving eve before the EPA team got to Spokane for their flights back to Denver. On the way, they talked about Gayla, about what had made her the way she was. There was so much they didn't know.

FROM THE TIME HIS LIFE STARTED on the cold, unforgiving plains of southwestern North Dakota, Perley Vatland never had anything easy. [3]

His parents were homesteaders, Norwegian immigrants. Mathias Vatland actually sent back to Norway for his mail-order bride, Raghnild Smedesang, and as it turned out he was extremely fortunate. Raghnild was a strong, devout, industrious woman.

The homestead was unproductive, partly because the land was poor and partly because Mat Vatland wasn't particularly ambitious. Indeed, the farm produced almost nothing but a few chickens, some vegetables from the garden and eight children, including Perley in 1912. The Vatlands spoke only Norwegian, so Perley didn't learn any English words at all until he went to school in the tiny town of Rhame.

Rhame was about half German and half Norwegian, but even the other Norwegian kids spoke some English, and Perley was teased constantly because he didn't. They called him "Patches" because of his mended hand-me-down clothing.

In those terrible years of drought in the late 'teens and early twenties, hundreds of homesteaders actually starved or froze on the northern prairie. The Vatland family survived, barely, because of Raghnild's force of will. She was a preacher in the Norwegian community's Church of Christ, and she worked tirelessly for her family.

"The Lord will provide," Raghnild Vatland told her hungry children, but by the time he finished the sixth grade Perley had grown tired of waiting for divine providence and left home to make his way in the world. He was 12 years old, and he rode the rails and found food and work where he could. He taught himself mechanical skills, and he learned to drive, and so he was never without work for long.

He met Margaret Rody, the daughter of a prosperous Montana farmer, and they were married in 1938. They settled in Fort Benton, near Margaret's father's ranch, and a year later, their daughter Eva was born. Their second daughter, Gayla, arrived four years later.

His status as a father of young children kept Perley out of World War II. He worked the winters as a mechanic in a Fort Benton garage, and in the summers he'd work on the wheat harvest. After the war, the Vatland family got a huge windfall. With a prosperous economy forecast, Margaret's father decided to expand his own ranching operation — and enable his children to get a start in the same business. He gave his two boys allotments of about $20,000 apiece — a princely sum in 1946 — to buy themselves some land to farm, and he did the same for Margaret and Perley.

All three families decided to settle in the Libby area. They were all flat-landers — Perley from North Dakota and the others from the broad Missouri valley near Great Falls — and the mountains held a powerful allure. Perley bought the old Vinion homestead just east of Libby, a half-section bordered by the brawny Kootenai River, with the Great Northern tracks and a road known as the East 5th Street extension alongside. The property included the lower pastures toward the river and a steep clay banked foothill of the big Cabinet range that looms above the town. Libby Creek tumbled into the Kootenai along the edge of the ranch. The farmhouse and outbuildings were on a little knoll just beneath the hill. Perley bought some cattle, planted some alfalfa and got the place operating.

For little Gayla, it was an exciting time. On the ranch, the possibilities for mischief seemed endless. She was forever taking off for the barn, or the pasture. Perley was scared to death of the fast-moving water in the creek and the river, and forbade the kids from going near it. Margaret, considerably more practical, took Eva and Gayla down to Libby Creek and taught them to swim.

Perhaps Perley's fear of water was prophetic. In the spring of 1949, a massive snowmelt sent the Kootenai leaping from its banks. Much of the

Vatland farm was flooded, and if the river had crested over the railroad embankment, the farmhouse itself would have been swept away. It might as well have been. When the waters subsided, Gayla's mother took her out into the ruined alfalfa field, and they found Audrey, Gayla's old pet yellow cow, and all the others, with their legs sticking up in the air, drowned.

With them died the Vatlands' golden chance. Perley and Margaret put the farm up for sale and moved the family into a little house in town, on Michigan Avenue just across the alley from the Zonolite Co.'s expanding plant. Perley took a job at the lumber mill, and Gayla enrolled in first grade. It was a little odd, living in town, Gayla remembers — all those people around all the time — but for the first time the Vatlands actually had indoor plumbing and a telephone.

The Vatlands weren't quite finished with the farm. After a year, the buyers discovered that they couldn't make the place pay, either, and Perley repossessed it. The buyers had planned on converting the farm to a dairy operation and had built a large, well-insulated milking shed. The old house was in rough shape, so the Vatlands moved into the milking shed for the winter. It was plumbed with a big sink on one end, and the rough concrete floor sloped sharply down to the drain, but it was well insulated and comfortable enough.

Just then Margaret's father decided his granddaughters needed a piano, and not just any piano — he bought them a magnificent old Steinway, right out of one of Montana's most famous landmarks, copper baron Marcus Daly's mansion in the Bitterroot Valley.

Other Montana families may have lived in milking sheds that winter, but the Vatlands were certainly the only ones with a huge black grand piano. Perley was delighted; he loved music and had taught himself to play the fiddle years before. So the family often gathered around the piano, and the girls quickly learned to play.

The next year, Perley managed to sell the farm again, and the family moved back to town, piano and all, this time to the house on Minnesota Avenue that would be Perley's home for the rest of his life.

Perley didn't like working at the lumber mill, so he took a job delivering fuel oil and kept his eye out for something better. That summer, he thought he'd found it when he successfully bid a contract to provide school bus service. He had to invest in a brand-new bus, but he figured to recoup that considerable expense by doing his own mechanical work and driving the bus himself, which he loved. His route took him up Rainy Creek Road, where he picked up the kids from the cabins at the Zonolite labor camp, and then all the way to the tiny town of Warland and back.

Margaret's family had been prosperous largely because of their thrift, and she had inherited the trait. She wasted nothing, making her girls' dresses, using every bit of food. With the income from the bus contract, the Vatlands found themselves in better financial shape than they had been since they'd bought the farm.

Unfortunately, somebody in Libby's power structure noticed that the newcomer Norwegian from North Dakota was actually making money, and the next year Perley's supposedly sealed bid for the school bus contract was undercut by a dollar. It was a disaster worse than the flood. Perley was forced to sell the year-old bus to the new operator for pennies on the dollar, and once again found himself unemployed. As fall approached, Margaret didn't have any money to buy fabric for the girls' school clothes. But she was determined that they would have them, so she opened an account at Montgomery Ward and got them two dresses apiece.

Perley talked with Margaret about moving the family to California, chasing yet another dream, picking oranges and making a new life. But even in such straits, Margaret was hesitant to leave. Her family was nearby, and Montana was the only world she knew. So Perley tried one more thing. On that school bus route, he'd seen the huge Euclid ore carriers at the Zonolite mine, and had thought that he'd love to drive one someday. He knew it was good, steady work.

So in that desperate autumn of 1954, Perley announced that on the next day, September 17, Gayla's 11th birthday, his gift to her would be starting a new job that would keep him in Libby full-time with the family. His new job was at the Zonolite mine.

It would be a while, he said, before he got the seniority to apply for a job driving one of the big trucks. He would have to start like everyone did, as a sweeper at the "dry mill," where the ore was broken up into a usable size.

Gayla was thrilled. She knew it meant the family might actually have a few more dollars to spend. But it meant more than that to her. At a time when she was suddenly losing the companionship of her big sister — Eva, starting her freshman year of high school, dropped out and got married — and nothing seemed secure, Perley's job gave her the precious knowledge that her daddy would be there for her. It made the world more certain. She knew that her best friend Margie Barney's father worked at the mine. Her new fifth-grade teacher, Mrs. Kair, was married to a miner, too.

For Perley, at age 42, it meant that after all the disappointments, he had a chance to make a steady wage and provide for his family's future. "If I work there twenty years I'll get a pension," he told Margaret happily. "We'll have that, and the Social Security, and I'll be able to retire."

GAYLA'S MOTHER WAS ABOVE ALL a practical, straightforward woman. If Margaret Vatland wanted to find out how to spell a word, she looked not in the dictionary but in the Sears and Roebuck catalog. Everything she needed to spell in her world was there.

As the family settled into life with Perley's new work at the mine, Margaret did not let the improvement in the family fortunes lead to sloth or wastefulness. She still made most of Gayla's clothes, and she still changed the bed linens on Saturday, washed on Monday, sprinkled the clothing on Tuesday, ironed on Wednesday and cleaned the house every day. It was a major irritation when the wind blew from the east on washdays. The clothing and sheets on the line would be fouled with dust from the mine, and she would have to wash them all over again.

The dust was an ordeal in the house every day, not just from the wind but also from the filthy clothes Perley wore home each workday from the mine. Margaret would sweep him off on the back stoop every evening before he came into the house, but the dust got all over everything anyway. In 1957, a traveling salesman demonstrated a Kirby vacuum cleaner to the Vatlands, and they bought it for nearly $400 — a staggering amount of money, more than a month's pay for Perley. But it seemed to help with the cursed dust.

Perley could play fiddle and guitar — and often on weekends he'd play in one of Libby's bars for a little extra money, and for the fun of it. Gayla would often go with him, as she had throughout her childhood; she was the one who inherited Perley's musical aptitude. When Eva was five, she had taken piano lessons for a time, and would come home and practice on the Steinway for an hour a night. The next day, when Eva was at school, Gayla would amaze her mother by playing whatever her big sister had played the night before. So by the time she was ten, she had actually performed in a dance hall, singing "Don't Sell Daddy Any More Whiskey," and then being tucked into bed in the back of the hall while the party roared on.

About a year after her dad got his new job, Gayla took a job of her own — at the Dome movie theater downtown. She ushered, and sold tickets, popcorn and candy. Gayla liked being able to make a little money of her own. At the same time her father was making about $2.50 an hour at Zonolite, she was paid 35 cents an hour. It was enough to feed her independent streak, and help with the family expenses, but the job did curtail her social life. If she could get to school dances at all, she would arrive late, and alone — and some of the girls would laugh and call her "Popcorn Annie" because she smelled like the movie-theater popcorn.

Still, it beat babysitting — Gayla *hated* babysitting — and it was social in itself, working at the theater. She saw everybody in town. Most evenings, the only police officer on duty would buy a movie ticket from her, then tell her to watch the police station across the street from her ticket booth. There was a light rigged on top of the station that would glow red if there was a police call, and she'd go get him out of the audience when the light went on.

Down the street from the theater was the J&J Dress Shop, with stock much more fashionable, and expensive, than they carried at J.C. Penney or Montgomery Ward, where most people bought their clothes. Often, Margaret would see something there that Gayla liked, and simply make it herself, but Gayla remembers that by the time she was fifteen, the owners gave her a charge account of her own, and she shocked Perley and Margaret by buying a $20 dress. Each week, she'd take her $5 or $6 pay check and give the women who owned the dress shop $2 or $3, until she had her bill paid.

Gayla's adolescence in Libby was quite complex. Despite her parents' financial stresses, she'd had a cheerful, happy childhood. But school, and her job, and Libby's hierarchical, whispering smallness all made their impressions on her. Gayla was asthmatic, and therefore not athletic, and her parents didn't push her toward extracurricular involvement at school, because they didn't understand it. You were in school to get educated, period.

As she got older, Gayla began learning the verities of class in Libby: The children of merchants and teachers and managers from the sawmill and mine were the most popular, the ones with the best clothes and the most friends. The gentlemen's and ladies' clubs that existed in the days of E. A. Alley were still very much present. The gentlemen's club met for coffee downtown at 10 A.M. every morning, and they ran the town as they saw fit. The ladies met separately, and passed judgments every bit as absolute. Perley and Margaret and, by extension, Gayla, were layered lower, as immutably as the geology of Zonolite Mountain layered vermiculite and asbestos. Growing up in Libby, you were pigeonholed early. Children of bosses would be treated like bosses; children of laborers would be treated like their fathers.

Gayla had always done well in school; she was very intelligent and even better at test-taking than she was at the study itself. From the fifth grade on, when she scored 141 on her IQ test, her teachers would always be saying to her, "You should be doing better." But that notion was constantly at war in her mind with the downward pressures she felt all around her, more subtle but just as cruel as the taunts Perley had endured from the other children on the North Dakota schoolyard forty years before.

Adults can be cruel, too. On the day Gayla registered for high school, her world there was defined, as bare and ugly as the mountaintop scraped away. The high school principal said to her, "I don't know why you're bothering to register. Your sister quit when she was a freshman and got married." In that instant of anger and shame, Gayla knew precisely where she stood, and her self-esteem plummeted. She looked around and realized that, yes, she was smart, but she would never be smart enough to escape the town's expectations. Yes, she was pretty, but she would never be a cheerleader; cheerleaders were the daughters of Libby's elite.

Even with a $20 dress, she was still Popcorn Annie, and she would never be allowed to feel confident about the way she looked. "You need to be careful with that red lipstick," other girls would tell her. "That blond hair makes you look cheap." Forty years later, one of her ex-classmates told her, "You were the best-looking girl at Libby High." "Hell," Gayla snorted. "Don't tell me that shit now. Why didn't you tell me then?"

She worked nights at the theater, and weekends playing piano with Perley in Libby's rough-and-tumble bars. They'd make $20 or $25 apiece for playing a few hours of music, and it was the highlight of the week for both of them. Kids growing up in the '50s in Libby lived the *American Graffiti* experience — hotrods, poodle skirts, rock 'n' roll music — and Gayla remembers it fondly. When she was 16, Gayla got her driver's license. Of course she didn't have her own car, but sometimes she'd get to drive Perley's old '49 Plymouth four-door sedan. It was always filled with dust from Perley's work clothes, but she was used to that, like everyone in Libby, and she never gave it a second thought.

Perley loved his job at Zonolite. Within a year, he got the job he wanted, driving one of the big Euclid dump trucks. The bosses took notice of his excellent skills as a driver, and soon they promoted him again, assigning him to operate a road grader, building, repairing and maintaining the roads that snaked across the mine site. He was very proud of the trust and responsibility the company placed in him, and he took it seriously.

Gayla remembers clearly the day in 1959 when Perley came home and told her and her mother about a new benefit at the mine. They were going to start X-raying the miners' chests, he said. "Margaret, they want to X-ray our chests and keep us healthy, and it won't cost a thing," he told his wife proudly.

CHAPTER 4

Les Skramstad and his "lady," the Fender jazz bass guitar,
are rarely too far apart. (Andrew Schneider)

W AY TOO MANY QUESTIONS *have to be answered, and an-swered quickly,* Peronard thought as he drove from Kalispell to Libby for the second time. He and Weis had to start identifying places for the gaggle of contractors he'd hired to begin sampling dirt, dust and air around Libby for asbestos.

At the same time, Aubrey Miller had to go to Spokane to have a doctor-to-doctor talk with Alan Whitehouse, the specialist in lung disease who had not yelled "the sky is falling," but could be sitting on the clinical evidence to prove that, in point of fact, it was.

Peronard didn't know what to think about Whitehouse.[1] Gayla and Les had told him that the physician had a lot of cases, and the *Post-Intelligencer* had quoted from a deposition supplied by the Kalispell lawyers in which Whitehouse said that more people from Libby were being diagnosed every month. It just couldn't be true. Could it?

It's a 298-mile round-trip from Libby to Spokane, no big deal in the mountain West where people travel that far just to go shopping. Mike Spence, Montana's chief state medical officer, was in the car ahead, driving as if the huge log trucks and tight turns were meant to be ignored. In October and November, the Montana physician told Schneider he was "way off base," and that if lots of people in "Libby or any other place in Montana were sick or dying beyond the norm, my office would know about it."

Spence's chances of knowing about the asbestos-related illness were remote, because, unlike Whitehouse, most physicians who saw the lethal shadows on the X-rays either didn't know what they portended, or didn't want to know.

Miller knew the basics of what clinical signs to look for and was hoping that Whitehouse had even more expertise. *Does he know what he's talking about? Is he a hack? Is he in it for the money, generating cases for some trial lawyer?* Miller wondered as he drove. Whitehouse really didn't want to talk. He said he was being harassed by Grace and he wanted to keep a low profile. But from his brief telephone conversation, Miller felt the Spokane doctor was more concerned with his patients than with anything else.

Miller, aged 40, liked the mountains.[2] He was taken with the beauty of this country, and even amused by the romping wildlife that makes driving an endless challenge. Clearly not the kind of road hazards found in his native Chicago, where he grew up and went to Rush Medical College.

His residency in occupational and environmental medicine qualified him to be the medical man on the Libby team. His seven years working for the Centers for Disease Control as a disease sleuth doing health hazard investigations made him precisely the person to be driving through the Idaho panhandle to see Whitehouse. He wasn't wearing the white, Navy-like uniform authorized for commissioned officers of the Public Health Service. He is in fact a commander, but jeans and boots made for a less intimidating impression, he thought. Which was good, because Whitehouse was already uneasy about why a federal government doctor and Montana's medical director wanted an afternoon of his time.

Whitehouse's office, shared with his partner, was snug.[3] In the corner were the trappings of his specialty — models of lungs, a mounted cross-section of diseased tissue, memorabilia from the tuberculosis outbreak in the '50s, and an oak plaque with a pin from Whitehouse's fractured hip. It's a reminder to be careful, he told Miller and Spence.

He talked casually about his background. Miller thought it sounded like he was being very modest about some of the pulmonary research he had developed for NASA while in the Air Force. He sat back in his 1898 high-backed oak rocker, listening to the young government physician, and tried to figure out whether Miller wanted the information on Libby for political or clinical purposes.

Whitehouse possessed more than 250 files on patients from Libby. He agreed to show them to Miller, and to discuss some of them, to a point. They talked briefly about individual patients' histories and discussed their pulmonary function tests — how well their lungs were working. Miller and Spence examined X-rays and some CT scans. In each case they discussed, Miller privately confirmed Whitehouse's diagnosis: The lungs were being destroyed.

As a disease investigator, Miller was impressed with Whitehouse's work. *He really knows his lungs,* he thought. Two things quickly became apparent: Whitehouse was very competent — he was a far cry from a hack — and there was nothing sinister or self-serving in his motives. As he perused Whitehouse's case records, Miller was very surprised. He realized that the team's initial assessment of the *Post-Intelligencer* stories, and the situation in Libby, was far off the mark. Here was proof — Libby asbestos was killing people. What Miller needed to know was the extent of the problem: Was it limited to miners?

Unfortunately, no, Whitehouse said. He held up the chest films of a person who reupholstered seats in some miners' pickups and cars. Then those of the wife of a miner who had only worked for Grace for a few months. Then those of someone who, as a child, had played on the ore piles near the ball field.

Miller's head was swirling. He really couldn't believe what Whitehouse was showing him: documented cases of non-occupational asbestos exposure. He didn't doubt the pulmonologist's diagnoses, but their significance was enormous. This was a public health crisis. If it had happened in New Jersey, Ohio, Massachusetts or just about anywhere but a remote corner of Montana, he thought, flares would have gone up and an alphabet soup of agencies would have descended instantly on the site.

No, he'd never reported it because Montana officials had to know what was happening. It wasn't a secret, Whitehouse said.

Spence sat quietly through the interview, saying almost nothing. Miller had literally hundreds of questions, but Whitehouse said he'd gone about as far as he would without getting permission from his patients to discuss their specific cases. And also, he added, a lawyer from Grace was due any moment for yet another deposition. "We can talk again," he told the public health specialist, "if my patients agree."

Miller drove to the airport, dropped off his rental and booked a flight to Denver, his mind racing with how he was going to tell Peronard that he had a much larger problem on his hands than they had thought.

He wondered who all those people were. Were they still alive? He realized that the anonymity that shields most public-health investigations might be impossible to maintain in Libby, because the town was too small and, apparently, too many people were sick.

He had only recognized one name as Whitehouse dug through his large pile of files. Skramstad. Was it Les, the old cowboy he'd already befriended? How sick was he?

LES SKRAMSTAD CAME HIGHBALLING into Libby, Montana, one May day in 1954 like Casey Tibbs riding a big bronc, wild and free and full of dreams and the joyous jolt of being seventeen years old.[4]

He and his best friend, Phil Nelson, were going to go and be cowboys, and if Les had had to sell his saddle to put gas in his '41 Pontiac, so what? That wouldn't stop them. There was another saddle down the road somewhere.

Back on the farm near Velva, North Dakota, the Nelsons had lived just down the road from the Skramstads, and Phil and Lester were best buddies growing up. Les's dad was a horse trader and a good one, so Les knew all about horses. But his family had been too poor to have any cattle — they raised a few pigs — and he wanted to be a real cowpuncher.

When Les was 13, the auctioneer's hammer came down on his family's struggle to farm in North Dakota. Les and his family found themselves sitting in an empty house that evening in 1950, not even a pot to cook dinner in, so they put everything they had left into the car and headed to Wyoming. After a while, his dad found work in Kennewick, Washington, and it was from there that Les and Phil launched their dreams.

They knew they could find good cowboying jobs down in Pendleton, Oregon, but first they wanted to visit Phil's parents in Libby. They set out from Kennewick early in the morning and drove east all day. They pulled into Libby in the wee hours of the morning and went inside to visit, never giving the weather a second thought. It was cold, but nothing bad compared to what they'd grown up with in North Dakota.

The next morning, Les thought he'd go down and look the town over. It was fourteen below zero, and he got in the car and hit the starter button, and got an ugly clunk in response. Lifted up the hood and the old six-cylinder flathead block was cracked the full length, about half an inch wide.

Les hooked up some heat lamps and thawed the motor out, and the crack seemed to narrow a little. He took it to a welding shop in downtown Libby, and the welder told him, "I don't know if I can fix that or not, but I'll try. Cost you six bucks." Amazingly, he welded it and it held together. But after Les paid for it, there wasn't enough left in his wallet to buy a tank of gas, so he figured he'd better stick awhile, and find a job, get some traveling money.

He was still a month shy of his 18th birthday, so he couldn't hire on at the lumber mill, but he found work surveying for a Forest Service crew. A couple of weeks later he got his first paycheck and thought, *Man, another few weeks of this, and I'm going to be cowboying.*

Then one evening, Les saw a pretty girl walking down the street, and soon he decided to stay in Libby awhile, and went down to the sawmill and hired on. He courted the girl, who was named Norita, and he fell in love with her, and with Libby, too.

Les and Norita were married in December 1955. The photos from back then show Les, six feet tall and thin and strong as a braided steel hawser, his deep-set eyes staring out toward the future like a raptor's, focused hard on his dreams.

Les and Norita moved into a little house on Minnesota Avenue, right across the street from Perley Vatland and his family.

In March of 1957, Norita gave birth to Laurel Lee Skramstad. Les was proud and happy, but after Norita took little Laurel to visit her family in South Dakota, he thought, *It's now or never.* So he went to his boss and said, "I quit." Norita remembers it all too vividly. A telegram from Les arrived at her mom's house: "I quit my job." No explanation.

By now Les had a '48 Pontiac. He put everything he and Norita owned in the car and a little trailer — a washing machine, Laurel's crib, the whole works — and drove south to Three Forks, Montana, where the Madison, Jefferson and Gallatin Rivers join to become the Missouri, and started asking after cowboying jobs. Finally he heard about a ranch that might be hiring. He pulled into the yard at ranch headquarters about nine o'clock one night, the little trailer bumping and swaying behind him. The rancher told him to go grab a spot in the bunkhouse, and he'd get to chase some cows in the morning.

As it turned out, "chase" wasn't the right word. Les picked himself out a decent horse, and spent the next fourteen hours trying to move a herd of Herefords who clearly didn't want to go anywhere. By the time they got the cows where they were supposed to be that night, it was nine o'clock and Les hadn't even had lunch.

He saw a house near the pasture where they put the cows — in rough shape, no paint, nothing around it but mud and rocks. One of the other hands told him, "That's what this outfit calls a ranch house. They've got a bunch of them like that, all over, and they just move the hands around to them as they're needed."

Les thought, *Holy hell, that's what Norita and Laurel and I are in for. I can't do that to them.* After a couple of weeks, he sent Norita a telegram. "Forget it," it said.

By that time, Les had done some basic math. Cowboying paid $150 a month, plus room and board. He didn't think they'd make it on $37 a week.

After a while he figured, *Well, maybe I'll head for California. Lots of money there, and maybe I can find something that'll pay enough to support us.* It was a thousand miles to Libby and then another couple thousand to California. He left the trailer with Norita and headed west. He'd ask for jobs along the way, and somebody would say, "I think so-and-so needs a hand," and he'd drive around looking, burning gas, and the money would just drain away.

He stopped near Glasgow, Montana, and even now that place brings a bitter twist to Les's face. He got a job mixing paint for an outfit who had the contract to paint stripes on the runways of a big Air Force base. The wind was blowing so hard that when he'd open a can it would blow the paint right out before he could dump it into the machine. He figured out how to allow for that, but then the wind dropped suddenly and he spilled five gallons of paint all over his boots.

The contractor had told Les he wouldn't be paid until the job was done. Les had been living on a Snickers bar and a hamburger every day, and finally he got down to 13 cents and he could only buy the Snickers bar. When the job was done the boss said, "The checks are on the way from California. You'll have to wait until they get here."

For two days, Les had nothing to eat at all. He was sleeping in his car down by the tracks, weak and waiting for his money.

The man who ran the paint machine was black — the first black man Les had ever encountered in his travels through the very white West — and he gave Les a doughnut, which still sticks in Les's mind as one of the most memorable acts of kindness in his life. Finally the checks came and Les gassed up and got out of town. He was ravenous, but his cowboy pride wouldn't let him eat in Glasgow. He got to the next town before eating everything he could reach.

He abandoned the job search and hightailed it for Libby, where his parents were living. "Norita and Laurel are here," his mother told him. They had taken the train to Libby — without knowing it, sailing right by Les sleeping in his car in Glasgow.

Now it was time to quit chasing dreams.

"I had a serious talk with myself right then, and another one with Norita. We had no money and I knew I had to stop right there and get a job. My pride stood in the way of going back to the mill, even though they would probably have hired me. I hired on for a few temporary jobs, and Norita got a job at the bank. I'll never forget that banker. He knew what kind of a fix we were in. We were too young to borrow money, neither one of us twenty-one yet. He just opened his wallet and handed Norita a hundred dollars."

They tried nearby Kalispell, a slightly larger town, for a year, and while they were there, Les worked in a garage, and he started playing a guitar, just for fun. Before long, he was playing — and singing — for money, something he would do steadily for the next forty years. He realized that no matter what else he did for a living, playing music would mean that he and his family would never be broke again.

He started out playing rhythm, but one day the lead guitarist said, "I'm going to the rest room, play lead for me," and soon Les was playing lead guitar and singing. Les — and the people he played for — favored the country stars of the time, as well as the classics: Hank Williams, Roy Acuff, Jim Reeves.

In May 1958, the Skramstads' second child, Brent, was born, and when Norita became pregnant the following year, it was clear to Les that what he really needed was exactly what he had scorned as an 18-year-old: a good, steady job.

The family moved back to Libby, and Les drove a logging truck for a while, then gritted his teeth and went back to the sawmill. But he had his eye on the Zonolite mine. At that time, in 1959, it had been one of the most reliable employers in town for more than thirty years. The sawmill and lumber yard employed a lot more people, but the jobs at Zonolite paid a few cents more, on the average, and they just didn't lay people off. Employment had been climbing steadily as the mine continued to increase its production. Jobs there didn't come up all that often, because men hung on to them once they were hired.

So when a temporary construction job at the mine came up, Les went to the Zonolite office downtown and talked to them about it. "It's only for thirty days; there's no guarantee you'd stay on," the hiring manager said. "What can you do?"

"Anything I'm told," Les said with his trademark quiet confidence. He realized the folly of quitting a full-time job to take a 30-day job with no guarantees, and he could imagine how Norita, pregnant with their third child, would feel about it. But he gave in to his impulse, and said, "I want that job."

With an irony that would become exquisitely clear in later years, the company made him get a physical, then signed him on.

Les would never forget that first ride up to the mine. He had no idea what to expect, and when he arrived, he couldn't believe his eyes. Everything — ground, trucks, buildings, people — was brownish-gray in color, covered with fine dust. It was like stepping into a sepia-tone photograph. Everything he could see but himself was the same color, and it wouldn't be long before he matched exactly.

When he reported to the construction office, the boss said, "Have you ever been up here at the mine, or in the mill?"

"No."

"Well, you're going to have some fun today. We're going to start you over at the dry mill, as a sweeper."

"I thought I was supposed to be on construction."

"Don't worry, we don't pay any attention to that. You start as a sweeper. You need to go over to the warehouse and get yourself a respirator, then head over to the dry mill."

So, just as Perley Vatland had done five years earlier, Les started his Zonolite career sweeping out the mill. That first day, he walked over to the warehouse and got his respirator. "Wear it if you can," he was told. He didn't exactly know what that meant, but he just fitted it together and put it on. Somebody directed him to the manlift — a foot-wide conveyor belt with steps on it — and told him to ride it to the top of the mill, seven floors up. "Start up there at the top and just sweep it all down," he was told.

When he got off at the top level, it was obvious what he had to do. The dust was more than a foot deep in places. Each floor had shovels and brooms, so Les set to with determination. But after about 15 minutes, his respirator was clogged with dust and he couldn't breathe.

He rode the lift down to the bottom, saw a couple of workers, and asked, "How do you clean these things out?"

"Oh, just use an air hose and blow them out, or you can wash them out with water," he was told. So he blew the fine, feathery dust out of his respirator, went back up and kept working.

By the time he'd finished one floor he'd cleaned his mask out four times. And of course the second-highest floor was twice as deep, because it held all the dust he'd swept down from above. By the time he got the second level done it was time for lunch. Les tried to clean as much of the dust from his head and face as he could. He found that it wasn't easy — the dust would cling to his skin. He looked around, and noticed respirators hanging on hooks all around the mill, and nobody else seemed to be wearing one.

When he went into the lunchroom, a couple of the supervisors were there, Tom DeShazer and Pete Watts, and a couple of the other miners.

"How do you like that dust?" one of them asked.

"That's the damnedest stuff I've ever seen in my life," Les responded with feeling, and the miners all laughed as though he'd told the funniest joke you could imagine.

"You don't worry about that dust," one of the supervisors said. "It's a nuisance, but there's nothing in it that will hurt you. You'll get used to it."

Les ate his lunch and went back to work.

He tried washing his respirator out, and that proved to be a big mistake. He'd tried to blow the moisture out of it, but what remained made it clog up faster than ever. So eventually his found its way to a hook like all the rest.

Each floor was worse than the last. Les's battle with the never-ending blizzard of dust was truly mythical in proportion, like Hercules cleaning the Augean stables. People would normally think of dust being light, but in such quantity it is surprisingly heavy. Finally he got the place swept down to the basement, where there was a waste conveyor that took the accumulation to the tailing pile. Of course, every time he moved the stuff, he sent more dust into the air.

When he got on the bus to ride back to town that night, he was covered in dust, just like everybody else. His hair was coated, his ears and nose were plugged up. His throat felt like sandpaper. The dust clogged his mouth and nose with what felt like thick brown syrup.

He cleaned up the best he could when he got home, and he didn't say much to Norita about his battle with the dust. He knew she wasn't very happy about his taking the job in the first place, and he didn't want her to be concerned.

He looked at his lovely pregnant wife, and hugged Laurel and Brent, and smiled. *It's okay,* he thought to himself. *I'll bet there's always something that needs doing up there. Sooner or later they'll move me to something else. And if I do a really good job at this, maybe they'll keep me.*

LIKE PERLEY, LES SKRAMSTAD grew to love his job. There was just something about working up on the mountain that drew the men close to one another.

For one thing, they shared the bus ride in the mornings from the parking lot where they met at 7 A.M. to the mine site. In the evenings, they rode back on the filthy old bus, tired, hungry, thirsty for the beer many felt they deserved after their hard work. Perhaps that was it, the work: the sense of shared toughness, having the collective grit and gumption to overcome the harsh physical challenges of cold in the winter, heat in the summer, the demands of the bosses, the pressure to produce and the dust, always the dust.

And there was the pride of getting it done, drilling the blast holes and loading the dynamite and caps and knocking down a little more of the mountain into usable chunks. Driving the Euclids, or "yukes," as they were known; running the conveyors and the skip track and the mill. Keeping all the machinery working, keeping the dust swept and watching the carloads of milled ore leave the mine, headed literally all over the world. And you had to trust the men you worked with, because one way or another, you put your life in their hands just about every day.

A man felt a part of something bigger than he was, something that was putting the food on his table, making a life for his family and his friends' families. You could take a measure of pride in that, yes sir — being good enough to beat the mountain, to beat the weather, to beat the dirt and the danger, to claim a piece of the Montana life for you and yours. And Les made good friends quickly on Zonolite Mountain.

He swept the dry mill for only about a week, and then he was put to work doing some maintenance on the skip track, a little railway that took cars from the bottom of the mill, where the operator would load them with the sparkling ore, freshly milled into thin pieces ranging from less than an inch to a couple of inches in length, to the storage bins, where they would be dumped and returned. The skip track ran continuously, and in order to repair the ties Les had to be very alert for cars on the tracks. The company put production over all else. He would hear the car coming down that steep track — *feel* it coming — as he worked feverishly on the ties. When it got there, he knew, he'd better not be in the way, because it wasn't going to stop.

The work on the skip track took another week or so. One day, on his way to the lunchroom, Les noticed a job posted on the bulletin board. The job was called "dump boss." Les hadn't even been up to where the actual mining was done, so he wasn't sure what the job entailed. But he thought he'd apply for it, just in case, because he was still worried about his status, which was officially temporary. He knew that anybody with more seniority than he had, which was just about everybody else on the hill, would beat him out. But his application, he thought, would show the company that he was interested in staying around.

Apparently, nobody else applied for the job, because Les got it.

When he found out, Les was nervous at first. If nobody in the whole place wanted the job, maybe it was particularly hard, or dangerous, or dirty. But as it turned out, it was a good job. It consisted of guiding the "yuke skinners," or drivers of the Euclids, as they dumped their big drawers of waste rock.

The job put him into contact with Orville Thorne, the superintendent of the mine operation, and they quickly became good friends. Thorny was a nice guy and was liked very much by the men who worked for him. For instance, he asked Les one day, "Would you like to join the credit union?" Les had no idea what a credit union was. Thorny explained that Les could get money taken out of his check for savings, and that if he ever needed to borrow money for anything, the interest rates were pretty low. And that's how Les managed to buy his first house.

The new job was just fine. "All I had to do was be alert," he said. He was there to direct the drivers to a safe place to dump their loads, and he was always very careful. The yukes themselves were pretty dangerous machines. Big Cummins diesel, five-speed gearbox, Plexiglas windows that were scratched up right away by the dust, and a crude seat. Not much for headlights, despite the fact that they were used at night. They were in use constantly, and the brakes were always worn. They held maybe 20 yards of waste rock, some of the pieces as large as cars.

Les would walk the perimeter of the site steadily, monitoring the stability of the waste. When a yuke showed up to dump its load, Les would walk alongside as the driver moved it into position and make sure the load got dumped in the right place. That was it. And he loved it. The work was outdoors, and a side benefit was getting to know all the drivers pretty well. They had a tough job, and they appreciated his help.

"I was content as a calf next to its mother, getting five or six square meals a day," Les said. "The job was great, and so were the people I worked with."

Every once in a while the mill would get a very high grade of vermiculite ore from the mine, and when that happened, the waste operation would all but come to a halt. At times like that, Thorny would come get Les and ask him to help with other tasks. One day he said, "You're going to help us with the blasting." He and Les took a pickup over to the bunker where the dynamite was stored, and Thorny began tossing boxes of dynamite into the truck bed. Thorny saw Les turn white, and laughed. "Don't worry, this stuff is perfectly safe. It's those little caps I've got in the safe up in the office you have to worry about."

Still, the huge dynamite sticks, two inches across and maybe a foot and a half long, made Les nervous enough. He helped drill about a hundred holes that day, and pushed six or eight of the big sticks into each of the holes, and they set the charges, and wired them together, and set the caps, and Thorny hit the plunger, and it seemed to Les like the whole mountain lifted up. A huge cloud of dust billowed out, and rocks the size of refrigerators flew through the air, and after a few more times like that Les told Thorny,

"You know, I wish you wouldn't put me on any more of those blasts. I just don't like it." And Thorny never did.

Meanwhile, another friend, Bob Cohenour, had been telling Les about what a good job he had down in the expanding plant in town. In the old corrugated shed built in 1943 to process ore for rail shipment, the company was experimenting, trying to find new uses for its product, and Cohenour was one of the hands who worked there. He urged Les to apply for a job there, but Les refused, saying he liked the job and working for Thorny.

It took tragedy to make him reconsider.

The fourteenth of December, 1959, dawned cold, and it had snowed a little bit overnight. By late afternoon, though, some of the snow had melted, and the surface of the road the yukes used between the mill and the dump site was greasy-slick. Les was working days that week, and just a few minutes before the end of the shift at 5 P.M., one of the yuke skinners, Gordon Torgeson, brought his rig in, dumped his load and said, "I'm taking these chains off. I can't stand them."

Les protested. "You've only got twenty minutes. The night crew will need them on anyway. Why don't you just leave them?" But Torgeson refused, and he unhooked the chains and removed them, and roared away.

Pretty soon one of the other drivers came burning up to the dump with no load in his truck. "Torgy's hit the bank," he yelled at Les. "Down by the office. Come on." So Les went down to see what had happened. Torgeson had lost control of the Euclid, and had been thrown out, and then run over by it. It was the first time Les had ever seen anyone killed, much less a friend.

Not one word was spoken on the long, dusty bus ride down the mountain that night.

Norita was in the hospital, and she'd just had their third child. They named her Gayla, because they liked Gayla Vatland, and her name. Les went to see Norita and little Gayla, of course, but he wasn't in much of a mood to celebrate.

After Torgeson's funeral, Les went down to the expanding plant and saw Bob Cohenour. Thorny had asked Les to take Torgeson's job as a yuke skinner. Les had driven the yukes from time to time, and even though he loved driving trucks, he didn't like driving the Euclids. He didn't think they were safe, and so he told Thorny he didn't want the job.

He asked Cohenour, "Is that job here still open?"

"Sure is."

"I'll take it."

The job included shifts on the millwright crew, as well as working around the experimental lab at the expanding plant. A fellow never knew what challenges would face him from day to day, and so he had to be good at just about everything.

It opened a new aspect in Les's life. He was pretty young, and while working around the farm was a good start, he hadn't developed a lot of skills yet — what's called simply being "handy" in Montana — and he was now working with a pretty handy crew. Cohenour, for example, was an expert welder and metal worker, and he made a point of teaching Les those skills. He also stressed something that Les had already seen, up close: It was a dangerous place to work. Safety was at the bottom of the list of priorities for the company, and you had to learn to look out for yourself and for the men you worked with.

The role of millwright was very important to the mine operation. The dust that covered everything was enormously abrasive, and it was hard on equipment of all kinds. Any part that moved would inevitably have problems; it was forever like rubbing sandpaper against sandpaper. Things broke all the time, and as millwright you were expected to know how to fix them. Downtime was not to be tolerated.

The only drawback to the job, in Les's eyes, was his foreman, a man named Dave Robinson, who would tell the crew to do things that they knew wouldn't work. They'd tell him, he'd insist, and sure enough, his way wouldn't work.

Robinson was royalty at Zonolite — his family owned the expanding plant for vermiculite in Great Falls, which was one of the biggest outlets in the state for Zonolite insulation. And he was married to the daughter of A. T. Kearney, one of Zonolite's original board members and for several years the board's chairman. The company had entrusted Dave Robinson with a job they considered vital: finding new, marketable ways to use both Zonolite and the other major raw material in the ore, the one now being discarded by the ton — tremolite asbestos.

Sometimes, this effort bordered on the absurd. Along with quite serious experimentation with animal-feed mixtures containing Zonolite, on February 3 a cook named "Mrs. Schermerhorn" baked at Robinson's direction several loaves of bread using various proportions of "No.4 feedgrade" Zonolite.

A report on the experiment found the results to be "certainly encouraging."

Mrs. Schermerhorn found that the loaves rose much more quickly than ordinary bread, and the report on testing indicates that for several days after baking, the bread did not develop mold when kept "in a filing cabinet in the office which has been humidified by a glass full of wet Vermiculite." The report does not include any comment on how the bread tasted.

The first time Les Skramstad ever heard the word "asbestos" was in 1960.

"I want you to go up to the mine and bring back a pickup load of asbestos," Dave Robinson said that day.

"What's that?" Les asked.

"Oh, you know, it's that grayish-white stuff that's around in the rock. That's called asbestos."

So Les and Bob Cohenour got picks and shovels and drove up to the mine in a short-box Dodge pickup. They ran into Thorny, who asked, "What are you fellows after?"

"We're supposed to get a load of asbestos."

"Oh, we got lots of that," he said. "Follow me."

So they drove up to one of the levels where the miners were working, and Thorny showed them how the asbestos lay across the other rock, in seams. He pointed to one. "That's probably the easiest to get right there, but if you need more of it, just let me know. It's everywhere up here."

So Les backed the pickup up to that seam. It wasn't hard shoveling — it was soft, almost soapy in consistency. It didn't take them long to get a load and head back to town with it. They didn't bother to cover the load with a tarp — why would they?

When they got back to the plant, they put down a sheet of Kraft paper, maybe 12 feet square, and dumped the load on it. They spread it out shallow so it would dry.

"Now, this has got to be plumb dry and pure," Robinson said. "You've got to get everything else out of it. No rocks, no vermiculite, no nothing."

It took them about two weeks of work. They found they couldn't put fans on it, because when it dried it would turn to dust and blow away. They put electric heaters around it, and got down on their hands and knees, right over it, picking rocks out of it.

The asbestos got very fluffy as it dried, and they were gradually getting it "clean." But they realized that in order to do so more efficiently, they had to come up with some method other than picking through it by hand. So they built a jig that would vibrate the stuff and shake out the heavier impurities. They had to run each batch through time and time again, but finally they got down to pure asbestos. They put it in 30-gallon garbage cans and closed them tight, so a draft wouldn't blow through and take it away.

Les remembers workers from the mine coming in and razzing him and Bob about their little project — particularly a friend, Don Riley, who would say, "You still playing with that stuff?" They'd take the tops off the cans and stick their arms in, and they'd go right through the stuff, clear to the bottom, and when they drew their arms out they'd look like they had feathers.

Les and Bob would brush them off and say, "Damn it, don't do that, we're trying to save that stuff." Finally, they took small sacks, like cement sacks, filled them and sewed them shut. That first time, they produced maybe 20 sacks.

Bob and Les were relieved when they got done with that load, because it was a nasty job. Of course, nobody had said anything to them about any danger, so they didn't wear respirators while they were cleaning the stuff, trying to get 100-percent obscenely pure tremolite asbestos.

But pretty soon, Robinson came back and said, "Go up and get another load of that asbestos. We've got so much of it up there, we've got to find a use for it. There's enough of it to last a hundred years."

Of course, Bob and Les were excited by that idea, because if they found a use for the asbestos, it could mean jobs for them and other men for a long time. So back they went, and Thorny said, "You boys after another load of asbestos? Well, you know where it is." They spent a full month shoveling and cleaning and packing the asbestos.

Robinson was an engineer of some sort, and he was full of ideas. He had one that Les actually thought made a lot of sense. Robinson wanted to develop a fire retardant that firefighters could take to a fire and spray on it, along with the water, and the asbestos and vermiculite would slow the fire down much more than just straight water. So they took No.4 ore, very fine stuff, and mixed it into a slurry and experimented with pumping it through a two-inch fire hose with a nozzle on it.

Here is Les Skramstad's worst nightmare, even worse than the month of inhaling the pure asbestos that probably sealed his own fate:

"We demonstrated this on several different occasions to people who came in from somewhere. I thought it could be the ideal product. This stuff didn't weigh anything, and it could be taken to a fire easily. So we were gung ho on it, and again we thought anything that was good for the company was good for our jobs. So we worked really hard on this."

He pauses for a moment. He can't tell the rest of it without choking up. It's easy to say he shouldn't have any guilt, this kind, smiling man who loves music, this principled man who would never hurt anyone if he could help it, who was just doing the best he could for his family. It's easy to say that he was following orders, that he had no idea what the stuff could do. But the guilt is in his eyes, the way they glisten, and in his voice as it cracks:

"And oh, Jesus, what I did was I sprayed that stuff all over near that building, over by the ball fields, on the trees and the brush to see how it would stick. Those ball fields, where everybody's kids played.

"Where my kids played."

LES SKRAMSTAD LEFT THE MINE after a couple of years. He would have stayed for the rest of his career, but Norita, ever restless in Libby, wanted to move back to Kalispell.

They did so, and stayed for five years, but eventually, they would return to Libby and raise their family there. Les worked at the Chevy garage, and played music nights and weekends, and the Skramstads quietly enjoyed their lives, their kids, and soon enough, their grandkids.

In early 1996, Les had a cough that he just couldn't shake.

He didn't think much of it. It had been a hard, cold winter, and he just figured he had a touch of bronchitis. But Gayla Benefield wasn't so sure. She started getting after Les. "You know how she is," he says now. "I'd cough while we were talking, and she'd ask me, 'Do you do that often? And have you had your lungs checked? How long did you work up at the mine? You better go and see the doctor, make sure you're okay.'"

She suggested that Les go over to see Dr. Whitehouse in Spokane. Whitehouse had already treated several people from Libby.

Finally, as much to get Gayla off his back as anything, Les made an appointment, and he and Norita got into their '89 Dodge and took the five-hour drive over to Spokane one spring day in 1996. Les was a little embarrassed about the whole thing when he got there. He told the nurse, "I don't feel sick."

Alan Whitehouse put him at ease right away. The doctor was middle-aged, and he wore a Western shirt and cowboy boots. He looked over Les's information and said, "So, you're from Libby, eh?"

"Yes."

"Well, I've got a pretty good idea why you're here."

"You do?"

"Yep. Take your shirt off, we're going to do a chest X-ray and a breathing test."

So they X-rayed Les, and then the nurse took him into a room and put him in front of a machine to measure how well his lungs were functioning. She put a mouthpiece in his mouth, and put a clip on his nose, so he wouldn't lose air that way. She had him breathe, in and out, slowly at first and then more rapidly.

After she was done, Les put his shirt back on and waited for the doctor.

About 45 minutes later, Whitehouse came back into the room and leaned on the examining table and said, "Well, you've got active asbestosis." No hemming and hawing, no bullshit. Les recalled the doctor telling him he had between five and ten years to live. He gave Les an inhaler and said to take a puff on it three or four times a day, and told him, "We'll want to check you again."

Les was stunned. He really didn't know what asbestosis was, but he knew he didn't feel bad enough to be dying. He hadn't worked at that mine for thirty-five years. How do you comprehend something like that? He took the inhaler, and walked out to the front desk and said, "Send me a bill," and he and Norita got in the car and started home. And he didn't say anything at all until they'd gotten almost halfway home.

He pulled over to the side of the road, and stopped the car, and shook his head.

"What's the matter?" Norita asked.

Les looked at her and said, "By God, you know, I believe I just got a death sentence."

U.S. Public Health Service physician and epidemiologist Dr. Aubrey Miller and EPA senior toxicologist Chris Weis worked tirelessly to understand why the asbestos contaminating Libby seemed so highly toxic. (Cold Truth)

P AUL PERONARD FELT like he was boxing blindfolded, trying to figure out how to attack an enemy he couldn't see. This stuff wasn't in 55-gallon drums, and it wasn't like the acid drainage from hard-rock mining that made creeks run red and green, like radiator water. He knew that he'd better get up to speed on asbestos, and fast.

He had help in this. Miller and Weis's medical and scientific training gave them a sound foundation, and they knew where to find the information the team needed. They were forever bringing Paul passages from the ample body of evidence that showed the lethality of asbestos, its use through history, and most important the enormity of the corporate coverup of asbestos dangers over the past century. As he read more, he began to realize the context he was dealing with in Libby. He was shocked to find that the case could be made that asbestos was the biggest corporate health scandal in U.S. history, dwarfing events like Bhopal; that hundreds, no, thousands of people had been killed from preventable exposure to an asbestos hazard that was systematically obscured by an industry determined to preserve profits.

Asbestos has been known to civilization, both for its miraculous properties and for its danger to health, for thousands of years.[1] Archaeologists studying the Paleolithic period of the Stone Age found asbestos fibers in debris dating back 750,000 years.

Greek and Roman stonecutters chided their slaves to avoid digging in quarries where deposits of peculiar silken fibers weakened the integrity of the stone. But slaves found that heavy pieces of rock could be easily shoved along a wall or stone walkway atop a path of slippery, wetted asbestos fibers.

To their puzzlement, they also found that when they tossed bundles of the thin fibers into the fire pits used for heating and cooking, the fibers were still there the next morning, unscathed among the cool ashes of the pit. They called the material asbestos, which some linguists say comes from a Greek word meaning "inextinguishable" or "unquenchable."

Others insist the name comes from a Latin word meaning "unsoiled." Romans wove the asbestos fiber into a cloth-like material that was sewn into table coverings and napkins. Supposedly, according to some researchers, these were cleaned by throwing them into a fire, where the asbestos cloth came out not only unscathed but whiter than when it went in — thus the name.

The Romans and Greeks did not have early versions of OSHA or EPA, but someone back in the time of Christ figured out that slaves weaving flax and asbestos into fabric were being sickened and killed. Pliny, the Roman historian, described the thin and nearly transparent membrane from the bladder of a goat or lamb being used as the world's first respirator to keep asbestos fibers from inflicting what Pliny called "the disease of slaves." This apparently had little to do with public safety, but rather the difficulty of replacing skilled slaves.

In 83 A.D., asbestos was used in Rome for the wicks of the eternal flames of the Vestal Virgins. Archaeologists say that the asbestos wicks on some of the recovered "virgin lamps," which were about the size of a softball, could still be lit when found in ruins more than a thousand years later.

It is thought that in 755 A.D., Charlemagne wrapped the bodies of his generals in woven asbestos shrouds before they were placed on funeral pyres so their ashes would not be mixed with those of the fire. Asbestos clothing was also used during this period as funeral clothing for the cremation of kings.

The French, German and Italian knights who fought in the first Crusades of 1095 A.D. to free Jerusalem developed huge weapons to break the sieges they encountered. Historians say a catapult called a trebuchet could fling huge rocks a great distance. It was made more terrifying and lethal when flaming pitch or tar was placed in bags sewn from asbestos fabric and launched over the city walls.

In 1280 A.D., Marco Polo wrote of finding garments "woven of a fabric which would not burn" in his travels in China. For centuries afterward, asbestos was little more than a novelty. But by the late 1800s, the British, Italians and Germans had found practical, commercial uses for what many were calling "the magic fiber." Almost every mechanical device invented and built had asbestos somewhere in the design. Motor vehicles, ships, trains, electric turbines, huge boilers and the massive web of piping that ran through most factories had coverings of asbestos.

The unique physical properties of the mineral made it a cornerstone of the industrial revolution. Asbestos can withstand the fiercest heat, and it is resistant to the strongest acids and alkalis and to rain, wind and salt water. It was described in sales catalogs of the early 1900s as being "feather light" but possessing "the tensile strength of steel."

In Italy, Africa and Canada, asbestos was unearthed more and more quickly as new mining equipment and techniques were developed.[2] It wasn't long before the increased use of the mineral took its toll on worker health, and physicians began to notice. In 1897, a physician in Vienna wrote that pulmonary problems in asbestos weavers and their families left no doubt that dust inhalation was the cause, reported Dr. Barry Castleman in his authoritative 1996 volume *Asbestos: Medical and Legal Aspects*.

A year later, in 1898 in Great Britain, the Lady Inspectors of Factories were the first to sound the alarm on asbestos dangers to workers because of "widespread damage and injury of the lungs, due to the dusty surrounding of the asbestos mill."

An Italian physician reported the deaths of 30 asbestos miners and workers in an asbestos-weaving plant. The same year, Castleman reports, there were 16 deaths from pulmonary fibrosis at a French asbestos textile plant.

Years after the asbestos industry proliferated in the United States in the early 20th century, many in industry and government continued to claim they had no knowledge of the dangers of asbestos. Yet in June of 1918, the Commerce Department published a study called "Mortality from Respiratory Disease in Dusty Trades." In it, the author, Frederick Hoffman, on loan to the government for the project from Prudential Insurance, made it clear that the dangers of asbestos were far from a secret. "In the practice of American and Canadian life insurance companies, asbestos workers are generally declined on account of the assumed health-injurious conditions of the industry," Hoffman wrote.

In 1930, North America's largest asbestos company, Johns-Manville, produced a confidential internal summary about medical reports of asbestos-worker fatalities, says Castleman.

Paul Brodeur, author of the landmark 1985 asbestos work *Outrageous Misconduct,* cited a 1932 letter from the U.S. Bureau of Mines to asbestos manufacturer Eagle-Picher that states: "It is now known that asbestos dust is one of the most dangerous dusts to which man is exposed."[3]

In 1933, Metropolitan Life Insurance Company doctors found that 29 percent of workers in a Johns-Manville plant had asbestosis. In the same year, Brodeur found, Johns-Manville officials settled lawsuits by 11 employees with asbestosis on the condition that the employees' lawyer agree to never again "directly or indirectly participate in the bringing of new actions against the Corporation."

Court documents show that in 1934, executives at Johns-Manville and Raybestos watered down an article written by a Metropolitan Life Insurance Co. doctor about the dangers faced by asbestos workers. A year later, the same two companies ordered the editor of *Asbestos Magazine,* a trade publication, to publish nothing about the hazards of asbestosis. In mid-1936, five large asbestos companies agreed to pay for studies on the health effects of asbestos dust, but they demanded that they maintain complete control over the reporting of the finding, Castleman found.

Court documents contain pages of confidential 1942 Owens-Corning corporate memos that quoted from and referred to scores of examples of medical literature on asbestosis and the health hazards of asbestos.

Other court documents gathered by Dr. David Egilman record accounts of a 1943 discussion in which Johns-Manville's president denounced managers of another asbestos company as "a bunch of fools for notifying employees who had asbestosis."[4] When one of the managers asked, "Do you mean to tell me you would let them work until they dropped dead?" the response was reported to have been "Yes. We save a lot of money that way."

Despite this widespread knowledge, in the early 1940s, asbestos went to war. Ads in *Life* magazine and the *Saturday Evening Post* proclaimed the ubiquitous fibers heroes of the war effort. By 1942, the War Production Board had declared asbestos a "critical war material," and soldiers guarded the stockpiles and asbestos manufacturing plants. Trainloads of the fibers, mostly from mines in Canada, were rushed to scores of factories, where they were transformed into thousands of miles of insulation, millions of gaskets, brakes, fabric and a thousand other products before being hustled to shipyards and plants where tanks and aircraft were built. The human toll from asbestos in the war was enormous. The government estimates that more than 4.5 million shipyard workers were exposed to asbestos during World War II, and thousands more during the Korean War.

Of course, GIs lived and fought while surrounded by the fibers. Sailors slept with asbestos-wrapped pipes beside their bunks. Tank crews and pilots worked wrapped in asbestos cocoons, and almost everyone breathed air through asbestos filters in their gas masks. And more than half a century later, sailors, airmen and merchant mariners are still dying from being exposed to asbestos. According to the U.S. military's own estimation, almost as many military personnel were killed from exposure to asbestos in World War II as by the enemy.

After the war, the industry's growth — and its deception — continued. In 1951, asbestos companies removed all references to cancer before allowing publication of research they had sponsored. The following year, Dr. Kenneth

Smith, Johns-Manville's medical director, recommended unsuccessfully that warning labels be attached to products containing asbestos. According to Castleman, Smith later testified: "It was a business decision as far as I could understand.... The corporation is in business to provide jobs for people and make money for stockholders and they had to take into consideration the effects of everything they did. If the application of a caution label identifying a product as hazardous would cut into sales, there would be serious financial implications."

Castleman cites a letter written by National Gypsum's safety director in 1953, intended for the Indiana Division of Industrial Hygiene, recommending that acoustic plaster mixers wear respirators "because of the asbestos used in the product." Another company official noted that the letter was "full of dynamite," and urged that it be retrieved before it reached its destination. A memo in the files noted that the company "succeeded in stopping" the letter, which "will be modified."

MEANWHILE, THE EXPOSURE to workers and consumers continued to grow. By the 1950s, it's doubtful that there was a home in the United States that didn't contain products made with asbestos.

Asbestos-lined barbecue mittens became a popular Father's Day gift. Irons, ironing board covers, hot plates, toasters, heating pads, hair dryers, the lining of some ovens and the motors in some refrigerators all contained the fibers. The outside of the house could be covered in asbestos shingles — both walls and roof. Inside, the kitchen and bathroom floors could be asbestos tile, the wallboards might be made with a blend of cement and asbestos, and the pipes twisting through the basement would often be wrapped in asbestos, as would the water heater and furnace.

Dad or his teenaged offspring, playing backyard mechanic, would be immersed in an invisible cloud of deadly asbestos fibers as he changed the brake linings or shoes on the family car. Public water was often stored in huge concrete cisterns reinforced with asbestos, and pipes made of the same material would be used to deliver the water to homes. The U.S. Commerce Department estimated that by the late 1950s, more than 3,000 products containing asbestos were being manufactured and sold in this country.

Peronard was shocked, and fascinated, by this wealth of information.

Considering all this, Peronard thought it was no surprise that asbestos exposure wasn't the primary concern of the mine managers in Libby, Montana. But as he and his team would also discover, those managers knew very well that the tremolite asbestos in the Libby ore was a hazard to everyone who came in contact with it, and they did not see fit to share that information with their wholesale customers, or consumers, or with the growing number of miners who found themselves short of breath.

Les Skramstad digs up pieces of vermiculite ore as he scrapes dirt on the old ballfield where Libby's kids played. (Gilbert Arias, *Seattle Post-Intelligencer*)

PAUL PERONARD was familiar with the concept of denial, but this was over the top. Libby town leaders and state health and environmental types were saying "What asbestos?" Yet Whitehouse's records and the others Schneider had found showed that hundreds had died and even more were sick. And Gayla's paper trail was persuasive. What he still couldn't understand was how all that dying could have gone on without somebody taking notice, raising hell, before now.

He needed more information. He needed a fuller understanding of how Grace pulled the vermiculite out of the ground and what they did with it.

Peronard, Weis, Gayla and Les sat around the makeshift conference table in the back of EPA's tiny storefront office at 501 Mineral Avenue.[1] Linda Newstrom, who ran the EPA information center, laid the few maps and aerial photos she'd collected on the table.

"This is how it worked," Les said, grabbing a couple of Forest Service topo maps. Gayla started making notes on a photo with a red grease pencil.

Gayla and Les lectured. Peronard and Weis listened. Back and forth they squabbled and bantered, and by the death of the second pot of coffee, the two environmental experts understood a lot more. The ore was strip-mined, milled at the mine to remove extraneous material and then trucked about a mile down to the bottom of Rainy Creek Road to the screening plant, where it was separated into the five different grades or sizes that Grace sold for insulation, fireproofing, lawn and garden products and other agricultural products. And they learned that a large series of conveyor belts carried the vermiculite across the Kootenai to an area called "the bluffs," where the ore was stockpiled and loaded onto rail cars.

Then the four headed out the door.

Gayla took Weis to the rail siding, to the city dump and to the land around the new nursing home, and showed him a half dozen gardens where the vermiculite still sparkled at the top of black soil — vermiculite that had been tilled under the ground a dozen seasons ago but had worked its way to the top again.

Peronard and Les walked through the frozen, barren soil of the old ball fields. The fields were the center of social life for generations of Libby children — along with the open-sided shed a hundred yards away where they swung on ropes to land in towering piles of soft, dusty vermiculite. The piles were gone, although ropes still dangled from the rafters, and outside, the field and everything around it glittered from bits of raw vermiculite and shreds of Zonolite.

"It would be kind of pretty if we didn't know it was a killer," said Les. He knelt by a dirt pile beside what was once home plate. His callused fingers gently brushed away at the dirt near the top, and he pulled out a two-inch-long piece of shiny ore.

"It looks like it's everywhere," Peronard said.

They walked across the field to what had been the export plant, where the ore was popped into Zonolite and bagged for shipment, where Les worked on his "pure asbestos" project, heaving in lungfuls of tremolite in the bargain.

They walked another hundred yards down the railroad track. With his boot heel, Les dug a six-inch hole in the dirt. Layers of vermiculite went to the bottom.

"It could be down a foot or more," Les said.

They weaved through piles of two-by-fours. The land was owned by the city and leased to Mill Work West, a retail lumber business.

"Move the wood and there's more of it," the old miner said.

Peronard wrote some more in his small notebook.

Les Skramstad sighed. "Seems like I tossed tons of this stuff out here," he said wearily.

BEFORE THEY SENT LES TO DIG a truckload of asbestos, before they made him "clean" it on his hands and knees, they knew.

Before they hired him in 1959 to sweep the dust that gathered in windows on each floor of the dry mill, they knew. Probably, even before they took Perley Vatland on in 1954 to sweep the same mill, they knew.

But certainly shortly thereafter, the men who ran the Zonolite Corporation knew that their employees, the men who did the dirty work at the mine, were in grave danger. And they did not tell the workers. Instead, they lied. And aided by the collusion of the state of Montana and the indifference of the federal government, they concealed the evidence.

Judged by the prevailing standards at the time, it is remarkable that the state government in Montana showed any interest whatsoever in the health and safety of its workers before World War II. The state actually began doing industrial-hygiene studies in many of its factories and mines, although the inspections were neither systematic nor frequent. A state inspector visited Zonolite "every few years," according to state records, but the war caused a long hiatus.

On August 8, 1956, Benjamin Wake, a young industrial-hygiene engineer for the state Health Department's Division of Disease Control, arrived at the mine for its first inspection since 1944, when only 34 people had been employed.[2] Wake found 100 workers on the job, although a few days earlier 40 men had been laid off for supposed lack of work, and most of them were called back soon after the inspector left.

For two days, Zonolite assistant manager Earl Lovick took Wake through the mine and mill. Wake gathered samples of dust from everywhere. Despite the mine's reduced production, and doubtless some preinspection cleanup efforts, he didn't have any trouble finding dust to collect. He used vacuum pumps to pull air into filters so the level of dust the workers were breathing could be measured, but the dust was so thick it often clogged the filters.

"The asbestos in the air is of considerable toxicity," Wake wrote in his report, adding that he found "enormous quantities of dust and inoperable exhaust systems." The company told him that the asbestos content in the dust ranged from 8 to 21 percent. There is no evidence, however, that the state determined for itself how much asbestos was in the dust.

Wake cited "poor policy in matters of maintenance and operation of this plant," and submitted a four-page list of repairs to ventilating systems, conveyors and other work areas that he considered mandatory to protect workers. He warned that "inhalation of asbestos dust must be expected sooner or later to produce pulmonary fibrosis ... pulmonary asbestosis, once established, is a progressive disease with a bad prognosis."

Wake returned two and a half years later, in late 1958, and again in 1960. Both times, he found that little had been done to protect workers. In 1962, the workforce had been increased to about 150 when he returned for his fourth inspection in six years. After spending three more days at the plant, he found that the dry mill was again "extremely dusty and in the need of repair and modification to reduce dust to safe levels." He found the concentration of dust, "especially asbestos," substantially higher than in earlier inspections, and for the fourth time he submitted a long list of changes needed to protect workers. Again, it warned of the dangers of asbestos.

Zonolite's bosses received the report, like all the others. Again, the workers were not told of the results. Wake's reports were all stamped "confidential." The cover pages carried this note: "This report is confidential and is not for distribution except to the management of the Zonolite Company." It is probable that the only way the state Health Department could gain access to Montana mines and factories for such inspections was to offer such a compromise — to keep the results confidential. But the effect was to make the state a co-conspirator with Zonolite — to know the hazards, and to do nothing. There is not a single indication in any of the surviving documents from this time that the state ever threatened, or even considered, the option of shutting down the vermiculite operation.

Wake's frustration shows through in the official documents from the time.[3] The inspections frequently allude to the fact that the dust problem had not been addressed by the company — first Zonolite, then Grace. In 1964, Wake's letter to Art Bundrock, then the union secretary at the mine, offers some insight into the reason he was powerless to fix the problems he saw. "The enforcement provisions of the Industrial Hygiene Act ... are very poor, and various provisions, over the years, from the attorney general's office have not strengthened the act," he told Bundrock.

It's not as though Wake's reports were the only evidence the company had of health hazards to its workers.[4] Indeed, the Zonolite Co. had its own file of X-rays of the entire workforce. On July 20, 1959, the doctors who had performed an X-ray screening reported to assistant manager Earl Lovick that out of 130 workers examined, 82 showed symptoms of lung disease. Workers were told nothing, and X-ray results were not given to their doctors.

In February of that year, the company was unable to avoid the first actual diagnosis of asbestosis. Most of the time, miners who experienced health problems would go to a doctor in Libby, and would be diagnosed with emphysema or some other ailment that had nothing to do with asbestos. But Glenn Taylor was diagnosed with tuberculosis, so he went to the state TB hospital, where doctors quickly determined that the disease that was robbing him of the ability to breathe was not TB but asbestosis. Taylor died in September 1961. His obituary omits any mention of the cause of his death.

EARL LOVICK WAS A TOUGH-MINDED, uncompromising man determined to make the best of his Libby roots.[5] Earl's father, Carl, was a sawyer at the lumber mill who died young of heart failure when Earl was only seven years old.

After high school, Earl attended Eastern Washington College of Education for a year, then Montana State University at Bozeman for another year. Then he went to war, spending the last three years of World War II in Africa, Sicily and Italy with the Army Air Corps, rising to the rank of captain. After the war, he completed a degree in accounting at the University of Montana, married his sweetheart, Eileen Dowling of Butte, and went to work for Zonolite in 1948 as an accountant. By the time Wake began inspecting the plant, Lovick was the assistant manager and part of Libby's power elite.

It didn't take long for this young churchgoing war veteran to establish his position. In 1953, just five years after starting work at Zonolite, he was elected president of the Libby Chamber of Commerce and was installed as Worshipful Master at the Masonic Temple. In a few more years, he became president of the Libby Lions Club, was elected to the Libby school board, and was appointed by the City Council to the planning and zoning board.

In May 1960, Libby's brand-new Little League field opened. Two hundred seventy-five boys in their Little League uniforms marched through town, led by the local Army reserve color guard, the Libby High School band, its twirlers and its majorette. The procession arrived at the new field on the edge of town, near the Zonolite expanding plant. Volunteer Brick Wollaston, known in Libby as "Mister Little League," announced that the field would be dedicated to its major benefactor, the Zonolite Corp., and would always be known as "Zonolite Field." The company's local manager, Raymond "Butch" Bleich, threw out the first pitch. Earl Lovick caught it.

But up at the mine, Lovick's duties were not always so pleasant. The chest X-ray program that had made Perley Vatland feel so well taken care of back in 1959 had been a company reaction to a new state law that would make employers responsible for industrial disease contracted by workers.

The tests, done at St. John's Lutheran Hospital in Libby, turned up some disquieting results. On July 20, 1959, Lovick wrote a memo informing Zonolite headquarters that of 130 employees who had been X-rayed, 48 men had shown lung abnormalities and eight probably already had asbestosis. The company did not share the results with the miners, or with any of the local medical community not involved in the testing.

It's clear, too, that Lovick knew exactly what was causing the problem. In a letter to C. A. Pratt, vice president of Western Mineral Products Company of Minneapolis, one of Zonolite's biggest customers, Lovick wrote, "Asbestos is a cause of asbestosis, which has been a matter of concern. There is a relatively large amount of asbestos dust present in our mill, and this is difficult to control."[6]

In the letter, dated June 14, 1961, Lovick warned Pratt, "There is, of course, asbestos present in the concentrates we ship to our expansion plants," and added that the greatest point of exposure for "your people would be in the unloading of cars," meaning boxcars of ore. Lovick's candor may have been due to the fact that L. J. Venard, Pratt's boss and the head of Western Mineral Products, served on the Zonolite board of directors.

Lovick also had received medical evaluations of Glenn Taylor and Eitel Ludwig, both of which concluded that their lung problems were due "almost certainly from asbestos content of the dust" at the mine.

The fact that he knew Zonolite employees were in severe danger didn't keep Lovick from his community activities. In the spring of 1962, one month after Wake's fourth inspection of the Zonolite mine, Lovick filed as a Republican candidate for state senator.

If his conscience was bothering him yet, it certainly does not show in the photograph that accompanied the story of his filing in *The Western News.* He looked like the prototypical small-town boss of the era — snowy white shirt, dark tie, dark suit with half an inch of white handkerchief peeking from the left breast pocket. With his slightly hunched shoulders, fleshy face, heavy black-framed specs and a hairline that had already begun its inexorable northward retreat, he looked older than his 42 years. And if humor ever visited those solemn features, it didn't show.

He promised to "work for sound government in Montana, representative of all the people." He lost the election, but his career would continue to flourish.

RIGHT AFTER WAKE'S INSPECTION in 1962, Zonolite had embarked on a project that would probably have increased the hygienist's concerns, had he known about it.

Even though Zonolite continued to show good profitability — in the fiscal year that ended in March 1960, the company earned $679,171 on total sales of more than $10 million — the managers continued to be obsessed with finding a way to make their biggest waste product — tremolite asbestos — into a moneymaker. Despite the lower estimates provided to Wake, Lovick pegged the amount of asbestos visible in the material to be mined at 32 percent, and he estimated that at production levels of 5,000 tons a year, the visible material alone represented between nine and ten years' supply.

Lovick reported to Zonolite headquarters that in the summer of that year, the vermiculite mill was shut down and converted to be used as a tremolite concentrator. He said various methods were tested to dry the slurry into a marketable product. Samples were "sent to prospective customers for testing and evaluation."

But in December 1962, Lovick complained to Zonolite president J. A. Kelley that the asbestos program was disrupting the vermiculite operation, and he also reported difficulty in hiring skilled people and getting the proper machinery to process the asbestos.[7] About seven weeks later, in February 1963, Kelley wrote back, chiding Lovick for his lack of appetite for the asbestos project.

"Your reports indicate a considerable downgrading of enthusiasm for this project," Kelley wrote. "I hope you're staying right behind it and keeping everybody's enthusiasm at a high pitch, so things don't bog us down, because we are missing a lot of business and opportunity for every minute of delay that takes place."

Of course, it's certainly possible that Kelley's zeal was due to the fact that Zonolite was about to be sold to W.R. Grace & Co., and he wanted to show off for the soon-to-be owners. It was Earl Lovick who took the phone call from Kelley, informing the Libby employees that the company's board of directors, in its last meeting, had formally approved the transfer of all assets to W.R. Grace & Co.

The acquisition by Grace certainly didn't hurt Lovick's career — indeed, the parent company was doubtless grateful to have competent managers in place. Lovick and Bleich became assistant manager and manager, respectively, of the Zonolite division of W.R. Grace.

Butch Bleich was six years older than Lovick. He couldn't match Lovick's Libby roots, but by the time Grace took over he'd lived in Libby for more than two decades. An Iowa native, he'd gone to work for Zonolite in Chicago as an engineer in the mid-'30s and shortly afterward had been transferred to Libby. Bleich also served in the Army Air Corps in World War II, and returned to Libby as mill superintendent after the war, becoming manager of the Zonolite operation in 1952. The workers at Zonolite liked him a lot. He was a working man through and through, and they understood that. And he was kind.

By the time Les Skramstad was hired, though, Bleich had very personal knowledge of Zonolite's health hazards. By that time he'd been "on the hill" for almost two decades, and he would pay a terrible price. "You could always tell Butch was around, because above any conversation you could hear his cough," Les remembered. Bleich's position as Zonolite manager did not protect him from the fate so many of the men who worked for him suffered. Five years after Grace took over, he died at age 55 of lung cancer.

When Earl Lovick and Dave Anderson and four other Zonolite men carried Bleich's casket out of St. John's Lutheran Church on April 3, 1968, Lovick had already been named acting manager. And after a decent interval — slightly less than two months — he was officially promoted to take Bleich's place.

Three months before he died, Bleich must have shaken his head when he got a memo from Grace's corporate safety chief, Peter Kostic. In it, Kostic suggested reassigning 32 Libby employees whose X-rays showed significant signs of disease to less dirty jobs. "If we minimize their exposure to dust ... chances are we may be able to keep them on the job until they retire, thus precluding the high cost of total disability," Kostic wrote.

One of those employees was Perley Vatland.

Perley, meanwhile, was happy with his job. In 1963, he was excited to learn that the mine was probably going to be purchased by a much larger company. He figured it had to be good news — it was a huge outfit with plenty of money. Everybody had heard of W.R. Grace & Co.

GRACE HAD EVEN LESS ROOM THAN ZONOLITE to plead ignorance about the hazards of asbestos.

In 1954, nine years before it purchased Zonolite, Grace bought the Dewey & Almy Co. and gave Bradley Dewey a seat on the Grace board of directors. With him came an uncomfortably intimate knowledge of asbestos.

Dewey's Multibestos brake-manufacturing plant in Walpole, Massachusetts, spurred a flood of asbestos-related suits in the 1930s, and Dewey had actually sold the plant because of the asbestos liability.

Dr. John Hawes studied the health problems of many Multibestos workers. In an article written about the study's results in the *New England Journal of Medicine* in 1937, Hawes wrote, "There is not the slightest doubt ... that asbestos dust is the most dangerous of all dusts ... and can produce total and permanent disability in a remarkably short time."

In 1965, a Grace internal memo reported that company air monitoring had detected asbestos "in downtown Libby on many dry days."[8] That becomes understandable after reading that, according to the company's own records, nearly 300,000 pounds of asbestos a day went through the dry mill. In 1969, tests showed that 24,000 pounds of dust a day were expelled from the large stack on the dry mill. The dust was about 20 percent asbestos, and had tested as high as 40 percent. So even at 1969 production levels, which were nearly doubled in later years, at least two and a half tons of asbestos was ejected from the dry mill stack *every day.* And there were several other stacks in operation.

The year before Bleich's death, Grace's insurance carrier, Maryland Casualty Company in Portland, Oregon, had told Grace that its "inability" to curb the asbestos contamination despite repeated warnings "through the years might be alleged at least to have constituted willful and wanton conduct."[9] The insurer also warned Grace that the practice of keeping confidential X-ray records that showed lung disease could expose the company to liability. "Certainly when an X-ray picture shows a change for the worse, that person must be told," a letter to Grace from the Maryland Casualty Co. said. "Failure to do so is not humane, and is in direct violation of federal law."

But the insurer urged Grace lawyers to do all they could to prevent the entry of the "confidential" state inspection records into evidence in a workers'-compensation case, cautioning the company to "keep them out of the hands of the Industrial Accident Board and through it, the general public."

Indeed, the company continued to do everything it could to keep its problem confidential.[10] In 1969, an internal Grace memo from R. M. Vining, head of the company's construction products division, to president Peter

Grace warned that tremolite "is definitely a health hazard." Vining told Peter Grace that "the vermiculite ore from Libby contains tremolite asbestos. This material is difficult to separate from the vermiculite at the mill and is usually part of the rock remaining in the concentrate when shipped." That same year, Lovick helped to complete a "Confidential Study of Zonolite/Libby Employees." Among the study's conclusions was that "although 17 percent of our 1 to 5 years' service group have or are suspect of lung disease, there is a marked rise (45 percent) beginning with the 11th year of service, climbing to 92 percent in the 21 to 25 years' service group. This suggests that chances of getting lung disease increase as years of exposure increase."

Judging from those figures, it seems "chance" was the wrong word. Work at Zonolite long enough, and lung disease was a virtual certainty.

IT IS HARD TO SAY PRECISELY WHEN Perley Vatland's breath began to slip away. No one knows which day it was that critical mass was reached in his lungs, which day he breathed another few million asbestos fibers that sealed his fate.

It's impossible to tell just when enough of those fibers became embedded to cause a reduction in the amount of air he could take in. We'll never know just when the tissue around those fibers became sufficiently inflamed, as his body tried every trick it knew to expel them, all unsuccessful, that it began to pain him. Even if they had wanted to, his doctors could never have said just when his lungs, pricked with so many tiny knives, began to scar over to the point at which they started to lose their elasticity, refusing to expand and contract quite as much as they had the day before.

But certainly that one day occurred sometime in the early '60s, and this strapping, smiling, flat-bellied, well-muscled man got a little less oxygen in his blood than he was used to getting, and he felt a little more tired that night than usual. Maybe he walked a little more slowly up the steps of his house at 1306 Minnesota Avenue, wearing his filthy work clothes, hungry for dinner and happy to see Margaret, who was waiting to brush the dust off him, help him out of those clothes and get him fed. Did he notice that he had a little harder time getting out of his recliner that night and walking to bed? Did he wonder what the little tugs of pain were? We will never know.

In 1966, Perley was finally worried enough about the growing pain and shortness of breath to go to the doctor: He was floored to be told that he had a serious heart condition and could die at any time. The doctor gave Perley a prescription for nitroglycerin tablets and told him to place a tablet under his tongue whenever he felt chest pains. What the doctor apparently didn't know, and Perley definitely didn't know, was that the Zonolite health screening in 1959 had singled him out as one of more than 40 miners with signs of lung disease.

By the time he was diagnosed, Perley had the job he loved most at Zonolite — running the road grader, making and maintaining roads on the mine site. But in 1968, his supervisors took him off the grader and gave him a desk job in the test lab, next to the dry mill. He hated to lose his job on the grader, but he knew he shouldn't be running heavy equipment if he was in imminent danger of a heart attack, and he was grateful to the company for accommodating him with a safer job. What he didn't know was that the company was acting on advice from Grace headquarters, moving employees with the worst lung symptoms into less dusty jobs in an effort to keep them working longer, thereby avoiding expensive disability claims.

In September 1961, at age 19, Gayla married a 1957 Ford convertible. At least, that's how she describes it these days. Behind the wheel was Gary Swenson, a big, handsome, blond Libby kid, just out of school himself. In marrying, Gayla fulfilled the Libby expectation for herself. It was simply what you did; nobody thought it was odd in the least. If Gayla had taken her grandfather up on an offer of college tuition instead, *that* would have been considered odd.

Six weeks later, Gary was drafted into the Army and stationed at Fort Lewis, near Tacoma. Gayla moved there to try to live with her husband, but it didn't work financially — they could barely afford to eat and buy gas. She went back to her parents' house, pregnant with daughter Jenny, who was born in April 1963.

Gary got his discharge from the Army on November 22, 1963 — the day John Kennedy was shot. The couple moved into a small house in Libby together, but the long separation had put too much strain on Gayla and Gary's marriage, and the following year they were divorced.

Then, in 1965, Gayla married David Benefield, a rangy, handsome Libby native she had known most of her life. Their daughter, Julie, was born, and in 1968, David took the job of manager at the local VFW Club in Libby. One of the first things he did was hire Les Skramstad and his band to play at the club.

The Skramstads and the Vatlands had stayed close in the years since they had become neighbors. Back in '59, Les and Norita had asked 16-year-old Gayla if they could name their second daughter after her, and she had been flattered and delighted. Les and Perley, formerly coworkers, would often get together and play music at the Vatland house.

The VFW was a bustling bar in those days, full of loggers, sawmill workers, miners and construction workers from the huge dam that was being built on the Kootenai River east of town. It was a raucous party until 2 A.M. nightly, particularly on weekends, when throngs would come to drink and dance to the sweet country sounds of Les's band. David's job paid well, but the barroom life was not healthy for marriage and family.

Gayla and David divorced — "I couldn't tolerate the drinking," she says — but six months later, David quit the bar, took a job in construction and they were remarried. Gayla found work as a union hiring dispatcher, keeping a priority hire list and sending workers to the dam project and other construction projects as the calls came in. She would usually have the hiring list — names and phone numbers — committed to memory. It was the same mental acuity that enabled her to ace tests and compelled her teachers to tell her she was an underachiever. "I presumed everybody could do that," Gayla says. David and Gayla lived a few blocks from Margaret and Perley. By 1971, David had taken a new job as a union representative, a position he would hold for many years, and their family life stabilized. In November of that year, after most of a difficult pregnancy had passed, Gayla was X-rayed and informed that she was about to give birth to twins.

Perley's health, though, was deteriorating fast.[11] He was forced to call in sick frequently, and the doctors repeatedly put him on antibiotics, supposedly to treat "walking pneumonia." He still had no idea that his lung disease had been identified by the Zonolite screening in 1959.

By 1973, Perley could not work anymore. Still, he got no answers. His doctor told him he could retire on disability because of a heart condition, the beginnings of rheumatoid arthritis and "a slight fibrosis of the lung."

By then, Perley had other friends who were sick and dying. He would sit out on his porch that summer with Gayla and talk about the other miners who were sick. The managers often said that the sick men had worked at a different mine before coming to Libby, and that was confusing. Perley had never worked in any other mine, but he still had no idea what was making him so sick, and he sure didn't want to think it was Zonolite Mountain that had cost him his health.

As Perley got sicker, he forced a reluctant Margaret to learn to drive, and she found work as an Avon saleslady. She was away from home a lot, and Perley seemed to hate to be alone. In the afternoons he would come over to Gayla's house for some time with his grandkids and some conversation. By the time he'd walked from his car into Gayla's yard he'd be exhausted. At night, he would have a few beers and become very sad. It was as if he could feel the life leaving his body.

Later that year, one of Perley's friends told him that his "fibrosis" might mean he could collect workers' compensation. David Benefield helped him file the papers, and David and Gayla drove him to Missoula for the required medical exam. It was the worst day of Perley's life.

He came out of the exam absolutely shattered. He learned that what the Libby doctors had been telling him all those years was bunk. His heart was normal and his arthritis was minor. His lungs, though, were nearly destroyed by asbestosis. The doctor told him he had two to ten years left, which proved optimistic. But it wasn't so much the prognosis that upset Perley — he already knew he was very sick — as it was the fact, unavoidable at last, that the job he loved and the company he trusted and admired had given him and his friends a death sentence.

He didn't know yet about his family.

Gayla kept working as a labor dispatcher. She sent men to work on the tailing dam on Rainy Creek, and on the new mill that was being built at the Rainy Creek area of the mine. She did not suspect that she was sending those men to the same fate her father was suffering.

Perley's afternoon talks with Gayla understandably became more bitter, and more bittersweet. Gayla knew she was losing her father, and he knew he was losing his life. For Perley Vatland, death, as life, did not come easy. He suffered terribly, and wasted away slowly. Perley died September 6, 1974. He was just five days short of having worked for the company for 20 years — the threshold for the pension he wanted so badly for his family. Instead, Margaret Vatland was left almost penniless, with a total of $37 a week in workers'-compensation benefits, payable for about ten years, and whatever she could make selling Avon products. She and Perley had dropped the life-insurance policy they had through W.R. Grace because the premiums had risen dramatically — at the same time his income dropped — when he went on disability.

Four years after Perley's death, Margaret wrote a letter to U.S. Senator Max Baucus protesting the way her husband's case had been handled by Grace and the state.[12] He had been awarded only the $148 per month in benefits from workers' compensation while he was alive — a ruling he was too sick to fight. It was hundreds of dollars a month cheaper for Grace and the state than if he had been granted a full disability benefit.

"He was sick for about eight years on the job, and more dead than alive for the 18 months after," Margaret Vatland wrote bitterly. "But I've managed to keep my home. I sell Avon, work hard at it." She finished by saying that even four years later, she didn't feel right about Perley getting "$147 or $150 a month for something so fatal."

Baucus asked the state workers'-compensation administrator to investigate. He did — for exactly one day. Baucus's letter was dated September 21, 1978. The return letter to Baucus from administrator Norman Crosfield, dated September 22, said simply, "From a review of the file, it appears that Mrs. Vatland is receiving the exact amount she is entitled.... Therefore, we would have to say that no further adjustment can be made in her case and that the case is being handled in accordance with the laws of Montana."

So Margaret Vatland, this proud daughter of a man of means who had fallen in love with a strapping, laughing young Norwegian, set her jaw and drove her little blue car through the frigid Montana winters of her widowhood, selling and delivering her Avon products. Just about every cold season, though, she'd end up in the hospital for a few days with a spell of pneumonia. And Gayla worried.

Obituary: Perley Vatland

Funeral services were held Monday, September 9, at 2 P.M. at the Vial Funeral Home Chapel for Perley Vatland, who died Sept. 6 at the St. John's Lutheran Hospital.

Vatland was born June 12, the son of Mathias and Raghnild Vatland in Griffin, N.D. He received his schooling in Rhame, N.D. He was married to Margaret Rody on Oct. 26, 1937, at Buffalo, S.D.

Vatland and his wife were wheat farmers at Fort Benton until moving to Libby in 1946. He was employed at Zonolite for 19 years. He served as an equipment operator for 14 years of this time and also spent the last five years as a shift assayer. He retired in 1973.

The Libby resident was well known as an old-time fiddler in the area and belonged to the Lutheran Church, the Sons of Norway and the operating engineers union.

Pastor Gerhard Kempff officiated at the funeral services. Iona Grundmann was the organist and accompanied the congregation as they sang "In the Sweet By and By" and "Softly and Tenderly."

—The Western News, September 12, 1974

PART 2: THE BATTLES

The stark Cabinet Mountains surrounding Libby. (Andrew Schneider)

The town's popular ballfield was just a foul ball away from huge piles of vermiculite waste, on which many kids played and became contaminated.
(Courtesy McGarvey, Heberling, Sullivan & McGarvey)

A S THE BOSS of EPA's Rocky Mountain region, Bill Yellowtail had heard a lot of off-the-wall requests from his people doing cleanups, but X-ray machines? Devices to test pulmonary function? A medical clinic? Never.

"Yeah. I know it's never been done, but we've never had a situation like Libby before," Peronard explained to his dubious boss.

"Think of it as an exit strategy," Miller quickly added. "It's the only way we can prove that the health problems there aren't as bad as some people believe."

Without even a pause, Weis chipped in: "Without it, we'll never be able to show that people aren't still being exposed."

Yellowtail shook his head at the tag-team approach, paused and said, "Okay. Let's talk about it."

They were in Yellowtail's conference room on the fifth floor of the South Tower of one of the several federal buildings that dot Denver.[1] Everybody with a dog in the fight was there, Peronard thought. There was Yellow-

113

tail; his deputy, Jack McGraw; Max Dodson, the regional asbestos expert; a gaggle of EPA press people; senior enforcement lawyer Matthew Cohn and his boss; and Peronard, Weis and Miller and the head of the emergency-response operation.

Peronard knew that all they really wanted to hear him and his team say was that the newspaper was wrong, that the reporter made it up or didn't understand what he was seeing. And that they couldn't do.

"The few things that we were able to check out showed the news reports were correct, at least so far," Peronard told the assembled bigwigs. "People are sick. Many have died. There's something to this." He let that sink in, then tried to soften the blow a little. "I don't think it's too big a deal. We might have some minor cleanup work at two locations — the export plant and there's something going on with the road near the mine. We'll do some more testing. It won't be a big deal."

The mention of a medical survey brought a hush to the room.

"If no one but the miners are sick, no one will believe us unless we have the medical data to show that," Peronard continued. "This is going to require something more extensive than we normally have done, not just questionnaires. We're going to have to go out and characterize the health of the population."

The EPA had never done that before. There had been some studies of lead levels in the blood of small groups, but not as part of an emergency response action. "Nothing like this," Weis admitted. "Not with thousands of people. Not with extensive X-ray. Nothing on this scale."

Yellowtail wasn't crazy about the idea, but he calmed some when the Libby trio started selling the testing as part of an exit strategy.

Miller and Weis had worked out the details of the medical survey on napkins at the MK Steakhouse outside Libby. They told Peronard what questions had to be asked, what tests needed to be done and what equipment was needed to do it.

"If you ever want to put this behind you, sir," Peronard told the regional administrator, "you're going to have to have hard data on how many folks are actually sick or affected. Miners and nonminers."

With visible reluctance, Yellowtail shrugged and gave the green light. Which was fortunate, because Weis and Miller had already started hunting for the proper medical equipment. Peronard was dickering with contractors to see how soon they could get a large trailer set up with electricity and plumbing to be used as a clinic for the screening.

The government agency that normally does this type of medical screening is the Agency for Toxic Substances Disease Registry, a research arm of the Centers for Disease Control. The relationship between ATSDR and EPA in the Rocky Mountain region was very shaky, Miller said. The health agency hadn't been very responsive to requests for help in the past. Nevertheless, Miller, who was still attached to the U.S. Public Health Service, called the ATSDR and told them what was needed in Libby.

"I was a team player and I invited them in and they blew me off, said they weren't interested," Miller told Peronard.

"Screw them. We'll do it ourselves," Peronard said, and the Libby trio continued buying medical equipment.

Things were going far too smoothly and moving too fast. But then, three weeks after the meeting, Yellowtail sent word that the screening was going to be turned over to ATSDR. "Period."

What happened?

Montana U.S. Senator Max Baucus wasn't sure EPA could move fast enough in getting the screenings going, so he wrote to Donna Shalala, then Secretary of Health and Human Services, who dumped it in the lap of ATSDR's headquarters in Atlanta. The health research agency was in the game whether they liked it or not.

ATSDR began calling Miller every day. "They think I'm a traitor for helping the EPA set up the medical screening, something ATSDR *now* clearly sees as its responsibility," Miller told Peronard. "They said it would take a year or so to develop a screening protocol and then probably another year to get the screening done."

But the EPA group already had a protocol and thought they could have their little clinic up and running in a few months. They also considered it far too important to let interagency bureaucracy screw it up.

But ATSDR was worried.[2] In an e-mail dated January 27, marked "FOR ATSDR EYES ONLY!!!," Susan Muza, the health agency scientist based in Denver, wrote to Dr. Jeffrey Lybarger, who headed ATSDR's division of health studies.

"We clearly have a long way to go in the terms of the 'joint team' concept," Muza wrote, then added: "Quite frankly, I am leery of the amount of influence that [Dodson] truly has over his team. Chris W. has been quite blunt that he is approaching this situation from the 'it is better to ask for forgiveness than permission' mind set, and is using Paul's authority to do whatever they decide they want to, including the health screenings."

She closed by saying that "some of Paul's comments" led her to believe that when Peronard says "we," it means "he is willing to include ATSDR, but only as long as he doesn't feel that we are holding him back."

By early February 2000, the vanguard of the ATSDR troops arrived in Libby, and with them came peace — more or less. Weis still grumbled that one ass with underwhelming credentials showed up far too impressed with himself, but the two agencies managed to play well together and they quickly focused on the task of documenting just how ill little Libby really was.

THE HEALTH STUDY THE TWO AGENCIES were contemplating was without precedent within the government.

But like all studies of asbestos exposure, it owed much to one courageous doctor. Despite the centuries of knowledge about the hazards of asbestos, and despite the proliferating asbestos industry, the U.S. medical establishment was remarkably silent on the issue until the 1960s, when that doctor refused to look the other way.

Irving Selikoff was born in Brooklyn in 1915.[3] He was Jewish and came from a poor family, reasons he believed prevented him from getting into an American medical school after he got his undergraduate degree from Columbia. But he was accepted at the Royal College in Scotland. After taking his medical degree there and serving an internship in Newark, New Jersey, he began what would be a 50-year career at Mount Sinai School of Medicine in Brooklyn.

He started as an assistant professor in anatomy and pathology, and also became known as an excellent consulting physician, never failing to give attention and empathy to his patients. While he was still in his 30s, Selikoff began pioneering research in the treatment of tuberculosis. With Dr. Edward Robitzek, he made a breakthrough in treatment of TB patients with antibiotics, for which he won the coveted Lasker Prize for Clinical Medical Research. The Lasker Prize is considered by many to be "America's Nobel," because so many of its recipients have subsequently won the Nobel Prize.

For most doctors, such recognition is the pinnacle of their careers. But Selikoff was only beginning the work that would be his biggest contribution to medicine and earn him international recognition — research on the occupational hazards of asbestos. His work on asbestos would become the foundation for a whole new field of occupational medicine.

In 1953, Selikoff had opened a lung clinic near his home in Paterson, New Jersey. Many of his patients were workers at the nearby Union Asbestos and Rubber Company factory. The brilliant young doctor was puzzled when 15 of his patients from the plant displayed similar breathing problems. Eventually, 14 of the 15 would die from what he suspected was asbestos-related disease.

Selikoff was stunned by the apparent toxicity of the fibers. He resolved to trace the medical histories of more than a thousand workers at the plant. Without any help from the company, he was able to find all but 50 of the workers. He discovered that as a group, the workers were getting lung cancer at a rate seven times what would be expected in a normal population. Workers were also dying of colon and stomach cancer at twice the expected rate.

Evaluation of the lung tissue from his diseased patients showed it was filled with millions of asbestos fibers. Selikoff considered this, and the results of his study, dramatic proof of the dangers of asbestos, and he tried to spread the word of the hazard. But lab analysis and autopsy results from a score of patients mean little in the world of medicine, and even less as a tool to convince huge corporations they were killing their workers. Mostly he was ignored, and manufacturers greeted his efforts with hostility. He published his first study in 1961, only to be derided by industry scientists. Selikoff did not hide his frustration at industry's lack of concern for the lives of workers. Often, only half jesting, he would threaten to teach a course called "Toxicology for Tycoons."

Selikoff realized that in order to make an impact, numbers mattered — huge numbers. So he gathered more and more medical and mortality records of workers who had been exposed to insulation years earlier in shipyards, boiler plants, insulation operations and other places where the "miracle fiber" had been or was still being used. He also gave X-ray exams and pulmonary function tests to 1,117 asbestos-insulation workers. He found evidence of asbestosis in 50 percent of them. Even worse, he found that among 392 men with more than 20 years of exposure, 339, or 86 percent, had developed the disease.

In April 1964, Selikoff published his major study in the *Journal of the American Medical Association*.[4] The magnitude of this work could not be ignored. The prestigious journal selected Selikoff's work as one of the 50 landmark articles in its 100 years of publication. Within a year, the first major international conference on the dangers of asbestos was held, and momentum began to build, but the industry and its customers continued to attack his work.

While they denounced his work publicly, company executives clearly paid close attention to everything Selikoff wrote and said.[5] A Grace corporate memo written November 22, 1969, illustrates the point as it discusses a presentation the doctor made three weeks earlier.

"[Selikoff] leveled very serious charges about the definite danger created by the use of sprayed fiber fireproofing. By the use of charts, he outlined the medical facts of the incidents of asbestosis, lung cancer and rare cancers of the chest wall and lining of the stomach among asbestos workers," Grace's T. F. Egan wrote in a memo to R. W. Starrett. "He then turned to sprayed fiber fireproofing in New York, showing the unchecked 'snow' throughout the downtown area. Special note was made of the World Trade Center. Selikoff stated they estimated 100 tons of fiber will be airborne in New York from this job ... and not one man spraying fiber today will be alive in 20 years. The officials of the international unions were there along with contractors and I know it landed like a bomb."

Grace's reaction in the last paragraph showed they were paying attention to the doctor.

"We must go all out to get asbestos out of Monokote at once," Egan wrote. Monokote was Grace's primary brand of fireproofing, where large amounts of asbestos fibers were mixed with a cement or plaster base and applied to steel support beams of buildings.

Selikoff passed the word with the zeal of a tent revival preacher. He told the press. He told Congress. He told the workers. Always, he spoke in terms that everyone understood. Many credit his work as the driving force behind the creation of the Occupational Safety and Health Act.

And after Selikoff's study was published, many doctors and scientists who had been content to take industry's word that it was not harming its workers began joining him in calling for reforms.

ONE MIGHT EXPECT THE MEDICAL COMMUNITY to be united in attacking a public-health scourge like asbestos.[6] But it is the same everywhere asbestos has killed people in America.

Doctors have either actively or passively aided industry in keeping a lid on the problem — misdiagnosing asbestos-related disease or opting not to confront companies when workers get sick. But it is equally true that in each location, some doctors, starting with Selikoff and continuing through today, have taken on both the companies and the medical establishment, if necessary, to raise the alarm.

Dr. Michael Harbut is one of the courageous ones who have added to Selikoff's legacy.[7] An assistant professor of medicine at Wayne State University in Detroit, Harbut has treated thousands of workers and family members with asbestos-related disease.

Most doctors don't stick their necks out like Harbut does. He knows why.

"If you go after a product that company X makes that makes people sick, then company X goes after you. And nobody sticks up for you," Harbut said. He has always spoken bluntly and clearly about asbestos, and the companies have indeed gone after him. He says he has been hounded by asbestos companies because of his court testimony on behalf of his patients.

In 1992, Harbut and two colleagues examined about 8,000 workers at the Ford Rouge plant in Michigan — the world's largest industrial complex. He was asked to undertake the study by the Occupational Health Legal Rights Foundation of the AFL/CIO.

"We found a lot of asbestosis among the autoworkers. Thousands of cases," Harbut said. The next year, as he was planning the next phase of the study, every agency that could decided to audit him. He was the target of a federal grand jury investigation. "The FBI showed up in my office and demanded all the information on the patients we had examined," Harbut said. "I refused.

"Medicare began two audits. Blue Cross and Blue Shield started an audit, and so did the Michigan Workman's Compensation Commission." All, including the FBI, were based on anonymous complaints, he said. The most bizarre was an audit started by the inspector general of the U.S. Agency for International Development.

Between 1989 and 1993, Harbut was the Chief U.S. Medical Adviser to Solidarity and for a while even shared an office with Lech Walesa.

"They were auditing me because I submitted a photocopy of an airline ticket for a flight from Warsaw to Gdansk," the besieged physician recalled.

"Eventually, everything was dropped. Medicare apologized. The U.S Attorney said there was nothing for them to prosecute, the state never came back, Blue Cross never mentioned it and U.S. AID decided the Polish photocopy was just fine."

Harbut used to work around the clock, seeing patients, talking to families, writing to medical organizations, urging them to take the asbestos problem seriously, trying to get taconite miners up on the Iron Range in northern Michigan and Minnesota to understand that tremolite in their ore was killing them.

The other obsessions in his life — his wife Laura, whom he met while treating her mother, and their four children — are the only reasons he has slowed down at all. "He is consumed with his desire to help these people," said *Post-Intelligencer* reporter Carol Smith after returning from two days with Harbut. She sat in the corner of his examining room as a seemingly endless stream of old men dragging wheeled bottles of oxygen came and went. "He knew every one of them. Big broad smiles would break out as they talked to each other. It was kind of magical. He was so empathetic, it was obvious that he suffered along with his patients," she said.

Harbut doesn't want to spend his time in court. He'd rather spend it helping his patients clinically. He tries not to take on any patients involved in litigation. But litigation is an occupational hazard for doctors who specialize in treating asbestos patients. He gets about 15 subpoenas a week for workers'-compensation cases or injury claims involving his patients.

"I'm obligated to stick up for my patients," he said. "That's my job."

Harbut is not willing to sit back and watch his asbestosis patients die. He is one of only a few physicians trying to treat the disease aggressively, hoping to find a way to change the course of a longtime killer. He is prescribing drugs called leukotrine blockers, originally approved for treating asthma, to treat asbestosis. "We know they block inflammatory mediators" — molecules that help trigger inflammation — "in the lung," he said. The new drugs appear to be helping some patients. "Patients feel better. We didn't make the scarring go away, but we made the good tissue work harder."

Meanwhile, Harbut asked the American Trial Lawyers Association to set up a fund for the study of improved treatment and diagnosis of asbestos-related diseases. "They [the lawyers] are getting rich off my patients," he said. After a year, ATLA responded to the request.

"No" was their answer.

Dr. David Egilman is also a pain in the ass to many American corporations who disregard the health of their workers.[8] He shares that opinion of himself, as do most of the corporate lawyers that try to trip him up. He is a medical doctor who specialized in preventative occupational medicine and a clinical assistant professor at Brown University.

He's got credentials. More than most. A medical degree from Brown University, a three-year residency in internal medicine, another three-year stint in epidemiology and a master's degree in public health from the Harvard School of Public Health. To pay off his medical-school bills, he served three years at the National Institute for Occupational Safety and Health. It was his first real exposure to occupational illness, and it did not take him long to get chewed out by his bosses for telling workers at the Fernald Nuclear operation in Ohio that they were being exposed to radiation because of what the company and the government did. It wouldn't be the last time he got in trouble for standing up for workers.

Many things set Egilman apart from the other physicians sitting in witness chairs in trials around the country where workers had been harmed by their companies. He doesn't hide behind his academic accomplishments; he still lays hands on patients — fewer these days, but still men and women whose lungs are leather-like from sucking down asbestos, or whose organs are failing because of exposure to vinyl chloride, beryllium, lead and a host of other by-products of "Better Living Through Chemistry."

He has worked at the request of both workers and companies and sees nothing unusual about it. "I don't testify for or against. I just present the facts. Just the facts, ma'am," Egilman says. The doctor sometimes works for free or reduced rates. He makes good money for his consulting and trial work and he works hard for it. But much of the money he gets for testifying — about $100,000 in 2001 — he donates to developing medical programs in Third World nations. He runs a nonprofit, called The Network, that serves as the development office for the World Health Organization. It is devoted to supporting nursing and medical schools that focus on training people to work in developing countries. "Because it should be done" is all he'll say when asked why he does it.

He has taught and published articles on the history of medical ethics and the duty to warn. Twice he has testified before congressional committees on the issue of medical ethics and corporate responsibility.

Egilman offers one of his few serious answers when asked why he has devoted most of his life to helping workers. "Companies should not be allowed to kill their employees, and if they do it, they shouldn't be permitted to get away with it," he said. "We are talking about millions and millions of men and women who died or were disabled because their companies put profit before safety or the government regulations were inadequate or both. How can I not be involved?"

Much of his passionate perspective on abuse of workers and human experimentation came from his father, a survivor of the Buchenwald concentration camp. Egilman runs a firm called "Never Again Consulting."

His first litigation involving asbestos was in 1986. The defendant was Owens Corning. "I testified about who knew what and when they knew it. That's usually what I'm asked to do," Egilman said. He researched the company's history and read thousands of pages of corporate documents that were produced during discovery.

"I told the court that the company knew a lot of bad things about the stuff they were making and they lied about it. They told workers it was safe," Egilman said. "They were worse than Grace in some areas. Owens Corning put nontoxic labels on their asbestos. Grace just refused even putting on a label, even though they knew there was asbestos in their stuff," he said. "You tell me. Which one was a bigger corporate bastard?"

He testified for five days, but the judge died. It was tried again the following year. The verdict was $26.3 million. "But it was reduced to about $3 million because it wouldn't be fair for a worker to get all that money," Egilman said sarcastically.

He says he really loves what he does. "It's intellectually stimulating. You get to see things that nobody else has seen. You get to see how these corporations make sausage. It's never pretty." His wife of 13 years, Helene, may believe he's nuts and so do his kids, he says. "But she never says that, and they love me." Many lawyers also question his mental stability, and Egilman does everything he can to further those questions. He has been known to show up at a deposition with a room filled with pinstripe-attired lawyers wearing his red Harvard tie, a blue dress shirt and a jacket, but beneath the polished conference table at which he sits, only shorts and Tweety Bird slippers. Now and then he'll show up wearing a dashiki.

Egilman has a poor opinion of Grace's lawyers.

"Some of them are dumber than a stick," he said, recalling a Grace trial in New York in 1994.

"Grace's lawyers not only asked me if I was a Jew and if my father was in a concentration camp, but if I was anti-Nazi. All true. I just couldn't believe they had the balls to ask me that," Egilman said, "but they knew I was going to testify that, in my opinion, it was poor corporate policy for a company to hire a convicted Nazi war criminal, who ran slave labor camps and did medical experiments, to be a senior consultant advising on how Grace could keep its workers healthy."

Gathering paper, corporate paper of all types, is almost an obsession for him.

In the basement of a building in Boston's Winthrop Square is the document repository that the Federal Court ordered Grace to establish after the company was convicted of lying to the EPA. It is a short and direct subway ride from Egilman's office 13 miles away. He has spent weeks there, and at many other companies' repositories, gathering all he can. "It's wonderful stuff that really offers insight into how companies work, and that can be frightening," he said.

"Grace did animal studies and proved that their vermiculite was dangerous, and then they didn't publish it. They hid it, and I thought they should take credit for their good work. Why should a mouse die in vain? I'm not an animal-rights person, because I really don't mind if the mice die and people don't. But I'm definitely not in favor of going out and killing a bunch of white mice, proving that the crap you're selling is potentially lethal, and then not using the useful information you get from it."

Corporate lawyers hate Egilman's website, which hypothetically he created for his students at Brown who take his courses in ethics, public health issues and corporate corruption. The web contains copies of tens of thousands of internal corporate documents that he has collected over the years from Grace, Bendix, Johns-Manville, Union Carbide and a score of other corporations. Plaintiffs' lawyers, government investigators, reporters and researchers have a field day with documents they never would have found any other way.

Egilman said the public doesn't understand the magnitude of corporate corruption. "When you focus on one apple at a time, it lets people think it's a bad apple. The problem is it's a bad barrel. It is the system that allows asbestos, beryllium, lead, vinyl chloride. It's the system that allows these products to be sold when it is known or knowable by the people who sell it that it is going to injure or kill people.

"People have got to change the system," he said. "I'm just doing my part."

CHAPTER 8

Don Kaeding, with his oxygen tank, joined more than 300 other townsfolk at the first public meeting to discuss the asbestos disease plaguing Libby. (Andrew Schneider)

I T IS NEVER EASY for an emergency coordinator to hear people talk about how frightened they are about whatever environmental hazard is endangering their community. But this December night in Libby, Montana, was like nothing Paul Peronard had ever seen.

In other emergencies, Peronard, Weis and Miller had told townsfolk about the statistical probability of being struck down by exposure to benzene, toluene, trichloroethylene or another of the thousands of industrial chemicals that the government has studied. They would discuss the scientific evidence: This solvent might cause birth defects, that chemical could cause tumors, laboratory rats died when exposed to that stuff. Could and might.

The deaths were in the abstract. Maybe something bad might happen some-day if we don't clean it up now.

In Libby, "maybe" did not exist.

Death and illness were sure things for a good chunk of the population. There was no room for doubt, Peronard thought, as he tried to count the number of people in the crowd who were clutching oxygen bottles.

Almost 600 people packed Libby's tiny gymnasium for a meeting.[1] No one is exactly sure who called the gathering, but officials from Libby, Lincoln County, the state and EPA all quickly jockeyed for time at the podium. The principal focus of the assembly — Peronard and his team — sat by themselves in the bleachers to the left of the stage. He, Weis and Miller sat on one step. Wendy Thomi and Diana Hammer, the two community coordinators, sat behind them. Linda Newstrom, the newly hired manager for EPA's Libby office and the only local, sat in the middle and kept a running commentary of who was whom, people they would all get to know — some of them all too well.

In addition to their oxygen cylinders to augment sparse breath from damaged lungs, many people carried a heavy load of pent-up anger. "In the local paper our health department says we have only one percent tremolite in our town. One percent of tremolite is not acceptable no matter what anybody says," Patrick Vinion yelled, slamming his fist on the podium. The noise echoed through the gym like a gunshot.

"One percent is tons of tremolite, and I guarantee it will kill your kids," he added in a near-whisper.

One after another, the people of Libby told stories of death and disease, and expressed fears for their children and their children's children. It was the first time Libby people had ever gathered to share their tales of what Grace had done to them. The first time a town left to die had confronted its killer in public.

A woman near Peronard in the bleachers tightly hugged two young girls nestled beside her, closed her eyes and shook her head.

Vinion despaired over the misinformation doled out to the miners and the community over the years about the danger from the pinkish ore that was supporting most of the town.

"When my father was a young man they told him, 'You can't eat enough of that stuff. It won't bother you.' He's dead. And when I started getting sick when I was younger, they told me, 'You never worked there. It's not possible. You can't get it that way.' Well, it's more than possible. I'm dying of it."

Mark Simonich, the head of the state's Department of Environmental Quality, admitted that "mistakes were made" by state agencies in the past. He urged people to tell their stories, but to be polite.

They were, for the most part, but the anger was never far below the surface.

Terry Smith, who lost both his parents to the asbestos, voiced concern that people were getting the wrong diagnoses. Many of the people walking around with oxygen bottles think they have emphysema, he said. His uncle and his father were both told that their breathing problems were from emphysema.

"When my father died, they figured out it was asbestosis," Smith said. "When my uncle died, they removed his lungs and found they were filled with asbestos.

"See a specialist. Find out what's really happening to you," he implored, and he was cheered loudly.

Flashing charts, graphs and old photographs of the mill and mine on the screen, Roger Sullivan told the crowd that Zonolite Mountain was still a killer.

The young lawyer explained how the largest stack in the ore-processing mill had put 5,000 pounds of asbestos into the air each day, and how the wind would disperse much of it over the town. He said the sparsely covered tailing pile, given a clean bill of health by state investigators, still contained five billion pounds of asbestos.

Many in the crowd gasped when he projected a huge blowup of a lethal tremolite fiber. Several people touched their chests. A couple hugged their spouses.

A day earlier, Grace chairman and CEO Paul Norris had flown into Helena with a bevy of lawyers and vice presidents and met with Montana governor Marc Racicot. They told state officials that they would participate in the Libby meeting, but they did not. Grace's representative, Alan Stringer, attended the meeting but did not speak.

Les and Norita both told the crowd that people had to keep the pressure on to protect Libby's children. "It is a death sentence, and there's nothing you can do about it," Les said. "Our biggest concern now must be the children of this town. We don't know if they have it, and we must find out. This lies dormant and then springs its ugly head up and it's full-blown."

Montanans are known to be stoic, keeping their emotions close to their vests. Not at this meeting. Grown men, many full-bearded, in hunting caps and heavy flannel shirts, gruff-looking loggers, miners and truck drivers, wept without embarrassment. One man, looking much older than his 60 years, pressed a plastic oxygen mask to his face. Tears streamed down both sides. "It's true. It's true. I know it, but this is the first time I've heard other folk talk about it openly," he sobbed. His wife hugged him hard. "Let him be," she said. "He'll be all right."

Peronard shook his head in disbelief. What he was seeing and hearing made him feel like his stomach was being ripped out.

"I can't tell you how bad I feel for these people. Everybody has failed them up to this point, and I'm going to make sure that stops," he told his colleagues. "We've got to do right by these people. We've never seen anything like this, and I don't know if I'll ever be able to look them in the eye."

Tony Berget, the mayor, still did not acknowledge the problem, or the pain people were feeling. "There is still a split in the town. A lot of people think Grace was good for the community, treated us well and did nothing wrong," he said. "Others are worried about real-estate sales and Christmas buying."

Don Judge, head of the Montana AFL-CIO, apologized for the union's lack of knowledge and help.

"We didn't understand what was happening," Judge said, and he turned to wipe tears from his eyes. "We knew that people had good jobs and good benefits and the community of Libby was thriving because of it. Only after the plant was shut down did we understand the extent of what had been foisted upon the workers of this community, their spouses and their children."

Judge added that "the government has the responsibility to those kids to make sure this town is clean. We're going to ride somebody's ass to make sure it's done. The children need to understand that they will be free to breathe the air, to drink the water, even play on the streets of this community. They need to understand that, so they can go back to being kids."

Gayla stood up and talked about the clipping from *The Western News* praising Grace for the cleanup of the mine site.[2] The clipping quoted Grace's Alan Stringer in glowing detail about the "incredible" job the company did in restoring the mine to such a pristine condition that the Montana Mining Association gave Grace an award of excellence. The article talked of elk grazing in the lush grass and trees that Grace planted.

"That's not what's up there," Gayla said, describing the towering, mostly barren tailing pile and the nearby pond, both of which, the state admitted, were full of asbestos dust.

"That's the dust that killed my dad. That's the dust that killed Mom."

AFTER PERLEY DIED IN 1974, Margaret Vatland found herself living alone for the first time in her life.

She liked her job selling Avon, and her customers liked her. She applied herself to it with the same determination that had seen her through a winter in a shed with her children, and it wasn't long before she was one of the leading Avon distributors in northwestern Montana. She liked talking to people; it helped take the edge off the loneliness.

For the first time in their lives, Margaret and Gayla were more like sisters than mother and daughter. They were all but inseparable. David was traveling a lot in his job, and Gayla welcomed Margaret's company and marveled at the change in her relationship with her mother. Often, Margaret would come over for dinner, and she joked that Gayla's house was the only place where she could sit down to a seven-course meal and still lose weight because of all the kids that needed to be served first. And if Gayla needed to drive over to Kalispell on the spur of the moment, Margaret would rearrange her schedule and go along.

Margaret especially liked visits from her grandkids. She was still trying to get the hang of cooking for one, and often in the evening she'd call Gayla and say, "I've cooked too much again. Send my best two grandchildren over here and help me eat this dinner." And Gayla, knowing it was a plea for some company, would do just that.

Especially in the first year or so after Perley's death, Margaret and Gayla and the kids would often visit the cemetery. And some nights, Margaret would be unable to sleep, and the fear would grow with the darkness, and she'd go out to the cemetery by herself. She'd sit by Perley's grave and ask, Why?

Still, Gayla was there to help her mother recover from the loss of Perley, even as she recovered herself. Margaret found herself depending on her daughter more and more — for companionship, for help with chores, even for advice as she received attention from some of Libby's older bachelors and widowers. Gayla took on the protective, almost parental role in their relationship.

Then, a year after Perley died, Gayla's own marriage came to an end again. She and David Benefield were in love — there was no doubt about that. But Gayla couldn't stand being taken for granted, or being placed in the stereotype of the traditional Montana wife. Women's liberation had not made many inroads in Montana by 1975. She felt that she was being treated like one of Dave's possessions, expected to raise the children, cook the meals, clean the house and be compliant, no matter what time he decided to come home. That just wasn't in her nature. She expected the marriage to be a partnership, and when she found it wasn't, she divorced him again.

Six months later, he came back to Gayla and said he wanted to try again. She wanted him in her life and in their children's lives, and so she accepted him back into the house — but only on the condition that he take a strong role in raising the children. And she refused to remarry. That changed the dynamic of the relationship, and it began to work much better for Gayla. Every year, Dave would ask her to remarry him. Every year, she would refuse. It was her declaration of independence, a small but significant defiance, a refusal to be anyone but herself ever again.

The winter of 1979-80 was bitterly cold, even by Montana standards, and many houses in Libby lost running water because of frozen pipes. Gayla's was one of them. Margaret's house still had running water, so Gayla would haul 50 gallons of water from her mother's house to hers each day. It's a challenge for a family with five children to survive on 50 gallons of water a day. Wastewater from baths or the dishes was used to flush the toilet. The kids found it was a real treat to go to Margaret's house for a hot shower.

On the morning of February 29, Gayla got the kids off to school, then took the family pooch to her mother's house to give it a bath. Which, as it turns out, was very fortunate. The power company was using a welder to "hot-shot" pipes, trying to thaw them, and excess power backed through the lines, through the old transformer at Gayla's house, and literally blew the house to bits. Suddenly, the family was homeless. They had been underinsured, and so they still owed money on the house that had been destroyed.

The family turned the disaster into an opportunity. A few years before, Gayla and Dave had made a small down payment on an eight-acre parcel of land on the Kootenai River, west of Libby. Now they made plans for a log house on the property, and that summer, they lived in two campers and a tent on the property and built the house together. The entire family pitched in. Dave's father had just retired, so he showed up for work every morning at the construction site. Margaret would come out nearly every day to help however she could, either by working on the house or by watching the kids. By September, the family was under a roof once again, and that Christmas Margaret gave Gayla a photo history of the entire project. Gayla hadn't noticed that every time Margaret had come out to help, she'd brought her little camera.

The early '80s were some of the best years of Margaret's life. Her brother retired, and he and his wife took Margaret on trips all over the country. She'd return with pictures galore, and one of her great pleasures was to sit down and show off her picture albums to anyone who wanted to spend the time to look at them.

Perley had always been a little morose at Christmas. He had very negative memories of Christmas as a child, and they permanently damaged his holiday spirit. But once he was gone, Margaret went crazy for the holidays, decorating, picking out her tree and trimming it, even buying a small organ for Christmas carols. Gayla would come into the house and hear Margaret belting out carols, off-key but joyful.

She did not change her housecleaning habits. Once a year, she removed the curtains and all the pictures from the walls, and scrubbed all the ceilings and walls. She scoured her floors on hands and knees each week, and refused all suggestions to get a dishwasher. Margaret kept her yard pristine, with never a weed in sight, and took pride in her vegetable and flower gardens. The vegetables would be canned each fall. Margaret had lived through too many tough times to waste anything.

But Gayla began to notice that her mother had a persistent, dry, hacking cough. Margaret would apologize and say that her dentures had caused it. But soon it became evident to Gayla that whenever Margaret was very active, she'd have a coughing spell, and then she'd be tired and out of breath for a while. By 1983, Gayla suspected that her cough was a sign of something more serious. She suggested that perhaps her mother had the same thing Perley had had, but Margaret shrugged that off and pointed out that Perley had never really coughed very much, which was true. In the later years his lungs had lost so much elasticity that it was all but impossible for him to cough.

Every winter since 1978, Margaret had suffered from what her doctors had called pneumonia. Each time, Gayla had asked them if Margaret could have asbestosis, and had received blank stares in return.

It is somewhere between scandalous collective ineptitude and outright collusion that miners with asbestosis just didn't get diagnosed by the medical community in Libby. But based on the medical knowledge of the time, it is much more defensible that people like Margaret didn't get diagnosed for many years. Asbestosis was known to be an occupational disease. The only known victims had been exposed in a mine or a factory or some workplace setting, so it seemed preposterous to Libby doctors that a widow, formerly a housewife, who sold Avon products for a living could have asbestosis.

In April 1985, Margaret was feeling very run-down. It seemed like she'd been fighting a cold since the first of the year. Gayla came to visit her one Sunday at around noon and found her in bed, so weak she couldn't get up. Gayla called an ambulance and got her to the emergency room at the hospital. The doctor who first saw Margaret, Brad Black, had the same reaction Gayla was used to seeing when she asked about the possibility of asbestosis.

It just didn't register with him. After all, this was a town, and a hospital, that were much used to seeing older people come to the hospital with pleural or respiratory problems. The winters were harsh, and people smoked. It was common for doctors to inform people gravely that their breathing difficulties were related to smoking — and most of the time, that made sense. But sometimes people who got that news were light smokers or had never smoked.

In Margaret's case, smoking was a handy scapegoat. During her time in the hospital that April, a chest X-ray revealed a spot on her lung. Her regular physician, Dr. Bardo, told the family it was lung cancer, cited her history of smoking and described the typical progression of the disease. He told Gayla and her sister Eva that Margaret probably would not be alive next Christmas.

When Gayla asked him if Margaret should quit smoking, he replied, "Why bother at this point?" He warned the family that Margaret should not see a specialist and get a lung biopsy, because he thought that would accelerate the cancer and shorten whatever life she had.

So Margaret went home, and went about her life. She sold Avon products. She went on a short trip with her sister-in-law. And she refused to discuss the diagnosis.

Eight years before asbestosis took Perley's life, he'd been told by Libby doctors that his heart condition could kill him at any time. Now Margaret had been given a similar sentence — and, as it turned out, it was similarly inaccurate. Gayla kept watching for the progressive symptoms the doctor described, and they just didn't appear. By the time the Christmas that Margaret was not supposed to see rolled around, she was actually feeling pretty healthy, although she'd lost some weight and some strength. Later, Gayla would attribute that mostly to worry over the diagnosis. Margaret never went back to the doctor who told her she was dying of lung cancer.

In fact, Margaret wouldn't go to any doctor. It was increasingly evident that she did not have lung cancer, but her health was deteriorating and she knew, in her heart that her worst nightmare was true: She was suffering from the same disease that had killed her husband.

She was angry and bitter toward Zonolite and Grace — for killing her husband, and treating him the way they did in the process — and she did not make any attempt to hide it. When her friend Louise Gidley's husband was dying of asbestosis, she'd told Louise to "nail the company." And Louise Gidley will swear today that Margaret's phone call was the catalyst that pushed her to call an attorney.

The problem with Louise's case against Grace was the same problem many others had: Under existing Montana law it was impossible to sue a company for damages if you had not been employed by the company for the last three years or more. But the Gidley case, together with that of Alice Priest on behalf of her dead husband, Virgil, was argued all the way to the state Supreme Court.

"Alice Priest was left without a husband, without a source of income, and it was clear that her husband's death had been caused by the asbestos, but Grace refused to pay her a dime," said Roger Sullivan, the Kalispell attorney who was to play such a key role in the Libby saga.[3] The state Supreme Court ruled, in effect, that Grace couldn't have it both ways: If it contended that people were barred from recovering under the Occupational Disease Act, it could not also successfully argue that they did not retain their rights to pursue a wrongful-death action. So Louise Gidley and Alice Priest won the right to sue, and suddenly, Grace's Libby legal problems multiplied.

Sullivan said, "It certainly opened up the courthouse doors for the workers in Libby and their widows. The state Supreme Court at that time was very conservative, but the fact that this out-of-state corporation was leaving these widows with nothing I think outraged even the more conservative members of the court."

As Margaret's illness progressed, she decided to try to sue the company on her own behalf. She consulted an attorney, Tom Lewis, who told her that based on her medical records, she had a good case — that the X-rays taken in 1985 actually showed evidence of asbestosis. He filed suit, and she received a $100,000 settlement in February of 1988. Of that, she actually received $67,500. Her first two purchases were a Ford Escort — the little car she was using for her Avon route was in terrible shape — and a new hide-a-bed sofa for her living room, which she started using immediately to sleep on at night. She never admitted to Gayla that climbing the stairway at night was getting to be too difficult. She would only say she was more comfortable on her new sofa.

Now that her real diagnosis had been disclosed, she felt able to discuss it with Gayla, and she confessed that she was terrified of dying the way Perley had. She'd been in the hospital room as he slowly suffocated and the doctors tried repeatedly to resuscitate him. Finally, though, she agreed to go see a doctor again, for the first time in three years.

The doctor she went to was blessedly thorough. Margaret hadn't had a Pap smear in 20 years. He ordered one, and discovered cervical cancer in the formative stage. He also discovered a mass on one of her lungs that he wanted to operate on, but the cancer was the top priority, and indeed that operation undoubtedly saved her life.

Finally, in October 1988, he operated on Margaret's lungs. Up to that point, despite Margaret's settlement, the doctor had doubted she had asbestosis. He had never heard of a non-occupational case. But lab reports on the biopsy he took confirmed what no doctor before had been willing to consider, much less admit: Margaret Vatland was slowly dying of asbestosis.

Among the many players in the tragedy of Libby are both varieties of asbestos doctors — the don't-rock-the-boat type and the get-mad, blow-the-whistle, fight-the-company kind. The do-nothings helped first Zonolite, then Grace, keep things quiet for years.

The companies were very savvy about being involved with the medical community.[4] When Zonolite got the results of its first screening in 1959, it invited every doctor in Libby to lunch to discuss them. "I think we only had six doctors in town," Earl Lovick would later testify, "and so it was no big deal to get them together." The doctors got the results, but the miners themselves never did.

Grace exerted tremendous influence on Libby's medical community. It donated heavily to St. Joseph's Hospital and always kept an executive on the hospital board. For many years, that person was Lovick.

Libby's doctors rarely diagnosed asbestosis, and it is a safe bet that many asbestosis cases were chalked up to pneumonia or emphysema, and blamed on smoking, because most residents did smoke. The doctors were at the upper end of the little town's enduring caste system – along with merchants, lawyers and executives from the sawmill and mine – and apparently were persuaded that what they were seeing was not asbestosis.

But even before Alan Whitehouse treated hundreds of Libby patients with skill, compassion and courage, another doctor tried to help the town's victims. In the 1970s and '80s, as pressure from various sources began to lift Grace's lid on Libby, a local doctor followed his conscience. It all but destroyed his life.

Richard Irons was the kind of doctor the government wanted to encourage to work in small towns with inadequate health care, and that's just what happened.[5] He graduated from Dartmouth in 1970, did a three-year residency at Virginia Mason Hospital in Seattle, and then went off "to become a citizen of the world." He traveled in Pakistan, Afghanistan, Nepal and Iran, working in church clinics and TB centers. He was always earning just enough to make it to the next country. "It was both wonderful and horrendous," he said. "I learned firsthand the value of good medical care to a community."

Then "it was time to grow up," Irons recalled. "I found I could get the government to pay off most of my med-school loans if I agreed to practice in a community that was medically underserved. A missionary friend told me about Libby." He came, and practiced family and internal medicine.

"It was a good life. I was sort of a respected member of the community, but that ended when I started asking too many questions about the workers from the Zonolite mine who were suffering from chronic obstructive pulmonary disease. These guys were sick, and there were lots of them. I'd ask the other doctors in Libby and Kalispell about it. They all had the same answer. The same words. 'Oh, they're miners, but they all smoke.' Grace said the same thing and said it was going to start a 'stop smoking' program," Irons said.

"I kept seeing things on the X-rays that were unusual. I remember going to Kalispell and showing some film to the radiologist. I put the films up on the light box, but he wasn't even looking at it. He told me, 'Don't make waves. Treat the mumps and measles and leave the guys from the mine alone.' He wouldn't say anything else."

Irons went to Seattle a few weeks later, and he took some of the films of his patients' chests to a radiologist he knew. "It took him ten seconds: classic asbestosis. He said a first-year radiology student could have spotted it."

Over the next six months, Irons saw 11 more men with the same symptoms. What worried him most was that three of them brought their wives, who were also sick. "I wrote to Henry Eschenbach, Grace's health director, in Boston and told him what I had found. I said that more testing had to be done on the workers and their wives because there was something seriously wrong in Libby. He wrote back bragging about the stop-smoking campaign and said Grace's studies didn't show any real problems."

Eschenbach wrote to Libby mine manager R. L. Oliverio and warned that Irons could be dangerous. He said Irons seemed to think that Libby Hospital was the "Mount Sinai of the West," referring to Selikoff and the hospital he would make famous as a center for asbestos research.

Grace started to send their men to other doctors in Libby and Kalispell. Irons would ask the other doctors what they were finding. "Nothing," they said. "Stop upsetting the game" and "making a big deal about some sick miners," Irons was told. But he couldn't accept that. He wrote again to Eschenbach and told him that three of the workers recently diagnosed by other doctors as having emphysema had never smoked.

"I never heard from him, but one of the mine managers stopped me a week later and told me to stop making waves. That was everybody's favorite expression. Stop making waves." By this time, every time Irons heard that expression, it was like a red flag in front of a bull. He wrote Irving Selikoff at Mount Sinai School of Medicine. He sent a couple of chest films and mentioned that some family members were showing symptoms.

Selikoff wrote him back quickly, saying it sounded like a serious problem, particularly the disease being found in family members. He confirmed that both chest films showed asbestosis, and he offered to come out and help Irons.

ON APRIL 3, 1979, Irons declared war.

He wrote to Grace, saying that workers were dying and more tests had to be done. He said that he wanted to do a health study. And Irons ended his letter by saying, "If I don't hear from you in the next several months I am prepared to proceed with this study.... I would at that point feel justified and required to make this information public."

"I was the Lincoln County Health Officer during those years, so I took my information to the county commissioners. They told me I was probably wrong and needed more evidence," Irons said. "One commissioner told me, 'We're not going to let you destroy one of the largest employers in town.'

"And he told me 'Stop making waves.' "

Irons began to get more cases. His patients were sending their friends. He gathered as much evidence as he could. He tried to show the county commission the new evidence, but they would not let him speak at a meeting. He called the Montana Health Department and they told him they didn't think there was a problem in Libby. He called OSHA and the Bureau of Mines, too, but no one was interested.

"It's hard to be an outcast in a small town," Irons remembered. "The wife of a Grace manager stopped me in the grocery one day. She screamed that I was a horrible man bent on closing the mine. She even cursed at me."

Grace had not yet begun to fight back, but when the blow came, it was vicious and effective. The Libby hospital accused Irons of drug use and revoked his hospital privileges — the kiss of death for a small-town doctor.

"They claimed I was using drugs. I was," Irons said simply. "It was pain medicine for my back which I had been using for years." He shook his head wearily. "Grace wanted me out of town, and the hospital was going to be their tool in achieving that."

Irons never did the study he threatened to do, and he left Libby.

"It really tore me up. I was a good doctor. I had lots of patients who cared for me. Grace and the town leaders couldn't keep me quiet, so they chased me out of town. Eschenbach and Grace lied — knowingly deceived their workers and the town. I can understand Grace's motivation. Money. But Eschenbach was a physician. He took an oath. How can he sleep at night?"

Alan Whitehouse remembers it well.[6] "Irons was driven out of town. I didn't realize this at the time, but he had a handle on this long before I entered the picture. I was aware of the problem in the miners, but I suspect he actually saw the contamination in the light of a risk to the entire community.

But Grace had the power to discredit him, and the hospital went along with it by trumping up allegations of Irons's misuse of pain medicine."

Whitehouse said, "He was a courageous guy who stood up to Grace and their lackeys in town, and they did their best to beat him down. This is Grace's method."

Brad Black is a pediatrician, so when he first came to Libby, he didn't come into contact with the asbestos disease in the normal course of his work. But for three years, he and Dick Irons worked in the same building, and they would take calls for each other. "Dick only made occasional comments about the asbestos problems. It was hard for him to talk about them," Black said. "It was real hush-hush then. You know, let's not stir anything up here. There was such an oppressive atmosphere. Grace supporters were in power all over town. The last thing they wanted was any discussion of health problems at the mine."

Black thought that Irons "was genuinely worried about the workers' health. Dick may have had his faults, but his ego was never looking for any glory of any sort. He had some personal problems and Grace dug into them, prodded the hospital to go after Dick. But whatever happened, it shouldn't cloud what he was trying to do for the miners. He told me the attack on his personal life was brutal. He just wanted to see justice done. When we talked before he died, he was glad that we were moving forward."

Irons worked at a couple of clinics in other Montana towns, then went back to Seattle for a while. Eventually he settled at the Menninger Clinic in Lawrence, Kansas, where he was associate director of the addiction recovery program. He died early in 2002 of heart failure, a colleague said.

Soon Alan Whitehouse became the doctor that the Libby victims knew they could trust.[7] After medical school, a hitch in the Air Force and a couple of years at Colorado University, where he was a fellow in pulmonology, he moved to Spokane and opened his practice in 1969. From the beginning, he would see patients from Libby. He was the first pulmonologist in Spokane, so patients from all around the area would come to him for lung problems.

"I got to know the docs in Libby, so I saw a smattering of cases. I didn't understand the full significance for probably ten years. I knew there was some asbestosis, and I knew there was some contamination, but I didn't even know it was tremolite initially," he said.

Grace actually referred some patients to him for review. He found that they had asbestosis, and indicated that to them, and to Grace. "In 1988 they invited me to tour the. mine, but then they suddenly changed their mind. There must have been something they didn't want me to see."

He soon found that the Libby cases didn't follow the classical pattern of asbestosis. "What bothered me all along was that these people were a lot sicker than their X-rays indicated. When you really delved into their pulmonary functions, you found they were really short of breath, and legitimately so." He would see people who said "I'm a little short of breath" or "I'm just getting older." Then, quite suddenly, those patients would show more and more symptoms of disease, quickly becoming more disabled. Then they would die.

"There was pleurisy, and a lot of lung cancers, and mesothelioma. It just became obvious that this was not just a minor problem. It was a real major problem."

For quite a while, Whitehouse said, "There wasn't a steady line of asbestos cases. I was seeing five, six, seven, eight a year. Mostly miners, and occasionally family members, so I knew that you could get contamination from heavy dust exposure."

Whitehouse said he became really alarmed in 1997, when for the first time he started seeing people who had absolutely no connection to the mine. "That really gets your attention," he said. He would try to figure out the exposure pathway of these patients. Most of the time he wasn't able to do so, but occasionally he did.

"There was a lady named Carol Graham whose exposure was upholstering the miners' vehicles. At that time it became evident that the whole town was contaminated, and we started getting a flood of cases." All that time, Whitehouse said, "I was the dumb shit who was the loose cannon, and I still am. I wear it as a mark of pride now. That's the way the medical community works. If you say something they don't agree with and you're not in the establishment, especially if you're a chest physician in Spokane, regardless of whether you're smart or dumb, you're stupid. You don't know what you're talking about because you're not in academia."

Whitehouse began talking about the unique pattern of disease, and doing research. "I created this huge bibliography, and as time went by there were more and more articles about tremolite." Now Whitehouse knows the tremolite in the Libby ore is one of the deadliest forms of the fiber.

When Whitehouse talks of Grace's "method," he is speaking personally. "I had a deposition in 1999. It was two weeks after I had a bypass operation. They didn't want to change it. I said okay. They took a phone deposition that took nearly all day.

"That really was a dumb thing for them to do, because at that point I said, 'These sons of bitches are never going to get to me.' They tried to kill me this time and didn't make it. They should have tried before my bypass, I might have croaked on them."

Whitehouse is fierce about doing everything he can for his patients, and to him that means doing everything he can to oppose Grace. "As long as you have companies like Grace that will buy off people, will buy off docs — the hired guns from the medical community — to say what industry wants them to say, the government can continue downplaying the asbestos hazard. Grace has had some real beauts over the years. There is only one of my patients who went to trial that their expert said had asbestosis. Everything else started with obesity, smoking or some other damn reason why the guy was short of breath. They get guys to say what Grace wants them to say. I can't be bought and they know that.

"In the early days, Libby's doctors may not have known what was going on. Today they know, they just don't want the responsibility of handling patients with complex asbestos disease." Whitehouse sighed. "There is nothing worse than dying of lung disease. Nothing worse. A lot of these people are stubborn. They hang on. They drive with their oxygen, they take their time, but there isn't much they can do. They're so short of breath, walking twenty feet from the waiting room to the exam room.

"These are solid, homegrown, American working people who have very few major aspirations outside of home and family, living in a nice place. They're very forgiving, and not particularly angry. They get beat on and they just come back for more. They're solid citizens. They take whatever is given to them, and say that's what life is.

"A patient of mine came to see me. He was seventy-seven or seventy-eight and he was really getting worse, and I told him. He went home and shot himself two weeks later. I don't feel good about that, because it was in direct response to my telling him. But I can't not tell them. I try to soften whatever I tell them.

"I can usually help people die in peace."

BY THE TIME THE MINE CLOSED IN 1990, Margaret Vatland was getting sicker.

Gayla finally convinced her to hire someone to help with housecleaning. Margaret was now on full-time oxygen, delivered through tubes in her nose. But in May of 1990, her doctors inserted a scoop into her trachea to deliver oxygen more directly. The scoop had to be cleaned twice a day, which was a very difficult and exhausting job for Margaret. She'd have to hook her nasal apparatus up to get oxygen that way for a while, then spray a substance down the scoop that would force her to cough up the mucus that had developed on the end of the tube. Otherwise, the tube would become blocked and she would not be able to get oxygen. After the coughing, she had to remove the tube from her throat and reinsert a sterile one.

By this time Margaret was taking a dizzying array of medications, which forced her into a very regimented existence. If she missed a pill, or if her oxygen hose became kinked, she would have trouble breathing or get lightheaded. But she handled those crises well, and clung fiercely to her independence.

One day Gayla found Margaret, exhausted, on Margaret's back step. Her car was pulled up into the yard, a hose and bucket next to it. Margaret had been washing her car when she accidentally closed the car door on her oxygen hose, at the same time locking her keys in the car. Some sick elderly people would have panicked. Margaret had reacted with remarkable calm and resourcefulness, disconnecting her hose at the waist, then gathering her strength and running to the back porch, where she had a spare tank. When Gayla found her, Margaret admitted she was too tuckered out to get her spare keys in the house, and asked Gayla to do so, and while she was at it, could she finish washing her car, please?

Margaret was an excellent cook, but as her disease progressed she frequently lacked the energy to fix anything. So on the days she felt good, she cooked large amounts and froze portions for the bad days. It was one more little way of hanging on to her independence.

But one by one, those little victories against the disease, won at such a cost in exertion and determination, would become impossible to maintain. Hard as Margaret fought, her disease followed its immutable pattern of agony and decline.

In 1993, Margaret realized she could no longer stay in the house that had been hers for 42 years. Too many "emergencies" happened, too many times she felt at risk because Gayla and Eva lived 10 or 15 minutes away. She couldn't maintain it or clean it, and now the upstairs was out of the question. She refused to consider an apartment, because she'd have to give her two cats away. Finally, Gayla helped her find a new mobile home with the living space concentrated in the kitchen and living room, which was convenient because of Margaret's limited mobility.

Margaret hated leaving her house, but she knew it was necessary. She and Gayla found a mobile-home court within three minutes of Gayla's house. And they got a nice carport and deck built around the home. Moving day was a sad one for Margaret, but all her grandchildren and their friends pitched in, and she was able to have lunch in her new living room and watch her favorite soap opera.

That day, Gayla realized how far Margaret had weakened. When the furniture was moved from her old house, Gayla found dirt where a healthy Margaret never would have tolerated it. This woman who had always insisted that paint would last for ten years if you washed your walls regularly could no longer do the most basic housecleaning.

By the next spring, another piece of Margaret's pride was forced into retreat. Shopping had always been a vital thing for her. It was a ritual, a marking of the rhythm of life, partly a chore, partly a chance for social interaction, partly an exercise in choice and control. On shopping trips with Gayla, she would steadfastly refuse to use a wheelchair or one of the electric carts that Rosauer's, Libby's biggest and best grocery store, provided. But by the time she and Gayla got back to the car, she would be exhausted to the point of tears.

After Margaret decided not to go shopping with her a few times, Gayla told her, gently, that if she didn't agree to use either a wheelchair or an electric cart, she would probably never get out of the house and see people again. So Margaret gave a little more ground, and it turned into a real blessing. Gayla helped her get a wheelchair, and figured out how to haul it around using a bike rack and bungee cords. It was a challenge for Gayla, pushing Margaret's wheelchair and the grocery cart, but she figured out how to do it. And once Margaret got over her shame at being seen in a wheelchair, she really enjoyed getting to see people again. Before long, she agreed to try the electric carts at Rosauer's. Soon, she was going to town three days a week with Gayla, and she was happier than she'd been in months.

The summer of 1994 was the worst wildfire season around Libby in many years. The little valley filled up with smoke, and what was an inconvenience for most was a life-threatening event for Margaret. There was no place to escape the smoke. Gayla duct-taped wet towels over Margaret's windows, and within a couple of hours they would be brown with smoke and would need to be changed. It minimized the risk, but still the exposure to the smoke took its toll on Margaret's diseased lungs. By the fall, she was much weaker. She could no longer do her own laundry, although she insisted on having the clothes placed in front of her so she could at least fold them before they were put away.

Often in the winter of 1994, she would call Gayla in the night, lonely and frightened. Dying wasn't what scared Margaret, it was what would happen before then. She had watched Perley fight for every breath over the last few days of his life. Margaret insisted to Gayla that she did not want to be resuscitated.

One day Margaret asked Gayla and her sister Eva to come over. She told them that she felt bad that Perley had not been able to leave anything to them, and then said that she'd found that she could legally give her daughters $10,000 apiece. Both of them protested, saying she might need the money for her care, but Margaret insisted. So Gayla and Eva simply decided to buy two $10,000 certificates of deposit with the gifts and let them draw interest, but be available if they needed them to take care of Margaret. A few weeks later, Margaret called them in again and said she didn't want them to be concerned about her burial costs. She had been so stressed by not having the money for Perley's funeral that she didn't want her daughters going through the same thing. She signed a check and told them to go to the funeral home and pay for her funeral in advance, which they did.

Gayla was spending more and more of her time with her mother. Of course it was hard on her and her family. But Gayla felt fortunate to be able to do so much for Margaret when she had not been able to help her father much at all in his last years. But with each little task — as she bathed her mother each morning, joking to her about her "tough old hide," as she ferried her to the store and helped her around the house, as she watched her mother suffer a little more each day — Gayla's anger toward Grace grew.

In February 1995, it looked as though Margaret's preparations had been made just in time. She was hospitalized with severe pneumonia, and the doctor warned Gayla and Eva that she was dying. Watching her, Gayla realized that what Margaret feared most was coming true. She was fighting for every breath, chest heaving. She was, in effect, nearly suffocating.

Gayla would go to the hospital each morning at 6 A.M. and stay with her until another family member could relieve her. Someone would be with Margaret around the clock. She could barely communicate, but she was fighting hard. Gayla would return at about 8 P.M. and stay until 1 A.M. or so, and during those night visits Margaret would talk about her childhood, about family, about dying.

But on the morning of her eleventh day in the hospital, Margaret asked to have the curtains in her room opened to let the sun in. Despite the doctor's prediction, Margaret was not ready to die. Gayla realized that her mother was getting better when she started calling Gayla at 4 A.M. from the hospital and asking her to come on down and get the day started. Gayla was understandably a zombie at that hour, and one morning at around 5 A.M., after she had cleaned Margaret's dentures, she started to put them into her own mouth, which both of them found pretty funny. They erupted with laughter, and Gayla realized it had been a very long time since she had heard her mother laugh. It was a wonderful sound.

The doctor met with Gayla and the rest of the family and confirmed that the immediate danger was past. But he also provided a reality check: Margaret could go home, but she could well be bedridden for the rest of her life, and she would probably not survive the next infection. He suggested that the care center would be a sensible option.

Gayla refused. She and her mother had made a deal: As long as Margaret was still mentally clear, she would not be placed in the nursing home. That meant Gayla had a lot of work to do, quickly. She had a wall removed from the living room of Margaret's mobile home, to make room for all the equipment she would need. She got an electric bed, a commode, and a privacy screen, and located qualified caregivers to help her. Margaret quickly determined the boundaries of her new life, and she adjusted to them quite well. She could still get into her wheelchair by herself, and could feed herself, and she was able to let people know what she needed. Quite forcefully. But her agreement with Gayla was that they would both try their best, and they did.

Some of the early caregivers were good, and some weren't. The job had so many facets — companion, medical monitor, personal attendant. Gayla had to sort all that out, and replace the ones who didn't measure up. Kim, the primary night caregiver, told Gayla that often Margaret would lie in bed and curse Perley for bringing home the dust, nearly shouting in her agony and anger.

As she took care of Margaret, Gayla tried to maintain a semblance of her own life, but a family member in the latter stages of asbestosis does not leave room for much else.

Gayla tried to reserve Wednesday nights for bowling with Dave, but Margaret resented it. She would call Gayla for help each Wednesday evening. Gayla understood Margaret's anger, but that didn't make it any easier.

Kim was one of the few caregivers who would stay with Margaret from start to finish, but that commitment would be sorely tried. The stress would build between her and Margaret all week, and by week's end Margaret would be ready to fire her, or Kim would vow to walk out forever. The first few times Gayla witnessed their Friday-morning fights, she was terrified. She knew it would be next to impossible to find someone else as good as Kim. But soon Gayla realized it was all part of the routine. Both of them simply needed to release stress and frustration.

After all, Margaret's life was truly nightmarish. Weak and in pain, this woman who had harvested wheat and taught her kids to swim in the creek was trapped in her bed like a butterfly pinned on a board. She was using a catheter and a bedpan now in order to save energy. Gayla got her a remote for her TV, but the shows did not bring her much pleasure. Gayla made video clips of Margaret's great-grandchildren, which only upset her because they showed how much she was missing.

In fact, the only time she smiled was when the great-grandkids came to visit. Because of the fear of infection, they had to wear surgical masks, and they couldn't stay for too long or she would get too tired.

Margaret worked hard to keep up her appearance. She was particular with her clothes — she dressed for the daytime and put on nightclothes in the evening — and she demanded that her earrings be changed each day. She also liked to have her hair styled daily, but washing it was an ordeal. But so was almost everything. Margaret's disease made it difficult to regulate her body temperature. Sometimes that summer she would be chilled despite the fact that it was 90 degrees outside, and would ask to be wrapped in blankets warmed in the dryer.

The emotional and physical realities of Margaret's care were daunting enough, but the financial realities were staggering. Margaret's care was costing more than $3,000 per month. By the summer, Margaret's funds were almost exhausted. Gayla cashed in the $10,000 CD her mother had given her and spent it within four months. Then Eva cashed her CD and added another $10,000 of her money. All was quickly consumed by the care. Meanwhile, Margaret's condition deteriorated. She never regained the strength she had lost in the hospital, and each month brought a new setback of some kind.

November 19, 1995, was Margaret's 77th birthday. As they had for the past several years, her children and grandchildren visited her, one at a time, each bringing a flower, and by the end of the day she had an enormous bouquet. It was probably the best day of the last part of her life.

The next month, though, Christmas didn't feel much like a holiday — just another evening in the flickering half-world of the dying. Gayla made sure her mother took the medicine that made this obligatory imitation of life possible. Kim came at 9 P.M., and Margaret settled in for another restless night, her mind if not her lips forming the sour supplication so well-known to the bed-bound: *Lord, please let this be the final indignity, the final struggle for half a breath. Merciful God, let this end before morning.*

The other asbestos-related diseases, particularly mesothelioma, which had killed Eva's husband in 1992, are quick by comparison. But there is no mercy in asbestosis, and the disease was not done with Margaret yet. In January 1996, Margaret's condition deteriorated and Gayla alerted the caregivers to make absolutely certain she took her sedative at night. Gayla was worried that she might hoard them and take them all at once. There were times when she regretted giving that instruction, feeling that since Margaret had so little control over her life, perhaps she should have control over her death.

By March, the family was broke again, and Gayla was forced to borrow $15,000 against Margaret's mobile home. Finally, nearly 17 months after she was first bedridden, Margaret got so weak that she and Gayla both realized there was no option but the nursing home. Gayla started to make arrangements. Margaret would be hospitalized for three days for a transitional period that was required before she could go to the care center.

Those last couple of days at home, Margaret was sad and lost. She called some of her family to her side and gave away many of her possessions, knowing she would never come home again. The next morning, Gayla came early to help her get ready for her ambulance ride to the hospital. Margaret was very worried about her old cats, and she made Gayla promise to have them put to sleep. She didn't want them running off and being scared and alone.

By the second day in the hospital, it was clear that Margaret was failing quickly. She drifted in and out of consciousness for nearly a week. One day, Gayla came in to find her crying. She had heard that the cats had indeed been put down. Gayla told her that David had brought them back from the vet's office to the house, and had dug graves for them down by the river. The grandchildren had come, and placed flowers on the graves. The kids only knew one prayer — "Now I Lay Me Down to Sleep" — so they said that, and then they wanted to sing a song, but the only one they all knew was "Happy Birthday," so they sang that. When Gayla told Margaret, they laughed and cried together.

On Sunday morning, June 24, the doctor called Eva and Gayla together. He said their mother had actively decided to die three days before. She was tired and ready to leave. He said that he was letting her go, and if either of them wanted more aggressive treatment, they could find another doctor. But they knew Margaret's wishes, and they agreed. The doctor said her time was short, and she wouldn't suffer as much as Perley had. She would just slip away.

Everybody in the family saw Margaret over the next couple of days. Providentially, her brother from Texas even showed up. He had not known that she was near death, but had wanted to come see her. Nobody said good-bye, but everyone enjoyed having some time with her. Gayla stayed with her until 1 A.M. on Wednesday. She was resting comfortably, and finally Gayla went home. She had been at the hospital around the clock for ten days. Gayla woke at 6 A.M. and knew something was wrong because Margaret hadn't called. She got to the hospital and discovered that her mother had slipped into a coma at about 2 A.M.

At 7 A.M. Margaret woke up briefly, squeezed Gayla's hand and said, "This dying is so tough, Gayla, so tough." She asked Gayla to have the children all bring one flower at her funeral. Gayla hadn't realized how much she'd enjoyed that little tradition.

Gayla reminded her of everyone who was waiting for her: Perley, her friends and her cats. When Gayla said "cats," Margaret smiled and drifted off again, and a couple of hours later she drifted away.

The evening after Margaret's funeral, a summer thunderstorm passed over Libby, and an enormous rainbow followed, starting at each end of the valley and slowly building a perfect arc. In the distance behind the rainbow, far down the Kootenai drainage, the thunderheads still rolled, and lightning flew in all directions, and Margaret Vatland's family knew she was finally at rest.

Obituary: Margaret S. Vatland

Margaret S. Vatland, 77, of Libby died Wednesday, June 25, 1996, at St. John's Lutheran Hospital after a long and courageous battle with asbestosis.

She was born on Nov. 19, 1918, at Maple Creek, Saskatchewan, Canada, to John and Lydia Samenock Rody.

Margaret moved to Montana with her family as a small child. She married Perley Vatland on Oct. 27, 1937, and they moved to Libby in 1945.

A wife and mother, Margaret also was a local sales representative for Avon. She also enjoyed gardening, caring for her pets, traveling and the role of grandmother and great-grandmother.

Her husband Perley died in 1974.

—*The Western News, June 26, 1996*

William Russell Grace traveled to Peru and began what would become a world-wide corporation by selling bird droppings. (Library of Congress)

W.R. GRACE & COMPANY had a less-than-fragrant beginning. Bird droppings were the company's first stock-in-trade.[1] William Russell Grace was born in Queensland, County Cork, Ireland, in 1832. At age 19, he fled the disease and starvation of the potato famines with thousands of other Irish. The young man and 180 other people arrived on July 20, 1851, at the port of Callao, Peru, which is six miles from Lima. They were to work on a sugar plantation owned by a British surgeon in desperate need of workers, according to a Grace historian, Lawrence Clayton. But even with the new arrivals, the plantation failed, as malaria ran wild through the Peruvian countryside. Many of the surviving Irish fled to Australia or New York or California's gold fields.

Grace stayed, intrigued by the people of Peru, their language and their country. The port of Callao bustled with ships — New England whalers, slave carriers, ships filled with fertilizer heading to Europe and others bound for California. Here, among the tall ships, the young Grace found work as a salesman for John Bryce & Company, the port's largest ship chandler. He excelled in determining what the ships needed and developed better ways to package the material. It took just two years for the young Irishman to become a partner in Bryce, Grace & Co.

The islands off Callao had, for hundreds of years, been the nesting grounds for countless pelicans, cormorants and other birds. The rainless coastal islands were covered in whitish-gray peaks towering hundreds of feet. The hills were not granite or sandstone, but guano, or droppings, from the birds. The foul-smelling material was rich in nitrogen and had been considered nature's finest fertilizer since the time of the Incas, who used it on their crops in the foothills of the Andes. Soon the entrepreneur was able to charter a dozen tall ships to continuously ship guano to both coasts of America.

In 1866, Grace and his bride moved to New York. Out of a small building on Wall Street, he chartered and ran ships from New York to all the countries along South America's west coast. The cargo holds were filled coming and going, and the profits made it easy for Grace to have his own ships constructed.

In 1867, the ship *Lillius* — named after his wife — was launched from the shipyard in Thomaston, Maine. Two years later, the *Agnes L. Grace,* named after his daughter born that year, was launched. Grace was well on his way to establishing the first freight shipping line to serve the Americas.

By 1872, Grace's business was widespread and varied. Steel rails and lumber were being shipped from both the eastern and western coasts of the United States to several South American countries building railroads. Locomotives and boxcars were soon being purchased and shipped by the company. By year's end, William formally chartered W.R. Grace & Co. into being.

A year later, the *W.R. Grace,* a 1,900-ton downeaster, was launched from the shipyard in Bath, Maine. The tall-sailed vessel was the star of Grace's New York-to-California run and made 12 trips around the Horn until it was wrecked in a hurricane.

In 1880, Grace, already known by his presence in the society pages, garnered more attention in New York when a steam-powered ferry on which he and his family were riding from Long Island to Manhattan exploded. Of the 350 souls on board, 50 perished in the flames. Headlines in the next morning's newspapers credited Grace and his wife with saving the lives of many. Grace had already been urged by the Tammany Hall gang to seek political office, and the wave of publicity was the perfect springboard.

The lower east side of Manhattan was filled with Irish, and their strong and well-organized voting bloc cut through other contenders in the city's fragmented Democratic party and eased William Grace into the mayoralty of New York City. Grace was the first Catholic and the first foreign-born citizen elected to that office. He was elected to a second term in 1884.

Grace attracted national attention for his zeal in doing the unthinkable — ending bribes, kickbacks and payoffs demanded of all companies doing business with the city. He impressed even his critics with the stylish manner in which he coordinated the burial of Ulysses Grant and accepted the Statue of Liberty from the people of France.

Back in South America, Grace and his offspring did more than meddle in foreign policy — they openly backed Peru in the War of the Pacific. The five-year war which began in 1879 pitted Chile against Peru and Bolivia, and, in part, was over the right to exploit nitrate deposits. Grace's ships shuttled rifles, carbines and Gatling guns from the warehouses of Winchester and Remington to the ports of Peru. In contrast, Grace apparently also cared for social reform. In 1898, he opened the Grace Institute in a large, old mansion in New York. The school, where 500 girls and young women had enrolled, taught not only cooking and sewing, but also stenography, millinery and bookkeeping.

In 1899, W.R. Grace & Company was incorporated in Connecticut.

By the turn of the century, William Grace had turned much of his energy to the construction of a canal in Central America. The need for such a pathway was obvious. It could cut 8,000 miles off a trip from New York to San Francisco. On August 14, 1904, a Grace ship was the first commercial vessel through the newly constructed Panama Canal. William Grace died that year and, three years later, his son, Joseph P. Grace, became the company's president.

While freight shipments had been the backbone of Grace's success for more than half a century, in 1917 the *Santa Ana* was christened as the first of the Grace Line passenger ships. In 1907, Joseph P. Grace turned his attention to the world of banking, and, seven years later, he established the Grace National Bank, forerunner of Marine Midland Bank. By the end of World War I, Grace was known as one of the world's largest commodities traders. The bank had offices in 150 cities, mostly overseas, and the Grace flag flew over hundreds of ships crossing all the world's oceans, their holds filled with coffee, tea, sugar, rubber and minerals.

On a clear morning in September 1928, Joseph Grace watched a tiny single-engine Fairchild monoplane with four passengers and a bag of mail take off from a racetrack in Lima. The fuel tank was down to vapors when the plane landed in a soccer field in Talara, Peru. This was the beginning of scheduled commercial air transportation along the west coast of South America and the launch of Panagra (Pan American Grace Airways). Grace kept 50 percent of the airline until it was sold to Braniff in March 1966.

J. Peter Grace became president of the company in 1945, at age 32. He would run it for almost a half-century, turning W.R. Grace & Company into a conglomerate. Although the company's focus remained on chemicals and packaging, Peter Grace moved the company into everything from sporting goods to fast-food restaurants.

According to a report by the *Los Angeles Times,* shortly after World War II ended and he took control of the company, Grace took a strong role in bringing a Nazi war criminal to this country. Otto Ambros, a German chemist, constructed and ran Hitler's synthetic-rubber-and-fuel factory complex at the Polish village of Auschwitz. He was convicted during the Nuremberg trials of 25,000 counts of slavery and mass murder, and was sentenced to eight years in prison. After three and a half years, he was freed — and Peter Grace hired him as a research chemist and asked Congress to allow his emigration to the United States.

An internal State Department document describes how Grace helped Ambros with a letter to the U.S. Ambassador to West Germany. In the letter, the corporate leader acknowledged that Ambros was a war criminal, but added that in the years he'd known Ambros, "We have developed a very deep admiration, not only for his ability, but more important, for his character in terms of truthfulness and integrity."

Grace also was involved in Project Paperclip — a post-World War II CIA-backed arrangement to remove classified information from dossiers so that former SS members and more than 900 Nazi scientists could emigrate to the United States. Hundreds of war criminals would find employment within government agencies and companies such as Grace.

In 1954, Grace acquired Davison Chemical Company and Dewey & Almy Chemical Company and became a leader in packaging products. So it was only logical that Grace would want to buy the world's largest supply of vermiculite, because of the mineral's many uses in packaging, construction materials and insulation. That supply, of course, was located on Zonolite Mountain in Libby, Montana. The February 28, 1963, edition of Libby's *Western News* trumpeted, ZONOLITE STOCKHOLDERS TO VOTE MONDAY TO APPROVE MERGER WITH GRACE CO.

The Zonolite stock price had been driven up by a good earnings year and by rumors of the impending merger. But much of Zonolite's strength in the negotiation came from the simple fact that they owned the mountain of vermiculite, a pile very conservatively estimated at the time of the sale to be enough ore to mine throughout the next fifty years at the current rate. The entire vermiculite industry had been built around the Libby deposit.

At the time of the sale to Grace, nearly half a century after Alley's discovery, more than three-quarters of the world's supply was still being produced in Libby. Grace saw even more potential. The Zonolite Corp.'s building-products division operated eighteen of its own expansion plants, in addition to selling ore to scores of other companies who processed it themselves. Grace would greatly increase that nationwide network of plants that made and distributed Zonolite insulation for attics and walls.

Of course, in buying the Zonolite assets, Grace also assumed all of the company's liabilities, an addition that would prove to be very expensive.

Les Skramstad was surprised at how much vermiculite was visible in soil collected from his yard and garden. (Andrew Schneider)

MORNINGS for Les Skramstad are a mixed blessing.

The old cowboy makes his way to the kitchen. He's usually a bit wobbly, but he braces himself against the counter and gets the coffee going, if Norita didn't beat him to the pot.

"Just making it to the table and I'm out of air," he laments.

Les sits down at the pine table and rests his head in his hand while he tries to catch his breath. He pours medicine into a cigar-box-sized machine sitting on the table. The label on the medicine box states: ALBUTEROL — A GREAT ADVANCEMENT IN BRONCHODILATOR THERAPY.

"All I know is that it makes breathing easier. That's what you worry about with asbestosis — breathing."

Medicated air flows from the plastic tube into his mouth. He takes breaths as deep as he can manage, trying to pull air into the asbestos-scarred tissue. Five, six minutes he sucks it in. His color improves. His eyes sparkle a bit. He's breathing easier. He makes it through the day in fits and starts. The slightest activity leaves him breathless again, and wheezing.

"He keeps at it. He won't give up," Norita said. "He'll go outside and work on the tractor for a few minutes, then sit down, catch his breath, and go back to the tractor and work another couple of minutes. Oxygen would help, but he'll never do it. To him it would be like giving up."

Each day that Les wakes up is another victory; each night another living hell.

It's hard to sleep when your lungs aren't pliable enough to breathe in the air you need to live. He tosses and turns. Norita gets even less sleep worrying about him. When he finally lies still, she lies there listening to hear that he's still breathing. His breaths are so shallow that she can barely see his chest rise, but she never mentions it.

Les is adamant about the oxygen.

"Dragging a tank of air behind you is like admitting that you're dying. Everybody I know who started on oxygen died a few months later," he said, pursing his lips and shaking his head.

"It's like giving in to Grace and saying 'Yeah, you killed another one.'"

"THIS IS A CASE ABOUT ASBESTOSIS, which is a fatal lung disease," Jon Heberling told the jury in his opening statement on May 13, 1997.[1]

He was in the Lincoln County Courthouse in Libby, more precisely the 19th Judicial District Court for the State of Montana, and he did not mince words. "Les Skramstad was diagnosed with asbestosis in 1995. His asbestos exposure was working at Zonolite here in Libby, from 1959 to 1961. He'll die of asbestosis."

Heberling, in his early 50s, still looked very youthful with his full head of blond hair with a few strands of gray.[2] Gangly at 6'1", he was soft-spoken but very effective in the courtroom. He had practiced law down the road from

Libby, in Kalispell, for 23 years, and he had won judgments for plaintiffs in all kinds of injury cases. But rarely had he had as much riding on the outcome of a case as he did in this trial. This was not just about Les and Norita. This was about all the miners and their families, and the other Libby asbestos victims who were waiting for justice.

Les didn't intend to take this case out of the hands of the jury, once they got it. He didn't intend to settle or sign a confidentiality agreement, and he didn't intend to back off an inch. Les Skramstad isn't an angry man by nature. Like many Montanans, he generally gives people the benefit of the doubt. Until he's shown otherwise, he'll think the best of folks.

But now he'd been shown otherwise. He'd been injured in a way that his doctors said would eventually kill him, and W.R. Grace had refused to take responsibility. He didn't just have a chip on his shoulder about Grace. He had the whole log. And he was determined to do everything he could to give them absolute hell, because he thought that's what they deserved. And Les Skramstad does believe in people getting just what they deserve.

So here he sat with Norita at his side, nervous as could be, listening to his lawyer tell a jury and a handful of spectators — Gayla Benefield and Norita's sister and one or two others — how sick he was. Les was out of his element, like a cowboy in a courtroom, which of course was exactly what he was.

Judge Michael Prezeau had greeted the jury that morning with an apology in advance. "This is a complicated case. It's been going on for a long time, with lots of issues and paperwork and things for me to consider. You determine the facts, but I have to consider the law, and the law can be sort of difficult to get a handle on sometimes." He said that he and the people in his court would do their best to make the jurors' service as pleasant as possible. "So if you would rather have maple bars than bear claws, let us know."

But the way Jon Heberling was setting out the case, it didn't seem like it was going to be that complicated. Les was sick. He got sick from working at Zonolite. Zonolite was purchased by Grace, who assumed responsibility for Zonolite's obligations. And the people at Zonolite (and later at Grace) didn't tell Les or the other miners about the danger they faced at work every day.

"The dust, which was everywhere, was twenty- to thirty-percent asbestos. Les Skramstad had no information on the serious health hazards of breathing asbestos fibers. The evidence will show that the company knew all along," Heberling said. "In 1959, before Les Skramstad went to work, the company did X-rays on all its employees, and thirty-six percent of them showed abnormal lung X-rays. The company did not tell the workers and did not tell Les Skramstad."

Then, using photographs and slides, he gave jurors a tour of the Zonolite operation, as it existed when Les worked there:

"The mining area is up here ... there would be blasting, and then the power shovels would put the ore into trucks and the trucks would come down the road.... The material was dumped into a conveyor that came down the steep hill to the dry mill. ... The mill had seven floors to it ... sort of like a seven-level sandbox toy. The material would be poured in the top and go down through the chutes and conveyors....

"Les Skramstad worked as a sweeper in the dry mill.... There will be testimony that the men that came out of the dry mill sometimes looked like snowmen.... It was hard to see a light bulb at ten or twenty feet because the dust was so heavy."

Then Heberling talked about the experimental lab, where Les worked on the project to take asbestos and clean the other material out of it, to make it one-hundred-percent "pure." And he talked about the work Les did in the dry mill and on the skip track as a millwright, and how he occasionally fired up the expanding furnace and "popped" vermiculite ore.

He told the jury a little about asbestosis, and about Les's health, and he said that Dr. Whitehouse would testify in detail about both. He mentioned rales, the abnormal crackling noises in Les's lungs when he breathed, from the scar tissue.

And then Heberling turned his guns toward the target — Zonolite, and by extension, W.R. Grace. He projected a page from Benjamin Wake's 1956 state report about the mine, highlighting the passage in which Wake said "the asbestos dust in the air is of considerable toxicity." And he mentioned that Wake's report had been stamped THIS REPORT IS CONFIDENTIAL AND IS NOT FOR DISTRIBUTION EXCEPT TO THE MANAGEMENT OF THE ZONOLITE COMPANY.

Short of protesting an egregious breach of the rules of law, it's considered bad form to object in the middle of an attorney's opening statement. But Gary Graham did not want the jury concentrating on what they'd just heard. So the Grace lawyer piped up. "Your Honor." He paused for a moment, then continued. "I hesitate objecting, but ..." He went on to make a technical point, that he had not been given notice that the document Heberling referred to was to be shown in the opening statement.

"The cat is out of the bag on that one," Prezeau said. Then he gave the jury a few minutes' break, while giving Graham a chance to look at any other documents Heberling intended to use in the rest of his opening.

Graham knew that the reference to Wake's report was accurate. But he was able to cast doubt on it by saying, "I'll just have to accept Mr. Heberling's assurance that he has made to the court ... that these are accurate documents."

Prezeau overruled the objection. The judge doubtless felt his own kind of pressure. He knew he had to be utterly impartial, in appearance as well as in fact. Before his appointment to the bench, Prezeau was an attorney at the Missoula law firm of Garlington, Lohn and Robinson, one of the largest and oldest law firms in Montana. It has built its practice and reputation representing corporations. Among its prominent clients are Anaconda Copper and the Milwaukee Railroad. And W.R. Grace & Company.

Gary Graham is a partner at Garlington, Lohn and Robinson.

He objected once more during his adversary's opening statement, when Heberling said, "The judge has ruled that we can only talk about conditions up to 1967.... We will show that a lot of the conditions [at the mine] that existed in '59 were not corrected by '67. There will be no evidence that they were corrected by '68, either, but that's how we're going to handle this. Otherwise we would have a case about the fifties, sixties, seventies — "

And Graham objected. "Beyond the scope of the judge's ruling."

Prezeau told the jury that they "should not infer that this was an ongoing problem beyond 1967. There won't be evidence of that.... I don't want the comment Mr. Heberling just made to cause you to infer that there is some artificial cutoff here." As the chest X-rays of many miners who worked at the mine after 1967 would attest, the judge's cutoff was indeed quite artificial. But Heberling pointed out that since Les worked there from '59 to '61, that period was enough for the jury to be concerned about, and he wrapped up his opening there.

Then Gary Graham stood up and did his best to counter the first impression that had just been left with the jury.

Grace couldn't have hoped for a better advocate. Graham was perfectly suited to the task. He knew Montana juries very well, for good reason. He grew up on a farm near Kalispell and went to elementary school in a one-room schoolhouse. He got his undergraduate degree from Montana State and his law degree from the University of Montana and, excepting a stint as a clerk for a federal judge in the 9th Circuit, had spent his entire career in his home state. He was handsome — square-jawed, gray-haired, with eyes that could sparkle with warmth or pierce like lasers — and articulate without being effete. He was a formidable presence in the courtroom.

"You have just been told that Zonolite and Mr. Earl Lovick were basically indifferent to their employees, were negligent in the manner in which they dealt with the dust problem ... and failed to act as they should have toward their employees in general and Mr. Skramstad in particular.

"That's simply not the case here. Earl and the company were concerned about the employees, their health, and took what steps they believed were reasonable and appropriate at that time. And we're talking about 1959 through 1961."

He hammered on that theme. It was the best one he had. "One other historical perspective we might put out was that Mr. Skramstad left Zonolite in 1961, and that was two years before Kennedy got assassinated, even.

"Not only was there less information in those days, but the information we did have was filtered through different personal experience ... that's really what this trial is about."

After giving a little early history, he returned to the we-didn't-know-it-would-kill-you concept. "The work at the mine and mill was clearly hard and dusty work, but it was honest work and it provided a lot of families in the Libby area with a livelihood in those days.

"As you will hear, the dust was readily apparent," he said. But he quickly added that the "outdoor work had the advantage of nature's ventilation" and "all of the information Mr. Heberling was talking about as to dust measurements and problems and so on and so forth was at the dry mill ... not the experimental lab, not the mine. Nowhere else."

As if that weren't enough.

Graham told the jury about the state inspections in the 1940s finding "nuisance dust" at Zonolite, and said that's why "old-timers" at the mine referred to it that way when they were questioned by newer miners.

In his effort to show that the company didn't know way back then that the dust was lethal, Graham knew he had to deal with the Glenn Taylor case — the miner who was diagnosed with asbestosis at the state tuberculosis sanitarium and died of it in 1959.

"The admission diagnosis, which you will probably see in this case, said 'possible asbestosis.' The final diagnosis was asbestosis, but there was a recommendation that to confirm whether or not this was actually asbestosis, a biopsy would be needed, and one was never performed," he said.

Of course, Gary Graham knew that back in 1986 Grace had produced an alphabetical list of all known employees at the mine and had attempted to estimate their exposure to asbestos, expressed in "asbestos years." Glenn Taylor worked for Zonolite for just over 14 years. Grace estimated his number of "asbestos years" of exposure during that time to be 1,356.

Then Gary Graham told the jury that, in effect, Les's exposure to asbestos was his own fault. "You will hear Mr. Skramstad's testimony that he was provided with a respirator, but chose to wear it around his neck."

And finally, he said he would show that Les's diabetes and his smoking were more to blame for his health problems than asbestos. "It's our contention that, to the extent problems exist as a result of any asbestos-related disease which he has, those problems are minimal" compared to the diabetes.

As his opening concluded, he poured a little sugar over his harsh words. "Earl Lovick ... will testify of his concern and the steps that he took to try to protect the employees. Lack of concern is not the motive for disputing Mr. Skramstad's claim. The facts and the evidence I've just discussed are the basis for disputing this claim."

IT WAS ONLY LUNCHTIME ON THE FIRST DAY of the trial, but Les and Norita already felt like they'd been through a war.

Now Heberling and Sullivan would lay out their case before the jury, and all they could do was hope that it would be convincing, even after Graham and the rest of the Grace team had done their best to pick it apart.

The first two witnesses, Don Johnson and Stu Cannon, were both former Zonolite and Grace employees. Both had asbestos-related disease, although Heberling and Sullivan were not allowed to get that fact into evidence. They described the physical layout of the mine, and talked about the dust, and the company's response to it. Both said the company did not warn them of any danger in the dust. Johnson testified about mill manager Harold Flatt, in the '50s, telling him and other workers, "It hasn't hurt anybody yet." And Stu Cannon testified that his boss, Ray Kujawa, told him, "I could breathe a ton of it. It could never hurt me." He also testified that Kujawa was in the dry mill a lot, but he never saw him wear a respirator.

Kujawa worked at the mine for 34 years. Grace estimated his exposure at 110 asbestos years, and he died of asbestos-related disease in 1988. Cannon, who worked at the mine only four years, from 1960 to 1964, was estimated at 97.03 asbestos years. Johnson worked on the hill for 33 years, and his exposure was estimated at 755.91 asbestos years.

When Graham's co-counsel Kelly Wills cross-examined Cannon, he asked, "It's true, isn't it, that you and your wife have sued W.R. Grace?"

"We have a case going, or pending."

"And it's true, isn't it, that you are making the exact same claim as Mr. Skramstad?"

"Your honor!" Sullivan said. "I wasn't allowed to establish evidence of his health condition, and now he's asking about that line."

"I don't need a speech, I just need an objection," Prezeau snapped. "And I'll sustain the objection."

As the cross-examination continued, Wills established that respirators were made available to Cannon and the other miners, but he couldn't do much else with him. Graham was similarly brief with Johnson. There was no percentage in leaving these obviously sick men in front of the jury for too long.

Heberling called Earl Lovick. He established his age — 76 — and took Lovick through his career at Zonolite and Grace — as accountant, assistant manager, manager of the Libby operation, and manager of administration at Libby. Lovick said that after his retirement, he helped Grace as a consultant, with an "epidemiologic study" and in a tax dispute with the state of Montana. Heberling also established that Lovick had testified in several trials and had been deposed at least 22 times. Lovick testified that Grace paid him $300 per day for preparing, being deposed and reviewing his deposition each time.

"Do you receive a pension from W.R. Grace?" Heberling asked.

"Yes, sir."

"Does that include health insurance?"

"I would object, Your Honor," Graham said. "That is irrelevant, totally."

"Sustained."

Heberling then peppered Lovick with questions. He took him through Benjamin Wake's 1956 and 1959 reports, getting him to admit that he did not do any further investigation of the asbestos hazard after receiving them, and that the company did not share the reports with the union, the safety committee or the workers themselves. He forced Lovick to testify about the Glenn Taylor case and the subsequent letter from the state sanitarium, and about the X-rays of employees taken in 1959, and that the results of that screening were not shared, individually or collectively, with the workers.

Then Heberling brought out Wake's 1962 report, which stated that no progress had been made in lessening the dust problem since the earlier reports. And he produced a January 1965 letter from Butch Bleich to Zonolite president J. A. Kelley discussing the state reports, in which Bleich wrote:

"In going over these reports, I can only say that it presents a very sorry record. There is some improvement indicated during 1964 but still totally inadequate."

Lovick testified that he "probably" disagreed with that letter, but Heberling pointed out that he had said in deposition he didn't recall disagreeing with it. Finally, he asked Lovick about receiving medical literature from Grace management showing a much higher incidence of disease among asbestos workers who smoked.

"You, yourself, quit smoking in 1972 or so, correct?"

"Yes, sir."

"And that was after you had a lung operation for removal of a pleural plaque due to asbestos?"

"Yes, sir."

"To your knowledge, did the company ever warn ex-workers like Les Skramstad not to smoke because they'd been exposed to asbestos?"

"No, sir, I don't know that."

Graham wanted Lovick off the stand. Repairing his testimony under the rules of cross-examination would not be nearly as effective as calling him later in the trial as Grace's witness, and so he told Prezeau, "We would reserve our questions, which will be, in light of this examination, very extensive, for our case-in-chief, Your Honor."

After short testimony from another former worker, Andrew Wright, who testified he never saw anyone wear a respirator in the mill, Les Skramstad took the stand.

Heberling got Les to tell the jury about Zonolite, about the work, the company, and the dust; about his family, and his diagnosis.

"At the time that you were hired, Les, did the company warn you that asbestos was of considerable toxicity to human beings?"

"I never heard the word 'asbestos' mentioned."

"What about the word 'toxic'?"

"Never heard 'toxic.'"

"What about 'health hazard'?"

"Never heard that one, either."

"During the entire time that you worked at Zonolite, did the company ever warn you that asbestos was toxic or harmful?"

Les bit off the words like a cold chisel bites rock. "Never one time."

At the end of the examination, Sullivan asked, "Les, if the company would have disclosed to you the toxicity of asbestos, would you have continued to work there?"

"Not another day."

Gary Graham did not ease into his cross-examination. He stood up and said, "Mr. Skramstad, had you learned that cigarettes cause lung cancer, would you have smoked another cigarette?"

"Well, probably not."

"And you did know that cigarettes caused lung cancer and you continued smoking, didn't you?"

"I don't know if I knew that for a fact or not. I seen it written on the side of the packages toward the end, but in the first days, there was none of that."

Now, having established his animosity to Les, and given the jurors the mental connection that it was Les's choice to smoke, and his choice to work at Zonolite, Graham switched tactics. He was nice as pie.

"I am going to ask you a few questions, and they are going to be a little bit — probably not as organized as the questions that your attorney was asking you, and I ask you to bear with me. And if you don't understand any of my questions, just be sure you let me know. And if you want a break at any time, just let me know and we can work that out with the court. Okay?"

"Okay."

"My understanding is you started out like I did, as a farmer, is that right?" Letting the jury know about his own background.

"My parents were farmers, yes."

He went over Les's duties at Zonolite, establishing that he did not work long as a sweeper in the dry mill. "You indicated that it was dusty in the experimental lab?"

"Yes."

"And it's correct that you don't know the makeup of that dust, isn't that right?"

A few minutes later, he asked, "You knew that the purpose of a respirator was not to have it hanging around your neck or hanging on a nail or in the locker or something, didn't you?"

Les replied, "To be honest with you, I don't know what the purpose was."

He asked Les some more questions about smoking, and about his diabetes, but he kept it short. He wasn't scoring enough points to offset the danger of engendering resentment among jurors for badgering Les Skramstad.

Sullivan took the opportunity for a short redirect. His last question was "When the supervisor told you to just go to the warehouse and get a respirator, did the supervisor then tell you that the company was well aware since 1956 that there was a serious health hazard in the asbestos dust at the Zonolite facility?"

"Objection, leading, asked and answered several times," Graham snapped, and Prezeau sustained the objection, but Sullivan knew the jury would remember that question. It was the last one of the day.

ROGER SULLIVAN AND JON HEBERLING had put in an enormous amount of work to get to trial on Les Skramstad's case.

In a way, it went all the way back to 1986, just a year after Roger Sullivan graduated from law school at the University of Montana and moved to Kalispell. Dale McGarvey, Allan McGarvey and Jon Heberling had been in a more general practice for a dozen years, but Dale McGarvey's dream was to take on cases involving issues of injustice. So when Roger was hired, McGarvey's firm took the great leap and specialized in plaintiffs' litigation. "We knew we were facing a wolf-at-the-door existence," Roger said, "because we only would get paid when we resolved the cases we were litigating."

They were an old-fashioned plaintiffs' firm. They did it all — investigate law, research facts, brief the motion, appear in court and try the case. When it went up on appeal, they went with it.

The firm had a signal success in the early 1990s that allowed them to take on the Libby litigation. A young woman came into the office and told Roger she was the chief accountant at a Columbia Falls aluminum smelter, previously owned by Atlantic Richfield, that employed more than a thousand workers. She said, "We have a problem. There is this profit-sharing agreement, and it's not being honored."

So Alan McGarvey and Sullivan looked into the case, and found that, sure enough, working men and women had lost tens of millions of dollars that were rightfully theirs. Finally, after years of litigation and chasing assets down all over the world, they reached a settlement that paid their clients $100 million.

In the late '80s, they had settled a couple of cases with Grace. But then they found what they considered the seminal documents in the case — the state Health Department inspection reports.

That discovery, combined with a new flood of clients who learned they were ill or dying, made the Libby cases Sullivan's and Heberling's main focus for the next several years. "The basis of our relationship with the people in Libby is personal," Roger Sullivan said. "We made repeated trips over there. We met people who were sick, who'd lost family members, those who worked at the plant and those who didn't." And now they were in the trial that they had to win — not just for Les and Norita, but for the other people in Libby who had their hopes riding on the firm, and on their rights under the law.

The next morning, Alan Whitehouse took the stand. He told the jury that he graduated from the University of Cincinnati College of Medicine in 1963, did his internship and residency at Duke University Hospital and had operated a pulmonary laboratory for the Air Force in New Mexico before opening his practice in Spokane in 1969. He added that he was board-certified in medicine and pulmonary diseases.

He told of treating hundreds of patients for asbestos-related diseases, including asbestosis, lung cancer and mesothelioma. He wasn't allowed to say how many of those were from Libby. If he could have, he would have said "more than 200."

He described asbestosis in detail — what it looks like on an X-ray and the other diagnostic symptoms, including rales, or crackling, in the chest caused by damage to the air sacs in the lungs. Then he talked about Les. He displayed one of the X-rays he had taken of Les, and pointed out the areas of "interstitial fibrosis," or fibroid growths, in the lower lungs. He also pointed out a thickening of the pleura, or lung lining, and irregularity along Les's diaphragm that indicated asbestos-related calcification. He told the jury that Les had rales and "poor breath sounds throughout his chest." Whitehouse also described the pulmonary-function tests that had been carried out on Les in his office, revealing about a 55-percent capacity in Les's exhalation.

After a barrage of technical questions, Jon Heberling finally got to the crux of it:

"What do you project is his life expectancy?"

"I think he's probably going to die within ten to fifteen years."

"Do you have an opinion as to what Les will likely die of?"

"I think he'll die of asbestosis."

It was nothing Les and Norita hadn't heard before, of course. Still, for them to have to sit there and hear Les's life, disease and likely death discussed in such terms was difficult. And listening to Kelly Wills's cross-examination of Whitehouse was worse.

"Given the fact that Mr. Skramstad's asbestos exposure ended more than thirty-five years ago and that it was thirty-five years before it was diagnosed by chest X-rays, that makes it less likely that his condition is going to progress at a rapid pace, isn't that right?"

"I don't know that."

"Well, the fact that his chest X-rays haven't changed over the past fourteen months would support a conclusion that it's likely his asbestosis will progress slowly?"

"I don't think you can draw that conclusion.... Many people with asbestosis will have sudden rapid changes.... I have observed it almost develop right under my nose where they've rapidly gone downhill."

"Doctor, it's not certain that Mr. Skramstad is going to die from his asbestosis or any asbestos-related disease?"

"Statistically it is."

Then Wills went through the medical-care plan that had been drawn up for Les, and made the doctor say that he didn't know exactly when Les would need each particular treatment, or how quickly the disease would advance. Whitehouse had testified about what Les probably would need; Wills demanded that he say whether or not there was a "reasonable degree of medical certainty" that various treatments would be needed. Whitehouse would not say that, but repeated that Les would probably need the treatments. That was the only point Wills could score, but he had probably succeeded to some degree in planting doubt in the jurors' minds about what treatments Les would need down the road. And that's all he was trying to do.

Over the next couple of days, Heberling and Sullivan put on the rest of their case. They called an expert in industrial hygiene, and experts in financial and medical matters who gave the jury their assessment of the money Les Skramstad would need in order to die of asbestosis as comfortably as possible. Wills and Graham picked and prodded at the witnesses, doing what they were supposed to do — trying to reduce their credibility with the jury.

After a tense weekend, Les and Norita were back in court Monday to hear their final witness, Don Riley, whose testimony was in the form of a video deposition from his hospital bed. He had died two months before the trial.

The only witness for the defense was Earl Lovick. Graham did his best to repair the damage from Heberling's questioning. Lovick testified that he didn't know about the experiments with asbestos in the lab that Les worked on. He talked about the fact that he'd told Dr. Knight at the tuberculosis sanitarium about eight minerals present in the ore, not just vermiculite and tremolite. He talked about the efforts he remembered to maintain the dust-control system in the mill, and stressed that respirators were always available, and that department heads enforced the wearing of them.

Then Graham tried a new tack. "We've talked about dust in the dry mill. Did you ever hear anyone tell the employees that the dust in the dry mill, or, for that matter, at any other location up there, was safe?"

"No, sir."

"Did the company ever authorize anyone to inform the employees that the dust was safe?"

"No."

That's not quite the same as protecting them from it, or even telling them it could kill them, but Graham thought it was better than nothing.

As Earl Lovick tried to put the best face on things under friendly questioning from Graham, he said something telling. He talked about the doctors in Libby at the time of the 1959 X-ray program, and about how easy it was to get them all to meet. "The doctors were generally pretty good about that. I think we only had six doctors in the town, so it wasn't any big deal to get them all together."

Graham finished by having Lovick testify that he considered many of the Zonolite workers friends, and that he was concerned for them, but that he had believed at the time that they were being protected. And he said if he knew then what he knew now, he would have done things differently.

On cross-examination, Heberling got back to his message very quickly.

"Isn't it true that from 1959 to 1961, the company never told the employees of the serious hazards of asbestos exposure?"

"Yes, sir."

"And the company never told the employees that the dust was 'of considerable toxicity,' correct?"

"No, sir."

"And the company never told the employees that thirty-six percent of the workers in 1959 had abnormal chests?"

"No, they didn't."

Heberling also succeeded in knocking down Lovick's testimony on respirators, pointing out that the dry-mill superintendent while Les worked there, Harold Flatt, not only claimed the dust was harmless but also did not wear his respirator much of the time. And as for the handling of Dr. Knight's inquiry, he asked Lovick, "You did not send him the existing samples of the dust analyzed for asbestos, did you?"

"No, sir."

"And in fact you told Dr. Knight, 'The dust in our mill has never been analyzed as such'?"

"Not by us it hadn't."

"It doesn't say 'not by us,' does it?"

"No," Lovick finally admitted.

At day's end, Prezeau asked Heberling outside the presence of the jury how much longer he thought he would need to spend with Lovick. After Heberling replied that he thought about half an hour, Graham said bitterly, "It's a lot of fun, beating up on a seventy-six-year-old man."

"The case is not against Mr. Lovick," Heberling replied. "It's against the company."

"Right," said Graham.

Heberling had actually squeezed just about all he could from Earl Lovick, and the next morning, after a few questions about the company's refusal to fund health studies, he turned the sole witness for the defense back to Graham.

By this time, Lovick had been before the jury for more than eight hours, and Graham knew the jurors' impressions were pretty much made, for good or ill. So after a short redirect, he rested his case.

Now just the final arguments stood between the jurors and the Skramstads' case. Jon Heberling spoke for Les and Norita, and despite apologizing to the jury for stumbling over his words, he spoke very well.

"Your duty as jurors places you above the rights of the parties as judges of the evidence, and you're also, in this one case, above the rights of W.R. Grace, which is not normal. It probably won't happen again. You have more power than the board of directors of W.R. Grace," he said. "We will not appeal to your sympathies. There is no right or need to do that. I would not humiliate my clients by appealing to your sympathies. Instead, we want to appeal to the facts and to your consciences."

He told the jury the same thing he'd told Gary Graham the day before: The case was not against Earl Lovick. "He will not have to pay a penny of what Grace may have to pay. The company is responsible for what he and others did at the time, and Mr. Lovick was not the only actor back in 1959 and '61. He just has the unfortunate position of having been the only survivor of the management team at the time, and he's a loyal company man."

He reminded them of Bleich's memo confessing to Zonolite's "very sorry record" of controlling the dust. "He speaks from his grave on that point," Heberling said.

Kelly Wills argued first for the defendants. "Now, Mr. Heberling ... indicated to you that W.R. Grace was not above the rights of you as individuals, that you're above the rights of W.R. Grace and that that won't happen again. He referred to W.R. Grace as a huge company. He referred to it as a company with a lot of resources. You've got to put that out of your mind. That's completely improper. W.R. Grace is an individual, just like Earl Lovick is an individual."

He told the jury they must "decide whether Earl Lovick and his co-workers were the bad actors that they've been accused of being, and you must decide this with hindsight, but with objectivity and fairness, putting yourself back to 1959 and what was going on in the industry in Montana in 1959." He added, "I'm convinced in my heart and my head that Earl Lovick and everyone else acted appropriately thirty-eight years ago, but you've all been determined to be competent to decide this case, so I'm not going to tell you how to do that."

He moved on to talk about some of the plaintiffs' witnesses.

"Now, Dr. Whitehouse, he's not a local doctor. He's not a Montana doctor. He's not a Libby, Montana, doctor. He's not a Western Montana doctor. He's a doctor from Washington." After that fervent appeal to xenophobia, Wills said, "He explained, after cross-examination, though, that the only medical care at this time that Mr. Skramstad was receiving was some periodic medical exams and an inhaler."

By contrast, he said Earl Lovick was "a real gentleman, in my book. He worked hard at W.R. Grace. I think he testified he did the best he could.... Now that he's seventy-six, he's being criticized for things that occurred over forty years ago. Plaintiffs' counsel has tried to make him look bad up here." He added, "You need to look into Earl's heart and soul, and I think you'll come to the same conclusion I did, and that is that Earl Lovick is an honest man who acted reasonably forty years ago."

As he wound to a conclusion, he said, "Look at Mr. and Mrs. Skramstad. They don't want your sympathy." He turned to Les and Norita. "You don't want their sympathy, do you?"

"Objection. Improper question," Heberling growled.

"Sustained."

Wills said, "I'll turn you over to my partner."

Prezeau broke in. "Before you do that, I'm going to give the jury a couple of minutes to stretch in place, and I'm going to meet with counsel." He took the attorneys into his chambers and said, "I'm not asking for any comments or argument.... We're halfway through closings, and I've heard things that I think walk the line of improper arguments. Both parties have said things. Jon mentioned something about what gets him, and Kelly mentioned that in his book Earl Lovick is a real stand-up guy." Prezeau looked at the lawyers and said, "I just want to make sure we don't do that anymore.... I'm just going to plead with you to keep things on the up-and-up, and that's all I wanted to say."

Gary Graham, with his Montana farmer's roots, played good cop to Kelly Wills's petulant and snarky cop. He soothed the jury with his soft-spoken, logical approach, saying he was going to divide the case for them into six questions: Why was it so dusty up there? Couldn't Zonolite do anything about the dust? Didn't Zonolite know the dust was toxic or unhealthy? Why didn't it tell its workers about this toxic dust? Why didn't it tell the workers about the effects of asbestos? And finally, if Les Skramstad got asbestosis from working at Zonolite, why didn't Grace just pay him instead of contesting his claim?

His answers were as facile as the questions. "Mines and mills of that nature are dusty. There's virtually no way to control the dust, particularly in the dry mill. It wasn't dusty all over, though." He pointed out that technology was much more primitive back then. He digressed from his question-answering to point out that from his testimony, a lot of the millwright work Les did at the dry mill was on weekends, and the machines wouldn't have been running then, so "the dust in the air certainly isn't a problem" without them running. Considering how much dust was in that seven-floor building and how long fibers stay suspended in the air, this was a questionable statement at best.

Then he strayed from the questionable to the downright misleading, saying that Zonolite did tell its workers that the dust was unhealthy. Never in this "answer" did he bring up the question of Zonolite's specific knowledge of asbestos, knowledge that wasn't related to the workers while Les was there, or for many years afterward.

Graham knew the letter from Lovick to Knight was one of the most damaging pieces of evidence, so he dismissed it by saying, "The State Board of Health is the one that came in and did the inspections that Zonolite is being accused of keeping from the state tuberculosis sanitarium. How much sense does that make? If you're going to conceal information from one state body to the other, it doesn't make very much sense to me." That is, of course, precisely what Zonolite did. And it worked. Knight never pursued more information from Zonolite because he never got the Board of Health reports that discussed asbestos in the dust.

"Now, probably the most troubling question for you as a juror is 'Why was it that Zonolite didn't tell the workers about the effects of asbestos?' That's something that's been raised over and over again.... As Earl said, knowing what he knows today, he would have done things differently in

1959." And finally, Graham said Grace shouldn't be liable because Zonolite "believed they were exercising reasonable care under the circumstances."

Heberling had one more shot, and he didn't waste it.

He closed by saying, "Did Zonolite conceal the hazards of asbestos exposure from the workers? Yes. That's sufficient for a punitive-damages verdict right there. Exposing Les in the experimental lab on the hundred percent asbestos project, where he's down on his knees filling these sacks with one-hundred-percent asbestos and the company knowing all the time that already thirty-six percent of the workers have abnormal chests and that asbestos is, indeed, toxic, and not applying the necessary dust controls, yes, that's an intentional disregard with a high probability of injury.

"You know, this case will be talked about for years to come, but every time — "

"I object to this argument. It's totally improper, Judge."

"Sustained."

But Heberling ignored both of them and rode it home: "Every time it comes up, you'll sleep well knowing that you served here and you reached what you considered to be a just result. Thank you."

The jury deliberated until after 11 P.M. that night, and came back the next morning and worked through another day, coming together on a verdict at about six o'clock in the evening of May 21.

The clerk read it to Les, and Norita, and Judge Prezeau and the attorneys, and to Gayla, watching from the gallery. "Lester and Norita Skramstad versus W.R. Grace and Company, a Connecticut corporation: On the issue of whether W.R. Grace was negligent, and, if so, whether W.R. Grace's negligence was a cause of Skramstad's injuries, we find for the plaintiff, Lester Skramstad.

"On the issue of whether W.R. Grace failed to provide Lester Skramstad with a reasonably safe place to work and, if so, whether the failure to provide a safe place to work was a cause of Skramstad's injuries, we find for the plaintiff, Lester Skramstad.

"On the issue of whether Norita Skramstad has been or will be injured by the loss of the support, aid, protection, affection and society of Lester Skramstad and whether W.R. Grace's actions were the cause of those injuries, we find for the plaintiff, Norita Skramstad.

"We find for the plaintiff, Lester Skramstad, in the amount of six hundred twenty-five thousand dollars. We find for the plaintiff, Norita Skramstad, in the amount of thirty-five thousand dollars."

It was not a total victory. The jury did not award punitive damages, and there was not enough money awarded to cover all of Les's projected medical expenses. But it was a hugely important verdict. Grace was found liable by a jury for the first time in Libby. The damages were significant, and many Libby victims would be helped by this verdict.

What Les and Norita didn't know that evening was that their legal ordeal was not over, and that they would never get all that the jury had found that they deserved.

CHAPTER 11

Over the decades, thousands of pounds of dynamite and black powder were
used to blast the vermiculite ore from Zonolite Mountain.
(Courtesy McGarvey, Heberling, Sullivan & McGarvey)

THE DISASTER OF ZONOLITE MOUNTAIN — the scope of the
contamination, sickness and death — was the single worst event
the EPA had ever encountered. Love Canal, Times Beach, Woburn, Silver Valley — no other came close.

But they did not yet know how bad it really was.

"Aw, shit," summed up Peronard and Weis's reaction late in January 2000
when Miller ruined their day.

Bill Daniels, a U.S. Public Health Service industrial hygienist in Denver,
had been searching the agency's enormous research library for anything on
non-occupational exposure from asbestos.[1] "There probably won't be anything on tremolite, but any cases of anyone who lived by a factory or plant
that used asbestos or lived with someone who worked there would be useful," Miller had told Daniels.

Daniels found a five-year-old article in the *American Journal of Industrial Medicine*.[2] Not only was it about asbestos; it was about tremolite, and people exposed to it other than workers. The authors of the study, Drs. Sharon Srebro and Victor Roggli, cautioned that tremolite was a risk not only to miners and manufacturers of tremolite-containing material but to those exposed to the end products. Miller read the more interesting parts of the study to his colleagues. There was the case of a 44-year-old man who died of asbestosis. As a child, he spent years playing in large piles of vermiculite waste rock at a plant across the street from his home.

Who was the man? Was it in Libby? they all wondered.

"We've got to track it down," Peronard said.

Miller found Roggli at Duke University Medical School. The pathologist said he found tremolite fibers in the victim's lungs. It was the next statement that floored Miller. The victim, Harris Jorgensen, was not from Libby. The pile of waste rock from the processed vermiculite was at the Western Mineral Products Company, across the street from the Jorgensens' home in Minneapolis.

The ore was from Libby.

A Minnesota lawyer had more information, Roggli said.[3] Miller found the lawyer and talked him out of Jorgensen's medical records and depositions with the victim and other workers at Western Mineral. Harris Jorgensen suffered long and hard with asbestosis and lung cancer. He died on June 22, 1991, his wife, Izzi, said. She talked about the dust from the plant covering everything — the clothesline, the car, the house, and her sons, Justin and Tim. She said she had to sweep them off when they came inside from playing on the same vermiculite pile as their father.

"Do my sons have to suffer also? It may be too late."

Dozens of people who lived near the plant were ill, Miller said. Minnesota health officials were trying to track down former workers at the plant and past residents of the neighborhood to get a grasp on how many might have died.

Peronard burrowed through a large stack of papers, trying to find the partial list of where in the country Grace shipped the ore to have it expanded. He was hoping that Minneapolis was a fluke. There were other factories in the neighborhood. Maybe something else was making these people sick.

That pipe dream floated out the window three days later when Miller brought in another pile of papers. These were old, back to the mid-'70s.

The documents — medical reports, questionnaires, X-ray evaluations — told a tale of workers at a plant in Marysville, Ohio, who began coughing up blood. It started with one, then another, but at the end of about six months there were a dozen workers at the O.M. Scott and Sons lawn-products facility that were showing signs of significant lung disease. Most had sharp chest pain, which worsened with coughing or deep breaths. Others, severe shortage of breath. All were coughing up blood.

Through their stethoscopes, doctors heard decreased breath sounds. The X-rays showed dense shadows. A needle carefully placed into the space between the two thin membranes lining the lungs found bloody fluid. Their diagnosis: bloody pleural effusion. The cause: probably asbestos.

But Scott didn't use asbestos in its products. Scott did use vermiculite. Lots of it. Trainloads carrying hundreds of thousands of tons of raw ore arrived like clockwork from Libby. Scott was Grace's largest customer of Libby ore, taking as much as 25 percent of the mine's total production. It was the lightly colored material in Scott's potting soil that held moisture and was coated with herbicides and fertilizers to improve lawns and kill bugs. The company even sold bags of straight vermiculite.

Scott reported to OSHA that its workers were getting sick. Physicians and industrial hygienists from NIOSH and Ohio universities swarmed over the plant. They tested the air. They attached air monitors to the workers' chests. They measured the asbestos in the dust. They found tremolite from Libby.

NIOSH doctors X-rayed all employees and found that one in four had lung abnormalities. It was this NIOSH report that had Peronard shaking his head. "This means that there could be people dying every place that Grace shipped that stuff," he said to Miller and Weis, as he threw the NIOSH report into the pile.

"Who said things couldn't get any worse?"

IN THE SUMMER OF 1959, the same year Les Skramstad started at Zonolite, Lee Joireman was 21 years old, and trying to get some money together
for college.

He got a job as a laborer at the Western Vermiculite Company plant at
the corner of Ash and Maxwell Streets in Spokane, Washington. His job
was hard physical labor — hauling tons of Zonolite ore from the boxcars in
which it was delivered to the expanding ovens at the Spokane plant.

He worked at the hot, dusty plant for only 23 months. Then he went on
to college and became a teacher. But 36 years later, with little warning, that
job shoveling Zonolite killed him.

Most of the students at the four middle schools where Lee Joireman
taught in Portland, Oregon, could not spell mesothelioma, much less understand the disease that took their favorite teacher in 1995.

Just before he died, he wrote his mother:

> *I kept my illness from you to spare you needless suffering. There is nothing*
> *you can do to help me, so I just felt it was best not to hurt you any sooner than*
> *need be.*

> *The chief doctor for oncology told me very bluntly that I can't think about all*
> *the years I won't get! He described an incurable type of cancer that I got from*
> *asbestos. It goes clear back to when I worked at Zonolite Insulation. It can lay*
> *quiet for between 30 and 40 years before it comes active. Of all the bad luck I've*
> *ever had, this one is the worst.*

For most of his life, Joireman's health was excellent. He and his wife,
Doris, bowled, bicycled and played basketball. But in late 1994, he began no-
ticing a fullness in his abdomen, swelling and shortness of breath. In January
1995, a doctor found cancer cells, and Joireman began chemotherapy. Every
third week, he would spend at least three days in the hospital to receive
the therapy, and paid the usual, miserable price: weight loss, vomiting, pain.
The chemotherapy did not stop the progression of the cancer, and finally
he heard the worst from his doctors. "We know there's no cure, only some
delay," he told his mother.

His wife quit her elementary-school teaching job to take care of him.

Arnie Joireman, one of Lee's three brothers, said that he worried when
his brother worked at the plant.[4] "I couldn't believe the amount of dust that

was pouring out of the vermiculite," Arnie says. "Lee was just covered in it. Even without the asbestos in it, it had to be hazardous. But it did have the asbestos in it, and no one ever told Lee or the other workers about it.

"It was the way they did business. They didn't want to spend the money to protect the workers from the asbestos, so they said nothing."

For 28 years, Joireman taught seventh- and eighth-grade humanities classes at four Portland schools. William Staub, a teacher at the George Middle School, said Joireman touched the hearts and minds of countless students.

"Lee was an outstanding teacher," Staub said. "He will remain one of the most significant individuals in thousands of former students' lives. It is an absolute tragedy that his personal talents and teaching skills, as well as his positive, warm personality, are not still at work in Room 417 at George Middle School. What a loss. What a man and teacher."

Grace settled a wrongful-death suit with the Joireman family in 1998. As a provision of the settlement, its amount was undisclosed.

FROM THE TIME OF EDGAR ALLEY'S earliest efforts to market his odd find, the vermiculite from Zonolite Mountain was sent across the country, and everywhere it went, its lethal partner, tremolite, went too.

Quickly, both the mine operators and their customers discovered that the easiest and least expensive way to handle the mineral was to ship it in its natural form — as ore — to expansion plants in at least 38 states and five Canadian provinces, where it could be "popped," or expanded, and used in a variety of products.

The heart of the expansion plants was the oven, where the vermiculite ore was baked at about 2,000 degrees Fahrenheit. The microscopic amount of water between the layers of vermiculite vaporizes and expands, or exfoliates, each piece of vermiculite into a puff 12 to 15 times its original size.

The material was then bagged and sold as insulation or soil extender, or mixed with clay, gypsum, commercial asbestos, and pigments to produce fireproofing and various other construction products, including wallboard. Some of it was made into a product called Verxite, a filler for animal feed. Over the mine's life, more than six decades, billions of pounds of vermiculite ore was shipped throughout the world. During the three decades it owned the mine, Grace made more than 92,750 shipments of Libby ore, totaling more than 15,782,000,000 pounds, according to invoices tallied by the EPA. The agency said many of the invoices are missing and the actual numbers could be considerably higher. Grace, EPA and OSHA records show that almost all of the ore was contaminated. Some samples tested were as much as 20-percent tremolite.

Documents collected by the government and Schneider showed that the ore was shipped by Grace to more than 750 locations throughout North America. Of those, EPA says that 293 sites were major users of the ore. Anywhere from 45 to 73 expansion facilities were, at different times, owned or licensed by Grace, the EPA reported.

Almost 9 billion pounds of the Libby ore went to Grace's own expansion plants. The remainder went to companies that made a wide variety of consumer and building products. The invoices show that O.M. Scott, the gardening-product company in Marysville, Ohio, was Grace's largest customer and purchased 1,061,000,000 pounds of Libby ore. 3M Company in Minnesota bought 77 million pounds, and Celotex Corporation of Fort Dodge, Iowa, used 41 million pounds of vermiculite in its plants. Cleveland Gypsum received 66 million and U.S. Steel Corporation took 10 million pounds of the contaminated ore.

With the exception of Scott, Grace's own expansion plants used far more than the average customer. 100 million pounds was delivered to the Grace plant in Phoenix. California Zonolite in Los Angeles used 123 million pounds. The plant in Albuquerque handled 134 million and Texas Vermiculite Company in Dallas processed more than 800 million pounds of the ore. The plant in Spokane where Joireman worked received more than 83 million pounds of ore.

The shipment of the lethal ore did not stop at the U.S. border.[5] The invoices showed that the vermiculite was shipped to Hong Kong, Japan, Australia, New Zealand, England, Ireland, France, Germany, Venezuela and Saudi Arabia. Canada received more than 1.5 billion pounds of Libby ore at 187 locations in Alberta, British Columbia, Manitoba, Ontario, Quebec and Saskatchewan.

As they did with their Libby miners, both Grace and the Zonolite Co. withheld information about the lethal nature of the tremolite from the men who unloaded it and processed it at sites around the world. Grace Construction-Products boss R. M. Vining, in a memo to Peter Grace in 1969, specifically mentioned the "health hazard ... at the expansion plants using the ore."

Grace would have an impossible time explaining why it didn't warn its customers and workers of the danger. It knew precisely how hazardous the fiber contaminating its vermiculite was. A May 1977 internal memo to Grace senior managers said, "Tremolite is classified as asbestos and regulated by the Environmental Protection Agency, Occupational Safety and Health Administration, the Mine Enforcement and Safety Administration, the Consumer Product Safety Act and the Toxic Substances Control Act as a carcinogen."

The number of workers and family members killed by asbestosis, lung cancer and mesothelioma at these plants will probably never be known, because of the transient nature of the workforce and because in many cases, as in Libby, the deaths were attributed to a litany of other diseases.

Even Grace had a difficult time pinning down the number of its own employees that were affected, much less the number of its customers' employees who were exposed. The Grace memo of May 1977 says, "Among expansion plant employees, the high employee turnover and a variety of past exposures make conclusions difficult." But one fact in that Grace report hinted at the scope of the danger: "Among 14 employees with 10 or more years of service in expanding plants which have used Libby ore, 28 percent (four) exhibited asbestosis."

The company had budgeted money to improve the safety of its expansion operations in Denver; Newark; Phoenix; Dallas; Portland, Oregon; Dearborn, Michigan; and Omaha. Yet Grace still failed to warn their workers in these plants and others.

Most of the workers never suspected the danger, because they were not told there was asbestos in the ore. The "nuisance dust" explanation was exported right along with the tremolite. Documents show that plant managers from Australia to Winnipeg were told there was nothing harmful in the ore.

"The enormity of the atrocities committed by Grace ... is too great to fathom," said Donald Judge, former president of the Montana AFL-CIO. "As we're just now discovering, it not only happened to the citizens of Libby, but dozens, hundreds, perhaps even thousands of workers throughout the nation are dead or dying because no one told them about the danger they were breathing."

Information gleaned from workers'-compensation offices, health departments, death certificates, government archives and thousands of court documents confirms that hundreds of workers at Grace's processing plants and those owned by their bulk customers did become ill and die from asbestos-related disease. And letters, internal company memos and reports show the extent of the coverup by Zonolite and Grace. In 1976, seven years after Vining's memo to Peter Grace, the company told the federal Occupational Safety and Health Administration that tremolite was not hazardous and did not cause cancer.

But in Lovick's 1961 letter to Pratt at the Minneapolis plant, he admitted that asbestos was present in the ore shipped to expansion plants.

Shortly after Grace bought Zonolite, the health-related queries from customers — and even from some government agencies — began to come more frequently. Even though U.S. health and environmental agencies mostly ignored the problem, the Canadian government was asking questions about the Libby ore as early as 1964.

That year, the health department in the Canadian province of Alberta raised concerns about the composition of a large quantity of dust from a Grace-licensed expansion plant in Calgary that used Libby ore.[6] They reported that in examinations of nine workers, seven of them had breathing problems. "This number of men with breathing abnormalities is most unusual and puzzling," wrote Dr. H. Siemons, director of Alberta's division of industrial health. He asked Grace if there were similar reports from other plants processing vermiculite. No answer to Siemons could be found in the thousands of pages of Grace documents Schneider had gathered.

The next year, investigators from the same department found asbestos in the dust, but their report was discounted by Grace's local management.[7] Three years later, in December 1968, N. F. Bushell, Grace's Zonolite manager in Vancouver, wrote headquarters about a worker in their Winnipeg plant who had asbestosis.

"There is asbestos in the ore that we receive from Libby. I'm afraid that we may still be exposing our employees to an unnecessary health hazard," he wrote, also asking if the company had measured the amount of asbestos in the air where the Zonolite was bagged. If not, he asked, when was Grace going to do so? "Get someone on this subject before we get closed down or slapped with some pretty large claims from employees or their heirs. It won't take many more biopsy reports before we get fingered," he wrote.

Also in 1964, Dr. W. E. Park of the Minneapolis City Health Department voiced concerns about the death of a worker at the Western Mineral Products plant.[8] He wrote to Pratt, the vice president who had been concerned about the asbestos problem since Lovick's letter to him three years earlier. Park told Pratt that the death of the worker, who "had long exposure to vermiculite dust, has renewed our interest in the importance of vermiculite dust in the causation of lung disease."

When they exchanged letters back in 1961, Pratt had pleaded with Lovick to do something about the hazard.[9] "If an effective improvement can be made at the mine in reducing the asbestos dust, this will of course benefit every plant that receives the ore and will minimize the hazards to hundreds of employees in the various plants."

"WE NEVER WERE TOLD A THING about that ore being dangerous or having asbestos in it. Nobody never told me nothing about this stuff being able to kill you."

That is the recollection of one Arland Blanton, a plant manager and superintendent of the vermiculite plant in North Little Rock, Arkansas, from 1951 until 1963.[10] When Schneider asked how he knew the ore from Libby was dangerous, Blanton's normally strong voice dropped to a whisper.

"I'm about the only one left," the 82-year-old man said. "Most of the rest of them are dead. The asbestos got them. All of them."

Blanton cast his memory back to the days when the plant was in high gear. "You wouldn't believe the dust from that vermiculite. It was so thick that you couldn't see your hands at times.

"I had a boy worked for me that lived in a house nearby and he used to say that he would have to shake his sheets out every morning to get the dust off.

"All of them, Zonolite and Grace, just said there was nothing in that dust that could hurt you. There's a lot of people dead today who would still be alive if we were told the truth about that ore."

Blanton said he does not know how many Little Rock workers were exposed to the asbestos. "We usually had about a dozen workers a day, maybe up to thirty when we ran three shifts," he said. "A whole bunch of men moved through there over the years. I wonder how many of them are still alive."

Not all managers at Grace's processing plants were so critical. "It was a good company," said Courtland Lowe, a former Grace regional manager in the Southeast. "Grace did everything they could to comply with all the laws and regulations at the time," Lowe said, declining to comment further.

Stephen Sheeran worked for Grace for 22 years in sales. He started as a salesman in the Dearborn plant and ended his career in 1991 as sales manager for the Dallas operation. Grace's vermiculite products sold very well, he said. "Millions of bags of that stuff from Libby was sold in Michigan as attic-fill insulation," he recalled. "They couldn't get it fast enough. Most of the homes in Flint are filled with it."

Now he has little positive to say about the company's management.

"They never told the workers the vermiculite was hazardous, or even the pure asbestos they were adding to some products. Never said a word, absolutely not," Sheeran said. "It was purely economics. It would have cost them money to make the operation safer."

He said the Dallas plant was in an area known as Little Mexico. Most of the workers there, he said, were blacks from a large community in a nearby neighborhood or Mexicans who had crossed the border to work.

"The Grace management had a stonewall attitude all their lives, and they don't think much of little people," Sheeran said. "The way they treated their workers was a huge injustice."

Sheeran recalled that at one point, the Libby plant started shipping the raw ore to Dallas with a coating of soybean oil, to avoid the railroad having to put a skull and crossbones on the bulk cars. "It all smelled like french fries when they expanded it," he said.

Robert Junker was the treasurer and superintendent of the Dallas operation where Sheeran worked.[11] In court documents filed in October 1991, he said that he had discussions with Grace about asbestos, "but we didn't discuss it with the men that worked in it" because Junker didn't want to "get them all shook up about maybe nothing.

"Some guy says you get asbestosis from asbestos, but that doesn't necessarily mean you do," he said. "I didn't want to cause a lot of uproar, because nothing was official. Nothing." He added, "You can't go out to a couple of black men on the line and tell them that they're going to die tomorrow from asbestos breathing and expect them to even come into the plant tomorrow. You just don't do it."

Junker worked for Zonolite and Grace for 31 years. He began as a bookkeeper for Zonolite in Chicago and then in San Antonio, and wound up running the Texas Vermiculite Co. for Grace. His view about telling workers of hazards matched his philosophy toward customers. "To tell the public about a potential hazard — that's what it is, a potential hazard — is kind of asinine," the plant superintendent said in his deposition. He added, "It's bad for business."

He said he mourned the day in 1973 when Grace ordered managers to stop marketing products with added asbestos. "We thought we had a good thing until they said it was not," Junker said. "It broke all of our hearts because it cut profits."

Robinson Insulation of Great Falls, Montana, owned by Dave Robinson's family, used the ore from Libby for more than half a century, from the 1930s to 1986. The ore would arrive in 40-foot-long boxcars, each containing 50 tons of vermiculite. As demand increased, 100-ton cars were used. About 2,000 tons a year were delivered to the small plant.

"It would take two men a day to unload, and it was extremely dusty," said Floyd Gebert, the plant's general manager, in court documents.[12] "There's always dust around vermiculite, whether it's expanded or unexpanded."

Although the workers may not have known what they were handling, Gebert said he knew, which was not surprising given the family's connection to the Libby operation. He'd also seen that there were hazard labels on the boxcars going to Robinson's plant in North Dakota, warning that the product might contain asbestos. "But you know, I never saw a sign on any of the cars that came to Great Falls," he said.

Gebert said the first official notice from Grace about the dangers of asbestos was in January 1973. He was told by his doctors in the early 1980s that he had asbestosis.

Out of the small workforce at the Great Falls plant, four people have died of asbestos-related disease and four others are diagnosed.

At least four employees of Burlington Northern Railroad who say they handled the ore from Libby have been diagnosed with asbestosis. Another died last year of mesothelioma, according to lawyers in Dallas and Houston who are representing the former railroad workers.

Edward Moody, a Little Rock lawyer who has handled the lawsuits of dozens of workers at Grace expansion plants, told Schneider, "Grace had no interest in protecting their workers. None. The documents prove it. Soon after Grace took over, they started giving annual physicals and X-rays to these workers," Moody said.[13] "Not one, and I've handled almost fifty cases, has ever been given a report from Grace on what the X-rays, breathing-function tests, indicated. Even if Grace knew they were sick, they never told them a word."

By the time Grace's biggest customer, the Scott Co., reported its sick workers to OSHA in 1978, Grace was deep into damage-control mode on the expansion-plant problem. A 1971 internal memo said that 20 of the expansion plants were in violation of pollution-control laws in their respective states. And a September 1971 memo dealt with the fact that the Construction Products Division could not afford to fix all the vermiculite safety concerns at the plants. The plan was to "tackle them singly, as they are forced to comply, and buy as much time as possible," the memo said.

In many instances, Grace plant managers were complicit in the cover-up.

"It is safe to say that I have procrastinated on answering this notice of violation," F. W. Easton of the Zonolite plant in Weedsport, New York, wrote in November 1971 to his superiors in reference to a pollution citation from the New York State investigators.[14]

In August 1971, the operator of a Zonolite plant in the San Francisco Bay area told headquarters he was nervous when pollution inspectors questioned him on how much #4 Zonolite ore — a particularly dusty grade — the plant was processing.[15] "I think our 'friendly inspector' will be by frequently for the next few weeks," he wrote, and added that the plant will be "getting as much #4 out at night as we can." When the inspector wouldn't be around.

Forty years after Pratt begged Lovick to do something about the dust, federal health agencies are cleaning piles of vermiculite from the Western Mineral site in Minneapolis, and the B.F. Nelson Company, 13 blocks away, which also used Libby vermiculite. Homes and parks nearby are also being tested.

Family members, backed by medical records and lawyers, have shown the state and EPA officials that more than 30 men who worked at the two plants, and four others who lived nearby, have died from asbestos-related disease. Dozens of others, including families who lived downwind from the plants, are ill with the same diseases. There are between 2,000 and 3,000 homes within a quarter-mile of the plants.

Aubrey Miller was horrified, not only by the nonworker deaths in Minnesota, but because those sites are the only vermiculite plants the team knew of where actual investigations had been done.

"What's happening in Minnesota might occur in dozens, if not hundreds, of other vermiculite-processing sites across the country," the physician said. "This is just the first place outside of Libby where health experts have made the effort to look.

"What's happening in neighborhoods around the hundreds of other plants that used this vermiculite?"

Lee Joireman, the teacher who contracted mesothelioma from his work at the Spokane expansion plant, kept a journal during the final stages of his illness. Some of those entries, reproduced here with the permission of his family, present a painfully vivid picture of how the disease takes its toll:[16]

> *Sunday, Sept. 24, 1995: It's so tiresome and depressing to be forced to sit around all day ... I took pain pills every four hours ... My poor Twerp (his wife Doris) has to keep busy to hide her suffering. I love her so much it*

doubles my depression to watch her and think about her "future." May God watch over her.

Monday, Oct. 2: The fluid in my lungs is collecting faster. I can't eat anything.... I feel very depressed that Twerp and I cannot do "normal" things anymore & make love, go on trips, go to the beach, movies with popcorn, walks, bike, etc. etc. etc.

Tuesday, Oct. 3: Had to be drained of 9 liters again. Doctors said it comes back a little quicker after each drain. My neck and head hurt so much.

Saturday, Oct. 7: Watched Mariners beat Yankees to tie 2 to 2 in best of five. Still taking pain pills every four hours.

Thursday, Oct. 12: Seems fluid fills up 24 hours after drained!! Difficult to breathe, sit, walk, etc. Feel weak and so useless! Please dear Lord, MERCY!!!

Saturday, Oct. 14: Bad Day! Stomach area swollen and presses hard on chest and back. Can't lay down or sit comfortably. Legs, ankles, feet terribly bloated and ache. Neck and head hurt. Why do we (Twerp & I) have to suffer so?

Sunday, Oct. 16: Life is very "meaningless" as I get weaker and ache so much. Please forgive me, but I do wish it were over to stop this useless suffering for us both!

Saturday, Oct. 28: Restless. Need two-hour pain pill. Nurse called and will check me.

That was Lee Joireman's last diary entry. He died five days later.

In this bucolic scene, the Kootenai River flows pass the mine entrance and storage sites. (Andrew Schneider)

PERONARD KNEW ONE THING FOR SURE: Zonolite Mountain was still heavily contaminated. Air-monitor sampling of the stiff breezes that usually flowed across the barren mine site showed the winds carried dangerous levels of tremolite fibers.[1]

The strong gusts that often corkscrewed off the surrounding mountains loosened enough asbestos-laden dust to quickly clog the air filter and frustrate the efforts of Peronard's contractors to track the spread of the poison.

"The mountain is a mess, and I don't know how we're going to keep the fibers from blowing off," Peronard said to Weis, who shrugged and replied, "We'll find a way eventually. We've got no choice."

Grace failed in its effort to establish grass and tiny tree seedlings on the stark mound that once provided 80 percent of the world's vermiculite. As Gayla so angrily proved to any state official she could rope, not a damned thing could grow on that hillside.

Peronard was going to have to worry about the mountain after he'd cleaned up the town. But he was determined to use the old mine site on the mountain to dump the thousands of tons of contaminated vermiculite and soil his contractors were scraping up at the screening plant, at the rail siding on the cliffs across the Kootenai and from the expansion and export plant in town.

In 1994, Grace had sold the mountain to a firm called Kootenai Development Corporation. The company, owned by Lum Owens, his son, Mark, and Jack Wolters, former vice president of Grace's Construction Products Division, planned to develop the land into a hunting reserve, and someday, the owners said, a housing development.

Peronard had been meeting frequently with Owens, the president and majority shareholder of KDC, about returning the toxic waste back to its source. His only other choice was to spend an extra five or six million dollars sending about 7,000 truckloads to a hazardous-material landfill in Spokane. It would be a 160-mile drive down a two-lane road already congested with hulking log trucks, winding through the center of a dozen communities in three states. Peronard knew that it was a no-brainer: A 15-minute run taking it back to where it came from was definitely the way to go.

Owens understood the logic of EPA's plans.[2] He gave verbal permission to enter the land for testing and would consider permitting the mine site to be used as a dump site, he said. Peronard found Owens to be a decent guy, very straightforward, and quite concerned about the toxic nightmare he now owned. He helped the EPA crew get some of the access they needed.

Peronard and senior EPA lawyer Matt Cohn spent a good bit of time fashioning an agreement to grant KDC protection against liability in return for allowing EPA to return the contaminated waste to the mine. Peronard and Cohn tried to explain the liability that came with owning the mountain, and they told Owens that it would be a good idea to sell it back to Grace so his company didn't get stuck in the legal quicksand of the cleanup.

Whether it was because of Peronard's suggestions or not, on July 14, 2000, Grace bought back controlling interest in the mine from KDC, a fact it shared with the EPA four days later. EPA's elation at having a cleaner legal path to Grace — the party responsible for the contamination — lasted only a few hours until a hand-delivered letter from Grace arrived that same afternoon.[3]

"What the hell do you mean Grace kicked us off the mountain?" Peronard exploded as he read the letter Cohn had just received.

"The EPA and its representatives, contractors, agents or guests are hereby forbidden from entering any KDC property," said the letter from David Cleary, Grace's senior environmental counsel.[4] Almost everyone thought it was a joke. It wasn't.

In Libby, Wendy Thomi, EPA's community coordinator, tried to explain to Gayla, Les and a handful of other activists that a company could put up all the "EPA Keep Out" signs it wanted to, but it wouldn't keep the agency from completing its cleanup. "I've never heard of it before, but it is Grace we're dealing with," she said.

In his office across the street, Grace's Alan Stringer offered his version.

"Look, we want to work with EPA and we always have, but they are demanding that Grace give them open access to the site, but they won't tell us what they want to dump up there. We can't allow the mine to be used as a dumping site for everything hazardous they can find in Lincoln County."

Kelcey Land, EPA's cost-recovery program manager, had sent Grace a one-page "consent" form with six short sentences dealing with sampling and the disposal of waste from other contaminated Grace sites "and other actions deemed necessary to protect human health and the environment."[5]

From Grace's corporate headquarters, vice president and chief spokesman William Corcoran added: "We don't understand what they want. What do they mean by access? We don't understand their letter."

Peronard was livid. "That's garbage and just about the stupidest thing I've ever heard," he said. "They know exactly what this is all about. They know that we're talking about only moving the poison they've spread all over this town back to someplace where it won't keep killing these people."

A day later, Grace's lawyer in Denver faxed Cohn another letter telling EPA that it didn't need access because it could use the Spokane dump.[6] It also demanded "appropriate and just compensation..." if EPA wanted to use the contaminated mine site.

Peronard's reaction: "I won't pay those bastards one damn penny."

Through the summer and fall, U.S. Justice Department lawyer James Freeman and his team continued to petition Grace for access, but to little avail.[7]

On September 14, the Justice Department filed suit against Grace in U.S. District Court in Missoula to allow the EPA full access to the mine. Grace responded by contending that there was no need for EPA to have access, the law didn't give it the authority and the demand for entry was "arbitrary and capricious," an accusation that Grace leveled against EPA at every opportunity.

On March 9, 2001, Chief Judge Donald Molloy ruled that the EPA was entitled to enter the property and that Grace must allow access for all purposes.[8] As far as being arbitrary and capricious, the judge said: "The EPA is entrusted by Congress and the President with responsibility for taking actions that usually feature a considerable degree of discretion. The EPA's discretion should remain as unfettered as possible."

In answering Grace's contention that EPA has no reasonable basis to believe that a threat from asbestos still existed, Molloy said: "The conclusion is as plain to see as the East Front of the Rocky Mountains." And the judge questioned Grace's newfound concern for the people of Libby. "Grace foresees dire consequences for the playgrounds of tender young schoolchildren, defenseless against the vicissitudes of EPA discretion," Molloy wrote. "Grace should have acknowledged this concern for the public long ago in the sordid history of asbestos and its harmful effects."

Grace offered no public reaction to the decision.

Not only did Peronard not have to pay Grace *one damn penny,* the company settled for a little over $2.74 million in fines. The judge could have levied a fine of up to $27,500 for every day access was denied. The total potential fine was around $5 million, so Grace got a bargain.

Normally such fines go into the U.S. Treasury. Not this time. Somehow, Cohn and his Justice Department colleague Freeman worked it so the money went to Libby to pay for medical care for the asbestos victims.

"There is something almost poetic about taking Grace's money and giving back to the people they harmed," Cohn said. "It's nowhere near what they need to pay for their care, but it's a start."

BY THE MID-1970s, Grace was already considering an exit strategy from Libby.

Several troublesome things were happening at once. Even with the introduction of the wet mill into the process in 1975, Grace knew that the Libby miners and millers were still being dangerously exposed, and the company knew that an increasing number of employees had abnormal chests, although it still had not told its workers that the asbestos in the ore was deadly.

The company had relatively easily fobbed off the State of Montana, promising after each successive Department of Health investigation to do more to protect workers. But the state was really the least of Grace's worries. More complaints about the ore were coming from bulk customers around the country. The Environmental Protection Agency, the Consumer Product Safety Commission and OSHA were all making noises about regulating asbestos, both in the workplace and in consumer products. Grace was very vulnerable in both areas. Also, the threat of litigation loomed larger and larger.

The company had some tough decisions to make.

On May 24, 1977, Grace executive E. S. "Chip" Wood set out the problem in a lengthy internal memo.[9] It is an interesting document for many reasons. Wood said the company's thinking about tremolite had changed: First, it was even deadlier than previously thought, as the confidential in-house mortality survey the company conducted in Libby showed; and second, government regulators were heading toward erasing the distinction between "commercial asbestos" and "non-commercial" asbestos like the tremolite in Libby.

Wood also disclosed in an offhand way, actually in an appendix to the main memo, that Grace was aware that exposures "can be high" in workers' homes. Despite this, and the fact that Wood admitted that current exposure to asbestos at the mine "still represents concern to us," new proposed safety measures at the mine included only "an employee education program" as well as efforts to further reduce exposure levels. No plans for additional showers or changing areas were mentioned. And apparently that education program did not extend to actually warning the employees that there was hazardous material in the dust, or sharing the results of the in-house chest X-rays directly with the miners.

Most of Wood's missive dealt with the business options for the company. "Divestment of Zonolite has been considered in the past and been judged impractical," Wood wrote, adding that the company thought no buyer could be found that was "capable of continuing to operate the business with adequate capital resources to give us an acceptable price ... as compared to other alternatives."

Another option Wood examined in detail was simply to close Libby and supply the company's nationally known Zonolite product line solely from the mine in Enoree, South Carolina, which had less tremolite contaminating its vermiculite ore.

"Closing of Libby and retrenching to South Carolina would require a drastic change in the basis on which the business is run," Wood wrote. "It is likely that we would be operating a regional business in the East, Midwest and Southeast, rather than the present national business for Zonolite products. This alternative, if required, would be expected to produce a high return but substantially lower after-tax profits."

Therefore, Wood wrote, "continuing to operate Libby ... is a preferred alternative, unless large amounts of capital are required to meet drastically tightened" asbestos regulations. In effect, he was saying, "Unless the federal government makes us cut down on the asbestos we expose our miners and our customers to, we'd prefer to make an additional $1.2 million a year, rather than voluntarily end that risk."

Wood's memo did not mince words. He identified seven specific risks to continued operation: harm to customers; harm to employees; product bans; label requirements; increasingly restrictive regulations and higher capital expenditure needed to meet them; adverse publicity; and finally, general liability to customers, employees and the public.

Wood said the largest risk to users came from attic insulation and masonry insulation. He said that tests a year earlier had shown "high concentrations" of fibers during simulated installation of attic insulation. Among the options he put forward was withdrawing the attic insulation from sale in the U.S. market, but continuing to sell it in Canada, where the market was huge because of the colder climate, and where regulation — and litigation — threats were not nearly so worrisome.

In terms of employees, the primary concern was still Libby, where the "employee education" plan and additional work to bring fiber exposures down were the primary remedies he offered. He also outlined some $721,000 in capital spending planned over the next two years to bring eight of Grace's expanding plants into compliance with existing OSHA regulations.

"There is a high risk that our products will be banned in several significant uses," Wood wrote. "We forecast that our vermiculite consumer products, namely attic insulation, horticultural vermiculite and Pool Base [used as a bed for swimming-pool installation] will eventually be banned by the Consumer Product Safety Commission."

This prediction did not materialize. Wood also assumed there was about a 30-percent risk that within a year and a half, Monokote, the company's fireproofing spray, would fall within a ban of fireproofing materials containing asbestos in five states. By this time, Grace claimed it had already removed commercial asbestos from Monokote, substituting vermiculite from Libby that carried tremolite contamination. "We are actively working on a vermiculite-free fireproofing material," he wrote.

Wood continued, "We believe that a decision to affix asbestos warning labels to our products would result in substantial sales losses." He added, "Based on advice from corporate counsel, our products do not require labels if OSHA limits are not exceeded in their intended use. We believe that all of our products fall below the limits ... thus avoiding the need to label our products." This was a particularly cynical business decision — based on the company's lawyers believing that they could get away with not labeling to avoid taking losses by letting customers know what was in the material. It was a decision made by many other asbestos-industry companies, including Johns-Manville, and also by some of Grace's own customers, most notably Scott in Ohio. In projecting losses from labeling, Grace specifically mentioned Scott. "Due to Scott's desire to avoid labeling Turf-Builder, Scott demand would fall by 30 per cent in 1977 (if Grace labeled its product) and continue to decline to 20 per cent of base levels by 1980. The basic assumption here is that Scott would attempt to maintain their 'natural' image and avoid labeling by substituting as much South African or Virginia Vermiculite ore as they could obtain," Wood wrote. He also estimated that ore shipments to Canada would cease altogether if Grace labeled its attic insulation.

The memo also shows that Grace believed lower exposure levels could be obtained — if the company wanted to spend the money. "We believe there is a very high risk that standards will become more restrictive," Wood wrote. "In addition to the $1.9 million we propose to spend between now and mid-1978 to comply with asbestos fiber safety standards, an additional $1 million is expected to be needed by 1980 in order to meet a projected OSHA standard" of .5 fibers per milliliter of air. The memo projected a 30-percent chance that an additional investment of up to $10 million would be required to reach a level of one fiber per milliliter at Libby ($3.7 million) and .1 fiber per milliliter at the company's expanding plants ($6.3 million). "Such a development would probably result in a decision to close Libby," he wrote.

"There is a risk that Grace will attract adverse publicity from national media concerning the presence of asbestos in vermiculite," Wood wrote. This was the publicity bomb that Grace knew it was sitting on. It would be 22 more years before the *Post-Intelligencer* stories touched it off. "This information is already being circulated within government agencies, and has been-reported on a local basis in connection with the Louisa County [Virginia] dispute over the mining of vermiculite ore," he added. "Future steps, such as the development of a case for continued sale of attic insulation to the Consumer Product Safety Commission, will increase the risk of widespread adverse publicity."

"The liability to employees is limited by the Workmen's Compensation laws," Wood continued, echoing the industry's reliance on laws that were supposed to protect workers but ended up protecting companies instead. "We should expect increased Workmen's Compensation rates in Libby as the number of disabilities increase," he warned. "The risk of liability to customers is heightened by the decision not to label our products," but he added that corporate counsel categorized that risk as "moderate." Finally, he addressed liability to consumers. "General public liability is a low-level risk with very high potential liability. While we have no evidence of any adverse effect of our products on consumers, neither can we offer convincing evidence that they are absolutely safe." He added that "a decision to label our consumer products would eliminate the risk of future liability while exacerbating the risk of claims from past use of the product."

Grace's upper management must have agreed with Wood's assessment of the situation, because the company continued to operate Libby for another 13 years after the memo was written. Also, sadly, it shows that Grace thought the government's determination to regulate asbestos to protect the safety of Americans was much greater than it actually proved to be.

There is no shortage of mind-boggling cynicism in the company's internal correspondence.[10] A November 26, 1980, Grace memo offers a rare glimpse at the inner workings of the industry's strategy against government regulators. Grace Construction Products Division executive R. H. Locke was summing up the company's options in dealing with a push by NIOSH to launch a new health study of Libby operations.

It is assumed NIOSH will submit a Libby study protocol ... in early January. "The principal options, which are not mutually exclusive, follow:

A. Obstruct and block, possibly even contesting in the courts. As I understand it, we'd lose and this is not exactly the image we try to project.
B. Be slow, review things extensively and contribute to delay. This might not be bad policy generally and it is possible that the new [Reagan] Administration's policies will make NIOSH more selective in how scarce staff resources are allocated after Jan. 20, 1981.

C. Publish a "pre-emptive epidemiological study." This could attenuate the resume-enhancement potential for NIOSH study personnel. This could also be a checkpoint for a subsequent NIOSH study when it is released.

D. Cooperate fully. This agency and its personnel have not always acted with high levels of professionalism on past studies. This option would save NIOSH time and effort, make their study more comprehensive and possibly rule out some inaccuracies. It would not necessarily make NIOSH's conclusions any more responsible.

E. Actively go upstream in NIOSH to personally repeat the same arguments, the first time immediately after receipt of the protocol.

F. Actively seek to turn off the sources of the pressure for the study by personally repeating the same arguments: Moreover, the sources may have supplementary reasons not fully shared by NIOSH.

G. Attempt to apply influence to congressmen, senators, lobbyists or others to get it turned off. However, it is not necessarily successful, can backfire and to be effective must be developed over long periods of time due to the trust required.

At this time I tend to favor a phased combination of options B, C, E and F.

THE SICKENING OF LIBBY was such a gradual thing.

Like a person with asbestos-scarred lungs that are slowly losing their capacity, a town that is slowly dispatching its miners to the graveyard, slowly increasing its per-capita use of oxygen tanks, slowly increasing its quotient of widows with shortness of breath, does not immediately realize what is happening.

And a town like this does not ask certain questions. Libby was built on the dust of hard work, on sawdust and rock dust. For decades, it had insulated its houses and aerated its vegetable gardens with the locally produced vermiculite, and watched its children play on piles of mining waste and on ball fields dotted with ore that sparkled in the summer sun. Libby proudly used Zonolite in building its schools and its stores and its railway station, and watched tons of ore carried by conveyor across the mighty Kootenai to the waiting trains, and accepted the certainty that dust came on the east wind.

So as more and more former miners died in the 1980s, nobody took much notice. People were more concerned about other news from Grace's operation. The mine and mill were closed for one-or two-week periods several times in the early '80s because of excess inventory. In March 1984, Grace laid off 44 miners, citing the bad economy and a declining demand for vermiculite resulting from a general slowdown in construction.

That was tough to take. Libby had seen painful times before. Growth in the lumber business that provided the bulk of the town's income was cyclical, very vulnerable to the vagaries of economy, politics and weather. But somehow J. Neils would always make sure the men got paychecks. If there was no work in winter, they'd send the men into town and have them shovel sidewalks, and figure out a way to pay them anyway. But Grace seemed less inclined to keep men it didn't need.

And as the '80s wore on, Dick Powell died, and Mickey McNair, and Herb Waltman, and Harry Ostheller, and Stuart Risley. Laura Johnson, who worked for Zonolite during World War II, died too. And the mountain claimed Roy McMillan, and Edwin Schnackenberg, and Derward Preston, and Jerome Ledum, and more.

In September 1990, Grace closed the mine. Poor economic conditions and low demand for vermiculite were the stated reasons. But in fact, vermiculite was still selling briskly, and was still being mined elsewhere by Grace, in the old Zonolite mines in Enoree, South Carolina. For many years, the Libby mine had been producing between 200,000 and 300,000 tons of milled ore every year. An estimated 55 years' supply of vermiculite ore remained in the ground on Zonolite Mountain – more than 50 million tons of raw ore — and the Libby mine was still providing 50 percent of the nation's supply.

A much more likely reason for Grace's decision to end Libby operations was the gathering storm of lawsuits — and the realization that, as relatives of miners started to get sick, the degree of contamination and the potential liability from asbestos claims were much greater than previously estimated.

For a while, most of the miners kept their jobs. Grace was anxious to get the buildings on the mine site demolished, and so the men were kept on to do that. And in the process, Grace made an ironic mistake. In their haste to get the buildings knocked down — they were of course heavily contaminated, and Grace didn't need evidence of working conditions left standing for all to see — the company, so used to taking shortcuts, disregarded regulations concerning the disposal of asbestos-lagged pipes. They left a pipe wrapped in asbestos sticking out of the ground, and it cost them half a million dollars in fines.

Company insiders must have shaken their heads in bemusement. Here these buildings were loaded with tremolite and the government was getting sticky about an asbestos-wrapped pipe? You had to kick the tremolite out of the way to see the stupid pipe on the demolition site. These government people were idiots.

After the demolition, Grace's Alan Stringer blamed state and federal regulation for the mine's closure, and he boasted about the company's contribution to the community.[11] He cited the $1 million per year in property taxes,

$4 million payroll, and $1 million in local purchases the company made. He even bragged about Grace's $1-million-per-year power bill.

"A viable use for a mineral has been eliminated," Stringer told *The Western News*.[12] "In today's regulatory climate it [the Libby mine] will never be permitted again.... The regulatory atmosphere has become so cumbersome and expensive that marginal operations can't be done anymore."

Obituary: Walter Baker, 71

Walter Baker, longtime Libby resident, died Saturday afternoon at St. John's Lutheran Hospital, following a long illness.

Baker was born May 31, 1912 to Louis and Emma Baker in Cass Lake, Minn., and came with his family to Libby in 1919, when he was seven years old. He graduated from Libby High School in 1931.

He married Lura C. Brindlehy, May 26, 1939 in Libby.

Baker was employed by J. Neils Lumber Company for 10 years, and at his retirement in 1972 had worked for W.R. Grace & Co. and the Zonolite Co. for 30 years. He was a lifetime member of St. John Lutheran Church at Libby.

Hymns by the congregation included "Rock of Ages" and "Jesus, Lover of My Soul"

—*The Western News, November 16, 1983*

Heavy and dangerous asbestos-contaminated dust covers vehicles and buildings at ore-processing buildings at the Zonolite mine.

"DON'T EVEN JOKE ABOUT IT," Peronard told Weis. "It's not even close to being funny."[1]

"I'm not joking. I found it," Weis said. "It came from MSHA. It's a study that EPA did twenty years ago on asbestos exposure at Libby. They knew it was killing people and they did nothing."

It was early February 2000. Two weeks earlier, Peronard had told his team they needed to find out anything that anyone else knew about vermiculite, tremolite and non-occupational exposures. So they sent out an all-points bulletin for information, and reams of paper started coming in from federal offices. Suddenly, Weis's office was filled with paper. His house and car were filled with paper. The team had boxes of documents stacked high in the Emergency Operations Center.

Peronard hammered away at the legal pissing matches with Grace and tried to keep the contractors for the emergency cleanup work on target. On any given day, between 30 and 100 men and women, dressed in white Tyvek protective clothing and full-face respirators, were using muddy yellow bull-dozers, front-end loaders, dump trucks and even picks and shovels to collect and remove contaminated dirt from the processing and transport sites of the old Zonolite operation.

Meanwhile, Weis was sifting through the scientific data, trying to pin down the best way to analyze the air and soil for asbestos, and Miller was bird-dogging anything he could find on the clinical prognosis of exposure to tremolite. The more the team read, the more disturbed they became. Then they found the worst of it. Within days, Weis and Miller had gleaned not one report, but four of them, all done under orders of EPA headquarters.

The Operations Center for EPA's Rocky Mountain Region is a window-less sixth-floor office in Denver where the on-scene coordinators, like Pero-nard, work when they're not in the field. A TV mounted in the corner was tuned to a muted CNN. Flip charts, a white board, maps and aerial photos occupied another. A coffeepot claimed the only free corner. Large color pho-tographs of earlier cleanup sites hung on the walls.

But the only things that held Peronard's interest were four documents that Weis and Miller had laid on a large table in the center of the room.[2] The titles of the reports alone might be mind-numbing to most. But certainly not to the Libby team:

> Priority Review Level 1 Report — "Asbestos Contaminated Vermiculite," June 1980.
>
> MRI-82 Report — "Collection, Analysis and Characterization of Ver-miculite Samples," September 1982.
>
> "Exposure Assessment for Asbestos-Contaminated Vermiculite," Febru-ary 1985.
>
> "Health Assessment Document for Vermiculite," September 1991.

The "Priority Review" and the "MRI-82 Report" were found deep in the files of the Mine Safety and Health Administration office in Spokane. The other two studies were buried in EPA's research library.

"We're out in the boonies groping for answers on asbestos in vermiculite, and everyone in headquarters shrugs and says they've never heard of it. Now these show up. What the hell is going on?" Weis asked.

"Keep reading," Peronard said.

Large sheets of white paper were taped to the walls, and long yellow pads were filled with notes and calculations as the trio burrowed in the reports. The combined 241 pages of the various studies were filled with the results of extensive sampling of almost every part of the Zonolite mine and mill, as well as the screening and export plant, including the exact spot where Les Skramstad probably breathed his lethal dose of asbestos.

Pages of exposure calculations detailed how much asbestos the workers in almost every job were exposed to at Libby, down to estimates for those running front-end loaders in the pit to workers in the dust-clogged processing mill. In sum, the reports' conclusions were clear: Vermiculite from Libby is loaded with tremolite asbestos, and the lives of the miners and everyone else who handles it down the line are at risk.

Peronard could not remember being angrier in his life. "When you put all these together, you've got the answers. You've got proof, vivid and unquestionable, that what was going on in Libby was a proven hazard and people were being killed.

"EPA, NIOSH, OSHA — the whole damn government — knew what was happening to the people in Libby and not a damn thing was done about any of it."

The reports cited specific findings that backed up what the three investigators and their contractors were finding 20 years later. One section said that miners and workers at various Grace expansion plants had been exposed to levels more than 100 times what OSHA then considered safe. A second concluded: "The available data indicate that workers who mine or process vermiculite from W.R. Grace & Company's Libby, Montana mine are exposed to asbestos levels that present a risk of serious asbestos related disease."

Another added: "EPA risk estimates, based on asbestos exposure, project that one of every 10 workers exposed to [the old OSHA limit of 2 fibers per cubic centimeter of air, which is written as 2 f/cc] for 50 years will die prematurely from asbestos-related disease." But on the page before that quote, the 1980 report said that asbestos as high as 245 f/cc was found in the mine and mill, a figure that Weis and industrial hygienists said translated into a death sentence for everyone who worked at the mine.

These were conclusions that Peronard's emergency response team was starting to reach with its own studies. They were also points that headquarters was adamantly insisting were wrong.

"This is criminal," Peronard said. "They botched the whole investigation, which would have saved twenty years' worth of exposure and lots of lives.

"We've been working our asses off trying to get an understanding of what happened here, why these people were killed, and nobody mentions that we knew these guys were swallowing asbestos and did nothing about it."

The various researchers, to whom EPA paid about a half-million dollars for the work, concluded that "the extent of exposure throughout the country from vermiculite derived from the Libby mine is likely to be large, considering that this source accounts for 80 percent of the vermiculite used in the United States."

The team's earlier discovery of the illnesses at O.M. Scott and in the Jorgensen family in Minneapolis were put into jarring perspective when Peronard read in the 1991 Health Assessment that "13,147,496 people who lived near Grace's exfoliation plants were at risk from tremolite exposure."

EPA had documented that tremolite asbestos caused disease and that millions of people stood a real chance of receiving a dangerous dose. But for two decades, the agency created to protect the public against environmental dangers warned no one, not a single health officer, not another agency, not the miners in Libby nor the people working at or living near the expansion plants. Not a soul was warned.

And even when the deaths and illnesses in Libby were finally made public, those in EPA headquarters who had ordered the early studies, or at least knew of them, didn't tell the team that was sent in to help what they knew about what killed the miners and their families.

"We've got people in headquarters who argue with us on almost every conference call that there can't be many, if any, non-occupational exposures," Peronard said. "They keep yelling that the science says that a lifetime of occupational exposure to asbestos is needed before you have to worry about getting sick from asbestos. Bullshit. Let them read their own damn report."

The 1980 report said: "Mesothelioma, a 'marker disease' for asbestos exposure, has occurred in persons with exposures as brief as one or two days and in persons with exposure as low as those found in the homes of asbestos workers and in the neighborhoods around asbestos mines, asbestos product factories and shipyards."

Weis looked up from the reports, caught Peronard's eye and shook his head. "What kind of game are they playing?" he asked quietly.

CHRIS WEIS WAS AN ADJUNCT PROFESSOR at the University of Colorado in Boulder. He taught toxicology.

The Center for Environmental Journalism is also on the campus, and every year they'd bring a bunch of reporters and editors in for a weeklong series of lectures on various environmental topics. Weis was always buttonholed to give a talk on "Why Small Things Matter," about things you can't see that make a difference in environmental problems.

So on May 26, 2000, a few hours after returning from Libby on a late flight, a very tired Weis stood in front of the visiting journalists doing his shtick.[3] It was his day off, but he liked talking about science and the environment. His talk was well-received. The question-and-answer session started off well. Until Scott McMillion, a reporter from the *Bozeman Daily Chronicle,* stood and asked Weis, "Aren't you part of the Libby team?"

"It was downhill from there," Weis said. "I just wanted to get out of there, but the guy wouldn't let up. 'When did the EPA find out? Doesn't EPA assess risk? What were the risks, Dr. Weis?' He was relentless, so I told him."

Five days later, on the front page of the Bozeman paper, McMillion quoted Weis: "More than 15 years before it took any concrete action, officials in the Environmental Protection Agency knew that deadly asbestos fibers were killing people in Libby," said the first paragraph in the story.

It was in the 13th paragraph that Weis discussed "death projections of almost 100 percent" for Libby miners. "If you worked at the mine you were probably going to die of asbestos-related disease," he told McMillion.

What might not have created a stir on the front page of the Bozeman paper became a bombshell on Capitol Hill when, the next day, a shortened Associated Press version of the story appeared on page A-6 of *The Washington Post.* Weis was oblivious to the firestorm searing the executive offices of EPA headquarters and the mob of bureaucrats lining up to get his head or at least a piece of his ass.[4]

He was 900 miles north, walking along the railroad tracks in a canyon near Alberton, Montana, where he had worked a mammoth train wreck a couple of years earlier. For reasons he said he couldn't explain, his cell phone, which had been useless all morning in the remote terrain, began to ring. The signal kept breaking up, but he could hear the person on the other end well enough to find out that he was from the office of EPA administrator Carol Browner and Weis was in more trouble than he could ever imagine. The voice on the phone said Weis had better have proof to back up the outrageous quotes in the *Post* or he was dead meat. Headquarters was circling the wagons.

Within hours of the Post story being read at Washington's breakfast tables, EPA had formulated and issued its official position on the reports, about which it had done nothing for decades.[5] An e-mail sent to the top EPA people at 9:29 that morning laid out the official line.

"Contrary to statements recently carried in the press, this study was made fully available to the public, was broadly disseminated and contained no information about the risk posed to workers at the mine." That was their story and they were sticking to it.

The Denver team couldn't believe that headquarters would continue to lie about something so important. And Peronard was broadsided with a tsunami of calls for Weis's job. Headquarters kept saying "that guy's out of control," and dumped on Paul for not being able to harness his own team. Peronard knew that Chris was 100-percent accurate. Would he have made Peronard's life easier if he hadn't said it, or if he'd said it more softly? Sure. *But what the hell,* Peronard thought. *You can't yell at somebody for sharing the truth on something that's well-documented. Our job isn't to lie to the public, the press or anyone.* That, apparently, was headquarters' job.

The question that Peronard couldn't get answered was, Why didn't EPA follow up on the studies, even when two of them called for a second phase in the original proposals authorizing the projects? Nobody official leveled with him, but some of the old-timers in headquarters told him the follow-up was never pursued because of the recommendations that J. Peter Grace gave President Ronald Reagan on reducing government interference in industry's business.

IN FEBRUARY 1982, at a White House press conference, Reagan announced with much fanfare that J. Peter Grace, Grace's CEO, would head the President's Private Sector Survey on Cost Control, which became known as the Grace Commission.[6]

In January 1984, Grace said his commission had created "thirty-six task forces, chaired by 161 top executives from around the country and staffed by over 2,000 volunteers that they provided. We came up with 2,478 separate, distinct, and specific recommendations which are the basis for the carefully projected savings ... of $424.4 billion over three years."[7] He added that the 47 volumes and 21,000 pages of the report "constitute a vision of an efficient, well-managed government that is accountable to taxpayers."

But Congress determined that the commission was dominated by white, male executives from Fortune 500 companies, and the report, for the most part, focused on the interest of these corporate leaders in getting government regulators off their backs. The watchdog group Public Citizen spent six months examining the internal letters and reports of the commission members and found open disdain for blacks and the poor.[8] Congress asked for information on the task-force membership and was repeatedly refused. "It is as if we were trying to get access to our first strike plans for an atomic war," said Rep. William Ford.

William Ruckelshaus, who was EPA's first administrator when it was created in 1970, was brought back by Reagan from 1983 to '85 after Administrator Anne Gorsuch Burford's near-destruction of the agency.[9] It was during his second tour that Ruckelshaus remembers asbestos becoming an issue and Grace's recommendations being doled out by the White House.

"The Grace Commission had a whole list of recommendations for EPA, some of which I thought made sense, some didn't. I thought some parts of it were okay and other parts were really biased."

Ruckelshaus questioned the propriety of Grace handing out environmental edicts.[10]

"If Grace's company owned that mine in Libby or had any other major involvement with asbestos, [Peter Grace] shouldn't have been reviewing actions dealing with regulation of the asbestos industry," he said. "That should have been something he recused himself of. It's okay for a private citizen to take on a review of that kind, but he should not be reviewing his own industry. Even if the things he said were sensible, it would have no credibility."

However, EPA researchers and historians in headquarters said they couldn't track precisely what recommendations Grace had made about asbestos.

Whether the reports were intentionally concealed or just buried in the billions of pounds of paper that Washington generates each year may never be proven. But the four studies they did find answered some questions for the Libby investigators, and raised many new ones. They confirmed the team's suspicion that tremolite was more lethal than other asbestos fibers, and presented stark, irrefutable proof of the danger to the rest of the country from Libby's poison.

The reports made it clear to Peronard that anyplace in the country you found vermiculite, you'd also find deaths from it. Since he and his team had arrived in Libby, Grace had insisted that unexpanded vermiculite ore had less than 1 percent asbestos content and wasn't dangerous. After the old reports came to light, the team started testing piles of vermiculite ore that it had been ignoring and found much higher concentrations of asbestos.

The revelations of the reports also made working with the people of Libby even more awkward. Schneider's original stories made it clear that some agencies knew about the deadly exposures and did nothing — OSHA, NIOSH and what was then called the Bureau of Mines. It was hard enough for the team members to look people in the eye knowing that they themselves were part of the same federal government that neglected Libby. But now Peronard and his crew knew that their own agency not only knew about the potential for death, but had studied it four times in 20 years and still did nothing.

Gayla, Les, Brad Black, staffers for Max Baucus, the Democratic senator from Montana, and a score of others that Peronard and the team had worked so hard to win over were now asking how the EPA could have betrayed them, lied to them.

Peronard met Steve Hawthorn, who was his immediate boss for emergency response, and Doug Skie, who was Hawthorn's boss, and Dodson, who was over everybody. "Guys, I ain't going back up to Libby, look those people in the eye and tell them that we did everything just fine," Peronard told them. "That's just bullshit."

Out of the grousing, an idea developed. On June 27, 2000, three senior EPA officials did something that no one could remember ever happening before.[11] They turned their agency in to its inspector general, to investigate how EPA had dropped the ball. In almost all cases, it's people outside an agency that blow the whistle — environmental groups, members of Congress, the public — but not this time.

"Questions have been raised by residents of Libby, government officials and concerned citizens regarding the federal government's decision record on the Libby vermiculite operation. These decisions were made more than 15 years ago when Federal policies regarding asbestos contamination, remediation and worker safety were being developed. The record of decision, particularly as it relates to EPA involvement with other federal agencies, needs to be reconstructed by an impartial entity," the letter to the inspector general said.

It was signed by Timothy Fields, Jr., the assistant administrator for the Superfund and emergency response side of the house, Susan Wayland, the acting assistant administrator for the Office of Prevention, Pesticides and Toxic Substances, whose section does pollution prevention and funded some of the old studies, and Rebecca Hanmer, who was the acting administrator for Region 8, replacing Yellowtail, until the incoming George W. Bush administration named a replacement.[12] They asked the inspector general to coordinate the investigation with other federal agencies which "had jurisdiction over W.R. Grace's Libby operation, including CPSC, MSHA and OSHA."

"We've got the IG to look into this. At least you can say that somebody's investigating what happened. You can do the cleanups and somebody else can determine whether something nefarious took place twenty years ago," Dodson told Peronard.

Dodson tried to convince him that the battle over why the old studies weren't released wasn't theirs to fight. They had a cleanup to worry about. "This is what we have an IG for," he told Peronard, but at that moment, the emergency coordinator would rather have solved it with knives in the street.

Three days later, Wendy Thomi, EPA's community coordinator, handed copies of the IG letter to Gayla, Les and the other members of The Community Advisory Group. The press had a ball, and dozens of papers gave the story the full treatment. The reaction to the IG request made many in headquarters cringe. A few predicted that little more than a whitewash would come out of it.

Dodson started weekly conference calls on Libby so the rest of EPA would know what was happening.[13] The expansion-plant issue made Libby a national issue, and he figured that if everyone was talking, there would be fewer surprises. And headquarters hated surprises. On each call there were usually representatives of each region that had a "Libby sister" or a Grace expansion plant, people from the Superfund, as well as John Melone, then director of the National Priority Chemicals Division in the Office of Pollution, Prevention and Toxic Substances. His shop hired contractors to research various pollution problems, such as the reports on vermiculite done twenty years ago.

Such conference calls are usually boring as dirt, but participants in the Libby calls found them to be great theater, especially when Peronard and Melone went after each other. The thin veneer of forced collegiality between them vaporized the first time Melone challenged Peronard on the old reports, shortly after they were discovered.

"They could have charged admission to that one," Weis said.

According to four people who were listening to the call, Melone repeatedly said that the Libby team was acting recklessly and that to characterize this vermiculite material as dangerous was contrary to science. Peronard wasn't shy in his response.

"So how come so many people are fucking sick and dying from this exposure? How come every time we stir the vermiculite up there are all sorts of fibers in the air?"

Word spread, and the next week even more people crowded around speakerphones in eight different cities. The working stiffs love it when someone in the field has the chutzpah to stand up to headquarters, and once again they were not disappointed. Melone said that Grace insisted that the asbestos in Libby ore was less than 1 percent and not a hazard. Peronard reminded Melone that he was the person who years earlier had ordered the MRI-82 study to be done. "Jesus Christ, guys," he said to those listening at headquarters. "How can you say that what we're finding in Libby isn't a risk? You concluded it was — twenty years ago."

The battle continued in the more private venue of e-mail.[14] In defending the study his office had ordered, Melone wrote: "Grace reported that their process changes would result in [very low levels of exposure to the workers.]" It is unclear to what extent that was ever verified. "We have merely recorded the assertion by W.R. Grace that their process changes resulted in dramatic reductions in exposures. There is no evidence that anyone disputed it at the time."

Peronard e-mailed back: "We dispute most of what Grace tells us, because in almost every case our findings don't support their claims."

In another exchange, Peronard wrote, "Your response reflects a hypersensitivity that is (and has been) most frustrating to deal with. This has been the case throughout my contact with you since Libby broke out."

Melone replied: "My sensitivity to the characterization is high, and you may call it hyper if you wish, because the earlier characterizations of this matter have been that this terrible outcome in Libby is due to the failure of HQ EPA, specifically this office, not notifying the region of key information or not acting as it should have."

Schneider, who had received the e-mails under a Freedom of Information Act request, tried repeatedly to interview Melone about his views on

Libby and the row with Peronard, but EPA's press office refused to make him available.

"There is no value in washing our dirty clothes in public," the press officer said with some rancor. Schneider raised the issue of fairness to Melone, to which the flack replied, "We'll decide what's fair" and hung up.

Gayla Benefield's tiny office in her log cabin beside the Kootenai River outside Libby became an early stop for government investigators and reporters of every ilk trying to understand the machinations of what W.R. Grace inflicted upon her community. (Andrew Schneider)

U.S. SENATOR CONRAD BURNS is used to getting a pretty warm reception when he travels to the small towns and rural areas across the very large state he represents. Montana's Republican junior senator is a rancher. He is unabashedly conservative, and so, in large part, is his constituency.

He once made a racial joke in Bozeman (about the trials of living in Washington, D.C., among so many blacks, only he didn't say "blacks"), and the *Bozeman Daily Chronicle* had the effrontery to publish it. His approval rating actually went up a couple of points statewide.

When he came to Libby, campaigning for reelection in the fall of 2000, the Lincoln County GOP put on a gala reception for him at the VFW. But at one table, a less festive group that included Les and Norita Skramstad, Gayla and Dave Benefield and Bob and Carrie Dedrick waited quietly to talk to Burns about the issue they cared about most — asbestos.

Finally, Burns came out of the back room at the club, where he was meeting with local Republican officials, and sat down at the table. Immediately, Carrie Dedrick began asking him to help the victims in Libby. At that, Burns did not respond to Carrie, but instead looked directly across the table at Gayla. He shook a big finger in her face and said, "Little lady, when you stop tearing me down is when I start doing something to help the people of Libby."

Gayla got her own finger — "the pointer, honestly," she would say later — wagging right back in the senator's face. She replied, "Sir, I have not been on your ass, or on TV talking about this, for six months, and you have done nothing in those six months, so don't try to use that as an excuse."

Burns tried another tack, telling the group that he had gotten W.R. Grace to provide millions for medical screening. In the same firm, polite voice, Gayla said, "You are mistaken. Grace is not paying for the screening. Our tax dollars are."

At that point, Burns decided to cut his losses, and got up and walked out of the room. Les had gotten up from the table earlier, and just happened to be standing quietly nearby when Burns came through the door and growled to an aide, "I had to come all the way here to put up with this shit?"

Conrad Burns would not be the last public official to feel the sting of Gayla Benefield's tongue on this issue. This ex-bartending, honky-tonk-singing grandmother was dedicated to doing all she could to help Libby's sick and bereaved. Justice? Her mother and father and hundreds more never got it. But Gayla was doubled-damned determined to find whatever measure of justice was left in the world and bring it to Libby.

Back in the '90s, Gayla gave up her own trial date twice to allow other claimants with advanced asbestos-related disease to get to court sooner. The district court in Libby permitted only one suit against Grace to reach the court calendar every three months, and at that rate, Gayla knew that Toni Riley, Andy Wright and Bob Graham would not live long enough to get any semblance of justice. There were more than 200 suits in the pipeline. Graham, a former miner, had mesothelioma, and Wright had asbestosis.

Finally, Gayla got a trial date she could keep, and as it got closer and closer, Grace attorneys made successively higher settlement offers. They had started, a few months after Margaret's death, by offering Gayla $10,000.

Of course, she said no.[1] A few weeks later they came back to her with a $20,000 offer. Roger Sullivan and Jon Heberling told her that the Grace lawyers said they didn't think she had a case, and that they were basically just giving her the money. She refused. A little while later they set up a negotiating session at the Venture Inn. Grace started at $35,000, and got to $75,000 by the end of the day. She became angry with Heberling and Sullivan for offering to settle for $175,000 that day. "The only way I'll take that is with both of your left nuts on a silver platter beside the check," she told the lawyers. "I don't want to settle this case. I want a guilty verdict."

Then, as the trial opened in November 1998, Grace offered $175,000, and Gayla got a chance to turn down the amount her attorneys had said they'd settle for. And she did. As the trial progressed, the offers to settle kept on coming. When Grace got to $400,000, Jon Heberling tried hard to convince Gayla to take it. That was more than he thought she'd get from the jury. Her case, a wrongful-death case, wasn't worth as much as Les's case or any case brought by a living victim. She said no.

A couple of nights later, the jury was deliberating, and Grace sweetened the offer to $500,000. The phone rang at Gayla's house. She was playing cribbage with Dave, trying to relax. Controlling her temper during the trial was not easy. Sometimes she'd wanted to reach out and choke Gary Graham, who was representing Grace in court. And that night came another insult: *The Western News* printed an op-ed piece praising Earl Lovick and all the good he'd done for the community. Of course the jury wasn't supposed to see it. Of course, they probably would.

Roger Sullivan urged her again to settle.

"I warned you I wasn't here for the money," she replied. "I still want a verdict. You can tell them to take their half a million dollars and shove it up their ass."

As the jury was about to come in, Grace, still desperate for confidentiality, offered Gayla $605,000, plus a letter of apology for causing her father's death. But they specified that she couldn't do anything with the letter. She couldn't put it on the Internet or show it around. She couldn't even frame it and put it on her wall.

Gayla knew it was a huge offer. She talked to her family, and then she talked with Roger and Jon. She told them that she wanted to turn it down, but she also realized that a goodly chunk of the settlement would be their money, too. "Can you get by on a little less income this year?" she asked them. They assured her that they could; it was purely her decision to make, they told her.

She made it: No.

The jury filed back into court. To Gayla, the whole courtroom seemed dark except for the place where the bailiff was reading. It was like there was a spotlight there. Everybody would tell her later that the lighting was normal, but that's the way it looked to her.

The jury found W.R. Grace liable for the deaths of Perley and Margaret Vatland.

They awarded Gayla and her family $250,000. "That part was almost immaterial," Gayla says. She got what she wanted — the judgment that Grace was guilty, and the freedom to recognize that publicly. And she let Grace know that her share of the money would buy a lot of phone calls and computer paper.

She went home and posted a note on a site dedicated to asbestos victims, saying she felt after the two weeks of trial as though she had "danced with the devil and spit in his eye!"

Before the court cases started, before Les got his verdict, many people in Libby quietly settled with Grace, signed nondisclosure agreements, and died. No one, not even their friends, knew the details of the settlements. Gayla understood that most victims would settle, and she understood that it was often the best decision. "Often, they felt like they were letting us down or something." But usually she told them: "Fine. Go enjoy your life. Take their money and enjoy it." She explained, "They knew, and I knew, what was coming down the line for them, and often the best thing was just to take that money and get a little pleasure out of the rest of their lives. Someone else can carry the torch through the court system." Gayla smiled.

"Someone like me."

MEANWHILE, the dying went on.

Toni Riley, Don Riley's sister-in-law, was a reserve deputy sheriff. She worked on Libby's ambulance crew, was a trained rescue diver and helped out fighting forest fires. She never worked at the mine. But that didn't keep her from being exposed to the asbestos. In 1995, she noticed she was often short of breath. A year later, she was diagnosed with mesothelioma. By 1997, she was in bad shape. "George," as she called her cancer, was winning the fight. As mesothelioma always does.

Heberling and Sullivan got her a settlement, which eased the final year and a half of her life. She died on December 4, 1998.

LES AND NORITA SKRAMSTAD WAITED patiently for their check from Grace.

But weeks, then a couple of months went by, and it didn't come. They wanted part of it to help out their kids a little bit, and so Les called Jon Heberling.

"There's a problem," Heberling said. Grace had filed a post-trial motion and brief with Judge Prezeau that contended the verdict did not conform to state law.

So the case file returned to Prezeau's desk.

Several more months went by. Prezeau had not ruled in the matter, so the payment was in limbo. "Don't worry, you're getting interest on it," the lawyers told Les.

IT WAS A RIDE THAT NO ONE WANTED TO MAKE but a ride that had to be made. It was clearly not the kind of togetherness that the Skramstad family savored.

On March 10, 1999, Les, Norita, their son and daughter, Brent and Gayla, and their grandkids, six-year-old Lester and two-year-old Makenna, all packed into Les's blue Chevy van. The 150-mile drive from Libby to Spokane seemed to take far longer than usual.

They made small talk, lots of it. They chatted about the amount of snow on the ground, the road, and whether the current thaw was for real. Was it really the end of winter? They talked about anything but what was waiting for them in Spokane — their appointment with Alan Whitehouse.

The physician had been tracking the deterioration of Les's asbestos-damaged lungs for years.[2] Now some of the rest of the family was going to get checked out. Now and then, Brent would have a hard time catching his breath. Gayla's cough sounded like hell all the time, and Les thought Norita was looking a bit peaked. He decided that he wanted Doc Whitehouse to "give them the once-over."

Norita and the rest of the family were apprehensive, hoping for the best but deep down, for some reason, not expecting it. Les played with his grandchildren in the waiting room as Norita and Gayla, after having their lungs X-rayed, now each sat in a tiny room, blowing into the plastic mouthpieces of the machines that measured how well their lungs were working. Brent was having his lungs X-rayed after having taken the pulmonary-function test twice. The testing completed, the clan gathered in Whitehouse's private office.

While the doctor went over his charts, there was little for the family to do but stare at the large X-rays that hung on the lighted view box on the wall. Norita could see some ribs and maybe the lungs, but she had no idea what it meant, or even whose chest she was looking at. Les stared in a different direction. He didn't want to look. He didn't want to know. But Whitehouse told them.

"That's what I'm supposed to do. I don't withhold things from my patients. That's not fair to them," the doctor said. "So I tell them what I see." Speaking calmly, in an almost matter-of-fact tone, Whitehouse ran his pointer over the varying shades of gray on the film, pointing out what was normal and what had been damaged by the asbestos fibers they'd sucked in. Les will always remember exactly what the doctor said that March afternoon:

Gayla's lungs looked "pretty clean." Norita "has asbestosis, but it's not serious yet." And Brent "has a full-blown, active case of asbestosis."

Les was devastated. "It was like a feller who's already sentenced to death being told he has to take his family with him to the gas chamber," he would say later.

As Whitehouse talked, Les kept stealing glances at his wife. Norita was afraid to look at her husband. They knew they would both burst into tears.

Whitehouse said most people don't get visibly emotional when they hear the news.

"Norita and Brent knew something was going on in one form or another — the trouble breathing, the pain," Whitehouse said. "Most of the time, people expect that you're going to tell them something that they don't want to hear but they pretty well know it's coming."

In medicine, it's rare that a physician will treat multiple members of the same family for anything other than a communicable disease — mumps, measles, chicken pox and the like. For a family to have several members with a disease that can be terminal is rarely seen. "It is unique, but not in Libby," Whitehouse said. "Les's family was one of the first, but after them, in late 1999 and 2000, a flurry of families from Libby came in and were diagnosed where several members had disease caused by asbestos."

The Skramstads' ride home was a lot quieter. Nobody wanted to talk about it, for fear of frightening the grandkids. And they still didn't know a lot about the disease then, Norita remembers — "like how fast it could spread and how it can make living a nightmare. Maybe we thought that if we ignored it, it would go away."

Les was already beating the hell out of himself, seeing this as proof of what he did to his family. "I knew he was going to react that way from the minute I told him about Brent and Norita's condition," Whitehouse said. "I told him that day and twenty times since that it wasn't his fault. He didn't do this to his family, Grace did.

"Norita and his children have all told him that it's not his fault, that he's not to blame, but Les will never believe that if he didn't bring all that asbestos dust home from the mine on his clothes, his family would not be sick. He's got too much anger to ever forget that Grace knew the dust was dangerous and never told anyone. I don't blame him. I'd be mad as hell, too."

Back in Libby, the kids got into their own cars and drove to their homes. On the ride to Havre, Lester, Brent's son, asked, "Dad, are you going to die?"

"We're all going to die sometime," his father answered.

"No. I mean are you going to die right away like granddad?" the six-year-old persisted.

Les said his grandson "looks at me funny when I start coughing. It's one of those little-kid looks that says he's afraid that I'm going to die right then and there, but he doesn't want to ask. When I catch my breath I give him a big hug and tell him that everything's going to be all right.

"But he knows it's not."

STILL NO RULING from the judge, still no money from Grace.

"Can't you do anything?" Les asked Heberling. "You know him. Can't you talk to the judge?" Before the trial began, Heberling and Sullivan had told Les that they knew Prezeau, and thought he was fair, so now Les figured that they ought to go see him. Heberling explained that it would be unethical to try to contact the judge while the matter was under advisement. So Les and Norita waited. A year went by, and still Prezeau had not ruled.

Finally, Les asked the lawyer if there was a way he could get an advance from Grace against the verdict. He knew he needed to do some work on his house. He wanted to build a carport so he'd be able to get to and from the car more easily when his mobility was even more limited. Heberling came back to him a few days later. "Grace is asking if you'll negotiate a settlement."

Les got even angrier. He'd been told he had a life expectancy of five to ten years, and he'd been without the money the court had awarded now for one of those years. He talked with Norita, and they realized that the verdict was worthless if he couldn't collect it. The lawyers would take 45 percent of whatever he recovered, plus expenses, which were estimated at $47,000. They weren't happy about the prospect of negotiating for part of something they thought was legally theirs, but ultimately they decided they didn't have a choice.

They settled for considerably less than the jury had given them.

"If he had just made a decision," Les sighed. "Even if he'd ruled against us, we could have taken it to the Supreme Court, but we were in limbo." After part of the award had been bargained away, Les tried to talk to the judge, to find out why he had not ruled. Prezeau's clerk told Les the judge wouldn't be able to discuss it.

Then, in June of 2000, Alan Whitehouse told another Skramstad kid, Laurel, that she, too, had asbestosis. She had been two when Les started at the mine. Her brother Brent had been just a year old. For Les, the tragedy was now complete — the company had poisoned him, his wife and his babies.

"If Les could have gotten his hands on a gun that day, he would have gone postal," Gayla Benefield says.

Obituary: Toni Riley, 54

Libby native Darlene J. (Toni) Riley, 54, died Friday, Dec. 4, 1998, at St. John's Lutheran Hospital after a long battle with cancer.

She was born on Nov. 9, 1944, at Libby, to Mark and Grace Burton Hall. Toni attended Libby schools and on Dec. 8, 1961, she married Vern Riley in Bonners Ferry, Idaho.

Toni had been a member of David Thompson Search and Rescue and an emergency medical technician with the Libby Volunteer Ambulance since 1985.

She was a reserve deputy with the sheriff's office for five years and worked for a labor union for three years, until she became ill.

Toni also worked at the Asa Wood School for two years as a teacher's aide. She enjoyed sewing, crocheting, hunting, camping and riding horses. She was a loving wife, mother, daughter and sister.

—The Western News, December 9, 1998

CHAPTER 15

Long, needlelike asbestos fibers can easily cause disease and death.
(Court documents)

THREE DAYS AFTER New Year's Day 2000, having survived all the end-of-the-world predictions for the millennium, Peronard, Weis and Miller returned to Libby ready to go to war. Unfortunately, their weapons — the regulations that control everything they do — were decades old.

During the 1960s, '70s and '80s, in fits and starts, individual government investigators or small bands of scientists would attempt to prod their respective agencies into closing a loophole, researching a new technique or modifying an outdated regulation, but if the toxin at the heart of any of these attempts was asbestos, chances were overwhelming that nothing meaningful would happen.[1] The status quo was good enough.

The Libby team was shackled to the official decision that there are only six types of asbestos and that only long fibers — greater than five microns — were dangerous enough to sicken and kill. (A micron, or micro meter, is 1/25,000th of an inch. A human hair is 100 microns wide.) The govern-

227

ment had bought off on industry's belief that the aspect ratio of the fiber, the relationship between its length and width, had to fall into narrowly defined ranges to be dangerous, and that broken pieces of asbestos called cleavage fragments weren't harmful, regardless of the toxicity of the asbestos they broke away from. The federal regulations also said that there really was no need to worry about any material that had less than 1 percent asbestos.

The asbestos industry was persistent in fighting any restriction the government felt was needed. In 1976, for example, while OSHA and NIOSH were pushing for asbestos exposure levels to be set at the lowest detectable levels, Grace representatives argued that tremolite, the form of asbestos that contaminates the Libby ore, wasn't a "commercial asbestos form" and therefore should be treated differently than other types of asbestos in the workplace.

In a letter to OSHA, Grace argued that "disruption of Grace's vermiculite business, which employs 1,300 people at locations in over 20 states, with an annual payroll of approximately $19 million, also would affect jobs in areas such as the construction industry where vermiculite products are used."

Now, 25 years later, Peronard and his team faced the outcome of Grace's successful lobbying. They had to confront rules that also established the analytical methods that could be used in hunting the elusive asbestos fiber. When trying to find asbestos in solid samples like soil, dust and insulation, nearly all asbestos laboratories use polarized-light microscopy, or PLM, which magnifies the fiber about 400 times. Adequate if you're looking for chrysotile, which was usually added in large amounts — 50 percent or more — to most products in which it was used. Tremolite, which wasn't intentionally added, but was a contaminant of vermiculite and other minerals, was usually found in much smaller amounts.

"Using PLM like the regulations demand is like trying to count cars on a road from 30,000 feet up. You can see the big trucks, but not the cars," Weis explained. "Where's the tremolite?"

And with the decades-old rules tying their hands, the investigators were having a hard time even finding the trucks.

CONTRACTORS FOR THE EPA, bundled against the piercing Montana cold with fleece vests and heavy flannel shirts under their white Tyvek hazmat suits, collected more than 700 samples of soil and dust from all over Libby and the former Grace property, often having to chip through frozen dirt and rock to get enough material to analyze.[2]

Peronard told the labs to work overtime. He needed to know how much danger the people of the town still faced. The demand for immediate answers came from the townsfolk, real-estate sellers and politicians. The reports of the PLM analysis began trickling in, and then gushed.

"What the hell is happening here?" Peronard asked his sidekicks as the trio pored over the piles of lab reports. "All we're getting are 'trace' amounts and a lot of 'non-detects.'"

Some of the places where the samples were collected were covered with vermiculite ore and the expanded Zonolite, and they were still coming up clean. More samples were collected and were sent to a different lab. The results were the same. EPA's hotshot National Emergency Response Team flew in from New Jersey, took samples from the same waste piles the contractors had explored and sent them to what they considered "the best laboratories on the East Coast." The results were the same. Nothing found. Days turned into weeks, and Peronard was climbing the walls as he fought to fend off demands from headquarters and Grace for the results of the testing.

Weis made several quick trips between Libby and the U.S. Geological Survey offices in Denver.

"They have the best mineralogists in the world and some of the hottest new analytical tools there are," Weis told Peronard. "Maybe they can help."

"Check it out," the boss said.

As would become his habit, Peronard was bluntly frank with the people of Libby.[3] Right up front, he told them that almost all the government's asbestos regulations dealt with occupational exposure or levels in a school where old asbestos is being removed.

"There is nothing, absolutely nothing that can help us evaluate the risk to the baby in Libby crawling on the kitchen floor in asbestos tracked in from the yard or from the Zonolite insulation that has fallen through cracks in the ceiling. We're doing the best we can, with what we've been given to use," he said at a public meeting in late January.

Weis added: "The risk models EPA uses are based on chrysotile and occupational exposure. Here in Libby we're dealing with tremolite and people exposed in their home, in the park, the schoolyards, their driveways. Most kids used to light a kitchen match, hold it under a piece of vermiculite ore and watch it pop off.

"How do you evaluate the risk from that?"

With the town's realization that the EPA was serious about the cleanup came a thousand questions. Knowing this, the team helped set up an advisory panel to help keep Libby people informed. Wendy Thomi explained that the agency would fund a facilitator for the group, and she agreed to help make it happen.

Mayor Tony Berget had seen his control of the Libby situation evaporate after EPA realized how far off base his assessment of the situation was. Now he tried halfheartedly to head this populist effort off at the pass. At the first meeting, he raised the question of whether the community really wanted such a group. Those present voted unanimously that they did.

The Community Advisory Group, or CAG, as it was called, proved to be everything Thomi had promised. Its meetings provided a good exchange of information, and they were also a focal point for the public discussion of something that was very private for too long. Often emotional, occasionally contentious, the meetings helped the town come to grips with the tragedy and plot a course for the future. By the second and third meetings, more and more victims were showing up, and often outbursts aimed at Grace came from the audience.

That doesn't mean the entire town got behind the EPA or was even willing to admit there was a problem. There's a far-right militia-type presence in Libby, and in the early days of EPA's investigation, a handful of militia members would come to the meetings and glower at the federal employees. "It was scary," said Miller. "But Wendy did a great job of communicating, just laying the facts out there."

BY MARCH, AN EARLY SPRING THAW had turned the soil being tested into mud.

Peronard was back in Libby and, to the annoyance of some of the ATS-DR team who worried about his candor, he shared his frustration at the mystifying test results with the 30 or so people attending the regular Thursday-night meeting of the CAG.

With no attempt to soft-pedal the problem, he admitted, "We just don't know what's going on.

"We're testing where we know there is asbestos and we're using the methods that EPA regulations allow us to use, and we just aren't finding a darn thing," he told the group.

With the patience of a Sunday-school teacher, Peronard explained the PLM analysis and what it was supposed to do. Gayla was among those listening that night, and a lightbulb went off.

"I remembered reading something about testing vermiculite, but I couldn't remember what," she said.

Well past midnight, she was still tearing through the binders holding the old Grace documents, and she found it: a June 7, 1973, memo from Julie Yang, one of Grace's scientists, saying that PLM wasn't telling her what she needed to know about the asbestos in the Libby vermiculite.[4] Yang wanted to use "scanning electron microscopy." SEM uses a microscope that can show very detailed three-dimensional images at magnifications up to 200,000 times, far greater than is possible with PLM.

It was a little after dawn that Gayla's phone call interrupted Peronard's push-ups in his room at the Super 8. And she quickly shared her findings.

Just three hours later, Weis called Peronard with more good news.

"We might have gotten a break at USGS," he said.

New USGS technology — visible infrared spectrometry — that NASA was going to use to evaluate the surface of Mars had been put on the shelf after the loss of two Mars-bound probes, in September and December of the preceding year.[5]

"They have this fascinating method that uses reflected infrared light," Weis said. "They told me that the technology might be useful for examining minute quantities of asbestos."

Taking them up on their offer, Weis handed them a bunch of the split samples from the earlier PLM testing. USGS ran 50 or 60 soil samples from Libby through the infrared scanner, and they reported a "strong signal" from almost all of them, meaning that the mineral composition of tremolite had been detected. Weis worried that the sensitivity of the Mars probe device was too great and that it was picking up on background minerals, so the USGS scientists put a few samples under their scanning electron microscope — the same technology that Grace's Yang had asked for.

Weis and the USGS scientists were shocked at what they saw: large bundles of fibers, along with minuscule fiber pieces and tremolite fibers so thin that they were only visible at the highest magnification of the electron microscope. They were everywhere.

"The samples were positive, the same ones that showed nothing under PLM, and I don't mean just a few samples, but most of them," Weis told a much-relieved on-scene boss that morning. "We're not losing our minds."

Grace immediately went on the attack. In the furor that followed the first *Post-Intelligencer* stories, Grace had said it would "do everything in our power to help the citizens of Libby." But that promise soon degenerated into acrimony and litigation. And the company's first battle strategy was to fight the test results on technical grounds.

"EPA does have methods for determining what is asbestos content, which have been peer reviewed and scientifically accepted for years and years," Grace spokesman Corcoran told *The New York Times*, "so we are trying to get some understanding of why, if those methods are good enough for every other situation, why are they not good enough for this one."[6]

Back in Denver, other USGS mineralogists started testing the samples with other sophisticated devices. Among the tremolite fibers, they found winchite and richterite, similar fibers with the difference of just one or two extra atoms. But these new tests were enough to technically set these fibers apart from tremolite.

"They even found fiber with winchite on one end and tremolite on the other," Weis said. "They found the fibers that were killing people. They were like twin cousins to tremolite, and I didn't give a damn what they called it."

But headquarters and Grace did.

Rockets aimed at Libby soared in from a half-dozen offices in EPA in Washington and from Grace's lawyers in the corporate offices in Maryland, in Denver and Memphis. All carried almost identical messages: The sophisticated microscopes that finally identified the fibers were not permitted under the aged regulations, and winchite and richterite were not among the six asbestos fibers that were government-regulated.

Therefore, EPA headquarters decreed, "we are not authorized to clean it up."

Therefore, Grace's lawyers argued, how can a company be accused of contaminating an area with fibers that aren't dangerous enough for the government to regulate?

The Libby team reacted neither calmly nor quietly to the input.

Sitting in the MK Steakhouse, ten miles east of Libby, Peronard, Weis and Miller were *not* enjoying some of Montana's best beef.

"These fibers, whatever they call them, are killing people," Peronard stormed. "What are we supposed to tell these people? 'There's no reason for you to be sick based on what the official literature says'? The reality of what's happening here isn't fitting the book science that we're stuck with."

"The whole thing is remarkably absurd," Weis said. "It's like *Alice in Wonderland,* but the mad hatters are in headquarters."

The contradiction between what Miller, Black and Whitehouse were seeing in the X-rays and CT-scans of the victims, and what the regulations were saying, was dangerous and driving the physicians crazy.

"According to the book, about eighty percent of these fibers are either too thin or too short to be counted as asbestos under the current rules," Miller said. "But there's nothing in the literature that says they're safe."

"They've got these fibers throughout their homes, on the floor, the chairs, the tables, everywhere. Their attics are full of it. Should they take comfort that the government says you're not in danger, but they go to Spokane and Whitehouse tells them they're dying?"

Weis showed his partners another message from headquarters.

R. J. Lee, who ran a large analytical lab near Pittsburgh and did a lot of work for Grace and the rest of the asbestos industry, sent EPA what would be the first of many letters insisting that what Peronard's analysis called asbestos fibers were in fact cleavage fragments or bundles of fibers.[7] But pathologists who have examined lung tissue of vermiculite miners and others exposed to tremolite who have died of asbestosis or mesothelioma have observed fibers broken from cleavage fragments embedded in diseased tissue.

"Even if Grace wants to call them cleavage fragments, there's no proof they're not toxic," Weis said.

On January 18, 2001, Grace's Corcoran wrote to Steven Herman, EPA's assistant administrator for enforcement, again complaining that EPA was being unfair to the company.[8]

"The current management of Grace had been in place for less than two years when the *Seattle Post-Intelligencer* stories about Libby ran. Prior to these news stories, we had no reason to believe that there was a continuing environmental problem in the community," the vice president wrote.

Corcoran ended the two-page letter sharing his views on Peronard and his team, accusing them of "taking positions regarding asbestos that EPA has never taken ... They have become legislators, regulators, and a research institution combined — and senior EPA management has allowed this to happen, and by its silence even encouraged it."

The heat was getting intense. A few others in EPA headquarters, including some political appointees who knew little or nothing about science, were being swayed by the expected arguments being made by Melone's shop and Grace. Something had to be done to get other experts — people willing to look beyond cobwebbed science — to weigh in on the fiber controversy, the Libby team believed.

With speed that dazzled everyone, by the third week in April 2000, EPA and USGS had convened a meeting at the federal center in Lakewood, Colorado. About 150 of the nation's leading authorities on asbestos mineralogy and health effects crammed into two meeting rooms to discuss the EPA's work in Libby and the size, shape and chemical makeup of asbestos fibers. "We needed to show headquarters that we hadn't lost our minds, that there were nationally recognized experts who agreed with the conclusions that we were reaching in Libby," Peronard said.

For the most part, that's what happened. EPA and USGS scientists and physicians joined colleagues from eight other federal agencies. Many agreed that the old asbestos rules were dangerously obsolete. The asbestos cat was slithering out of the bag that industry had shoved it into decades earlier.

Michael Beard, a former senior chemist at EPA for 26 years, was in the crowd.[9] He was the principal investigator in a study done by Research Triangle Institute in 2000 that warned of the danger of the government using outdated analytical techniques. Beard was interested in hearing the group's reaction to the thousands of tests done for EPA that showed the asbestos killing the people of Libby was tremolite and actinolite.

But at the conference, geologists from other government agencies who had also analyzed the Libby ore disagreed. One said there were minute amounts of sodium and manganese in the Libby fibers, making them technically richterite. Another said they had found a bit of iron in their sample, so the fiber had to be winchite. Again the mantra was repeated: "Neither fiber is among the six the government classifies as asbestos."

"Who cares?" Beard snapped at his colleagues with the disarming smile that only a Southern gentleman could muster. "You've got at least 192 people who died and hundreds more made ill in Libby from what has been diagnosed as asbestos-related disease.

"They don't care whether it's actinolite, tremolite or buffalo-girl-won't-you-come-out-tonight. Whatever it is, it caused disease. If the fiber isn't one of the six regulated types of asbestos, the folks in the government have got to realize it can't just be ignored."

Mineralogists, including many for USGS, had determined that dozens of different minerals had asbestos-like characteristics. It was years of continued cajoling and pressure by industry lobbyists that kept more types of asbestos from being researched and added to the list.

MELONE AND MOST OTHERS from headquarters showed no sign of joy at Beard's statements.

But finally the anger from Melone made sense.[10] Someone at the conference had slipped Peronard a copy of a 32-page "white paper" that the Office of Prevention, Pesticides and Toxic Substances (OPPTS) and others had done for the White House. The report, issued May 1999, was directed to the World Trade Organization and presented what was supposed to be the

United States' current opinion on the dangers of asbestos. It was to be offered as a third opinion in a malicious diplomatic battle between France and Canada over banning asbestos. Most of the report was composed of boilerplate from the asbestos regulations of EPA and OSHA. The conclusions were that chrysotile caused cancer and all asbestos fibers had the same toxicity — they killed and sickened equally.

Melone was adamant that the assumptions in the report should be taken as gospel.[11] He was displeased not only with the indications coming out of work in Libby, but also with a decade's worth of research done by Arnold Den, senior science adviser for EPA's San Francisco office. They were dealing with large areas of land in Northern California where homes and schools were being built on soil heavily contaminated with naturally occurring tremolite. He had other sites near San Francisco loaded with chrysotile. Both Den and the Libby team were concluding that tremolite was more toxic than the familiar chrysotile fiber around which all the regulations were written.

In a March 30, 2000, e-mail to 15 top EPA people, Melone wrote that EPA must "have a single agency position on these issues or we're heading for real trouble."[12] He said the report prepared for the White House "constitutes the most recent statement of EPA policy."

Then Melone quoted from page three, paragraph five of the White House report: "In the view of the United States ... a regulatory approach that treats all forms of asbestos on par with each other is scientifically justified."

In short, Melone didn't want new research to get in the way of an old theory that his office supported.

"His message was clear. Everyone pushing to update the science, techniques and regulations on asbestos had better toe the line," Peronard said. "The problem is that we had hundreds of deaths in Libby that caused us to question the dogma."

The conference took a lot of the wind out of headquarters' sails, Peronard said.

"Melone was going to have a harder time telling everyone that we were cavalier and reckless and our actions were not supported by the science that was a quarter of a century old," he said.

Grace also had people at the conference.

"They were very, very quiet," Weis said.

Grace got even quieter on April 10, 2001 — the day the entire Libby team was ordered to Washington to receive EPA's Silver Medal for its work in Montana. Miller, being a commissioned public health service officer, received a medal suitable for wearing on his dress uniform, and Peronard was also named by headquarters On-scene Coordinator of the Year.

"We didn't get any cards of congratulation from Grace," Weis said. "I wonder why."

THE FEBRUARY 11, 2000, EDITION of the *Post-Intelligencer* carried a story by Schneider and Smith that began: "Almost everyone believes that the mining, production, sale and use of asbestos in America has been banned.[13]

"Almost everyone is wrong."

The flood of phone calls and e-mails from outraged readers was expected. What wasn't were the calls from two professors teaching public health at a California university and occupational medicine in Boston. They were positive that Schneider and Smith had lost their minds. This was echoed over the next few days by about two dozen state and federal employees, including those working for OSHA, EPA and the Defense Department, all of whom insisted that there was a ban. A woman who said she worked for Senator Patty Murray called to ask if the story was true, and if so, could Schneider send the Washington State Democrat any more information than what was in the story? At least, he thought, someone in Washington seemed upset about the ban being overturned, *if it had been.*

Common sense said there had to be a ban.[14] Even *The Wall Street Journal* and other major newspapers were reporting that the cancer-causing fibers had been banned years earlier. But despite a valiant effort, they weren't.

William Ruckelshaus recalled that one of the first things the virgin agency did was to start the battle for the ban.[15] "As I recall, there was solid science to support it. I think there was even agreement within the agency, and that rarely happens." The two-term EPA boss paused for a moment, then added: "Asbestos was clearly bad stuff, and trying to regulate it was very contentious and fraught with all sorts of battles. EPA's scientists would reach a conclusion that supported the need for tighter controls or lower exposure levels or whatever. Then scientists hired by industry interests would often present a completely opposite interpretation of the same issue, showing, in their opinion, that tighter regulation wasn't needed.

"Sometimes it boiled down to who had the more powerful friends."

In the late 1970s, EPA's health and toxicology specialists began urging their bosses to do something about the abundance of asbestos-laden products being sold throughout the country. Epidemiologists and other medical sleuths had tallied the body count of thousands of workers and their family members. With the support of then President Jimmy Carter, they had documented the risk to the public from exposure to consumer products containing the deadly fibers and extrapolated the number of funerals that would continue to take place if asbestos was not banned.

The asbestos industry did not sit silently by as the EPA and OSHA worked to control the product it was mining, producing and selling. The industry's lobbyists doled out enormous campaign contributions to influential members of Congress to thwart or at least water down the agency's effort to ban the moneymaking fiber. Still, the EPA experts soldiered on through the political and scientific minefield.

When Chuck Elkins became the EPA's director of the Office of Toxic Substances in 1986, the team he took over had already been working on the asbestos ban for more than five years.[16] Given the effort his office was putting in on the work toward the ban, it is all the harder to understand how the agency managed to overlook the huge health implications of the 1982 and 1985 EPA-commissioned reports on Libby and its vermiculite. But no action was taken either time to address the immediate public health hazard. Still, the ban was the asbestos fighters' primary focus.

"It took about ten years and about ten million dollars to put the ban together," Elkins said. "But the science and medicine backing it were solid and clearly supported that at least ninety-four percent of all asbestos products should be banned."

In July 1989, the EPA issued landmark regulations that banned the manufacture, importation, processing and selling of almost all products containing asbestos. The ban was to be implemented in three stages over nine years. This, the agency said, would permit industries using asbestos to find safe alternatives. Almost instantly, United States asbestos manufacturers, supported by the governments of Canada and Quebec province, sued the EPA. Two years later, on October 18, 1991, the 5th Circuit Court of Appeals in New Orleans — known for its friendliness to industry — overturned the ban.

"It was not unexpected," Elkins recalled. "The Canadians felt the ban was an anti-Canadian effort by the United States. We couldn't convince them that the EPA staff doesn't have the foggiest idea about foreign policy. This was strictly a public-health issue."

The three-judge appellate court did not take issue with the EPA's painstakingly crafted scientific and medical opinions on asbestos's health hazards. Rather, the judges faulted the agency for technical errors in its cost-benefit analysis on the new regulations. Of course, this fact didn't prevent the Canadians from insisting that the court had ruled that EPA failed to prove that asbestos was dangerous.

The staff that developed the science and legal justification for the ban was devastated. It was the first time in 14 years since the Toxic Substance Control Act was passed that the agency had actually used it to protect the public health. A decade of work was negated. EPA staff members sent a blizzard of memos to then administrator Bill Reilly, telling him that asbestos was still killing people and that the court ruling wasn't going to make that tragic fact disappear.

"Asbestos poses an unreasonable risk to human health and nothing can be done to diminish its lethality but banning it," one team of scientists wrote.

Reilly, who had in his short tenure frequently angered the first Bush White House by putting environmental health issues before political niceties, supported the concerns of his staff.

On February 6, 1992, the EPA's general counsel asked the Justice Department to appeal the overturning of the ban to the U.S. Supreme Court.[17] Nothing happened. In fact, Justice never officially replied to the thoroughly documented ten-page plea.

"All we got was a verbal reply from Justice saying the administration didn't want to go forward, and by 'administration' it was fairly obvious they meant the White House," said Melone, who directed EPA's National Program Chemical Division during the Clinton administration.

Many members of the EPA's technical staff still say the rejected ban should be taken before the Supreme Court. They believe that the 5th Circuit's opinion would be overturned now. Melone agreed with his staff on the chances of victory, but said the decision to appeal the ruling "would have to be made at a level a lot higher than me."

SINCE THE OVERTURNING OF THE U.S. BAN, Canadian diplomats and scientists have turned their efforts toward the World Trade Organization, fighting efforts around the globe to ban the fibers.

Some U.S. diplomats are as puzzled as EPA officials in trying to pin down why the Canadians are so zealous in their defense of a Quebec industry that employs fewer than 1,600 miners.

"It's politics," explained Steve Guilbeault, an environmental specialist with Greenpeace in Vancouver, B.C. "It becomes understandable when you know the desire of the federal [Canadian] government to gain as much public support in Quebec as it can. Its support of Quebec's asbestos miners must be visible to prevent the sovereignist movement from using the argument that the federal government is in no position to defend the interest of the Quebec population."

In the United States, the asbestos lobby continues to wield enormous power over the decision-making process.

"Look back over the decades. When the health of industry became more important to the White House than the health of the public, protecting its citizens from asbestos and other toxins was something that just didn't happen," said Dr. Richard Lemen, former assistant surgeon general and deputy director of NIOSH.[18] He was an observer and participant in many of the early battles to regulate asbestos until he left the government in 1996.

"The industry has a responsibility to tell the truth but a poor record of doing so," Lemen says. He cited the documented cover-ups of the '30s through the '90s, and added, "They are going on to this day, thanks to politics." He added, "No one is willing to go up against the asbestos companies. Meanwhile, the public continues to get exposures that kill."

EPA's asbestos experts continue to see valid reasons for concern. In late 2003, huge quantities of asbestos products were still moving through this country's commerce. The USGS, which monitors all commercial activities involving minerals, says that in 1998 more than $300 million worth of asbestos products were exported or imported, including pipes, construction materials, floor tiles, abrasives for cutting and grinding, and aircraft and automotive brake parts. EPA officials remain concerned that most people, even workers who routinely use products containing asbestos, don't know that there is no ban to protect them.

"People knew about the ban when we were trying to do it in the late '80s, but unfortunately they didn't get the message that the ban was overturned in 1991," said Neil Pflum, asbestos coordinator for EPA's Region 6 in Dallas.[19]

"Almost everyone thinks they're still protected," he added. "People just don't know that the ban was overturned."

In 2000 and 2001, Pflum tried to determine how much of a problem there could be from what was still being imported and sold. He found that more than 3,000 products on the market still contained asbestos.

"The whole idea was to go out and see if we could find asbestos, and if we found any, see if the manufacturer warned the consumer that the product contained asbestos," Pflum said.

He tested 20 different categories of products — a total of 50 individual samples — of material commonly used in the construction of schools, homes and public buildings.

"Three categories of products came back hot, containing over one percent asbestos," Pflum said. "Four others came back with traces of asbestos."

He refused to publicly identify the brands of the hot samples, those products that testing showed were at or above EPA's 1 percent action level.

"More work has to be done," he said.

A press person in EPA headquarters responding to Schneider's request for a comment on Pflum's work told him she knew nothing about the work in Dallas, then added: "Why would EPA test that stuff? Asbestos is not being used anymore."

Patty Murray knew that wasn't true. Anna Knudson, her investigator and a legislative staffer, gave the Washington senator the proof. Knudson has amassed thousands of documents on asbestos regulation and its lethal history. She had sought and received help — lots of it — from Peronard,

Weis, Miller and Keven McDermott, all of whom thought asbestos must be banned.

On July 31, 2001, the senator chaired a hearing of a subcommittee of the Senate Health, Education, Labor and Pensions Committee on Asbestos Exposure and Workplace Safety.

"Asbestos was not banned," Murray told a packed hearing room.[20] "Today, it is still in consumer products. It is handled by workers every day. And it's still a health danger. However, the government is not doing all it could and all it should to protect consumers, people who live near plants that use asbestos-contaminated material and those who work with the deadly fibers.

"Lives can be saved if we pay attention. Now."

It had been decades since the dangers of asbestos had been raised in the halls of Congress. And everyone knew that for the second-term senator — nicknamed the "Mom in Tennis Shoes" — it was a very long shot that she could do anything to tighten the government's control of asbestos.

"You've got to try. You can't just ignore it," the senator told Schneider in her office after the hearing.

PART 3: THE SPREAD

EPA investigator Keven McDermott crawls through a Seattle-area attic that's heavily insulated with Zonolite. (Paul Kitagaki Jr.)

CHAPTER 16

Vermiculite ore is seen before it is "popped," or cooked at 2,000 degrees, into Zonolite. (Gilbert Arias, *Seattle Post-Intelligencer*)

F OR MONTHS AFTER the first stories ran in the *Post-Intelligencer*, letters, phone calls and e-mail continued to flood the paper.[1] Every time another magazine or TV network picked up the tale of Libby, the surge would increase and hundreds of Internet users would pluck the stories off the newspaper's website or one of a hundred other sites that linked to the stories.

Many people who had lived in or near Libby and had moved on, never knowing the dangers, contacted the newspaper to say they now knew why some loved one had died. They included the widow of a man who had worked as a logger for two summers while in college, the sister of two men who had worked on the Libby dam project and the grandmother of a woman who used to drive from Sandpoint, Idaho, to Libby every year to pick gallons of huckleberries near the mine.

Schneider could tell when the foreign media — BBC, CBC, Australian Broadcasting, Japanese television, *The Irish Times* — were running stories on Libby because e-mails from overseas would show up. Most of those who contacted the paper were asking questions that Schneider, McCumber and Carol Smith couldn't answer. The journalists referred them to McDermott at Seattle's EPA office, or to Peronard, Weis or Miller. Others who wrote expressed outrage at Grace and the government. The tragic stories kept coming.

From Oregon, the wife of a U.S. Forest Service horticulturist e-mailed to say her husband used vermiculite, "tons of it," for years while planting seedlings. "He died three years ago. It was a godsend because he couldn't walk 20 steps or breathe without oxygen for the last two years he was alive. The doctors said he had asbestos in his lungs and we never knew how it got there."

A man from Tennessee called to say his family had been building swimming pools for years and used vermiculite as a base for pools. "My dad and my granddad died from lung problems. Two of my three brothers are having trouble breathing. I don't feel so good, but I'm afraid to go check it out. The doctors always say it's emphysema, but none of us smoke and never have. Is it the vermiculite?"

A California woman wrote to say that her partner of 40 years had just died and the doctors said she had mesothelioma, but couldn't figure out where she was exposed to asbestos. "For years she used vermiculite mixed with a little cement to make her sculptures. She had big bags of different types of vermiculite all over her studio. Is that what killed her?"

Schneider, Smith and McCumber were stunned by the calls and amazed at how many people had some kind of contact with vermiculite. The question most frequently asked by hundreds of readers was "Can I still use the stuff in my garden?"

Sitting in McCumber's office, the trio debated that question.

"Well, sure they can. Can't they?" asked Smith. "The mine has been closed for years."

"It's got to be out of the pipeline by now," McCumber added. Schneider nodded, but for once said nothing.

"What," growled McCumber.

"There are garden products with vermiculite all over the place. Where the hell is it coming from? How do we know it's clean?"

"Yeah," Smith added, her eyes flashing. "What if the other mines also have contaminated vermiculite?"

Things became more bizarre an hour later, when someone called the paper and said Chubby and Tubby, a small chain of Seattle hardware stores, was selling large bags of Zonolite vermiculite. On the top shelf of the tall racks holding garden supplies were eight large heavy paper bags, maybe three or four feet tall. W.R. GRACE & CO was stamped on the sides. ZONOLITE CHEMICAL PACKAGING was printed across the front in green ink.

"Everybody buys it for the garden. You get a lot for the money," the store clerk volunteered as he stood on a ladder to get a bag. But Schneider was still trying to figure out how someone could be selling Zonolite nine years after the mine at Libby had closed.

Smith and Schneider continued their shopping spree for lawn products. Home Depot, Ace Hardware, Lowe's and a large grocery store supplied all the samples they needed. Schneider backed his Jeep into the lower parking garage in the *Post-Intelligencer* building, unloaded the bags onto a tarp and lined them up. There were four different brands of lawn fertilizer, potting soil, "Pure Vermiculite," "Garden Starter," "Flower Food," a bag of vermiculite kitty litter and the tall sack of Zonolite. Twenty-two samples were taken, labeled and shipped to Lab/Cor. Five split samples were sent to a second lab for backup. Schneider and Smith went off to the coffee shop to chat with McDermott about the paper's newest venture into the world of vermiculite.

She surprised Schneider. EPA was doing its own testing of lawn products.

"We had no choice. All these people who had read or heard about the *Post-Intelligencer* stories wanted to know whether it was safe to use other products with vermiculite," McDermott said. "We just didn't have the information on whether there was asbestos in these products or not, so we decided to test them. I don't know what we're going to do if the stuff comes back hot. People will just go crazy."

After a moment's pause, McDermott added: "The public has a right to know whether common household products are safe or contain cancer-causing ingredients such as asbestos."

"When will you have the results back?"

McDermott said the basic screening was done at EPA Regional Laboratory, across Puget Sound, in Manchester. They were still waiting for the more sophisticated TEM results to come back from Lab/Cor.

"I don't know when we'll get those back. They said they have to finish your damn samples first," McDermott said with mock anger.

Two days later, the newspaper got its results back from Lab/Cor and the other lab.[2] Eleven of the 21 samples — including the cat litter and three bags of straight vermiculite — came back clean, no asbestos detected. Four had very low levels. The remaining six ranged from moderate to high levels of asbestos. The fiber was tremolite, the same that killed the miners and their families in Libby. Two of the five samples sent to the second lab were found to contain asbestos.

"Now what the hell do we do?" McCumber asked, perusing the lab results.

Smith looked at Schneider and shrugged. They all knew that asbestos was too dangerous to be in consumer products, but if it was, it should be labeled. None of the bags was labeled. They also knew that asbestos, undisturbed, is usually not a health hazard.

"If the fibers aren't airborne, if people can't breathe them in, then what are the health risks?" Schneider questioned.

"Remember the calls we got from those people whose relatives died after using vermiculite in nurseries and tree lots?" Smith reminded him.

They went into Schneider's combination office and toxic dump and pulled the six bags from which the samples containing asbestos had come. Four were major national brands. The other two the reporters had never heard of. The potting soil was damp. No risk of releasing fibers until it dries out. The pure vermiculite and fertilizer and plant food were dry and dusty.

"We can't sit on this information," McCumber said. "Don't we have an obligation to the readers?"

"Of course we do, but unless we run simulations of people using this stuff and take air samples, we don't know how dangerous it is. What are we going to tell them?" Schneider asked.

They decided to try to hire a lab to run some simulations of the asbestos-tainted product for the newspaper and see if the fibers went airborne. Meanwhile, Smith called the makers of the lawn products that came back positive in the testing. All insisted that they didn't use vermiculite from Grace and that therefore their products could not have asbestos in them. But one manufacturer thought for a moment, then said, "Let me check."

Schneider called Grace.[3] The company, which sold millions of bags of vermiculite attic insulation and for decades was the nation's largest producer of vermiculite for horticultural products, almost all from its mine in Libby, repeatedly said there was nothing dangerous in its products. That's a claim Grace maintains today for vermiculite being mined and sold from its mine in Enoree, South Carolina.

Corcoran, Grace's vice president for dealing with the press, asked for the tracking number printed on the bottom of all Grace products.

"I'm sure it's not ours, but I'll get back to you," Corcoran promised.[4] He kept his word. An hour later he reported that the big bag the *Post-Intelligencer* bought at Chubby and Tubby contained vermiculite from the mine in Libby and was packaged at a Grace plant in Santa Ana, California, in August 1991, "most likely on the third shift." He said he was surprised that "a product discontinued eight years ago is still available today" and added that he had no idea who was selling the material, but it wasn't Grace. "Chemical packing material," he said, "is not now, nor was it ever, intended to be sold in lawn-and-garden sections of home-improvement stores."

Schneider told him that the newspaper's testing of the material found levels of almost 5 percent asbestos — five times the 1 percent level that EPA designates as a hazardous material.

He refused further comment unless, as he'd requested a dozen times during the earlier Libby stories, the *Post-Intelligencer* would give him its test results. As he always did, Schneider offered to overnight Corcoran a sample of the stuff so that he could have it tested himself. The vice president said goodbye.

Going back over old e-mail from readers, Schneider found that Zonolite Chemical Packaging Vermiculite was still being sold in southern and eastern Washington, Oregon, Michigan, Missouri, Texas and Georgia.

A mile south, in downtown Seattle, McDermott was having an identical discussion with her colleagues about what their responsibility was to the public. Jed Januch and Dave Terpening sat in McDermott's cramped office on the ninth floor of EPA's Region 10 office — the Investigations and Engineering unit. They kept passing around the TEM lab results that they had just received. The trio were investigators who normally handled hazardous dumping and waste sites and problems with the old, familiar, well-researched, fully vetted chrysotile asbestos. Not something called tremolite, which only a handful of people, outside of Paul Peronard's team in Libby, seemed to know anything about.

"We may not know everything about the tremolite or likelihood of exposure in using these products, but we do know that there's asbestos in them, and a lot in the Zonolite. How could we not tell the public?" McDermott asked.

She remembered a call a few days earlier from a Seattle woman, "She was in tears, saying that every spring she'd buy a few bags of vermiculite and dump it on the kitchen floor and let the kids play in it while she made up bags of potting soil. 'What have I done to my children?' she asked, and I couldn't tell her," McDermott said. "We're being inundated with calls from people who want to know if it's safe, if they can garden. They're frightened, and we've got to tell them what we know."

EPA's problem was made more morally difficult because their scientists across the Sound in Manchester had already figured out that the vermiculite was dangerous. While McDermott and Januch were running their tests in a far corner of one of the laboratories, a technician, watching Januch pour the vermiculite into a testing box, told the pair that if they needed more, there were barrels of the material in the next building. McDermott went to check it out. And there were barrels and large boxes filled with vermiculite, packaging remaining from containers of samples and chemicals shipped to the scientists for evaluation. Because of its cushioning and absorbent qualities, vermiculite has been used for decades as padding for shipments of liquids.

"We won't use it anymore for shipments received at the laboratory," Gerald Dodo, an EPA chemist and contract officer, told McDermott. "The coolers and boxes they use to ship samples to us are packed with vermiculite. We just don't want people here to deal with it, because the exposure could be dangerous. A simple painter's or dust mask isn't going to do anything to stop asbestos fibers, so it would be better not to deal with it at all," Dodo said.

Back in Seattle, McDermott and her gang were talking themselves into a decision. "It would be immoral not to tell the public when we know something is dangerous. That's what we're supposed to do in this agency, isn't it?" she asked Bill Dunbar, the spokesman for Region 10 who had joined the debate.

"Hell yes," Dunbar said. "The Zonolite packaging material you tested came back hot and our own lab won't use the stuff. It's unfair for us to have that knowledge and protect our own workers and not give the public the same consideration," he added, and went off to set up a meeting with Chuck Findley, Region 10's deputy administrator.

The decision might have been made a bit easier because as McDermott and her crew gathered the material for the meeting with Findley, Schneider called and said the *Post-Intelligencer* was running a story the next morning on the Zonolite and the garden products and the fact that EPA had found similar results.

Findley listened. He asked McDermott if she was sure of the facts, sure of the testing, then said, "Just tell them what you know. Don't go beyond it. Give them what they need to make the decision themselves." Findley had been with EPA long enough to know that headquarters was going to be less than pleased when it heard about the news conference.

Dunbar thought the same thing. Normally, he knew, the agency chewed on things forever before people in headquarters got comfortable enough to say anything to the public.

For a news conference discussing that some consumer products sold across the country might be harmful, the turnout was underwhelming. Two television stations, the Associated Press and Smith from the *Post-Intelligencer* stood on the plaza beside EPA's building, in front of a folding table with jars of Zonolite and vermiculite lawn products.

McDermott played it short and straight.

"There may be asbestos in products containing vermiculite, and if you mess with it and the fibers become airborne it could, ten or twenty years down the road, lead to asbestosis, lung cancer or mesothelioma," she said.

Dunbar's boss, Melanie Luh, cringed when McDermott answered a reporter's question. "We work under the assumption that there is no safe level of asbestos exposure. Asbestos is like a time bomb. Once you've been exposed, you don't know how your body will respond over time," McDermott said.

The weekend was quiet, but the calm was not destined to last. The cable networks and the wires had picked up the *Post-Intelligencer's* story and EPA's news conference. On Monday, Dunbar walked into his office straight into what he called a "shitstorm."

"What the hell did you do on Friday?" screamed a headquarters' spokeswoman's tinny voice over the speakerphone in the conference room.[5] "Why didn't you warn us? What right do you have to do that?" she bellowed. The rant went on and Dunbar, who had only been on the job for 15 months, thought a lot about not having any civil-service protection for another eight months.

The next several months wouldn't get much easier for Findley, Dunbar, McDermott, their lawyer Richard Mednick or the others involved in chasing asbestos in consumer products.

"Headquarters was clearly worried that we would force them to take a position on something they would have rather ignored," Dunbar said. "We understand that the life in headquarters differs greatly from what we in the regions face. Headquarters is a more theoretical place where the politics is all-important and keeping peace with everyone — Congress, the White House, the lobbyists — is paramount. They wouldn't want to get the American Vermiculite Association angry. They want to study things to death so they offend the fewest power brokers with any statement or action they take.

"In the regions, trouble can walk right in the front door and we've got to handle it. Then. You can't blow people off when they've got toxic drums leaking into their water supply. Things are just different in the field," Dunbar said.

At headquarters, Seattle's little adventure was generating dramatically different views. The top people, mostly political appointees, and some of the career people who saw their mission as protecting them, were outraged. E-mails flew between carpeted offices demanding that heads roll in the Pacific Northwest outpost.

"We're already swamped with keeping Peronard and his cowboys in Libby under control, and now we have this debacle with asbestos in consumer products. Asbestos? That's the last thing we need. What are those people doing to us?" said an internal memo the press office wrote to John Melone.

But others in smaller offices or tiny cubicles in headquarters saw it differently. Some privately cheered. Many of them were the scientists and technical experts who knew that the agency had been negligent in addressing the asbestos problem. They praised the Seattle group for either their courage or their stupidity. The bell could not be unrung.

GRACE WASTED LITTLE TIME getting on the phone demanding the heads of McDermott and Dunbar and insisting that headquarters discredit their conclusions.

It sounded like a great idea to many higher-ups, but too many people were watching. The national media were still calling the press office's minions every day.

Meanwhile, at the laboratory on the Sound, Januch and other Seattle team members had installed air-monitoring equipment in a 3'-by-4' sealed plastic enclosure and emulated a home gardener using the vermiculite products. The tests showed that with normal use, asbestos fibers were set free — in some products, a lot. Consumers might be in danger, albeit slight. But people who worked with vermiculite in their jobs, and there are many of them, could face significant exposure.

But this was something that headquarters had ordered them to keep the lid on. And that order was repeated almost daily.

McDermott and her team crafted a thoroughly documented report on what their testing had found, why they did it and what the agency knew about the dangers of vermiculite from studies done years earlier.[6] Headquarters read the Region 10 report with the same scrutiny afforded Florida's hanging-chad ballots in the 2000 presidential election. The bosses in D.C. were outraged that McDermott would admit, in writing no less, that the agency had investigated tremolite-tainted vermiculite in 1982 and 1985, determined it was dangerous and done nothing about it.

"I have some serious concerns about this report," Melone wrote in an e-mail to McDermott.[7] "There are sections in it — historical and others — which are not relevant at all to our testing of vermiculite. What is the purpose of these sections? They seem to raise more questions about who did what when and just foment the debate of what happened long ago. We are trying to put that behind us.

"Why do you feel the need to explore the past in this report?"

McDermott stuck by her guns and said the public needed the information on what EPA knew earlier. She felt that it was important that, decades earlier, EPA had reported that 32 million people who used garden fertilizer and another 74 million who used vermiculite-containing lawn products faced potential health risks from asbestos in the material. It had also warned of possible dangers from potting soil, kitty litter and Zonolite attic insulation. Still the gag order from headquarters was repeated.

Tom Simons, who worked in headquarters' chemical-programs section, reminded the Seattle office that the inspector general was investigating why EPA failed to do anything.[8] "Given the upcoming investigation, it is the agency's policy now not to discuss the history — either verbally or in writing. Therefore, there should be no history section in your report," he wrote.

The same day, Richard Mednick, the associate regional counsel for the gang in Region 10, fired a strident note back to headquarters: "It appears that EPA Headquarters is trying in many ways to stifle Region 10's upcoming dissemination to the public about a factual history of asbestos. If, as you represent in your e-mail messages, the refusal to provide the public with any type of history about asbestos is now an official 'Policy' of EPA, then I am interested in receiving (from you) a copy of the written 'Policy' to that effect which is signed by the administrator."[9]

He also suggested that headquarters get off McDermott's back, saying, "… she knows how to do her job, and I don't think it's appropriate for individuals at EPA headquarters who seem to know very little about the work of being a civil investigator to tell Keven how to best do her job."

Several days of silence from headquarters was finally broken with the order not to release any of the report. "The issue must be studied further," Melone said.

EPA hired Versar Inc. to conduct the new tests of a wider selection of lawn products purchased throughout the country. As it happened, Versar was familiar with the hazards of vermiculite. It was the same consulting firm that EPA had used in 1985 to investigate vermiculite in consumer products. Nothing was ever done with the results of that report or of three others that had also documented that the tremolite asbestos, which contaminates the vermiculite, caused cancer, asbestosis and mesothelioma.

The final EPA report — a blend of Region 10's and Versar's work — had been examined, rewritten, toned down and peer-reviewed by almost everyone in EPA who could spell "asbestos." It was to be released in early July. But after a July 6 meeting at agency headquarters with members of the vermiculite industry, the EPA agreed to do more tests and risk assessments. The meeting included senior EPA officials; scientists from Versar; officers of The Vermiculite Association (TVA); representatives from the Scotts Co. and the Schundler Co., two of the nation's largest producers of lawn and garden products; and representatives of Grace and Virginia Vermiculite, who run the country's two largest vermiculite mines.

The industry group didn't like what it heard and told EPA that the report shouldn't be released. Nor were they shy about expressing concern over EPA's methods of testing. "Based on comments made at the meeting, The Vermiculite Association has grave concerns that the planned Versar report of the testing may inappropriately emphasize Versar's few findings of asbestos and thus be misconstrued by the public," association president Michael Allen wrote to Melone on July 18.

It was more than a month before EPA felt it was safe to release the report. There was no fanfare from headquarters but a lot of screaming from the industry. EPA's report found asbestos at a level that could pose a potential for exposure in five products, among them Earthgro's Best Vermiculite,

Hoffman's Vermiculite and two samples of Ace Horticultural Grade Vermiculite. In addition, 17 others contained trace levels of asbestos.

But was it dangerous?

The intricate assessments of the risk of using asbestos-contaminated vermiculite show that home gardeners who use the product once a year for 30 years face a negligible risk of contracting cancer from the asbestos. The real risks were to commercial gardeners, foresters, nursery workers and people using bulk vermiculite on a regular basis. The health assessment portion of the study said workers could face a greatly increased cancer risk, depending on the material used. Preliminary assessment for the workers' group calculated a risk that could mean as much as one additional cancer for every 100 workers using the tainted vermiculite.

"Our general benchmark for taking action is when we start to see numbers that exceed one additional death per hundred thousand to one in one million. That's when we become somewhat concerned," said Stephen Johnson, then EPA's deputy assistant administrator for the Office of Prevention, Pesticides and Toxic Substances. "If we start to see numbers of one added death in one thousand to one in ten thousand for the general population, then those numbers are of real concern to us."[10]

So the risks were clearly dangerous enough to be of "real concern" to the agency, but what would EPA do? an official spokesman was asked.

"Yeah, our people in Seattle found something that might be a problem, but EPA doesn't have regulations to cover what's sold to consumers or safety in the workplace. That would be the job of the Consumer Product Safety Commission and the OSHA," the spokesman said.

CPSC responded with: "Not my job."

"We have nothing to add to what EPA has said," CPSC spokesman Russ Rader said. The fact that EPA said "notifying consumers of risks is the job of the consumer agency" did not appear to impress Rader, who refused to say why it wasn't his agency's job.

OSHA and other sections of the Department of Labor expressed concern at what they characterized as a surprisingly high exposure threat to workers. But as government is wont to do, OSHA ordered NIOSH to do its own study of vermiculite risk to workers. It would be three years before the policy people in NIOSH permitted a watered-down, cautionary note to be posted on the agency's website.

ROBERT PARKS HAS A GREAT VIEW of Puget Sound and part of the Seattle skyline from the second floor of his white wood-frame house.[11] But he doesn't make the trek to the second floor much anymore. He has only one lung, and that one is filled with asbestos.

"It's a battle walking on level ground, but it's a nightmare going up the stairs," said the 73-year-old retired aircraft mechanic.

"I never could figure out where I was ever exposed to asbestos. Boeing kept the hangars free of that stuff. I never had any wrapped around the pipes. And I never worked with it," Parks said, pausing to catch his breath.

A few days earlier, he had read the *Post-Intelligencer's* story about asbestos in garden products, and he saw a word there that triggered something in his mind. So he drove a mile or so down the road to the EPA regional laboratory, which happened to be in his small waterfront community of Manchester. He walked up to the desk, pulled a small jar out of his pocket and waited. Finally someone noticed him. The lab doesn't get much walk-in business.

"Is this the stuff that the paper's been writing about?" he said, shaking the dice-sized pieces of silver-and-tan fluff. "Is it asbestos? My attic is filled with it."

Now, shortly after dawn, Parks and Schneider held a ladder as Keven McDermott climbed through a two-foot-square opening into his attic. Decked out from head to toe in protective coveralls, surgical gloves on her hands, her face fully covered with a respirator, McDermott slithered from rafter to rafter, picking her perches with care to avoid falling through Parks's ceiling. The beam of her flashlight swept over a scattering of empty red-and-black paper bags labeled ZONOLITE ATTIC INSULATION. The bags also carried the label 100 PERCENT VERMICULITE, below two smiling cartoon characters saying, "Just pour ... and level."

Parks squinted up at the green ceiling, trying to figure how far the EPA investigator had progressed. "There's quite a bit of it up here," McDermott said, her voice muffled by the filters over her nose and mouth. She filled clean plastic bags with the fluffy, expanded vermiculite from several places around the darkened attic. She placed the samples and her gear in a large yellow "asbestos hazard" bag and climbed back down the ladder. Parks eyed the bag warily. "I read about Zonolite in the paper and thought maybe that's what happened here," he said, tapping his chest. "In 1970, I dumped 130 bags of that Zonolite up there."

The Zonolite came from a company called Vermiculite Northwest, which ran vermiculite expansion plants years ago in Spokane and Portland. That company, along with producers of millions of other bags of Zonolite insulation, used vermiculite from Libby. McDermott found that the Zonolite contained asbestos.

PERONARD LOOKED AT THE PICTURE of Keven McDermott crawling through Robert Parks's attic in full hazard gear. *Good for you,* he thought, and shook his head. *How many more like this guy are out there?*

For Peronard and the Libby team, the insulation, along with the expansion plants themselves, were really the sum of all fears — the way the mine, despite whatever cleanup they did in Libby, could go on killing people across the country for years to come. He knew from the expansion-plant data that Grace had given EPA, and from the long-buried reports, that millions of tons of the insulation had been spread throughout the country. Which meant it must be in millions of homes. The testing his team had done showed that tremolite fibers were sent airborne with just the slightest disruption. The agency needed to get more information on this, and fast.

Grace defended its insulation by saying that while there may be large quantities of asbestos airborne while the material is being installed, asbestos is only harmful when there is repeated exposure over years. But as early as 1972, investigators at NIOSH reported that a heavy one-time dose of asbestos may be as harmful as the cumulative effect of lower doses over many years. And of course, Miller and Weis were already convinced that tremolite was much more lethal than chrysotile asbestos, which was the fiber in most of the studies cited by industry.

Peronard didn't know what EPA would do about the national problem. But he damn sure wanted Zonolite out of the attics of Libby. That, he told himself, was one he'd go to the mat on. Aubrey Miller would not let this rest, either. The danger was clear to him, and it was unconscionable. He began lobbying Dr. Hugh Sloan, an assistant U.S. surgeon general, and finally Sloan decided Miller was right. People had to be warned. And so, in August 2000, he threw the weight of his office into the fight.

Sloan issued a warning: Asbestos-contaminated vermiculite insulation in millions of homes across the country poses a "substantial health risk" to anyone who works in the houses' attics.[12] "Internal company documentation and recent testing of residential insulation material reveals that even minimal handling by workers or residents poses a substantial health risk," Sloan wrote in a request for help from other federal health experts.

In his letter to Linda Rosenstock, the director of NIOSH, Sloan said recent investigations documented that even casual handling of the insulation can generate airborne exposures up to 150 times the level considered safe by OSHA for workers.

Among the documents to which Sloan referred is a risk assessment conducted by Grace health experts while the mine was still open. The company experts estimated that 30,000 additional lung cancers would result from exposure to asbestos by those "involved in the application of our products." Sloan asked NIOSH to examine the risk to nursery, construction, insulation and other workers who use vermiculite end-products and to issue a nationwide warning, a "hazard alert," cautioning workers of the potential dangers of these products. He also asked NIOSH to update its earlier studies on the asbestos-tainted vermiculite to examine the progression of asbestos-related disease, and to determine whether tremolite was more toxic than earlier believed.

Grace lawyers wasted no time in denouncing Sloan's letter to top officials in a half-dozen federal agencies.[13] "He based his letter on certain confidential information that he should not have had," one Washington lawyer complained shrilly in his letter to the Department of Health and Human Services. But Sloan's warning was supported by testing done by EPA, scientists hired by plaintiff's lawyers, and Grace itself. All reported that during simulations of a homeowner or craftsman working in the attic — installing a fan, a light fixture, or a vent; installing phone line or cable; or just moving boxes around — analysis of air samples found asbestos levels that ranged from 4.5 fibers per cubic centimeter of air to 12.50 f/cc. All these findings exceed EPA and OSHA's safe limits by a factor of several hundred times.

Nobody is sure how many homes contain Zonolite. Estimates range from 15 million to 35 million. But according to the EPA and U.S. Justice Department's tally of Grace invoices, the company shipped billions of pounds of tainted ore to more than 750 processing plants throughout North America. Most of those companies produced attic insulation. Homebuilder and construction associations cite studies that average people, especially those living in older homes, go into their attics at least three times a year. Eventually, old insulation has to be replaced. Remodeling, rewiring and a score of other home renovations could disturb the old Zonolite. Of course, so could demolition.

Dr. Henry Anderson, the chief medical officer and epidemiologist for the state of Wisconsin, said that he agrees the public must be warned. "In order to safeguard public health, it is essential that homeowners with Zonolite insulation, and those contractors who may be called upon to work on it, be warned about the presence of asbestos in the product," said Anderson, who has been studying the health effect of asbestos for more than 25 years.

Grace has always insisted that there was nothing hazardous in the insulation. The printing on the Zonolite bags said "Contains no harmful chemicals" and that "masks, gloves or special [safety] equipment" were not needed. But thousands of pages of Grace correspondence, memos and reports obtained by the *Post-Intelligencer* show that the company was well aware of the asbestos in the insulation and the health hazards it presented. In the May 24, 1977, memo he wrote to Grace senior officials, Executive Vice President E. S. Wood reported attic insulation generated the highest levels of asbestos of all the vermiculite products tested, generating levels of 15f/ml, when OSHA's ceiling for exposure was 10f/ml. Three years later, Grace did additional simulations in which ten separate samples of insulation from its Weedsport, New York, plant were tested.[14] All ten exceeded government safety limits.

Grace documents reveal that the company felt it could defend itself by showing that even the high exposures its own testing found were within the limits that OSHA set for workers. That may have been true at the time, but those exposures and the levels found after testing contaminated homes in 2002 are 150 times greater than OSHA's present worker exposure level, court papers show.

Most of the many studies done on the health effects of asbestos exposure centered on the worker being exposed hundreds of times a year for dozens of years. But studies by NIOSH, the EPA and private medical investigators in the 1970s and '80s cautioned that "single bursts" and "peak episodic" exposures to humans can cause cancer and asbestosis. Other Grace documents from 1977 showed that the company was aware of reports that "even brief exposures, presumably at high levels, can later produce mesothelioma."

"The hazard of these [high, short-term] exposures is aggravated and worsened when the release or disturbance occurs in an enclosed space such as an attic," Anderson, the Wisconsin health chief, added.

Even though OSHA was made aware that thousands of workers were handling the contaminated vermiculite at factories and work sites throughout the country, there is no indication in public records that it ever weighed in on the asbestos hazard.

Grace's Corcoran said the company maintains that Zonolite insulation, as well as Grace's other vermiculite-based products, present no health risk to consumers. In 2000 and again in 2001, Grace distributed a statement about some of the products it manufactured during the '70s and '80s.

"It was well known to regulatory agencies and many of our customers that minute quantities of naturally occurring asbestos were in our products. We are making this announcement to make sure that everyone hears the facts from Grace," said Paul Norris, the company's chairman, president and CEO.

After the *Post-Intelligencer* stories, class-action suits were filed across the country to order Grace to notify homeowners of the potential dangers.

CHRISTOPHER LADERA has been vacuuming insulation out of attics for 12 years without realizing he may have been exposing himself to deadly asbestos.[15]

His Seattle company, EnviroAire, specializes in residential insulation removal, does about 700 homes a year in the Seattle area and runs into vermiculite insulation at least three or four times a month. "I didn't think it posed any threat to us," Ladera says. "Now I think I might have been exposed."

Ladera, 38, once worked in a law firm that handled asbestos cases. He knows what exposure to asbestos can mean. "Yeah, I'm worried," he says. "I know the end results can be really bad."

He's also worried about his family. "I share my laundry with them, and there's dust everywhere on my clothes," he says. "I have a five-year-old and a twelve-year-old, and it could be possible I've exposed them to asbestos."

According to court records, many people have died from exposure to the insulation.[16] In 1951, Edward Harashe headed to the hardware store to make his one-story white house in St. Louis, Missouri, a little warmer. He came home with 20 bags of Zonolite insulation, hauled them to his attic and spread the loose, silvery-tan, popcorn-like insulation between the joists. "I shoved it through a trapdoor in the ceiling and spread it around the floor," Harashe recalled in his testimony. "There was dust everywhere. My eyes, ears, nose, hair, everywhere."

Harashe didn't feel well but didn't find out why until he went for a medical screening at his union hall on a muggy morning in August 1990. His X-rays showed suspicious shadows in his lung. A biopsy identified them. The father of four and grandfather of ten had mesothelioma. He died at age 68, some 40 years after being exposed to Zonolite. A court found that the home-improvement project killed him, and Grace's Zonolite was to blame.

Herb Conklin was one of hundreds of talc miners in upstate New York sickened by asbestos in a Vanderbilt talc mine. Conklin's wife, Margaret, makes sure he takes his medicine, some of which fills the basket on their kitchen table. (Renee Byer, *Seattle Post-Intelligencer*)

SCHNEIDER AND MEDICAL WRITER CAROL SMITH sat in the small windowless room that had become the heart of the *Post-Intelligencer's* continuing asbestos investigation. Wide steel shelves were bending under the weight of zipped plastic bags filled with soil, rock, vermiculite ore and other samples gathered at mines and expansion plants.

Shelves on the other wall overflowed with bags of attic insulation, potting soil, vermiculite expanders, lawn food, fertilizers and cat litter. Schneider insisted on saving the samples in case the lab results they published were ever challenged. Fortunately, Steve Smith, the *Post-Intelligencer's* lawyer, agreed, or those editors who disapproved of having a toxic dump in the newsroom might have succeeded in getting the office condemned.

They sat at the desk, which was covered with piles of lab reports, empty sample bags, small shovels, two charging air pumps and a box of filter cartridges.[1] Schneider tried to add order to the mess so he and Smith could have a few inches of space to package up the new samples to be analyzed. "Don't stir anything up. God knows what you're releasing into the air," she said, only half kidding. "You're so old that you'll die before the asbestos gets you. I, on the other hand, am in my prime, and don't forget it."

Schneider put up with Smith's kidding because she was a gifted writer who painted beautiful word pictures and cared as much about the victims they had encountered as he did. Also, it was fun to watch her lose her lady-like demeanor when she knew a company or government agency was lying to her.

McCumber appeared in the doorway, watching the sparring. Glad he wasn't in the middle of it for a change.

"This is the last batch of drugstore items we're sending for testing," Schneider said. "J. D.'s going to crap when he sees I've spent two hundred and eighty-seven dollars for makeup, medicine, foot powder and tampons and the first batch came up clean."

Yes. Tampons. The reporter had discovered that several companies, including Grace, had filed for patents where the design called for the use of asbestos. However, they could find no evidence that such tampons were ever manufactured or sold in the United States.

For weeks, Smith and Schneider had gathered items that hundreds of readers, responding to the earlier stories, had insisted contained asbestos. Four of them sounded like they knew what they were talking about. Mark Germaine, a physician-scientist from California; a former U.S. Food and Drug Administration investigator; a makeup model; and a nurse from Boston all named some of the same brands. The only thing the consumer products had in common was that they all contained talc.

Earlier, sitting at a large table in the conference room covered with newspaper, the two reporters had collected dabs of medicated ointments, a scoop of $40 body powder, scrapes of the powder in compacts and eye shadow, three brands of medicated powder, the powder from a condom, and the insides of tampons. Sixteen samples, neatly labeled and carefully packed into a heavy plastic pouch, were ready to go to Lab/Cor for analysis. The lab offered a price break for 20 samples.

"Let's do the crayons," Smith said, spotting a familiar yellow box on a shelf. "The scientists said they use talc to make them."

"Okay. Label them, bag them and put them in the pouch," Schneider growled, muttering under his breath about the things he did to keep his partners happy. Three days later, the results from Lab/Cor popped into Schneider's computer fax program. The report from the EPA-certified lab stated that no asbestos was found in 13 of the drugstore items. In three others, only minute levels were detected.

Schneider stared at the last page in the report. The four crayons. He read the numbers again. And then once more, before he bellowed, "Carol, David, you're not going to believe this."

The green crayon had nothing. But the yellow, Carnation Pink and Orchid wax sticks were loaded with tremolite asbestos.

"What in the hell is going on?" McCumber asked. "Asbestos in crayons? It can't be." Maybe it was a fluke, something wrong at the lab. The trio agreed to courier four more crayons over to a different analytical lab in Seattle and pay extra for a rush analysis. Those results came back the next morning. Two crayons were clean. Two others were contaminated with tremolite.

"Maybe it's just Crayolas sold in Seattle," Smith ventured.

"Let's get them from other parts of the country," Schneider said.

"And all the other brands we can find," McCumber added.

The newspaper's budget was destined to take more abuse. Soon the three were calling friends and relatives throughout the country, giving them the paper's Federal Express number and asking them to buy a box each of all the different brands of crayons they could find. By week's end, Schneider and Smith were again sitting in the conference room, this time sorting crayons. Most were manufactured in Malaysia, China, Indonesia or Mexico. Three brands were made in the United States. Batches were labeled as to the location purchased and the manufacturer and sent to two different labs.

Lab/Cor was asked to use TEM. Of course, it was more expensive. The three days needed to complete the analysis dragged on forever. "Stop calling us or we'll never get them done," Robert Fisher, the chief scientist at Lab/Cor, finally told Schneider. But when they finally arrived, the second set of results were the same: Three major brands of crayons — scribbled with and nibbled on by millions of children worldwide — contained asbestos.

Of 40 crayons from the three largest domestic manufacturers — Binney & Smith, makers of Crayola; Prang, a division of Dixon Ticonderoga; and Rose Art — 80 percent showed asbestos above trace levels. None of the crayons from Malaysia, China, Indonesia and Mexico were found to contain asbestos.

The next question to answer was, So what? Did the presence of asbestos in crayons mean a health risk? Asbestos causes cancer and asbestosis, but in order to do so it must enter the body. Inhalation is the most common and well-researched exposure pathway, but ingestion — eating, drinking or otherwise swallowing the fibers — is a less-researched exposure route. But as a multi-agency team of federal health experts had concluded in 1987: "The potential hazard should not be discounted, and ingestion exposure to asbestos should be eliminated wherever possible." Was exposure from either route possible with the fibers held in the waxy substance of the crayon?

Of course, children eat crayons.[2] "Everyone who has a child knows that everything goes into the mouth," said Dr. Michael Harbut, director of the Center for Occupational and Environmental Medicine in Detroit. "The old shoebox, or whatever a child uses to keep their old crayons, has a layer of bits of wax and crayon shavings in the bottom. This gets all over their hands and into their nose and mouth. If there's asbestos in that wax, you've got the potential for a real health hazard."

Or as Dr. Philip Landrigan put it, "It's just imprudent to put a product as manifestly hazardous as asbestos in material such as crayons. The way you use crayons is to abrade them. That's how they transfer the color. In the course of using them, the risk exists that some of the asbestos fibers are liberated and can be inhaled by a child whose face is close to the paper. It's not sensible."

Landrigan, pediatrician and director of the Center for Children's Health and the Environment at the Mt. Sinai School of Medicine in Brooklyn, said, "This is not a circumstance where you go through the rigorous toxicological and epidemiological studies. You just get it out of there."

A Consumer Product Safety Commission spokesman said the agency had never heard any hint that crayons might contain asbestos.[3] "We are surprised that it's there, and we're in the process of getting hold of companies to find out what they know about what's in their crayons. We're having discussions with them now," said Ronald Medford, assistant executive director of Hazards Identification at CPSC. "We're trying to figure out what's going on. How much is in there? Where is it coming from? And what's the risk as a result of its being there?"

Landrigan said it was not time for the CPSC to be subtle. "The commission loves to persuade manufacturers to adopt voluntary codes," he said. "They hate to put the hammer on people. But they should put the hammer on manufacturers for something like this."

Watching kids at a preschool, Schneider saw a wide range of activities with crayons that, knowing what he knew, concerned him. He saw some children who enjoyed sharpening the crayons down to a nub, pausing only to color long enough to break off the point before sharpening again. He also saw kids burrow their heads into crayon containers, sniffing the distinctive crayon scent. According to Binney & Smith, a Yale University study documented that the aroma of crayons was among the country's 20 most recognizable smells.

Which brought up another point: This was not a story to be undertaken lightly. This was not like telling people the insulation in their attics or the fireproofing in the steel buildings where they worked or the brake shoes on their cars were capable of killing them or others. Those facts were outrageous, but more easily explainable. But you were asking people to make an enormous cognitive leap, to understand that the same poison that killed thousands of shipbuilders and World War II veterans was present in their children's toy box.

Few things in our culture are more closely associated with American family life than a box of Crayolas. If the newspaper was going to tell its readers, and the country, that one of the best-loved symbols of happy childhood was potentially lethal, it had to be prepared to deal with a wide range of negative reactions — certain wrath from large corporations, doubtless followed by a massive spin-control campaign. And worst of all, the paper had to expect that this was a story its readers would not *want* to believe was true.

On the other hand, it was an enormously important story, the sort of story that newspapers were supposed to do. If crayons were toxic, people needed to know about it. For the obvious reason: to protect their children. But for another reason: because it would represent an enormous hole in the safety net that people assume is out there in modern life — a hole in the way toxic substances are regulated, and the way those regulations are enforced. It represented a violation of the trust people had — in products they knew, and in the government. In a way, it was the most dramatic example possible of how pervasive asbestos still was, when most people assumed it had all but disappeared from American life years before. All that was fine, Schneider, Smith and McCumber thought. But what was colloquially known in newsrooms as the post-publication shitstorm was still going to come, they knew, and this time it would be a monsoon.

J.D. Alexander had been promoted to a corporate job and it was just Roger Oglesby's third month in the publisher's office when Schneider knocked on his door, shook his hand and told him, "We're running a story this week saying Crayolas and other crayons contain asbestos."

Oglesby didn't blanch.[4] Or gulp. And he showed only the briefest look of "what the hell have I gotten into here?"

"I just have three questions," the new boss said. "Is the reporting solid, is the testing accurate and is it all on the record?"

"Of course," Schneider assured him.

"Then go with it," Oglesby said, and was already on the phone calling McCumber as Schneider left his office.

In the *Post-Intelligencer's* first crayon story, Tuesday, May 23, 2000, industry representatives spoke cautiously.[5] "We are in the process of looking at all of our materials," said Tracey Muldoon Moran, a corporate spokesperson for Binney & Smith, which makes Crayolas. "With the information that we have today, we do believe that our products pose no health threat, but we have already begun to investigate alternatives to the material being questioned — the talc — so we can properly address any potential concerns customers might have."

Ronald Shaffer, Dixon Ticonderoga's chief operating officer, says his company was concerned with product safety. "We are collecting all of the information from our suppliers that provide the talc, trying to see what they know is in it."

But a trade association paid by the industry to certify materials as non-toxic was less cautious.

"There is no asbestos in crayons," said Debbie Fanning, executive director of the Art and Creative Materials Institute. "The [Institute's] toxicologist evaluates the products, and if there was asbestos in crayons, he'd be right on top of that. We check for lead in crayons, and asbestos is that much worse."

The Institute's toxicologist, Dr. Woodhall Stopford, said that his earlier analysis of Crayola, Prang and Rose Art crayons showed no asbestos at all. But he couldn't specify when those tests had been done, and he finally admitted, "We don't analyze crayons for asbestos, and I doubt that we ever will."

He said that "I basically don't allow any detectable asbestos in products I certify," but then added, "We don't analyze talc that goes into crayons for asbestos, because I'm not aware of any talc in our program that has asbestos in it." Stopford suggested that the labs used by the newspaper were "confused" as to what they were seeing under the microscope. The government-certified laboratories, which routinely do work for the EPA, stood by the test results. Twenty-five companies that produce about 100 different brands and packages of crayons are members of the Institute, Fanning said. Membership costs between $450 and $41,000 a year, depending on the size of the company. Members are then permitted to use the Institute's logo, mandated by the government, which says CP NONTOXIC. The three domestic brands in which asbestos was found all carried the Institute's seal.

Other doctors weighed in with worried reactions. Dr. Michael McCann, a chemist and industrial hygienist who founded and directed New York's Center for Safety in the Arts, said the industry must take action immediately. "The crayon particles can get into the lungs.... Does the child's body temperature melt the wax? There are lots of questions that must be answered promptly." He added, "Once an issue like this is raised, it's up to the industry to prove it's safe, not the other way around. I don't believe products are innocent until proven guilty."

Dr. Samuel Epstein, professor of environmental and occupational medicine at the University of Illinois Medical Center and director of the Cancer Prevention Coalition, said, "Childhood exposures to carcinogens are responsible for a very significant incidence of adult cancers. And that is also an overwhelmingly neglected area [of medicine]."

Dr. Harbut added, "The metabolism of young children is such that they are even more sensitive to toxins. Levels of asbestos exposure that would do minimal harm to an adult can cause serious disease in a child after the latency period has run its course."

The consumer reaction to the May 23, 2000, story was immediate and enormous. The *Post-Intelligencer,* the crayon manufacturers and the Consumer Product Safety Commission were all flooded with calls from worried parents. The day the report was published, the CPSC announced it would do its own testing, and it cautioned parents that they might wish to keep their children from using crayons until the government's tests were completed.

Fanning and Stopford of the industry-sponsored Art and Creative Materials Institute repeated their blanket denials, as if saying no could make it so, and again called into question the accuracy of the *Post-Intelligencer's* testing. Stopford insisted that the labs must have found "a non-asbestos form of tremolite."

"That's not the case," said John Harris of Lab/Cor in Seattle, who did many of the tests.[6] "There is asbestos in the crayons we tested — tremolite and anthophyllite."

Meanwhile, Binney & Smith launched a hurried counterattack. Two days after the *Post-Intelligencer* story appeared, the company announced that it had hired an independent laboratory to test its crayons, and that the lab had given Crayolas a clean bill of health-no asbestos content. The laboratory, R.J. Lee Group of Pittsburgh, said it had tested two crayons and found them both to be free of asbestos.

The *Post-Intelligencer* stood by its stories, and its tests, but reported Binney & Smith's findings, and the company's accompanying statement: "These findings reaffirm the commitment to safety we've upheld for nearly 100 years."

And then the *Post-Intelligencer* discovered something interesting about the lab that had done the testing for Binney & Smith: It had a long list of asbestos-company clients.[7] The *Post-Intelligencer* found that Richard Lee, president of the R.J. Lee Group, had confirmed under oath earlier in the year that he had testified for asbestos companies more than 250 times, and had been paid more than $7 million for doing so. Schneider asked Binney & Smith if Lee's heavy involvement with the asbestos and talc industries met its definition of "independent." The company declined to answer the question.

The storm had hit, and the industry tests put the paper very much on the defensive. But more evidence supporting the *Post-Intelligencer's* story was on the way. On Friday night, three days after the stories ran, ABC News's Bill Blakemore hit the national nightly news with the results of the network's own tests: ABC's lab found asbestos as well. The *Post-Intelligencer* now had company out at the end of the long limb from which it was hanging. And by the end of the next week, more than a dozen labs analyzing crayons for various school districts had duplicated Lab/Cor's results.

The clincher came almost three weeks later, when the CPSC announced the results of its testing: Government scientists had also found asbestos in the three major brands of crayons. Immediately, Binney & Smith, Prang and Rose Art announced that they would accede to the agency's request and remove the contaminated talc from their crayons. Rose Art announced that it had already removed the talc from almost all of its products. By the time the CPSC announced its results, the *Post-Intelligencer's* attention was focused on where the contaminated talc had come from — and what the paper found bore an eerie resemblance to the situation in Libby, Montana.

THE ASBESTOS that the *Post-Intelligencer* found in crayons was there because a powerful company had been able to find ways to influence — and ultimately change — government safety regulations.

It is a company that forty years ago marketed the asbestos content in its product, and now flatly denies it's there-just like the denials of the Art and Creative Materials Institute, just like the denials by Grace's managers in Libby when miners asked what was in the dust that was choking them. It is a company whose president bragged to his workers that he had a U.S. senator in his back pocket.

The company is the R.T. Vanderbilt Company, owner of a huge complex of talc mines in upstate New York, and supplier of talc to the three crayon-makers whose products were found to contain asbestos.

The revelations that followed the newspaper's crayon discovery were a major embarrassment to the federal government, but they were not a surprise. A government-sponsored study first found large quantities of asbestos in Vanderbilt talc a quarter of a century ago. Those results have been confirmed time and again by other scientists, pathologists and health experts. They have been confirmed for decades in the dying gasps of talc miners. But since that time, under heavy pressure from Vanderbilt, the government has created a hole in its regulations big enough for the company to drive its ore trucks through.

Through Vanderbilt's efforts and with the government's acquiescence, the debate has been shifted from the medical records of the company's workers to an argument about mineralogical semantics. It is an unconscionable triumph of power politics over science and safety. Here's how it happened. Talc has been mined and milled in the soft-rock farmland of St. Lawrence County, New York, since 1878, when Henry Palmer opened the first talc mine in America. It was a primitive open-pit operation at first. An underground mine was added, with the talc being raised from the shaft by a horse-drawn bucket. From the first, the talc was used in making paper and paint. By the end of World War II, the county was honeycombed with deep shafts and pits — some mom-and-pop operations, others producing thousands of tons of minerals. The miners extracted not only talc but zinc, lead and other minerals. Asbestos was commonly known to occur throughout. In 1942, the Saranac Laboratory documented that anthophyllite, tremolite and four other fibers were plentiful in the mines.

In 1948, the Gouverneur Talc Company was formed as a subsidiary of the R.T. Vanderbilt Corp., a mineral and chemical supplier that had been operating since 1916.[8] Vanderbilt quickly became a major player in the area's talc mining, and bought up several smaller operators. In 1966, a book published by Vanderbilt to mark the company's 50th anniversary described the importance of the talc and asbestos mixtures it sold.

But in 1970, the Occupational Safety and Health Act created a new government agency charged with protecting workers — OSHA. And in 1972, the new agency set its first regulations limiting worker asbestos exposure. Tremolite found in talc and vermiculite was specifically included in the regulations.

By 1974, OSHA was under attack, fighting for its very life.[9] The Nixon administration, sympathetic to business, faced a hostile, Democrat-controlled Congress that was urging tougher regulation. But President Nixon was mindful of the complaining he was hearing from businesses, and Vanderbilt was lobbying hard. During the Watergate hearings, a 1972 memo from George Guenther, the first OSHA administrator, to Nixon was revealed, outlining "the great potential of OSHA as a sales point" to enlist business support for Nixon's reelection and calling for suggestions from the staff about how to promote the advantages to industry of four more years of a "properly managed" OSHA.

Just two weeks before he resigned, Nixon spoke at an economic conference in Los Angeles, decrying the "burdensome over-regulation" of industry.[10] "Where regulatory agencies, because of obsolete rules, have the effect of restricting production rather than encouraging it, those rules need to be changed," Nixon said.

Nixon's successor, Gerald Ford, was no less interested in making government friendlier to industry, and at the same time, Vanderbilt was strongly lobbying Congress and protesting to OSHA that its ore contained a non-harmful variety of tremolite. That year, OSHA granted Vanderbilt "temporary relief" from its asbestos standard.

Nevertheless, on January 2, 1975, a Vanderbilt executive wrote a letter to the Georgia Pacific Corporation in Portland, Oregon, stating that[11]

> ... in the course of our assuming the business of the former International Talc Company, we will continue to market five fibrous (asbestiform) type talcs previously supplied by them.... We intend to label bags containing these products with an Asbestos CAUTION label as follows: CAUTION PRODUCT CONTAINS ASBESTOS FIBERS. AVOID CRE-

ATING DUST. BREATHING ASBESTOS DUST MAY CAUSE SERI-
OUS BODILY HARM.

As you know, the mineral fibers present in these grades, which make
them industrially useful, are the asbestiform varieties of those minerals
normally contained in commercial talc, and consequently fall under Section 1910.93a, the OSHA Asbestos Standard.

This letter is the last known time that Vanderbilt officially acknowledged
the asbestos content of its talc. From that point on, despite study after study
that found asbestos, Vanderbilt denied its presence.

John Kelse, manager of Vanderbilt's Corporate Risk Management Department, explained the discrepancy by saying, "At that time [the early
1970s] there was no one here at Vanderbilt that had good mineralogical expertise or a full understanding of what OSHA's regulations were about."[12] He
added that "the people here didn't understand that there are two varieties of
tremolite.... [T]hen they hired a mineralogist who said, 'What are you doing?' so they stopped" putting on the warning labels.

But the change in tactics went far deeper than labeling. Over the next
three decades, Vanderbilt developed and refined a highly successful strategy:
Deny that the asbestos is there. If confronted with evidence of fibers, declare them "non-asbestiform," and never let up in pressuring both regulatory
agencies and politicians.

Vanderbilt's message sounds plausible. Its literally fatal flaw is found in
the cemeteries of Talcville and Balmat and Hailesboro. It is beyond dispute
that generations of miners have gotten lung diseases in the talc mines of St.
Lawrence County. But for hundreds of these men and their survivors, justice
has been as hard to get as a good breath of air.

In Montana, a key state supreme court decision allowed the people of
Libby the right to sue. In New York, in a similar case, the decision went
the other way. In 1999, New York's highest court decided that the talc mining companies, including Vanderbilt, could not be sued because state law
requires claims to be handled through workers' compensation. So men like
Herb Conklin have no recourse.

Schneider found him at home near Edwards, New York, with his wife Margaret.[13] An American flag hung from a pole in the driveway, which was covered in soft white rock, tailings from the mine.

"I worked for the mines for thirty years to the day," said Conklin, now in his late 70s. He ran a rock crusher, drove ore cars, and fixed heavy machinery. "I did about everything that could be done at the mines, and all of it in dust so thick you couldn't see ten feet," he said. "They claimed the dust was safe, non-asbestiform. Vanderbilt called it nonfibrous, nothing that would harm us. They posted signs on the bulletin board saying the government doctors, the guys from NIOSH, were wrong, that it wasn't dangerous," he said bitterly.

Conklin and other miners Schneider interviewed were critical of mine inspectors for being too cozy with the company. "They always called two or three days before they came out to tell the company they were on the way, and for the next two or three days we shoveled, swept and wet down all the dust we could find," Conklin said.

In 1978, he realized how much he had been harmed. "I was climbing up a ladder to work on the roof of the barn, and all of a sudden I couldn't breathe," he said. As his disease worsened, he and Margaret were forced to sell the 35 cows that they milked twice a day to put aside money for retirement. Conklin dropped his head and rubbed his eyes, and Margaret clutched his arm a little tighter. "It was wrong," he said wearily. "If Vanderbilt didn't care enough about its workers, why didn't the government step in?"

"It didn't matter what they called it, it was dangerous. It is killing us."

About a mile away, on the main street of Edwards, two other Vanderbilt veterans sat in an immaculate living room and compared notes on life in the mine, and what came afterward. Charlie Minkler spent almost half of his 65 years working for Vanderbilt. Bill Fuller, who is 68, put in more than 26 years in the mines, part of it with Vanderbilt. They tried to recall the young men with whom they started work at the mines. After a litany of "He's dead," "He's gone," and "Nope, he passed also," the men became quiet.

"I guess I'm lucky," Minkler said in a soft, raspy voice. "Of the fifty-two guys I began with at the mine, all but three are dead and most of them died young, in their forties and fifties."

"Cancer took a bunch of them. The rest of them just couldn't breathe."

Minkler and Fuller talked about their friends who must use tanks of oxygen to make it through the day. "Once they get on that oxygen, they won't be around much longer," Minkler says, shaking his head.

Fuller uses a portable device that forces oxygen into his lungs. He uses it about every six hours. "I can't walk to that window without stopping," he said, "and that's no way for a man to live."

Both men echoed Conklin's bitterness, not only toward the company but toward the regulators.

"We know why Vanderbilt lied about the danger. It would be bad for business and no one would work for them," said Fuller. "But what about the government? Why don't they care? This asbestos, or whatever Vanderbilt wants to call it, is not a secret. The graveyards are filled with proof that those fibers are dangerous."

What makes them madder than anything is that the company doctors hid the illness from them. "It wasn't as if they didn't know," said Minkler. "Hell, just look at our fingers. They're clubbed. Everybody's are like that. It's a sign the lungs aren't working." Clubbing, a bulbous distortion of the fingertips and nails, is caused by a prolonged period of inadequate oxygenation.

"They knew we were sick. We took company physicals every year," Minkler said. "They knew whose lungs were shot, but they wouldn't tell us and they wouldn't send us to a specialist."

"There have been many claims of finding asbestos in our mines, but when we've been able to analyze those claims, we've not been able to confirm it," said Vanderbilt's Kelse.

The Syracuse law firm of Setright and Longstreet spent years gathering depositions and other evidence on behalf of 139 talc-country miners or heirs of miners who died from asbestos-related disease. Because of the state's high court's ruling, none of those claims will get anywhere. Those depositions, medical records and company documents show repeated examples of exactly what Minkler complained about — company doctors telling workers for years that they were healthy, when X-rays locked away in company files showed lungs filled with asbestos or tumors.

"We probably didn't believe that the X-rays showed asbestosis," Kelse said when asked why the company withheld the information. "You can't do mineral analysis on an X-ray."

DR. JERROLD ABRAHAM is director of environmental and occupational pathology at Upstate Medical University in Syracuse, New York.

He has fought the battle over asbestos in talc for many years. His cluttered office in the crowded, red-brick pathology building is probably one of the world's largest storehouses of knowledge on the health effects of the fine white powder. The two rooms house an eclectic accumulation of voluminous file folders, overfilled cabinets and floor-to-ceiling shelves stuffed with medical charts, death certificates, studies on talc going back to the 1920s and hundreds of slides carrying slivers of miners' organs.

"It doesn't bother me that Vanderbilt can get away with not calling the fibers what they are — asbestos," Abraham says.[14] "What should bother everyone is that Vanderbilt and the government say they're not harmful."

Abraham added, "Our medical center is the referral center for people from the area where the mines are. We found several cases of mesothelioma in the miners, and we've done studies on what we've found in lungs of the sick miners. Of course we find lots of talc, but there are also significant amounts of asbestiform tremolite."

Kelse acknowledges that Abraham is "a good pathologist," but says, "Vanderbilt has never said that overexposure to our talc or anyone else's talc is safe. It isn't. Talcosis is different from asbestosis. But there's not much difference in the X-rays."

Abraham peers over the top of his glasses at a dozen microphotographs spread atop a long table.

"These are fibers from the mill at the Vanderbilt mine," he says, holding a photo up. "This is from the lung of a Vanderbilt miner," he says, reaching for another. "They're identical. Anyone can see that. My findings in reviewing the autopsy lung tissues of these miners show disease attributed to asbestos by any competent medical standard. You get OSHA and the mine inspectors to say why they don't believe it's asbestos."

"Our position," John Kelse says, "has always been, just call the stuff what it is. Whatever the health effect that's demonstrated as a result of overexposure to these fibers, you regulate it and control it to avoid those health problems."

But regulation is precisely what Vanderbilt has fought for three decades.

The battle began in earnest during the summer of 1973, when NIOSH issued a health-hazard evaluation for one of Vanderbilt's customers, Fortune Industries in Chelsea, Michigan. NIOSH told the company that the tremolite from Vanderbilt's talc exceeded OSHA standards and advised Fortune to find a replacement for the talc.

Vanderbilt was alarmed, and began campaigning to get the tremolite in its talc excluded from the standards.[15] It won the temporary reprieve in 1974, but by 1975 a study done for the federal government by Walter McCrone Associates in Chicago examined seven talc samples from Vanderbilt mines and reported finding tremolite asbestos in all of them.

"The asbestos mineral present ... is definitely asbestiform by any definition of the word," the report said.

In January 1977, Vanderbilt knew time was running out. It sent a letter to Secretary of Labor Ray Marshall, saying that OSHA's proposed standard "will in all likelihood result in staggering losses to the R.T. Vanderbilt Co. and directly jeopardize a $30 million manufacturing facility [with] 175 employees." But later that year, OSHA reversed itself after preliminary studies showed an increased incidence of disease among Vanderbilt's miners. Still, the company fought on, and the government did not take direct action.

In 1980, the company's miners called for help. The union knew its members were dying, and they asked NIOSH for a health-hazard evaluation on Vanderbilt. NIOSH demanded company records, and identified 710 men who worked with the talc from 1947 to 1978. The Institute conducted a health study of those men and found the death rate from lung cancer to be twice the normal rate, and the death rate from non malignant respiratory disease to be three times normal.

As the bureaucracy ground on toward the final establishment of new health standards for asbestos, the company, after a decade of struggle, appeared to be cornered. It immediately criticized the NIOSH study, but the damage was done, and the company knew the report would have a serious impact on OSHA's asbestos standard.

One development cheered Vanderbilt — the election of Ronald Reagan and the change of administration that resulted at the Department of Labor and OSHA. But the 1980 report still stood, and Vanderbilt realized it would have to be countered directly.

In 1984, Institute records show, Vanderbilt contacted John Gamble, an epidemiologist assigned to NIOSH's Division of Respiratory Disease studies in Morgantown, West Virginia, to express its concern again about the 1980 report and its expected impact on the definition of asbestos that OSHA was about to make into law.[16]

Over the next few years, NIOSH investigators later found, there were more than a dozen private meetings between Vanderbilt and Gamble and Bob Glenn, who headed NIOSH's respiratory disease division. Those contacts, never officially reported to Gamble's and Glenn's superiors, included meals and travel at Vanderbilt's expense, and meetings directly with Hugh Vanderbilt, the company's president. The scientists embarked on an unauthorized study of their own.

This "project" was intentionally concealed from other NIOSH staff and the Institute's director, investigators later found. There was no research protocol and no peer review.

Since it was unauthorized, Gamble's work would not be of any value to Vanderbilt unless it was somehow made public. So, according to the investigators, the scientists in the Morgantown lab "developed a strategy" to have Vanderbilt request an updated health-hazard evaluation, to supersede the 1980 study that the company hated so much. Glenn received the request and immediately assigned it to Gamble. Just two weeks later, Gamble submitted a "preliminary" 22-page report to Glenn. It criticized most of NIOSH's findings in the 1980 study.

Meanwhile, on June 17, 1986, OSHA finally issued its new health standard. It defined the fibers NIOSH had found in its 1980 study as asbestos. Three days later, Vanderbilt filed a challenge for review to the U.S. Court of Appeals. It also brought more political pressure to bear.

United States Senator Lowell Weicker and United States Representative Stewart McKinney, both Connecticut Republicans, fired off a letter to Secretary of Labor William Brock. "If these regulations are allowed to go into effect on July 21, 1986, R.T. Vanderbilt Co. Inc., which we have written on behalf of for over 10 years, will be forced to shut down," they told Brock in the letter. On July 18, three days before the new standard was to go into effect, OSHA backed down again, granting Vanderbilt another temporary stay.

Two weeks later, Dr. Donald Millar, NIOSH's director, learned of the rogue study when Hugh Vanderbilt and a lawyer showed up at the agency's Atlanta headquarters to pick up the study, armed with a Freedom of Information Act request. Glenn had hand-carried the material to Atlanta so Vanderbilt could get it so quickly. Other NIOSH scientists quickly raised concerns about the way Gamble's report was done. Regulations say such an evaluation must have input not only from the company but also from the union and other concerned government agencies. But in this case, all the information used came from Vanderbilt. Other troubling departures from policy were found, including Gamble's bypassing the chain of command and reporting directly to Glenn.

In December 1987, Brock called Millar and said he had just met with Vanderbilt officials. He wanted to know why OSHA had not been told about Gamble's study, and questioned what NIOSH's position was on its 1980 report and how it was defining asbestos. Millar quickly wrote to OSHA, saying that "the NIOSH definition and policy regarding asbestos has not changed."

The next year, Vanderbilt employees got a note from the company warning, "We are certain that ... labeling our product as asbestos as required by the OSHA regulations would lead to a rapid loss of our business.... Our operation could not survive the stigma attached to such a label." About that time, Hugh Vanderbilt came to the mine to rally his workers. That day, the mine captain gathered all of the day-shift miners and millers in the carpentry shop. Attired in a dark suit and tie, Vanderbilt stood before the talc-smeared miners and told them not to worry about the debate over the asbestos definition. Everything was under control, he told them.

Miners' depositions later varied over how much money Vanderbilt said he had already spent fighting the new regulations — hundreds of thousands or millions of dollars. But all agreed that Vanderbilt then told his workers that if all else failed, he had a senator in his back pocket. He made a show of patting his wallet, and said none of the miners had to worry about their jobs.

The jockeying continued. But on June 8, 1992, OSHA announced that it had decided to eliminate the part of its standards that would have regulated the asbestos found in Vanderbilt's mines, based in part on "certain NIOSH staff memos which have recently been brought to its attention." Dr. Richard Lemen, a former associate director of NIOSH and a former assistant surgeon general, said that Gamble's study was "a low point to the morale of the institute, but ... the institute took quick steps to assure such behavior would not recur."

NIOSH and the inspector general for the Department of Health and Human Services launched the investigation of Gamble and Glenn, which culminated in "appropriate disciplinary action." Glenn denied to the *Post-Intelligencer* that he and Gamble had been fired, but both left the agency. Gamble could not be reached for comment.

NIOSH also convened a board of scientific counselors to review their report, and the board's findings supported the original 1980 study. But one NIOSH official said the impact of Gamble's "spoon-fed study" on OSHA was "a bell that couldn't be unrung." In 1994, the new rules were finalized, omitting any regulation of the fibers in talc.

OSHA's decision has left miners, other workers and consumers at risk ever since, Lemen said. "The fact that these fibers, which are respirable, can get into the lungs, can cause disease, but are not regulated, means that these miners and the people who use their products are not being protected under federal standards as they should be."

Dr. John Dement, who headed the team that did the 1980 NIOSH study, agrees.[17] "There's a lot of semantics being played again in regard to the definition of asbestos, but the lung and [its lining] doesn't care about what it's called. That mine has asbestos fibers of biological significance which have caused, and most likely continue to cause, health problems for the miners and others exposed to them."

DR. GEORGE WINEBURGH had no intention of raising hell when he moved to upstate New York in 1982 with his wife and four Labrador retrievers.

In fact, he was looking for a nice, quiet place to practice medicine — an antidote to the 16 pressure-packed years he'd spent in New York City's largest hospital. But raise hell he did.

He was eager to start his job as the radiologist at Ogdensburg's Barton Hepburn Hospital.[18] "I thought this was going to be a piece of cake, you know, no stress, a handful of cases, a great change from the big city," he said. "Boy, was I wrong."

But the same skills that made Wineburgh attractive to the hospital soon spurred him to ask some questions. Each morning, he looked through the pile of X-rays waiting on his desk. They'd be from the patients examined overnight in the emergency room, usually for assorted trauma, aches and pains and heart problems. Among the cracked ribs, bruised kidneys and clogged arteries, Wineburgh was frequently finding something unexpected: the distinctive shadows of lungs damaged by asbestos. "I kept seeing four, five, six cases every single week, week after week, classic asbestosis," Wineburgh said.

He questioned the other doctors in the community.

"All the clinicians that I asked said, 'Ah, they're just smokers. Yeah, they're miners, but they're all smokers. That's the reason, so we don't mess with them,'" he said.

But Wineburgh was certain that what he was seeing was asbestosis. "It's distinctive," he says. "If you know what you're looking for, there's no way to confuse it with something else. Asbestosis is one of fourteen [X-ray] findings that is unique, that can be one thing and nothing else." After three months, he had X-rays from 50 patients that he considered evidence of asbestosis. Other doctors still insisted it was emphysema from smoking, and they claimed they had the pulmonary-function tests to prove it.

"But the numbers were all wrong, completely opposite of what they should have been," Wineburgh said. "Emphysema is called an obstructive lung disease, and the lungs are over expanded. With asbestosis the lungs are small — restrictive lung disease — completely opposite numbers. There should be no confusion."

He became more and more uncomfortable about the reaction he was getting. "I didn't like it. It smelled. Nobody wanted to stand up for the miners. Nobody was being clinically objective. It was like they were under the thumb of the mining company," he recalled. And as the numbers of X-rays showing disease increased, so did his frustration. "These miners were desperate," he said. "They weren't getting any better, and they weren't getting any answers. Some were dying. Doctors were telling them to stop smoking, but some of them never smoked."

Wineburgh alerted the unions.

"They were supposed to stick up for the miners," he said. "But they said they had been told that if they raised a stink, demanded that the safety regulations be followed, management said they would close down the mines. So they, too, did nothing. Just breathe in, breathe out, and keep working."

Then Wineburgh sent the 50 cases to the state health department. "Asbestosis is a reportable disease. You guys have the authority," he told them. "So here you are."

The state shipped the X-rays to the Selikoff Institute for Occupational Medicine at Mt. Sinai Hospital in New York City. There, a specialist confirmed that Wineburgh was right in almost all of the cases. Then the health department contracted with Wineburgh to lead the examination of all the X-rays taken of people aged 40 and older between April 1982 and March 1983 at six hospitals in a two-county area. About 22,000 films of 9,442 patients were examined. Wineburgh and his team found chest abnormalities in 500 patients. Those X-rays, in turn, were evaluated by what the health department called "an internationally recognized" expert.

This expert found that 71 percent of Wineburgh's 500 "were indeed consistent with chest abnormalities indicative of asbestos exposure," said Dr. Edward Fitzgerald, who co-wrote the state's report and is assistant director of the state's Bureau of Environmental and Occupational Epidemiology.

Lengthy interviews were conducted to pin down work histories. The largest number of the patients with diseased lungs worked in talc mining or milling. The next-largest group afflicted were workers in the paper mills, which used large amounts of talc.

The state "jumped in immediately," said Thomas DiCerbo, the associate director of New York's Division of Occupational Health. His department sent physicians upstate to meet with local doctors "to alert them to what they should be looking for." His department also met with the R.T. Vanderbilt Co., the owners of the mine. They "agreed to talk to us, and we explained our concerns," DiCerbo said. But he would not say whether the state thought there was asbestos in the mine's talc, and no enforcement action has been taken against the company.

For his efforts, Dr. Wineburgh lost his job.

"My contract with the hospital was canceled three days before it was to be renewed," he said. "Most of the medical community thought I was a troublemaking traitor. Working with the Health Department of New York State to try to get help for hundreds of miners made me a traitor to the physicians of two counties."

Wineburgh is now practicing in the Midwest.

"Finding those sick New York miners changed my life," he said. "I'm a lot poorer now. I have to work a lot harder than I should at my age. Would I stick my neck out again for those guys? Of course. That's how medicine should be practiced."

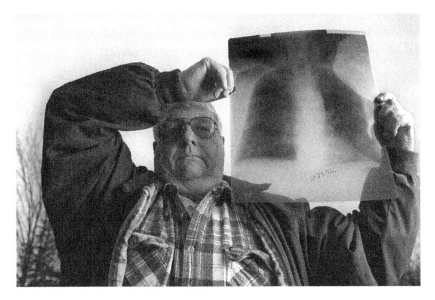

CHAPTER 18

George Biekkola mined taconite in northern Michigan, where mine
management insisted there was no asbestos in the ore. But his X-ray, and death
certificates of other miners, said the danger is real.
(Paul Kitagaki Jr., *Seattle Post-Intelligencer*)

SCHNEIDER'S PHONE RANG one afternoon in mid-March 2000.[1]
The Libby stories had been out for months, and he was still chasing
a zillion leads. Asbestos was truly everywhere, if you judged by the
flood of e-mails and phone calls he and the paper got every day.

So when the voice said, "Mr. Schneider, I'm Davitt McAteer, and I've
read your stories about Libby," Schneider didn't exactly jump to attention.

But he sure did when the voice added, "I'm in charge of the Mine Safety
and Health Administration. We really blew it in Libby, and I will make damn
sure that it doesn't happen again."

At first, Schneider thought it was a prank. Administrators of federal
agencies don't often call reporters and volunteer the fact that lives could

have been saved if the agency had done what it was supposed to do. But as he soon found out, Davitt McAteer was an unusual administrator.

"I had a hard time believing what I was reading," McAteer continued with absolutely no prompting. "So I had all the reports pulled on Libby and found out it was true. What I found bothered me a great deal. We could have done more. We should have done more, and we didn't."

Schneider thought he'd died and gone to heaven. Every new sentence was dynamite.

"We failed to detect, failed to alert and failed to remedy the situation," McAteer went on in a rush. "We can't bring those people back, but we can make changes in how we operate so we don't have any revelation of preventable deaths twenty years from now. I want to ensure that this is not happening today in any of the mines we're responsible for."

Twenty minutes later, Schneider sat in McCumber's office and talked about Davitt McAteer. It didn't take long for them to agree: Schneider had to get on a plane and interview the assistant secretary of labor face-to-face. "I hate to give him a chance to back off what he told you on the phone, but you have to go," McCumber said.

"I've got to watch his lips move while he says it, and we need to make sure he's who he claims he is," the reporter said, reaching for an airline schedule.

In forty-eight hours, the interview was done, and McAteer had backed off on exactly nothing. In fact, he'd been even more emphatic in person. He told Schneider that he had ordered special inspections at all mines in the country where asbestos could be present. It was a surprisingly long list: the nation's only operating asbestos mine, near King City in central California; vermiculite mines in Louisa, Virginia, and in Enoree and Woodruff, South Carolina; at the talc mines in Gouverneur, New York, Dillon, Montana, and Ludlow, Vermont; at rock quarries in Sparta, New Jersey, North Branford, Connecticut, and near San Jose, California; and finally at mines across the tops of Minnesota and Michigan that produce taconite, a form of iron ore often contaminated with tremolite.

At each mine, the inspectors attached small, portable air pumps to the workers while they did their normal jobs. The filters from the vacuum pumps were examined at OSHA's laboratory in Salt Lake City, and the fibers of asbestos were counted. Some of the tests showed levels less than MSHA's permissible exposure limit. That did not satisfy McAteer, even though some mine operators boasted that the tests gave them a clean bill of health.

"These say the air testing came back below our limit," he said, waving a stack of test results. "But MSHA's limit is twenty times higher than OSHA's limit. There could be twenty times more asbestos fibers in the sample than OSHA's limit and it could be legal under our regulations. How can we say that's safe?"

The safety standard used by MSHA was 27 years old, he said. Back in 1989, the agency had tried to bring the asbestos-exposure limits down to OSHA's standards. The industry flooded the agency with protests. W.R. Grace said there was no need to lower the permissible exposure limits for vermiculite mines, because it claimed there was no asbestos in its South Carolina operation. Libby would not close until the following year.

The Asbestos Information Association, the industry lobbying group, cited medical studies that they said showed the risk of asbestos exposure in the mines was minimal. But almost all of those studies came out of industry-funded projects.

Some of the miners on the front line had a different opinion on the prevalence of asbestos.[2] In April 2000, in LTV Steelworkers 4108's union hall in Eveleth, Minnesota, Senator Paul Wellstone leaned against a wall and listened to the gripes of his constituents — miners of taconite from the sprawling, black pits of the eight steel companies along Minnesota's Iron Range.

"Our men are dying because of asbestos in the ore and the government isn't doing anything," union president Dave Trach told his senator.[3] "Hell, the MSHA inspectors give the companies a warning before they come to inspect, and the supervisors have time to wet the ore down to keep the asbestos dust from being collected in the air samples. They shuffle the men to areas of the mine that have less asbestos and put up red caution flags around the areas they were just working in, making believe they're out of bounds."

Wellstone, who would die in the same town 30 months later when his campaign plane crashed on an icy October morning, was bothered by what he heard. Actually, "pissed off" is a more accurate description. "What the hell are they doing?" the senator asked. "Their obligation is to protect the miners, not warn the company they're coming. Sometimes I have to wonder whether these agencies care at all about the people they're paid to protect."

The popular senator dropped his voice to almost a whisper and said: "Pray for the dead and fight like hell for the living."

The miners, who were straining to hear, asked those closer to the front what Wellstone had said. He repeated it and told them it was the creed of Mary Harris Jones, the Irish-born American union organizer who fought in the 1880s and 1890s for the safety of miners.

"Where is the Mother Jones of today?" Wellstone asked. "Someone needs to fight to protect you guys."

About 270 miles east, in Michigan's Iron Range, George Biekkola of L'Anse, a taconite miner almost completely debilitated from asbestos disease, was wondering the same thing.[4] In July of 2001, Biekkola told a Senate hearing chaired by Patty Murray on Workplace Safety and Asbestos Contamination that asbestosis from tremolite contaminating the taconite ore he mined for the Cleveland Cliffs Iron Company had left him with only one-third of his lungs functioning. He told the senators that he had collected more than 200 death certificates of other miners who died of asbestos-related diseases.

"Companies will tell you that asbestos isn't a problem. 'Go back to work, George. There's nothing to worry about,' the mine would say," he explained. "Senators, they lied. We need to worry about asbestos — and we need our government to protect us — because businesses, on their own, won't always do the right thing."

McAteer and Celeste Monforton, chief of MSHA's health division, tried. "The efforts to prevent the new standard were pretty much made by the same people making the same statements they made in defending Libby," McAteer said. "They said, 'Our asbestos isn't bad asbestos.' And 'Those fibers are too short or the wrong shape to be harmful' and 'Our mining process doesn't result in the kind of asbestos exposure that would cause the disease.'"

CELESTE MONFORTON CONVINCED HER BOSS that she had to talk to miners who had been hurt, and Peronard had told her Libby was the place to go.[5]

She flew in for a meeting of health experts. While medicine was the topic in the VFW's meeting room, she sat with miners in the club's bar, which was dark, except for the lights over the pool table and a blinking sign over the bar for Moose Drool beer.

She shared her boss's angst that the Bureau of Mines, the predecessor of MSHA, had blown it. Repeatedly. The reports by Benjamin Wake in the '50s and the later ones by other inspectors never got to the workers, and more disturbingly, apparently generated no attention when they finally got to headquarters, weeks or months later.

Monforton's hope was that the old miners could tell her things that weren't in the old files. She twisted a curl of her dark hair and her eyes shone with anger as she listened to their stories. Les wasn't bashful and gave her an earful. When he told her that he had brought the death home to Norita and his kids, she laid her hand over his and fought the need to weep.

"I need to talk to other miners," she pleaded, and Les took off in search of his former colleagues.

Several miners she shared beer with that afternoon had mentioned that federal mine inspectors gave Grace three or four days' notice before they showed up to examine safety conditions. The same charges made by the Iron Range miners, but a Libby miner added a new wrinkle.

"We never had a chance to talk to the government inspectors. Our bosses would shoo us off if we tried to approach the man, and none of them seemed to have any interest in actually talking to the workers. Hell, we would have told them about cleaning up the place before they arrived, but they never asked," said Butch Hurlbert. Tall and handsome, the former steelworker and rodeo roper is still a poster image of a cowboy, but his three years working at the vermiculite mine was enough to damage his lungs so that even saddling one of his horses is an agonizing endeavor.

MSHA's files do not show why the effort to make the exposure standard more meaningful was dropped in 1989.[6] But MSHA was again developing a proposal for a health standard for asbestos that would lower the permissible exposure to the OSHA level. "I'm sure we'll be hearing from the industry as soon as the word gets out," said Carol Jones, director of MSHA's Office of Standards. "There is no doubt the miners will be safer if we can reduce the exposure," Jones said. "When you have a carcinogen like asbestos, you want to have no exposure at all."

But Jones, McAteer and other government experts perform a delicate balancing act — lower the standard as far as possible, but keep it high enough so mines can still operate. OSHA's limit of 0.1 fiber per cubic centimeter of air still permits exposure that is estimated to cause three or four cases of cancer per 1,000 workers.

"We have to go to a level which won't close the mines," she says. "So that's the reason the zero-point-one fiber still has significant risk, because we couldn't go any lower, because we couldn't drive everyone out of business." That level sounds like a tiny amount, but Jones put it into perspective. "That's 100,000 fibers per cubic meter. We breathe ten cubic meters of air in a workday if we're working hard, so that's a million fibers. And, with asbestos, research allows that, in some cases, just one fiber could get into one cell and cause it to become a tumor cell. It multiplies, and you've got cancer."

McAteer told Schneider that he had sent his inspectors back again to take more air samples as well as actual ore samples. He said he wasn't worried about hostile mine operators. "We have authority to take samples when and where we believe dangerous exposures might exist, and that is precisely what our inspectors will do."

A RUMBLING EXPLOSION at Consolidated Coal Company's No.9 mine, eight miles from McAteer's home in Farmington, West Virginia, shoved him into the world of mine safety in 1968.

Then a law student at West Virginia University, he stood a somber vigil for days with the rest of the small town, watching the rescue effort, hoping that boys he went to school with, their fathers and grandfathers would somehow survive. Twenty-one miners were rescued, but 78 were entombed in the deep shafts as the mine was sealed to halt continuing explosions.

Almost immediately, McAteer found Ralph Nader, whose reputation as a consumer advocate was spreading, and offered to run a team of law students to investigate mine safety in the state. When that report was published five years later, West Virginia passed laws that changed the way mines were regulated.

When McAteer took over as the head of MSHA he didn't have to wait long to be challenged by powerful mining interests.[7] He hadn't had time to hang mementos on his new office walls in 1994 before Republicans in Congress began clamoring for MSHA to be gutted, its staff cut by 60 percent or eliminated altogether. But McAteer persevered and actually strengthened the agency. "That's why he got the job," said his boss, Labor Secretary Robert Reich. "Davitt comes from a mining family, and he cares deeply and passionately about what happens in those mines," Reich said. "He knows more about mining, the technology and the dangers than just about anybody I've encountered. He says what he believes. It's not easy in Washington to tell it like it is, but if you are telling the truth, giving an accurate portrayal of reality, and you have technical competence on your side, then you're unassailable. That's the way he operates, and he thrives on challenges."

McAteer said he had made the health of miners a prime focus of his agency, which wasn't easy. "If we had an epidemic of safety problems the magnitude of Libby, with hundreds of miners dying, we'd take some action immediately. But with health problems, it doesn't happen right away, and it gets pushed back and pushed back and pushed back until something forces it to the front again. Meanwhile, lives that could have been saved are lost."

Safety problems are usually easily fixed, he said. "You have a conveyor belt with a guard missing, you can put the guard back on. A broken piece of equipment causes an accident, you can repair it. But solving health problems is nowhere near as simple. There's a latency period where you don't see the impact for fifteen years, typically. So it's a lot harder to get people involved, be they the miners, be they the mine operators, be they my own agency people."

Less than a month later, an MSHA employee made a key discovery that dramatically increased the amount of asbestos discovered during air testing. The agency's staff had been frustrated for a long time by inconsistencies between what they heard anecdotally and what the air tests were showing. They knew miners were getting sick, but their tests did not demonstrate why. Chris Findlay, an industrial hygienist and analyst in MSHA's headquarters, kept going over the database of test results and all he saw was a stream of "non-detects" — no asbestos. Something, he thought, was not right here.

Before coming to MSHA, Findlay had worked with the Defense Department. He finally realized that the tests he'd done at Defense had been conducted at a higher airflow rate. The MSHA inspectors were following the procedures in an outdated handbook. "It didn't make sense," he said. "The more samples you collect, the more asbestos you'll get for analysis." An e-mail to all MSHA offices that March suggested that the airflow in the vacuum pumps be doubled and a new, more effective collection filter be used.

"There is no doubt," McAteer said, "that if we were able to apply these new techniques earlier we would, without question, have reduced exposure that led to illnesses, and we would have done a better job of protecting the workers. The reality is that we didn't. I can't fix that, but what I can fix now will be fixed."

"This is not Libby, where it's way after the fact," Monforton said. "These are real bodies, real miners, still working today at mines contaminated with asbestos in the talc, vermiculite and taconite. We won't ignore what's happening."

"ARE YOU THE GUYS that did the stories on the vermiculite mine in Montana?"

"Yeah, that's us," Schneider told the unfamiliar voice on the phone.

"Well, why the hell aren't you looking at the other vermiculite mines?" the caller suddenly charged. "Don't you care about workers that are being exposed today?"

He said he worked at a place called Virginia Vermiculite, mining "the same damn stuff they mined in Montana." He said he was worried that he was sick and so were some of the "old guys" who had dug the ore from the strip mine only two hours south of the White House.

"How do you know there's asbestos in the ore?" Schneider asked.

"Because some of these old guys can't breathe and one of the professors from the university saw it in the microscope," he blurted. "And all the samples that W.R. Grace took showed asbestos right here and that's why they sold the place."

He wouldn't give Schneider his name and wouldn't or couldn't share the name of the professor, but he eagerly offered to mail some samples of the ore to the newspaper. "All you want. Lots of it." The miner did not hide his frustration and anger when Schneider told him not to send the ore, "because we really have no way of documenting where it came from."

"We'll have to get our own samples if we chase the story," Schneider tried to explain.

"What are we supposed to do in the meantime while you're making up your mind?"

Schneider's suggestion that he call the Virginia Health Department or MSHA was answered with scorn. "They won't do anything. They don't care, either." And the phone slammed down.

Back in McCumber's office, the discussion of the call was frustrating for both reporter and editor.

"We can't be the asbestos cops for the whole country."

"But if we don't do it, who will?"

"You've got a point."

Nevertheless, Schneider admitted that they had too much to be followed up on from Libby and its expansion plants to put a new story on the front burner. They agreed to take a look at the mine near Louisa, Virginia, when time permitted.

A month later, Schneider was in Washington again, chasing documents and a dozen interviews. But a quarter-inch of snow had immobilized the nation's capital and government offices were closed. With time to kill, Schneider drove the 97 miles down to Louisa.

He stopped at a convenience store for plastic bags and spoons for sampling and then at the Louisa Police Department for directions to the mine.[8] The desk officer drew a quick map and then mentioned, as an afterthought, that the mine shipped its ore from a rail siding a couple of blocks away. "If you want more information, go find a lawyer named Rae Ely. She's always raising hell about that mine," the officer volunteered.

No rail cars waited at the siding, but vermiculite ore, now a familiar sight to Schneider, was strewn on the tracks, sparkling in the bright winter sun. On a concrete pad, in a short-walled bunker, was a three-foot pile of the ore. Schneider scooped a few spoonfuls into the bags, sealed and labeled them and headed off to the mine. There, he cursed the NO TRESPASSING signs and turned around. The *Post-Intelligencer's* lawyer, Steve Smith, was fond of saying, "Trespass and we can't do a damn thing to protect you."

Back at the convenience store, he found coffee to neutralize the nine-degree wind-chill and a phone book to get a number for the lawyer the cop had mentioned. In front of the store was a large dump truck. Its whitish-gray load was uncovered. It looked like the same ore from the siding. Schneider, obviously looking guilty, quickly went back outside and brushed some of the material from the truck's tailgate into a bag, stuffed it into his pocket and returned to the store.

Pouring more coffee, he asked the only other guy in the store, "What's in the truck?"

"Vermiculite. Why do you care?" the driver asked with about as much warmth as the outside air.

"Just wondering," Schneider tap-danced.

"Go wonder someplace else," the driver snarled.

Rae Ely's law office was just a couple of blocks away in a small house on Main Street. "Sure. Come on in," she said. "I don't know what I can do for you, though." Schneider looked around her cluttered office. The walls were covered with maps of Louisa, the county and Historic Green Springs. There were aerial photographs of Virginia Vermiculite and Grace's mines in Enoree, South Carolina. The tops of shelves, filing cabinets and most other flat surfaces, including her desk, were covered with bags and jars of vermiculite ore and the expanded stuff. It reminded Schneider of his office in Seattle. Amid the organized muddle Schneider spotted another 8"- by-10" photograph. It was of the mine at Libby.

"Oh, I think we have a lot to talk about. Let's start with this," Schneider said, pointing to the photograph of Zonolite Mountain. Ely paused for a moment, looked at the Montana photo, then at Schneider. She shrugged and said: "I took it about twenty-six years ago when we were fighting to keep W.R. Grace from opening a vermiculite mine here. Some government guy told me that the miners were getting sick from asbestos in the vermiculite, and I wanted to see what it looked like." Schneider blurted out a streak of questions. "Who was the guy? What agency did he work for? What else did he tell you?"

"Shut up for a minute," Ely said, bringing their relationship to a more comfortable level. "Hell, I don't remember. It's been decades. Let me see what I can find." She pawed through file drawers crammed with paper. Schneider spotted a thick folder in the back of one of the drawers labeled NEWS STORIES. Reaching around her, he pulled it out. It was filled with yellowed clippings of articles from *The New York Times, The Washington Post,* the Richmond newspapers and the Associated Press, stories about her fight in the '70s to keep the Commonwealth of Virginia from building a prison on 200 acres abutting the Historic Green Springs district. Other pieces of paper, frail with age, told of Ely's battle to prevent Grace from opening its mine.

More clippings from society pages and magazines — including *Penthouse* — showed photos of Rae at age 34, with her 80-year-old husband, retired Army Col. Hiram B. Ely, standing in front of their Tuscan-style mansion. The stories told of how Ely and her band of volunteers overwhelmed Grace, getting the company not only to agree not to mine the Louisa vermiculite, but to donate the land to the Department of the Interior as a protected easement around the historic district.

"Yep," Schneider said, "we've got a lot to talk about."

A week later, back in Seattle, McCumber and Schneider looked at the results from the analysis of the samples collected in Louisa. They weren't hard to interpret: All four samples showed tremolite asbestos above the 1-percent level, meaning that under EPA standards the ore was a hazardous material. They looked at each other and nodded. Now there was no question: Louisa was a story that had to be written.

IT IS SUCH AN UNLIKELY STRUGGLE: a posse of Southern widows and maiden ladies waving history and epidemiology like twin Colt .44s, facing down a former EPA bureaucrat who just wants to mine his vermiculite, undeterred by decades of evidence that it is heavily contaminated with tremolite.

The Ladies of Green Springs are descended from families who carved farms out of hickory and oak forest near Louisa in the 18th and 19th centuries.[9] In 1720, Col. Richard Morris built a mineral spa near the center of the five-by-six-mile oval that is Green Springs. Thomas Jefferson touted the spa's "medicinal virtue," as he took his own medicine at Boswell's Tavern with the likes of Lafayette and Patrick Henry.

Boswell's is still serving liquor, and for the most part, Green Springs has been virtually untouched since the Civil War, or, as it was known in these parts, the War of Northern Aggression.[10] Almost every knoll and high spot in the rolling valley between Charlottesville and Richmond has a classical home. The houses range from modest colonial farmhouses to palatial ante-bellum plantation homes. Add in icehouses, smokehouses, kitchens, barns and slave quarters, and the number of historic structures exceeds 250. "The early American architecture is preserved in harmony with the landscape, and the proximity of each to the next make up a whole property much more significant than any individual part," the Interior Department declared in deciding to bestow a historical designation on the entire area.

But anywhere from five to 90 feet below the same coveted ground are huge veins of commercial-grade vermiculite, including more than 70 pockets between 300 and 500 feet wide. To Robert Sansom, owner of Virginia Vermiculite Limited, it was a geological treasure chest worth more than $150 million, and he was determined to dig it out, mill it and sell it. He was a formidable adversary in a place where political connections are as much of the history as the fine old piles of brick on the hillsides. Sansom worked for Richard Nixon in the West Wing, and for Henry Kissinger at the National Security Council. And from June 1972 to February 1974, he was an EPA assistant administrator.

Rae Ely and the Ladies of Green Springs could care less about his bureaucratic bona fides. They just want him to stop tearing up their corner of the world. Most of these women still run a few dozen head of cattle, or produce enough hay, wheat and corn to pay the property taxes. And they refuse to yield. Ely has led the fight for three decades.

In the late 1960s, W.R. Grace & Co. began seriously evaluating the area for its potential as a source of vermiculite. By that time, the company already knew that the Libby operation, which they had bought just a few years before, was seriously contaminated with asbestos. So Grace was eager to find a better supply of vermiculite, the miracle mineral that had so many industrial uses.

By 1972, the company had drilled nearly 3,000 test holes in the fertile valley.[11] "There is no other known vermiculite deposit, or series of deposits, in this country or worldwide, that has anywhere near the potential ... of the Green Springs Area," wrote Grace evaluator Lewis Hash to the head of Grace's Zonolite vermiculite division. So Grace bought the mining rights to more than 1,400 acres around Green Springs. But by the next year, the company had analyzed even more samples and knew the other half of the story: The ore deposit was contaminated with tremolite, just like Libby.

In May 1974, while Grace officials debated what to do with their paradoxical holding, the Interior Department designated the neighborhood as a national historic landmark. The ruling emboldened the Ladies of Green Springs in their effort to stymie Grace. Several of the Ladies bought a few shares of Grace stock, enough to get into the stockholders' meeting, where they confronted company president J. Peter Grace with their pleas not to mine the historic site. "We got polite, patronizing smiles and not much more," recalled Ely.

But in 1976, then Interior Secretary Thomas Kleppe wrote to Grace, saying the company's plans for mining Green Springs were "incompatible with the cultural and scenic values of the area," and urging the company to donate the land as a buffer around the historic site.[12] The company did not respond.

Rae and her band of belles became experts on the health effects of asbestos, and they kept relentless pressure on Grace. But even as they laid siege to the multinational giant, another enemy attacked. Robert Sansom quietly bought mining rights from a family within the historic district. In the late '70s, he began mining operations, and he quickly followed that with a courtroom challenge to the historic designation itself. In 1980, a federal judge ruled that the Interior Department was out of line in granting the protective status, and that the agency's regulations did not give it authority to "save" Green Springs or any other historic site.

The women raced 100 miles north and invaded the Capitol, buttonholing any member of Congress they could find in the marble corridors. In record time, and by unanimous vote, Congress added a few words to the Interior Department's statutes that protected not only Green Springs but also hundreds of other sites that the agency had previously declared to have historical importance.

"Mrs. Ely is a tenacious woman," Sansom told Schneider, barely concealing his anger. "She's riled up the Ladies of Green Springs for years over this. She just never stops."

In 1991, Sansom offered to buy Grace's holdings in Louisa County. The offer was rejected. A year later, without mining a single bag of vermiculite, Grace donated the land to Historic Green Springs Incorporated in return for a significant tax write-off and the promise that it would never be mined. The company — citing a judge's gag order — still declines to say whether the presence of asbestos in the ore had anything to do with its decision.

But by that time, Sansom had obtained mining rights to two more historic farms and the Virginia Vermiculite operation was going around the clock. Sixteen-ton trucks lumbered along State Route 22 to the rail siding in Louisa, where the ore was shipped around the country, just as it was from Libby.

Sansom pushed hard for the right to expand his mine. Heated debates ensued throughout the county.[13] The danger of asbestos in the ore — which Sansom vehemently denied — became a frequent topic, and concern over it brought new supporters to the Ladies' cause. One of those was Steve Lucas. He and his family live a stone's throw from the mine. The buffer of Eastern white pine that Sansom planted to mask the mining operation from the view of passing motorists does little to halt the noise and dust that flow over Lucas's 500-acre farm.

"When the wind is blowing from the mine, our place is covered in this fine dust," he said, running his finger through the tan powder covering a windowsill on his front porch as his five-year-old daughter Hannah gazed quizzically out the window. "I worry about letting my daughter play outside. I worry about the livestock that graze on grass covered with this. How much asbestos is in this stuff? How much harm is it doing?"

Lucas is nicknamed the "Cowboy Poet" for the poems he posts on the Internet, and as he pulled a weathered Stetson low on his brow and folded his lanky six-foot-plus frame over his mechanical steed – an all-terrain vehicle — he looked the part. He headed over the hill to see what Virginia Vermiculite was up to. He stopped just over the crest, looked down and shook his head. Below, a yellow crane and earthmovers clattered across the soggy ground. The lip of a 70-foot-deep pit was just 50 feet from the back porch of the old house on the neighboring property.

"So much for historic preservation," Lucas said.

Sansom stunned local residents — and legal scholars — in 1995 when he sued both Grace and the Historic Green Springs Inc. in federal court, seeking $21 million in damages and the land Grace gave away.[14] He alleged that the giveaway was a violation of the Sherman Antitrust Act. Sansom maintained that Grace and the Ladies of Green Springs conspired to prevent him from acquiring the vermiculite-rich land, thus "depriving America's consumers of the right to this valuable mineral," he told the *Post-Intelligencer*. "Somebody violated a law, and we should have our day in court. And the consumer has an interest in this because they like to plant tomato seedlings and poinsettias and live in fireproof buildings and use cattle from [rail] cars that are covered with blankets of vermiculite," Sansom said.

The preservationists, having used up much of their savings, turned to bake sales and quilting bees and roasting 200-pound hogs. They set aside their privacy and allowed gawking strangers — even Yankees — into their museum-like homes to hustle money for the growing legal bills. For five years of litigation, Grace stood shoulder to shoulder with the Ladies of Green Springs. But a month before the trial's end, in October 1991, Grace settled all claims with Sansom, and is believed to have paid him almost $2 million.

The one remaining accusation, "conspiracy to monopolize," was left for Green Springs' widows and spinsters to defend. Seattle lawyer Charles Montange provided hundreds of hours of free legal work, and finally, in 2001, the case was decided in Green Springs' favor.

Sansom appealed, but in November 2002, he lost on appeal as well.

He took it to the U.S. Supreme Court.

On April 28, 2003, the high court refused to hear the last-gasp appeal of Virginia Vermiculite.

"We have thought it was 'over' in the past, only to have the fools continue to press on in the face of all odds. So, today, nearly eight and a half years after it first began, it is truly *OVER,*" Ely e-mailed to her supporters.

"The cost of all of this has been sickening, but their intention to crush us failed. We are weary and broke, but still standing."

ALTHOUGH THE LADIES prevented him from getting the Grace land, Sansom has mined steadily for more than 20 years. During that time, MSHA had routinely sent out a team of inspectors every six months.

Never had its inspectors reported finding any asbestos, even though the agency had received reports of its presence.

"We had received complaints that workers were ordered to conceal it, cover it up, so our inspectors couldn't find it," Monforton told Schneider. "But all we had were suspicions."

But after the *Post-Intelligencer* stories energized the agency, things changed. The miner who had called the *Post-Intelligencer* did indeed follow up by calling MSHA, and he found that the agency did care, after all.

Monforton took the call one afternoon in February or March. The caller told her he was worried about the safety at the mine, that he and the other miners were working in large veins of what he thought was asbestos — like up at Libby. But management kept telling them not to worry about it. He was afraid to come to Monforton's office, and he asked if she would meet him in Louisa.

A couple of weeks later, early on a Sunday morning, she met him at a gas station and followed him to a house. They were both nervous — the miner because he knew if the mine found out he was meeting with MSHA it would be his job "and maybe worse"; and Monforton because clandestine meetings with miners really weren't in her job description.

Sitting at the kitchen table, they drank coffee and talked. He hadn't been to a doctor, he told Monforton. She got the impression that in his mind, he figured he'd been exposed and had worked there long enough to get sick. And he told her about other workers he thought were sick. He said he knew there was asbestos in the mine but wasn't sure it was dangerous. "I just need to know," he told her. "Maybe it's okay, like the managers tell us, but maybe it's like that vermiculite mine in Montana and we're all going to die."

They went out to his car and the miner handed her four containers of vermiculite ore. Then he drew her a map of the mine on a piece of yellow legal paper and talked about where the samples in the bags and jars had been collected. Monforton promised to have the samples analyzed, but told him they could not provide the basis for any enforcement action, because the agency did not collect them.

She took them back and showed them to Davitt McAteer. They didn't really know what they were looking at, so they sent the samples to the OSHA lab. A few weeks later, Monforton was in Charlottesville — a stone's throw from Louisa — on vacation. That didn't stop her cell phone from going off.

"My contact at the lab called and she had the results back. When she started to tell me the percentages, my hands were shaking. I just couldn't believe it. All along, I was thinking that this was just some hysterical worker. Obviously, he wasn't."

From her hotel, she called McAteer. "You will never believe this," she told her boss. "That stuff that that worker gave me? It's like ninety-nine percent tremolite."

McAteer told her to hold on and he got Ernie Kestrel, the head of metal and non-metal mining, his deputy and a couple of other people on the speakerphone. He said, "Celeste, just tell them. You know, you don't have to say how you got these samples or anything, but say what it is."

She did. Then she asked, "What are we going to do? You know we have to go out to that mine."

They strategized a little, discussed whom they would send and when they would go. And in the ensuing weeks, they began to mobilize for an inspection that would change the very nature of the agency.

Then Monforton met with the miner one more time.

"He brought a more detailed map that showed the areas where the asbestos was, and how they usually concealed it from the inspectors, and the area of the mine where the digging was being done. Places they didn't want MSHA to go," she recalled. "I almost filled up a notebook with details."

Finally, they were ready. MSHA's special team of industrial hygienists gathered in a motel near Louisa with Monforton.[15] First, Rocky McKinney from the coal side of MSHA. "He's from West Virginia and has dealt for years with coal operators and knows every trick in the book. And in his mind, coal operators are no different than Virginia Vermiculite operators.

They all are the same," Monforton said. She showed him the map the miner had drawn, and gave him the other details. Two others — Galen Trabant from Denver and Bill Pomeroy from Duluth — soon joined them.

It was 6:30 P.M. when they arrived at the mine — after the day shift and, they expected, after the management had left. They found the worker in charge of the night shift, showed their IDs and then went to work. It wasn't long before the worker called manager Ned Gumble and said, "MSHA's here."

By the time Gumble arrived, the three inspectors had spread out across the mine, gathering samples like mad. It was July, and the sun set late. When Gumble came, he was furious and demanded to talk to the inspectors. They talked, and then informed him they'd be back the next day. Which they were, at first light.

Gumble was very distressed that he couldn't control where the guys were going and what samples they were taking, the miner told Monforton. She thought, *This is a team of sharp people who know how to do their jobs and won't put up with intimidation, and they're doing the kind of inspection we should always do. But we don't.*

The team collected 12 samples of ore and rock from all over the mine and mill, even scooping a jar of ore from the back of a truck headed for a customer. Also, the inspectors took 30 samples of the air the miners were breathing and 10 samples of air in other areas of the mine pit and processing operation.

In early October, the agency announced the results. Asbestos was found in all 30 of the miners' air samples. Four samples contained asbestos in quantities higher than the 0.1 fiber per cubic centimeter of air deemed legal by OSHA, but all were lower than the 2 fibers per cc that MSHA regulations permit. All 12 bulk samples showed the presence of tremolite or actinolite. Seven of them showed asbestos at extremely high levels, several between 95 and 99 percent asbestos.

MSHA cited the Louisa mine for three violations of federal health and safety regulations: failure to notify workers of the risk; failure to take action to prevent worker exposure; and failure to provide protective equipment, clothing and warning signs. The agency further enraged Sansom by sending two staffers to Louisa to brief the company's workers on the findings before announcing them publicly. The agency also took the unusual step of offering free X-rays and lung-function tests to the company's two dozen workers and as many former workers as they could find.

"If the miners want it, we will bring in a mobile testing unit. We'll do it at the mine or in the Wal-Mart parking lot, any place they're comfortable. This is really all we can do for them," Monforton said. "We will give these poor guys everything we can. They have to make the decision of whether they want to work there or not. It's their lives we're dealing with.

"I wouldn't want anyone I loved working there with asbestos at that level without a lot of protective equipment," Monforton added. "The potential for exposure goes well beyond the mine. We are concerned about exposure to the environment, to those people who have been using waste rock from the mine for years around their homes and businesses, and to workers in companies elsewhere in the country who are exposed ... in products they're making and selling."

The agency notified EPA, OSHA and the Consumer Product Safety Commission about the amount of asbestos found at the mine. "Once the ore gets off mine property, we no longer have jurisdiction over it," McAteer said. Industry analysts estimated that Virginia Vermiculite was selling about 100,000 tons of the ore a year. Sansom's customers included makers of construction products such as drywall, plaster and fireproofing, and horticultural companies that use vermiculite in planting operations and soil enhancers.

"The tragic lesson that we learned from the vermiculite miners in Libby is all the proof that anyone should need that exposure to asbestos, if not controlled, will result in asbestosis, mesothelioma and lung cancers," Monforton said. "Those who contract those diseases will die. If that isn't reason to halt these exposures, then nothing is."

The agency's findings came after years of Sansom's declarations that his vermiculite was asbestos-free. Those claims had been echoed by the Vermiculite Association, which had stoutly maintained that all vermiculite ore, except for that produced in Libby, was free of asbestos.

As administrations change, so do the federal agencies, and so does enforcement of asbestos regulations. Over the past six decades, it's been proven time and time again. Now, under the younger President Bush, Monforton and McAteer are long gone, and so is their shame over what MSHA allowed to happen, in Libby and elsewhere.

What happened to their efforts to lower the exposure limits? What happened to all the test results after they changed the testing procedure, the ones that showed asbestos exposures over the agency's limits? The new head of MSHA, Assistant Secretary of Labor Dave Lauriski, spent 30 years in the coal-mining industry before coming to government. He has refused repeated requests for interviews on the agency's current approach to the asbestos issue.

Monforton is now at George Washington University, completing a graduate program in public health and working on a research project involving the abuse of science in corporate action and government regulations. She remains proud of what MSHA accomplished while she was there.

"We dropped the ball at Libby and hundreds, perhaps a lot more, are going to die because of it. I just felt that history couldn't be allowed to repeat itself," she said. "You see so many examples, whether it is environmental or occupational, where people were harmed and there was actually information that people knew, but no action taken."

On July 31, 2001, at the behest of U.S. senators Patty Murray and Hillary Rodham Clinton, the Senate Committee on Health, Education, Labor and Pensions held a hearing on workplace safety and asbestos safety and workplace contamination. A former Louisa miner, David Pinter, testified.[16] He was a heavy-equipment operator and mechanic who worked at the mine for 22 years. "Every day I worked in clouds of dust.... never was I given any protective clothing or respiration equipment," he told the senators.

He talked about the day the MSHA inspectors came to the plant. He remembered hearing them say, "This looks more like an asbestos mine than a vermiculite mine." He said that when MSHA returned with the results, they told the miners they needed protection as well as shower facilities. "They also made management put red flags and orange cones to mark the dozens of veins of asbestos which crisscross the property."

He said no respirators or protective clothes were ever issued to the miners.

"On Inauguration Day, January 20, 2001, the bosses at the plant were joyful and ordered all the red flags and orange cones removed ... and the workers were told to excavate through the asbestos as they always had." He said he heard Ned Gumble say, "We don't have to worry about MSHA anymore. From now on they'll be behind us every step of the way. They won't cause us any more trouble."

Pinter concluded by testifying, "Everyone talks about what a tragedy Libby, Montana, was and how it can never happen again. Well, it is happening again right now. It is happening under your noses just two hours from where you are sitting. It is probably too late for many of us, but you need to shut the mine down and require the company to thoroughly decontaminate the mine and mill site. You also need to require the company to disclose every location where they spread their waste rock and to clean up those sites, too."

It takes months to decontaminate a onetime nursery and vermiculite screening plant downhill from the mine. (Andrew Schneider)

IT HAD BEEN TWO MONTHS since three EPA officials busted their own agency—turned it in to its own inspector general.[1] Now, on August 14, 2000, five federal inspectors arrived in Libby, looking not for asbestos but for something even harder to grasp — why the EPA failed for decades to protect miners and their families from the deadly fibers.

Peronard was surprised. He knew how unusual such a response was. Go to the field? Actually talk to the people harmed? That's a hell of a sign that someone is serious, he thought.

Every federal agency has an inspector general, appointed by the president and confirmed by Congress, to serve as a watchdog. Their investigations are normally bloodless — conducted by phone or letter or by reviewing mountains of paper. But there they were, the inspectors — or auditors, as they prefer to be called — in Libby, sitting face-to-face with victims of the actions of Grace and the inaction of their own agency, which had admitted that it knew for decades about the deadly hazard spewing from the mine and from scores of processing plants throughout the country.

For three days, they took notes in living rooms, motels, coffee shops, schoolrooms — anywhere they could get people to tell them stories. Twenty-two of the men and women who came to give information to the inspectors at one meeting had parents, other relatives or friends who had died from asbestos-related disease. Twenty-one of the people sitting in the red chairs of the brightly colored school auditorium were themselves dying because of exposure to the lethal fibers. Once-strong men sat next to their women — wives and mothers sickened by the asbestos the men brought home. All of them made it clear that they were more concerned about what the EPA is doing about the problem today than about what happened 20 years ago.

Frances Tafer, the leader of the IG's team, told the group that their mission was to determine who in the EPA knew about the hazards, when they knew it and why nothing was done. "It's like putting together a huge puzzle and you may have some of the pieces we need," Tafer said, pleading for help. "Send us an anonymous box of documents, call our free hot line, invite us to your home. We need the right pieces to put this puzzle together so we can ensure it doesn't happen again."

She said she knew that in the '70s and '80s, EPA health experts were among the parade of federal investigators who dropped by this bucolic corner of northwest Montana to visit the world's largest vermiculite mine.

"Yeah. They came, saw and did nothing. And lots of people died because they did nothing, and a bunch more of us will be heading to the graveyard before our time because they did nothing," Les said in an angry whisper, the loudest volume he could manage with his decimated lungs. Norita nodded her head in agreement and held tightly to her husband's arm.

"On one hand we've got all these dead bodies, our relatives and friends. On the other, we've got all these covered-up government documents. What are the real answers to why the government let the people of Libby die?" Bob Dedrick asked. "We don't trust anyone anymore. Not doctors, lawyers or the government. We've just been hit, betrayed, too many times. We are fighting some very, very rich people with very powerful friends. All we have is us and the truth and a handful of EPA workers who care a lot," Dedrick said, and pointed to Peronard, Weis, Miller and the rest of the Libby team leaning against the wall in the back of the room.

The government auditors took copious notes and shook their heads occasionally at the comments they were hearing, even though they knew that most of the complaints were well beyond the scope of their inquiry.

"We don't have the authority or the ability to unravel everything that happened here," team member Eileen McMahon told the group. "We will give you our full efforts, but even though we report to Congress, we can't force any other agency to do anything."

"Can you protect the cleanup here and the people that look like they care enough to do it right from being cut off at their knees by EPA headquarters or the White House?" asked Gayla. "Can you keep them from killing your own investigation?"

Tafer looked uncomfortable and said she couldn't comment, but added, "If we don't finish the report, you'll know about it."

For white-collar, bureaucratic types, the auditors impressed many of the Libby victims with their efforts. During their four days they worked dawn to dark, and the sun sets late in Libby in the summertime. They got out of their pin-striped suits and into durable pants, sneakers and boots as they toured some of the asbestos-contaminated sites where Grace processed and shipped the ore.

"This is what it's all about. This is vermiculite," Jim Stout said, holding up a piece of ore for the inspector general's team to see and photograph.[2] Stout worked for the URS Corporation, which managed the cleanup project for Grace at the old expansion plant near the center of town. He was not at all bashful about telling the auditors from Washington that he and EPA didn't come close to agreeing on how much asbestos had to be removed from the site for it to be considered decontaminated.

"We only find a trace of asbestos and EPA is all over us saying we have to remove it. Hell, it's only a trace. Why go to all that effort for a trace? Kids go to school all day in buildings that have traces of asbestos and that's no big deal," Stout snarled. The auditors just nodded.

Les, who had tagged along with the visitors, watched the cleanup technicians Stout was managing go in and out of the old expanding plant in full protective equipment — white Tyvek head-to-toe coveralls and respirators that covered their faces.

"As I recall," Les told Stout, "I worked in that plant for more than a year and the company never gave me a moon suit to wear."

They walked past the large, open-sided building that Grace used to store huge piles of Zonolite waiting to be bagged and shipped. It was where most of the kids in town climbed and played in piles of the ore. It's also where many apparently sucked in the tremolite asbestos fibers that are killing them today.

When an auditor asked about the tremolite, Stout amazed them with his answer. At first they were sure he was joking, but he wasn't.

"We don't deal with tremolite in the United States. The only place you find it is here in Libby. We're really only worried about three kinds of asbestos — chrysotile, crocidolite and amosite. The rest don't matter much."

The auditors, who had studied the federal regulations governing asbestos before hopping on a plane, looked mystified. A couple of supervisors from Stout's cleanup company were suddenly examining the clouds, and Due Nguyen, the EPA guide for the tour, quietly rolled his eyes and said nothing.

All government agencies list six types of asbestos as cancer-causing and thus regulated. They include the three that Stout mentioned, but also anthophyllite, tremolite and actinolite. The latter two contaminate the Libby vermiculite. "Tremolite and actinolite are not really a big deal. They're not used much, and I never really heard about that anthophyllite," Grace's project manager added as the auditors edged closer to their cars.

"See? See what I mean? Grace is still denying that there's a problem," Les told one of the auditors standing near the contaminated building. Stout turned red in the face, and as he walked away from the crowd, he said that although he was sorry Skramstad was sick, "he's a hell of a troublemaker."

That night, another group of residents told their stories at the school auditorium. Clinton Maynard, whose father and grandfather worked at the mine and died from asbestos, got in the last word of the evening. "What happened in Libby in the last century can still happen elsewhere in America today, and it shouldn't be allowed to," Maynard said.

"If industry can thwart government's responsibility to the workers, then we are not any safer than workers in a Third World country. Will what you people are trying to do make any difference? Can you get the other agencies to protect the workers and their families, or will thousands more die because government doesn't care?"

The auditors said they would do what they could, gathered the new documents they were handed and returned to their motel. They knew the sun rises early in Libby.

WITHIN A WEEK of EPA's auditors leaving Libby, a team from the IG's office of the Department of Labor showed up to start its own investigation of the early snafus there.

Patricia Dalton, acting inspector general for the Labor Department, said their investigation could force an examination of federal policies governing asbestos exposure that may have put at risk tens of thousands of workers who mine or handle vermiculite, talc and other contaminated minerals. Her team sought out 17 former miners and convinced them to share what they had seen and what they knew. Dalton's investigators would focus on the actions or lack of actions going back to the 1960s by OSHA and MSHA. Both are parts of the Labor Department.

"The job of the Department of Labor is to protect America's workers," Dalton said. "Our concerns are whether there are systemic problems in either OSHA, MSHA or both that may have taken root in the past. There can be no shortcuts tolerated when it comes to the health and safety of workers," she added.

Physicians and union officials who deal daily with workers dying from asbestos exposure urged the inspector general to get to the root of what they say is the most serious problem: how OSHA determined which asbestos fibers it would regulate.

"A decade ago, George Bush's OSHA made a decision to define these asbestos fibers as if they were almost harmless. We applaud the Department of Labor for starting an investigation of that decision and its consequences," said Mike Wright, health and safety director for the United Steel Workers of America.

The mine at Libby closed in 1990. But suspected asbestos contamination at other mines — vermiculite mines in Virginia and South Carolina, talc mines in New York and taconite mines in the Iron Range of Minnesota and Michigan — continued to concern health experts who had seen workers suffer with asbestosis and asbestos-related cancers.

OSHA says workers cannot be exposed to more than 0.1 asbestos fibers per cubic centimeter of air, a limit OSHA admits will still cause some cancers. But MSHA's regulations allow miners to be exposed to 20 times the limit set by OSHA. "This disparity just isn't sane," said Dr. Michael Harbut, the Detroit physician who has treated thousands of workers with asbestos-caused diseases. "The inspector general clearly faces a difficult task, but it is one of enormous importance. One that, over the years, could save the lives of millions of workers."

Peronard was glad that all the Washington bigwigs had come to town.[3] The rest of the government needed to know what happened here, and frankly, he hoped it might take some of the attention off the problems he was having with the cleanup.

It wasn't going nearly as fast as he had hoped.

He had to retest the dozens of homes and businesses that had been tested for asbestos during the first six months using the new analytical methods refined by USGS and Weis and Miller. A few homeowners were starting to grumble about the lack of visible progress and the retesting that had to be done. Some said they saw it as EPA reneging on its promises, just as they'd expected. This was a charge that Peronard would hear over and over, regardless of how well things were going.

"I do understand," he said. "But it sure is hard at times. In every emergency response, people always want us to come in, clean up everything overnight and get the hell out of town. That rarely happens anywhere, and with the amount of asbestos dumped on Libby, it sure isn't going to happen here."

People were taking their time asking EPA to test their homes. First 55, then another 81, then another 165 requests came in. Eventually they would do most of the 3,500 homes and buildings in Libby, then start to address the same problem in the little town of Troy, ten miles west.

By May, the tests of gardens, driveways, attics and homes were coming in "hot" and heavy, with hot being the operational word. But with the results came a puzzle. They were getting big hits of tremolite everywhere in the dust samples, but the air samples taken inside the homes were coming back clean. That could be great news — that the continuing danger to people living in Libby was lower than they might have expected. But Peronard didn't really believe that, and neither did Weis and Miller.

"With all the asbestos being detected in the dust collected from the same houses, we would have expected the levels in the air to be higher," Weis told Peronard. He and Miller argued that the air samples coming from stationary collection devices in the main living areas of the homes might not be reflecting what people were actually breathing. The hum of the air pumps was low, but irritating enough that most people left their homes while the air was being tested.

The trio agreed that the air had to be tested while people were in their homes, doing what they usually did, or they'd never learn how much asbestos they were breathing. It took a few days, but they were able to find some volunteers who agreed to wear the battery-operated air samplers while they lived their lives — watching TV, cooking, ironing, making the beds, playing with the kids.

The team thought it was too risky to have the volunteers do the second part of the test, wearing the pumps while being more active — like sweeping, vacuuming and dusting. They put the families into a motel and had contractors wearing protective clothing and respirators simulate the more active household chores.

Three days later, Miller, Peronard and Weis sat at a corner table in the Libby Café, half a block down Main Street from their storefront office. Purple smears on the large white china plates were all that remained of the featherweight huckleberry flapjacks. The café's creation tops Libby's very short list of culinary delights. But food was the last thing on the minds of the EPA trio this late-summer morning.

Larry, Moe and Curly, as Gayla lovingly calls them, passed around yesterday's batch of hate mail from headquarters. One challenged the new testing methods they were using, and another dumped on Peronard for being "too candid" in his public statements. They showed Schneider some fan mail, e-mails from people in headquarters and in other regions that urged them to "hang in," and "fight the good fight," and "don't let the bastards wear you down." But they told the reporter that if he named any of the authors of the "atta boy" notes, it would be a career-ender. "Or at least their lives would not be pleasant," Weis added.

Peronard and Weis's cell phones both began ringing. The latest tests of the air samples were in. In eight of the 11 samples taken from the pumps worn by the families, asbestos was found well above the level that OSHA said was safe for workers. Of the 17 samples from the filters attached to the contractors doing the heavy housework, asbestos was found in 16, and in seven the numbers of fibers were at dangerous levels.

"Well, finding asbestos is nothing to be happy about, but at least it shows we're learning enough about this tremolite to make some right decisions," Peronard said, and asked Pauline for more coffee, please.

The cleanup at the old screening facility was finally moving. Fences had been erected around the property at the bottom of Rainy Creek Road, between Highway 37 and the river. Dozens of workers in white Tyvek suits and masks crawled over the site that Grace had sold to the Parker family for a home and nursery. Mud covered much of the bright-yellow dozers and graders as the wranglers guiding the heavy equipment followed a carefully scripted plan that would remove tons of heavily contaminated soil while still contouring the land so it wouldn't erode into the Kootenai.

Meanwhile, Stout said the cleanup Grace had been ordered to do at the former expansion and export plants on the edge of town had been completed in great shape. But soon after the cleanup ended, Les Skramstad infuriated Stout, angered Grace and embarrassed EPA when he showed up at a visit to Libby from the new governor, Judy Martz, with a quart jar of vermiculite ore he said he gathered on the decontaminated site.

"Grace thinks he planted it there," Peronard said to Schneider. "But knowing Les, he probably found it right where he said he did. I think he sees his mission in life as keeping us on our toes, and most of the time I'm happy about that. Most of the time."

Grace's unsuccessful effort to keep EPA off the mine site, too, had slowed things down while EPA fought it out with the company, and eventually won. It was like pouring glue over EPA's cleanup efforts, and that's why it irked Peronard so much.

But Grace was playing games on all fronts. A week earlier, the Libby team's personal EPA lawyer, Matt Cohn, had come tearing through the door to Peronard's Denver office, shutting it far too hard, and yelled, "How in the hell could this have happened without me being told?"

"What?" said the team leader, now on his feet.

"This," Cohn said, as he waved a copy of a Grace June 2000 10-Q, a quarterly report that all major firms must submit to the Securities and Exchange Commission. In it, a corporation must report profits and losses, the salaries of its top people, pending lawsuits and a hundred other facts the government believes that stockholders should know. On page 24 of the official filing, Grace discussed a class-action lawsuit brought against the company on "behalf of all owners of real property situated within 12 miles from Libby …" for contamination and loss of property rights from the vermiculite mining. To which the worldwide conglomerate said, "Grace has no reason to believe that its former activities caused damage to the environment or property."[4]

It was the next sentence in the filing that had Cohn laughing with Peronard.

"Grace has agreed with the [EPA] to remediate or pay the cost to remediate two sites in Libby formerly used by Grace operations …"

"That is just crap. They're fighting us every step of the way on the cleanup," Peronard said. "How can they say this?

"I know Grace has decades of lying to its workers, to the communities their plants are in and to every government agency they encounter, but this is so blatant I can't believe they have the audacity to try it."

"Then I gather it's not true?" Cohn chided.

"Out, while you can still walk," Peronard joked.

Cohn again wrote to Grace's Lund saying that EPA knew nothing about the reported agreement and that if the lawyer had any proof to please send it to him quickly. Cohn also suggested that if the filing was in fact inaccurate, the SEC should be told "to assure that the public is provided with accurate information."

It was November before Lund wrote back stating that "no formal legal documents exist between EPA and Grace ..." and they would change the wording in their next SEC filing.

But the agency's relationship with the chemical company would become even more contentious. In the legal sparring that marked the relationship between the regulator and the corporation, Grace and EPA had requested hundreds of thousands of documents from each other. Grace had just delivered about 700 cardboard boxes to the offices of a contract law firm it used in Boulder, Colorado. The boxes were stacked on row after row of high steel shelves, and Peronard, Miller, Weis, Cohn and Kelcey Land had just begun the first of what would be weeks of examining the documents. But it ended soon after it began.

Weis was digging through three boxes of shipping invoices and bills. These particular documents were of vital interest to both EPA and Justice, which were already investigating where in the country Grace actually shipped billions of pounds of asbestos-tainted vermiculite ore.

"There's something on this paper," Weis said, shaking a fine, tan powder onto the table. All the documents in two of the boxes were covered with the powder.

Peronard, who was in another part of the large room, was convinced that Weis, Miller or Cohn was playing games, until he saw the dusty material.

"Don't touch it until we get the powder analyzed," the team leader said, ending the document search for the day.

The tests came back and showed the papers were covered with tremolite.

Corcoran, Grace's VP for handling the press, told the *Post-Intelligencer* that the company was "having our experts look at these tests that were done and the results. Until we know what this means, the boxes will be quarantined."[5]

On April 18, 2000, Cohn wrote to Lund and told him that tests of the dust-covered shipping papers showed they were contaminated with asbestos at "levels which may be of concern."[6] He urged the lawyer to tell his employees who also handled the documents about the potential danger.

Peronard wondered whether things could get any sillier. And the answer was yes.

His days were filled with complaints from locals who felt they were being cut out of the cleanup money that was being spent. "Everybody with a truck within a hundred miles of Libby is sure that they should be getting paid to haul the contaminated soil, but they don't like it when I tell them that to work for the government they must be bonded and have insurance," he said to Gayla and Les after a Thursday-night CAG meeting. "Most of them just got pissed and wouldn't even stay around long enough for us to tell them how to get bonded."

Peronard continued his rant: "Hell, there are rumors all over the place about how we hire our contractors. Last week, the Libby gossip network was overflowing with the fact that EPA was only hiring Spanish-speaking drivers. Spanish in Libby? Come on."

He, Miller and Weis couldn't just focus on Libby.[7] Responding to the tenacious prodding of Washington senator Patty Murray, headquarters had finally put out an order in June to its regional offices to inspect all former Grace or Zonolite expansion or vermiculite processing plants in the states for which they were responsible. And the Libby team was getting swamped with calls.

"Some were asking for technical help, which Chris and Aubrey offered gladly. Other callers — from people in our own agency — felt obligated to tell me how stupid they thought the order was, and why look for trouble? I guess they never took the time to read the EPA reports from the eighties that said millions of people lived dangerously close to these plants," Peronard said to one of his contractors.

"I wonder how good a job they'll do checking it out."

E-mail between the regions and headquarters showed that many regions had blown off the order to inspect the old plants. From what Schneider learned in interviews, some did no more than "windshield survey," looking over the cup of coffee or soft drink they were holding, and out the car's window. Not seeing a mountain of vermiculite or a pile of bodies, many inspections were reporting "nothing found."

But even some of the most diligent investigators sometimes missed the danger. It happened in Denver, the supposed Mecca of all information on vermiculite. An EPA team, including Peronard and Weis, checked out a former Grace plant. The warehouse-like building was now being used to process and package corn syrup, and everything inside was freshly painted, carefully cleaned. The ground all around the facility was paved and well maintained. After two hours at the site, the team reported "nothing found."

Unfortunately for Peronard and his gang, a Denver television station, Channel 9, trying to get a local angle on the Zonolite problem, did its own inspection of the site and found a 15'-by-10' rock swath at the end of the paving. The lab the station hired reported that it was asbestos-containing vermiculite and stone.

"Oh yeah," Peronard admitted somewhat sheepishly, "tailings and unex-foliated vermiculite. The test showed it was seventy percent Libby tremolite. We all checked the plant and its grounds carefully. What we didn't do was walk around the perimeter. That's where the stuff was."

PERONARD'S DAYS IN LIBBY were always long, as were his visits. He was spending more and more time in Montana.

A quick trip up to solve one crisis usually turned into a week, usually followed by another week, and sometimes another. On past assignments he had almost always been able to get home on weekends. Not always in Libby. When he did get home, Libby and its problems were always right there. In his face.

He called Tracy and the kids regularly, but often his calls to Tracy included a plea for her to solve some computer glitch, to somehow fix a file that he couldn't open on his laptop in Libby.[8]

"Tracy is somewhat of a computer whiz, and I ask her for help often enough that my bosses call her the free tech support."

At one point, her computer assistance gave her and her husband a few awkward moments. "I was having some problems manipulating some data files and I had e-mailed them home for Tracy to sort it out for me," Peronard recalled. "She fixed the problem and sent them back to me with a somewhat racy note attached."

"Okay, so it was highly suggestive," he added, rolling his eyes. "I guess I should have gotten home more often."

Because of the litigation with Grace, everyone in EPA who worked on the Libby project — except for the lawyers — had to turn copies of all their e-mail over to Grace as part of the discovery process. Peronard's private love note became public and also became part of the mountain of evidence that Grace collected to use in its suit against EPA.

The note was far too good for Grace to leave alone. Nine months later, as Peronard was being deposed by Grace's lawyers, he was asked about an EPA contractor that he had fired for sexual harassment. True, he admitted, we got him out of Libby quickly. At the next break, a Grace lawyer grabbed Justice Department lawyer Jim Freeman and EPA's Cohn. She dropped her voice to a conspiratorial whisper and said that Peronard had his own problems with improper sexual contact and using government computers to send inappropriate sexual material. She had an e-mail to prove it.

Freeman and Cohn looked at each other, forcing themselves not to laugh, and told the soon-to-be-disappointed Grace lawyer that the computer on which the steamy note had been written was someone's personal computer and not the government's. Peronard was not the author of the amorous words, but the recipient. And it was not written by a government employee, but rather by Mrs. Peronard.

Grace never mentioned the note again.

Lascivious note or not, there were times when Paul's long absences made it hard for Tracy to like her husband a lot, even though she loved him. The first year was particularly rough, she admits.

"This wasn't like any other cleanup project he'd done. When he'd come home on the weekends I could tell he was stressed out. The strain was enormous, everyone pulling him in different directions.

"He wasn't a lot of fun. He wouldn't talk about what was happening in Libby, but it ate away at him. He couldn't sleep at night and was a real grouch when he was up. This just wasn't the guy I married.

"I wondered what I was doing wrong. Finally he said it wasn't me, it was the job, and he didn't want to dump it all over me or the kids. Finally, he started talking about it. Sharing his frustrations about how slowly the work was progressing, the silly things that Grace was doing, the back stabbing from headquarters. Most of all, he was being eaten up by what was happening to the victims, people whose names he knew who were dying, and that was something he could do nothing about.

"When he started talking, things got a lot better. It was again fun having him home."

You'd think that Peronard, a man who loves the mountain West, would have taken some personal time to get closer to some of the natural beauty that encircles Libby. It just wasn't to be.

"The people here were great, and they would tell me they wanted me to know there was more about Libby than its asbestos problem. They were desperate to show me it was a good and beautiful place where they lived, to share their secret fishing hole, the best place to hunt, places just to unwind and see the beauty," he told Schneider as they walked through the bluffs, where the vermiculite was conveyed across the Kootenai.

"I knew it was beautiful, and it made me feel so guilty, so bad for what happened here. It always felt to me like I should be making things happen and happen faster. It wasn't my time and place to have fun."

IN MARCH 2001, seven months after their interviews in Libby, the inspectors general of EPA and Labor issued their reports.

Both said their agencies needed to do a better job of protecting both workers and the public from deadly exposure to asbestos. The Labor Department inspector general cited deficiencies in MSHA's efforts to protect miners of vermiculite, talc and iron ore from asbestos fibers.

EPA's inspector general, Nikki Tinsley, acknowledged that her agency had studied asbestos in Libby years ago, but that even the dire predictions made in those reports "did not result in regulations or other controls that might have protected the citizens of Libby."[9]

The IG concluded that the failure to take action in Libby was due to "ineffective communication," "fragmented authority and jurisdictions within EPA and between it and other agencies" and, of course, "other priorities."

Peronard, Weis and Miller had bet that EPA's failure to take action after it found the Libby problem would be blamed on communications problems.

"Did you really think the IG would come out and say the miners in Libby were allowed to die because of recommendations in the Grace Commission report?" Peronard asked Miller.

"If we only knew what went on behind the closed door of the commission, I bet we'd have all sorts of answers," the team physician replied.

Tinsley said that EPA still wasn't doing a "proper job" of detecting and preventing exposure at other operating facilities where the ore or rock was contaminated with the same type of asbestos. And, she added, the agency must address any other asbestos-contaminated mines and situations similar to Libby.

The shortcomings cited by the Labor Department inspector general were just about the same as those enumerated a year earlier by MSHA administrator Davitt McAteer and his special assistant Celeste Monforton.[10]

The assistant secretary of Labor and his colleague tried to implement a variety of what he called "very obvious changes" between the time the *Post-Intelligencer's* first stories on Libby were published and when McAteer and Monforton were replaced by the incoming George W. Bush administration.

They had begun advising miners of the hazards of asbestos, had dramatically modified techniques used to collect samples, and had undertaken extensive tests at a score of vermiculite, talc and taconite mines where asbestos is believed to be a contaminant. But both McAteer and Monforton knew that what they had begun would be little more than eyewash unless other crucial steps — changes in the safety regulations — were taken.

The inspector general said the mine agency should lower its limit for asbestos exposure for miners and bring it in line with OSHA's more protective limit for non-mining workers. That miners should be prevented from wearing asbestos-contaminated clothing home and thus potentially exposing their families. And the IG recommended that techniques used to analyze asbestos samples at OSHA's main laboratory be undated to use the more sensitive transmission electron microscopy (TEM) method.

When the report came out, MSHA had an acting assistant secretary who, through his spokeswoman, told Schneider that the changes could not be done without rule-making, which had to wait until MSHA had a new boss.[11] President Bush had named Dave Lauriski to the job. Lauriski had run a Utah-based mining consulting firm and was chairman of the Utah Board of Oil, Gas and Mining. Some in the agency doubted whether such a mining-industry stalwart would push for more stringent regulations.

But they knew that the biggest roadblocks to the improved safety regulations would come from the Bush White House. All new regulations — for any agency — must receive the blessing of the Office of Information and Regulatory Affairs under the White House's Office of Management and Budget. Bush appointed John Graham to run the powerful OIRA. Graham had run the Harvard Center for Risk Analysis and was strongly denounced during his confirmation because of what his critics called "strong and highly questionable" relationships with industries that funded his center.

One of the strongest challenges came from Public Citizen, a consumer-advocacy group in Washington. It said that Graham's center had been financed, in part, "by industry groups that fight enforcement of health safety and environmental safeguards." Public Citizen president Joan Claybrook added, "The president has nominated someone intent on eradicating basic government safeguards to head the very office charged with overseeing them."

Almost two years after the inspectors general's reports were issued, their recommendations have yet to be implemented. Of course, it takes time to get laws passed, but based on three years of actions by the Bush administration to overturn rules aimed at reducing pollution and regulating logging and mining, public-health advocates believe chances are slim for the passage of any new regulations that could place demands on industry or help to identify another Libby before the dying begins.

CHAPTER 20

Paper masks do little or nothing to protect from the enormous numbers of
asbestos fibers released when grinding brakes.
(Meryl Schenker, *Seattle Post-Intelligencer*)

THE AUTOMOBILE HAS BEEN AROUND for a little more than a hundred years — almost exactly as long as asbestos has been recognized as a hazard in the workplace.

For most of that time, asbestos has been a key component in auto parts — in clutches, exhaust manifolds, cylinder heads and gaskets. But by far the biggest automotive use – and the biggest hazard — is in brake shoes.

Just as the general public believes that asbestos is illegal in consumer products of all kinds, most mechanics believe that asbestos was banned in brakes long ago.[1] Schneider, McCumber and the *Post-Intelligencer's* medical writer Carol Smith initially assumed that was true, too. So did almost everyone Schneider and Smith interviewed during a four-month investigation — including some of the government officials charged with protecting workers. The reporters interviewed 143 repair-shop managers and owners, auto-parts salesmen and mechanics across the country, and 137 of them said there was nothing to worry about because the government had outlawed the use of asbestos years ago.

That is not the case.

Even though auto and parts manufacturers have known of the hazard for so many years, the fibers are still killing mechanics — and because the government is doing nothing to stop it, the number of deaths is expected to rise.

The truth is that millions of brakes on cars and trucks today — and millions more waiting on parts-shop shelves across the country — contain asbestos fibers that can kill mechanics. And even though federal health and safety officials acknowledge the risks, none of them have taken action in the past decade to warn the nation's 750,000 mechanics of the risks they face every day. The same lack of accountability Schneider found in Libby has left most regulators in the government unaware of the problem, or unwilling to admit it still exists. And for more than ten years, the government has stayed silent instead of warning mechanics that their jobs could be killing them.

Schneider and Smith did extensive testing of dust in garages nationwide; air monitoring of mechanics' environments during brake jobs; and a survey of brake products on the market.[2] They collected samples of dust from floors, work areas and tool bins in 31 brake-repair garages in Baltimore, Boston, Chicago, Denver, Richmond, Washington, D.C., and Seattle. The results were horrifying: Asbestos, mostly chrysotile, which has been used for decades in brakes, was detected in 21 of the locations. The amount of asbestos in the dust ranged from 2.26 to 63.8 percent.

EPA personnel entering any area where asbestos contamination of material present is 1 percent or higher are required to wear protective suits and full-face respirators. "If those measurements are valid, that's a very concentrated source of asbestos in the dust," said Aaron Sussell, an industrial hygienist with NIOSH in Cincinnati. "At those levels, it's not going to take a lot to put asbestos into the air at a hazardous level."

In several repair bays, Schneider duct-taped air monitors onto willing mechanics. Analysis of the air sampling found that mechanics were being exposed to large amounts of airborne fibers. Out of air samples taken during nine brake jobs, analysis revealed significant amounts of asbestos in six.

"Assuming the samples were properly collected, the results indicate some workers' exposure was about forty-three times higher than what is recommended," Chris Weis told Schneider. "At those exposure levels, the theoretical risks to those mechanics would be about one-point-five increased cancers for every ten workers." Weis said those estimates were based on exposures continuing for a whole career.

Bill Rice is 60, and his is one of those careers.[3] He figures that by now, it's too late to protect against asbestos. He's been doing brake work for more than half his life, managing or owning seven auto shops in the Puget Sound area. "I probably swallowed so much asbestos in the old days that I'm fireproof," he jokes, his laughter a bit forced.

Rice was one of the few mechanics who were willing to participate in the *Post-Intelligencer's* air monitoring program, and who were also willing to talk about their experiences. He refused the offer of a respirator, as did the other eight mechanics who agreed to be tested. With his bare hands, Rice wrestled a brake drum from the rear wheel of an elderly bronze Buick and dropped it to the floor. It clanged on the cement, and a cloud of black dust puffed up into the air. "There's a lot of dust in the drum," he said. "That's why I drop 'em — to get most of that stuff out."

Mechanics need a clean surface to remount the new brakes. "When I started doing this back in 'sixty-four, we used a whisk," he said, preparing to hose down the exposed brake surface with water. "I should be wearing a mask," he admitted with a nervous laugh. Dust, forced into the air by the stream of water, swirled next to his face. "But then, nobody does."

Rice handed the drum off to Larry Carpenter, 35, who turned it on a lathe to restore its shape. Carpenter wore a paper mask for the job, something he never used to do. But it offers little or no protection against the tiny fibers. He admitted that he's worried now about asbestos. "I've been doing this for eighteen years and I never thought about it," he said. "All the manufacturers, all the after-market parts suppliers, everybody who sells parts — that's all you heard: no asbestos."

Analysis of the old brakes Rice removed from the Buick showed 55 percent asbestos. The dust that covered his clothing and hands, and the floor and work area, contained more than 17 percent asbestos. The air monitoring showed dangerous levels of the cancer-causing dust in the air he was breathing. Rice was sobered by the test results. "This stuff can be killing you and you'd never know it until you were dead," he said.

IN THE 1970s AND '80s, the EPA, OSHA and the Public Health Service were all concerned about the asbestos-caused deaths of thousands of mechanics who worked on brakes and clutches.[4]

Blunt and graphic descriptions of the cancer dangers were produced and shipped to all public high schools and vocational-technical schools in the United States in 1986, and 1987, said Steven Johnson, EPA deputy assistant administrator for the Office of Prevention, Pesticides and Toxic Substances. The warnings stated: "Asbestos released into the air can linger long after a brake job is done and since asbestos can spread 75 feet from the work area, it can be breathed in by everyone inside a garage, including customers. Asbestos can be carried on work clothing, contaminating the family car and home. This can cause asbestos disease among family members."

But since then, government safety efforts have stagnated. Federal research programs to find ways to control asbestos exposure among auto workers have screeched to a halt. The government simply quit paying for them. Priorities have changed. Interviews with state and federal occupational health and safety agencies garnered the same comments: There is no indication that autoworkers are still being harmed by asbestos. But the same agencies reluctantly conceded that they hadn't checked. In the last decade, the entire federal government had not done even as much testing as the *Post-Intelligencer* did. Interviews with state and federal officials uncovered only a handful of inspections during the past five years specifically for asbestos exposure of brake workers. None was found in which air sampling was done.

"We don't know how many cars that pull into service stations to have their brakes relined have old asbestos linings. We don't know whether these workers are being exposed. We just don't know," said Peter Infante, OSHA's director of the Office of Standards Review in the Clinton administration.[5] "If you don't do air monitoring, you can't determine compliance."

EPA's Johnson said his agency "is concerned for anybody exposed to asbestos." But he admitted the agency had not gone out and done any testing.

In 23 states, OSHA has given the responsibility for worker safety to state governments. But the president of the association representing those state programs, Keith Goddard, said he was unaware of any of them who were looking at asbestos exposures in auto-repair shops.

The newspaper contacted a dozen of the states and found that all but one of them believed the problem of asbestos in brakes no longer existed. "We haven't targeted it because it's mostly gone," said Barry Jones, manager of enforcement for Oregon's OSHA. Other state enforcers said the same thing. Bob Andrews of North Carolina's OSHA program said, "Most brake pads don't have it anymore."

Schneider and Smith checked to see if that was true. At a Seattle outlet for a national parts chain, a salesclerk said, "None of the brakes we sell have asbestos. It was banned." The clerk invited Smith into the storeroom to see for herself. The first box of brakes the clerk handed her was plainly marked "contains asbestos." When she pointed that out, he told her the interview was over and asked her to leave.

The reporters bought sets of replacement brake pads for eight different models of cars and light trucks. Four were labeled as containing asbestos, two had no markings and two were marked "asbestos free."

Laboratory analysis found that three of the four labeled as containing asbestos contained chrysotile, and one of the unmarked sets contained large amounts of tremolite and actinolite asbestos. One of the "asbestos free" sets also contained tremolite, at lower levels. Evidently, the tremolite was present because many manufacturers use vermiculite as filler in brake pads. Ironically, some makers have used larger amounts as a substitute for chrysotile asbestos.

Hundreds of different styles of replacement brakes continue to be made with asbestos, and mechanics continue to play Russian roulette with every brake job they do. It is estimated that as many as 15 major companies manufacture brakes for new cars, as do between 25 and 50 "mom and pop" operations. Identifying those companies is difficult. In many cases, manufacturers' names and addresses do not appear on the packaging.

Schneider contacted six manufacturers.[6] Only one, the nation's largest producer of brakes and the maker of the well-known Raybestos brand, agreed to talk on the record. "There may be a perception that asbestos doesn't exist in brakes being sold today, but it does exist, and in significant numbers of products sold by various manufacturers, including us," said Alan Morrissey, vice president of product development for Brake Products Incorporated in McHenry, Illinois. "We would like to see asbestos in brake linings banned by the government. It will be safer for everyone. Nevertheless, by next year [he said this in 2000] we will no longer produce any asbestos-containing brakes. It's our decision."

However, in July 2003, Schneider checked three auto-parts outlets and was told that they were still selling brakes distributed by Raybestos that contained asbestos.

Brakes that the company sells under the Raybestos brand all carry warnings to avoid dust. "The reason we have warnings on all our boxes, whether they have asbestos or not, is that one never knows which fiber in the future will have the potential of having some untoward health problems," Morrissey said.

While the EPA's short-lived ban on asbestos products was in place, U.S. automotive manufacturers worked feverishly to develop substitute friction materials for brakes. And while the automakers were working on the problem, EPA devised a new strategy.

"The agency came up with the idea of enlisting the support of industry on a voluntary approach to agree to reduce exposure and prevent pollution by phasing out the use of asbestos in new vehicles," said the EPA's Johnson.

For months, the manufacturers and the EPA exchanged letters, faxes and phone calls. The largest U.S. manufacturers backed the effort, and others jumped aboard. A few makers who weren't asked, like Mercedes Benz, called EPA and signed on. By September 1993, every major manufacturer of cars, trucks, buses and motorcycles — 44 of them — was poised to formally agree to stop using asbestos after November of 1994.

But the Asbestos Information Association was not happy, and AIA chairman Bob Pigg did little to hide the group's displeasure.[7] "Since these asbestos brake parts can be produced, used and repaired safely, there is no reason for EPA to seek termination of their use now or in the future," Pigg said at the time, adding that "workplace controls would protect any worker who might come in contact with asbestos."

EPA officials told Pigg that they were concerned about the "high probability" that workers would not follow the protective rules, and that "consumer [do-it-yourselfer] exposures are likely to be more intense than occupational exposures." By November 1993, final documents were drawn up, with places for each of the 44 chief executives to sign. A press conference to unveil the agreement was scheduled.

But two days before the deadline, the initiative fell apart when the asbestos industry threatened to sue all parties to the agreement. "It was very, very close," Johnson said. "In the middle of it the AIA raised huge issues about this being antitrust. It's clear that they threatened the manufacturers and informed us that the asbestos industry saw this as an antitrust violation.

"All the manufacturers got very cold feet and said they were no longer interested in a voluntary approach."

The EPA scrubbed the effort, and the government's asbestos fighters took another loss, becoming even wearier and more discouraged. "They tried to do it as a rule, and that didn't work. They tried to do it voluntarily, and that didn't work. What else was left to do?" Johnson asked. "To say that it's frustrating is putting it very mildly."

Even in the comparatively liberal Clinton administration, efforts to battle asbestos were shot down by EPA's top management, agency workers said. EPA administrator Carol Browner, in one of her early speeches after taking over the agency, told staffers that asbestos was a problem of the past and to put it behind them, agency sources said. Browner would not comment. As for other agencies, Consumer Product Safety Commission spokesman Russ Rader said, "Our [defining] legislation prohibits us from regulating car parts." He said that such responsibility falls to the National Highway Traffic Safety Administration. But an NHTSA spokesman was unaware that asbestos was still being used in brakes. "That hasn't been allowed in brakes for some time," said spokesman Tim Hurd. "We don't test for asbestos in car brakes. It's not covered by any of our safety standards."

NHTSA does ask brake manufacturers to certify that their brakes meet certain performance requirements, such as stopping distances, but does not require brake manufacturers to list the materials used in their brakes. Even some government scientists and doctors who specialized in researching asbestos exposure to autoworkers admitted they didn't know asbestos brakes were still being sold.

"I'm surprised there was asbestos," said Dennis O'Brien, acting deputy director of NIOSH's division of applied research and technology, when told of the *Post-Intelligencer's* testing. "I thought the EPA had banned it ten years ago.... In addition, I thought the product liability would have forced it off the market."

"The government is not doing its job," said Richard Lemen, the former U.S. deputy surgeon general. "OSHA should have been testing. NIOSH should have been testing. And EPA should have been testing. For them to say there is not a problem based upon the fact that they've done no testing is irresponsible."

Even without the agreement, most new vehicles are now sold without asbestos brakes. Replacement parts, as well as all the asbestos brakes on the road, are the biggest problem now.

In a 1993 internal memo, EPA officials decried "scores of mom-and-pop operations rebuilding brakes with asbestos," and said, "There seems to be little accountability or control that we or any other agency can put on this segment of the automotive industry."[8] The memo continued, "We have no reason to believe that [the companies] will ever voluntarily stop using asbestos. The profits are too great. The controls are too loose." The memo warned that unless asbestos was forcibly removed from replacement brakes, "deaths from asbestos-related diseases 20 or 30 years down the road will be counted in the tens of thousands."

Bob Pigg, the president of the AIA trade group, insists that there is no danger in asbestos brakes. "The public's exposure to asbestos, if any, is just negligible. There is no public-health risk from using asbestos as a friction material, absolutely none at all," he said.

Dr. William Nicholson, professor emeritus at Mount Sinai School of Medicine in New York and a leading authority on the hazards of asbestos in brakes, agreed with the assessment in the EPA memo.

"It's an intolerable hazard," he said. He estimated that about 6 million mechanics have been exposed to asbestos since 1940, and that those exposures are now resulting in about 580 asbestos-related excess cancer deaths a year. Within ten years, the expected rate of mesothelioma deaths alone will be 200 per year from exposure to brake dust, he said.

Other experts acknowledge that for every case of mesothelioma that is diagnosed, there may be dozens of cases of asbestosis. The number of deaths caused by exposure to asbestos from brake products had been expected to peak sometime around 2012, but since asbestos is still in brakes being sold today, it could mean that the deaths will continue to climb. "This would push the peak back," Nicholson said. He paused, and added, "Cancer from asbestos is a horrible way to die."

PATRICK DENNIS KINE knew the dangers of asbestos all too well.[9]

"These kids working at gas stations have got to understand that there's still asbestos in brakes. They can't see it, feel it, smell or taste it, but it's going to kill them just like it's killing me." On August 25, 2000, twelve days after making that statement, Kine died, without doubt a victim of the more than 5,000 brake jobs he had performed over 20 years.

The 65-year-old Olympia, Washington, resident was a clown — a real one, red nose and all. His sense of humor endured through the nightmare of his illness. So did a deep caring for others that drove him to spend as much time as he could warning young mechanics of the danger they still face. After two decades of running his own auto-repair shop in Spokane, Kine spent 26 years teaching auto mechanics to hundreds of youths. He would warn his students about the danger of asbestos, but in March 1998, that theoretical danger became reality in his life.

It was a tightness in his chest, a hard time getting a full gulp of air, that sent him to the doctor. "First I thought I had a bad cold, or the flu, but I couldn't shake it," Kine recalled, but the X-rays showed he had something else. "The next morning I was flat on my back in the hospital and they were draining this yellow gunk out of my right lung. Lots of it," he said.

Ultrasounds and CT-scans revealed a huge mass between his right lung and his ribs. A biopsy, to get a sample of the mass, became major surgery.

"They started up front," Kine said, pointing to his chest, "and wound up going all the way around to the back and up over the shoulder blade. They were trying to get around the mass, but it was everywhere. It had grown through and all around my ribs."

He had mesothelioma.

"I knew what it was. It was in the handouts I gave to my students. It was what I warned them about — the ultimate harm that asbestos can do to you if you're sloppy working with brakes and clutches," he said. "And now I'm dying from it." The survival period for mesothelioma is usually eight to 12 months after diagnosis. Kine made it almost two years. He fought hard — the surgery, chemotherapy, and dozens of radiation treatments. They slowed the growth of the cancer, but they couldn't stop it.

"I'm not afraid of dying, but I'm terrified of leaving Donna alone," Kine said, fighting back tears as he thought about his wife of 42 years. His thoughts turned to the rest of his family — his daughter, two sons and four grandchildren. "I don't want to be a burden, but I really wanted to watch them live their lives," he said. But the clown couldn't stand to be sad for long, and he quickly changed the subject. "The worst thing about the chemotherapy is that it changes the way things that you've loved all your life taste," he said. "My favorite was shortbread animal crackers, but now they taste terrible. Coffee, which I used to almost inhale, tastes ghastly.

"Life is just funny."

He thought back to when he first learned that asbestos in brakes could kill. "I guess it was in eighty-three or eighty-four," he recalled. "We got these flyers from the EPA or OSHA or some government agency, telling how dangerous asbestos was and how much was contaminating the average guy doing a brake job. It just didn't make sense. I'd been messing with asbestos for years, and so had every other mechanic I knew. No one ever told us it could kill you."

As he debated how much attention to pay to the federal warnings, the National Automotive Education Association sent him another batch of pamphlets for his students. "They were serious. This asbestos was bad stuff. I started thinking back to all the old mechanics I knew, but I didn't know a lot of old mechanics. Most of them had died of breathing problems or lung cancer, and some of them had never smoked," he said.

Quickly, he added the asbestos dangers to his curriculum.

He remembers telling his students that medical researchers said a short, heavy exposure could result in mesothelioma developing 30 or 40 years later. "I don't think it sunk in," he said. "These kids were convinced they'd never die, especially not from something they couldn't see. But I kept hammering at them." He became an auto-repair evangelist, spreading the word of the dangerous fibers every time he stopped at a gas station or garage. "God, they were bullheaded. I remember when I was young. I thought nothing could harm me."

Long before he was diagnosed, he wondered about his own exposure. During the 20 years when he ran his own repair shop in Spokane, he was doing four or five major brake jobs a week. "There was asbestos dust all over the place," he said. "We'd sand the brakes, file them, drill them, grind them, and we and everything around us would be covered in that black grit. I'd blow my nose and it would be black. I'd wash my hair and the tub would be black."

He was angry at the car companies and the parts makers. They never warned anyone, he said. "Not a damn word. Not one. Never," he recalled. "Even in the early nineties the parts salesmen were saying it was much ado about nothing. How could they possibly keep something so deadly a secret?"

He said he also didn't understand why the government became so quiet. "I was just amazed. The government was so serious about getting the word out in the eighties. Then it just stopped, silence, like someone turned off the faucet," he said.

Kine didn't quit trying to spread the word. "I'd go to these gas stations and see the kids covered in dust. They would just shrug. They probably thought I was an old fool." But it became easier to make his point after his surgery. "I'd lift my shirt and show them the scars, and then they'd pay attention," he said.

Kine was proud when students came back to visit and introduced him to their wives and kids. But he wondered, looking at them, if they were going to get sick. "My students were not the ones that were going to MIT, but they were going to be damn good mechanics. But would the job kill them?"

As the tumor grew, Kine became weaker, but he kept fighting it off. He had one more thing he wanted to do. In June 2000, the National Model Railroad Association and the Circus Model Builders were having their annual convention in Boise, Idaho. Trains and circuses were two of Kine's loves. "They go together because in the old days all the circuses traveled by railroad," he said. He had an extensive model-train collection, and he wanted to show it off one more time. But he also wanted to be Red Nose again. For years, as Red Nose the Clown, he had entertained hundreds of children.

Kine went to Boise, oxygen bottle trundling behind him, and he was Red Nose one more time. "It was hard, but it was worth it," he said. The disease was taking its toll. On August 13, he went into the hospital for the last time. He was suffocating from the fluids in his lungs, and the cancerous mass had grown so large that it was blocking his intestines. That night, he talked about the importance of getting the word out, about asbestos and brakes.

"I hear the burst of an air hose and I cringe," Kine said. "Even with my eyes closed I can see the clouds of dust, and now, when it's too late, I can almost see the invisible fibers of asbestos. I know they're in there. I wish I could do more, but I'm going to die here. EPA, OSHA, someone has got to warn these kids that they're working with death. If the government doesn't do anything, no one will."

Two weeks later, he was dead. And three years later, the federal government still has not renewed its warnings about asbestos in brakes, and the prospect of actually removing the hazard is more remote than ever.

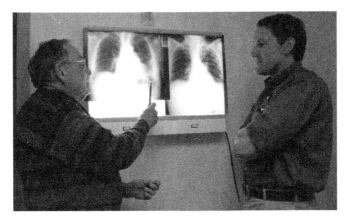

Drs. Alan Whitehouse and Brad Black toiled in the town's asbestos clinic to meet the heavy parade of new victims of the deadly fibers. (Andrew Schneider)

I F YOU WERE WITH the federal government and cared about how asbestos killed and sickened, Libby was the place to be in the late summer of 2000.

A parade of rental cars from the airports in Kalispell and Spokane shuttled in more than 65 physicians, toxicologists, researchers, regulators, investigators, and an assortment of paper shufflers from more than 16 federal and state agencies. They all packed the Super 8 and Venture motels so they could attend a three-day conference on "Asbestos and Public Health."

The speaker list was impressive and contained many of the government's top thinkers in the world of asbestos and health, and just enough bureaucrats to keep the laughter down.[1] Many had communicated with one another by phone or e-mail for years and found it humorous that they should finally meet at a VFW club not far from the Canadian border. Rebecca Hanmer, the acting regional administrator, opened the show and was followed quickly by a presentation to clarify "the roles and responsibilities of federal, state and local agencies." This was useful to the people of Libby, who now knew which agency to ask for what. For the government participants it was a subtle reminder to stay on their own turf.

Drs. Henry Falk, assistant administrator of ATSDR, Assistant Surgeon General Hugh Sloan and Pat Cohan, a registered nurse skilled in asbestos issues, talked about long-term health care. Weis, Dan Crane, who runs OSHA's lab in Salt Lake City, and Galen Trabant, one of MSHA's sharper mine inspectors, discussed how non-occupational exposure could be avoided. They did, in fact, acknowledge that it was probably too late for most of those in the audience.

Dr. Susan Kess, a senior physician from ATSDR, discussed asbestos and children, and Brad Black gave tips on living with the disease. Dr. Jeffrey Lybarger, the director of the ATSDR's Division of Health Studies, explained how the upcoming medical screening would be handled, and Peronard told them how the sampling was going. There were five sessions on grief and stress, something almost all the local people in the room knew all too much about.

"I don't know about this touchy-feely stuff," one old miner said. To which a woman sitting next to him too loudly replied, "Shut *up* and sit *down.*"

During the lunch break, Keven McDermott walked into the attached VFW bar. She spotted Dan Crane sitting in front of a bank of gaudy poker machines, and the EPA investigator offered him a drink. Crane, a physical scientist who headed OSHA's Physical Measurement and Analysis Branch, is his agency's analytical expert on asbestos. Many, including several at the conference, thought he was evil incarnate, the man who thought polarized-light microscopy, or PLM, was the answer to everything. The man who refused to use TEM or any more sophisticated analytical method to test ore and dust from mines. His critics said that when it came to asbestos, Crane had OSHA in his hand, and that as OSHA went, so did the other agencies.

People in his own agency who sent him dust to examine for asbestos from gas stations where brakes were changed had their samples returned from Salt Lake City marked ND, non-detect. Yet when they sent the other half of the split sample to a private lab doing TEM, the same brake grindings often came loaded with the deadly fibers.

However, chat with him for a few minutes and it becomes apparent to most that he's smart, in his own way he cares, and he's not evil.

"Bullheaded would be a better way to describe him," McDermott said. "He told me he wasn't advocating PLM because it was best, but because that was what the regulations demanded be used."

Crane told Schneider, who was just listening for a change, that he'd rather use TEM.

"Of course it's better. But it costs a lot more," he said. "Maybe triple what PLM does, and it takes longer to do." "But what if your techniques fail to detect the actual danger that the miner or autoworker is being exposed to?" the reporter asked over the sudden din of a nearby slot machine spewing out tokens.

"Simple," Crane said. "Change the regulations."

McDermott reminded him that the asbestos industry had blocked new analytical methods for years and was now screaming bloody murder over what Peronard was doing in Libby and the analysis of garden products her team was trying to complete back in Seattle. Crane just shrugged. He started to say something, but then just shook his head.

After lunch, a panel of people from Libby made it vividly clear why everyone had gathered in the VFW. Two men and three women talked about their illness and the loved ones they'd lost. The pain of living with lungs that never allowed you to take a full gulp of air; of no longer being able to hunt, hike, shovel snow, work or make love; of wondering how soon you will be too weak to get out of bed, and who will take care of your spouse when that happens.

The stories were not new to those in Libby, but most of the government visitors sat frozen in the hard metal chairs, staring, some eyes blinking back tears. They were physicians and scientists, people who deal with death and suffering, yet they appeared shocked as the five survivors talked about what Grace did and what the government didn't.

"This is what it's all about," said McDermott, who had actually gotten her boss's permission to come to the conference from Seattle.

Richard Troast, an EPA senior scientist, and Patty Smith, an environmental scientist, were to explain how they assessed the dangers in a site like Libby. Smith got about 20 seconds into her presentation and tears poured down her cheeks. With deep sobs she tried unsuccessfully to thank the five for sharing their stories.

Watching the reaction, Les said, "Okay. Okay. Maybe some of these people do care."

Peronard, leaning against the wall beside Les, added: "It looks like some of them are finally starting to understand what really happened here."

"This is clearly *the* place to be if asbestos is your game," Miller told Peronard. "If we're going to get the upper hand on the disease here, we're going to need everything these people and their agencies can do and a lot more. We're going to have to continue trying things in Libby that have never been tried before."

IT WAS ALMOST LIKE A VIDEO-ARCADE GAME — make the bowling ball knock the tenpins down. [2] But it wasn't in an arcade; it was in one of the 15 testing rooms cramped into the two trailer-like buildings hurriedly erected across the Libby street from St. John's Lutheran Hospital.

It wasn't a teenager jiggling a joystick that was making the ball move, but an old miner who had worked on the killer mountain for 17 years. He sat in the small room blowing into a plastic mouthpiece connected to a spirometry machine, an instrument that measures the volume of air entering and leaving the lungs. The harder the old man blew, the faster the computer-generated ball would move toward the pins. It was supposed to be rapid and forceful, but the man's asbestos-encrusted lungs lacked the power to move the ball much at all. He reached out and touched his green oxygen tank parked beside him and tried again to move the ball as the pulmonologist from the Denver hospital cajoled. He was one of about 50 people who showed up to be screened that warm July day in 2000. And others followed, 30 to 60 per day, seven days a week at first.

The sparring between ATSDR and EPA over what had to be done, why and how soon, was nasty at first, downright uncivil. [3] The reason, explained Sharon Campolucci, who directed the testing program, was that each agency had a different way of working, different priorities, a different understanding of the problem. The health researchers normally hammer out methodical, carefully conceived protocols, checked and rechecked and reviewed by many before being released to the field. At times, this has taken a year or more. EPA wanted it done now, and Peronard, Miller and Weis weren't shy about showing their displeasure.

It could have gotten much sloppier, but Campolucci quickly saw the need for urgency. As the deputy director of her agency's Division of Health Studies, she had 70 people — physicians, epidemiologists, environmental health scientists, computer programmers, statisticians and others — whom she could call on, and she did.

"I had at least half of them working in Libby," Campolucci explained proudly to Schneider. "It was such a high priority for us that we took everybody here off of other projects to put them on Libby. We had to, because EPA had data showing that people had been exposed. We had reports from the local medical community of people being ill and we needed to get some answers. And get them fast."

She told people to take research projects they'd been working on for weeks or months and put them all on the back burner.

"We'll answer to those congresspeople or communities who call when the time comes, but now Libby is the number-one priority," she told her staff in the Atlanta headquarters.

The plan or protocol for the screening was meticulous. All were standardized to eliminate criticism down the road. All the X-rays were shot in the exact same way, taken with the same equipment, all read by the same independent, specially trained X-ray evaluators (called B-readers). The lung-function studies were all done by pulmonologists and staff from National Jewish Research and Medical Center in Denver, which Campolucci considered the number-one respiratory hospital in the United States. The "exit strategy," which Peronard, Weis and Miller had convinced their bosses was necessary to show that only the miners were killed and sickened and let the government get out of Libby quickly, had become the largest emergency medical screening ever attempted in the nation.

"The absolute biggest," Campolucci added. "It was also done very, very quickly, but in a way that was completely scientifically valid."

ATSDR was expecting fewer than 2,000 people, but 6,149 people were tested between July and November of 2000. And more would follow. EPA and ATSDR wanted to test all former Grace or Zonolite workers in the Libby area, all household members of former employees, and anyone who had lived, worked or attended school in the Libby area for at least six months before December 31, 1990.

"What about those who lived or worked here for a while and moved on?" Gayla asked Miller one day early in the screening. "There were just thousands and thousands of men and women who worked here for years on the dam and highway projects. What about them? What about all the railroad guys?"

Miller and Campolucci expanded their search. Several former Libby miners had moved to Elko, Nevada, where the winters weren't as harsh and where new mines were opening as Grace's Libby operation was shutting down. EPA paid for an ad to run in the *Elko Daily Free Press*.[4]

Did you live or work in Libby, Montana, before December 31, 1990?

Did you work for W.R. Grace in the vermiculite mining industry there?

It mentioned the free screening and gave Wendy Thomi's telephone number.

Seventy former residents of Libby, now living in Elko, signed up for the medical screening. Another 400 called in from California, Washington, Oregon, Colorado, Utah and British Columbia wanting to sign up for the program after hearing from friends or reading stories on the *Post-Intelligencer's* website.

Peronard wasn't getting all the money he needed to do the job properly. In early 2000 he had requested $14 million for work in Libby. Headquarters only approved $9 million.

"What they sliced out was money to track down and screen former Grace employees and Libby residents who no longer live here," the cleanup boss told U.S. senator Max Baucus. On May 31, Baucus, the Montana senator who fights hard and openly for Libby, was in town trying to get an update on the cleanup. It didn't take long before Gayla cornered him to tell him about EPA's money problem.

"Paul's got to have that money. Now. Those people have got to be found," she said, forcing herself to be as polite as possible.[5] One of Baucus's entourage scampered to get a number for Tim Fields, the top dog in EPA's national Superfund program. Baucus punched the number into his cell phone, waited for an answer and, according to accounts in *The Western News,* talked Fields out of enough money to find and screen people who had left Libby. Within days, Peronard and ATSDR had an additional $650,000 earmarked to offer screening to those who had left.

Peronard told Miller and the ATSDR team that the levels of asbestos showing up in the testing of the former Little League field were running high — dangerously high in some spots.

"Remember, it was right next to the expansion plant. If kids played there two or three games a week, they could be right in the middle of it. They've got to be tested."

ATSDR said yes and quickly modified part of its "Say Yes to the Test" campaign to urge the now-grown Little Leaguers to come in for a screening. Business continued to be brisk at ATSDR's testing. Those who had signed up for the screening had to confront a 30-minute face-to-face interview with a professional questioner that ATSDR hired from the Chicago-based National Opinion Research Center. They were asked dozens of questions. Did they work at the mine? If so, how long and at what job? How long did they live in or near Libby? Did they play in the vermiculite piles or at the ball field near the expansion plant? Did they smoke?

"Detailed knowledge of their work and home background and earlier health problems is vital if we're going to understand how dangerous this exposure was and what the younger generations might face," explained Miller.[6]

Next they took the bowling-ball lung-function tests, then went across the street for X-rays of three different views of the lungs. The X-ray films were reviewed first by a local radiologist and then by three independent B-readers. Because of a few people's fear that in the past some doctors in Libby had worried more about Grace than about their patients, ATSDR made a point of stressing that the three radiologists doing the final read were not from Libby. Campolucci told the participants that chest X-rays alone cannot detect asbestos in the lungs, but that they are the most reliable way to identify changes in the lungs and lining of the lungs that might be the result of asbestos exposure.

The screening brought something very important to Libby — the Center for Asbestos Related Disease, or the CARD clinic, as it became known. Screening equipment was installed there, and the clinic began diagnosing and treating patients with asbestos-related disease. It quickly became invaluable to Libby's victims, and in it Dr. Brad Black, as its director, found the perfect way to contribute his energy and knowledge to the community.

By October, ATSDR started mailing out the results of the testing. The X-rays and a report from the B-readers were sent first to the patients' personal physicians. A week later, the patients received the letters.

"It was like waiting for your draft notice during the war," said Les, who already knew how sick he and Norita were before the testing. "It was like going out to the mailbox — that long walk — hoping that the long white envelope from the government wasn't there."

Residents who were really sick didn't have to wait months to find out, said Jeff Lybarger, Campolucci's boss. Those whose X-rays showed serious abnormalities were told as soon the radiological results came back. Between 300 and 500 letters a week were going out, and about a third of the recipients were urged to see their personal physician for a follow-up. Rick Palagi, the chief executive officer of St. John's Lutheran Hospital, was worried about the few physicians in town getting swamped with patients being told by ATSDR to see their own doctors.

"We are not diagnosing asbestos-related diseases," Lybarger reminded everyone.[7] "The X-rays and function tests tell us whether there are indicators of disease. The patient's private physicians have to make the call as to what the symptoms mean, or refer them to a specialist who can."

Some doctors in town were referring some of their patients to Black at the CARD clinic, which was already packed with more patients than it could handle. Black and Pat Cohan, the program director, found themselves working nights and weekends.

"There just really isn't any choice. These people need to be seen by someone who understands the disease process, and it's just too far to send them all to Spokane to see Alan [Whitehouse]," Black told Miller.

Whitehouse pitched in when he could, but his list of patients was growing as more people found out how sick they might be.

It wasn't as though there was much doubt that lots of people in Libby were ill and that many had already died from asbestos-related disease.[8] But even the statisticians in ATSDR's Atlanta headquarters were surprised at what they had found when they examined the causes of death in Libby in the 20 years between 1979 and 1998. Like a macabre early Christmas present, on December 12, 2000, ATSDR released its report, "Mortality from Asbestosis in Libby, Montana." Among the findings was that the death rate in Libby from asbestosis was 40 times higher than in the rest of Montana and 80 times greater than in anyplace else in the country.

HENRY FALK joined ATSDR in late 1999, just in time to run into the Libby buzz saw.

Congress created ATSDR to respond to health crises at Superfund sites, but never before had the agency experienced anything like Libby.

"We see people who may have been exposed to chemicals that might affect them in the future. We see people who are at increased risk for illness because of exposure to chemicals, but at no other site have we seen the extent of health-related findings as we've seen in Libby."[9]

Campolucci put it in plainer words.

"I have never been surrounded by so many people who were sick. Never. Never."

A SECOND ROUND OF TESTING was conducted during the summer of 2001, and an additional 1,158 persons were tested.

A total of 7,307 people had been screened by the time ATSDR pulled the plug on the screening part of the Libby operation. On August 23, 2001, the health agency reported that 30 percent of the people tested — almost 2,000 men, women and children — had possible lung abnormalities that could indicate early stages of asbestos disease.

The former miners were the hardest hit. Lybarger told the CAG that almost half of the former Grace employees — 159 of 328 — had signs of disease.

ATSDR is a small but hectic agency with only 400 employees and about 1,000 different projects in some stage of completion. After the 9/11 terrorist attacks and with new Homeland Security demands, the agency fought hard to stay on-target in Libby. Henry Falk was somehow always able to get the funds that were needed. Campolucci's colleagues said she burned the oil well past midnight, night after night, making sure the alarming conclusions that they were coming up with were based on the correct information.

"I was stunned by what we actually found looking at those X-rays and the lung-function tests and reading those interviews. We all had a sense that people in Libby were sick. But we didn't begin to have a picture of what was really going on.

"The national average for these diseases in a community is two percent or less, and we're coming up with eighteen percent, twenty percent, thirty percent in that little town. Oh, my God," Campolucci said.

Miller's view was the same. "I was expecting no more than ten percent. This is a remote population in an obscure corner of Montana. So we're faced with the questions of whether the tremolite fibers are more toxic than we believed or that the exposures were unbelievably high. Or both."

Every month during the testing, Campolucci flew to Libby for a week or more.

"Yep. The good old Super 8, the Libby Café and Marsha's for the Thursday special. It was great. ATSDR needed a face up there, someone for people to talk to, to yell at, and that was me," she said with no rancor.

The relationship between the health-research agency and EPA grew less hostile, more collegial. A bottle or two of Moose Drool beer had been shared among members of the two agencies. "When government workers from one agency are putting in 60- and 70-hour weeks and they see another government group that cares enough about the problem to also work their tails off, it's difficult to be pissy with one another," Peronard said. Campolucci agreed.

And the commitment that ATSDR had for the people in Libby seemed to grow.

"It was because of what they were finding," Kathy Skipper, the chief of the ATSDR communications office, explained to Schneider when he asked why the agency jumped into Libby with such intensity.

"What made Libby so dramatic for our people are the numbers. They're powerful, dramatic and tragic, and the evidence is in black and white," explained Skipper. "The number of people that died just because they needed a place to go to work is an American tragedy. I believe in our way of government and our capitalistic system, but I also believe that Libby never should have happened. No one should pay this kind of price for a job," she said.

Many of those whose work kept them in ATSDR's headquarters often grilled those returning from Libby for information on the town, the land, the people and, most often, on how men deal with having brought poison into their houses that can kill their wives and children. How do they live with that?

PERONARD FILLED his huge plastic cup with almost the entire carafe of fresh brewed coffee, frustrating those behind him in line for the liquid gold.

He sat at the scarred worktable in EPA's Libby office as his science and medical advisers scanned the latest screening figures from ATSDR.

"The numbers are huge, but you know they're going to grow," Weis said, looking at the hundreds of people who refused to be screened even though they met the criteria.

Miller told them that that was the least of the problem.

"It's the kids and the teenagers that just worry the hell out of me," the physician said, tossing down the breakdown from the health researchers. "We know that a bunch of those kids have been living with asbestos in their homes for their entire lives, even those who were born after Grace closed the mine. They'll be the next generation of Grace's victims, but their disease won't show up for years. Lots of them may die. The only thing we don't know is how many."

Campolucci feared the same bleak outcome, and she urged Falk to find money to continue the screening for several years.

"This prognosis just makes it crystal-clear that there has got to be some long-term health care setup for these people," Miller told his partners when they saw the numbers.

Grace's promised medical-insurance program for anyone diagnosed with disease had proven to be hit-or-miss. The insurance was available to former Grace employees, spouses and children of mine and mill workers, and anyone else who lived or worked within a 20-mile radius of the mine or mill for at least 12 consecutive months at any time before January 1, 2000, the company said when announcing the program.

To be eligible, a person must have been diagnosed with an asbestos-related lung condition.

It looked great on paper, and the public statements made by Grace VP Corcoran sounded like a great deal. The medical program will pay 100 percent of the "reasonable and customary amount" for services and supplies, including prescription drugs, for conditions including asbestosis, lung cancer, pneumonia, influenza and bronchitis, Corcoran told *The Western News*. "For people diagnosed with asbestosis, the list of covered conditions also includes heart disease and cancer of the larynx, stomach, gastrointestinal tract and esophagus.

"Once a person is enrolled in the plan, it will provide coverage for asbestos-related illnesses for life," said the corporate vice president. "It's intended to be generous."

"Sometimes they're generous. Just sometimes," a frustrated Black told Schneider. "We run into serious problems when Grace's agents say a patient doesn't have the disease.

"I've got people who we know are sick, the films and CT-scans show it, and those running Grace's insurance programs refuse them, saying they're really not sick."

In April 2001, Baucus came back to Libby and held a formal U.S. Senate field hearing. Gayla testified at Baucus's hearing with passion and precision. But not an hour after the hearing, the EPA told Gayla it had found asbestos at Plummer Elementary School in Libby. Vermiculite tailings had been used as a base for the school's ice-skating rink.

Gayla was horrified, and her anger flared anew. For many years, kids had played on the rink in the summertime, when it wasn't frozen over. And nine of her 11 grandchildren had attended Plummer School. For parents and grandparents already terrified that Libby's children had been exposed, it was an outrage on a whole new level.

Peronard's cup of problems continued to overflow. Earlier in the year, Gayla had given Kirby Maki, the superintendent of Libby's schools, a Grace memo from July 8, 1981, about testing that the company had done for asbestos-tainted mine tailings at the high school. Maki immediately wrote to Peronard, asking that EPA inspect and, if necessary, remove vermiculite tailings from the running tracks of both the city's middle school and high school.

"Grace knew that there was trouble with the tracks," Peronard told the boss of his contractors.[10] "We got the Grace memos showing that tests that they did in 1981 proved that the runners were stirring up dangerous levels of asbestos. Grace apparently even put an air pump on one of the runners and found the kids were being exposed to asbestos levels higher than anything OSHA would allow for workers. And they never made those findings public."

The memo said: "Fiber concentrations were surprisingly high ..."

Peronard wondered what else Grace did that he didn't know about yet.

In June, Gayla was given another reason for anger, as if she needed one. She and Dave got their results back from the ATSDR screening. Both of them were diagnosed with lung abnormality.

With her level of exposure, Gayla had expected that she would be diagnosed.[11] But Dave's condition was evaluated to be more severe than Gayla's, which really enraged her, because Dave had chosen, years ago, not to work at the mine. *He shouldn't have it,* she thought. *Another Libby victim with no personal connection to that damned mine.*

Brad Black found himself fighting Grace even harder over its insurance plan in the beginning of 2002. For a mild man, his anger raged. Forty-three people had applied for coverage between January and March, the physician told Schneider over lunch at the Hidden Chapel restaurant, one of only two eateries in Libby with tablecloths. "About sixty percent of them were declined coverage by Grace. Declined. Period. That's almost two out of three. There is absolutely no medical logic to what they're doing.

"These people have no place to turn."

EPA became the new biggest employer in the Libby area. Handling hazardous material, including the asbestos-contaminated debris and soil, paid better than almost any other work in that part of Montana. (Andrew Schneider)

I N THE 150-YEAR HISTORY of W.R. Grace & Company, April 2, 2001, was a new low.

Paul Norris, Grace's CEO, announced that the company was declaring bankruptcy. He blamed some 325,000 asbestos suits pending against Grace, and said the company had already paid out more than $2 billion to clear asbestos claims.

Of course, in most of the suits Grace was named as a defendant along with several other companies, in the scattershot approach so favored by many asbestos lawyers. Unfortunately, the bankruptcy did not just affect the hundreds of thousands of suits in which Grace was a drive-by codefendant and the plaintiffs had only the threat of disease. It also crippled hundreds of claims related to Libby and the expansion plants, where Grace was the only defendant and the plaintiffs were very sick, or bereaved.

The Libby victims were thrown into turmoil. Hundreds of victims and their families still had lawsuits pending, but now it appeared Grace was "judgment proof." And nobody knew if the bankruptcy meant that Grace would stop making payments for medical care. The company had promised $250,000 a year to Libby's hospital and established the medical-insurance program for victims. At the time of the filing, 200 people had already applied. The number was expected to soar after the screening results arrived, and it did.

"It is especially sad for Libby, because these people were Grace's own workers and families," Kalispell lawyer Heberling said. "Now Grace is attempting to hide from its responsibilities to them."

Grace said it "plans to work closely with asbestos claimants and other creditors in order to address valid asbestos claims." But the company provided no details.

Just a week before, the EPA had sued Grace to recover the first $10 million in Libby cleanup costs. In the *Post-Intelligencer* story on the bankruptcy, Schneider quoted Peronard as saying, "We budgeted between $14 million and $16 million for this year, and it now becomes a problem of getting that money. It's looking more and more like taxpayers will pick up what Grace drops."

But Matt Cohn and Justice Department lawyers were already examining Grace records to see whether the company had moved assets into other holdings before the bankruptcy to protect them from asbestos cleanup or litigation expenses — an allegation vehemently denied by Grace.

THE GATHERING IN THE UNION HALL had more the atmosphere of a retirement party than an all-day medical screening to determine whether the old-timers were dying of yet-to-be-detected asbestos disease.

These men and a handful of women had put in 20, 30 or more years on the assembly lines of the Boeing, Ford and General Motors plants on the outskirts of St. Louis. In July of 2001, Schneider moved to St. Louis. He and his wife, Kathleen Best, took editorships at the *Post-Dispatch*, Schneider in charge of investigative projects and Best as assistant managing editor for metro, state and regional news.

But Schneider couldn't get away from asbestos. Soon after the move, he walked into the St. Louis union hall for Local 837 of the International Association of Machinists and Aerospace Workers. With the functionality of an Army induction center, various rooms in the union hall had been converted into stations where nurses and medical technicians were creating medical files on the workers. At two desks, technicians tested pulse and blood pressure. Three other desks were set up to extract medical histories, as far back as the workers could remember. Almost half of the men answered, "If my wife were here she'd know" to many of the questions.

In another part of the makeshift operation, the most experienced surveyors were coaxing workers to remember every job they'd ever had. Especially any job that might have put them, at any time, anywhere near asbestos in furnaces, boilers, pipes or production lines or in any operations where asbestos was being stored, used or removed. Even walking beneath or by asbestos in any form was "important," the workers were told.

The crucial piece of hardware in this operation was a 60-foot-long burgundy trailer parked outside the union hall's main door. The trailer, with ASBESTOS TESTING and a toll-free number painted on each side, was driven up from Mobile, Alabama. For reasons that the driver couldn't explain to Schneider, Alabama is the home base of at least a dozen of these $100,000 screening units, run by eight separate firms.

"We were in Nashville and Indianapolis last week, and we'll be in Milwaukee, Dayton and Latrobe, Pennsylvania, next week," the driver said, proudly showing Schneider a map covered with scores of dots. "It has been a great year, and it's only half gone."

The "mobile clinic" has several examination stations separated by faux paneling. In addition to the X-ray machines and its processing equipment, there are two stations with tubes attached to monitors and computers which are used to perform pulmonary-function tests. If an X-ray shows a shadow in the lungs, the workers are given the pulmonary-function test before being sent back inside the union hall to see a physician.

For a group in their late 50s, 60s or 70s, the workers looked healthy. There were the expected complaints of heart disease, high blood pressure, cataracts and an assortment of cancers of various parts of their bodies. But none complained of lung cancer or great difficulty breathing or any of the other symptoms of asbestosis or mesothelioma. Why were they at the screening?

Two men and a woman told Schneider they had actually worked with asbestos insulation years earlier and thought it was smart to get a checkup. Sixteen other workers or retirees Schneider talked to admitted it might be a way to add a little cash to their retirement funds.

"I saw the notice in the union newsletter and said 'Why not?'" said an automotive worker from Ford. Sitting on the tailgate of his shiny, new Chevy pickup and lighting a fresh cigarette off the one he had just finished, he added, "It's better than the lottery. If they find something, I get a few thousand dollars I didn't have. If they don't find anything, I've just lost an afternoon."

Standing nearby, a Boeing worker ten days from retirement volunteered, "The lawyers said I could get ten or twelve thousand dollars if the shadow is big enough, and I know just the fishing boat I'd buy with that."

When asked if he'd ever worked with asbestos, he said, "No, but the lawyers say it's all over the place, so I was probably exposed to it."

Schneider told three of them that it could cost $300,000 to $500,000 to treat lung cancer or mesothelioma, and asked if they were worried about signing away their rights to ever sue again if they actually got the disease. None of the three said anything. What about those guys who really have the disease and can't get any money because of frivolous suits? Schneider asked.

"Tell them to get better lawyers," a Boeing worker said, and walked away.

Two of the junior lawyers for the Illinois firm that set up the screening hovered around the men being questioned at the various desks. One of them was actually rubbing his hands together.

"We're here because the union president called us and asked if we'd set up the screening. We're doing it as a favor," said the lawyer, who looked about 18 years old. Schneider weaved through a maze of folding chairs in the main meeting room and found the president. "He said what?" the union leader questioned. "Hell, they called me a half-dozen times to let them set this up. I didn't think it could do any harm, and maybe some of the guys would get a little money. But it was the lawyers who wanted to do this."

Two weeks later, the young lawyer called Schneider at the *Post-Dispatch* and reported that about half of 105 members examined at Local 837 and about the same percentage of 500 other workers or retirees examined the same week at two other union halls "came back positive for asbestos-related disease."

One out of two is far higher than anything found in Libby.

When asked whom his firm was going to sue on behalf of these 300 newly discovered victims, the lawyer answered in blunt honesty, "Anyone who made products with asbestos who hasn't gone bankrupt yet."

If their claims work like most of the others that are spawned by mass screenings, suits will be brought against between eight and 20 different companies who, at any time, sold products containing asbestos. For those with suspicious shadows on their X-rays — perhaps pleural plaque — they may settle for between $400 and $800 from each of the companies sued. If asbestosis can be claimed, the money could double or triple. For lung cancer or mesothelioma, it would be a big payday. It is rare that any of these cases ever goes to trial.

Not all trial lawyers use such tactics. The early Libby victims probably never would have had their day in court if it were not for McGarvey, Sullivan and Heberling. Scores of trial lawyers bust their tails to help clients screwed by the system. The public views the antics of the stars from A *Civil Action* and *Erin Brockovich* and believes it's all fiction. But when these small firms go up against the government or a mammoth corporation like W.R. Grace and its hundreds of lawyers, it is truly David against Goliath.

Going through 40,000 pages of documents to prove who lied, or meeting a terrified whistleblower late at night in an out-of-the-way place to try to turn him into a public witness, becomes commonplace. So, for some good lawyers, does taking a reduced fee so a sick miner will have enough money to live on.

But these aren't the lawyers clogging courts across the country with tens of thousands of suits filed on behalf of clients who feel fine, who have no symptoms of illness and may never become ill.

Frail old men hooked to oxygen, awaiting death in small communities around the Vanderbilt talc mines in New York and near the taconite mines along the Iron Range in Minnesota and Michigan, are the losers in the litigation sweepstakes. And, in 20 years, so may be the emergency workers from the World Trade Center attack, and those who lived and worked in lower Manhattan, and an unknown number of people exposed to the deadly fibers from the tainted Zonolite insulation in their attics.

"Too many lawyers are dedicated to filling their own pockets rather than getting justice for their clients," said Dr. Michael Harbut. "They come into town, set up a screening operation in a union hall, get these guys to sign an agreement, which gives them a few dollars and the lawyers a lot more. But to get those few dollars, the miners sign away any future rights to sue if they should become fully debilitated.

"It is criminal and must be stopped."

AROUND THE TACONITE MINES in Minnesota's Iron Range, Schneider found miners doubly victimized — by the asbestos-laden taconite ore and by the bogus screenings.

David Trach, the president of a group of retired LTV Steel miners, and Joe Scholar, a member of a state advisory committee on miners being exposed to asbestos, sat around a conference table in Steelworkers 4108's union hall. They said a study released in 2000 showed that a third of the tested LTV taconite miners have some type of asbestos disease. But Trach and Scholar didn't need a study to know that. Drive through any of the tiny towns that border the black taconite fields and men can be seen dragging their wheeled oxygen tanks behind them as they slowly shuffle down the sidewalks.

"Nobody wants to put the blame where it belongs, on the steel companies who have known for years that the taconite we mine is contaminated with tremolite," Scholar told Schneider. Trach added: "These lawyers don't want to sue the mines who let us do work in that tremolite dust without ever telling us it was asbestos. They'd rather go after twenty other companies who made asbestos brakes, gaskets, insulation, pipe coverings, anything. They're an easy target, and the lawyers say they pay off without having to go to court. So some of these guys get a few thousand dollars from companies that probably had nothing to do with why they have asbestosis or mesothelioma and it doesn't change a damn thing. These out-of-state lawyers make big bucks, and the next generation of miners, our sons, keep working in that contaminated ore."

Dr. David Egilman has testified as an expert witness in more than 100 trials, "mostly on behalf of the injured worker," but also on the side of several asbestos companies. "Some lawyers are great, and their efforts to help people injured by chemicals, asbestos or dangerous practices in the workplace may, in many cases, be the only way to eliminate the hazard," said Egilman, a specialist in occupational medicine. "But all too often, these medical screenings are little more than rackets perpetrated by money-hungry lawyers. Most workers usually don't know what they're getting involved in."

Plaintiffs' lawyers typically receive 25 to 40 percent of a settlement, and even though the settlements are small, the numbers add up to big money.

"The lawyers promise them money if they sign the papers," Egilman said. "They may get a thousand dollars or fifteen hundred dollars, but what happens years later when the shadow on the X-ray develops into full-blown asbestosis and the poor guy has to spend five thousand dollars a month on medication and oxygen? You can't go back and sue the same companies. The lawyers pull out a copy of the agreement you signed ten years earlier saying you would not sue the asbestos company again in return for the pittance you got."

Egilman is worried that the screenings can be dangerous.

"The first rule of medicine is 'Do no harm,' and the screenings can do harm in a variety of ways," Egilman said. "The first harm is to the actual person being screened, who can be unnecessarily frightened by being told they have a disease, when they don't really have one, or being told that their risks are greater than they may actually be.

"The second harm is that some of these screenings may misdiagnose people. Someone went through a screening. There was a nodule noted on the X-ray. That information was given to the lawyers and never got to the patient. It was months before the fellow was actually diagnosed, and by that time it was too late. Had the screening not gone on, the person probably would have died anyway, but he might have gone to a real doctor who might have diagnosed the problem in time to prolong that poor bastard's life."

Back in Denver, the lawyers for EPA and Justice were putting in incredible hours. Their efforts were quixotic, more common to starry-eyed rookie lawyers than to seasoned barristers for the federal government.

The EPA's Cohn, Andrea Madigan and Kelcey Land and Justice's Jerel Ellington, Jim Freeman and Heidi Kukis were excited by the legal challenges that Grace was throwing at them.

"At times I get the feeling that we're standing in front of one of those machines that pitch baseballs and the machine is firing at the highest speed," Cohn said.

The claim from Grace that it would never conceal its assets held little water for the lawyers in the Denver federal building.

Cohn couldn't believe the level of deception he encountered with Grace — not only in the company's dealings with EPA, but in their statements to regulators and to the public. In 19 years with EPA, he had never seen anything like it. For almost two years, the EPA and Justice lawyers in Denver put in hundreds of hours of research, quietly hunting through thousands of company documents and government filings. The grueling task of following the money and private corporate dealings gave Ellington, Madigan and their colleagues much of what they needed to prove that Grace was going to try to conceal its money before the bankruptcy court split up the pie of its assets.

Roger Sullivan and his Kalispell firm had shared extensive evidence collected for two years documenting Grace's business restructuring long before the company's bankruptcy filing.[1] As early as Gayla's trial in 1998, Sullivan and his firm had been worried that Grace was concealing funds. They hired Professor Sally Weaver, a specialist in corporate law from the University of Montana, to analyze all the company's SEC filings, annual reports and other documents on its corporate reorganization. It was Weaver's analysis and hundreds of other documents that Sullivan gave to Madigan. By then, the government lawyers had teamed with forensic accountants who specialized in tracking convoluted money transfers and company acquisitions.

Finally, their case was ready. There was real concern that Grace had squirreled away an enormous amount of money, hiding it in another of its companies called Sealed Air, makers of bubble wrap. The brief they were preparing alleged that the money, perhaps as much as $2 billion, was veiled from the bankruptcy court so it wouldn't be available to pay creditors, including asbestos claimants and the federal government, Schneider reported in the *Post-Dispatch*.[2]

EPA wanted money not only for the cleanup at Libby but for contaminated sites across the country that Grace took 99 pages in its 1998 SEC report to list.[3] Grace said its liability for these sites totaled $230 million. EPA bean-counters thought it was closer to a billion dollars.

Some of the people involved in the effort to file the unique intervention were concerned that it would be quashed at the last moment by bosses at the Justice Department or EPA headquarters. It was obvious that the George W. Bush White House had strong opinions on the harm that asbestos suits were doing to large corporations. Not just Halliburton, which was run by Dick Cheney before he became vice president, but also to scores of other companies. The administration had been working with Republicans in Congress on legislation that would restrict the ability of asbestos victims to file lawsuits.

In May 2002, Halliburton agreed to pay about $4.2 billion to settle 374,000 claims for harm from asbestos and create a trust to handle future claims. However, according to the *Wall Street Journal,* Halliburton said in a report filed with the SEC in August 2003 that it may have to renegotiate the deal because a new wave of complaints brought the total asbestos claims it faced to 425,000.

Back in Denver, no one stopped the government lawyers from intervening in Grace's case. Perhaps, some thought, because official Washington was distracted by the Enron debacle. The company's record-shattering bankruptcy that turned it into the ultimate symbol of corporate excesses was steaming to a boil just as Ellington and Madigan's team was putting the final touches on its brief to intervene. Even the most zealous asbestos-industry supporter in the administration or Congress knew it would be unseemly to get caught preventing government officials from pursuing an honest accounting from a corporation that may have contributed to the deaths and illnesses of thousands. In the third week of May 2002, the Justice Department filed papers with the court saying that Grace had fraudulently concealed its assets in new companies it set up before filing for Chapter 11 bankruptcy protection.

The lawyers asked the court to let the government intervene in the company's bankruptcy proceeding because "Grace allegedly removed billions of dollars of assets against which parties who were injured or damaged by Grace's asbestos-containing materials had claims," the court documents said.

In Libby, word spread quickly about the government's action against Grace. Some were excited, some skeptical. Many said they had more urgent concerns about Grace. On the same day the government filed its suit, pharmacists in Libby were forced to tell many of their customers that the insurance program that Grace had established with much fanfare two years earlier was now refusing to pay for some of their medication and oxygen.

"The list is long. Painkillers, blood pressure medicine, about fifteen to twenty different drugs are suddenly being kicked back by Grace's insurer," pharmacist Wendy Dodson told Schneider.[4] "Many of my customers can't afford the large amount of medication that is needed to live with these asbestos-caused diseases. If they stop taking it, the medical consequences could be dire.

"But nothing Grace does surprises anyone in Libby anymore."

And in November 2002, just days before going to trial, Sealed Air Corp. settled with the U.S. government and with the Creditor's Committee who brought the suit and agreed to transfer more than $500 million in cash and nearly another $500 million in stock to the bankruptcy court holding Grace's assets.

American industry has paid out an estimated $53 billion to workers and consumers injured by asbestos in their products or operations.[5] The long-term predictions are even more dire, with actuarial firms saying that the total costs of asbestos suits will eventually reach $200 billion to $250 billion. By mid-2003, 67 major companies had filed for bankruptcy protection since 1982 because of millions of asbestos suits. The bankruptcy automatically excuses the companies from lawsuits against them. More than 8,400 companies are or have been the targets in suits involving harm from asbestos.

In a 1999 case before the U.S. Supreme Court, Justice David H. Souter called asbestos litigation an "elephantine mass."[6]

Over the last several decades, Congress has considered a number of bills aimed at creating a system for resolving asbestos claims outside the judicial system. The Democrats, backed by trial lawyers, have consistently blocked any changes in the law.

In 1977, New Jersey congresswoman Millicent Fenwick, in whose district was Johns-Manville, introduced legislation which would have established a federally administered central fund for asbestos victims.[7] There was never enough support on Capitol Hill to turn the proposal into law. In 1980, Johns-Manville moved its headquarters to Colorado. The same year, former Colorado senator Gary Hart introduced the Asbestos Health Hazards Compensation Act, which would have barred victims of asbestos disease from filing suit. It met a similar fate.

In 2000, the Fairness in Asbestos Compensation Act hit Washington. The bill, backed by the asbestos lobby, would have set up a government agency — the Office of Asbestos Compensation — under the Justice Department to control an industry-financed Asbestos Compensation Fund to pay claims. However, those claims would have to meet a new set of medical criteria that would bar even some of the sickest people in Libby from filing suit.

A DELEGATION FROM LIBBY, including Gayla, Les, Alice Priest, Robin Redman and Roger Sullivan went to Washington in the first week in March 2000 to show lawmakers debating the "fairness bill" what it is like to be dying of asbestosis.

They found themselves watching a legislative tornado of name-calling, dueling experts and frenzied lobbyists.

"This is worse than watching someone make sausage," Gayla told Schneider.

The legislation the Montanans came to oppose was a highly contentious package of laws promoted, for the most part, by GAF Corporation, Grace and others in the asbestos industry. For almost three years, this bill and earlier versions had been pushed hard, mostly by Republicans on the Senate Commerce and the House Judiciary Committees. Like that of most legislation, the verbiage sounded noble and beneficial. The bill's sponsors insisted it would end the logjam of hundreds of thousands of victims waiting for their day in court and prevent personal-injury lawyers from pocketing large chunks of the settlements.

The opposition — mostly unions, victims groups, consumer coalitions and the Association of Trial Lawyers of America — says it should have been called the "Asbestos Industry Relief Act," because it would have prevented thousands of terminally ill victims from filing suit for holding the industry accountable for the disease they had contracted.[8]

The bill called for government-approved doctors, using medical criteria defined in the law, to be gatekeepers, issuing a pass to qualifying victims who wished to sue or seek a government-ordained settlement.

The battle over the proposed legislation got sloppy, even by Washington standards.[9] More than $6 million was spent in lobbying by both sides, and the conflict grew far beyond Republicans snarling at Democrats. Industry lawyers and victims' lawyers denounced each other as ambulance-chasing hacks delaying the process to increase their fees. Doctors, some of them industry consultants, developed the medical-screening criteria for the law. But other physicians, including some nationally recognized pulmonary and cancer specialists, called the proposed standards "antiquated," "exclusionary" and "barbaric."

As with many legislative debates, those voting on the compensation bills must deal with facts, statistics, history and interpretation that are often provided by lobbyists. For example, the language for the bill originally presented to House Judiciary Committee Chairman Henry Hyde was written for the Illinois Republican by a Harvard Law School professor working with an asbestos industry-funded group.

Most members of Congress admit it is often difficult to put a face on the people affected by legislation being debated. For two days, the group from Libby showed any committee member who was willing to meet with them precisely who would be affected by the legislation.

"We're just working stiffs from Libby, but three or four hundred people in our tiny town have got the disease, and the legislation that's supposed to help us out won't do a damn thing for almost any of them, including those that are close to dying," Les told various committee staff people.

Alice Priest was 72 and had been diagnosed with asbestosis a year earlier, 17 years after her husband Virgil died from it. She dragged a wheeled canister of oxygen behind her as she shuffled across the marble floors of the congressional buildings she visited. Her neighbors lugged three extra tanks of oxygen. Robin Redman was 44. She and her brother and sister all have asbestosis, also from the dust on her father's work clothes. He died in 1998.

Gayla didn't know she and David had the disease yet, but she told the members that her mother and father had both died slow, painful deaths from the asbestos-caused disease. "The law, if passed, would have excluded all of these people from any protection," Gayla said, indicating her friends and their families. "The medical criteria and lengths of exposure that the asbestos industry wants included would just slam the door shut. There would be no place to go."

On the second day of their visit, Roger Sullivan quietly herded them into the House Judiciary Committee hearing room.[10] Hyde looked up, spotted the group, looked hard at Alice and her oxygen tanks, grabbed his gavel, hammered the hearing adjourned and left the chamber. Schneider, who'd covered Washington off and on for 20 years, stood in the corner of the meeting room, shook his head in amazement and burst out laughing. He couldn't help it. These cowpokes from Libby had forced Henry Hyde to flee. Who would have believed it?

At least one member of his Judiciary Committee did not hesitate to speak out. "The people of Libby have been let down by one government agency after another over the years," said Massachusetts Democrat Marty Meehan. "Those who could have stepped in, made Grace do the right thing and provide some relief, instead passed the buck and pointed the finger elsewhere. Now the regulators are beginning to make up for it. But the damage is largely done." Meehan spoke about the fact that the tainted Libby ore was sent to hundreds of processing plants around the country. "One of those plants is in my district," Meehan said.

On June 18, 2002, on the Senate side of the Capitol, Patty Murray introduced another asbestos-related bill. The Ban Asbestos in America Act, she explained, would legislate what the EPA had tried to do administratively almost a decade earlier — pass a ban on products containing asbestos. She acknowledged that her bill might take years to pass. "A successful year is having the bill introduced, having a hearing on it and educating my colleagues in the United States Senate to the fact that asbestos is not yet banned," she said.

The Judiciary Committee had been expected to approve Hyde's bill the same week Murray held her first hearing. Hyde had anticipated a quick vote to send his legislation to the House floor.[11] But it didn't happen. Public reaction to the *Post-Intelligencer* series and the resulting investigations by EPA, the Labor Department and other federal agencies increased the visibility of the debate, reported that week's issue of the *Congressional Quarterly Report.* "With all those red flags out there, I question why we're rushing into marking up this bill. I could see an argument for moving ahead if we had at least done all we could to get to the bottom of these medical criteria and see what they mean for flesh-and-blood human beings like those here today. But we haven't," Meehan said, pointing to the four people from Libby.

Senator Baucus did his part to fight the bill that would exempt asbestos companies from paying punitive damages to asbestos victims. "I'll filibuster in the Senate any attempts to bail out asbestos companies at the expense of victims. That's not fair, and I'll fight it tooth and nail," he said.

The bill never made it to the floor for a vote *that year.*

Clothing at a T-shirt store near the collapsed Twin Towers is coated with toxic dust. (Kevin Manning, *St. Louis Post-Dispatch*)

I N THE EARLY 1970s, Irving Selikoff was outraged about asbestos fibers being released into the air of lower Manhattan from the fire-proofing being sprayed during the construction of the World Trade Center.[1]

The physician who was the father of occupational and environmental medicine warned New York officials that a hundred tons of asbestos fibers were "falling like snow" from steel skeletons of the rising towers.

He told union health experts that not one man of the thousands who worked on or near the spraying would be alive in 20 years. Those protests led to bans on the spraying of asbestos fireproofing on new construction across the country.

Imagine how Selikoff would have felt about the asbestos in the air on September 11, 2001. Like the rest of America, Paul Peronard, Chris Weis and Aubrey Miller were riveted to their televisions that morning. They watched the impact and collapse of the towers over and over and over again until the horrible reality was etched in their brains. And they all thought about Selikoff and his predictions for the World Trade Center.

Among the thousands of Grace documents that Schneider had collected as he hunted for the truth on Libby were hundreds that dealt with the company's efforts to get asbestos out of the Monokote fireproofing they were selling to the New York Port Authority contractors for use in the towers, for the new Macy's store and the terminal at Newark Airport.[2] The Libby team, their lawyer, Matt Cohn, and his Justice Department colleagues had gathered even more paper, including Port Authority documents showing that Grace's Monokote 3 — a mixture of asbestos and cement — was sprayed all the way up to the 40th floor in one of the towers and the 64th in the other.

Other Port Authority papers showed that Monokote 4 — a mixture of vermiculite and gypsum plaster that Grace insisted was "asbestos-free" — was used as a fireproofing and was still contaminated with cancer-causing fibers.[3]

Lawyers from the Port Authority said that Grace had stopped adding chrysotile to the fireproofing and instead used vermiculite from Libby and from its vermiculite mines in South Carolina. Shipping papers show that tons of the tainted vermiculite were brought in by rail to plants in New Jersey and New York state, which processed it into fireproofing for the towers.

In November 1981, a photograph of the towers was displayed in a full-page ad in *Asbestos Magazine*, a trade publication. "The bigger the building, the more important fireproofing becomes," the ad read. "That's why today's buildings have asbestos-cement walls and even floors containing asbestos.... You'll also find asbestos sealing plumbing joints, insulating heating pipes, electric motors and emergency generators. Asbestos. We couldn't live the way we do without it. When life depends on it, you use asbestos."

"WE WATCHED THE DUST CLOUDS boiling after people running from the collapsing buildings, their faces coated grayish white. You knew they were sucking in lungs full of asbestos and God knows what else," Weis said. "We had to do something."

They did, or at least they tried.

The information being shared at the daily 1 P.M. conference calls with the White House, EPA top boss Christine Todd Whitman and her regional administrators was frightening for many reasons.[4] Some of the people listening in at headquarters and in Denver were shocked when the EPA Region 2 team in New York, running the cleanup, reported that its sampling was showing 3 to 4.5 percent asbestos. The Libby team cringed when New York reported, "It's no problem."

Dr. Phil Landrigan also cringed. He headed the Mount Sinai Medical Center's department of community and environmental medicine, which Selikoff had started decades earlier.

"There were hundreds of tons of asbestos-loaded fire retardants on the steel trusses of the lower floors. Now the fibers are floating all over the city," Landrigan said. "The emergency workers are going to suffer from increased disease, and the amount of fibers probably being inhaled by those living and working in lower Manhattan presents serious questions for their future health."

Nevertheless, two days after the attack, Whitman was guided through the scene of destruction and confidently announced: "I am glad to reassure New Yorkers ... that their air is safe."

It was clear that the New York EPA did not have the expertise to evaluate, let alone handle, the asbestos contamination. Their work logs and reports showed they were taking far too few samples and none from the inside of the condos, apartments and offices that packed lower Manhattan. The most alarming issue was their use of 20-year-old technology — PLM, or polarized-light microscopy — to analyze the samples.

The thousands of samples analyzed at Libby should have shown the New York team that they were missing too much by not using transmission electron microcopy, or TEM, or the new NASA technology Weis had adapted with USGS. Being forced to deal with the tremolite in Libby, which permeated everything, including the homes, Peronard, Weis and Miller knew how to find and analyze asbestos. They, working with USGS, had developed and repeatedly proven techniques that the rest of EPA had never used. They offered this knowledge, and manpower, to help in New York.

For his work in Libby, Peronard had under contract 130 of the country's best scientists for collecting and sampling asbestos.[5] The laboratories used to analyze the material happened to be within a 20-minute drive of the smoldering ruins in Manhattan. By September 15 and 16, most of those scientists had volunteered to pack up and go to New York. "No one ordered them. They just wanted to help. We all did," Weis said.

One of the contract scientists got into Manhattan and found places for the Libby team to work and sleep. Peronard, Weis and Miller had found a dozen electron microscopes to use, and they began packing cases of equipment they would need and wrote a plan for the testing. By September 18, they were ready to go. They could have 30 experienced teams on the ground by the next day.

Some members of the crew from the New York region were eager to have the help. They admitted they were overwhelmed and over their heads.

"This is not the time for posturing or ego trips. We're dealing with life and death here, and those guys from Libby know how to do it," a New York supervisor told Schneider in a call to the St. Louis *Post-Dispatch*, where he now worked. "This asbestos is a whole new world to us. We can't play games. It's not right. It's not fair to the emergency workers and the people living and working there."

The people in the field may have wanted the help of the Libby team, but their bosses sure didn't. Richard Caspe, the deputy regional administrator, stiffly declined the help. Joe Laforara, who headed EPA's national emergency response team in Edison, New Jersey, was far less subtle. Using the difficult-to-misunderstand language favored by some New Jerseyites, he told the Denver team and its scientists to "fuck off."

The New York on-scene coordinators, desperate to fathom what the dust meant to the workers and residents in the city, were angry that "the gutless wonders calling the shots would rather have us stumble around looking for the answers than swallow their pride and let those guys from Libby bring what they know to this disaster," a coordinator told Schneider weeks later. He and others, he said, called Peronard to thank him for the help he, Miller and Weis were slipping them on the q.t.

"I thought this was remarkable given the pressure they were under, and the fact that it was their city that had been attacked, and that they were being played as pawns in the political games that went along with getting folks back to normal," Peronard told Schneider.

"Talk about being in the barrel; I felt for them," Peronard continued. "They were getting just the opposite treatment that our team in Libby was getting. Where our management sent us to Libby to get the job done, with a lot of autonomy and then backup when push came to shove, the guys in Region 2 were being micromanaged in the worst way. They were put in a no-win, no-authority, you-be-the-patsy position."

THROUGHOUT FALL AND WINTER, EPA, the city and the state continued to paint a rosy picture of the asbestos problem at the World Trade Center site in its public pronouncements.

The pulverized glass, metal, plastic and concrete in the cataclysmic dust cloud that billowed from the towers would not present a long-term risk to those sucking it in. Nor, the agency said, was there a real problem from the deadly, invisible asbestos fibers from the thousands of tons of asbestos fireproofing or from asbestos products in floors, walls and ceilings. Almost nightly, network news showed video of apartments and offices with inches of the fine dust coating floors, walls and furniture. But still EPA was taking no inside samples.

From the first, federal officials seemed more interested in reassuring the public than in confronting the dangers. The government, and the EPA in particular, seemed to be interested in minimizing any cleanup and maximizing both the appearance and reality of things getting back to what passed for normal. "Wall Street must reopen" was the order from the top.

"The agencies ... made it a priority to get the lower-Manhattan financial and stock markets up and running at any cost," said Joel Shufro, executive director of the New York Committee for Occupational Safety and Health, which represents more than 250 unions.[6] "In so doing, they allowed thousands of people to be exposed to substances that haven't even all been identified, let alone quantified."

A year later, Schneider would get documents showing that the White House was controlling the statements Whitman and others made on the health hazards confronting those who worked or lived near Ground Zero.[7] The order, "which was repeated almost hourly, was to get Wall Street up and running. Unless the stock exchange is on fire, the Street must be opened," a senior member of Whitman's staff told the reporter.

Even some of the senior political appointees in EPA, FEMA and Health and Human Services were outraged at being forbidden from sharing what they knew about the dangers that existed because of the dust.

"It was the worst of all worlds," an investigator from EPA's Office of the Inspector General told Schneider in January 2003 as they were comparing e-mails and memos on the emergency communication they had both acquired.

"It was like warning that loose lips sink ships," the investigator said of the documents. "The cloak of security was being thrown over many of the most innocuous statements that those on the senior agency conference calls wanted to release. They made it seem that it would be like giving aid and comfort to Osama bin Laden to tell people in New York that their government really didn't know how dangerous the dust they were breathing was to their health."

Documents from the White House Counsel on Environment Quality showed a repeated pattern of downplaying the hazard to health even when the sparse information available showed just the opposite — to the extent of ordering the headlines of government news releases changed completely so no threat or hazard was ever conveyed. The documents made it clear that asbestos was to be treated like a curse word.

Nevertheless, experts inside and outside the EPA were saying that the number of people at risk of asbestos-related disease was grossly underestimated. Evaluations by teams of leading asbestos researchers showed the increased risk to people who live, work or study in homes or offices that have not been properly decontaminated could be as high as one additional cancer death for every ten people exposed. But the EPA, OSHA and other agencies ignored such assessments.

There was no disputing that the dust made thousands of New Yorkers ill. For months after 9/11, people were plagued with severe sinus infections, asthma attacks, nausea, headaches, rashes, bloodshot eyes and severe cough-ing, nicknamed "Ground Zero cough." Those problems were not indications of asbestos exposure. They were caused by the pulverized concrete, fiber-glass, metal and other debris in the toxic dust storm and smoke that inun-dated lower Manhattan and parts of Long Island and New Jersey.

Official statements made by government health and environmental ex-perts at all levels downplayed the dangers, even obvious ones. For example, the New York City Health Department was asked a logical question: Was the heavy concentration of dust from the collapsed buildings presenting any additional risk to pregnant women and young children? The department's official answer in one of its advisories was: "No. Pregnant women and young children do not need to take additional precautions." Many pediatri-cians, neonatologists and respiratory specialists cringed at that government guidance. But at the time, a spokesman for the city health department told Schneider that the statement was based on information from EPA. "They or the CDC are basically telling our people what all this dust and asbestos means to everyone's health," he said.

It was August 2003 before the *Journal of the American Medical Association* would publish an article on a study by researchers at Mount Sinai Medi-cal Center that said its preliminary research had shown that dust from the World Trade Center collapse may have resulted in smaller babies — about a half-pound less — among pregnant mothers who were in or near the disaster area.

One of the realities that make asbestos so hard to track and so easy to ignore is that the disease has a latency period of 10 to 40 years — the period of time from when a fiber is inhaled and becomes embedded in lung tissue to when a person begins showing signs of illness. "Those exposures may have grave adverse public-health consequences, but we will not know exactly what those consequences are for decades," Shufro, the New York Commit-tee for Occupational Safety and Health leader, told Schneider.

For weeks, EPA, OSHA and their state counterparts said that only low levels of asbestos were found in the air outside. "The public faces little or no danger from asbestos," agency heads echoed. Most major news outlets parroted this "good news." But in New York, Schneider was getting a different picture as he spoke to government and civilian scientists and physicians hired by unions, tenant groups, contractors and New York political leaders.

Schneider was fortunate. His new editor, Ellen Soeteber, just like Alexander and Oglesby before her, saw nothing wrong with letting him chase a story across the country that other journalists were ignoring. Back to New York he went.

EPA continued to cite publicly that its sampling was finding asbestos at less than 1 percent and using that as proof that there was no danger. That belief in itself was dangerous. The work at Libby showed that far lower asbestos levels could create harmful exposures when the dust was in the air.

"Concentrations well below the 1 percent ... [of] asbestos have been found to generate hazardous airborne exposures in the breathing zone when disturbed," Miller wrote three weeks after the attack in a lengthy list of suggestions requested by Kelly McKinney, an assistant commissioner of New York City's Health Department.

Miller took a page from what he, Weis and Peronard had proven in the living rooms of Libby. He strongly urged that when apartments and businesses were tested, sampling be done while tasks such as walking, sweeping and dusting are simulated. Without these simulations, you have no clue what people may actually be exposed to, the doctor said.

The experts Schneider followed took hundreds of samples, many inside apartments, offices and condos.[8] Using soft brushes and microvacs, they swept fine powder from hallways, stairwells and heating vents into special sample jars. Powerful vacuum cleaners with special filters tight enough to trap the invisible asbestos fibers were run over industrial-grade carpet and the finest Oriental rugs, down cheap sheets hung over windows by college kids and through the weave of brocade drapes costing $400 a yard. Air pumps connected to filter cartridges hummed as they sampled air from a living room filled with huge leather couches on Trinity Place; a nursery, newly decorated in three shades of pink for twin sisters on Barclay; and a loft just off Broadway furnished with four king-size futons and shared by six medical students, who were never home at the same time.

Schneider was sure he was going to observe a sudden death as he toured several rooftops with a scientist who said she was very afraid of high places. The reporter wrapped one end of her safety rope around his waist as she leaned much too far trying to scrape dust samples from cornices and the heads and wings of two gargoyles. Neither one of them enjoyed the experience.

For the first several months, EPA did not collect these types of samples, because, as in Libby, the agency said its regulations didn't permit cleaning private dwellings. But this didn't stop the civilian experts. They used the newest electron-microscope technology and fiber-counting protocols — precisely what the Libby trio had offered while the fires were still burning. The civilian specialists found far more asbestos fibers than did government investigators. These private experts — all regularly hired by the government as consultants — found levels in the dwellings that were alarming to many authorities who tried to assess the health risk faced by New Yorkers.

Fortunately, EPA's ranks are dotted with people like Peronard, Weis, Miller and the Seattle office's Keven McDermott, who do not automatically trust the pronouncements of the bureaucrats and politicians. Cate Jenkins is one of those who place science and the public trust over politics and expedience.

"These eminent asbestos researchers brought state-of-the-art methods to lower Manhattan and ... what they found with the new technology is dramatically different than what EPA and New York State reported," said Jenkins, a senior chemist in the agency's hazardous-waste division.[9] "For every asbestos fiber EPA detected, the new methods used by the outside experts found nine," she said. "This is too important a difference to be ignored if you really care about the health of the public."

Jenkins, a 22-year veteran of the EPA, talked about the asbestos levels that researchers Eric Chatfield and John Kominsky found in apartments and condos near the collapse that had not been cleaned or had been cleaned improperly.

"If people continue living and working in places that still have dust in the carpets, furniture, drapes and heating and cooling system, these fibers will continue to be resuspended," Jenkins explained. "The elevated risk could be from around one in a thousand extra cancers to maybe as high as one in ten."

Four other federal health experts — two toxicologists, an epidemiologist and a physician — from the EPA and the Centers for Disease Control studied the data gathered by Chatfield, Kominsky and a team headed by Hugh Granger of HP Environmental in Virginia. They agreed with Jenkins's interpretation. "The concentrations of asbestos in settled dusts inside homes in Libby are comparable to the settled dusts inside the buildings in lower Manhattan," Jenkins said.

She and others in the agency are questioning why, if Libby is dangerous enough to be declared a Superfund site, the EPA is shrugging off even higher levels in New York. "It is unfathomable to believe that EPA can stand behind antiquated science when a report on Libby, issued by the same agency, irrefutably documents the validity of the new methods," Jenkins said.

While EPA may not have wanted to admit the need for a thorough federal cleanup of the entire affected area, it did think enough of the hazard to make sure its own offices in lower Manhattan were thoroughly decontaminated. Asbestos levels in those offices were tested not with the decades-old PLM technology but with newer, more accurate TEM analysis.

EPA insisted it wasn't its decision to clean its offices. "It wasn't our idea. The General Services Administration made us do it," said Bonnie Bellow, the EPA spokesperson in New York.

"Yeah, right. Of course," a supervisor at GSA, the government's landlord, told Schneider. "The only cleanups done in that building were ordered by EPA."

Many federal employees, contract scientists and physicians believe that the lack of action on asbestos from the towers' collapse was a reflection of the government's long-fought internal disputes over what kind of asbestos is dangerous and how many fibers of what size it takes to sicken or kill.

The dust storm that crashed through Manhattan on September 11 blew in windows and doors many blocks from Ground Zero. Air-conditioning units on rooftops and in windows sucked pounds of dust into apartments and building ventilation systems. Some apartments had inches of gray dust covering everything. Most others within blocks of the attack had floors, walls, window coverings and furniture covered in a fine, powdery film.

At Ground Zero, hundreds of environmental and occupational health specialists tried to keep the emergency workers in the still-smoking hole protected, and tried to diminish future exposure to asbestos and other dangerous material. But many of the approximately 340,000 people who live in the lower part of the island believed they were abandoned and, at the least, fed conflicting information by federal, state and city officials on how to avoid asbestos exposure.

"It's like all of us who live down here really don't matter to anyone in any government. We've pretty much been left to fend for ourselves," said Steve Swaney, who, with his wife, lived in a Battery Park apartment.[10] The Swaneys' patio doors were open when the buildings collapsed. Their one bedroom apartment, like many of the 238 others in their 15-story building, was covered in dust.

Those with insurance paid as much as $10,000 to have professional asbestos crews clean their apartments, Swaney said. The landlord cleaned the rest. "But there was still dust all over the place, and we couldn't get anyone to tell us how much asbestos was still there," he said. So the tenants paid to have the dust analyzed, and the dust contained levels of asbestos above 1 percent, which the EPA considers unsafe.

The landlord sent in another cleaning crew.

On the streets nine floors below the Swaneys' balcony, men in air tanks and moon suits slowly waddled behind and beside huge gushing mobile water tanks and purring SuperVac vacuum trucks. The bizarre ballet was precisely orchestrated to wash out, suck up and capture the most minute pockets of dust from Battery Park's promenade, playgrounds and sidewalks, and even from children's sandboxes in the park.

But Swaney, a 58-year-old computer consultant, had a sick wife. Her ribs were sore from hours of gagging, coughing and choking from the same dust that EPA crews so carefully removed on the street out front. He wonders why the crews working on the street were so meticulous, using microfilter vacuums, wearing protective clothing and respirators. But in his apartment, the three-person pickup band of day laborers the landlord hired used brooms, dustpans, old mops and buckets, and everyday vacuum cleaners.

"They didn't even have masks," he said. "My wife had to find masks for them."

He wondered what government officials knew about the dust that they weren't sharing.

"To those of us in the middle of this, it's obvious that there is a conscious effort not to put out the facts," said Swaney, who heads his building's tenant association. "I don't know whether it's the White House or the governor's mansion or the mayor's office, but someone doesn't want this truth about asbestos getting out. They don't want to close down lower Manhattan. We're talking about a lot of money, a lot of jobs. That's okay, but is it safe to live here?"

Swaney and his wife moved out of lower Manhattan.

"Christie Whitman says it's fine to return to our homes," he noted. "She's the EPA boss. Should we not believe her when she says our apartments are safe? But how does she know?"

Les Skramstad had an opinion on that, and he wasn't shy about sharing it.

"It's the same damned government babble and half-assed decision-making that led to half this town being either dead or dying from asbestos," Les told Schneider as the old miner watched Whitman in New York on TV. "You'd think what happened here would have taught the government why it's important not to sweep this asbestos under the rug.

"Twenty or thirty years from now, when those New Yorkers start falling over dead, some young government bureaucrat will get all choked up apologizing for what the EPA and others didn't do.

"That's what they did here."

THE EPA SAID it couldn't test apartments and offices.[11] None of the thousands of tests that the agency cited as showing the asbestos risk was minimal were taken inside the buildings and rooms where people live, study and work.

"That's just not our job, and we have no policies or procedures for doing that type of testing," said Bonnie Bellow, spokeswoman for the EPA's Region 2 office in New York. "We've never had to worry about asbestos in houses before."

Granger, of the Virginia company HP Environmental, said, "To ignore testing the indoor environment for asbestos defies logic. Outside, the normal air movement dilutes and dissipates asbestos concentration. Inside, the fibers are trapped by four walls. They constantly get resuspended just by occupants walking on carpets, closing the drapes or having the air conditioner or heat go on or off."

In October, the EPA and OSHA were still putting out information to residents saying that if dust from the collapsed towers was in homes or offices, "people should be sure to clean thoroughly and avoid inhaling dust while doing so." State and federal agencies warned about the toxic material and asbestos in the dust and quickly told people to wear masks if they found dust when they returned to their homes.

More than 1,800 volunteers from the Southern Baptist Church, the Salvation Army and other groups who cleaned hundreds of apartments wore plain paper or cloth masks. No one told them that of the 29 most available brands of masks on the market, only one contained filters fine enough to stop asbestos fibers. But state and federal asbestos-removal regulations demand that the cleanup be done by personnel wearing special respirators and full head-to-toe protective suits and gloves, and that the waste be disposed of only at authorized sites.

The EPA and New York Health Department point fingers at each other as the source of the misleading information. Bellow admits that the EPA's website initially linked to incorrect guidance for office and apartment landlords and renters. "It wasn't our information. It was from the [New York] state or city health department, and we removed it from our website," she said.

"Obviously, our asbestos program was overwhelmed by a catastrophe of this magnitude. We are usually only concerned with asbestos from renovations and building demolition." But a check of EPA's website after Bellow's comments found that the same links were being used.

When it came to the bureaucrats issuing medical information on asbestos, the contradictions were even more glaring. The New York City Department of Health told residents that "asbestos-related lung disease results only from intense asbestos exposure experienced over a period of many years, primarily as a consequence of occupational exposures." But the EPA's own experts as well as physicians at the CDC and private research centers have shown that a single, heavy dose of asbestos can be enough to cause lethal disease.

"They keep calling it a 'trace.' This implies to the public that there is no hazard from it," said Dr. Jerrold Abraham, director of environmental and occupational pathology at Upstate Medical University in Syracuse.[12] "If you're talking about pure chrysotile asbestos, there are ten billion or more fibers per gram, or about a fifth of a teaspoon. Their whole measuring and reporting system needs to be made more honest."

The EPA's Bellow tried to answer the criticism.

"We didn't see ourselves as the primary source for information on what the health implications were. We're not a health agency," she said. But Walter Mugdan, EPA's top lawyer in Bellow's regional office, had a different opinion.[13] A major part of the agency's mission assignment for the disaster response was "environmental monitoring to help determine what short- and longer-term health risks were presented by the terrible events of that day," the regional counsel said.

EPA headquarters, long in turmoil over asbestos issues, has repeatedly declined to discuss these topics.

Granger, the HP Environmental scientist who has studied the importance of risk communication, said the ball was dropped. "We are talking about the very lives of these people and those they love," he said. "Because of the misleading or completely inaccurate government information and guidance, people don't know where to turn or whom to trust."

In fact, thanks to some courageous scientists from the U.S. Geological Survey, not usually an agency primed to respond to emergencies, the federal government had very detailed information about the contents of the dust cloud. They just refused to allow the scientists to share it with the people who needed the information.

The USGS scientists used a sophisticated sensing unit designed for exploring the terrain of Mars and Jupiter to analyze the dust.[14] It was the same technology they had used months earlier to help EPA get an accurate picture of how much tremolite asbestos polluted Libby. Weis called in some IOUs with people in Washington and got the Air Force to agree that it would not shoot down a NASA DeHavilland Twin Otter while it made 16 passes over Manhattan. Poking through a hole in the plane's belly was an infrared spectrometer. The USGS scientists and the NASA pilots repeated their flights on September 18, 22 and 23, and they hustled the information they got to the EPA. Back at the USGS laboratories in Denver, a dozen scientists in almost as many different specialties worked around the clock with the samples. They found not only asbestos, but an alphabet soup of heavy metals. The biggest surprise was that they found that the dust was much more caustic than believed, with some samples showing pH levels comparable to that of drain cleaner.

Immediately, USGS passed the information up the chain of command, to EPA, to FEMA, and to the management group guided by the White House, which met every morning, either in person or by conference call. The White House group knew the danger that USGS had identified. The scientists had told them. But those on the front lines of protecting the health of the public and the workers cleaning up the site said they were never given that information. The groups responsible for the safety of the thousands of men and women on the rescue and recovery groups were never told about the contents of the dust.

The first clue New Yorkers got was on February 10, 2002, when the networks picked up Schneider's story on the cover-up from the *St. Louis Post-Dispatch.* And it hit the fan. Physicians and union officials couldn't believe the government knew and told no one.

"We've not heard from the EPA or anyone else releasing information on specific pH levels in the dust, and that's information that we all should have had," said Carrie Loewenherz, an industrial hygienist for the New York Committee for Occupational Safety and Health.

"I'm supposed to be in the loop, and I've never heard any specific numbers on how caustic the dust actually was," said Dr. Robin Herbert, codirector of the Mount Sinai Center for Occupational and Environmental Medicine. "There's a large segment of the population here whose physicians needed to know that information that USGS submitted [to EPA]. Exposure to dust with a high pH could impact everyone, but especially the very young, the very old and those with existing pulmonary disease."

She added that physicians are "struggling to reconcile the health problems they're seeing with the exposure data they're being given. The high pH of the dust may be a part of the answer. ... Any credible information the government had relating to health issues just should have been released," she said. "There is no justification for holding it. You don't conceal the information from those who need it."

The EPA's Cate Jenkins again blasted her own agency over its refusal to disclose the information. "The pH levels the USGS documented were far too high for EPA to ignore. They insisted that all the information regarding health and safety was being released to the public. Well, that's not true. There's nothing, internally or in public releases, that shows the agency ever disclosed specific pH levels."

On October 16, 2002, a year and a week after the help of the Libby scientists was curtly refused, a new EPA team finally permitted to oversee the testing and cleaning of thousands of New York's apartments and businesses made the trip to Libby to see how it was done.[15] The EPA deputy regional administrator from New York, Cathy Callahan, brought toxicologist Mark Maddaloni and on-site coordinators Joe Ingaldi and Eric Johnson. They were concerned about the job they'd been assigned, and some of them were worried that too many people may have returned to their residences before the contaminants were properly removed. Peronard shared that concern.

"Callahan is sharp as a tack and she's got the guts to stand up for her crew. They give a damn about people who may be living in a world of asbestos fibers," Peronard told Schneider as the Libby boss guided his Yankee visitors over to Brad Black's clinic to see X-rays and CT-scans of the lungs of Libby. "They're getting grief for decisions that were made by politicians and image-makers. All they want to do is clean up as many apartments as they can. But all of us are worried that for some, the cleanup may be coming too late."

The day after Christmas 2002, EPA issued yet another report on the contamination of lower Manhattan. As usual, the executive summary, which is all most people read, painted a rosy picture and concluded there was little health risk to residents or workers in the area other than those who were exposed to the initial dust plume. The heart of the report said that the EPA was still working to clean up asbestos from apartments near the attack site and added that potential exposure levels in some dwellings were up to 150 times the level considered safe.

At 3 P.M. on the following day, December 27, 2002, dozens of residents of lower Manhattan gathered in front of the EPA building on Broadway. They were protesting the closing of the EPA hot line for requesting cleanup of World Trade Center dust. "EPA's outreach has been atrocious," said Sudhir Jain, president of the World Trade Center Residents' Coalition. "They're not properly conveying to people the long-term health risks of living with these contaminants in their apartments. And the longer people are exposed, the greater the chance they'll have serious health consequences like cancer later on.

"New Yorkers deserve better."

The week of Labor Day 2003, 19 months after the *Post-Dispatch* published its stories on the White House pressuring EPA to tone down the dangers to emergency workers and residents of lower Manhattan, Nikki Tinsley, the agency's inspector general, released her report on what she found in New York.

A firestorm of criticism erupted instantly. At least three congressional hearings were scheduled. Demands were made by top politicians that the Justice Department investigate the White House's involvement in the alleged cover-up.

The leaders of the 19 unions representing EPA employees across the country demanded that the "president pledge to never again order EPA to tell less than the whole truth about a public health emergency."[16] They denounced the White House for ordering vital information on the dangers after the terrorist attacks to be withheld from the public. They charged that "unwarranted and inexcusable interference ... by politicians reporting directly to President Bush caused rescue workers and residents to be exposed to health risks that could have been, indeed should have been, avoided.

"Instead, the Bush White House had information released, drafted by political appointees, that it knew to contradict the scientific facts. It misinformed. And many rescue workers and citizens suffered. Some citizens now face the long-term risk of asbestos-related lung cancer as well as other debilitating respiratory ailments as a result."

By March of 2004, the Mount Sinai Medical Center for Occupational and Environmental Medicine had examined 9,229 men and women from the estimated 40,000 individuals who participated in rescue and recovery operations at Ground Zero. Almost half of those examined — 4,200 — the physicians reported, had long-term respiratory illness or injury related to their often-heroic effort.

We're not talking about asbestos-caused disease in this group of men and women. The first symptoms of that painful path to death won't surface for 15 years or more. The illnesses diagnosed at Mount Sinai were a result of inhaling caustic chemicals, ground metal, glass and concrete.

The tragedy is that if the government had behaved humanely and released the information on the hazards instead of concealing it, the workers who toiled for months amidst the death and destruction could easily have been protected, instead of becoming victims themselves.

Gayla, frustrated that she couldn't get lawmakers in Montana to heed the health crisis in Libby, decided she might do more if she became a legislator.
(Andrew Schneider)

THE TRANSFORMATION of two bar singers into activists may seem improbable. But it was fueled by the kind of anger that burns hot and changes the shape of a person for life. Lose your mother and father. Get duped into contaminating your wife and children, and get handed your own death sentence in the bargain. You won't have any problem getting motivated to fight.

"Les and I can stand back-to-back and fight to get something done about this asbestos," Gayla was fond of saying. "We bunch up real good. I'm loud and rough and say what I'm thinking. Les speaks softly and weighs his words, but don't cross either of us."

At first, the two simply fought to get the town to notice the victims' plight, and tried to get the politicians and bureaucrats to make sure their kids weren't in danger. But they couldn't get much traction in Libby. Peronard realized that until the *Post-Intelligencer* stories came out, it had been a long, hard road for Les and Gayla. They were shouted down by those who didn't believe, or didn't want to believe, that there was a health problem.

But with the burst of publicity, that changed quickly. Suddenly, they were the two most sought-after advocates for asbestos victims in the country. Reporters from *People, McCall's, USA Today, Mother Jones, Men's Journal,* and assorted TV newsmagazines stuck microphones and tape recorders in their faces. The fire of their anger still burned hot, and now the flames were visible nationwide.

Les was determined to see Libby cleaned up and safe for his grandchildren and the generations to come. After the stories came out, when Grace volunteered to clean up the export plant, he was skeptical. He didn't think it was possible to decontaminate the building. He was convinced there was so much asbestos in that building that it would never be clean. So when Grace pronounced it clean, Les went down there with the editor of *The Western News,* Roger Morris, and showed him literally piles of dust that had been missed. He kept after Peronard and the others at EPA, and finally, sure enough, they realized the building was still contaminated, and it was demolished. He went through much the same process with the expanding plant, where he used to work. But first, the current tenant, a small sawmill operator, needed to have his equipment moved to another location, and that move took literally years. Les gritted his teeth, day after day, as he passed the old building where he had labored on his hands and knees to produce "clean" asbestos for the Zonolite Corporation.

Norita took Les's seat on the CAG, because he knew he'd get too angry to be effective. But he kept lobbying EPA and doing everything he could to press the advantage that national publicity had finally given them. "He's in our face and he won't let us slow down," Peronard said. "He cares desperately about what the exposure has done to his family, and he still fights the battle for the rest of the town."

Gayla, meanwhile, was turning herself into an eloquent spokeswoman, a one-stop media resource center, a repository for documents, and a cyber-whiz able to knock out PowerPoint presentations and surf the Internet with equal ease.

"The last thing in the world I ever thought I'd buy was a computer. Hell, I could barely handle the remote for the TV," she said. But now a corner of her bedroom/office had expanded into her worldwide communications center. There's the computer, monitor, scanner, CD burner and a dozen other gadgets that she says she mastered by "trial and a hell of a lot of error."

"Thank God for the Internet," she says. "If you're fighting the government or a company like Grace, it's the best weapon available for leveling the fighting field. It gives you a voice, a way to communicate, a source for information. It can damn sure make you hard to ignore."

When EPA and ATSDR first began to discuss the screening program, the EPA asked her to attend a conference on the subject in Cincinnati with Brad Black, Aubrey Miller, Chris Weis and Alan Whitehouse. Her passionate advocacy for a full-on survey helped the EPA win an early argument against surveying only those in Whitehouse's case files.

The Cincinnati conference was the first of a string of far-flung appearances for Gayla. Close on the heels of that conference was the testimony on the Asbestos Fairness Act in Washington. Gayla hadn't been home from Washington long when she was asked to help in the investigation of a vermiculite mine near Dillon, Montana, that had applied for permission to expand its operations. She and several other Libby residents went to Dillon and spoke at a public meeting. It was there that Gayla first ran into the R.J. Lee firm, the same company that tested crayons for Binney & Smith and found them "asbestos-free." Sure enough, Lee said it had done a study of the tremolite at the Dillon mine and proclaimed it to be a "safe" form.

"Bullshit," said Gayla.

The following month, in June 2000, Gayla went to San Francisco to make a presentation to a conference of community advisory groups from cleanup sites around the nation. The message from Libby was mixed this time: Gayla gave her presentation about the mine and the sickness it spawned, and was quickly followed by Mayor Berget, who tried to explain away the problems while promoting Libby as a tourist destination. Then Ron Anderson from the Lincoln County Sanitation Department gave a talk on the history of the mine. Fortunately, Brad Black followed up with hard numbers on the dead and dying.

Everywhere she spoke, Gayla found shock and anger at the Libby story. The same was true the next month, when she flew to Brazil to make a presentation at an international asbestos conference. There, without the mayor trying to provide counterprogramming, Gayla's presentation was all the more dramatic, and she was greeted with a standing ovation and embraces from an audience that had been moved to tears. It was an amazing moment for the woman who was scorned by her principal at Libby High School and told she'd never amount to anything.

While she was in Brazil, Gayla got a phone call asking her to come to Warwick, New York, where a quarry known to have tremolite in the rock was trying to reopen after being shut down for 40 years. In the intervening years, the town had grown all around the quarry. After five days at home, she went to Warwick and appeared at a packed meeting in the town's gymnasium.

She was preceded on the podium by the supporters of the quarry, who announced that the tremolite in Warwick had been studied by a prominent scientist and found to be "safe." And the scientist was none other than R. J. Lee. Gayla got up and told the crowd about Libby, then about the Dillon mine — and R. J. Lee. Again, she got a standing ovation, and the effort to reopen the quarry failed. Through it all, Gayla insisted she wasn't interested in fame. She had made her grandchildren a promise that she would do everything she could to make Libby, and everywhere else, safer from the hazards of asbestos than it had been for her and her children.

Of course, back home in Libby she had been getting hate mail ever since the stories broke. A group of businessmen actually considered suing Gayla and Les for hurting the town's image. But none of this slowed Gayla down for an instant. Ever since her days as "Popcorn Annie," Gayla had been used to meanness from certain quarters in Libby, and this was no different.

"These are the ones that really hurt to read," she told Schneider, opening an e-mail from a woman in Alabama whose father worked on Libby Dam and died of asbestosis.[1] Just below it in the queue was another from the daughter of a man who worked at Grace's mine in South Carolina. She wrote that both of her parents had died from asbestos-related disease, just like Gayla's, even though Grace had said there was no tremolite in the South Carolina ore.

"After reading about Libby, now I know what really killed my parents," she wrote.

Another came from the wife of a Burlington Northern Railroad man who worked the trains that shipped ore from Libby. She wrote frantically, saying her man could barely breathe, and where could she find a doctor who cared, and was her husband going to die?

Gayla answered those e-mails after midnight, when the phone wasn't ringing and she had time to think. Most people, she realized, just wanted information, and they had no other place to turn. As the *Post-Intelligencer* reporters did, she heard from many who had lost someone they loved from Zonolite insulation and never knew where the exposure came from until they read the newspaper stories or saw accounts on TV.

Meanwhile, Les Skramstad had developed a new friendship — with the governor of Montana.

The previous governor, Marc Racicot, whose two cousins had asbestosis and who had played on the piles of vermiculite himself as a child in Libby, did little for the town while he was in office. Gayla and Les tried and tried to make an appointment with him, but couldn't get on his calendar. So one day when they knew he was talking with Grace officials, they drove to Helena and ambushed him, demanding to see him. Racicot spent five minutes with them, looking at his watch nervously the whole time, and nothing came of the visit.

Racicot was prevented by law from running for a third term, and when he was succeeded by Judy Martz, also a Republican with a pro-business record, Libby's victims didn't expect much from her, either. A big decision was waiting in the wings for the new governor. Under federal law, each state gets to designate one environmental cleanup site in the state for the federal government's National Priority List, or Superfund, thus bypassing months or years of federal red tape. No governor had ever used that power in Montana, and pressure had been mounting from victims and advocates to name Libby as a Superfund site.

At first, Martz was lukewarm at best on the idea of using Montana's "silver bullet" to put Libby on the Superfund list.[2] A lot of Chamber of Commerce types in Libby were dead-set against it; they figured it would be terrible for business. And, of course, they were Republicans who'd supported Martz for governor. But Les Skramstad decided not to take everybody else's word about Judy Martz.

One night, at a CAG meeting, the director of the state's Department of Health came to give the group an update, and after the meeting Les buttonholed her and said, "All you say the state's planning to do, it sounds really good, but I want to know if the governor is really going to do anything or not."

"Well," she said, "I've got an 800 number right here on my card that will get you in contact with her." "Give me that number," he said. The next day, he dialed it, and got not the governor, but Myrna Ornholt-Mason in the governor's office.

"I am Governor Martz's citizens' advocate," Ornholt-Mason said.

"Well, that is nice, but I really need to talk to the governor," Les said.

"Well, I can't connect you directly, but I'll transfer you to Lynn Staley. She's the governor's scheduler."

"What can I do for you?" a new voice asked Les crisply.

"Well, I need to talk to the governor, and not on the telephone. I want to meet with her in person."

"She's awful busy."

"I realize that, but I need to talk to her about this asbestos problem in Libby."

"I see. Well, I'm looking at her schedule." She named a day a couple of weeks distant. "Would that work? I can give you fifteen minutes."

"No," Les said. "I can't drive 700 miles for fifteen minutes."

"Well, is it just you, or will there be others coming?"

"No," Les said, "I think I'll bring Norita, my wife, and Brent, my son, and his wife, Julie. And Gayla Benefield. And her daughter might come too. And there might be another one or two of us."

"Holy smokes, that's quite a few of you."

"We're in a desperate situation here, and we need to talk to the governor about it."

"I tell you what, we'll give you half an hour."

"We'll take it, and thanks." Les called Gayla right away.

"You got half an hour for a personal talk with the governor?"

"Yep."

"Well, I'll be damned."

When the day arrived, Les was nervous as a cat. The group arrived at the Capitol more than two hours early. Les had no idea where to go. He finally found the right office, and told the receptionist who they were, and that they had an appointment with the governor at two.

"That's quite a while from now," she said.

"I know, but I wasn't going to be late."

When the time finally came, Martz came out, greeted them and ushered them into her office. Les walked right up to the head of the table and sat down beside her. Judy Martz is tall, gray-haired and down-to-earth. From the first moment, she and Les clicked. The news media were there — TV cameras, microphones. Les hadn't expected any of that, and Martz sensed that. She said simply, "I'm anxious to hear what you have to say."

Les, sitting probably two feet away from her, max, looked her in the eye and jumped right in. After he'd explained the situation in broad strokes, he said, "So you know I have asbestosis. I brought it home and gave it to my wife, Norita, and she's here to tell you her side of it. I gave it to my son, too, and he's here, with his wife, to talk about their family. I gave it to my daughter, too, but she's in Wisconsin and couldn't be here. This is affecting all of us in a serious and very dreadful way."

Then Martz listened to Norita, and Brent, and Gayla, and asked some questions, and Les talked some more. Pretty soon it had been an hour, not half an hour. Les kept contrasting Martz with Racicot in his mind, and she seemed so much more genuine. He thought she had a caring, compassionate nature. And the whole time they were there, she never looked at her watch.

In December 2001, Judy Martz came to Libby.[3] She held a press conference to announce that she was invoking the "silver bullet" on Libby's behalf, to get the town on the Superfund list and get some help. For someone who had been a conservative Republican right down the line, it was a courageous thing to do. She talked about the people of Libby, and she singled out Les and Norita Skramstad and said they were instrumental in changing her mind on the Superfund.

Two months later, Martz invited Les and Norita to Helena for her State of the State address to the Legislature, and during her speech she talked about her decision on Libby, and the state's ongoing responsibility there. And she asked Les and Norita to stand and be recognized. So don't bad-mouth Judy Martz within earshot of Les Skramstad. You'll have a tussle on your hands. Now framed personal notes and autographed photos from Martz hang on Les and Norita's walls. And every once in a while the phone rings, and it's Governor Judy, wanting to chat.

Martz acknowledges that she and the old cowboy with the toothpick in his mouth and Resistol on his head are a bit of an odd couple. But she says, "There's nothing phony about Les. He says what he thinks, and he's given me an earful from time to time, though it's usually something I need to hear. He's a genuine man. And I had been raised the same way. And in some ways, Les reminded me of my own dad — his honesty, his frankness, his illness.

"I trust Les. And every time I talk to Les, I'm reminded of what W.R. Grace did to Libby."

Les says he's still puzzled by the relationship. "Ever' now and then I get the feeling that she must think she's talking to another Les, someone smarter, someone with more clout, someone she has to make believe she cares about. I've got years of having Libby's mayor, city councilmen and county commissioners just sneer when I talked about the danger here from asbestos. They'd just blow me off as some kind of pain in the ass. Now I've got a governor calling to see what I think should be done.

"Life is sure funny."

MEMORIAL DAY 2002 brought more white crosses: fourteen rows of fourteen and five extra.[4]

Thirty-eight more than the year before. They covered the northeast corner of the Libby cemetery from block 12 to block 14, from almost the road to the edge of Parmenter Creek.

The day was gray. Ashen clouds obscured the Cabinet Mountains. Far off in the distance a peak, snow-covered and bathed in sunlight, lit up the horizon. "It's like Libby," said Les. "Gloom and darkness covers everything, like the death and pain we all live with, but far away, out of reach, is a shining bright light, like the hopes we have for our children and those who follow us."

The ceremony for the asbestos victims was still three hours away.

The veterans had finished their salute. Twenty-one shots fired by an honor guard echoed under the low-hanging clouds. Tight-fitting old uniforms stretched over potbellies, but the veterans stood taller than in years past. They talked of the terrorist attack and the men and women fighting in foreign lands. Many of Libby's citizens have little tolerance for the government — any government — but do not for a moment question their patriotism.

Dozens of American flags flapped in the breeze along the fence bordering the cemetery. Flags of the states and of the military units that went to U.S. wars stand post at the corners of each block of graves. About 200 people milled around the tombstones, many laying pink and red and purple bouquets at gravesites. The cluster of crosses was unadorned, plain by comparison. Only five of the 204 had flowers. Dena Crill made it six when she knelt and affixed a sparkling blue ribbon corsage to the cross that bore her father's name — Don Kaeding.

A tall man in a brushed leather coat stood at the end of a line of crosses. He paused for as long as it took to read the name before moving to the next. You could see him quietly mouthing the name and moving with almost military precision the three short steps to the next one. Right to left, to the next row. Left to right, another row. All 14 rows. He stopped to read a large wooden sign in front of the crosses: *In memory of the miners, their families and community members that have passed on.*

"Nope," he answered when Schneider asked if he knew the miners or their families.

"Nope," he added when asked if he was from Libby.

Why was he here?

"Someone has to care about these people," he said softly in a slight Texas drawl. "Someone has to care," he repeated as he walked away.

A few others walked quietly among the crosses. Most of them knew what they were facing. They had lived with their fathers, mothers, siblings, spouses and children dying slowly as the invisible fibers scarred their lungs until breathing was impossible. They had witnessed the agony up close. For too many, the sound, smell and pain of death were far too fresh.

Les and Norita had set up a microphone and a portable amplifier under a cedar. Les hobbled over the uneven ground to a nearby picnic table to catch his breath. Norita walked beside him and just a bit behind, in a good position to grab him if he stumbled, but she didn't touch him, just watched closely as he leaned heavily on his cane.

The air hung heavy in the Kootenai valley. It was the kind of day when Les and others with their lungs shot to hell fight for every breath. For Les it was worse, because he was still too stubborn to start using oxygen. "Nobody suckin' air out of those tanks lives for too long," said Les. "I've got too much more to do before I give it up."

He watched the crowd trickle in and scanned the crosses. They were laid out alphabetically, and Les tried to figure where Skramstad will go. *It'll be somewhere back near the creek,* he thought. The water was running wild and frothy, brought almost to flood stage by days of heavy rain.

Then it was noon and the crowd was as large as it was going to get. Les pulled himself up and walked slowly to the mic to welcome about 80 people. "This is a happy day and also a sad day," he said. "Happy because we are together. Sad because each one of these crosses represents someone who has died from asbestos."

The Pastor Cam Foote of Libby's Troy Baptist Church moved to the microphone, looking slightly bewildered. None of the dead were members of his church. Most were Lutherans. But he was the Council of Churches' representative to the Citizens' Advisory Group, so he knew how asbestos killed.

"Many dear persons have been torn from us ..." he said. But he was new in town and knew few of them. He turned to his Bible and read Paul's second letter to the Corinthians, first chapter, then said, "We are not here to honor the fallen. We are not here today next to two hundred crosses to shake an angry fist toward God. We are here today because there is a sense of helplessness. We are here to express sadness for shortened lives" — laughter denied, picnics never held, words never spoken.

Families, what was left of them, stood in clusters. Les, Norita and their daughter Gayla stood together, their arms around each other. Five-year-old granddaughter Makenna clung to Les's legs. A few feet away, Dena Crill held tightly to her husband Mike. Her grown son, Andy Faris, stood close. Her mother, Louise Kaeding, sobbed quietly, staring at the cross of her husband, Don, who had died six months earlier.

Alice Priest stood by herself. She breathed deeply, adjusting the oxygen that flowed from the small belly-pack tank into the plastic tubes by her nose. She was happy she was no longer tied to the long, green oxygen cylinders she'd been shackled to for three years.

It was as if Foote was speaking of her. "We are also here to express our sorrow to the survivors who are now alone. And we are here because we are in empathy with the people still walking but afflicted with asbestosis and asbestos-related diseases. We will care for you." The time had come, Foote said, to stop huddling privately in small groups to mourn the dead. Strength for the living and peace for the dead would be found in a public sharing of grief.

"We hereby remember by name and ask God's blessing ..." The sun broke through the clouds as Foote spoke, but was swallowed up again as Bob Wilkins, the former union president for the miners, shuffled slowly to the mic to read the roll of the dead.

"Emmet Adkins, Morris Ahrenkiel, William Airth ..." Wilkins read, his voice a barely audible, hoarse whisper. "Donald Dutton, Ed Dutton, Walter Dutton." Two worked at the mine, one at the lumber mill, but the tremolite took all three lives.

He read the names of Gene Lyle and his two sons Jim and John, all miners for Grace.

"Alice McQueen, Walter McQueen, Edward McQueen, George McQueen." Wife, husband, two sons.

They strained to hear Wilkins's whisper above the sound of the rushing stream.

"Dorthe Noble, Harvey Noble." Wife and husband. He worked at the mine and brought the tremolite home to her on his work clothes.

"Ed Orr," croaked Wilkins. He stopped, shook his head and handed the list to his son Don. The young man's strong voice ricocheted off the trees.

"Margaret Vatland, Perley Vatland."

The tall stranger in the leather coat was back, standing apart from the crowd. Close enough to hear, but on the other side of the road, alone. As the names were read he lifted his face to the sky. He was facing in the direction of the mine, but he couldn't have seen the 4,200-foot-tall Zonolite Mountain even if the clouds were not hanging low to the ground. His eyes were squeezed tightly shut as the names rolled on.

When asked, he said he was 68, but he wouldn't give his name. "I just can't talk about this," he said, and pointed to the crosses. "God knows it's horrible, but I worked for Grace all my life and there's nothing I can say." He walked away as Don Wilkins continued to read.

"Bud Vinion, Rae Vinion, Jack Vinion." Another family, lost to the mine. And finally, "Ted Wright." The last name on this year's list.

Gayla Benefield stood alone, leaning against the thick trunk of a tree. "The crowd is larger this year because more have died, but we're still by ourselves," she said, more sad than angry. "There's no one here from the town except those who have lost kin. Not the mayor. Not the city council. None of the Lincoln County officials.

"Superfund, congressional hearings, dozens of network news specials, hundreds of newspaper and magazine stories, and most of this town still wants to believe that nothing bad happened in Libby."

GAYLA DECIDED TO RUN for the state senate.[5] She knew it would be an uphill fight, but she had been urged by several people in the state Democratic Party to give it a try.

The seed was planted in November 2001 when Montana attorney general Mike McGrath came to Libby and met privately with Gayla and Les. He suggested to Gayla that she run, and at first she thought, *That's the last thing I need.* But she began to think about it: Could she do more from the inside than peering in from the outside? She thought the legislature needed someone who knew what had happened to the people of Libby. Running for office from a community where you are both despised and respected was clearly a crapshoot. She admitted early in the campaign that she was a long-shot candidate.

Logic would say that she had a great platform from which to campaign. After all, for years, she and Les stirred the pot to hold Grace accountable. The EPA finally rushed to town and had thousands of tons of asbestos contaminated soil hauled away. HHS sent teams in to examine more than 6,000 people for asbestos-related disease. With almost two-thirds of the families in and around the tiny town either having kin who had been killed by the disease or a relative now dying of it, the candidacy of a woman who screamed loudly enough to get the government to pay attention ought to be a strong one. But logic and Libby don't always get along.

For all the people in Libby who will benefit from her zeal, there are just as many who scorn her for bringing shame and unwanted attention on their community. Her most fervent critics are Libby's good-old-boy group, the ones who defended Grace for years. For a long time, Gayla believed that the antipathy that many in Libby had for the asbestos problem — and to her for publicizing it — would fade as EPA's cleanup progressed. She thought that after the Superfund designation had been won, she could contribute the most in Helena. She was hard to intimidate — make that impossible to intimidate – and she wasn't going to sell out to anybody. McGrath and others told her she could change the system. And that was irresistible.

So in late January 2002, just before the final deadline, Gayla put down $15 at the county clerk's office and filed her intention to run for the senate from Lincoln County. By August, she was running from sunrise to long after dusk, racing from CAG meetings to CARD meetings to EPA's public briefings on the cleanup while popping her head in at every businessmen's club, civic meeting or union gathering that would have her. The invitations came in from Troy, Eureka and Yaak, but few from Libby.

She sat on tractors, poked her head out of car windows, waved to the sparse crowds watching whatever parade or festival was happening in Lincoln County — Libby's Nordicfest and Logger Days, or Troy Days or the Eureka fair. "I thought the smile would freeze on my face and my wrists were going to break off from my little royal wave," she said. Donations trickled in. Slow and small.

The state Democratic Party virtually ignored Gayla. But the Republicans ran eight commercials a day on the local radio station for the two months leading up to the election. Gayla made her own campaign signs and buttons to save money. She burned up a printer running off thousands of leaflets. "We don't make much of a deal about running for office until it's time to vote, then honey, watch out," she said as she arranged the jars of red and blue paint and a three-by-four-foot white board on her kitchen counter.

Gayla never thought her Republican opponent, Aubyn Curtiss, was an easy target. She'd been in the legislature since the '70s and was a career politician who had never been defeated. But Curtiss's record was easy to run against. The *Missoulian* reported that Curtiss asked Racicot to mark the state's National Guard helicopters with distinctive numbers because, Curtiss said, her constituents felt threatened by black helicopters flying over their property. After the FBI swarmed into Lincoln, Montana, to arrest Unabomber Ted Kaczynski, Curtiss introduced legislation requiring the FBI to get permission from the local sheriff before taking any action in their county. Racicot vetoed the bill.

At age 78, Curtiss used a campaign photo that looked like it was taken 25 years earlier. She refused Gayla's requests to debate, and at one joint appearance she fell asleep sitting on the stage. Gayla, meanwhile, used her campaign brochures to urge improved education, levelheaded approaches to increasing logging, and greater accountability from the state government in all areas, especially the $450 million in tax incentives given to out-of-state companies, which brought not a single job to Montana.

Her advisers, both locally and on the state level, told her to avoid mentioning asbestos. She ignored them. "What am I supposed to do, make believe that half of Libby hasn't been killed or sickened by the stuff?"

Whenever Gayla spoke during the last month of the campaign, she would close with a discussion of what she had done in the asbestos issue. She would look her audience straight in the eye and inform them that she had stood up to Grace. That the children of the community would no longer be exposed to the fiber from simply playing like children. "Our schools are now clean. Football players and the track and baseball teams don't have to worry about being contaminated," she reminded them. "Now we have a treatment center and a medical plan." She would add that even though it was too late for her parents, or even for her husband and herself, she hoped that her children and theirs would not die from asbestos.

Still, when some of her opponent's supporters claimed that she'd disrupted people's lives, it stung. By midsummer, rumors started circulating that the Stimson lumber mill — Libby's largest employer — would close. The chatter in George's Deluxe Barber Shop was that workers with asbestosis were suing the mill for damages. The week before the election, mill owners announced that they would shut down two days after Christmas. The closure, management said, was because there was no market for the type of plywood Stimson produced. But back at the barbershop the blame was laid on asbestos and Gayla.

The Republicans were handing out bumper stickers that said "… and no I don't have asbestosis." They were designed to go below the "I love Libby" stickers that were popping up everywhere. Governor Martz e-mailed Gayla to express her dismay "that such a bumper sticker might originate or be distributed from a local Republican headquarters in light of the high emotions that exist within a community struggling to come to terms with the number of individuals affected by an asbestos-related disease."

Gayla was endorsed by Lincoln County's only newspapers — the *Tobacco Valley News* in Curtiss's hometown of Eureka and *The Western News* in Libby, where editor Roger Morris said he appreciated Curtiss's "years of service but it's time to get more aggressive and not on things like black helicopters, jackbooted thugs in the federal government and the much-feared UN invasion from across the Canadian border."

He allowed that Gayla "is not widely appreciated for her efforts to get the asbestos-contaminated vermiculite cleaned up in the Libby area. But think about it. She sued Grace and won. She could have easily sat back and minded her own business. But she cared too much for the health and safety of the community. And she has been working just as hard to help the community recover. I think she will funnel that type of energy into the biennium session of the legislature and drive the opposition crazy — both Republican and Democrat."

On the Saturday before the election, bright-red postcards showed up in mailboxes throughout Lincoln County. On the front was a photograph of two men kissing, surrounded by large white type asking, "Is this Gayla Benefield's vision for Montana?"

Gayla blew up when she started getting phone calls. Not just over the card, which was paid for and authorized by a fundamentalist Christian group in Falls Church, Virginia, but the fact that it was timed to show up in mailboxes on Saturday. "That's when the kids are home to pick up the mail," she seethed. Months earlier, she had told the Montana Family Coalition that she would not oppose same-sex marriages. "I stand by that. That's what I believe. But this postcard two days before the election is just wrong."

On election night, Gayla and about 25 other Democrats and their supporters sat in the smoky bar of the Elks Club waiting for Lincoln County's paper ballots to be counted. Sitting shoulder to shoulder with Les under the heads of seven dead elk, Gayla told the tale of a Christmas cactus she kept after her mother died.

"The girls got all the other plants, but no one wanted the cactus. It was ugly, but you couldn't kill it. It just hung in there. Ugly and bare of blooms.

"But in November of 1998, just as the trial was starting, the buds, for the first time, started showing. By the last day of my trial, it was in full bloom. It was absolutely covered with beautiful red blossoms, just covered. It bloomed again the week the stories came out in the *Post-Intelligencer,* and then nothing again until this week."

On election morning as Gayla left to vote, the cactus, sitting on a ledge by a large window in the dining room overlooking the icy Kootenai, was in full bloom. She told her supporters that night, "I don't think it's a sign that I'm going to win, but rather that things are going to be okay regardless of what happens."

At 10:39, Marianne Roose, a county commissioner, rushed in from the county building across the street where the votes were being counted. Gayla, with a beer in one hand and a cigarette in the other, peered over Roose's shoulder as she read the tally.

Yaak. Gayla, 35. Curtiss, 63.

Northwood Lake. Gayla, 190. Curtiss, 394.

Libby. Gayla, 294. Curtiss, 557.

"I may get my life back," Gayla joked, "or maybe not."

Her husband, David, poured her another beer, hugged her and said, "She pissed off a lot of people, but it looks like a lot of the people who voted against her have kin who have the disease. It just doesn't make sense."

"That damn postcard sure didn't help."

11:18. Roose returned with more numbers.

Bull Lake. Gayla, 193. Curtiss, 464.

County Commissioner John Konzen sat at the end of the bar, shaking his head.

"Gayla ruffled a lot of feathers when she started this battle against Grace, and many of them never forgot," Konzen said. "It will probably be years down the road before people appreciate what a champion Gayla was for this community and how much she did to protect the lives of everyone. It's going to take a long, long time."

By midnight all the votes but Eureka's were counted and there was no way she could win. She hugged Les and Norita and her daughter Jennie and walked out into the cold of a Libby midnight.

She stopped by her car and, for a moment, was quiet. Then she looked up. "I sometimes dream about waking up in the mornings, and stretching and just wondering about what will I do for myself that day. Refinish some furniture, clean the house, work on the quilt. Just do something that doesn't involve the Internet, e-mail, rushed phone calls or researching what the government should be doing for Libby.

"It's silly but I want to make a quilt. I've got the strips all cut and ready to sew, but I've never had time to put it together. Tomorrow is another day. Which is good, because this one wasn't a lot of fun," she said, and drove home.

First the townsfolk paid little attention to the wooden crosses erected each Memorial Day in Libby's cemetery. But as the crosses increased in number, so did the concern. (Andrew Schneider)

I T LOOKED LIKE the government had finally learned its lesson about the need to tell people about the dangers of asbestos from Libby.[1]

It was April 2002, and after months of internal agonizing, bureaucratic soul-searching and scientific arm-wrestling, the EPA was finally on the verge of warning millions of Americans that their attics and walls might contain Grace's deadly asbestos-contaminated insulation. The announcement had first been scheduled for late 2001, then again in February of 2002, then March, then April. It was to accompany EPA's long-awaited declaration of a public-health emergency in Libby.

The emergency declaration, which had never been used by any agency, would authorize the removal of the disease-causing insulation from about 800 homes in and around Libby. Of equal or even greater importance to many, especially those dying from asbestos-related disease, the emergency plan would provide long-term medical care for those stricken by the disease.

It had been a long struggle. Peronard and his team had been bombarded with questions from Washington like, "Are the risks to those people really that great?" and "Your numbers must be off. They're way too high." They had been asked by bureaucrats why the government should care about long-term health problems in Libby.

"Most of these poor bastards here are sick and dying because the government failed them decades ago. If we don't have a moral obligation to help them now, who the hell does?" Weis snapped.

Miller added, "We just about forced them to go through the health screening so we could understand how many of them are sick and how toxic the stuff really is. We needed that information. But because they got screened, two thousand or more of them came up with signs of disease, and they will never be able to get insurance from anyone."

Peronard sighed. He thought his team was right to be angry with the foot-draggers at headquarters. "They just don't get it," he said, shaking his head. "The asbestos levels that the contractors are pulling out of these homes doesn't leave anything to the imagination. Even if we could clean every damned tremolite fiber from every surface inch of Libby, people here are still going to get sick and die because their attics and walls are filled with Zonolite."

The team members had gritted their teeth and complied with every request for proof of the contamination and documentation of the hazard. In this they'd been aided by the unprecedented, incredible job ATSDR had done. The space-age technology that USGS had brought to this remote corner of Montana had supplied newer and more detailed information on the tremolite. All of this supported the need for the public-health emergency declaration.

The Libby team believed they had the strongest possible ally — their big boss, EPA administrator Christie Whitman, was concerned about Libby and what risks the asbestos-contaminated ore might pose for the rest of the country.[2] Her staff said she was infuriated when EPA's inspector general issued the report that said the agency had dropped the ball decades ago.

"She wasn't angry because EPA got caught dropping the ball. She was outraged that the agency had dropped it at all," said a Whitman confidant. "She swore it would never happen again, at least not on her watch."

Before the report came out, Whitman had already apologized to Libby.[3] On September 7, 2001, she stood in front of a packed town hall and told the townsfolk that she was there to ensure that the cleanup is "done right and done thoroughly and we're not going to leave until it is."

She added: "Because of what we found in Libby, we are reviewing all the scientific information about health risks posed by asbestos. We want to know if there are other problem areas out there, and if there are we will take the appropriate steps to address them." She said the agency would increase its education and outreach on potential risks associated with vermiculite. "We want everyone who comes in contact with vermiculite — from home-owners to handymen — to have the information to protect themselves and their families." But back at her headquarters, the decision to declare the public-health emergency was not without conflict.

Responding to a Freedom of Information Act request from the St. Louis *Post-Dispatch,* the EPA and the Justice Department released thousands of pages of documents on Libby. When Schneider walked into the conference room in the Justice Department's Denver office, he thought it was Christmas. Nine huge file boxes crammed with paper. Five feet away, a copy machine. What else could any investigative reporter want?

The documents were hard to track at times, but they clearly revealed the battles between different offices within the agency. Hundreds of e-mails, scores of "action memos" and piles of "communication strategies" for how the announcement would be made illustrated the split within the agency.

To Schneider, the documents painted a picture of politics being placed before science.

Long threads of e-mail showed internal EPA debates over how peril-ous things actually were in the Montana town and why the Libby team was insisting that tremolite was more dangerous than chrysotile.[4] Alan White-house was in a unique position to answer that last question. Not only had he treated 500 people from Libby who are sick and dying from exposure to tremolite in the vermiculite, he also had almost 300 patients from Washing-ton shipyards and the Hanford nuclear facility who are suffering health ef-fects from exposure to the much more prevalent chrysotile asbestos. White-house's comparison showed that the toxicity of the tremolite from Libby is far greater. "Tremolite is ten times as carcinogenic as chrysotile and probably one hundred times more productive of mesothelioma than the commercially used chrysotile," he said.

The proof of the dangers of Zonolite can be found in the graveyards of the northwest corner of Montana and in the homes of hundreds who are sucking on tanks of oxygen to make it through the day. But the proof of the potential hazard to the millions more that have the contaminated material in their homes and offices can be found in EPA's own files and those of other scientists who have studied the material, including scientists working for W.R. Grace.

At Grace's plant in Weedsport, New York, ten air samples were collected on July 11, 1977, during simulations Grace ran on its own insulation.[5] The numbers of asbestos fibers in all samples were hundreds of times above the limit that OSHA set for workers. Yet, on April 3, 2002, Grace wrote Whitman insisting that the insulation was safe.

In April 1997, the Canadian Department of National Defense reported studies of the Zonolite insulation at a World War II–era base in Manitoba.[6] The report showed asbestos levels so high that workers dismantling the base were ordered to wear the highest level of protective equipment.

The files also contained Weis's study from December 2001.[7] "The concentrations of asbestos fibers that occur in air following disturbance of [insulation] may reach levels of potential human health concerns," Weis wrote. He added that the levels exceed "OSHA standards for protection of workers and exceed EPA's normal risk for acceptable excess cancer risk for exposed humans. Actual risks may be even greater than estimated."

The U.S. Public Health Service reported on August 1, 2000, that "even minimal handling by workers or residents poses a substantial health risk," with exposures from tremolite fibers in the air up to 150 times the current level OSHA allows for workers.[8]

No one knows precisely how many dwellings are insulated with Zonolite, but memos from the EPA and ATSDR cite estimates of between 15 million and 35 million homes.[9] The EPA and the Justice Department gathered thousands of invoices and shipping records from Grace that show that at least 15.6 billion pounds of vermiculite ore was shipped from Libby to

750 plants and factories throughout North America. Between one-third and one-half of that ore was "popped" and sold as insulation.

BY THE SPRING OF 2002, there was a gradual, albeit reluctant, acceptance in the agency that Libby's homes had to be cleaned. The emergency declaration had to be issued. The danger to the people in Libby was so great that the insulation had to be removed.

While EPA lawyers and the Superfund team smoothed out the language of the declaration, the agency's wordsmiths and image people molded the language of the announcement to stress how endangered and unique Libby was — which downplayed the national nature of the problem.

But many health experts in the government weren't buying that. Yes, Libby is unique because of what has already happened there. But they saw that the largest continuing hazard was from the Zonolite insulation, followed closely by exposures from the hundreds of processing plants and manufacturing facilities that turned billions of pounds of contaminated Zonolite into consumer products. The Zonolite, in fact, managed to scare the hell out of everyone in the agency — the physicians and scientists because of the implications for public health, and the bureaucrats and the bean-counters because of the implications for the budget.

In a memo written on February 22, 2002, the Office of Pollution, Prevention and Toxics said "the national ramifications are enormous" and estimated that, if only 1 million homes have Zonolite and any other asbestos, such as floor or ceiling tiles or wrapping on boilers and pipes, "aren't we put in a position to remove their [insulation] at a national cost of over $10 billion?"

The memo questioned the agency's strategy of claiming that Libby was a "unique" situation and the EPA's claim that the age of Libby's homes and severe winter conditions require a higher level of maintenance that leads to increased disturbance of the insulation. It's "a shallow argument," the memo said. "There are older homes which exist in harsh or harsher conditions across the country. Residents in Maine and Michigan might find this argument flawed."

Still, EPA had promised that this time around it would do the right thing. In a meeting in mid-March of 2002, Whitman and Marianne Horinko, the head of the agency's Superfund section, met with Peronard and his colleagues. The two bosses asked tough questions, and apparently they received the right answers. Whitman and Horinko agreed that the notification and emergency declaration should be made.

So, by early April 2002, news releases had been written and rewritten. Lists of governors to call and other politicians to notify had been compiled. Internal e-mail shows that discussions were held on whether Whitman would go to Libby for the announcement. It could be a major media event, the press office argued, positive stories for a change after the hammering the agency took over its actions following the terrorist attack. But the declaration was never made. On May 9, over Horinko's signature, EPA quietly announced that the homes in Libby would be cleaned, but no mention was made of the long-term health care that came with the public-health declaration, nor of the warning to homeowners elsewhere in the country.

The White House had been informed of the planned declaration, as it is of all major agency activities. Its Office of Management and Budget had been kept apprised of EPA's progress, but in late April the White House's financial watchdog ratcheted up its involvement. It didn't want the declaration to go forward.

Just days before EPA was set to make the declaration, it was blocked by the OMB. Both OMB and EPA acknowledge that the White House agency was actively involved in the decision on the declaration, but neither agency would discuss how or why.[10] EPA's chief spokesman, Joe Martyak, said "contact OMB for the details." OMB spokesperson Amy Call said, "These questions will have to be addressed to the EPA."

Call said OMB provided language for EPA to use, but she declined to tell Schneider why the White House opposed the declaration and the notification of the public. "These are part of our internal discussions with EPA, and we don't discuss predecisional deliberations," Call said. Both agencies refused *Post-Dispatch* Freedom of Information Act requests for documents to and from OMB.

The question about what to do about Zonolite was not the only asbestos-related issue in which the White House intervened with the EPA. In January 2002, in an internal EPA report on problems with the agency's much-criticized response to the terrorist attack on New York City, a section on "lessons learned" said there was a need to release public-health and emergency information without having it reviewed and delayed by the White House.

"We cannot delay releasing important public-health information," said the report. "The political consequences of delaying information are greater than the benefit of centralized information management."

William Ruckelshaus says he had his problems with the White House — and specifically OMB — when he headed the EPA.[11] OMB was created in 1970 to assist the president in the development and execution of his policies and programs. The White House department has a hand in the development and resolution of all budget, policy, legislative, regulatory, procurement and management issues on behalf of the president.

"The president never called me personally on any of these issues," Ruckelshaus recalled. "The pressure could come from industry pressuring OMB, or if someone could find a friendly ear in the White House to get them to intervene. But these issues, like asbestos, are so technical, often so convoluted, that industry's best chance to stop us or modify what we wanted to do would come from OMB."

There was a limit to the White House interference Ruckelshaus said he'd accept.

"When I was there, if there was a health problem, we dealt with it," he said. "If the White House objected, let them object. If you're running EPA or any other agency, you always have to bend to political pressure, but not when it comes to an issue of public health."

He says it's logical that EPA is worried about the public's reaction to learning they might have dangerous products in their homes.

"The demand that the government do something about it becomes overwhelming," the former administrator said. "I never felt that was a reason not to warn people that there was a danger. If you haven't decided what the government's role ought to be in correcting it, then argue that out, but that's a separate question as to whether we ought to alert people to a danger.

Your first obligation is to tell the people living in these homes of the possible danger. They need the information so they can decide what actions are best for their family. What right does the government have to conceal these dangers? It just doesn't make sense.

"When the government comes across this kind of information and doesn't tell people about it, I just think it's wrong, unconscionable not to do that."

Schneider made repeated requests over several weeks to speak to Whitman, Superfund boss Marianne Horinko, or anyone with firsthand knowledge of why the notification wasn't made. Finally, in late December, Martyak called Schneider and said Horinko was on a train and he would connect her on a conference call.

Horinko is respected by many in the agency, and by the Montanans she met in Libby, as someone who understood the issue. She joined Whitman in approving the declaration. She was willing to clarify anything she could, she said over her cell phone. Schneider believed her. Schneider asked, "Why did OMB intervene and kill the declaration?" She started to answer, but immediately Martyak cut her off.

Then Horinko began to explain why the public wasn't told about the danger in their attics, and again the senior spokesman interrupted.

"Ms. Horinko can't answer those questions off the top of her head," Martyak said. "Wait until she's back in the office and we'll call you."

The call never came.

IT WAS A COLD NOVEMBER NIGHT in Libby, and Peronard's last public meeting was not going to be fun.[12]

Over the past three years, he had been on the hot seat scores of times playing teacher, cheerleader and chaplain to the beleaguered Montanans who had learned the hard way what it meant to be betrayed by the government. He had their trust and confidence now, and the town believed he would never lie to them.

Peronard had been warned that people were expecting an answer to why the public-health emergency declaration was killed.

"I'm going to have to do a hell of a dance on the head of a pin," Peronard told Schneider as about 50 people settled into the metal folding chairs in the town hall. Some leaned on canes. Others sucked oxygen out of portable tanks. A couple had the more stylish and concealable "belly packs," which held only a short charge of air.

The meeting began with the issue of whether the trees in the National Forest near the mine were contaminated with asbestos. The Forest Service had been asked to free several hundred acres for logging and said it depended on what EPA said.

"Testing of the trees is on our list two years down the road," Peronard said. "We felt that it was more important to get the town and homes cleaned first."

A half-dozen loggers in the crowd booed and moaned.

"Is that asbestos going to prevent us from ever earning a living in Libby?" a logger yelled.

"If the town wanted the trees tested, we'll try to move it up. We want to do what's needed here," said Jim Christiansen, who had taken the cleanup over from Peronard and was already playing peacemaker. Christiansen's hands were full of problems not of his making. Budget cuts and problems had slowed the cleaning of houses to a crawl, and he was being dumped on by many.

A woman grabbed the mic and asked, "Why are you leaving us, Paul? Does that mean that EPA is abandoning us?"

"Jim is going to do a great job, and he's better trained for long-term cleanup than I am. It's his specialty," Peronard said. "I was supposed to be up here for the emergency phase, and never before in the EPA has that phase lasted this long. I will stay involved. I promise."

The warm and friendly tone disappeared.

"Why didn't we get the declaration? EPA promised us," said a man with his Stetson pulled low over his eyes.

"I obviously don't have a satisfactory answer for you. We pushed as hard as we could and we got half a loaf. We're going to clean the homes now and, hopefully, eventually we'll find some way to get the long-term health care that's needed."

Norita took the mike.

"Paul, you know we need the health care. You know that. EPA was ready to give it. What happened?"

"Marianne Horinko, she runs the Superfund program in the country and she ended up signing the document without the declaration," Paul said, not looking at Norita.

Even with the microphone, Les's hoarse whisper could barely be heard:

"We had a meeting with Ms. Horinko, right here, and she made it real clear that because of deaths we had, and the sickness, she understood that we really needed this help, this medical care," Les said. "Are you telling me she made the decision not to do this? Is that what you're telling me?"

"I left the regional office with the recommendation for the public-health emergency. Ms. Horinko got input from all sorts of people, maybe some asked for and maybe some not, and signed the document without the medical-care provision in there. I'm not in a position to tell you why she decided that was the best thing to do."

"Who does she work for?" bellowed a voice from the rear.

"Ms. Horinko works for Ms. Whitman. Ms. Whitman works for George Bush."

The man in the rear cut him off with the one question Paul did not want to hear: "Could this have come from the White House?"

Peronard had his face buried in his hands.

"Yeah," he said, finally, looking up. "If you look in our administrative record, there are two e-mails — redacted e-mails — where there is specific language on the topic coming out of the Office of Management and Budget.

"It's a career-limiting statement, but I just got to say that in my heart I don't believe that direction came from Ms. Horinko or Ms. Whitman."

The documents that Schneider had copied in the Justice Department's conference room supported Peronard's belief. There were far more than the two OMB e-mails he had mentioned. Dozens of pages of not only e-mails, but letters and policy statements showed the intensity of OMB's efforts to micromanage, if not kill, EPA's effort, especially any reference to Libby's long-term health problems and the risk to millions from the attic insulation.

The language the agency planned to use in its announcement had gone back and forth between the White House and EPA headquarters for days.

A word was changed here. An entire section removed there. References to potential dangers downplayed everywhere they appeared.

The frustration became almost intolerable at EPA headquarters, and in Denver and in Libby. The announcement was set for April 5, and the last-minute preparations were frantic. Martyak, the agency's communications czar, was driving everyone crazy. He decided the announcement would be released in Libby over the signature of Region 8's acting administrator Jack McGraw, who had actually flown to Libby to unveil the long-awaited decision. Martyak believed that the more distance there was between the announcement and Washington, the better it would be, others in the press office told Schneider.

On April 4, drafts of the news release were being sent to Rich Lathrop, the regional press officer, and to Wendy Thomi in Libby. The first draft was followed by a second, a third, a fourth. Neither Lathrup nor Thomi was happy with the wording.

"I'm not going to send this out," Thomi told Schneider. "Most of it's not true. It's not fair to the people in Libby. The stuff is misleading. It's not right that the EPA lie again to those people."

She refused to put the release out, turfing it back to Denver.

McGraw was still in Libby. Waiting.

It didn't happen. Headquarters backed off.

Three weeks later, McGraw received an action memo from headquarters.[13] It was a legal document that the regulations require to be completed whenever policy decisions are made or new programs started. It outlined what the agency was prepared to do for Libby.

Peronard, Cohn and the others refused to sign it.

"I wasn't going to put my name on it," Peronard said. "It wasn't what I'd been promising the people in Libby for two years. Not even close. It wasn't even legal."

McGraw signed it as headquarters had ordered. "He had no choice.

"We were all ordered to be good soldiers and shut up," Peronard told Schneider.

On May 2, the action memo was shipped back to headquarters with McGraw's signature on the last page. When it was returned to Denver two days later, McGraw's signature page was still attached, but the White House had inserted last-minute changes in the document.

"There were seven changes that OMB demanded be made, and they were," Peronard said. "And headquarters didn't even have the guts to tell the man whose signature was on the document that the wording had been significantly changed."

Even though the *Post-Dispatch* story on the White House intervention was published between Christmas 2002 and New Year's Day, a time when people are usually too busy to read newspapers, the reaction was explosive. The story ran in dozens of papers, and CNN, MSNBC and Fox streamed it for days.

Senator Patty Murray reacted with anger to the *Post-Dispatch* story when it was played across the front page of the Sunday *Seattle Times* and *Post-Intelligencer.*[14]

"It is appalling that the government refuses to notify millions of home-owners that they and their children may be at risk. There may be as many as 35 million homes today that have Zonolite insulation in their attics and walls. People are most likely being exposed to asbestos fibers and they have no knowledge of it.

"We, the government, the EPA, the administration have a responsibility to at least let people know the information so they can protect themselves if they go into those attics. The people at risk go beyond the families and their kids. We also have people who go into the attic to do repairs or installations of some type who can be unknowingly exposed to asbestos. They can take the fibers home on their clothing and expose their own families.

"EPA's answer that people have been warned because it's on their website is ridiculous. If you have a computer, and you just happened to think about what's in your attic, and you happen to go to EPA's web page, then you get to know. This is not the way the safety of the public is handled."

In Seattle, EPA investigator Keven McDermott said, "Someone has got to tell people that this problem exists."[15] It had been back in early 2000 when McDermott and scientists from the Seattle regional office tested Zonolite from local attics and found the asbestos contamination.

"I continue to get calls from people who have just learned about the problem from a friend or something they saw in a newspaper and they are terrified about what they may have done to their children," she said. "How can we not tell people about this?"

EPA headquarters was doing damage control. Whitman, being the kind of good soldier she had been every time the White House blindsided her, fell on her sword and said the decision on killing the public-health emergency was all her fault. And headquarters erupted when it learned that the communications between the White House and EPA were among about 8,000 documents released under Schneider's Freedom of Information Act request.

Martyak was intent on finding who had put the incriminating documents into files that Schneider or any other reporter could get their hands on.

"To say they were upset is a significant understatement," Cohn told Schneider. "When I made the decision, I didn't think I was putting my job on the line. I thought it was the right thing to do. It was the only thing that explained why a public-health emergency wasn't declared. From my perspective, the law says you're supposed to have a record showing how decisions were made."

Cohn was less than happy with his agency's final decision.

"My concern was looking at the law, we were denying the people of Libby an opportunity which the law provided, and if we didn't declare the public-health emergency, that opportunity would be gone," the senior government lawyer explained.[16] "We have an obligation to these people. The government knew this was a problem decades ago and did nothing."

On May 8, 2003, EPA finally released its warning to the millions of people that may have Zonolite Attic Insulation in their homes and businesses.[17] EPA's plans did call for a major news conference and follow-up appearances on the morning TV shows and the cable networks by senior agency people explaining the dangers.

Unfortunately for those who needed the information, the same morning that the insulation announcement was to be made, Christie Whitman decided to tell the world that she was quitting EPA. Little or no media attention was paid to cancer-causing insulation that day. EPA officials promised that the word would get out that "every major home improvement and hardware chain in the country has agreed to widely distribute EPA warnings on the danger of the insulation." But when we checked 40 national chain stores in nine states in May 2004, not one manager questioned said they had ever received anything from EPA to distribute.

Even though Grace shipped millions of pounds of Zonolite north of the border, Canadian health officials were as lackadaisical as EPA in warning of the dangers of the asbestos-containing insulation. That changed almost instantly in May 2004 when it was confirmed that four members of one family living on the Ojibwa reserve north of Winnipeg were all found to have mesothelioma. Their only exposure to asbestos was from the vermiculite insulation in their home, Health Canada said. The agency promptly flooded the Internet with warnings.

A CRISIS FOR ASBESTOS VICTIMS everywhere came with the swearing-in of the Republican-controlled 108th Congress in January 2003.[18]

Plans to introduce Asbestos Fairness Bill II were already making the circuit on Capitol Hill in the hands of optimistic industry lobbyists. Roger Sullivan, Gayla and Les tried to figure what they could do to modify the bill's language to protect the people of Libby and others exposed to tremolite.

"The draft legislation that I've seen is all predicated on medical criteria written for those exposed to chrysotile," Sullivan said. "It bases the claims on chrysotile disease, which has a progression from detection to serious impairment of twenty percent. Whitehouse's work clearly shows that the progression rate from tremolite is seventy-six percent, almost three times as serious. If this Congress wants to tear apart the ugly, greedy underbelly of trial lawyers who are abusing the system, let them find a way to pass legislation that acknowledges the distinction that tremolite is far more toxic and fast-developing. If this distinction is not recognized, the people of Libby will be hurt again by their government."

Orrin Hatch, not Henry Hyde, carried the ball this time. In May 2003, after months of fruitless negotiating, the Republican senator from Utah finally went back to his initial plan — setting up a $108-billion fund, underwritten by industry, to pay all asbestos claims for the next 25 years. Insurance companies would pay in $45 billion and major companies that have been sued would pay in another $45 billion. The rest of the money, he said, would come from smaller companies, existing asbestos trusts and interest on the fund.

The problem with the proposal, its critics say, is that it's not nearly enough money. The AFL-CIO said the fund should be at least $200 billion and have a federal or business backstop in case money runs out before all victims are cared for. And, as with the first "Fairness" bill, the medical criteria Hatch proposed would eliminate many real victims.

At almost the same time, May 5, Murray offered up her asbestos-ban bill for another try at the gold ring. She had more supporters this time, and asbestos was in the news because of Hatch's bill. The Ban Asbestos in America Act was on the Senate docket again. Then, on June 4, Murray upset Hatch's applecart when she testified before the Judiciary Committee that it made no sense to legislate a ban on asbestos victims suing the responsible companies when asbestos was still being imported and used in this country.[19]

"Why on earth does Congress allow thousands of tons of asbestos to continue to be put into consumer products every year? This is the elephant in the room for this legislation. It is the most obvious, yet least discussed, aspect of asbestos," the Washington Democrat said.

Polite as she always is, Murray nevertheless stunned Hatch with her criticism of his legislation.

"The bill only covers workers exposed to asbestos on the job, and ignores everyone else," she said to a hushed hearing room. "Anyone who works on their brakes at home, anyone who is exposed to vermiculite insulation in his or her attic, anyone who is exposed simply by living near an asbestos-processing facility, would be left out.

"If we are going to cap the number of people who can be compensated, the least we can do is stop adding to the problem," said Murray. "If we are going to protect corporations far into the future, we need to protect victims far into the future by banning asbestos once and for all."

Anna Knudson, who did most of the research for Murray on the asbestos problem, joined other Senate staffers, who worked late into the night, night after night and often into the early morning, hammering out a compromise, or something enough people wouldn't gag on, to get the "save the industry" bill passed.

Politics is always a game of compromise. Hatch, realizing he needed all the votes he could muster, reluctantly agreed to add Murray's ban proposal into his bill. But he didn't get a convert in the feisty lawmaker. Murray blasted the restrictive provisions of his bill on the very day the two measures were joined. She showed the Senate judiciary Committee pictures of two young brothers, Justin and Tim Jorgensen, climbing a pile of Zonolite. Their father, who worked at the Minneapolis expansion plant, died at age 44 from asbestosis and lung cancer. But Murray said, "Under the bill being considered, if Justin and Tim ever got sick from asbestos, neither one would receive a dime because they were not exposed to asbestos on the job."

The AFL-CIO, which had nothing to say on the last fairness bill and had remained silent for most of the year, finally lashed out against Hatch's legislation. Peg Seminario, the AFL-CIO's director of occupational safety and health, said the medical criteria would exclude too many people. As Murray had said, the AFL-CIO echoed that to ignore those who were exposed to asbestos outside the workplace was unacceptable.

The American Thoracic Society kept saying it was going to unveil its view on the bill's medical criteria, but it still hadn't done so.[20] Harbut pushed his organization to release the position that it had debated internally for months. "They have to release it now, when it's needed and might have some real value," Harbut told Schneider. Finally, it did. And again the Senate staff members huddled all night to make changes.

On July 11, the legislation that would prevent victims from suing asbestos companies for damages, unless the government agreed, came out of the Judiciary Committee. The vote was ten for and eight against. Baucus said the bill would exclude Libby residents and former Grace workers from the restrictive medical-criteria requirements in the bill. Anyone who had worked at the mine or had lived within a 20-mile radius of Libby for at least a year before December 31, 2003, would be exempt from the requirement that anyone seeking compensation had to prove significant exposure to asbestos.

The legislation assumes that Libby residents and Grace workers had significant exposure to asbestos, the Montana senator said. The bill, if passed, will give a victim with mesothelioma, the most lethal of the asbestos caused cancers, $1 million. Ten other levels of asbestos-related diseases have been included, most with payouts well below the $1 million mark.

A much-watered-down version of Patty Murray's ban-asbestos bill was added as an amendment. The bill was immediately renamed the "Hatch Ban Asbestos in America Act."

Some of the concessions that Hatch's staff had demanded were important. Murray's original bill required that legislative attention be paid to naturally occurring asbestos — like the tremolite in vermiculite, talc and taconite. In Hatch's version, there was no mention. It was like Libby had never happened and the talc, taconite and vermiculite miners still digging asbestos-contaminated ore from the ground today were of no consequence. It was far from a sure thing that Hatch's bill would make it to the Senate floor for a full vote, let alone get enough votes to pass.

Opposition to the bill was strong and apparently growing. Lobbying by both sides was fierce. Vermont senator Patrick Leahy, the ranking Democrat on Hatch's committee, still had doubts about the proposed law.

"I still feel that victims are giving up too much to guarantee finality to those who are responsible for the diseases they inherit," he told reporters the day after the committee vote.

That same week, it was learned that the major corporations targeted in the majority of the asbestos claims — Halliburton, Honeywell International, W.R. Grace and eight other companies — would save about $15 billion if Hatch's bill was passed, according to transcripts of Leahy's statement.[21] Companies that had already agreed to pay $21 billion to the families of those who had died or were dying from asbestos-related disease could renege on the hard-fought-for agreements. In the end, they would have to pay only $6 billion under Hatch's plan. The senator and his senior Judiciary Committee staff refused to discuss the matter with Schneider.

As the Senate left for its August recess without Hatch's bill having reached the floor, many of the Utah senator's most generous and avid supporters were openly turning on the legislation.

The very lobbyists who pushed most strongly for the legislation — the insurance industry — were jumping ship, fearing they would be asked to kick more money into the fund. By late September, the unions were getting vocal with their criticism, and with the approaching presidential campaign, no one wanted to offend the unions. Even with the incessant prodding of Senate Majority Leader Bill Frist, the Fairness Act failed to harvest enough support to get to the Senate floor for a vote in 2003 and again during the first half of 2004. Frist promised it would pass "at some point."

And more new pressure came from new figures released by USGS, which showed that asbestos imports had increased over the past decade. Some items, like asbestos brakes, soared almost 100 percent.

Patty Murray's disdain for many provisions of the asbestos legislation had become more apparent. Other members of Congress were troubled that Hatch's removal of asbestos-tainted ore like vermiculite, talc and taconite from his version of Murray's Asbestos Ban Act had gone too far.

Whether Hatch's bill passes or not, the Washington State Democrat said she has no doubt "about the need for the U.S. to enact a ban on asbestos, including naturally occurring asbestos. I will continue to push for a ban until this country finally does what the rest of the industrialized world has done and bans asbestos once and for all."

She will not forget what happened to the people of Libby and others exposed to asbestos from Grace's ore, she said.

Les's voice was always raspy, but by the time his disease progressed, his gentle tones were down to a whisper. (Courtesy Skramstad family)

WHAT HAPPENS, AS TIME PASSES, in a town where the covenants of basic humanity have been broken? Where good, hardworking people have been used as a commodity to be mined like a mineral, then tossed aside like waste rock? Where families have died and are dying in bunches? Where victims suffer not only the pain of slow suffocation but also the insults of the ignorant, because they had the courage to protest, and the guilt of the damned, because they have passed on their suffering to the people they love the most?

Fortunately, we have few places to observe the progression of such a thing. Somehow it seems all the more obscene that this hell would be visited upon one of the most beautiful places on this planet, Libby, Montana, with its perfect glades of evergreen and rushing snowmelt, and its little enclave of people who have used hard work and endurance to avoid the gabble and grime of the cities.

So what happens as time passes? The sick get sicker. More of them die: a few each year right now, but many more will follow.

Memorial Day 2003. Eight new white crosses. Don Kaeding read the names of the dead in 2001, and his name was on the roll that Bob Wilkins read in 2002.[1] This year, Wilkins's name was one of those read by his son, Don. Very few people attended. No town officials. No TV crews, and no reporters — not even anyone from Libby's own papers, *The Western News* and the *Montanian.* Les and Gayla, a handful of others. "I guess they all think the problems are solved, the danger is passed, and all the vermiculite has been removed," Les said.

Memorial Day, 2004, 225 crosses this time, but four more died during the week the crosses were up.

"The terrifying thing is that there are probably thousands of others and we'll never know about them," Gayla told Les as they pulled the white crosses from the ground.

In one sense, the worst of Libby's plague years have passed, the time when the monster from the mountain was killing people and nobody stood up and stopped it. Now some brave, determined people have fought back, and what they have done should stop the killing, if the EPA's vigilance continues. But that won't happen today, or in five years, or in ten. So in terms of the actual number of dead, the worst is yet to come.

Nobody knows when people will stop dying of asbestos-related disease in Libby, or even when the disease will peak. If the EPA cleanup is effective in removing the hazard, that point should come within the next 20 years or so. But in the meantime, many more people are going to get sick.

Brad Black says, "It's hard to get the majority of my patients to admit they have it. They are very stoic. The work ethic in this town is very strong, and the loss of self-esteem is painful to watch. It's the fact that they can't put in a full day's work, that they can't do all the work at home. Fix the roof, cut the wood, shovel the snow. Things that defined, in their minds, who they were."[2]

Alan Whitehouse added, "It's going to take a lot of screening to look for the things that you can treat — pleural effusions and lung cancers — and find them early enough so you can do something about them."

The problems of Grace's spasmodic health-insurance plan continued to drive Black and Whitehouse up the wall. Too much of their time was being spent sparring with Health Network America — Grace's New Jersey–based insurance carrier — for better treatment of their patients covered under the much-hyped "Libby Medical Program."

"It's gone well beyond fighting for who's covered and who's not. Now we battle to get the meds they need to make their lives bearable. They want to disallow the use of oxygen at night for some of these people. Oxygen? Can you believe it?" Black asked.

One of their patients, a man near death from mesothelioma, just received his last hospital bill, of $4,000.

"Grace paid three thousand dollars and he got stuck with a thousand. That's an enormous amount of money to people in Libby," Black said.

"But the ultimate in audacity is this," the doctor said, waving a letter from J. Jay Flynn, a vice president for the Grace insurance carrier. "They won't pay this guy's medical bills, but they're eager to pay for his autopsy."

The letter said: "W.R. Grace has agreed to pay for the full cost of autopsies on deceased members of the LMP. The family will have no out of pocket expenses."[3]

Normally, Black is a quiet man, but he is outraged at the decision not to declare a public-health emergency in Libby. "We're going to have to find another way to get money to care for these people. It's identical to what happened last time the government abandoned the people of Libby."

THE LEGAL SKIRMISHES between Grace and EPA moved on to the big stage at the end of 2002.[4] Grace was fighting EPA's insistence that it pick up the tab for $55 million that the agency had already spent to clean up the mess the company had made in Libby. Grace said that EPA was wrong in just about everything it had done — that its actions were arbitrary and capricious and not based on good science — and said it didn't have to pay. Negotiations failed, so early in 2002, the Justice Department lawyers in Denver filed suit to collect the money. The suit was dumped in the lap of U.S. District Judge Donald Molloy, the same jurist who had so colorfully rendered a decision against Grace in the access case.

Since he had turned the ongoing cleanup over to Christensen, Peronard had been working with Cohn and the rest of the legal team, preparing for this lawsuit. He knew that this was it — the real test. All the marbles tossed into one circle, he thought, winner takes all. Knowing better than anyone what Grace had done in Libby, and having been stonewalled every step of the way in trying to clean it up, Peronard was motivated on a visceral level. More practically, he knew that if the EPA lost the suit, the rest of the Libby cleanup would be endangered, and it would be a long time before headquarters let any on-scene coordinator operate like he had. Too many people in Washington were still denouncing his methods, and too many people in headquarters were always nervous.

Besides, he thought, if we lose, Grace will walk away and leave the taxpayers to pay for cleaning up their mess. And that isn't right.

The government lawyers knew they had a fight ahead. It would be a classic David-and-Goliath showdown. The government's legal team of Cohn, Andrea Madigan and Kelcey Land, the enforcement specialist, from EPA and James Freeman, Heidi Kukis, Mark Elmer, David Askman and Corrine Christen from Justice. Five lawyers, one paralegal and Land going up against as many as 48 lawyers and 40 paralegals or assistants for Grace, at least according to legal bills for the period that it submitted for payment to the bankruptcy court.

Grace wanted to drag out the battle as long as possible. First, the company asked Molloy for a change of venue to Delaware. When that was refused, Grace asked for a trial date two or three years down the road. EPA said it wanted the case heard within a year. Molloy set a trial date for January 2003.

Cohn was very pleased. He knew that the longer the wait for the trial, the more Grace would try to wear the government team down. But this was exactly what the government team wanted. It would start a waterfall of events that swept the case along rapidly. Depositions were taken of all the key witnesses on both sides. Motions were made. Briefs were written and filed, facts were agreed upon. At the same time, Cohn, Peronard, Miller, Weis and Land had to respond in writing to hundreds of formal criticisms from Grace about EPA science. Grace's charges and EPA's responses formed a record upon which Molloy would base his decision concerning the appropriateness of EPA's actions.

The government took over two suites in Missoula's Doubletree Inn as its war room. Workstations were built and computers were brought in, along with copiers, a fax machine, shredders and, of course, reams of paper. The walls were covered with witness lists, chronologies, the main issues and a thousand other facts that no one wanted to forget. And the tables that lined the walls were filled with black binders containing all the evidence and exhibits in the government's case. Grace had a similar but larger operation in another hotel four blocks away.

The courtroom was about sixty feet square, and modern. Very modern. The lawyers had flat monitors in front of them that showed all the exhibits being discussed and a running transcript of the trial. Cohn was impressed. Quite an operation — in Missoula, Montana, no less.

The big Irishman on the bench fit the room perfectly. Molloy looked utterly judicial.[5] Graying hair and a significant, but neatly trimmed, mustache framed a frequent smile that confused and concerned the plaintiffs and the defense equally. The attorneys who came before Molloy knew he would brook no nonsense or silly legal games. There was never any doubt that he listened to every word uttered in his court.

On December 16, both sides flew to Missoula to hear Molloy issue the rules for the rapidly approaching trial. But that wasn't the only action, nor the most important one, that the judge took that winter afternoon. Each side had filed a variety of motions, including requests for summary judgment. Such requests pop up in many civil trials. The judge is asked to remove an issue from consideration in the trial because one side or the other doesn't have the facts or evidence to support its case. Judges rarely grant motions for summary judgment. Usually, judges decide to hear whatever case is presented, weak or not, before making a decision.

So as the government lawyers sat before Molloy at a long table to the judge's right, opposed by Grace's phalanx on the left, they weren't expecting much when Molloy said he'd made his decision on their summary judgment request.

Then he said that he was granting the government's request, that Grace had failed to show that its allegations against EPA had sufficient merit to continue the case. The courtroom was completely silent for a few moments. Peronard and the government lawyers were taken aback, but certainly no more than the Grace team was. The company's lawyers looked at one another, rolled their eyes, shook their heads, and stared at the ceiling. Then they asked Molloy for a clarification.

He said that EPA's cleanup procedures in Libby were legal and warranted, and that the agency had acted properly in establishing that contamination in the town represented an imminent and substantial threat to the public health and welfare.

The government team never got to use the dozen or so expert witnesses they had tracked down or the thousands of pages of documents collected and evaluated showing that the science they were using was solid. Peronard could barely contain himself. It was like having a baby in a smooth delivery, he thought, when you were expecting a breech birth. Our science and methods stand. It was a hell of a Christmas present. It was the second time he had faced Grace down before Molloy, and the second time he had prevailed.

Molloy went over the numbers with both sides. His ruling meant Grace would pay $32 million for emergency work done in Libby by the EPA and for the medical screening undertaken by ATSDR between November 1999 and December 31, 2001.

The remaining $23 million was still at issue. Grace insisted that EPA and ATSDR had spent too much money, or calculated costs improperly. Molloy said they could fight that out at trial before him from January 6 to 9, 2003. Most of the government's team worked through the holidays getting ready for the trial. Even though the issue of Grace's overall liability had been settled, this was an important step, too. Peronard knew that $23 million would clean a lot of asbestos from a lot of houses.

The three days of presentations before Molloy were relatively uneventful.[6] Both sides called experts in cost control, and went over, almost line by line, expenditures, overhead and other financial issues. Molloy said he would rule on the remaining money later in the year. On August 26, 2003,

Molloy issued his final ruling in the cumbersome case. The decision was a half-inch thick, but the conclusion was simple: Grace was ordered to pay the entire $54,527,081.11. Six weeks later, Grace filed an appeal of Molloy's ruling.

LES HAS BEEN MARRIED to Norita for forty-seven years, and he has been married to a Fender bass for thirty-six of those same years.[7] Now he sits on his porch swing and holds her, gently. "She plays so, so sweet," he says, running callused fingers over the fret board, inlaid with pearl chips by a friend, and the four thick steel strings. He has teased life's own rhythm and his family's living from them for a long time.

Les has taught his children to make music. Brady Skramstad plays drums and bass, Brent plays bass and lead guitar. Sloan and Gayla are singers. Norita used to accompany them on an old upright piano, but now it's been passed on to Gayla, and to the grandkids.

Les still sings, when his lungs will let him. He sits down during his gigs now to conserve his strength and his breath. And when he decides to sing, it's not the nasal twang some country singers employ, but a rich baritone like warm maple syrup on a winter morning. The disease will take it, eventually, but as long as Les is alive, he will sing every note in his mind, sweet and true.

And Les is alive, this morning, or "still on the right side of the dirt," as he puts it. "Every day I wake up, lay there and try to take a breath, try to see how much air I can suck in, see if there is enough so I might kid myself into believing I might make it through another day. So far, I've done it, but there have been some days that I would have bet against me.

"The real painful thing is that every time I can't catch my breath or I get dizzy or too weak to sit up, I just start thinking about my kids and what kind of hell I've sentenced them to live. Thanks to Grace, they'll live in hell just like I am, and like Norita. There is no way in the world that I can convince myself that the other kids won't get it."

Les takes as deep a breath as his lungs will let him. "I'm not afraid of death. I'm not afraid of dying, but I can't handle the idea that I'm going to leave Norita to face this same damn death without me. I made her sick. I brought that poison home from the mine. I should be here to care for her, and I won't be."

Norita carries her own pain, but talks about it even less than her husband does. Obviously, she worries about their children, but she's being eaten away by watching Les deteriorate. Still, she knows he's tough as the North Dakota landscape he comes from.

"He was strong, quick on his feet, nimble as they come," she says. "Now every step is an effort, but he keeps trying. He'll go out to mess with the tractor or snowplow and it can take him fifteen minutes to walk fifty feet. He'll take a few steps and find a tree or table to lean on to catch his breath, walk a few more and have to find some place to sit down for a bit.

"You can't stop him. That's the way Les is. He has to try. He has to make the effort. He'll never stop. Not while he's still alive."

In 2002, Les achieved one personal triumph: The expansion building where he worked — where he sucked in so much poison — was finally torn down. "But the site's not cleaned up yet," he says, and the old stubbornness returns to him, the set of the jaw, the cold blue gaze.

He is picking his fights carefully these days. As Gayla has found, it gets tiring, fighting for people and getting nothing back. "Sometimes you look around in this town, at the cleanup and the CARD clinic and everything, and you think, 'I don't need any thanks, but I sure would like a little support,'" Les says.

Right now, his big concern is a permanent memorial for the victims. There's a lot of controversy in town about where to put it. Gayla wants it up on Rainy Creek Road. Others want it at the cemetery, or out on the edge of town somewhere. There's a lot of resistance to putting it where Les wants it — right smack dab on Main Street, where people will see it and remember it. On his worst days, Les doesn't believe it will happen at all. "I'm afraid it will die on the vine. The last thing the Chamber of Commerce and the realtors want is any kind of monument to the people who died here. It just wouldn't be good for business."

Peronard is worried that Les will die bitter. "I reckon he has the right, but I hope he avoids it. I'm so sorry for the pain and grief he has, but sometimes I think it makes him focus on the problems left without appreciating the good progress that has been made. For example, I hope he can appreciate, when he's arguing about how to handle Zonolite insulation in walls, that a little over a year ago I didn't think we'd get to do Zonolite removals at all.

"All this is easy enough for me to say. My lungs are clear, my family's healthy, my community isn't a Superfund site with a long list of casualties. I don't have to worry whether my government or Grace will shortchange us once again."

On a 100-degree day in July 2003, Les sat in front of a small fan with Norita, sweating and reading a letter from Max Baucus about Hatch's bill.[8] The acrid smoke from the fires burning this summer – on all sides of Libby-Glacier National Park, in Idaho and along the Canadian border — was making Les's labored breathing even more difficult.

Some of the progress that Peronard mentioned was happening: the Skramstads' house was finally cleaned by the EPA in September. But on this stifling July day, Les was indeed bitter, there was no getting around it. Reading Baucus's letter, he got angrier and angrier, and finally he threw it down on the table. The fan blew it away. "There's no sense reading the rest. What it means is they've gotten away with murder," he said. "Nothing will happen to Grace. Nothing.

"Grace should have been brought to trial on criminal charges. They did what Hitler did, they systematically killed us and they knew they were killing us and they did nothing to stop it," the old cowboy raged. "I won't give up. I won't be quiet. Everyone else in this town can think I'm nuts, but when I shut up and go away like a lot of people want, it will be when I'm buried. I'll die without Grace ever saying they are sorry, and so will everyone else."

In her speech back in December 2001, announcing that she would use her "silver bullet" to put Libby on the Superfund list, Governor Judy Martz said, "A new day is dawning in Libby. It will dawn on the strengths of the people that call this town home. People like Les Skramstad." And the strength of Les, in his frail, asbestos-ravaged body, is that in the finest tradition of the cowboy, there is simply no quit in him.

After a few minutes, he settled a bit. "Thank God, I still have my music."

IT WAS A SATURDAY NIGHT like hundreds of others, and Les was doing what he loved. The old bass guitar shone brightly under the colored gels of the spotlights, and so did he. The tiny silver angel pinned next to the feather band on his Resistol hat glistened. The turquoise, purples and blues of his Western shirt shone like an unbalanced rainbow.

"Your cheatin' heart," crooned Les, deep and sweet.

Stella Sharp was 75 years old and Les had agreed to play at her party, and the VFW Club was swinging. Some of Stella's older friends were dancing up a storm, gliding through a two-step like they'd been doing it all their lives, which they probably had. A handful of kids danced — five-, six-, and seven-year-olds. Looking not a bit out of place.

Les hammered out "Pick me up on your way down" and sounded fine, not like a man whose lungs were close to useless, almost as rigid as a football, unable to expand to suck in a lungful of air. But if you looked closely, you could see his lips were right up to the microphone, the amplifier turned up to max. When the others on the stage picked up the refrain, Les drew in a dozen small breaths between teeth clenched into a wide smile, then came in on the lead just perfectly.

He finished "Rodeo Clown" and swept right into "Old Flames Can't Hold a Candle to You" before the dance floor could start to clear. His longtime buddy, Ron Masters, picked up his guitar and sang. His lungs are also scarred. Masters was born and raised with his brother and sister in a house along the railroad tracks that carried trains shuttling the ore and expanded Zonolite from the mine. All three family members "have it," as they say in Libby.

"We finally got a name for our band: 'Life Without Air,'" said Les, only partly joking. His daughter, Gayla, 41, took the mike and belted out "What Part of No Don't You Understand?" The crowd loved it, and so did Les.

His back was ramrod straight. One heel of his tan boots was locked over the bottom rung of the stool, the other flat on the floor, tapping slightly in time with the music and backing up his daughter's gravelly but dulcet tones: "I need someone to hold me when I cry."

Ninety minutes is a long time for a set for even a much younger band, but they paused only when the bartender brought out a tray with five double shot glasses of whiskey and set them next to Les. The universal Montana sign that it's break time.

"Those days are long gone," he said, glancing at the liquor. He painfully eased himself off the stool and gently down the two steps from the stage, holding on to the wall for balance, grabbing a chair back to hold himself up.

"It just doesn't hurt when I'm playing," he said, and reached out to Norita for support. She easily moved in and hugged him close to her. A long hug.

"I do it carefully so no one thinks he needs help," Norita said. "He's a proud man, and I do what I can to help him keep his pride, but it's just getting harder for him to walk, even with the cane."

Others came up to pump his hand and slap his back for the fine music. He thanked them, grinned and clutched Norita even harder. The second set filled the dance floor again.

Gayla Benefield and her David moved gracefully around the floor. Couples who had to be in their 70s two-stepped around the perimeter with a speed and grace that made you sure they were wearing skates.

Some folks got tangled in the intricate turns, loops and dips they attempted. A couple fell to the floor, and everyone laughed, including them. "When the government took whiskey away from the Indians, they should have pulled it away from the Norwegians also," Gayla Benefield said. "We do okay on beer, lots of it, but don't give us that hard stuff, because it makes us crazy."

It was midnight when the babysitter delivered Makenna to Norita. The beautiful little five-year-old clung to her grandmother. She beamed when she saw her mother and grandfather singing. It took only a wave from Gayla to get her on the stage, and no coaxing at all to get her to sing.

Clutching the mike, decked out in pink cowgirl boots, Makenna brought the celebrants to their feet as she sang "God Bless America" in a startlingly big-girl voice, perfectly in tune.

Three generations of Skramstads singing on the stage. Les cried.

"I'm glad I lived to see this," he said.

GAYLA BENEFIELD LOOKED DOWN at the rainbow of colors on the three sheets of paper she had spread out on her kitchen table.[9] She explained the marks in short sentences separated by long sighs.

The papers represent her family tree, and it is dying.

"The seven red marks are those who have died. It includes my mother and dad.

"The thirty yellow marks are those who have been diagnosed with the disease, and that includes me and my husband.

"The green and the gray are the fourteen whose X-rays show abnormalities or who are at high risk.

"The blue and purple are the ones that frighten the hell out of me, that may be the most tragic of us all. Eleven kids who went to Plummer School and a day-care center that was lousy with the fibers."

Sixty-two members of Gayla's immediate family are either dead, dying or in danger from the tremolite asbestos of Zonolite Mountain.

Gayla has had plenty of time to think about the years since she and Schneider started snapping at each other, and she guided him toward one of the biggest stories of his career, and Libby was changed forever. Every time she asks herself, "Would you do it again?" the answer is a resounding yes.

She turned 60 in the fall of 2003, the same age Margaret Vatland was the first time Gayla had to call the ambulance to take her to the hospital with pneumonia. She feels she has given herself and her generation in Libby the choice of ending up like their parents, or, knowing what they are carrying in their bodies, doing their best not to die in the same manner. But for Gayla Benefield, the biggest accomplishment is raising awareness that may save some of the lives on her color-coded chart, and in other family trees.

"Whenever I wonder if we did the right thing," she told Schneider, "I look at the facilities that we have available now. The CARD clinic, the screenings, the research. If only those had been available when either Mom or Dad was sick! How wonderful it would have been to take Mom to a clinic that would not only monitor the progression of her disease but treat it for what it is instead of hiding behind politics and greed.

"If anyone in Libby wakes up with a fever or congestion, one phone call, one trip to the CARD clinic, and within hours we are being treated for the very thing that shortened so many lives — infection.

"Nationally, we have made inroads despite the political climate. Even the staunch supporters of corporate America cannot deny that there is a problem with asbestos exposure. I cannot agree with their solutions, but at least we're talking."

On September 17, she sat in a Kalispell tattoo parlor. It was her 60th birthday, and she was having the artist tattoo a daisy and a butterfly on her shoulder and a pair of red lips on her hip.

"It's going to be useful when I'm in the nursing home dying from the poison that Grace inflicted on me and everyone else," Gayla said. "I may not be able to talk, but every time they roll me over, it will be clear that I want Grace to kiss my ass."

She lamented that two more people died that week, bringing the total for the year to at least ten. Working with Drs. Black and Whitehouse, she's thrown herself into doing all she can to get a medical research program into tremolite started at Libby.

"It's for the kids and grandkids in Libby — the next generations — and all those other people across the country exposed to the damn fiber," she said. "We've got to find a cure for this disease."

Gayla admits she is tired. But says as much as she wants to "put this whole damn tragedy behind me and let other people knock their heads against the walls," she's still up to her tattoo in battles.

She's on EPA's citizen's and technical advisory groups as well as the CARD board. Her loud mouth and Jim Christiansen's persistence appear to be the biggest obstacles to EPA further gutting the cleanup money. On June 9, 2004, EPA officials made a big show of returning $4 million of the money they had previously taken. They again pledged that "Libby is one of EPA's top priorities for cleanup nationally." Gayla and Les looked at each other and rolled their eyes.

ON JUNE 2, 2004, Gayla's youngest daughter, Stacey, 32, called her. "She told me she had received her report from the ongoing screening in Libby.

The report stated that she had an abnormality on her right lung and should see her physician."

Gayla felt her anger at Grace swell once more.

"I feel for every parent who learns that it isn't only our parents' generation and our generation that will feel the effects of the tremolite," she said.

"Maybe this is just a blip on the X-ray, but I have heard this story too many times, from too many people, to believe in miracles anymore."

LES AND GAYLA ARE NOT the only people concerned about asbestos who are feeling fatigued. Across the country, people inside the government, like Peronard, Weis, Miller, Keven McDermott and Matt Cohn, and outside, like Harbut, Whitehouse and Egilman, are uncomfortably aware that most of the bosses in the current administration do not have the stomach for asbestos reform.

In Gouverneur, New York, the R. T. Vanderbilt Co. continues to mine "tremolitic talc," and its miners continue to die. On its website, it tells prospective customers that "early health studies did suggest that an overexposure to Vanderbilt talc might pose a lung cancer risk similar to asbestos. However, after more discriminating studies were completed, it became clear that the lung cancers were not linked to the dust exposure." Discriminating in the fashion of R. J. Lee.

By midyear, it became obvious that EPA had finally tired of Lee's analysis consistently reporting that asbestos did not exist in whatever samples his company was analyzing or, if it was found, that it wasn't harmful.[10] On June 19, 2003, Michael Cook, the head of EPA's emergency response program, told all of the agency's Superfund managers to "thoroughly review any site management decisions for asbestos contamination where analytical data generated by asbestos testing laboratories associated with RJ Lee Group, Inc. were critical." Cook's memo cited two pages of concerns with the lab's methods.

In August, the Justice Department's Thomas Sansonetti and James Freeman filed a brief with the court handling Grace's bankruptcy. It urged the court to exclude Lee's findings that Grace's Zonolite Attic Insulation was not harmful. It also challenged Grace's statements to the court that Lee, "the world's foremost expert in minerals characterization," had been "asked by the EPA to devise a standardized protocol for the analysis of vermiculite." Not true, said EPA and Justice Department lawyers.

Criticism aside, Lee continued to show up at EPA and other venues representing Grace and other companies concerned with asbestos regulation.

The Consumer Product Safety Commission, which was rousted from more than a decade of torpor on the issue of asbestos when the *Post-Intelligencer* revealed the problem with crayons, has apparently fallen back to sleep, with no initiatives planned regarding asbestos in consumer products.

Binney & Smith quietly entered into an agreement with a Chicago law firm that filed a class-action suit against the crayon-maker after the *Post-Intelligencer* stories.[11] In a simple, clean and legal extortion, the lawyers pocketed $600,000 and Binney & Smith agreed to reformulate its crayons to exclude talc (which it had already agreed to do) and placed ads in *USA Today*, *Parade* and *Parents Magazine* that included coupons for 75 cents off on boxes of Crayolas. No mention of talc, asbestos or the suit was made in the advertisements. The total coupons printed carried a face value of $45 million, but almost certainly only a fraction was redeemed.

In Louisa, Virginia, Rae Ely watches the vermiculite trucks continue to roll from Robert Sansom's Virginia Vermiculite, unmolested by regulators.

MSHA continues to maintain that it is going to make changes that could prevent the lethal exposure to the miners it is supposed to protect. But by mid-2004, the mine agency continued to flout the safety changes demanded by the Labor Department's Inspector General. Some in the agency say that McAteer's replacement, David Lauriski, will do nothing meaningful to reduce the amount of asbestos that miners are exposed to every day.

Meanwhile, in April of 2004, Michigan taconite miner George Biekkola died of asbestosis.

No agency of the government has issued any health warning regarding asbestos in brakes or other auto parts. Asbestos brake shoes are still legal, still available and still on cars nationwide. Ask a mechanic, and the chances are good that he will tell you earnestly, "They took that stuff out of brakes years ago." But Schneider reported in the *Post-Dispatch* that even as auto-industry law firms try to force EPA to stop releasing 20-year-old warning materials to mechanics and automotive students, the U.S. Commerce Department reported that the importation of asbestos products — mostly brakes — has increased 300 percent in the last decade.

EPA and ATSDR scientists have been painfully blunt about their concerns for the health of millions of people that either worked at Grace's vermiculite processing plants across the country or lived close to the plants.

"In the eighties, EPA reported that about thirteen million people were possibly at risk from what the reports described as continuous, high-level exposure to asbestos. Thirteen million people and we've done nothing," Peronard said. "These are people that we've got to find. We owe it to them."

ATSDR took on the job, and in early 2002 it launched the bureaucratic-sounding National Asbestos Exposure Review. But little was bureaucratic about the effort. Teams of physicians, epidemiologists, statisticians and other health experts from ATSDR's Exposure Investigation and Consultation Branch had 250 plants to examine. This was not a paperwork exercise. They actually went to the field, sometimes with state health officials. They took samples, examined the facilities, walked the neighborhood. Got their hands dirty.

By mid-2003, they had hoped to complete initial surveys of 28 plants in 22 states. These operations were checked first because each had received at least 200 million pounds of Libby vermiculite ore from the 1920s to 1990. Some in EPA anticipate embarrassment that may ensue from ATSDR's findings if they show that many of the sites EPA regions declared clean are still dangerous. The contamination of the sites across the country may be even greater than the health agency knows.

At a meeting in late September, at an empty ski lodge on a 9,700-foot peak outside of Denver, about three dozen EPA asbestos experts and state health officials from across the country gathered to compare notes on what they really knew about tremolite asbestos. Almost all were veterans of Libby or other communities with tremolite contamination.

"It was like a fellowship, belonging to a very small and elite club of people who have lived through the hell of the asbestos wars," said Seattle's Keven McDermott.

The group debated the government's inadequate definition of asbestos; analytical protocols based on old technology and other technical and bureaucratic issues that make the asbestos battle harder to fight.

McDermott and her partner, Jed Januch, got everyone's attention when they explained a new technique they had used to evaluate a Zonolite expansion plant in Spokane.

The soil surrounding the once-heavily-used plant came up clean or with only trace amounts of asbestos detected using traditional EPA testing methods. However, when the pair disturbed the soil with shovels and earthmoving equipment, surprisingly high levels of asbestos were measured with air monitors.

"This will bring into question the accuracy of all the testing that EPA has done at the hundreds of Zonolite sites around the country, as well as the work that ATSDR is about to release," said Aubrey Miller. "There could be dangerous spots all over the country that no one has picked up on yet."

ATSDR said it is aware of the Spokane technique and is talking with the Seattle investigators. The new testing method could help them determine what risks exist now from the old plants, and what risks existed in the past for people who worked there or lived nearby. The agency wants to add their names and contact information to its Tremolite Asbestos Registry. That does sound bureaucratic, but Dr. Henry Falk, assistant administrator for ATSDR, insisted it's far from it.

"There is an inflammatory process that goes on in the body once the asbestos fibers are there, which inexorably leads to complications ten, twenty, thirty, forty years down the road. Soon there may be drugs which can halt that progression," Falk told Schneider in July 2003.

"Anything that would prevent the progression of the inflammatory process would serve as a preventative for the people who have asbestos fibers in their lungs or in the pleural surfaces," Falk said. "This would be especially valuable to those that don't have clinical symptoms now, but were exposed to tremolite."

He said major advances in biotechnology and pharmacology in just the past few years have had an impact on inflammatory processes.

"My hope is that sometime in the near future, some smart scientist some-place figures out a way to intervene in the inflammatory process that goes on in the lungs from the asbestos fibers."

The registry, he said, will allow them to find all the people that need it.

"It would be terrible if a treatment actually came forward that could re-tard the development of this disabling and often fatal process and we couldn't find the people that needed it."

The job of finding these workers and residents will fall to Sharon Cam-polucci and her team in Health Studies. She said the hunt won't be as daunt-ing as it appears.

"There are lots of ways to find these people," Campolucci said. "First, you start with whether there were any company records at all. If you can find two people who can tell you two more names, who can tell you two more names, who can tell you two more names. That's how you do it."

The release of the first handful of ATSDR studies of the expansion plants in 2003 created quite a stir in Washington, Baltimore, Chicago, Denver, Southern California, and Weedsport, N.Y. While the health agency found that minimal contamination remained at the sites, ATSDR urged, with a bluntness rarely seen, that the thousands of people who worked at, or lived near, the Zonolite plants see a doctor to determine whether they had an asbestos-related disease. "Even if you only washed a worker's clothing," a spokesman urged.

By mid-2004 ATSDR was still plodding through the remainder of the 28 sites on the hot list. Budget cuts across the health agency were responsible for the slow pace.

"We'll find the money. This is too important not to be done properly," Falk told Schneider.

Marc Racicot, the former governor of Montana with sick relatives in Libby who did so little for the asbestos victims, embarked on a lucrative Washington lobbying career after he left office, including representing En-ron. After working as chairman of the Republican National Committee, keeping his lobbying job too for a time, he took on a new challenge in 2004: directing the Bush-Cheney reelection campaign.

CHRIS WEIS AND AUBREY MILLER moved on to big new challenges. Both went to Washington to give advice on the decontamination of the Hart Senate Office Building after the anthrax letters. But no matter what else they were doing, they kept a weather eye on the situation in Libby.

Aubrey Miller became EPA Region 8's chief medical officer and toxicologist. He hopes that someday he can feel good about the accomplishments in Libby, the assignment took a toll. It made him more cynical and impatient with what he calls "government lip service and doublespeak," as well as with corporate deception. The more he found out about the compromises inherent in the country's health and safety regulations, the more disturbed he got. "It's appalling that workers, their families, and others in the community were, and continue to be, knowingly allowed to be exposed to asbestos, especially given that the hazards have been so well-known for decades," he said.

Miller got to know quite a few people in Libby who were sick, and some who have since died, and the effect of that will always be with him. "It is their stories, their handshakes, their gazes and their trust that resonate in my heart" and keep driving him toward his goals, which remain unchanged. They are to eliminate all remaining unsafe exposure pathways, to try to get people the health care they need, and to help guide future research to increase knowledge and eventually find effective treatments.

Weis also told Schneider that he feels privileged to have had the opportunity to meet and to help the people of Libby, "even if we were too late for so many."

He acknowledged the "bitter struggles" within the agency, even some that are still raging, "but in the end, in its own strange way and perhaps even unwillingly, the agency has supported us. Thanks to a few key people in critical places and times, we were able to keep moving forward in the face of threats, backhanded comments, personal attacks and political power plays.... With all its warts and bumps, the EPA is unique. Since Libby, I find it hard to say I'm proud to work for the agency anymore, but I wouldn't work anywhere else."

Chris Weis became senior toxicologist for EPA's National Enforcement Investigation Center, a small, high-powered group that provides the forensic science in major investigations for the agency and develops emergency response plans for terrorist attacks. He showed up at the Super Bowl, the G-8 Summit and other high-security events, but just shrugged when asked what he was doing.

He remains hugely grateful to Peronard for his support and leadership. "Early on, and without much discussion, we made a pact that we would use science and facts to get to the truth. And we were going to share that information with anyone who would listen and some that wouldn't. It was the only way we were going to live with ourselves after this thing was over.

"We knew it would be painful, but we had no idea how much suffering we would expose."

Paul Peronard began to disengage from Libby, handing control of the cleanup over to the capable Christiansen. But he worried. He worried that Jim's budget would be stripped. It happened. The $35 million they'd requested for cleaning Libby in 2003 was gutted to $20 million and then down to $17 million. On November 13, 2003, Christiansen told Libby citizens that the cleanup of their homes will take longer because his budget was cut another $2 million. Also, money EPA had earmarked for asbestos research has disappeared. Peronard worried that the daily grind would wear Christiansen down, but he knew that his replacement had solid experience running big cleanups, and that he would handle whatever came.

In March 2003, Peronard was feted at a going-away party at the Red Dog Saloon, near the tiny town of Yaak. He had broken his hand practicing tae kwon do that day, so he didn't feel tip-top, but he sat on a red vinyl barstool in front of a video poker machine and downed beers, pizza and chicken wings with Les and Norita, Gayla and Dave, Brad Black, many of his contractors, the mayor and other local officials.

And Tony Berget, the mayor who initially told the EPA team that there was no problem in Libby, presented Paul Peronard with a large wooden ceremonial key to the city.

For Peronard it had been a good year for accolades. He'd already been named On-Scene Coordinator of the Year by the agency he'd fought with so fiercely and represented so well. But in April 2002, on the stage of the historic Warner Theater in Washington, EPA administrator Christie Whitman presented Peronard with the Administrator's Award for Excellence, for his leadership and his dedication to the people of Libby.

It is a very significant award, given rarely. The 14-inch crystal obelisk was etched with the EPA seal, Whitman's signature and the words PRESENTED TO PAUL PERONARD. When Whitman presented it, she called Tracy, Ove and Tristan Peronard up to the stage, too.

She asked Tracy how she put up with Paul. Good question.

Back home in Denver, Tracy asked the kids if they knew Paul was a hero because of his work. They thought she was being funny. But in Libby, Alice Priest, who lost her husband and then her breath, will tell you he is. So will men who can't walk 20 feet without resting halfway, and so will women whose children go to Plummer School, and so will people who walk the cemetery early in the mornings and quietly curse the deception and neglect that put their family members in the ground.

Tracy was very proud of Paul. But she has a secret fear that he will wake up in 20 years and be sick from Libby asbestos. She worries that he didn't handle the asbestos carefully enough early on, before he knew how bad it was. "And he and his guys were always in the middle of that stuff," she told Schneider. "When he was doing other cleanups, they tested his blood once a month to see if he had elevated lead levels. The scary thing about asbestos is there is no way to test him to see if he is going to get sick in the future.

"I know that is a selfish thing to worry about."

On June 27, EPA boss Christie Whitman resigned from the agency, after amazing many that she tolerated so long being the White House's environmental scapegoat. President Bush named Marianne Horinko as acting administrator until his new choice for administrator, Utah governor Mike Leavitt, made it through the confirmation process in late October. EPA staffers caught up in the controversy over asbestos said that some of the headquarters' pressure dissipated in July when chief EPA spokesman Joe Martyak announced he was leaving government to join a Washington lobbying firm.

Peronard has moved on to other high-profile assignments, but he is always eager to rush out to an emergency. He waded the swamps of East Texas and Louisiana as part of EPA's response team for the Columbia explosion. But his mind is never very far from Libby.

Obelisk or no obelisk, Paul is still angry that it had to be as hard as it was in Libby. "Hell, it shouldn't have ever come about this way. A bloody newspaper had to get us to do a job that should have been done twenty years earlier.

"But that is not a very constructive lesson. I guess what I've really learned is that people count. In a world where money and politics have so much sway, it is not enough to have an organization with responsibility. It takes people within an organization with a desire to figure out what's right, and the balls then to stick out the fight and make it happen. But even that isn't quite right. You've got to know the system and how to work it. It isn't Don Quixote slashing at windmills that is most effective. It's Machiavelli with a sense of integrity and conscience."

He worries for the town; that in spite of the cleanup it may lose its vitality. He hopes that someday, the major topic of conversation in the Libby Café is the fishing in the Kootenai and the view of the Cabinet Mountains, not who has gotten sick or how bad business is because of the publicity. And he hopes that the divide between victims, advocates and the business interests is finally healed.

"Any sense of smugness I might have had about my role up there in Libby was wiped out one day about two years ago, when I watched Al Kaeding shop at Rosauer's Grocery Store. Two steps and stop, gasp. Pick up a head of lettuce, wheeze, adjust the valve on his oxygen tank, slump over and lean on his cart. I watched him for about an hour, and he covered maybe three aisles.

"He sort of brought it all into focus for me. Too many sick people, too much pain. No victory to be had here.

"I always felt I was a day late and a dollar short.

"Al, who was a veteran, was as good-natured a man as I've ever met, who I reckoned rarely if ever complained about anything. He died, probably in pain, a couple months short of his twenty-fifth wedding anniversary. I saw an obit in the paper shortly thereafter, and for some reason it got to me. I cried like I never have.

"How do I feel good about my part in that?"

Still, Peronard believes his team did some good things in Libby, cleaned up a lot of asbestos, fought off innumerable attacks from W.R. Grace &

Company, and moved a hell of a lot of bureaucratic inertia from his own agency out of the way.

He's just one man who did what he had to do. And Libby, Montana, after enduring 75 years of unspeakable greed, carelessness and indifference, worse than all the poison that ever poured from the torn sides of Zonolite Mountain, was damned lucky to have him.

PART 4: THE CATASTROPHE GROWS

*Chapters 27-33 updated by Andrew Schneider
in 2016 with frightening news of the asbestos tragedy*

Les's granddaughter Makenna and her father, Bob Cody, lay roses on Les's pine coffin. (Andrew Schneider)

Les Skramstad turned from a sweet-singing cowboy to a man agonizing because he brought home the asbestos that sickened his wife and children. (Andrew Schneider)

New Year's Day 2007 –

SCHNEIDER PRETTY MUCH HATED all predawn phone calls and just knew that the one that woke him at two in the morning this first day of 2007 was not going to change his mind. First, he was sure that the deep, gravelly whisper he was hearing was an obscene call.

But then he finally deciphered: "This is Les, in Montana. Happy New Year," the caller rasped. "I'm not going to make it a lot longer. I just wanted to thank you and McCumber and say goodbye."[1]

An awkward pause, too damn long, as Schneider frantically stumbled for the right thing to say, for anything to say.

"It's okay. I'm ready," said Les, finally breaking the silence.

"My homemade coffin is about as done as it's going to be. The pain is so damn bad at times that I take it out on Norita and that won't do," he added, words loaded with sadness, interrupted by gasps of air.

IN THE NINE YEARS SCHNEIDER KNEW LES, he watched him morph from a sweet-singing, soft-spoken cowboy into a politically savvy activist and, finally, a man agonizing because he believed that he'd given a death sentence to his wife of 50 years and at least three of his children.

He talked about needing to live long enough to make sure Norita would be cared for and to "sit in the front row [at Grace's trial] and look into the eyes of those bastards who killed or made sick so damn many."

Les would say he dreamed about a long row of wooden gallows built on the lowest terrace of the pit of the abandoned vermiculite mine on Zonolite Mountain.

"On those gallows, I'd see swinging the bodies of all the company bosses who knew they were killing us, who knew they were killing our wives and children, who knew they were killing this town and other towns where their poisoned ore was handled. They knew it and they hid it," he said.

"I may go to hell for what I've done to my family but those guys from Grace will be there with me. I hope I live long enough to see them swing."

But he didn't.

Twenty days later, almost to the hour, on January 21, Lester Lewis Skramstad, 70, died peacefully in his own bed as mesothelioma stole his last breath.

On January 29, his polished, handmade white pine coffin, dusted with lightly falling snow, sat over a hard-dug hole in the frozen Montana earth. Most watching kept it together until Les's granddaughter, Makenna, laid a hand and a red rose atop the wooden casket.

The tears flowed.

While the asbestos fibers killed Les before the trial, he savored that he lived long enough to hear the announcement of the criminal indictments against Grace and its gang.

Few thought it would ever happen.

For nearly five years, EPA and Justice Department civil lawyers in Denver had pursued W.R. Grace for a variety of environmental transgressions related to its operation of the vermiculite mine on Zonolite Mountain. All were civil actions and limited to financial sanctions.

Almost everyone wanted more.

IN THE WINTER OF 2001, two years into the cleanup, Paul Peronard, Aubrey Miller and Chris Weis gathered at the MK Steakhouse, 10 miles of icy road east of Libby. The three EPA warriors had just left another meeting where townsfolk demanded to know why the government hadn't jailed Grace officials.[2]

"Grace has been telling the same lie for over 40 years," Peronard lamented to his colleagues. "They still maintain that insulation and other products made from Libby vermiculite has little or no asbestos in it. The courts have ruled that people have died because Grace concealed the danger from their workers, from the town and from their customers."

Peronard understood the town's frustration. "What Grace did was criminal," he said. "There's got to be more that the government could do."

The trio and others who had watched people in Libby deteriorate and die said fines were not enough. They wanted government criminal investigators to take a look.

IT WAS FEBRUARY 2004 before the Libby team members, including Kelcey Land, an EPA financial forensic specialist who had cataloged tens of thousands of Grace internal documents and shipping invoices, were convinced they could present solid evidence of Grace's wrongdoing. They wanted to give criminal investigators the opportunity to decide whether this was a case worth pursuing. They were ready.

Daniel Horgan, a senior EPA criminal investigator; his boss, Lori Hanson; and Linda Kato, the Criminal Investigations Division's top lawyer, gathered in a conference room in EPA's Denver office. For almost two days, Peronard, Miller, Weis, senior enforcement attorney Matthew Cohn, and others presented documents to their colleagues from the criminal side. They showed old aerial photographs of the vermiculite mine with white plumes spewing from the processing mill, Grace documents and court exhibits showing that about 5,000 pounds of asbestos fibers fell on Libby every day the mill operated.

With precision and passion, they explained that one fiber sucked into the right place in a human's lung could eventually kill the person. They passed around folders of documents showing that Grace knew its product was hurting and killing its employees and their families. They explained why they believed that Grace had lied repeatedly in response to EPA questions. They handed out copies of letters from a Grace vice president to former EPA Administrator Christine Whitman, insisting there was no danger of cancer-causing contamination in attic insulation made with Libby vermiculite. Then they presented Grace reports showing that its tests had proved the insulation was dangerous.

They had a journal article by Dr. David Egilman, a specialist in occupational and pulmonary medicine and one of the first physicians to write that the vermiculite-mine workers were at risk. Egilman reported in Accountability in Research that in 1976 Grace funded an animal study that the corporation hoped would prove that its vermiculite did not cause mesothelioma, the usually fatal cancer uniquely associated with asbestos exposure.

But, the Massachusetts physician wrote, the study proved just the opposite and Grace told neither its workers nor regulators.

The information in his "Corporate corruption of medical literature: Asbestos studies concealed by W.R. Grace & Co." would not be known publicly for years.

Wrote Egilman, "These actions were intentions, and were motivated by Grace's conscious decision to prioritize corporate profit over human health."

Assistant U.S. Attorney Kris McLean of Missoula told the Libby team to keep working. Leading the effort were Horgan; Bert Marsden, another criminal investigator, and Susan Zazzali, an environmental engineer from the EPA's Montana office. Because of the complex financial issues, Internal Revenue Service Special Agent John Nielsen was added to the team.

ON THE EVENING OF MAY 10, 2004, bearing a huckleberry pie, the foursome ended up in the home of Gayla Benefield. Over the past five years, lots of visitors had knocked on her door to discuss asbestos-tainted vermiculite and W.R. Grace.[3]

The western larch log house beside the Kootenai River had hosted scores of newspaper and magazine reporters and photographers from nine countries, would-be authors, documentary filmmakers and television crews from every major network.

But the four visitors that evening were different. All were federal agents. At least two carried guns. Also clustered around the kitchen table were Les and Norita Skramstad; Mike Noble, a miner whose mother and father were killed by asbestos, and LeRoy Thom, who was the last union president before Grace closed the mine.

By the time Gayla had made her second pot of coffee, they'd gotten down to business. The investigators had done their homework. Before arriving in Libby, they had spent a couple of days at the Kalispell office of McGarvey, Heberling, Sullivan and McGarvey. These lawyers represent hundreds of people suing Grace for deaths or illness from exposure to Libby vermiculite. The lawyers shared their Grace documents with the investigators. They had told the federal agents their next stop should be Gayla.

The questioning continued late into the night. The pie was gone and the coffee pot, cold. The investigators left after admitting that getting an indictment was a long shot.

DRESSED IN DENIM OR KHAKI AND BOOTS, the feds at first attracted little attention as they scurried around Libby and surrounding Lincoln County throughout the summer of 2004. As the number of people they questioned grew, so did the notice their presence generated. But people were trying to keep it quiet.[4]

"No one was mentioning they'd been questioned, or if they did it, they whispered," Gayla said. "We were all terrified that word would leak out and Washington would kill the investigation."

All those who understood its consequences were concerned about the rapidly approaching five-year statute of limitations. An indictment had to be issued by late November 2004 – five years from the date the *Seattle Post-Intelligencer* began publishing its Libby investigations and Peronard's group arrived in town. An investigation like this normally would take two to three years. They had only months left.

In the EPA team's war room, about 200 miles southeast in Missoula, flow charts and financial notes covered the walls. A mind-blowing computer system designed by people at the Justice Department allowed them to search three million pages of Grace documents. Evidence, including depositions of Grace officials taken over years of civil suits, was piling up, but also growing was the anxiety over being shut down. The angst was never more palpable than when the investigators were summoned to Washington in mid-October.

There, Justice Department lawyers from the Environmental Crime Section evaluated the investigators' progress, debated what else was needed to proceed with the prosecution and offered help.

In Billings, Montana, U.S. Attorney William Mercer told investigators to keep at it. They made trips from coast to coast and north to south, questioning former and current Grace officials, workers and others. Twelve- to fifteen-hour days became the norm.

On October 29, as federal law demands, the Justice Department notified Grace that it and several of its current and former officials were targets of a criminal indictment. The investigators and prosecutors were making last-minute fixes to the indictment, but the November deadline loomed. The presidential election had some team members holding their breath.

THE PRO-BUSINESS STANCE of President George W. Bush's administration was no secret, and going back to Ronald Reagan's days, Grace was often a White House favorite. Vice President Dick Cheney's past involvement with Halliburton and the company's estimated $4 billion-plus tab for asbestos claims that had been filed over the years were discussed over a lot of beer, but team members shrugged it off because there was nothing they could do about it.

David Uhlmann, then chief of the Justice Department's Environmental Crime Section, kept telling the Libby investigators that "Political considerations never come into play in criminal cases."[5]

No one really believed that.

Right after Bush was reelected, the investigators made their last presentation before the federal grand jury that had long been weighing indictments against Grace. The two dozen jurors met in Missoula the first Wednesday of every month, for two or three days. The statute of limitations was about to expire. There was no sign of the indictment.

"The deadline had come," Gayla said. "None of us knew what was happening, but we expected the worst."

BUT AT THE CRAMPED OFFICE of the federal investigators, new information, corporate papers that appeared to be vital to proving Grace's wrongdoing, suddenly showed up. Some came from Grace itself under discovery demands, others from lawyers who had previously sued the corporation.

Documents indecipherable because of age or damage became readable because of a Tom Clancy-like gee-whiz technology that most likely came from a spooky lab that often did its magic for the Secret Service. Forensic financial analysts finally cobbled together asbestos exposure estimates from more than 125,000 samples of water, air, soil, dust and tree bark collected by an army of government and contract scientists.

But how could the clock be stopped?

The answer came from Uhlmann's environmental crime group in Washington. Tolling, it was called. An infrequently used doctrine allows an approaching deadline to be placed in limbo for a short while, if the accused agrees. And Grace did.

Why would a corporation decide to give prosecutors more time to develop charges against it?

Grace didn't volunteer an answer, but most companies agree to tolling to have more time to try to harvest political IOUs to get the indictment dropped, or to work out a plea bargain, or just postpone what they know will be bad publicity.

THE "WHY" DIDN'T MATTER to Horgan, McLean and their associates. They had more time - more trips, more interviews and another run at the grand jury in January, and, at the most, one more in February. The jurors were going to end their long examination of the evidence against Grace February 2.

They either voted to indict Grace and its officials on that date or the indictments would be dropped.

The federal team wasn't sure it would even make it that far. When President Bush made the first of several speeches on January 5, 2005 on the immediate need to halt "abusive asbestos suits," he said they were harming "some of this country's leading companies."[6]

Two weeks later the team was in Washington when the president raised the "asbestos problem" at a White House news conference.

"Obviously, there are some things we need to do to make sure that America is a good place to continue to risk capital and invest. That's why I'm urging the Congress to pass legal reform. You might remember, one of the first issues that I addressed after election was legal reform, asbestos reform, class-action reform, medical liability reform," the president told reporters on January 26.

The Libby investigators and lawyers knew Bush wasn't referring to criminal suits. But they weren't sure the political appointees in the EPA and Justice Department would understand the difference.

On February 2, in his State of the Union address, Bush again brought up the asbestos problem.

"To make our economy stronger and more competitive, America must reward, not punish, the efforts and dreams of entrepreneurs. Justice is distorted, and our economy is held back by irresponsible class-actions and frivolous asbestos claims – and I urge Congress to pass legal reforms this year," the president said.

EARLIER THAT VERY SAME DAY, the federal grand jury in Montana had handed down the indictments against Grace.

U.S. District Judge Donald Molloy, whose disdain for U.S. attorney William Mercer was palpable and widely known, refused to let Montana's top federal cop make the announcement at the federal courthouse.

So, at 2 p.m. on February 7, 2005, a few blocks away outside the Missoula County Courthouse, Mercer held up the 49-page indictment and said: "A human and environmental tragedy has occurred in Libby. This prosecution seeks to hold Grace and some of its executives responsible for the misconduct alleged in this indictment."[7]

Skramstad and Benefield beamed as they thumbed through the pages of the thick indictment.

The Justice Department called it "one of the most significant environmental criminal indictments in U.S. history." Grace and seven of its current and former executives were accused of multiple charges, including criminal conspiracy, obstruction of justice, wire fraud, and knowing endangerment.

What this means, the government said, is that Grace knowingly released asbestos into the air, and therefore placed miners, their families, and townspeople at risk, and defrauded the government by obstructing the policing efforts of various agencies including the EPA. All this, the government charged, increased Grace's profits and allowed the corporation to avoid liability for damages it inflicted upon thousands of people. They were accused of knowing that the ore from Libby was deadly and concealing the danger from workers, people living near the plants, and the government. That lethal ore ended up in plants across North America, and in attic and wall insulation in millions of homes and businesses.

ACCORDING TO THE JUSTICE DEPARTMENT, Grace could face a fine of up to $280 million, which is twice the amount of profits the government says the company made from the Libby mine. Also named in the 10-count indictment were Henry Eschenbach, Grace's medical director; Jack Wolter, a former executive for Grace's construction products division; William Mc-Caig, former general manager of the Libby mine; Robert Bettacchi, a senior vice president of the company; O. Mario Favorito, Grace's top lawyer; Alan

Stringer, former manager of the mine, and Robert Walsh, former Grace vice president. If convicted, they faced possible prison terms of up to 15 years for each of several counts.[8]

Skramstad and Benefield and some of the federal investigators were not shy in insisting to anyone who would listen that Grace's executives should be standing trial for homicide.

There are several reasons why that wouldn't happen. The main one being the Clean Air Act does not provide for homicide charges.

Even if convicted of all charges, the Grace bosses wouldn't hang, as Skramstad had hoped, but they could face many years in a federal prison.

"It's not as good as hanging, but even prison is more than I ever thought I would see happen to those bastards," Skramstad said.

Grace denied the charges and said it looked forward to setting the record straight in court.

When Mercer wrapped up his announcement at the Missoula County Courthouse he said that the trial could begin within three months.

He was not even close.

U.S. District Judge Donald Molloy both shocked and thrilled observers with his rulings and comments during the 10-week criminal trial of Grace and several of its executives. Court watchers' opinions differed depending on whether they thought the worldwide corporation was right or wrong in its actions in Libby. (Kurt Wilson, *The Missoulian*)

IT WAS 1,477 DAYS LATER – at 8:28 on the morning of February 23, 2009 – when the sound of Judge Donald Molloy's gavel boomed through a packed courtroom. On the second floor of the Russell Smith Federal Courthouse in Missoula, the oft-delayed criminal trial of W.R. Grace & Co. and its top officials had finally begun.

Optimism for a guilty verdict against Grace and its officials for what the EPA called the "the biggest environmental crime in history" soared high that day among the prosecution team and the Libby residents crammed sardine-like on the courtroom's oak benches. Almost all had seen or heard of the thousands of Grace documents that to most readers clearly established that the company and its top employees knew that the vermiculite ore being blasted out of Zonolite Mountain was pervaded with high levels of an extremely toxic form of asbestos. And that Grace letters, memos, and reports, spanning decades, showed that the corporation's executives at the highest levels knew that the Libby miners, their families and even the townsfolk who never visited the mine were being sickened and killed in numbers never seen in the United States.

The majority of the incriminating papers were signed by the men sitting along the right wall of the courtroom in a line of chairs reserved for the accused. They were grim-faced, dressed in dark suits like their lawyers, unlike those Montanans sitting in the gallery, attired in fleece and flannel. The corporate officials worked hard to avoid being caught even peeking at the locals, most of whom were from Libby. Their eyes never left the judge.

Molloy had been the arbiter of years of legal sparring between Grace and the federal government.

ON DECEMBER 21, 1995, President Clinton appointed Molloy to fill a vacancy in the Montana U.S. District Court. Seven months later, with the blessings of the U.S. Senate, the son of a copper miner from Butte became judge for life, a term Molloy said was "a wise decision the Founding Fathers made so judges could make unpopular decisions."[1]

Many of his court-watchers say Molloy comes across as the kind of judge you'd like to hear your case. At times stroking his handlebar mustache, Molloy beams as he talks of his Irish heritage, that he's the father of five and that he flew F-4B Phantom fighter-bombers in the Navy, often off the aircraft carrier John F. Kennedy. Molloy was called the "greenest judge in the West" for his environmental rulings, which infuriated loggers, hunters, off-the-road enthusiasts, and others.[2]

He earned the scorn of ranchers when he blocked the killing of gray wolves in Montana and Idaho by keeping them on the Endangered Species List. He halted logging in sections of various national forests to protect endangered grizzly bears, and he forbade the use of ATVs, snowmobiles, and other motorized vehicles on parts of government-owned land, including the Gallatin National Forest, the nearly two million acres of federal land adjoining Yellowstone National Park.

In an effort to protect endangered fish and plant life, Molloy angered firefighters and worried many homeowners in fire-prone mountainside communities when he ordered the Interior Department to conduct detailed environmental studies of the harm caused by aerial spraying of red plumes of toxic fire retardant on forest and brush fires.

Some of Molloy's previous decisions against Grace showed the judge was willing to stand up to the giant corporation. For example, on April 27, 2003, Molloy ordered the company to pay the government $54.5 million. It paid for some of the cost of EPA's investigation into what Grace had done to the community and the agency's removal of a fraction of the asbestos contaminating homes, schools, and roads in Libby and nearby communities.

Nevertheless, Kris McLean and the rest of the prosecution team, both in Montana and in the Justice Department, privately fretted over the barely concealed scorn that Molloy had for the state's U.S. attorney. Many in Montana's legal community said Molloy's anger at William Mercer was spawned soon after the federal prosecutor went to Washington in May 2005 to become a senior aide to Attorney General Alberto Gonzales. Almost instantly he was named the chairman of the Attorney General's Advisory Committee, which advised Gonzales on policy matters.[3]

Soon after Mercer's arrival in Washington, President George W. Bush, who had appointed him as Big Sky Country's top federal cop in 2001, nominated the Montanan to be associate attorney general, the third-highest person in the department.

Molloy did little to conceal his fervent belief that Mercer was violating a federal law by holding two jobs – about 2,000 miles apart – and not residing in the state where he was U.S. attorney. The judge said Mercer averaged three days a month in Montana.

McLean's office mates said Molloy's visceral disdain for their boss grew along with Mercer's influence and perceived stature in DOJ.

On October 20, 2005, Molloy wrote to Gonzales urging that Mercer be replaced in Montana because he was violating the agency's residency laws and his office wasn't doing its job, thus clogging the court system.

Twenty-one days later, Gonzales replied to the judge, saying he had given careful consideration to Molloy's concerns, but was refusing his demand because Mercer was not violating federal law.

MERCER AND MOLLOY'S LONG DISTANCE fencing match became local when Mercer showed up in 2006 to comment on a case the judge was hearing.[4]

Tristan Scott, a talented Montana journalist, reported in The Missoulian on a loud, angry clash in Molloy's court over Mercer interfering with a state case by trying to bring federal gun possession charges against a man who had served his sentence years earlier for killing another man in a bar fight. The state had put the man – owner of a multimillion-dollar construction business – under "intense supervised probation" because of his gun collection. The local prosecutor said the accused had a "clean record for years."

Reminding the U.S. attorney that it was a state case, Molloy said: "What is the federal interest in prosecuting this case?

"Your job is not to get convictions. Your job is to ensure that justice is done. I think that's just a real problem for you. You're not pursuing justice. You're pursuing statistics," Scott reported the judge saying to Mercer.

"You have no credibility," Molloy said. "None."

As Scott wrote, the judge denounced the operation of Mercer's team in Montana: "You're in Washington, D.C., and you ought to be here in Montana doing your work. Your office is a mess."

Mercer continued to work in D.C.

The Washington Post reported that Mercer, in November 2005, had Republicans in Congress add language to the reauthorization of the USA Patriot Act that would explicitly make dual jobs like his legal. The Congressional Research Service said Mercer was DOJ's front person at the time, directing changes in the renewal of the act. Wording by DOJ was added to the legislation's more than 342 pages and allowed the attorney general or his designee to exempt federal prosecutors from residency requirements. This, so they can take on "dual or additional responsibilities."

Things got politically uncomfortable in Gonzales's department in 2007 as Congress scheduled hearings into the questionable firing of seven U.S. attorneys, allegedly to make room for White House favorites.

According to the *Post*, Mercer was one of eight Justice officials about to be subpoenaed by congressional investigators to testify in his alleged involvement.

Before that could happen, on June 22, 2007, Mercer resigned from his DOJ position and returned to his job in Montana.[5]

Most of the lawyers Schneider asked said Molloy's hatred of the U.S. attorney didn't present a notable problem when Mercer's assistant, McLean, had appeared before the chief judge in earlier cases. However, all acknowledged that with reporters from most of the national news organizations crowding the back two rows for the trial, this case could be different.

CHAPTER 29

The ten-week criminal trial of W.R. Grace and its officials in federal court in Missoula, Montana, took its toll on many, yet Gayla Benefield and Norita Skramstad hung in for almost all of the testimony. (Andrew Schneider)

THE CRIMINAL TRIAL of W.R. Grace & Co. was filled with both blistering arguments and sleep-inducing science. It overflowed with legal theater and often-puzzling rulings. Some bizarre edicts by U.S. District Judge Donald Molloy were immediately overturned by higher courts, yet he continued to run the trial as he saw fit.

Schneider was in the courtroom and hallways every day of the 10-week proceedings and delivered his coverage online, first in "Secret Ingredients," his blog at the *Seattle Post-Intelligencer*. After the newspaper was closed, his reporting from Molloy's domain spread across the country in his own blog, "Cold Truth."

These excerpts capture the most revealing actions reported from the federal courthouse in Missoula, Montana, during that spring in 2009.

THE TRIAL:

February 20, 2009

After just a day and a half of questioning, a jury of 12 and three alternates were accepted by the federal judge, the prosecutors and defense lawyers to sit in judgment of W.R. Grace & Co. and its senior executives in what the government called the largest environmental crime in U.S. history. For their role in this legal drama, the jurors are paid $40 a day. The 15 came from a jury pool of 80 winnowed from 400 men and women from throughout Western Montana.

February 23

At 8:28 a.m. Monday, a sound that many thought they'd never hear echoed through a packed federal courtroom as U.S. District Judge Donald Molloy gaveled the start of the oft-delayed criminal trial of Grace and its top officials.

In an overflow room on another floor, Norita Skramstad sat on a hard wooden bench, listening to Molloy tell the jury about the charges the government had brought against the international chemical company.

She held a tan felt Resistol cowboy hat in her lap. It was her husband's. Les Skramstad died because of the asbestos he sucked into his lungs while he worked for the mine. Norita and three of their four children are also sick, their lungs damaged by the asbestos dust most likely carried home on Les's work clothes.

"He made me promise that I'd bring this hat to court if he died before the trial," Norita said, running her fingers over the eagle feathers and the tiny silver angel on the hat band.

Les's anger would have been evident if he'd lived long enough to attend. He fought hard and long for the people whose lives were destroyed by what he saw as the heartless actions of Grace and its predecessors on Zonolite Mountain. Today, those people were the topic of discussion in the courtroom.

The trial's first day was like a game of legal show and tell, with government prosecutors Kris McLean and Kevin Cassidy given two hours for an opening statement. David Bernick, Grace's top lawyer, also got two, and the lawyers representing the five former Grace executives got four to present their opening.

The judge told the jury his name was Don, he's been on the federal bench for 13 years, and "I love what I do and especially the trials."

The opening statements followed.

These are the presentations lawyers practice over and over, the words that tell the jury what they're going to show and how they'll do it. It's the chance to get the jurors on their side early, to win them over with charm, knowledge and the understanding that they're only getting paid $40 a day.

McLean told the jury that Grace "endangered the health of hundreds, if not thousands" and individual executives "chose profits at the expense of people's health."

He listed where the dangerous ore and mine tailings were used in Libby, including a high school running track, the skating pond at the elementary school, and youth baseball fields. And he explained the Grace documents the government would use to prove what Grace knew and the secrets the company kept.

McLean said the government would prove that Grace knew for decades that the ore and products made from it posed serious health hazards to the miners, their families, and residents of Libby and nearby Lincoln County. And, he added, Grace hid the risks from workers and government regulators.

Prosecutor Cassidy talked about the five Grace executives by name and described them as decision-makers and top officials who were clearly aware of the dangers but took active steps to conceal them from workers and the government.

Several of the jurors were watching the defendants across the courtroom. Two of the accused were looking straight at the jury and the other three any place but.

Grace's lawyer Bernick disputed almost everything the government alleged, emphasizing that Grace did not conspire to hide the asbestos problems in Libby and that they were widely known by everyone, including the Environmental Protection Agency, for years.

"There is no question that miners and their families suffered tragic losses as a consequence of the operation of this mine," Bernick said, which spawned puzzled looks throughout the courtroom.

The style of McLean and Bernick differs as greatly as their individual missions on Molloy's battlefield.

McLean has done an exquisite job of bringing the criminal allegations before two sessions of the grand jury, through the brier patch that needed to be navigated to appease the judge and finally before the jury today. He's solid and knowledgeable, and like most federal prosecutors, he shuns glitzy playing for the jury.

Watching Bernick during his two-hour opening statement, it was quickly apparent why Grace is paying him $1,000 an hour, plus.

He used huge, colorful charts, almost constant hand gestures and expressions, raising and lowering his voice to emphasize his view or discredit a point made by the government. The jury hung on almost every word.

Quite a showman.

February 24

If Grace lawyer Barbara Harding got a buck each time she leaped out of her chair to object to a question the prosecution had asked their witness, she probably would have made more today than the $40 each juror got paid to hear her. Depending on which side of the courtroom you sat on, Harding was either tenacious or obnoxious. But regardless of what you call her, she was doing what any good defense lawyer would do and that's keeping the opposition from straying from what the judge says the trial is all about.

In this case, that path is very narrow.

To the pain of many Libby residents in the spectator seats, the government cannot address the decades of dangerous practices at Grace's mine on Zonolite Mountain. Nor can prosecutors discuss that the company allowed thousands of pounds of asbestos fibers spewed from a vermiculite processing mill at the mine six miles away to inundate the town of Libby.

Rather, the government must focus only on harm that occurred after the federal Clean Air Act and its "knowing-endangerment" provision were enacted in 1990.

Harding repeatedly interrupted the questioning by prosecutors McLean and Cassidy and griped that the question wasn't relevant.

Judge Molloy played referee in his long, black robe and told McLean and Cassidy to "be precise about the dates these events happened." The jury got its first peek at some Libby residents sickened by exposure to asbestos at the mine, in the air or soil, or from the Zonolite insulation leaking into the house.

Kelly O'Brien, who worked at a mental health center in Libby, told jurors that the vermiculite was all over. "When the washer or dryer were on the spin cycle, it would shake the insulation from the ceiling and there would be piles of dust on the machine."

Seven of the witnesses said they had asbestos-related diseases, four had lost spouses or siblings.

Vernon Riley told of his wife, Darlene, dying of mesothelioma. "I had her just two and a half years after she learned she had that cancer," he said, his soft voice cracking.

Defense lawyer Harding asked every male whether he'd ever changed brakes on his own car or truck, a common chore for men and boys in the West. She asked three witnesses if they knew that brakes contained asbestos.

This is an amazing admission for someone representing a company that sold asbestos, because in courtrooms throughout the country, the asbestos industry had denied for years that asbestos in brakes is harmful.

February 26

It's bizarre and a bit prickly to sit in a federal courtroom and watch a story that you broke a decade ago, then chased with about 240 follow-ups and a book, being played out in front of you.

It becomes surreal when the judge talks about the book from the bench and defense lawyers introduce excerpts into evidence, and then do dramatic readings to the witnesses for the prosecution, and then ask if the published statements were accurate.

That's pretty much what happened Wednesday at the criminal trial of W.R. Grace. The prosecution's most knowledgeable witness, Paul Peronard, EPA's on-scene coordinator for Libby, sat in the witness chair and listened to comments he made years ago which I quoted in the first edition of this book.

Peronard was the prime target of Grace's defense team, which wanted him to be banned from testifying — or at least discredited. Neither happened, but Grace lawyers were able to convince Judge Molloy that Peronard could only testify about his actions, and then only within a narrow time span.

The 23-year veteran of the EPA held his own and kept his cool. His straight-talking answers drew occasional smiles from some jurors and scowls from members of the defense team. But even he was startled when defense lawyers started reading back comments he made years earlier.

The first was from a *Seattle Post-Intelligencer* story from 2005 which discussed Peronard and Drs. Aubrey Miller and Chris Weis having a dinner at the MK Steakhouse on an elk-clogged road 10 miles out of Libby.

The trio had just left a late-night community meeting where residents were seething that the international chemical company that owned the polluting mine had not yet been brought up on criminal charges.

"Grace had been telling the same lie for over 40 years," Peronard said in the *P-I's* report. "They still maintain that insulation and other products made from Libby vermiculite has little or no asbestos in it. The courts have ruled that people have died because Grace concealed the danger from their workers, from the town, and from their customers." Peronard understood the town's frustration, the lawyer read.

"What Grace did was criminal," he said. "There's got to be more that the government could do."

A murmur went through the spectators.

The lawyer asked Peronard whether he had made that comment, and, if so, was it accurate.

"It's pretty much what I said," Peronard said.

The defense lawyer then read a section from "An Air That Kills," where Peronard and his team are sorting through documents from Grace and the government:

"When you put all these together, you've got the answers. You've got proof, vivid and unquestionable, that what was going on in Libby was a proven hazard and people were being killed. EPA, NIOSH, OSHA – the whole damn government – knew what was happening to the people of Libby and not a damn thing was done about any of it."

The lawyer jumped ahead a few paragraphs.

"This is criminal," Peronard had said. "They botched the whole investigation, which would have saved twenty years' worth of exposure and lots of lives.

"We've been working our asses off trying to get an understanding of what happened here, why these people were killed, and nobody mentions that (the government) knew these guys were swallowing asbestos and did nothing about it."

This time, the lawyer asked if Peronard still believed that the actions of both Grace and the government, including his own agency, were criminal.

"Absolutely," Peronard said. "This is why we're here today."

The lawyer asked if his candor had gotten him into trouble. "At times," he answered modestly.

What he didn't volunteer was that much of the trouble he and his team repeatedly found themselves in came from Grace, the asbestos industry, and its defenders in his own agency, Capitol Hill and the White House.

He never doubted that Grace had painted fluorescent bull's eyes on his back and those of Miller and Weis.

Letters, e-mails and memos from Grace and other players in the asbestos world, denouncing the actions, findings and conclusions of the threesome, fill files in every federal agency that deals with public health, and the archives of the Bush White House's Office of Management and Budget.

Grace may end up not being held accountable for the tragedy at Libby when this trial is over, but it will not be because Peronard and his gang weren't doing their jobs.

February 27

The first week is over. Jurors headed home. Some lawyers flew back east while most are, and will be, cloistered until Monday in their hotel war rooms trying to sort out the ramifications of Judge Molloy's numerous head-spinning decisions and orders. And there were many.

One of the new wrinkles has to be the action this morning by the U.S. 9th Circuit Court of Appeals, which tossed out Molloy's much-debated interpretation of the Crime Victims' Rights Act. Before the trial started, his honor ruled that 34 Libby residents who were scheduled to testify for the government couldn't enter the courtroom because it hadn't been shown that they were victims of criminal actions by Grace.

Depending on how Molloy reacts to the higher court decision, it could make next week a little spicier.

But getting back to this week, courtroom chatter said the prosecution was more seriously damaged, especially with the severe restrictions on what Peronard, the government's top witness, is permitted to testify about.

But prosecutors McLean and Cassidy did a lot of skillful tap dancing and on-the-fly maneuvering in skirting Molloy's land mines to keep Peronard's testimony moving.

The prosecution led the EPA on-scene coordinator through seemingly endless questions on what his agency had asked Grace and what the chemical giant had replied. There were displays of aerial photographs of locations in Libby tainted with the asbestos-contaminated vermiculite or mine waste.

Defense lawyers were doing a very accurate, nonstop imitation of "Whack-a-Mole" throughout Peronard's testimony. The government could barely get a question asked before one, two or three Grace lawyers popped up with objections.

David Bernick got his turn to cross-examine Peronard late in the day and it wasn't pretty. None of the jurors dozed off.

Grace's number-one barrister hammered away at Peronard, his machine-gun-paced questioning attempting to rebut or at least dilute the effectiveness of every point the prosecution may have scored with the jury in establishing the obstruction of justice charge against Grace.

The center of the argument was a questionnaire called a "104-E" that I'm sure the jurors will come to despise. Companies involved in investigations into alleged illegal handling of hazardous material are required to complete the multi-page form.

Bernick repeated almost every statement Peronard made in answer to Cassidy's earlier questions about the 104-E.

In reference to one section of the document dealing with where Grace stored waste from the mine, Peronard responded to Bernick's version of what he had said with "You've got to be kidding me. Those are your words and I think they're nonsense."

When the normally unflappable EPA on-scene coordinator bit his lip and tried to show Bernick why he was mistaken, Grace's lawyer would snarl "Unresponsive," followed instantly with another question.

Peronard jabbed at Bernick at one point, "You keep saying I knew about it and I didn't."

Molloy admonished them to play nicely but the loud gamesmanship continued until the courtroom clock mercifully struck 5 o'clock and week one ended.

March 1

Missoula, Montana, has more than its share of high-end eateries but most of the cheaper ones are worth a visit. The absolute best burger in the world comes off the tiny grill at the scruffy Missoula Club, or a breakfast of brains and eggs and other memorable fare I also recommend at the Oxford Saloon and Café.

The pinstripe-suited army of W.R. Grace lawyers, paralegals and assistants are expected to pump hundreds of thousands of dollars into the local economy over the next four months as they ply their trade in the federal courthouse. Grace and the five former top executives on trial will get stuck with the tab for the classy restaurants, hotel suites and condo.

The "Briefcase Brigade," as Matthew Frank of the *Missoula Independent* calls them, are being paid $200 to $1,000 or more an hour. That's not just courtroom time. Many of the visiting Easterners are spending some of those bucks looking to adopt a bit of Western motif. Pearl-button shirts and Stetsons were prime acquisitions. However, I heard two of the well-paid lawyers lamenting that they could find no snakeskin boots in Missoula.

March 2

Even court personnel and defense lawyers seemed a bit stunned Monday when Judge Molloy ripped into government prosecutors, blaming them for every problem but global warming. It didn't take a legal scholar to figure out that the judge was royally angered at a ruling on Friday by the 9th Circuit U.S. Court of Appeals.

The higher court overturned a February order by Molloy that barred witnesses from Libby who were also victims of Grace's alleged criminal action from watching the trial before they testified. The appellate court made it clear that Molloy had violated the provisions of the Crime Victims' Rights Act and had to let the people watch.

On Friday, Molloy had suspended the trial and ordered Assistant U.S. Attorney Kris McLean to have 34 witnesses in the courtroom this morning to testify. They would do so before the judge and not the jury and then return at a later date to testify for real in open court.

But when Molloy slammed the gavel, there was no sign of the witnesses. There wouldn't have been the original 34. Some had already testified and, McLean said, several were dropped from the witness list. This, because Molloy had severely restricted the evidence that the government could present against Grace.

"They could not be here today for many reasons, including the fact that they have determined that they just do not want to be here. No one wanted to make two trips to Missoula to testify," McLean told an incredulous judge. He added that the matter was moot.

"It's not moot," bellowed Molloy, adding that the appellate panel had ordered him to listen to the testimony of all witnesses so he could determine if later they had changed their opinions based on what they had heard from other witnesses.

"Let's get something straight here," Molloy said. "This case has been going on for too long.

"And it has been delayed, delayed, delayed. And it's going to get tried. And it's going to get tried in accordance with the procedures that have been around in this country for over 200 years," said the judge.

You could see the white knuckles of those sitting at the U.S. attorney's table. Neither they nor McLean said a word, but you had to know that everyone wanted to scream that the endless delays were caused by Molloy.

In the weeks before the trial the judge had repeatedly taken Grace's position on the admissibility of witnesses, evidence, and science the prosecution planned to use. Those rulings were so devastating to the government's case that McLean took the dangerous and uncommon action of challenging Molloy's orders to the appellate court.

The higher court overturned Molloy almost every time, as they did on Friday, and some Missoula lawyers think today's tirade was payback.

The judge told McLean that he had warned the government as long ago as four years and several times since that this witness issue would surface. "You did nothing," Molloy said.

One of the defense lawyers put his hand over his eyes, as if blocking something obscene or unpleasant.

"They just don't want to come. The witnesses have decided that they don't want to sit here for three to five months. What would you have me do?" McLean asked the judge.

The judge said he didn't want the community of Libby thinking that this process is somehow tainted. "This is a public process. And there are rights that the defendants have, believe it or not. And it's going to be a fair process," Molloy said.

It turned out that the only witnesses who really wanted to watch all of the trial were Melvin Parker and his wife, who had bought acres of asbestos-contaminated, riverfront land from Grace. In fact, the motion to the appellate court was filed on their behalf. More than a dozen other witnesses said they wanted to see a portion of the testimony, but not enough to give Molloy a preview. The Parkers finally told McLean that they would not attend so the trial could move ahead.

Molloy didn't like this idea either. Instead, he ordered McLean to put the Parkers on the witness stand the following day, rather than as the prosecution's last witnesses as planned.

McLean had no option but to agree.

March 3

EPA's Paul Peronard ended three days of intense questioning. Even with Judge Molloy's stringent restrictions on topics that he would permit Peronard to address, and the jack-in-the-box antics of the defense team bounding out of their seats with endless objections, lawyers in the courtroom told me the EPA agent did more than hold his own and that the Montana jurors believed him.

I don't know what Grace's lawyers thought. However, after lunch, Peronard was sitting by himself in the almost empty lobby outside the courtroom door. David Bernick, Grace's lead lawyer, sauntered by, saw the man he'd been grilling two days, donned a broad smile, whipped his arms apart and bowed two or three times. Peronard looked puzzled.

By midafternoon, Melvin Parker was on the stand. He was a key government witness that Molloy required to testify today, rather than at the end of the batting order as McLean had planned.

Parker bought 22 heavily contaminated acres of land at the base of Zonolite mines from Grace to use as a plant nursery, mushroom farm and winter storage area for 118 RVs and cars. He was to be a main player in McLean's effort to prove the knowing endangerment charge: that Grace knew the land was contaminated and kept it secret.

The jury seemed willing to accept Parker's answers to McLean's questioning. They smiled at the white-haired forester's folksy replies. He talked about how he bought all the land and the buildings outside Libby from Grace in 1999. He explained how his wife, their daughter, and her husband worked at the nursery.

The government tried to introduce a photo showing Parker's granddaughter playing in the yard, but Molloy upheld Grace's objection.

Parker said he was assured by Alan Stringer, Grace's man in Libby, that there was no hazardous material in the site, which he bought two years after Grace closed the bedeviled vermiculite mine.

He said he first learned that there was asbestos in the vermiculite covering his land in the November 1999 stories on Grace's operation in the *Seattle P-I.*

Stringer, Parker explained, showed up and said he was very disappointed in the *P-I* reporting and would "do anything it took, anything at all, to make it right."

Stringer was also indicted in this case but died before trial.

To McLean's last question, Parker said he had an asbestos-related disease.

Defense lawyer Thomas Frongillo methodically set about dismantling the government's witness.

He spent almost an hour getting Parker to discuss various million-dollar deals that he tried to craft with Grace, including buying hundreds of acres of forest land bordering the mine and, at one point, even the mine itself. They also went over the bidding war the Parkers had with Grace when the company wanted to buy back the contaminated nursery property. Parker testified that he found an offer from Grace for more than $900,000 "insulting" and also refused a $1.2 million offer. That was almost 10 times what he had paid for it.

It brought scowls to the faces of some jurors and soft moans from spectators when the lawyer had Parker repeat the answers he had given earlier to McLean about not having a clue that there was asbestos in the vermiculite.

Parker turned a bit surly and mumbled when Frongillo asked him about language he had written in his offer to Grace to buy the mine land seven years before the *P-I* stories. In that offer, he mentioned the presence of asbestos-type material on the property.

It became more painful to watch when the lawyer, who apparently did a lot more homework than the prosecution, pulled out a sworn deposition by Parker taken during a civil suit he brought against Grace.

Again, Parker contradicted many of the statements he had made to McLean.

Frongillo was just beginning to ask Parker about the 5,000-square-foot house that EPA had provided him when Molloy ended the session. The cross examination resumes in the morning.

March 4

Of course, no one will know the outcome until the jury hearing the W.R. Grace trial issues a verdict three, four or five months from now, but the 15 jurors and alternates were given a lot to consider today as the second week of testimony ended.

The day began with defense lawyer Frongillo continuing to paint Melvin Parker, the owner of Raintree Nursery, as an opportunist swirling in million-dollar payouts from both Grace and the EPA because the 22 acres he bought from Grace was heavily contaminated with asbestos.

Frongillo got Parker to admit that he and his wife, Lerah, had received $1.5 million from the EPA for his house and belongings when the environmental experts told him it was too contaminated to live in. The lawyer described a series of letters from EPA to the Parkers saying they would only be given the money if they truly didn't know the land was contaminated — something Grace maintained they did know.

In response, Assistant U.S. Attorney McLean did a surprising job of trying to resurrect the shredded image of Parker, who had been one of the government's primary witnesses to show that Grace knowingly endangered residents of Libby.

McLean beat the defense to the punch by having Parker explain to the jury why he and his wife refused offers from Grace to buy back their tainted land. They rejected Grace's offers of $1.2 million, then $2 million. Parker explained that when Grace finally asked "what do you want," his wife said, "$10 million." Grace declined.

He quickly added that he and his wife weren't being greedy. Rather, they were trying to explain to Grace that "money wasn't the issue" because he said they didn't know what the future would bring for him, his wife, his daughter and granddaughter – everyone who played or worked in the asbestos-tainted vermiculite at the nursery.

Lerah Parker took the stand, resolute and well-prepared and far more strident in her answers at first than later in the questioning. McLean had her describe eight photographs she'd taken of her grandchildren and others playing in the yard at the nursery.

She cried softly as she went through the photos, describing what the children were doing and pointing out all the vermiculite in the area.

Every attempt to introduce a photo into evidence was met by an immediate objection by the defense. Judge Molloy permitted only one of the eight photos — the one showing no children — into evidence.

The person who has the greatest actual knowledge about the health of the people of Libby and Lincoln County was sworn in to testify for the government. Dr. Alan Whitehouse, the pulmonologist from Spokane who has treated more than 10,000 patients in his 35-year career, was the first physician to identify a serious asbestos disease problem among the residents of Western Montana.

He walked the jury through 30 minutes of X-rays and CT scans of Libby patients, pointing to blurs of differing shades of gray and identifying them as asbestosis, mesothelioma, scarring and the other asbestos-related diseases he routinely finds.

Most of the jurors were trying hard to follow, some trying to trace with their fingers the scans of cancer or plaque on the screens before them.

Whitehouse showed the films of the Parkers' diseased lungs. The couple watched them flash on the 42-inch flat screen in front of them in the spectator section. Mrs. Parker seemed to shudder a bit. Her husband just stared unmoving at the images. McLean fashioned his questions with painful care to elicit numbers on the sick people in Libby and Lincoln County and avoid the nonstop objections by Grace lawyers.

Whitehouse explained that there were about 2,400 people being seen at Libby's Center for Asbestos Related Disease, but about 600 were not showing symptoms. Of the remaining 1,800, a quarter were miners, a quarter were members of miners' families, and the remaining half apparently got the disease from just living in Libby.

"Libby has the highest mesothelioma rate in the nation because there is so much asbestos floating around," Whitehouse explained as three Grace lawyers rose to object.

The disease, which has no cure, is rare in the rest of the country.

The cross examination was predictable as Grace's star, David Bernick, did the job.

He started by acknowledging that Whitehouse was the chest specialist for most of the people in Libby and then quickly asked how much money the doctor was making testifying on behalf of the patients who had sued Grace before the corporation had grabbed bankruptcy protection.

Bernick then challenged Whitehouse's ability to identify environmentally caused disease and to predict the spread of the disease. He hauled up the traditional debate between physicians and epidemiologists that defense lawyers have used for years.

Whitehouse angrily said epidemiologists deal with numbers and physicians lay hands on patients. "Real people with pain and fear," he said.

Some jurors nodded in apparent agreement.

Bernick said that other people reading the X-rays and CT scans of his patients didn't always find the same problem. Again, Whitehouse said radiologists deal with images on film while he and other physicians actually sit across from the patient.

The afternoon ended with Bernick challenging Whitehouse's contention that the amount of illness in Libby is severe and will last for decades. As proof, the Grace lawyer quoted from an old study by the Agency for Toxic Substances Disease Registry, the worker health research arm of the Centers for Disease Control.

That study, Bernick said, showed Libby was no worse than the rest of the country when it came to asbestos-caused deaths. Whitehouse said the study of miners from 1979 to 1988 was flawed, and used bad science and death certificates that mischaracterized the cause of death.

Bernick attempted to mock Whitehouse, expressing surprise that he would have the nerve to question the august and lofty scientists of this leading government health agency. The doctor stood firm by his numbers.

March 10

It took Judge Molloy just 14 words this morning to respond to hours of yammering Monday by Grace lawyers who wanted a crucial government witness to be prevented from testifying.

"Defendant's joint motion to exclude the expert testimony of Dr. Aubrey Miller is denied," wrote the judge.

After the specialist in occupational and environmental medicine spent more than six hours testifying, it was obvious why the defense wanted him gagged.

Miller had methodically and gently explained to the jury precisely how he reached the conclusion that Libby was contaminated with asbestos fibers from the vermiculite in Grace's closed mine.

The doctor, in his U.S. Public Health Service Navy dress uniform with the four gold stripes of a captain and three rows of medals, walked the jury through dozens of Grace corporate documents, studies done by the EPA and other agencies, and the work of scientists in the U.S. and abroad. To say it was technical and potentially confusing is an understatement, but the jury appeared to get it.

Lead Prosecutor Kris McLean doled the questions out at a measured pace. Miller, who was assigned as medical officer for EPA in the first team sent to Libby, cited study after study that showed the asbestos that contaminated the community was different, more toxic, more friable or more easily disturbed than other types of asbestos fibers.

Miller referred to Grace correspondence from the sixties, seventies and eighties that showed the company and some of the officials on trial were told of the dangers of the asbestos tainting their vermiculite. He read portions of other studies from the company's own scientists and other more recent work that reported that dangerously high concentrations of lethal fibers were easily released.

The physician also guided the jurors through the extremely complex morass of exposure limits and risk assessment jargon, even making the alphabet soup of acronyms used by the government (PEL, STHL, TEM, etc.) somewhat understandable.

It was a Whack-a-Mole Day again with defense lawyers popping up about every two minutes with an objection. McLean seemed unperturbed.

At one point, five of Grace's legal team leaped to their feet at the same moment to prevent Miller from answering a question asked by McLean.

I'm sure neither side loved the judge today, but isn't that the way it's supposed to be?

While the jury was still at lunch, Grace's lawyers exploded over the exhibits that Miller was using to support his expert opinion.

They charged that McLean was using Miller to get into evidence documents and exhibits disallowed when On-Scene Coordinator Paul Peronard and pulmonologist Alan Whitehouse testified last week.

David Krakoff, the lawyer for Grace medical director Henry Eschenbach, charged that the government was using Miller's testimony as a "drivethrough of the entire fraud case through this one witness."

Krakoff said that Miller was referring to "dead people who we have no way to question."

Grace's Bernick asked the judge, "How in the world are we going to cross-examine this witness? We'll be up all night figuring that out."

The question came across as a bit of theater from a lawyer who probably could successfully cross-examine a boulder — and knows it.

With the jury back, Miller took another quick tour of asbestos hot spots in Libby – the screening and export sites Grace used, the ball fields, running tracks and play areas at the town's three public schools.

He explained how EPA employees, wearing vacuum-driven air samplers, simulated a child digging the dirt, and a person raking the ground and mowing a lawn.

Asbestos was found in all samples, Miller said, and added that even when trace amounts of asbestos were found, it translated into hundreds of thousands or even millions of fibers in areas where they could easily be inhaled.

Miller said he concluded that there was — and is — an imminent health hazard which could lead to continued disease and death in and near Libby.

While the defense sharpened its swords to cross-examine the doctor, Krakoff renewed his complaints about Miller's testimony and asked the judge to restrict what the jury can consider. Molloy told him to make a motion and he'd consider it.

An identical motion was filed by the defense this afternoon asking Molloy to strike all the testimony previously given by Dr. Whitehouse.

March 11

By the end of testimony today, I was thinking that some of the jurors and many of the spectators were beginning to believe that the federal government was more guilty of concealing the asbestos dangers in Libby than the international chemical company that's on trial.

Most of the day was spent watching Grace lawyer Bernick trying to skewer Miller. But the environmental and occupational medicine specialist dodged almost every thrust.

Bernick's mission was to discredit Miller in the eyes of jurors and taint the hours of fairly persuasive testimony the doctor had presented the day before.

He accused Miller of concealing facts from the jury, such as not describing all facets of the asbestos disease that killed a Libby woman in 1987.

It was clear that no one had collected the information when Margaret Vatland died, but that didn't prevent Bernick from barking, "You didn't tell the jury, did you?"

It became his mantra for the morning.

Bernick demanded that Miller explain why the EPA had declared Libby an emergency cleanup site when it didn't have the proof of the danger.

And with machine-gun speed, he followed with: Wasn't it the only way EPA could get cleanup money from headquarters without first completing a complex study in the risks facing townsfolk?

If he wanted Miller to stumble, it didn't happen.

You had to wonder whether the prosecution team had been superglued to their chairs. Assistant U.S. Attorney Kris McLean rose only once to object to Bernick's haranguing, as opposed to the 60-plus objections the defense had launched the day before.

Miller refused to let the defense limit his answers to complex or multi-part questions to a simple yes or no. But a dozen or more times Bernick cut Miller off with a cry of "not responsive," and asked the judge to have Miller's comment struck from the record.

The Grace lawyer practiced the competitive sport of cross-examination with a wireless mike in one hand and red and black markers in the other.

His footwork was masterful and he deserved points for agility as he slid between the podium – the area where Judge Molloy and the court stenographer want lawyers to ask their questions – and an enormous whiteboard on a shaky easel so he could draw a line or two, then write a date, a word or a phrase.

By the afternoon questioning, it seemed that the 4-by-8-foot whiteboard was angled towards the judge and Miller, and it appeared only three or four jurors could see Bernick's intricate artwork.

It was almost 4 p.m. when defense lawyer Thomas Frongillo took his shots at Miller. He pushed for answers, but was somewhat more courtly.

He walked Miller through the timeline that Molloy set for the knowing endangerment counts in the indictment, the most severe of the eight charges brought against Grace and five former executives.

He questioned the language used in EPA plans for announcing the results of the first asbestos testing in town, and then raised an issue that McLean could have gone all month without hearing again.

Frongillo questioned Miller at length on four studies discovered by the Libby EPA team that showed in painful detail that Grace wasn't the only party in this trial that had kept secret the asbestos dangers confronting Libby and its citizens.

He quoted from studies funded by EPA in the 1970's and 1980's, which, in great detail, told of the asbestos in the vermiculite, the risk to workers, the community and consumers using or exposed to the tainted vermiculite Grace sold throughout the world.

EPA wasn't alone in concealing the asbestos danger. Frongillo asked Miller about studies by the Occupational Safety and Health Administration and the Consumer Product Safety Commission, also done in the seventies and both promising regulations and warnings on vermiculite products from Libby. Neither delivered.

The lawyer shook his head, lowered his voice a bit and asked Miller if it wasn't true that EPA had known of the asbestos danger in Libby almost as long as the agency has existed.

Frongillo said EPA was founded in 1970. Grace admitted it had asbestos in its vermiculite in 1971.

The judge adjourned for the day before the doctor could answer.

March 12

Dr. Aubrey Miller began his third day of testimony confronting issues that had been debated and fought over long before charges were even filed in this case, namely, what is asbestos?

Grace lawyer Thomas Frongillo took a unique approach to the question. He asked the judge to permit him to introduce five separate regulations or rules from EPA, OSHA, the Mine Safety and Health Administration, and the Consumer Product Safety Commission, along with one federal law passed by Congress.

And then he read a section from each document that identified "the federal six" — the minerals that the government regulates as asbestos. He read off: tremolite, actinolite, anthophyllite, chrysotile, amosite, and crocidolite.

He repeated the list four more times and asked Miller if he heard any mention at all of "winchite" or "richterite." Grace's lawyers say the U.S. Geological Survey has determined that winchite or richterite comprise 95 percent of the fibers in Libby.

"As far as I'm concerned it's all asbestos," Miller said, echoing the views of almost all of the public health experts who have observed the illnesses and death in Libby up close.

April 14

Two former officials of an enormous Ohio company and Grace's largest customer testified that their firm was the first to openly complain about its workers being sickened by asbestos in the vermiculite from Libby.

The executive from what was called the O.M. Scott & Sons Co. – the nationally known plant and turf fertilizer company – offered a straightforward presentation of what their firm did between 1978 and 1980 when workers at their Marysville, Ohio, plant, 30 miles northwest of Columbus, were diagnosed with bloody pleural effusion.

The symptom is a dangerous indicator of possible future significant asbestos-related disease such as asbestosis or mesothelioma, a cancer caused by asbestos exposure.

Grace shipping documents gathered by the EPA show that the company, later known as Scotts, received more than 4,500 shipments of vermiculite ore from Libby. With it came the asbestos contamination that eventually made Scotts workers sick.

Assistant U.S. Attorney Kris McLean began the questioning with Sergeant Chamberlain, who was the purchasing agent and director for Scotts for almost half a century. The white-haired man spoke strongly about being surprised when placards warning of asbestos started showing up on the rail cars carrying vermiculite ore from Libby.

Chamberlain said Grace officials told him repeatedly that they were trying to reduce the amount of asbestos contaminating the ore. He said he told them he wanted "No asbestos. Period."

The second to take the stand was John Kennedy, former general counsel for Scotts. It was interesting watching Grace's lawyer, David Bernick, trying and failing to muscle another lawyer during cross-examination.

Kennedy offered chapter and verse on the help that Grace offered Scotts after the workers got sick.

While the testimony of these particular witnesses was vital to the prosecution's hope of proving the conspiracy charges, it was just as important for Bernick to show that the government was told about the hazard at Libby. At times he scrawled arrows, lines and dates across two large whiteboards on easels he had again set up in the courtroom.

The next to testify was epidemiologist Kathleen Kennedy, who had worked for the National Institute for Occupational Safety and Health, the worker safety research arm for the CDC.

From 1979 to 1981, Kennedy headed the government research team at the U.S. Bureau of Mines and its subsequent agency, the Mine Safety and Health Administration, which eventually studied asbestos exposure among Grace workers.

Bernick seemed frazzled. Almost every document he showed Kennedy she said she had never seen before. She stalled Bernick's efforts when she repeatedly replied that she couldn't answer many of his questions because she either wasn't at the meeting he was referring to or couldn't recall what it was he wanted her to remember.

The fact that 30 years had passed didn't make the Grace lawyer any more willing to accept her denial.

After the lunch break, Grace's lawyers told Judge Molloy that they will provide documents that prove that government prosecutors intentionally concealed evidence that defendants had a constitutional right to have.

After jurors were released for the day, the lawyers and Molloy quickly targeted the integrity of Robert Locke, a former Grace global vice president for its construction division. The defense team alleged that when he testified late last month, Locke had perjured himself by repeating statements that may never have been made.

Locke had testified that he told Robert Bettacchi, one of the five indicted Grace officials, that selling land in Libby "was a real bad idea; we should just plant grass and keep people the hell out of it." According to Locke, Bettacchi replied, "Buyer beware."

Locke's statements in March contradicted his testimony before the grand jury hearing the Grace indictments in 2005, where he reportedly said, also under oath, that he had never discussed the properties with Bettacchi.

Judge Molloy said that Locke's testimony was wrong, and the government knew it and did nothing. "I think he's perjured himself. If not he's coming as close as I've ever seen," said the judge, speaking of Locke.

Locke's reputation plummeted further when the defense disclosed documents and e-mail showing that Locke said he was offered an immunity deal in exchange for the testimony, but claimed he turned down the agreement.

Grace's lawyers said they also found correspondence from EPA Special Agent Robert Marsden urging Locke to turn down the offer because it would mean more to the jurors.

Bernick, seeing that Molloy was already significantly displeased with Locke, took his time at the podium to broaden the allegations of misconduct to perhaps include the entire government team.

He requested that Molloy order delivery of the paper trail by showing the prosecution's communication with all the witnesses to see how far the alleged prosecutorial misconduct might range. The defense lawyers said disclosure of that information could affect if and how the remainder of the trial unfolds.

Defense lawyer Thomas Frongillo jumped into the fray, saying the tainted evidence damages the integrity of the U.S. criminal-court system as well as the constitutional right of due process of the Grace officials on trial. With unrestrained emotion he talked about the indictment of knowing endangerment against his client, Robert Bettacchi.

Frongillo said the 15-year sentences that can come with the country's most serious environmental criminal charge could force Bettacchi, if found guilty, to spend the rest of his life in prison.

"And this," he added in his comments to Molloy, "is based on tainted evidence."

Every lawyer who spoke invoked the Brady Doctrine, which demands that prosecutors disclose exculpatory material to the defendant, and pointed out that violation of Brady violates the defendant's right under the Due Process Clause of the constitution.

Bernick called it a tainted case and claimed that the evidence has been manipulated, and Frongillo added that the fairness of this trial has been irreparably discredited by the prosecution.

Assistant U.S. Attorney McLean countered that the defense was misrepresenting the letters from Marsden by failing to read the back side, which, he said, put the matter in context.

April 15

The prosecution has called fewer than half of the potential witnesses on its original list, and today McLean announced the loss of another key witness. Toxicologist Chris Weis, the government's top expert on how and to what degree people were exposed and sickened by asbestos from Grace's mine in Libby, will not be permitted to testify.

Overnight, the Grace team had filed a 10-page brief objecting to Weis taking the stand.

The motion concluded that "the Court should preclude Dr. Weis from testifying, because his testimony would violate the Confrontation Clause and because his testimony is outside the scope of his expert disclosures and wholly cumulative" to what other witnesses presented.

Grace has repeatedly invoked "the Confrontation Clause," which basically says the accused must have the opportunity to confront those presenting evidence against them.

In a case like this where you're talking about over 70,000 individual asbestos samples taken over five or more years at hundreds of different locations in and around Libby and the Grace mine, it would be impossible to identify and bring hundreds of lab technicians in to testify.

Weis, long a target of Grace's team, was expected to testify on a wide range of vital points that court watchers believe the prosecutor needed to prove his case.

For example, many of the topics which Dr. Aubrey Miller was barred from discussing by the judge, such as levels of asbestos exposure, were to be addressed by Weis.

One of the most puzzling parts of this tale is that the prosecution didn't even file an argument to Grace's devastating motion.

The U.S. government has fielded only four lawyers, two investigators and very few assistants for what the Justice Department calls "this most important of trials." Grace's legal team has scores of people on its payroll and present in the courtroom or nearby war rooms.

Every day, Grace's top lawyer, David Bernick, promises the judge another selection of fresh motions and legal briefs for his reading pleasure.

Bernick has made no secret that Grace is taking every shot it can to throttle the government before his client begins its defense. He warned Judge Molloy this afternoon that a wave of new motions is coming.

They are expected to challenge McLean's few remaining witnesses, allege prosecutorial misconduct and seek an acquittal for Grace.

April 15

With the deadline for wrapping up its part of the trial just three court days away, the prosecution continues to try to prove its conspiracy charges against Grace.

Dr. James Lockey, an authority in occupational medicine and a specialist in pulmonary diseases, walked the jury through two studies he did on workers from O.M. Scott, a quarter of a century apart.

But first, Lockey, a professor of environmental health and pulmonary medicine at the University of Cincinnati, explained in great detail and simple terms the anatomy of an asbestos fiber. He also walked the jury through the potential minefield of why tremolite and other Libby fibers are more toxic than more commonly found commercial asbestos – chrysotile.

He described his two studies of workers at O.M. Scott that he had completed by that time. This work showed that even low doses caused bloody pleural effusion in workers' lungs.

During his cross examination, defense lawyer Bernick set up his drawing boards on easels, and with a fistful of colored pens tried to draw a human lung and had the doctor walk him through the various sites of asbestos-related disease. He endlessly drew wiggles and graphs to argue with Lockey about what the physician's studies showed.

Repeatedly Bernick tried to get Lockey to say his research proved that low exposure to tremolite cannot cause asbestos-related diseases. And repeatedly the doctor told the lawyer he was wrong.

The Grace top lawyer finally got to where he was heading all afternoon, or so it seemed. All that was missing was a drum roll.

Bernick showed that the first Scott study talked about tremolite fibers, but in the second study, 25 years later, where many of the same workers were re-examined to show progression of the disease, Lockey referred to the Libby fibers as winchite, richterite and tremolite.

Bernick beamed widely, and he continued hammering away at the same old canard that Grace has been flogging for years, namely that a number of laws don't list winchite and richterite as asbestos.

Lockey, as many other witnesses have tried to say before him, began to explain that it didn't matter what they called the fibers. They were all long, thin, and lethal.

But objections flew.

April 16

Special Assistant U.S. Attorney Eric Nelson began the day by questioning Fred Kover, a career EPA industrial hygienist, who had read reports from Grace about asbestos in its products as far back as the 1970's and early 1980's.

Kover was then supervising the group that handled mandatory reports from corporations under the Toxic Substances Control Act of 1976, which requires all companies involved with hazardous material to immediately inform the EPA Administrator.

Nelson had Kover walk the jury through the law and explain several EPA reports and documents that dealt with what information Grace gave the government and when.

In Grace lawyer Bernick's cross-examination, he again set up his whiteboards and for two-and-a-half hours tried to prove that his client gave the government all the information needed.

Bernick roamed all over the playing field, asking rambling, protracted questions, more like he was making closing arguments to the jury than trying to elicit answers from an opposition witness.

The questions were often repeated and, in many cases, his efforts to lead the witness appeared obvious.

In one exchange, Bernick asked Kover if EPA reports on tremolite asbestos from Libby in the early eighties marked "a sea change" in EPA attitudes in how the agency viewed Grace information. The retired EPA official didn't give the answer the lawyer wanted, so Bernick repeated the question again, and again, and finally a third time.

The same theatrics were repeated for another 20 or 25 documents, letters or reports, and again Kover testified that he'd never seen any of them before.

April 17

The seats in the federal courtroom in Missoula were packed and more people filled the doorway Friday to watch Grace lawyers battle to end the largest environmental criminal trial in U.S. history before it ever gets to a jury.

David Bernick was the conductor for today's symphony. Grace's main lawyer had promised to lead a two-prong attack against the government. If successful, either prong would be a fatal blow on the chances of the trial continuing.

All morning Bernick worked to convince Judge Donald Molloy to banish the entire government team for prosecutorial misconduct.

His primary target was EPA Special Agent Robert Marsden, one of the handful of government investigators who for more than four years found witnesses, gathered their stories, and got documents to verify their allegations for this trial.

Marsden had handled several witnesses, but Grace's gun was aimed at his handling of Robert Locke, a former company vice president and key prosecution witness.

Bernick used the shtick that makes him worth what he's paid – machine-gun-paced questions shooting all over the target as he tries to force the witness to agree with Grace's view of the world. He even had his flip chart, despite the jury's day off.

The lawyer smoothly repeated what had been discussed in court for weeks – Locke hates Grace, he's hard to handle, he wants Grace to fall hard — all things that Grace itself knew long before the indictments, because Locke had filed civil suits against the corporation.

What Bernick didn't do, according to several of the lawyers who packed into the courtroom, was demonstrate misconduct.

This was slammed home repeatedly by the cross-examination of Marsden by Assistant U.S. Attorney Timothy Cavan, from Billings, Montana.

Cavan is a tall man with a deep, solid voice and a take-no-prisoners style of questioning that challenges Bernick's statements head on.

This was the first time in the seven weeks of testimony that a government prosecutor openly and directly contested the veracity of Bernick's tirades. Grace's lawyer was visibly bothered by his legal wizardry being questioned.

In the end, Cavan showed that Marsden did his job the way government investigators are supposed to.

But the consensus of many watching Friday's proceedings was that Judge Molloy's opinion is the only one that matters in this Montana courtroom.

Bernick and fellow Grace lawyer Thomas Frongillo, who also questioned Marsden, both demanded that the Department of Justice intervene in this trial because of their claims of misconduct.

Bernick also argued the charges against Grace and its five former executives should be dismissed. Molloy was not subtle about his leanings.

The chief district judge ended the day by talking about an event early in his career, when, as a young lawyer, he "saw federal agents absolutely destroy a home during a search. It was not right. Somebody in the Department of Justice needs to have the courage to do what is right."

April 21

Just what constitutes asbestos is a question that already has made its way from Montana to the 9th U.S. Circuit Court of Appeals and back again. But that didn't stop the argument from arising again this week in the Missoula courtroom.

On Monday, Assistant U.S. Attorney Kris McLean asked Judge Molloy to take "judicial notice" of the definition of asbestos, allowing a well-established fact to be introduced without the traditional presentation of evidence and testimony.

The prosecutor wanted Molloy to accept and read to the jury the definition of asbestos handed down by the appellate court, which ruled that asbestos was grayish in color, non-combustible, composed primarily of impure silicate magnesium, and fibrous.[1]

McLean also asked the judge to read to the jurors the rest of the appellate court's September 20, 2007, ruling on the subject. The three-judge panel found that Molloy was wrong when he "improperly limited the term 'asbestos' to the six minerals covered by the civil regulations."

But Molloy only gave McLean half a loaf. He read to the jury the physical characteristics of asbestos outlined by the appellate court, but declined to mention that the 9th Circuit also had ruled that the definition of asbestos "need not include mineral-by-mineral classifications."

That left open the argument that long has raged over the asbestos found in Libby. And both sides were quick to join that battle again.

McLean introduced into evidence carefully sealed jars with asbestos-containing vermiculite from Libby. He then asked senior U.S. Geological Survey Geologist Greg Meeker to walk the jury through the movement of glaciers over Libby 14,000 years ago.

Meeker was the first to determine that the amphibole asbestos found near Libby – long, thin, dangerous fibers – was a mixture of tremolite, winchite and richterite.

Frongillo, the lawyer representing former Grace VP Robert Bettacchi, cross-examined Meeker and quickly moved to the argument that none of those three fibers were among the six forms of the mineral commonly considered dangerous.

Even if the jury remained confused about what asbestos is, the government pushed hard to prove that the health effects for the people of Libby were beyond dispute.

Prosecutors ended their day with testimony from Dr. Richard Lemen, a former assistant U.S. surgeon general and past deputy director of NIOSH, the workplace safety research arm of the Centers for Disease Control.

Lemen is an epidemiologist and specializes in identifying the sources of disease. And he quickly got to the point the prosecution wanted made.

"Yes, there was an imminent risk of (asbestos) exposure to the people of Libby," Lemen said.

Lemen said asbestos was all over Libby. And the more asbestos people are exposed to, the greater the accumulation of the lethal fibers will be in their bodies.

Grace lawyer Bernick and Lemen sparred vigorously and loudly over epidemiological studies on the victims in Libby.

Lemen stood his ground and refused to parrot Bernick's words.

"Stop," Molloy bellowed at Lemen. "You're here to be a witness. I don't want to have to intervene with every single question. If you want to be a lawyer, go to law school."

April 24

Grace lawyers filed a 75-page motion outlining their reasons Judge Donald Molloy should end the criminal trial against the company and its former executives now.

On the 74th page the lawyers wrote: "CONCLUSION: The indictment must be dismissed with prejudice."

The phrase "with prejudice" means the specific case the government brought against Grace cannot be brought again.

The Grace team claims intentional and unending misconduct by the prosecution. "Dismissal is the only appropriate remedy," the defense lawyers insisted.

These section headings in their motion offer a glimpse into what the company hopes the judge will agree to:

The Government Directs Its Experts To Mislead The Jury And Seeks To Conceal Its Own Malfeasance.

The Government Deceives Its Own Witnesses And Obtains Misleading Testimony From Them.

The Government Systematically And Recklessly Deprived Defendants Of Their Right to a Fair Trial.

The Government Has Shown A Reckless Disregard For Defendants' Rights.

Meanwhile, elsewhere in the clerk's office, Molloy left a ruling filled with bad news for the prosecution.

No one expected Kris McLean's team was going to savor Molloy's decision on what exhibits the government could enter into evidence, but his honor outdid himself. Molloy ruled that the jury would be permitted to see only seven of the government's 54 exhibits.

The 54 were just a fraction of the hundreds of documents that McLean wanted to introduce, but they had realized that they stood no chance of getting the rest past the judge.

Molloy, in his ruling, said the prosecution's indictment "appears to have been drafted as a historical compendium of the defendants' alleged wrongful acts, without regard as to whether those alleged acts relate in any way to a federal criminal offense.

"Most of the exhibits suggest some knowledge of dangerousness on the part of the defendants, but there is already ample evidence in the record on that point," Molloy wrote.

Molloy said the government used the "notice of dangerousness as a pretext through which it can present irrelevant and prejudicial evidence of the serious health problems of company employees."

April 27

The number of defendants in the W.R. Grace criminal case dropped by one today as the prosecutors said that because of restrictions on what evidence they were permitted to introduce, they could not prove their conspiracy case against former Grace senior vice president Robert Walsh.

They told Judge Molloy that they were dropping conspiracy charges related to Walsh. The freed man was met with tearful hugs from some family members and defendants waiting outside the courtroom.

The rest of Monday was semi-high drama before a packed courtroom, and the bottom line was that Molloy is considering dropping the remaining charges in the nation's largest environmental crime case ever.

"One thing I can do is declare a mistrial," the judge said at one point.

Molloy is faced with two sets of defense arguments: one, that prosecutors failed to prove their case, and so the defendants should be acquitted, and the other, that the government has engaged in repeated misconduct by misleading jurors and concealing evidence.

Grace's defense team – starting off with a two-hour plus speech by lead lawyer David Bernick – presented reasons all charges against the company and its former executives should be dropped.

Bernick claimed rampant prosecutorial misconduct and that the charges lacked merit and that prosecutors had failed to prove their case. He urged Molloy to pick any of those reasons to dismiss the case.

Assistant U.S. Attorney Timothy Racicot argued for the government and repeated many of the same responses that have been used against Bernick's allegations before.

"Bernick talked about our weaknesses for over two hours and only mentioned two documents," Racicot told the judge.

He acknowledged that mistakes have been made in disclosing some evidence, but that they were not grounds for dismissal.

Molloy said the prosecution "put in 40 years of discombobulated evidence that they don't understand themselves. That's the problem with a 50-year-old case."

"I know, your honor," Racicot said.

"Others do not," Molloy added.

"Trying to split hairs and justify unprofessional behavior will not work," he said and added, "From the get-go, I trusted Mr. McLean. My trust probably kept me from doing what I should have done."

A few minutes later Assistant U.S. Attorney McLean took the podium and appeared infuriated by the charges that the defense had thrown at him all day – lying, suborning perjury and more.

"I have never misled or lied to a jury," McLean told Molloy.

"I'm standing here to answer your questions about my conduct," he said to the judge.

Molloy said nothing for a while.

"I don't have any other questions, Mr. McLean," he said finally.

"Are you sure?" the prosecutor asked.

"I'm sure," the judge replied.

April 29

Molloy began the day two hours before the jury was seated with prosecutors McLean and Kevin Cassidy defending their case to the judge, who had been asked to toss it out for lack of merit and evidence.

"This case looks like a complex matter, but at its essence it's really quite simple. It's a matter of right and wrong," said McLean.

They had shown Grace's wrongs, or at least as many as they could with Molloy's severe restrictions on what material and witnesses he'd allowed to be used by the government. McLean said there are 100 acts that support the charges of conspiracy, and the government has proven 82 of them.

And with precision and straightforwardness that was missing through much of the past eight weeks, the prosecutors methodically flashed through Grace documents that spanned 30 years.

McLean adroitly laid one document upon another, showing documents that had been presented before but now were offered in a more telling manner.

Before calling in the jury, Molloy made a blitz of brief announcements and shocked many in the courtroom by announcing first that he had decided that he would not dismiss the case for prosecutorial misconduct as Grace's defense team had requested.

I had believed that judges always tipped the players in their cases about major decisions they were about to make. But most of the lawyers and defendants whose faces I could see looked bewildered or stunned.

"The parties have put before the court a range of remedial options," the judge said.

The most drastic is to dismiss the charges, either with or without prejudice. "But dismissal on the basis of prosecutorial misconduct is not warranted here," Molloy explained in his ruling.

The next option is for the court to declare a mistrial. "The defendants have shown no interest in a mistrial, as it would allow the government the opportunity to start anew and, in essence, benefit from its failure to fulfill its disclosure obligations by receiving the proverbial second bite at the apple," his honor explained.

The third possibility is to strike the testimony of prosecution star witness Robert Locke in its entirety as a remedy for the government's alleged violations of full disclosure requirements of Congress and the Supreme Court.

Molloy made it clear he believes that Locke lied while testifying, and information about him was withheld from the defense until late in the trial.

The judge said that the defense would be given another shot at Locke for a very limited cross examination, and he would tell the jury that it must ignore much of Locke's testimony on senior Grace VP Bettacchi, who Molloy believes was "targeted" by Locke.

At 10:18 on the second day of the eighth week of testimony, the prosecution rested.

David Bernick wasted no time bringing the first defense witness, former Grace executive VP Elwood "Chip" Wood.

Wood was a good witness, got a few laughs, played well to the jury, but rarely looked at them. Bernick directed him well as he walked the jury through a list of actions Grace had taken to remedy its tremolite asbestos problem.

He asked about the government's charges, but Wood denied that there was any conspiracy.

"I can't imagine that I would not have been aware of some such conspiracy if it were happening," he said.

Wood vigorously denounced and discredited a key memo from Locke, which talked about how Grace would stall or thwart an investigation of the Libby mine by NIOSH, the federal worker safety agency.

Wood said he learned of Locke's memo and "did a slow burn" for weeks, adding, "It corrupted everything we were trying to do."

Bernick then guided the former top boss into explaining that Grace had notified the federal government of the health problems at the mine.

Wood said that the study was "hard evidence that you have an asbestos related problem."

In his cross-examination, prosecutor Kevin Cassidy skillfully regained some of the lost ground when he showed that 10 years after Grace learned that 41 percent of its Libby miners who had over a decade on the job had asbestosis, the company was still telling EPA that it had no data to document there was a health problem.

Cassidy also got Wood to admit that he had hired Locke for another job when Wood was made a president of another Grace operation, and he volunteered that Locke did good work.

When Locke was called to the stand for the questioning ordained by the judge, Bernick was ready. His grilling of Locke was merciless.

He pushed Locke until he admitted that he was wrong when he had testified weeks earlier about the number of meetings he'd had with the prosecution team over the past five years.

Bernick repeatedly hammered away trying to get Locke to admit that he had a "special relationship" with the prosecution. Four, six, eight times. More. And Locke wouldn't be forced to use that two-word phrase that Bernick has used throughout the trial to support his allegation of misconduct.

April 30

By the time the jury gets to decide guilt or innocence in the W.R. Grace criminal trial next week, they will have far fewer charges to consider.

Citing court-imposed restrictions on witnesses and documents that created the inability to introduce enough evidence to prove guilt beyond a reasonable doubt, prosecutor McLean dropped all charges against defendant William McCaig, former general manager of the Libby mine.

Judge Molloy quickly interjected that his "restrictions" came from the law, the Supreme Court, the Constitution and not something cooked up in his chambers.

"I'm not making this up. I don't go back in my chambers and say, 'Gee, how can I screw this thing up?' I'm trying to follow the law," the judge fired back.

Leaving the courtroom, McCaig shook hands with McLean and others in the prosecution team, and his lawyers hugged several of the defense team remaining to continue the fight.

May 4

For me, it was surreal to see W.R. Grace Vice President William Corcoran on the witness stand in the Missoula courtroom. He is the boss of public and regulatory affairs for the worldwide company, which means he deals with the press and Congress, and because of years spent on the staff of U.S. Senate and House committees he's well suited to do both.

He and I both became involved with Grace in 1999, and that's when we met. Corcoran told the jury on Thursday that neither he nor Grace's new CEO had ever heard about the problems in Libby, Montana, until the *Seattle Post-Intelligencer* wrote about them just before Thanksgiving of that year.

Off and on for much of the last decade Corcoran and I would often thrust and parry over what his company had done and how I was reporting it.

On April 10, 2002, Corcoran wrote a now-famous letter to then-EPA Administrator Christine Todd Whitman. He told the EPA leadership that Zonolite Attic Insulation, which was made from asbestos-tainted vermiculite from Grace's mine in Libby, was not dangerous. According to the environmental agency's assessment of Grace shipping papers, ZAI was installed in as many as 35 million homes and businesses across North America.

In his letter, Corcoran wrote that the insulation poses no risk to human health or the environment and contains "biologically insignificant amounts" of asbestos fibers. But according to tests and studies run by Grace and later confirmed by the EPA, the insulation can be dangerous as hell.

To a point, Corcoran is correct, ZAI presents minimal risk if it's never touched or disturbed. But if the vermiculite is disturbed during installation, by a child playing in the attic, or a cable or telephone installer or anyone doing even minor renovations, high levels of asbestos fibers will be released.

The government obviously thought it was untrue also as the criminal indictments cited direct quotes from Corcoran's letter to support the prosecution's obstruction-of-justice charges. When Prosecutor McLean showed Corcoran copies of the studies Grace had done that confirmed the hazard, the company spokesman said he had never seen them before.

Corcoran offered another example of his candor when Grace lawyer Bernick was questioning him and mentioned the head of EPA's emergency response team and Grace's arch-villain, Paul Peronard.

Not only did Corcoran admit that he knew Peronard but that he'd first met with the EPA emergency response expert on a cleanup in Georgia years earlier when the Grace executive represented another company. Several Grace lawyers winced when Corcoran volunteered that they'd gotten along and that Peronard had done a good job.

The defense finally brought out its scientific heavyweight, Dr. Suresh Moolgavkar, a Seattle mathematician and epidemiologist, who quickly attempted to discredit the work of Drs. Aubrey Miller, Alan Whitehouse and James Lockey.

The trio of government witnesses all have hands-on experience in Libby and with its people. Moolgavkar, who has been an expert witness for Bernick and Grace for years, said he had not done original research on-scene in Libby, but rather had just recalculated the work of Lockey and other scientists. From this, he said he concluded: "There is … no evidence of an increased risk at Libby from environmental exposure."

His statement might make one wonder about the hundreds of people in Libby's cemetery and nearby hospitals with asbestos related disease who never worked at the mine or lived with miners. Or about the almost 2,000 who showed some level of lung impairments when the government tested 10,000 or so townsfolk from Libby and nearby Lincoln County years ago.

By early afternoon, David Bernick's target was again EPA criminal investigator Robert Marsden and his alleged "special relationship" with discredited witness Robert Locke.

With a theatrical delivery, feigning disgust that a Shakespearean player would covet, Bernick read from innocuous e-mails between Marsden and Locke as if they were confessions of drug dealings, or selling little children or possessing weapons of mass destruction.

Few dispute that the prosecution screwed up its obligation under law to promptly get information and documents on Locke — a former Grace official and crucial witness — to the defense and they've been punished for it. But that has nothing to do with the deceptive picture Bernick has painted for the jury on the spurious "special relationship."

I shared with seven legal experts examples of language Bernick used as the basis of his accusation. All concluded that the e-mail indicated that Marsden's actions were appropriate, completely professional and just the way investigators routinely work to maintain contact with a witness. There was nothing "special" about it, they all said.

May 5

Defense attorney Thomas Frongillo said plagiarism proves the key prosecution witness has lied, and began questioning Melvin Parker to attempt to prove it.

Frongillo, who represents former Grace Senior VP Robert Bettacchi, questioned Parker, who built a plant nursery on the site of the former Grace screening plant at the base of the road to the mine.

Frongillo's intent was to show that Parker "flat-out lied" when he said he didn't know that the mine was contaminated with asbestos that was harmful to humans.

This was a path that other lawyers had tried to go down with little or no success.

Frongillo, who served 10 years as an assistant United States attorney in Boston's ruthlessly competitive legal playground, pressed Parker hard about when he learned about the asbestos.

The nurseryman said it was in the *P-I* series on Libby in November 1999.

"Not so," Frongillo said, and he showed the jury a 1993 report from Patrick Plantenberg, a Montana State official who worked on the mine reclamation. The lawyer also read a paragraph from a lengthy report that specifically outlined the risks from asbestos.

Plantenberg said he had spoken to Parker in September 1993 and sent him a copy.

Parker insisted he had never received the document.

Frongillo, who had kept his cool over the past 10 weeks, was getting hot and Parker was unbending and loud in his denials. Sparks were flying.

The defense lawyer said he knows that Parker received it because he had plagiarized the language describing the asbestos danger in a management plan Parker had submitted to Grace when he and his wife wanted to buy the old mine.

The words were almost identical. Nevertheless, Parker vociferously and repeatedly denied that he lied.

Frongillo slowly shook his head and returned to his seat.

After 10 weeks of testimony and theatrics, the defense in the Grace criminal trial rested today at 3:10 p.m.

The last witness in the seemingly endless ordeal deserved the honor of having the last word. Paul Peronard started and headed the EPA's emergency response in Libby and had the integrity and courage to push for the criminal investigation that led to this trial. He also started the trial as the prosecution's lead-off expert.

What was bizarre today was that Peronard was called by the defense. Grace's top lawyer, David Bernick, paced around the defense's half of the cluttered courtroom, rubbing his hands together in anticipation. He was going to take another shot at discrediting Peronard, showing him to be a cowboy who was scorned by his EPA bosses in Washington.

Bernick first tried to get Peronard to admit that he thought of himself as a "king," a statement attributed to him during earlier testimony.

Peronard had been asked, cajoled and pressured to return to Libby after his initial stint there as on-scene coordinator to try to sort out the endless and often angry disputes over the cleanup of homes and property that had erupted after his departure.

Not one to blow his own horn, all Peronard would tell Bernick was that he wanted to ensure that he would have enough authority to get the job done.

Bernick let it drop and went on to the issue he thought would blow the on-scene coordinator out of the water.

Waving them like a flag, Bernick held up copies of e-mail from John Malone, a member of EPA's headquarters staff, criticizing the actions and recommendations of Peronard and his teammates, Dr. Aubrey Miller and toxicologist Chris Weis.

Malone didn't like the Libby team and did not have much good to say about EPA regional headquarters in Denver, from where the Libby operation was controlled. He repeatedly denounced plans to remove dangerous Zonolite Attic Insulation from Libby homes and charged that Miller and Weis were using bogus science.

Bernick was gleeful as he tried to get Peronard to admit that Malone's e-mails were proof that headquarters opposed the team's plans.

"Not so," Peronard said again and again as Bernick repeated the same question. Malone, Peronard said, did not speak for headquarters.

What Peronard did not explain were the reasons underlying Malone's efforts to stifle the Libby operation. Peronard and his colleagues knew that Malone had headed the crucial, and embarrassing, 1982 and 1985 EPA studies of the tainted vermiculite from Libby. Rather than take actions at that time to order Grace to stop exposing workers, their family members and the town to lethal levels of asbestos, Malone stuck the reports on a shelf.

No one knows if lives could have been saved if Malone had paid attention to the very real dangers clearly flagged in the studies he monitored.

Peronard also didn't tell the jury that at the same time that Malone was writing e-mails denouncing his team, EPA's administrator was awarding Miller, Weis and Peronard for their outstanding work.

Peronard was permitted to leave and the judge told the jury: "I believe you have heard all the testimony you're going to hear in this case."

The jury beamed.

May 6

It took an hour for Judge Donald Molloy to give the jury its instructions.

Earlier he asked both the defense and prosecution to object to or accept each of the 50-plus instructions. Grace's side objected to many of them. The government didn't like a handful, but Molloy said the language stood as written.

Since the judge barred the public and press from a point-by-point debate with the lawyers last night, the public may never know what arguments were made.

There were one or two surprises in the judge's order to the jurors. He told them that they should be aware that EPA headquarters did not give Grace lawyers e-mail from John Malone, a headquarters pollution policy worker who repeatedly denounced the actions of Paul Peronard and his emergency response team.

Several of Malone's e-mails and statements had been shown to the jury yesterday, and the defense treated them as the Holy Grail in proving that everything EPA had done was wrong and not based on science.

What the jury was not told was that Malone had retired years earlier and the agency's computer system routinely purges e-mails that old. Nor were they informed that Malone's science background was minimal compared with scores of others in his department who supported the Libby cleanup.

Nevertheless, Molloy made it sound like the unavailable e-mail was concealed intentionally to the detriment of two of the three remaining defendants — Jack Wolter and Robert Bettacchi.

The judge also told the jury to ignore comments made by prosecution witness Dr. Alan Whitehouse when he predicted that illnesses would continue to surface. The jurors were also told to not consider Whitehouse's statements on the source of the asbestos-related disease that has killed and sickened hundreds of his patients.

Whitehouse continues to diagnose and treat these people. When the mine was still open, Grace itself sent miners to Whitehouse.

May 7

After 10 hours of almost nonstop closing arguments Wednesday, the W.R. Grace criminal case has gone to the jury.

The closing argument offered few surprises, with the lawyers on both sides performing as expected.

The courtroom was packed to the point of being uncomfortable and became hot enough to warrant judicial notice when Molloy mentioned that the building's air conditioner shuts off at six.

The jury paid attention. Most were making notes up until the end. One juror, who always laughs at Grace lawyer David Bernick's antics, was enjoying himself fully as the comedic lawyer really hammered it up in his closing with wild gestures and his weird emphatic pronunciation of words.

Paul Peronard and others from the EPA sat in the rows in front of me, and it was painful to see the muscles in their necks become taut as they listened to statements they knew were outright lies or distortions being offered as gospel.

Five U.S. marshals and bailiffs were ordered to the front of the courtroom, raised their right hands and swore to keep the jury sequestered, and moments later they ushered their new charges out of the courtroom and into seclusion somewhere.

There is nothing more the defense or prosecution can do. They've all taken their best shots, and now it is truly in the hands of the jury.

Never to step out of character, Bernick barely waited for the door to close behind the last juror before he was on his feet demanding that Molloy dismiss the charges, issue new instructions to the jury, hang the prosecutor or just do something. He was outraged at statements Assistant U.S. Attorney Kris McLean made during his rebuttal to the closing arguments.

Like a father trying to calm errant teenagers, Molloy twice reminded defense lawyers that there was still a "Rule 29" motion pending. The motion would allow the judge to dismiss the charges after the jury issues its verdict.

Looking around the courtroom, most lawyers, investigators, court watchers and reporters had puzzled expressions on their faces – somewhat like long-distance runners when the race is over. What now?

May 8

A juror wept as a clerk stood before U.S. District Judge Donald Molloy and reported that W.R. Grace & Co. and three of its former executives were not guilty of charges brought by the government. The nation's largest environmental crime trial in history had ended.

The trial took 10 weeks, and the clerk's reading of the verdicts of the jury's six men and six women was done in just three and a half minutes.

Saying it was the longest trial he'd ever been involved in, Molloy dismissed the jurors, who deliberated for less than two days, and said: "It is, I think, truly a reflection of how we are supposed to govern ourselves. Ultimately it is the people of the community who have to make a decision."

The verdict, joyful to some and painful to many, was no surprise. Most of the observers in the court gallery expected, at the most, a guilty verdict on only one of the eight counts, obstruction of justice.

The heavy charges of conspiracy and knowing endangerment that carried long prison sentences were dropped early as Molloy imposed repeated restrictions and limitations on what evidence and witnesses the prosecution could use.

"It's unfortunate that so much evidence was withheld from the jury by (Molloy's) evidentiary rulings," said David Uhlmann, who led the U.S. Justice Department's environmental crime section when the Montana U.S. attorney's office worked to bring the charges.

That withheld material included "some of the most compelling internal memos written by W.R. Grace officials about the harmful effects of their mining operations," Uhlmann added.

Picking his words with care, he said: "Many questions now linger about what would have happened if the trial had been conducted in a manner that was fair to everyone involved."

Uhlmann was the top environmental crimes prosecutor in the country until two years before the trial, when he joined the faculty of the University of Michigan Law School as a professor and director of the Environmental Law and Policy Program.

Speculation is rampant on why the government lost.

People talked about the prosecution being heavily outnumbered.

It had fewer than a dozen lawyers, investigators and support personnel. Grace fielded 50 or more and almost daily swamped the court with motions and briefs cranked out around-the-clock by their scores of paralegals and junior lawyers. The prosecution had most of its team working to midnight and beyond almost every night just to respond to the avalanche of paper.

Others weighed the impact of Molloy sitting mute day after day while Grace's superstar lawyer unleashed unsubstantiated, inflammatory accusations of misconduct by members of the prosecution team.

We can try to compare the effectiveness of Grace lead lawyer David Bernick's fiery, dramatic, comedic performances as he trashed witnesses and prosecution alike to the low-key, soft-spoken questioning of lead prosecutor Kris McLean.

For weeks, lawyers who had watched McLean in earlier trials said his "solid delivery" would win the day. Two Montana lawyers working for Grace as local counsel told me repeatedly that a Montana jury would never be impressed with Bernick's antics and "scrawling over whiteboards larger than himself."

It was admirable that prosecutors McLean and Kevin Cassidy kept their self-control throughout the ordeal. Through a bombardment of often-unsupported accusations fired almost continuously by Grace's defense team and often the judge himself, the pair defended themselves, yet maintained an air of civility that had been discarded by both the court and their opponents.

Many believe that the jury's verdicts were guided by the blatant disdain that Molloy heaped upon McLean and his case day after day.

Uhlmann said, "It's also hard to know how much the jury was influenced by (Molloy's) hostility to the government's case.

"It always was going to be a difficult case, and the way the trial was conducted made it all the more difficult."

Of course, the reason for the not-guilty verdicts may just be that W.R. Grace was totally innocent of all aspects of the poisoning of Libby and its people.

Wall Street thinks so. Shares of the company rose more than 30 percent almost instantly on the news of the acquittal.

"We at Grace are gratified by today's verdict," said company president Fred Festa. "We always believed that Grace and its former executives had acted properly and that a jury would come to the same conclusion when confronted with the evidence."

Sputtering mad Gayla Benefield, the most vocal critic of Grace, concluded that "They've gotten away with murder again, and that's just the way it will always be.

"I think of my family and friends, dozens of them, who died because of exposure to asbestos from Grace's operation and I really pray for the day that someone, anyone, can tell me why they are not guilty," she told me.

But Uhlmann cautioned that no one should lose sight of the fact that it was a tremendous accomplishment to investigate and prosecute Grace.

"While the outcome is disappointing, the only tragedy in this case is what happened to the town of Libby, Montana," he said.

CHAPTER 30

EPA's Keven McDermott, left, and Jed Januch decontaminate colleagues who were gathering soil samples from the yards of homes near a vermiculite processing plant in Spokane, Washington. Hundreds of these asbestos-contaminated facilities exist across the country. (Andrew Schneider)

T HE PEOPLE WHO CAME TO KNOW the stoic Montanans had a hard time accepting the jury's acquittal of W.R. Grace and its leaders. They had watched as life after life ended in drawn-out suffocation from the asbestos contaminating Zonolite Mountain and Libby.

For many of the surviving friends and family, the not-guilty verdicts ended any hope of what they craved: official revenge against the mammoth corporation.

For others, though, the acquittals boded ominously for protecting the lives and health of millions of people living nowhere near the vermiculite mine – nor Montana.

Among those most concerned were the doctors intimately familiar with Libby's fibers. Even they initially underestimated the risk.

Six years after the Grace acquittal, emerging research now confirms that the toxicity of Libby asbestos – with even minimal exposure – can sicken and kill at rates thousands of times greater than previously thought.

Dr. Alan Whitehouse was the first to recognize the unique danger of the Libby asbestos. He was the only pulmonologist between Minneapolis and Seattle 45 years ago, and physicians throughout Idaho, Utah, Eastern Washington and Northwestern Montana sent him almost all their chest cases.

"It didn't take long to know that the stuff from the mine was really bad," said Whitehouse, who began researching patients from Libby in the early 1970's.

For decades before he became the lead chest expert at Libby's Center for Asbestos Related Disease, or CARD, Clinic in 2005, Whitehouse's practice centered on patients exposed by their occupations throughout the region, such as the more than 51,000 workers at the sprawling Hanford Nuclear Reservation, 130 miles southwest of his Spokane office.

During the Cold War, the plant's workers refined the plutonium for almost all of America's nuclear arsenal. Like most industrial complexes, Hanford had chrysotile asbestos insulating pipes, boilers, furnaces and in scores of other applications all over the 500-square-mile site. A portion of the complex – Hanford Reach – is now operated by the National Park Service.

Over the years Whitehouse treated more than 500 patients, almost all sickened from exposure to chrysotile. This most-commonly-used lethal fiber has a latency period – the time from first exposure to the appearance of symptoms of asbestos disease – of 10, 15 or 20 years.[1]

Whitehouse knew that chrysotile problem well: "Asbestos is a very slowly progressing process. For disease to become apparent takes years and years and years," he said.

When the Zonolite miners and their family members started showing up at his door 36 years ago, Whitehouse quickly realized he was dealing with a different and far more toxic type of asbestos.

He said he had about two dozen patients whose disease had progressed from minimal to severe in just a year or two.

"Their X-rays had dramatically changed, their pulmonary function went down the tubes and they became very sick. Some of them died," Whitehouse said. "If you look at enough of them, you begin to see patterns and you learn things just from looking."[2]

DR. AUBREY MILLER, CHRIS WEIS and other health experts looked at Whitehouse's findings as they dug anxiously to sort out what was causing the suffering and death in Libby. They were stunned.

"Whitehouse's numbers were so out of line with everything we thought we knew about asbestos that we found his conclusions hard to believe," said Miller. "We went through every patient record he was permitted to share with us and the proof was there. His assessment of this previously unknown danger was right on target."[3]

Many of the federal health experts who rushed to Libby in 1999 and 2000 joined Whitehouse calling for urgency in protecting people nation-wide from exposure to the toxic fibers from Libby. Yet decision-makers in their agencies refused to heed the pulmonologist's early warning and even the appeals of their own specialists on the scene.

Wanting another expert to double-check his startling findings, White-house teamed up with Dr. Arthur Frank, head of the Department of Environmental and Occupational Health at Pennsylvania's Drexel University School of Public Health. The pair of experienced researchers re-analyzed Whitehouse's early findings and examined the deaths of patients at Libby's asbestos clinic.[4]

"We examined the deaths of patients at the CARD clinic between 2000 and 2010 that were attributable to asbestos-related disease," Whitehouse said.[5]

He had documented that 127 of the 203 deaths, or 63 percent, were caused by asbestosis.

"What is so important is that we showed the death rate from asbestosis is dramatically higher than any death rate previously described from chryso-tile," he explained.

Whitehouse and other physicians believe that the actual number of deaths from exposure to contaminated vermiculite in Libby is likely significantly higher because of missed diagnoses, incorrect causes of death or missing medical records.

Nevertheless, several health experts told Schneider that Whitehouse's work showed not only an asbestos mortality rate higher than chrysotile's, but also higher than ever known to be found in studies of the other five regulated types of asbestos – amosite, crocidolite, tremolite, anthophyllite and actinolite. His studies also sent up the first painfully bright red flare warning of the dangers from the mineral from Libby.

In late 2015, a study of Whitehouse's findings was being finalized for publication.

FURTHER PROOF OF THE EXTREME DANGER of Libby asbestos was revealed in a scientific journal in January 2015. But this time, the evidence was a long way from Libby: It was in Ohio.

This remarkable research started back in 1980, about 2,000 miles east of where Whitehouse hung his shingle, when Dr. James Lockey got his first professional exposure to Libby asbestos. He'd been out of medical school for eight years and was already boarded in a fistful of medical specialties but was working on a Master of Science degree in environmental health at the University of Cincinnati. At the time, the university offered the nation's only advanced program in occupational medicine.

"I had to do a thesis to graduate and my mentor (Dr. Stuart Brooks) had just been asked by what was then called O.M. Scott & Sons to determine what was sickening some of its workers. He assigned that to me as my thesis project," said Lockey.

For 14 years, millions of pounds of ore were shipped by trains and trucks from Libby to the Scotts plant in Marysville, Ohio. Scotts, one of the nation's major sellers of lawn and plant food, ran the material through its eight 1,000-degree furnaces and the vermiculite was popped into the shiny particles that the company used as a carrier for pesticides, chemicals, and plant and lawn food.

In the seventies, Scotts said 12 of its workers had been diagnosed with pleural effusions, a buildup of fluid between the chest wall and the lung. As federal regulations required, the company reported this unexpectedly high number to the Occupational Safety and Health Administration as well as the EPA.

The feds surveyed the workers for more than a year and couldn't conclusively pin down the cause of the disease. Yet investigators admitted there was reason for concern and suggested a more comprehensive and formal study.

Meanwhile, the company stopped using the Montana ore after its executives heard comments at professional meetings and from the industry grapevine about reported asbestos contamination of Grace's vermiculite.

Enter Lockey and his colleagues.

In 1980, they shuttled between the university and the Scotts plant, two hours north of the campus. At the ends of their stethoscopes were 513 Scotts workers.

They took chest X-rays, and did spirometry (measuring how much air a worker could inhale and exhale, and how quickly he could do it) and about every other pulmonary function test that was in use back then.

They found that 2 percent of the workers had documentable asbestos disease. Scotts insisted that it used no asbestos in its plant or its products. However, for years, tiny pieces of silver vermiculite sparkled in many of the items the company sold.[6]

"We told the company that the Grace vermiculite from Montana did indeed have asbestos minerals in it, amphiboles, and although the number of workers that had changes in their chest X-ray were relatively small, the finding was crucial to understanding the health risks its employees faced," said Lockey.

"It was our recommendation that the ore from Libby not ever be used again at that facility."

LOCKEY MOVED ON to the University of Utah, where he headed the Occupational Medicine Clinic and researched the hazards of manmade fibers.

Grace ceased operations at the Libby mine in 1990. It was about another nine years before the *Seattle Post-Intelligencer* told the world about what the company had done.

As the word spread of the *Seattle P-I's* disclosures in 1999, federal specialists and consultants swarmed into Libby. The health professionals who knew the most about the machinations of Libby's asbestos – Miller, Weis and Whitehouse – carefully read Lockey's work from 1980 on the Libby Zonolite sickening the Scotts workers, and the swapping of knowledge and opinions began in earnest.

With funding and urging from the federal government in 2004, Lockey went back to check out the men in his initial Scotts study group who were still alive and willing to participate.

He knew that there was no further exposure to Grace's contaminated product at the Scotts plant and he wasn't convinced he would find anything striking.

This time Lockey's team was 11 radiologists, statisticians, epidemiologists, industrial hygienists and physicians from his university's departments of Environmental Health and Radiology. They were joined by Dr. Vikas Kapil, medical officer from the Centers for Disease Control.

"When we went back and looked at that population some 14 years later, there was a dramatic increase in the number of chest X-ray abnormalities. It went up from essentially 2 percent in 1980 to 29 percent in 2004," Lockey said.

Lockey and many of his colleagues were amazed at the findings, not just because the increase in asbestos disease was about 1,500 percent, but because the study showed that the exposure those workers endured – the total amount of asbestos they sucked into their lungs – was astoundingly low.

"There was nothing in the medical literature that indicated" that the type of fibers in the Libby ore "would cause this type of abnormality at this low cumulative exposure," he said.

The exposure rate that he calculated was so far below the level that OSHA deemed safe for workers that he was concerned about the accuracy of the work.

"These changes were occurring at very, very, very low exposure levels and we did question the data. We looked at our results every possible way we could to see if we were somehow doing some type of misclassification.

It was accurate but just far, far more dangerous than anyone could believe," said Lockey.

"This fiber is persistent in the lung and in the chest cavity, causing a continuous lung inflammation. Even after the patient is removed from exposure this process continues and continues."

In 2012, Lockey again re-examined the survivors of the initial group he studied 30 years earlier, but this time, instead of using the traditional chest X-ray, he used high-resolution CT scans with the pulmonary function tests.

The results were even more shocking.

Of the 191 workers evaluated, 106 of them, or 55.5 percent, had asbestos-related changes of the tissue lining the lungs or the lungs themselves.

The results of Lockey's third study of the same Scotts workers were published in the Journal of Occupational and Environmental Medicine in January 2015.[7]

Lockey, now an emeritus professor of environmental health and pulmonary medicine at the University of Cincinnati, said he was greatly concerned by the health impact of even a low-level exposure to the fiber from Libby.

"The longer you live after this type of exposure, the more likely you are to have more and more significant adverse health issues. You will likely become impaired because you're going to develop a mesothelioma or lung cancer. This fiber does not stop. It continues its impact on the lung years after last exposure. Death is a likely outcome so it is imperative that any and all exposure to this Libby asbestos be prevented," Lockey said.

World Health Organization scientists keep adding to the list of malignancies caused by asbestos exposure.[8] Its International Agency for Research on Cancer now includes cancers of the larynx, ovaries and colon. The work on the extreme toxicity of Libby's fibers by Lockey and Whitehouse makes this growing list of potential disease sites even more fearsome.

But researchers looking beyond the anticipated respiratory effects of Libby asbestos have documented other unexpected and startling consequences of exposure.

Jean Pfau was a professor of immunotoxicology at Idaho State University, researching whether environmental exposures can cause immune system dysfunction.

Her interest in studying the people of Libby began soon after CDC's Agency for Toxic Substances and Disease Registry performed its 2001 screening of 7,307 residents of the area.[9]

The health research agency found that almost 7 percent of those tested reported that they had been diagnosed with an autoimmune disease. This means the body's immune system was attacking its own tissue or organs.

The ATSDR said the reported cases "far exceeded the expected prevalence of less than 1 percent." The federal investigators had questioned those they had screened on whether they had lupus, rheumatoid arthritis, or systemic sclerosis, which can trigger possible failure of the lungs, heart, kidneys, and gastrointestinal tract.

More research was needed.

Dr. Stephen Levin, a director of the Mount Sinai Selikoff Centers for Occupational Health in New York, obtained a federal grant to establish the Libby Epidemiology Research Program and conduct several studies of the hazard of Libby asbestos. Levin quickly recruited Pfau and others working on Libby health issues.

Meanwhile, Pfau; Curtis Noonan, associate professor of epidemiology at the University of Montana's Center for Environmental Health Sciences; and Theodore Larson, an epidemiologist with ATSDR, kept investigating.

The researchers began by taking serum from blood of 50 middle-aged Libby residents with asbestos disease and tested samples for antinuclear antibodies. The ANA test measures the amount and pattern of antibodies in a person's blood that work against the natural immune system.

They did the same with blood samples from 50 people from Missoula, a city 200 miles south that had no asbestos contamination problems.

The study, published in 2004, showed the link between the antibody levels and asbestos-related diseases in the Libby samples. [10]

"The folks from Libby had at least twice as many positive samples as those in Missoula," said Pfau.

"The ANAs from the Libby subjects were not only present, but they were high – really, really high – suggesting the presence of significant disease.

"There was six times the expected prevalence of rheumatoid arthritis in Libby, sixteen times the expected prevalence of systemic lupus, and eight times the expected scleroderma."

The researchers questioned whether exposure to other asbestos fibers would also cause the dramatic increase in autoimmune diseases.

Levin provided serum samples from his patients at Mount Sinai School – pipe insulators and steamfitters who were exposed almost exclusively to chrysotile asbestos.

"No significant increase in ANA was found among the Mount Sinai chrysotile patients," Pfau said.[11]

"The material from Libby carries a unique and severe hazard. Thus having Zonolite in your attic is very different from having chrysotile asbestos in your floor tile."

Examining the effects of Libby asbestos on other autoimmune diseases like multiple sclerosis and type I diabetes was added to the growing list of research.

Pfau told Schneider that she's calling it the Libby Disease.

"Everything about this material from Montana is extremely unique and unexpected, especially the symptoms, the severity and the rapid progression of the disease."

Aubrey Miller said Pfau's findings are of major significance and "the work shows exposure to Libby asbestos is likely triggering unexpected levels of autoimmune diseases as well as hiking the occurrences of lung diseases."

Pfau said she's amazed at how far and wide the illnesses and deaths from Libby asbestos have spread.

"I talked to a lady recently whose mother-in-law died of mesothelioma, her husband has rheumatoid arthritis, and her daughter suffers with several other immune disorders, and she's calling me because she's concerned that asbestos is just causing this rampant disease through her family," she said.

"I'm now getting calls like this all the time."

Pfau is now a professor of immunotoxicology at Montana State University in Bozeman. In late 2015, she and her colleagues had six studies being reviewed for publishing and an ever-growing list of new questions for which they were seeking answers.

WHILE PHYSICIANS and health researchers were investigating an asbestos disease process unseen before, Greg Meeker, a geologist and mineralogist with the U.S. Geological Survey, was digging deeply to determine the chemical composition of an asbestos fiber that wasn't among the six identified and regulated by the government.[12]

"Some of the issues of contention had been simmering for decades, such as what constitutes the shape, size and physical origin of a regulated asbestos fiber," said Meeker, who found himself battling with Grace, other mining and manufacturing industries and their lawyers, and government colleagues of all specialties.

Meeker recently retired after 24 years with the USGS. He and his colleagues had determined that the extraordinarily harmful asbestos fibers from Libby contained winchite at one end, tremolite at the other end, and richterite in the middle. However, Meeker told Schneider in late 2015 that to his great dismay, the fibers from Libby were still not listed in the government regulations. This means that there is no federal control or monitoring of this fiber's use or presence.

Why this particular chemical mixture is so lethal is not yet known. But the work of Whitehouse, Lockey, Levin, Frank, Miller, Weis, Pfau and Black has presented undeniable proof that this contaminant of Libby vermiculite is far more deadly than any other asbestos fiber yet identified by the government.

It wounds and kills far more quickly, and from minuscule exposure.

These researchers concur that the danger to the millions of people who have Zonolite in their homes, schools and businesses borders on the inconceivable.

A few stores have closed and about the same number of new ones have opened. With the exception of a large metal eagle at one end, Libby's main street remains much the same over the years. (Cold Truth)

THE EPA INSISTS that its obscure website on the dangers of Libby vermiculite is all that's needed to adequately inform tens of millions of people that the stuff in their attics, walls and yards could sicken or kill them.

EPA is wrong.

Pulmonary expert James Lockey illustrates: He was having dinner with a health scientist who knows hazardous substances and the dangers of asbestos.[1]

His host asked Lockey to come see the renovations underway in his very old, charming house. As they walked into one room, Lockey saw piles of vermiculite scattered on the floor.

When he asked about the vermiculite and the potentially associated hazards, his friend said: "Yeah, it was in the walls here," Lockey recalled.

"Most of it was already swept up and disposed of, but it was amazing to me that my friend knew of this exposure risk but did not use respiratory precautions," Lockey said.

"If a knowledgeable person like that, with extensive expertise in dangerous material, including asbestos, doesn't acknowledge through personal actions the hazard from vermiculite, how does the government expect the general population to take precautionary measures based on the current limited public education program?"

Aubrey Miller shares Lockey's concerns. And the government physician echoed the views of many others worried about the risks to people who most likely don't read the websites of EPA or CDC or any other federal agencies.

Schneider remembered a morning with Les Skramstad. Les was sitting at his kitchen table holding a huge coffee mug that Norita had just topped off. The miner said: "Grace put food on the tables of the people of Libby. But it also put asbestos in their lungs." That morning he was raging about the much-hyped warnings on government websites. "Useless, that's what they are. Even if you have a computer, who the hell would know to look there," he said, slamming his empty cup on the table and earning a glare from Norita.

Miller explained, "The warning really needs to get out to places where people congregate and in a way that they can understand this pervasive material and the risks to themselves and their lives."

There was and still is a learning curve in understanding how lethal Libby's unique asbestos fibers really are.

Additionally, public health and criminal investigators and statisticians know that this dangerous product is in homes, businesses and schools a long distance from Libby. Thousands of Grace invoices, shipping papers and sales reports revealed the massive multinational company shipped by rail and road 15.6 billion pounds of Libby's disease-causing vermiculite to more than 750 plants and factories throughout North America.[2]

An EPA study in the seventies – which was ignored by the agency's headquarters – reported that about 18 million people lived close enough to Grace's vermiculite processing plants to breathe asbestos-containing dust night and day.

It has been about 15 years since the EPA concluded from Grace's paper trail and interviews with former Zonolite sales staff that "there may be anywhere from 15 to 52 million" homes, schools and businesses nationwide contaminated with the lethal insulation from Libby.[3]

"The analysis of Zonolite distribution shows that the insulation was pretty much evenly sold from coast to coast, most heavily across the tier of Northern states – from New England to the Pacific Northwest," toxicologist Chris Weis said.

EPA statisticians geographically plotted sales at least as far south as Jacksonville, Fla., and deep into the Canadian provinces.

But if numbers on spreadsheets aren't enough proof that this killer is everywhere, ask Paul Peronard.

The boss of the Libby cleanup continued after that project to coordinate EPA's response to manmade and natural calamities throughout most of the country. All too often, he told Schneider, he encountered the asbestos-tainted Libby vermiculite in other emergencies far from Montana. For example, in the aftermath of the massive floods that devastated Minot, North Dakota, "we cleaned up over 350 properties with Zonolite in piles on the side of the road."

EPA regulations prevent its personnel from entering private homes, but he saturated the community with fliers warning of the danger of Zonolite "and people started bringing it out to the curb in bags and clearly marked," he said.

"We teamed up with OSHA and handed out hundreds of respirators and did a whole bunch of training to the volunteer groups. Still, I know hundreds of folks got exposed to the asbestos during the cleanup." And that was just one part of one town.

Coordinators from the Federal Emergency Management Agency and investigators from the U.S. Public Health Service say Zonolite insulation is routinely found in debris fields after hurricanes, tornadoes, and even in the charred remains of wildfires.

The physicians and scientists who battled to control the spread of Grace's deadly product pushed EPA to live up to its mission: to protect human health and the environment.

When it came to Zonolite, they got promises. Over the years, three consecutive EPA administrators said exactly what the public health community wanted to hear – we'll notify the homeowners, we'll tell cable installers, contractors and home repair workers.

In the end, EPA leaders did nothing.

ON JUNE 17, 2009, five weeks after W.R. Grace and its executives were exonerated of all charges of criminal wrongdoing involving its vermiculite, then-EPA Administrator Lisa Jackson and Health and Human Services Secretary Kathleen Sebelius went to Libby.[4]

As Montana's U.S. Sens. Max Baucus and Jon Tester squeezed into camera range, Jackson and Sebelius announced that Libby would finally get the long-awaited declaration that it had a public health emergency. The declaration would authorize the difficult and extremely costly removal of the asbestos-tainted vermiculite permeating the town and its homes. Of equal importance, it would make the government responsible for ensuring the delivery of continuing health care, including the medication needed to fight the related diseases.[5]

It was the first time anywhere in the country that an emergency declaration of this type was made. But the good news for Libby did not extend to the millions of others endangered by its vermiculite. The two cabinet members paid only passing note to the wider hazard.

Jackson told the seven reporters at the poorly promoted event that there "are many towns and cities across the U.S. with vermiculite insulation in their homes and commercial buildings." She added that dangers are still present in and near the hundreds of former vermiculite processing sites where ore from Libby was turned into insulation.[6]

Jackson urged the public to "become educated. Just don't disturb it. Treat it like asbestos. We're just asking people to use common sense and protect themselves and their families," the EPA boss told the reporters.

A few weeks later, when Schneider asked how Jackson or anyone in the agency expected homeowners to know they could be at risk, the administrator's spokeswoman said she'd get him an answer. He's still waiting.

None of the carefully crafted nationwide radio, television and newspaper public service warnings on Zonolite were ever issued. The promised leaflets and posters outlining the unique hazards were never sent to do-it-yourself or hardware stores or home improvement chains.[7]

As of 2015, nothing has been done.

DURING ITS 45-YEAR HISTORY, the EPA has often been the whipping boy for corporate special interests. Intense battles were fought between the agency and Monsanto, Dow, BASF, Bayer and other chemical giants over regulation of their high-profit toxic products.

But political interference with EPA's efforts to clean up toxic nightmares grew during the last decade or two.[8]

Members of Congress from both parties said the fight to control exposure to the lethal asbestos fibers from Libby set new records for political intrigue. Email and other inter-agency documents that Schneider obtained clearly laid out continuing White House intervention, partisan stalling and industry meddling during the entire George W. Bush-Dick Cheney presidency.[9]

For the eight years he occupied the Oval Office, Bush repeatedly ranted against asbestos litigation and protective changes in regulations. The White House Office of Management and Budget thwarted attempts to institute Libby's Public Health Declaration and other efforts to protect the public from Zonolite.

"The political component surrounding Libby reached new peaks during that administration," Libby cleanup boss Paul Peronard said.[10]

He attributed the increased meddling to "the broader implications of asbestos lawsuits, asbestos claims and the amount of people affected. Certainly the politics during the efforts involving Libby were on steroids. You know, just the notion that the White House was reviewing plans for cleanup is a unique and troublesome thing."

It's almost natural to blame Republicans for the government's failure to warn the public about asbestos. However, President Obama has been in office for almost two full terms and still there's no public warning on Zonolite.

"If I had Zonolite in my house I would want to know it, and if I knew it, I would do everything I could to get it out of there," said Peronard.

Many find it absurd and inexplicable that an argument made years ago in EPA headquarters remains the bulwark of the internal opposition to notifying the public: If we tell them, they will expect the government to pay to decontaminate all their homes.[11]

One email Schneider was allowed to read in October 2015 said that EPA's entire 2016 agency budget of $8.6 billion "would pay for the cleanup of fewer than 2 million homes" out of the estimated tens of millions that could need work.

NOBODY IN THE PUBLIC HEALTH COMMUNITY pushing for Zonolite notification expects the government to pick up the bill, except in Libby. They do want the government to do its duty and warn the people who live in contaminated houses.

"When it comes to vermiculite, the government has advanced the concept of benign neglect to an art form of previously unimagined heights," said Dr. Michael Harbut, an internationally recognized expert in the diagnosis and treatment of diseases of the environment and workplace.[12]

Harbut said he is concerned not only with the millions of families in the U.S. but the hundreds of thousands of others in countries where Grace shipped the poisonous vermiculite insulation.

With more than three decades of researching lethal mineral fibers, Harbut said, "There is data which shows that even the simple act of placing boxes in attics which have been insulated with vermiculite can release an amount of carcinogen adequate to cause cancer."

He called the government's vermiculite websites almost meaningless to the millions of owners of contaminated homes and the people who work in them.

"They are painfully inadequate and are of no useful value to those who don't understand that the vermiculite insulation they live with can sicken and kill them," said Harbut, clinical professor of internal medicine at Detroit's Wayne State University.

The only government warning for workers in these asbestos-contaminated homes comes from a brief report from Patricia Sullivan, an investigator with the National Institute for Occupational Safety and Health.[13]

In 2007, she reported that "increases in asbestosis and lung cancer mortality highlight the need for better understanding and control of exposures that may occur when homeowners or construction workers – including plumbers, cable installers, electricians and insulators – disturb loose-fill attic insulation made with asbestos-contaminated vermiculite from Libby."

Almost all the scientists who have studied the effects of Libby asbestos believe the threat of harmful exposure is increasing as the homes containing this insulation age.[14]

"They're being renovated. New wiring is being put in as the aging wiring becomes unsafe. Internet wiring and cabling is being installed in these attics, as well as exhaust fans and various types of winterization," said toxicologist Weis. "All of this activity – even the most gentle action – disturbs the asbestos, endangering not only the workers but spreading it through the homes."

Even if attics are well sealed off from the rest of the house, EPA and its outside asbestos consultants have found asbestos-contaminated vermiculite dust seeping through wall switches, ceiling-light fixtures and fans, and sometimes through the dried-out joint tape in ceilings and walls.

The anger is almost palpable when the government gang who fought to protect lives in and around Libby talk about their agency's continued failure to do anything substantive about dangers elsewhere in the country.

"In order to protect themselves, people must know two things," Weis said. "The first is that asbestos can kill you and second is that it's likely that you're being exposed to asbestos."[15]

To prove his point, Weis tells of a woman in Colorado who ran a flower shop.

"She made a practice every Friday of putting a single rose in a small vase filled with vermiculite and passing those out to customers who would come by and take them home.

"The woman who ran that family business came down with mesothelioma. She died. Handling that small amount of vermiculite from Libby killed her," said Weis.

Yet no one – not the federal agencies, not the states and certainly not W.R. Grace – is telling people living with or near Zonolite to beware.

Some of the nation's top experts in the lethality of mineral fibers like asbestos and taconite gather at EPA's Gitche Gumee Conference Center in Duluth, Minnesota, to review the latest research on these killer fibers. From left, Ron Dodson, David Berry, Chris Weis and Aubrey Miller prepare their presentations. (Andrew Schneider)

T HE PAINFUL REALITY for people in public health, occupational safety, and environmental protection is that government action that costs money rarely will happen until you can point to a large number of bodies.

That's the reason these experts want a tally of the mortality and morbidity of those exposed to Libby asbestos. They hope that real numbers documenting the scope of the carnage might force the EPA and other government health and safety agencies to actually do something to protect those not yet affected by the killer mineral.

"It has got to be understood that the disease and deaths from this asbestos haven't abated and won't end with the decontamination of Libby and the surrounding area," said Aubrey Miller, the first federal physician to arrive in the poisoned community in 1999.

When Miller first got to Libby after the *Post-Intelligencer* stories broke in 1999, the newspaper had identified 192 people whose deaths could be certainly attributed to vermiculite pulled from the nearby mine.[1] A year later Schneider reported that the death count exceeded 400.

The newspaper stopped counting.

And more than 15 years later, the body count is still reported by almost everyone as 400 souls.

London's *Daily Mail, The Huffington Post,* The Associated Press, *The Wall Street Journal* and a few score of other news organizations seem comfortable assuming that the dying stopped at 400.

"The death toll attributed to Libby is just the very small tip of a very large iceberg," said Miller.

This contaminated vermiculite product is in millions of homes, and millions more people have encountered it while living near or working at Grace's Zonolite processing plants, said the senior Public Health Service physician.

"Throughout the country, the number of people sickened or killed by it is clearly enormous. We are talking about tens of thousands," he said.

Brad Black, of the Center for Asbestos Related Disease Clinic, said he watches closely what's being reported by other physicians and health departments near Grace's former vermiculite processing sites around the country.

"Most likely more than 20,000 have died as a result of their exposure to Libby amphibole, and this number will continue to climb since most don't have a clue as to the hazard from all the Zonolite out there," he said.

Toxicologist Chris Weis calls tens of thousands a conservative guess:

"What is terrifying is that there are ten times that number of people still at risk from exposure to Libby asbestos in their walls, attics, and most likely don't know it."

SO WHY DO WE CARE about the number of asbestos victims?

"The ability to point to those sickened or killed – to count the bodies – is often the only way to embarrass the government into doing its job, to protect the public from a risk that is as real as is this fiber from Libby," Schneider was told by Dr. Stephen Levin, medical director of the Mount Sinai Irving Selikoff Center for Occupational and Environmental Medicine.[2]

Levin was among a group of physicians, toxicologists and other researchers sitting around a stone fireplace in the cedar-paneled main room of the Big Horn Lodge in the spring of 2003. The rustic inn on the Bull River, about an hour south of Libby, was a unique venue for the first formal gathering of health professionals concerned about the people struck down by Grace's vermiculite. Montana wildlife sauntered around and above the lodge, but inside debates over what had happened in Libby and what to do about it raged passionately.

"There are people who need the help of the public health community if they are to obtain any justice and the care they deserve for harm they suffered from corporations chasing the largest profits they can make," said Levin.

He called W.R. Grace a corporation that is "an obvious example that harmed its workers, its consumers and the communities they operate in."

Levin, the physician who fought long and loudly to get care for the thousands of first-responders sickened by the toxic dust of the World Trade Center attacks, said in a 2004 telephone interview that "just looking at the vermiculite exposure potential nationwide, it's obvious that the ultimate number of deaths (from Grace's Zonolite) will surely surpass the death count inflicted on New York City on and after 9/11."

He went on: "The real value of knowing the numbers is to help us identify the people who have been harmed, and to detect others with the same diseases as early as possible, while there is still a chance to cure them or at least improve the quality of the lives they have left."

EVEN WITH HIS YEARS OF EXPERIENCE documenting the extreme dangers from Libby's asbestos fibers, James Lockey said that when he's dealing with regulatory agencies that know the hazards, they still demand proof.[3]

"People tend to bury their heads in the sand and say, 'I'd rather not deal with it.' If the harm is not blatantly apparent, (they'd) rather let somebody else deal with it fifteen or thirty years down the line. This is not how public health should be delivered."

Sometimes knowing the numbers accomplishes nothing. Levin, Miller and Weis pointed to the 1985 EPA report that stated 13,147,496 people who lived near Grace's vermiculite production plants were at risk from asbestos exposure.[4] This number does not include the millions of homeowners at risk from their insulation. Yet this report sparked no action from EPA headquarters.

Analyzing personal injury lawsuits is often a way to quantify the magnitude of harm from a toxic exposure.

When Grace declared bankruptcy in 2001, its CEO, Paul Norris, said the company was forced to do so because of 325,000 asbestos suits pending against his company from people allegedly sickened.

What's the number of Zonolite-related suits today?

In late 2015, the hub of the personal injury litigation universe for victims of Grace's vermiculite was still the McGarvey law firm in Kalispell. Its founder, Dale McGarvey, has slowed down a bit, but the quartet of corporate dragon-slayers he left behind – Allan McGarvey, Jon Heberling, John Lacey and Roger Sullivan – continued successfully fighting the wars.

It was this group of small-town barristers who, in May 1997, shocked Grace's brigade of dark-suited lawyers when they made history persuading a jury to convict Grace for the illness that eventually killed Les Skramstad and Margaret Vatland, the mother of Gayla Benefield.[5]

But when asked to provide an estimate of the numbers of victims or lawsuits to help quantify the harm, the McGarvey firm declined.

Schneider also questioned 14 law firms in 11 states that heavily saturated cable television with ads touting their ability to sue corporations on behalf of individuals harmed by asbestos. He also tried to interview many of the expert witnesses these lawyers used. Like the McGarvey firm, none would say how many cases for injury or death from Zonolite they had brought or had in the pipeline.

All admitted, to one degree or another, that Zonolite insulation is the golden egg from the Grace goose.

The absence of information on the spread and disease mechanism of the Libby fiber is compounded by a shortage of physicians who know that a century-old respiratory disease still exists and how to identify it if they actually look for it.

"The asbestos disease we have dealt with here doesn't fall in line with the traditional view on how asbestos sickens and kills," said Brad Black.

Traditionally, only the occupational medical specialists considered asbestos exposure when they encountered a patient with lung disease. Medical books, even today, call it only a "worker's disease" triggered by heavy, occupation-level, continuous exposures to asbestos fibers. The risk was contemplated only in people who work in dust every day.

It is the rare general practitioner who asks a patient, even one with lung disease, if he or she was ever exposed to asbestos.

And, even if they did, the asbestos damage from Libby's fibers doesn't follow the typical pattern.

"Because of the nature of Libby's disease, instead of getting the big, thick plaques or scars, patients here present a very thin layer along the chest wall called a lamellar. It's thin enough that if you don't use the right techniques, you'll miss it. It'll totally disappear," said Black.

MICHELLE BOLTZ is a nurse practitioner who returned home to Libby after four years providing medical care in an Inupiat Eskimo village above the Arctic Circle that was also near an asbestos-contaminated mine.[6]

In the Libby CARD Clinic, she supervised the screening of new patients and told Schneider she was amazed at how aggressive the Libby asbestos disease was. Eight members of her family had been diagnosed, including her parents and grandparents and her husband's parents. None of them ever worked at the mine.

She did a lot of lecturing on Libby's asbestos to medical groups throughout Montana and nearby states and was troubled about how little is known.

"There's still a lot of confusion, missed diagnoses and misunderstanding the disease process within this community," Boltz said. "So if we haven't come that far here in Libby, I guess we shouldn't be surprised that nationally, medical providers are not recognizing the unique manifestation of this disease and people are likely dying because of it.

"I am convinced that the number of cases identified nationwide is just going to explode if we can educate providers about how to recognize and treat this disease."

WHEN IT COMES TO DUST-INDUCED lung disease, a lot of physicians, even the occupational medicine specialists, believe it is an old issue and that they learned all they needed in medical school.

"They think they know everything they need to know about it," Lockey added, "yet most are unaware that the same materials are now being utilized in other ways that are presenting renewed risks for the workers and the public who are exposed to it.

"Unless they are cognizant of that, they're not going to see it – they're not going to ask the right questions and patients with asbestos disease will go undiagnosed," he said.[7]

For decades, occupational medicine specialists and pulmonologists rushed to the chest X-ray as the initial screening tool to detect lung injury from asbestos, talc, silica, and other fibers sucked into the lungs.

There is nothing easy about accurately evaluating a chest film or scan, especially if it's early in the disease process. The average radiographic image has far more than 50 shades of gray, perhaps thousands of subtle variations.[8]

Most of the physicians following Libby patients were aware that X-rays were not that sensitive for picking up early changes in somebody's lung or pleural membrane, and CT scans became the diagnostic tool of choice.

"There just aren't enough doctors who know what they're doing to go around," said Michael Harbut, co-author of the American Thoracic Society's most recent criteria for the diagnosis and treatment of asbestos-related diseases.[9]

For decades, actually until pulmonologist Alan Whitehouse showed that people with no connection to the mine were contracting asbestos disease, the illness was always considered an employee safety issue, a matter for workers compensation and corporate lawyers.

Because of the money involved in these medical-legal and employment situations, Harbut says, he has seen too many cases where obsolete, archaic diagnostic techniques are used to determine the presence or absence of these diseases. Sometimes the use of these techniques is unavoidable. Often, it's intentional.

"Simple chest X-rays are utilized much more often than CTs of the chest, and even more often than the appropriate type of CT for the chest. Primitive breathing tests are utilized over more sophisticated complete pulmonary function testing, and blood testing for mesothelioma is still in its infancy," Harbut said, adding:

"The failure to use the latest, most telling diagnostic tools on these asbestos patients not only impedes the progress of science and the art of medicine, it costs life and well-being."

Dr. Brad Black sits in the Libby Café savoring the headline "Libby now safe from asbestos." "We've waited a long time for this," he said. (Andrew Schneider)

O N THE EVENING of December 8, 2014, to the surprise of even the scientists involved, EPA finally released its highly debated findings on remaining Libby asbestos health hazards – both in the little Montana town and across the rest of the country, where the distinctively lethal fiber lies in millions of family homes, ready as ever to kill.

That winter night was typical for the northwest corner of Montana – damned cold.

Perhaps that explained why few people showed up in the Ponderosa meeting room in Libby's town hall to hear the long-awaited report on how safe Libby had become after the government spent hundreds of millions of dollars and 14 years scouring asbestos-contaminated vermiculite from the community.

About a third of the 26 attending were from the EPA – either managers of the cleanup or authors of the 425-page "Toxicity values and Human

Health Risk Assessment for Libby amphibole asbestos." As ponderous as the name was, the question it was to answer was pretty simple: Had enough asbestos been removed from the town to allow people not yet sickened to safely live there?[1]

The EPA team, working with their National Center for Environmental Assessment and other health experts, also released a toxicological review called an Integrated Risk Information System.

The exposure calculations in the IRIS were specific to the unique chemical composition and characteristics of the asbestos fibers found in Libby's vermiculite.[2]

There was no doubt among the people of Libby that the asbestos contaminating their town was harmful. The town cemetery and the always-filled beds in the hospital held all the proof needed. But the government demanded more. The IRIS was required if new protective environmental laws and worker-safety regulations were to be instituted, not only by EPA but also other federal, state, local and international health organizations.

The evaluation documented the relationship between exposure to the asbestos and the specific risk from inhaling, ingesting, or even absorbing the toxic material. It also identified and quantified potential cancer and non-cancer hazards such as asbestosis and thickening of the lung lining.[3]

Having an IRIS for a toxic material also opened the door to let health regulators and their cleanup crews determine things like the danger from contamination and how clean is clean.

GAYLA BENEFIELD LOOKED AROUND the near-empty meeting room and said the sparse showing was because most of the townsfolk "were tired of listening to anything EPA had to say and not understanding much of what they did hear."[4]

This time EPA made sure its message was clear and understandable. In the front of the room, among the whiteboards, easels and projection screen, stood Rebecca Thomas, the manager of Libby's Superfund cleanup project; David Berry, senior toxicologist; Deborah McKean, the project's lead toxicologist, and Christina Progess, who was leading the cleanup of the abandoned mine.

Schneider was sure he could hear a collective sigh of relief as Thomas introduced the team. Few people in her agency, in other federal health agencies or in Libby itself thought this assessment would ever get released. Grace, political appointees in federal agencies, and scientists-for-hire had fought for years to stifle the reports.

Thomas admitted that she and her colleagues were holding their breath, expecting a phone call or e-mail any moment shutting them down.

Thomas, an engineer with 23 years in the agency, said she and the team had never been involved with anything that survived the level of scrutiny that plagued this effort.

The industry angst was spawned when then-USGS geologist Greg Meeker and his colleagues found the Libby asbestos was different from the six asbestos fibers regulated by the government. Meeker reported the fibers permeating the vermiculite from the Grace mine were made of winchite, richterite and tremolite – a chemical combination never before identified and one whose health effects were just starting to be recognized.[5]

An enormous amount of new science had to be conceived, confirmed and reproduced for the IRIS and the risk assessment to protect EPA's conclusion from intense criticism from a lengthy parade of skeptics, highly paid corporate scientists, lobbyists and politicians. Industry knew that the issuing of the IRIS would permit the government to finally crack down on dangerous exposure from the same fibers in other vermiculite products.

"It's been very frustrating at EPA, and I'm sure much more so for the community members, waiting for the science to really understand what exposure to Libby asbestos really meant," said the project boss.

Toxicologist David Berry shared a brief look at the research and said the agency had collected 3,100 activity-based air samples under more than 150 exposure scenarios. This was done to measure the level of asbestos experienced by people living and working near the tainted Zonolite. It included the comic-looking but deadly serious sight of scientists in protective respirators and Tyvek clothing pedaling tricycles, playing softball, sweeping, vacuuming, climbing trees and gardening.

The IRIS formalized what Libby residents had known for decades. The asbestos contaminating its vermiculite was a killer. And now its identity could be tracked, regulated and perhaps outlawed.

The broad implications of the highly technical IRIS and the risk assessment may not have been easily grasped, but most in the audience responded to the findings about the safety of their town with nods of understanding.

"The concentration – the amount – of asbestos fibers in the air in Libby today is about 100,000 times lower than when the mine and its processing facilities were in operation," Deborah McKean, the team's lead toxicologist, reported.

The scientist added that the concentration in the center of Libby was about 90 asbestos fibers in a cubic meter of air. She said a person could breathe it every day for a lifetime without any likely adverse health effects.

McKean stressed that the EPA still had more work to do and that the risk assessment had confirmed that the cleanup strategy was a success, but had not given Libby a completely clean bill of health.

EPA remained concerned about the 800 properties the agency was not allowed to decontaminate. Some of the property owners belonged to one of Montana's militias, or were running a meth lab or just did not want anything to do with the government.

Thomas said that refusing to let EPA dig up their property was rational when the agency didn't have enough science to decide how clean was clean enough.

But since the reliability of EPA's science had been proven, the agency worried that homes not cleaned could recontaminate areas now asbestos-free.

She said they were considering enlisting health departments to order access to contaminated private property in nearby Troy, Montana; Lincoln County, and Libby.

Reflecting on the work in Libby, McKean, former director of an EPA laboratory that tracked substances like anthrax for Homeland Security, said Libby was a different and often painful undertaking.

"It has been quite an emotional experience working side-by-side in Libby with the folks that have survived this health crisis for 20 or 30 years or more," McKean told Schneider after the meeting. "There is enormous satisfaction in knowing that what we do will affect the health of their children and their children's children."

The team is highly experienced and all have encountered serious environmental crises, but Libby was different, they said. "I've never worked on another project where there have been so many illnesses, and even deaths associated with the contamination," said Thomas.

At the mine site from which the contamination spewed, Project Manager Christina Progess was still working with her team to figure how to keep the remaining asbestos from spreading outside the mine.

She told local reporters that Grace was cooperating and $250 million of the corporation's money had been designated to pay for the work she deemed necessary. But making the mine site safe could cost more than that, and EPA wanted Grace to pick up the entire tab.

The price tag for cleaning up Libby – mostly paid with taxpayer dollars – will easily top $1 billion, the project managers said.

EPA had quickly replaced Grace as Libby's largest employer with dozens of clean-up crews, truck drivers and heavy equipment operators, all dressed in white Tyvek protective gear, combing every hiding place in town for asbestos.

By the beginning of 2016, EPA reported it had spent at least $570 million removing more than a million cubic yards of asbestos-contaminated building material and soil from Libby and Troy, and hauling it to a safe landfill. That's about 71,000 large dump-truck loads from more than 2,275 homes, businesses and public areas in both towns. Of the 8,072 properties in the towns, 772 still had yet to be inspected.[6]

LIBBY'S ASBESTOS CLINIC HAS EXPANDED dramatically and is seeing more than 6,800 patients a year, said its director, Dr. Brad Black. About 3,900 have been diagnosed with some level of asbestos-related disease, including the doctor himself.

Black said he had seen many advances in diagnosing and treating asbestos disease, but after more than a decade of watching the machinations in Libby, he is concerned about the "sinister side" of politics and medicine.

The onetime pediatrician turned asbestos expert said, "It has become un-comfortably clear that if enough money is offered, you can get an expert to say anything, and that includes too many physicians."

Often, the gatekeepers for detecting abnormalities in the lungs from as-bestos are a group of physicians certified by the government as "B-readers." The difficult, complex testing process for certification includes accurately reading 125 government-selected chest X-rays. Insurance companies, work-er compensation boards and judges often hang their decisions about the health of a worker on the finding of these specialists.[7]

But the professionalism and loyalties of a B-reader, a radiologist, pulmo-nologist, or the local practitioner sometimes can be bought by lawyers for either the defense or the plaintiff. Medical virginity is often sacrificed for the big bucks paid to physicians willing to give the desired reading of an X-ray or scan.

LIBBY IS PROSPERING IN SOME WAYS. It is now promoting itself as the City of Eagles because of the massive metal sculptures that adorn the town as well the real birds soaring above. Houses and vacation properties are sell-ing well in and around the area, real-estate agents reported in 2015, saying they were being scooped up by people other than Californians – who were known to buy anything.

The town still does little to capitalize on its natural beauty and the almost limitless opportunity for fishing, hunting, hiking, kayaking and other out-door activities. So the stream of travelers along Route 2 pretty much stops only for gas and fast food, then speeds out east to Glacier or north to Canada, missing out on the Libby Café's magical huckleberry flapjacks.

AT THE BEGINNING OF 2016, Gayla Benefield was still tracking the dev-astation caused by the Libby asbestos by tallying the dead and dying in her own extended family.

"Fifteen have been killed by the disease and 35 others have been sickened by that damn asbestos, and others are going for more exams soon," she told Schneider. Among those claimed by Libby's asbestos was Gayla's husband, David.

When the *Seattle Post-Intelligencer* first reported on Libby, most people in the town had no idea that the person next door also had asbestos disease. They kept it secret; didn't want to talk about it. They rarely, if ever, took their oxygen tanks with them, so they didn't go out much.

"Now it's different. No one is embarrassed," Gayla said. "They drag or carry their tanks with them everywhere, and it's not uncommon to stop in an aisle in the grocery or at the post office and gush over what a nice, compact O2 system the other person is carrying, just like you might talk about a new golf club someone had."

The secrecy over what was killing the town is gone, she said.

"Today, everyone knows what happened, what causes the sickness and death, what to look for and what to medically do about it," she said.

IN JANUARY 2016, MORE THAN SIX YEARS after the trial of Grace and its leaders, Libby veterans Aubrey Miller, Chris Weis and Paul Peronard were still questioning the failure of EPA and other federal health agencies to do anything meaningful to protect the millions still being exposed to Libby asbestos.

Peronard continued to lead emergency assaults on toxic disasters and Miller and Weis were both senior advisors to Linda Birnbaum, the director of the National Institute of Environmental Health Sciences – Miller for medicine and Weis for toxicology.

The three were still circumspect about what they're up to, but those who work with them said they continue to zealously battle government bureaucracy and corporate corruption on behalf of public health.

These men were the first feds sent to figure out what was happening in Libby. After just weeks on the job, they discovered their own agency had documented the dangers to Libby, its miners and people across the country 15 years earlier. Yet the agency had done nothing to shut down the mine nor the hundreds of Zonolite processing plants across North America.

They worry that it will happen again.

"After spending all that time watching the people in Libby suffer horrible, slow deaths from exposure to this fiber, it's painful, really difficult for me and others who worked this cleanup, to know that we're not doing enough to educate those across the country who face the same fate and don't know it," said Peronard.

What makes EPA's official apathy even more inexcusable to them and other health experts is that the agency is ignoring both the detailed scientific proof from Drs. Whitehouse and Lockey and its own, hard-fought scientific research for the IRIS, all of which show that the asbestos from Libby is far more deadly than any other asbestos fiber yet identified.

In January 2016, the media office at EPA headquarters declined to comment when Schneider asked whether the current administrator, Gina McCarthy, or any other headquarters official had made public comments on dangers posed nationally by exposure to vermiculite from Libby.

When asked after all these years what they've done to alert the public, all EPA officials did was refer Schneider to the vermiculite page on the agency's website.[8]

Greg Meeker, the former USGS geologist and mineralogist who fought so hard to help the public health community understand the peculiar characteristics of Libby's asbestos, still wonders why the federal government has yet to include the killer fiber in its list of regulated asbestos minerals.

SOME THINGS INVOLVING LIBBY have changed. O.M. Scott now calls itself Scotts. Grace dropped the W.R. from its name.

Makenna, Les and Norita Skramstad's red-haired granddaughter, whom Schneider last saw as a 10-year-old, laying a red rose on Les's coffin, has graduated from high school.

Dr. Stephen Levin, the medical director of the Mount Sinai Irving Selikoff Center, the first expert to pronounce that what he saw in Libby "is not your grandfather's asbestos-related disease," died in 2012.

Judge Donald Molloy took senior status in August 2011. As of January 2016, the cantankerous jurist was still on the federal bench and still garnering headlines. Neither Molloy nor any of the jurors in Grace's criminal trial ever replied to Schneider's requests for an interview.

Schneider's co-author and friend David McCumber, while running Hearst Newspapers' Washington bureau, took another look at the status of the efforts to ban asbestos in this country.

He wrote about EPA Administrator McCarthy telling a group at Georgetown University how much her agency had accomplished in its four decades of existence.

"In the '60s, our rivers were burning, future Superfund sites were popping up all over, smokestacks were spewing black soot, and cars were fueled by leaded gasoline," McCumber reported her saying. "We have tackled our environmental challenges in ways that sparked American ingenuity."

McCumber wrote that the one thing the EPA boss didn't mention in the 2014 speech was that it is legal today to import, manufacture and sell asbestos and products containing it – just as it was at the creation of the EPA in 1970. And asbestos-containing material remains in millions of U.S. homes.

In October 2007, with great fanfare, the U.S. Senate unanimously passed Washington Sen. Patty Murray's Ban Asbestos in America Act.

The bill originally imposed a total ban on asbestos, and that's the version that the public health experts supported in their testimony.

For years, Murray fought to get her colleagues in the Senate to join the rest of the modernized world and outlaw the lethal fibers. People were dying by the thousands, and deaths in a new generation might be prevented. But industry and the Bush White House didn't want the U.S. to follow the 50 other countries that forbid or restrict the importation, use and sale of asbestos. Lobbyists for America's largest industries swarmed over Capitol Hill, called in IOUs and dumped millions of dollars to fight the ban.

Even so, Murray and her co-sponsor, fellow Democratic Sen. Barbara Boxer of California, thought they had it in the bag. But sometime between much cheering for the restrictions in the final hearings and the vote in the Senate, where the legislation passed overwhelmingly, it was watered down to useless.

Many asbestos-containing products weren't banned at all. Changes to the fine print gutted the protection from the legislation and gave industry an open door to continue using the toxic material. Murray, who privately told some who testified for her bill that she was genuinely shocked by the alterations, has never agreed to talk publicly about what happened.

"The human cost of congressional inaction is reprehensible," said Linda Reinstein, the co-founder and president of the Asbestos Disease Awareness

Organization. Reinstein, whose husband died after an agonizing three-year battle with mesothelioma, said more than 50,000 people are supporting or following her educational organization.

"Seven ban-asbestos bills have been introduced, but none have passed both chambers," she said. "The environmental disaster in Libby, Montana, should have been a significant wake-up call for Congress, but instead, lawmakers fall prey to the pro-asbestos trade associations who lobby for inaction."

IT'S CALLED THE ZONOLITE ATTIC INSULATION TRUST. Some call it a gift for Grace. Others say it's an enormous payday for lawyers. But no one thinks it's a panacea for people whose homes and businesses are contaminated with Zonolite, the vermiculite insulation mined in Libby and laced with deadly asbestos fibers.

For those homeowners who know they have Zonolite in their homes or businesses, the trust is a way to get a small amount of cleanup money from Grace.

The trust was spawned in 2004 by three lawyers who had ramrodded efforts to bring class action suits against Grace on behalf of an estimated 120,000 households with Zonolite insulation. But because Grace entered Chapter 11 bankruptcy in 2001, the suits were blocked.[9]

It took ten years for Grace's complex, multi-faceted bankruptcy to be settled. In February 2014, the bankruptcy court signed off on two Grace-funded trusts to provide compensation to thousands of people harmed by the company's products.[10]

By the end of its 20-year life span, the Zonolite trust could have as much as $140 million to distribute, minus 25 percent (or $35 million) for lawyers' fees and operating expenses, said Ed Cottingham, who runs the trust.[11]

Lawyers for Zonolite victims – in Libby and elsewhere – said the $140 million is a fraction of what Grace might have been forced to pay out had the bankruptcy and creation of the trusts not prevented individuals or their survivors from suing the corporate giant.

By the beginning of 2016, Cottingham said, 794 claims had been settled for a total payout of $2,597,409.

The trust will pay up to $4,125 for cleanup costs and replacement insulation. But interviews with 15 asbestos abatement firms across the U.S. found the actual cost of properly removing asbestos from a typical, three-bedroom home can range from $8,700 to more than $46,000.

Cottingham said there are many reasons Grace agreed to pay just a portion of the cleanup cost. "In short, it was the best that could be achieved," the trustee said.

The majority of those who filed claims were on the initial list of class action claimants. Cottingham said he is trying hard to pass the word of the danger from Zonolite to others but is "not having much luck."

For example, he said, the trust mailed information to the leaders of each state's real estate association and no one responded.

"Unfortunately, those folks don't seem particularly interested in hearing about things that might gum up a sale. It's like they don't want to hear the 'A word,'" Cottingham said.

He showed Schneider an extensive list of other organizations – government and private – that he contacted about the available money. Out of the scores of groups, only three replied.

Of course, as experts keep saying, the multitude who live with contamination from Zonolite don't know it.

The trust's funds would serve more people if it advertised the hazard in major media outlets across the country. That's what EPA said it would do a decade or so ago.

"If the government doesn't have the stomach or resources to remove Zonolite from the millions of homes across the country you could at least educate people about it, make them aware that they may be living with the dangerous material," Peronard said.

THE OTHER TRUST THAT CAME from the settlement of Grace's bankruptcy is for past and future personal injury claims. The spokesperson for that trust said the designers of the trust believe more than 500,000 people may be eligible to file a claim for injury or death.[12]

Lawyers representing injury claimants said the trust will pay settlements of only $180,000 for mesothelioma down to $2,500 for asbestosis, a fraction of the settlements that cases against Grace which have gone to court have received. But as with the attic insulation trust, bankruptcy action prevents injured parties from suing Grace.

KEVEN MCDERMOTT SPENT YEARS on EPA's front lines listening to many in the Pacific Northwest who lived or worked with asbestos-contaminated vermiculite. Now retired, she vividly remembers the pain these people lived with.

"I heard mothers weeping because they felt their babies were doomed, fathers raging that the homes they worked so long and hard to buy were filled with an invisible poison.

"What troubles me most is the uncertainty and dread that haunts their lives to this day," she said. "Every cough or chest cold brings the old fear. Has the asbestos finally worked its evil magic, quietly destroying their lungs?"

The still-fiery activist Gayla Benefield said she hears from people frightened about living with Zonolite:

"I still get calls from strangers who saw my name somewhere and said they had just put an exhaust fan or some cable in their attic and saw a Zonolite label on some of the bags. They ask if their family member or friend died or got sick because they had that stuff in their house."

She and McDermott share similar concerns about the government's inaction.

"There is not a reason in the world why the government shouldn't warn them, really tell them what to look for and help them understand what might be making them sick. They deserve to be told what may be in store for them, and it isn't pretty.

"Suffocation is a horrible way to die so we can only pray for quick death," Gayla said.

THE EPA'S CLEANUP NEGLIGENCE goes beyond contaminated homes and businesses.

Grace shipped billions of pounds of its contaminated ore from Libby to more than 700 sites in 40 states. The EPA was concerned enough about the potential danger at 266 of Grace's former vermiculite processing plants to order its 10 regions to conduct extensive inspections. Some conscientious regional inspectors analyzed soil and dust samples from every location they could find. Many others did little more than what were called "dashboard inspections," never getting out of their cars as they drove by the sites. In some states, they did nothing.

And even the properly done inspections "were flawed," the Government Accountability Office reported in 2009 after studying EPA findings. The investigators for Congress concluded that EPA may not have identified the actual hazard of the sites because the agency "did not adequately understand the toxicity of the asbestos in the Libby ore" and needed to use more accurate sampling methods.[13]

Processing plants were using ore that contained as much as 26 percent asbestos, an enormously unsafe concentration by anyone's calculations. Yet the Congressional Research Service found that in most cases, EPA didn't warn state or local health officials of the potential risks.

The GAO investigators concluded that "any facilities processing Libby ore which previously were inspected may not be safe."

Alarmingly, this analysis was made long before the EPA issued the IRIS and before the landmark studies by Whitehouse and Lockey. Yet, EPA has not ordered additional inspections.

LOOKING BACK AT ALL THOSE WHO SUFFERED and died from exposure to Libby's asbestos, it's obvious that most of them didn't have to pay that horrible price.

Of course, Grace bears much of the blame for those unnecessary deaths. But it's equally clear that if federal or Montana health or worker-safety authorities were doing their jobs, far fewer lives would have been lost – or would be lost in the future.

Bureaucrats in the EPA admitted being terrified at the estimated billions of dollars needed for a cleanup of the millions of homes that are still dangerous. But warning the property owners by radio, television and newspaper and fliers at hardware and home improvement stores was estimated by the agency to cost, at most, $410,000 – pennies a home.

Still, nothing has been done. And Peronard, Weis and Miller fear that EPA leadership will once again look away as thousands die preventable deaths.

In 2016, Schneider asked EPA's press office in Washington again for a statement on why the agency wasn't doing more to warn the millions who have Zonolite in their homes. Was EPA at all worried about the thousands of additional deaths that are predicted to come from that exposure?

The press spokeswoman, whom he's known and respected for years, said, "I'll take your queries," which is Washingtonese for "Don't hold your breath."

Gayla stops by Les' grave often, and she says she hopes her former activist partner is resting peacefully. "The battle against Grace is over and all that's left for Libby is the dying." (Andrew Schneider)

If You've Encountered Zonolite

WHAT SHOULD YOU DO if you know, or believe, that you're living or working with Zonolite?

Answers aren't easy to come by – at least, answers that reflect the full scope and severity of the problem. The EPA and other government bodies dangerously rely on informational websites alone to warn millions of home-owners and businesses – and the cable installers and renovators working in those structures – of the hidden hazard that may exist. At the time this book was published, some of those inadequate government websites had not been updated in years – and, more disturbingly, none addressed what we now know about Zonolite's high level of toxicity, proven by Drs. Alan White-house and James Lockey.

Having said that, if you know or believe Zonolite is present, some of these websites may serve as a starting point by providing a limited amount of useful information about how to protect yourself, and how to identify and deal with the toxic substance.

"Protect Your Family from Asbestos-Contaminated Vermiculite Insulation"
http://www.epa.gov/asbestos/protect-your-family-asbestos-contami-nated-vermiculite-insulation

"NIOSH Recommendations for Limiting Potential Exposures of Workers to Asbestos Associated with Vermiculite from Libby, Montana"
http://www.cdc.gov/niosh/docs/2003-141/default.html

"ATSDR's fact sheet on vermiculite consumer products"
http://www.atsdr.cdc.gov/asbestos/vermiculite051603.pdf

Libby Vermiculite Insulation: A Guide for Homeowners, Homebuyers, Home Inspectors, Real Estate Professionals, Residential Contractors and Tradespersons
http://www.amazon.com/Libby-Vermiculite-Insulation-Professionals-Tradespersons-ebook/dp/B00LNEO4PO
Reviews are mixed on this short Kindle book by Daniel Erwin, but like the government websites, you should know it exists.

Source Notes

Prologue:

1. The federal government ... Schneider's interviews with Les Skramstad and Gayla Benefield. Unless noted otherwise, all of Les Skramstad's and Gayla Benefield's comments are from Schneider's and McCumber's interviews with them between September 1999 and the present; and September 1999 to September 2003 research and interviews for 173 stories published in the *Seattle Post-Intelligencer* and the St. Louis *Post-Dispatch*.

2. On this day ... Re-creation of 2001 Memorial Day ceremony from interviews by McCumber with participants and review of videotapes of the event.

3. Undertaker ... Lyrics from "Will the Circle Be Unbroken," a Pentecostal hymn written in 1907 and updated and recorded in 1935 by the Maybelle Carter family as "Can the Circle Be Unbroken." In 1972, it was featured on bluegrass music's first million-selling album in a version by the Nitty Gritty Dirt Band.

Chapter 1:

1. A man who has fallen ... Scenes throughout this chapter that describe the EPA team receiving the order to go to Libby are based on Schneider's interviews with Paul and Tracy Peronard, Aubrey Miller, Chris Weis, Wendy Thomi and Bill Yellowtail.

2. Environmental reporter Robert ... Discussion with *Seattle Post-Intelligencer* reporter Robert McClure about the Montana Environmental Information Center's concerns about possible problems at Libby based on notes and Schneider's recollections.

3. The law offices ... Schneider's interview with Kalispell lawyer Roger Sullivan.

4. She waved a document ... September 1999 Montana Department of Environmental Quality report on Grace's restoration of the Zonolite Mountain.

5. She saw a legal ... September 1999 legal notice in *The Western News* on returning the balance of Grace's reclamation bond to the company.

6. What was really bothering ... June 12, 1992. *The Western News,* a short article on three suits being filed against Grace by the families of three miners.

7. "Ah, what the hell ... " Sept., Oct., Nov. 1999. Schneider's discussions on asbestos-testing methods with Keven McDermott and Armina Noland from EPA's Region 10 office.

8. A reporter trying ... Schneider's interviews with physicians or their nurses who had treated Montana asbestos victims in hospitals or clinics in Denver, Salt Lake City, Portland, Seattle, Boise and Spokane.

9. Scanning the numbers ... Oct., Nov., Dec. 1999. Schneider and McCumber's discussions with J. D. Alexander, former publisher of the *Seattle Post-Intelligencer,* about the scope of the stories and the cost of testing material for asbestos.

10. "KTNY Libby ..." August 1972. "All I Need Is the Air That I Breathe," The Hollies.

11. Carrie Detrick leaned ... Sept., Oct., Nov. 1999. Schneider's interviews with Carrie Detrick.

12. Art Bundrock worked ... Oct., Nov. 1999. Schneider's interviews with Helen Bundrock.

13. Post-it Notes ... 162 death certificates of Libby miners and family members.

14. He was stunned ... Oct., Nov. 1999. Schneider's interviews with John Wardell, EPA's Montana representative, on why he did nothing about the Libby miners.

Chapter 2:

1. Peronard and his team ... December 1999. Schneider's interviews with P. Peronard, C. Weis and A. Miller on their first tour of Zonolite Mountain and an interview with Grace's Libby representative, Alan Stringer.

2. It was the summer ... Schneider and McCumber compiled the history of Zonolite Mountain and the beginning of Edgar Alley's vermiculite operation from stories and advertisements in *The Western News,* material from the Libby museum, county historical society and personal collections covering the period of January 1918 to December 1959.

3. Montana, like most of the West ... The information on the geologic history of western Montana and the formation of Zonolite Mountain came from research of USGS reports and academic studies compiled by Kathleen Best and from interviews with noted geologist Art Montana, retired chairman of the Department of Earth and Space Science at UCLA.

Chapter 3:

1. She was still seething ... The "Libby Team's" first meeting with Gayla, Les and Norita was re-created from interviews with the participants and EPA notes on the meeting.

2. Gayla went back ... "alpha list." W.R. Grace, April 11, 1986. A 38-page, single-spaced list of every Zonolite Mountain miner, manager and employee, their employment history and a calculation of their exposure to tremolite asbestos.

3. *From the time ...* McCumber compiled the history of Perley and Margaret Vatland from interviews with G. Benefield.

Chapter 4:

1. *Peronard didn't know ...* May 7, 1999, deposition of Dr. A. Whitehouse for use in suits against Grace and discussing the scope of disease he found in Libby.

2. *Miller, aged 40, liked the mountains....* Schneider's interviews with Dr. A. Miller on his background, training and how he joined the U.S. Public Health Service.

3. *Whitehouse's office ...* Schneider re-created Miller's first meeting with Whitehouse from interviews with the participants.

4. *Les Skramstad came highballing ...* Schneider and McCumber interviewed L. Skramstad on his work at the mine and how he found out he had asbestosis. Also used court documents and depositions prepared for his case against Grace.

Chapter 5:

1. *Asbestos has been known ...* Source material for history of asbestos included documents and studies obtained from the National Medical Library at the National Institutes of Health, the National Archives and the files of the Congressional Research Service.

2. *In Italy, ... Asbestos: Medical and Legal Aspects, 4th edition,* by Barry I. Castleman, Aspen Law and Business, Englewood Cliffs, N.J., 1996.

3. *Paul Brodeur ...* From *Outrageous Misconduct: The Asbestos Industry on Trial,* by Paul Brodeur. Pantheon Books: New York, 1985.

4. *Other court documents ...* Schneider's interview with Dr. David Egilman on his collection of asbestos-industry corporate documents and his experience in testifying against corporations accused of knowingly harming their workers.

Chapter 6:

1. *Peronard, Weis, Gayla and Les ...* December 1999. Schneider's observations of P. Peronard, G. Benefield and L. Skramstad on tour of contamination in Libby.

2. *On August 8, 1956 ...* Aug. 8, 1956; Jan. 12, 1959; June 7, 1960; April 19, 1962; April 11, 1963; and May 11, 1964, inspection reports of vermiculite mine in Libby by Benjamin Wake, industrial hygiene engineer from Montana State Board of Health.

3. Wake's frustration ... April 13, 1964, letter from Montana industrial hygiene engineer B. Wake to union officer Art Bundrock.

4. It's not as though ... July 20, 1959, confidential study of X-rays sent to E. Lovick showing that 92 percent of Libby's senior workers have lung disease.

5. Earl Lovick was a tough-minded, ... E. Lovick's background obtained from court documents, *Western News* articles and depositions.

6. In a letter to ... June 14, 1961, letter from Lovick to C. A. Pratt, president of Western Mineral Company in Minneapolis, admitting, "There is a relatively large amount of asbestos dust in our mill and this is difficult to control."

7. But in December 1962, ... December 1962 memo from Lovick to Kelley at Grace headquarters on disruption to vermiculite production caused by the company's order to mine asbestos from Libby and develop new uses for the material.

8. In 1965, ... Grace memo on air monitoring in Libby citing volume of asbestos-laden dust generated by the mine.

9. The year before ... December 16, 1969, Maryland Casualty Company letter to Grace warning that failure to notify workers of their illness is "not humane and in direct violation of federal law."

10. Indeed, the company continued ... June 24, 1969, report from R. M. Vining, president of Grace Construction Products Group, to J. Peter Grace; and October 1969, "Confidential Study of Zonolite/Libby Employees."

11. Perley's health, though, was ... August 31, 1973, letter from E. Lovick to Grace headquarters about P. Vatland's illness and compensation claim.

12. Four years after ... December 28, 1973, Montana Workman's Compensation form on P. Vatland.

Chapter 7:

1. They were in Yellowtail's . .. December 19, 1999, Libby team's meeting with EPA Regional Administrator Bill Yellowtail re-created by Schneider's interviews with participants and review of EPA meeting notes.

2. But ATSDR was worried.... January 27, 2000, ATSDR e-mail from Susan Muza, Denver, to Dr. Jeffrey Lybarger, Atlanta.

3. Irving Selikoff was born ... History of Dr. Irving Selikoff from library of Mount Sinai School of Medicine in Brooklyn.

4. In April 1964, ... "Asbestos Exposure and Neoplasia" by Irving Selikoff, in the *Journal of the American Medical Association,* April 1964. One of the first articles to link cancer to environmental causes.

5. While they denounced his work ... November 22, 1969, Grace memo from H.

A. Brown, vice president of Grace's Construction Products Division, to R. M. Vining about Selikoff becoming interested in illness at Libby's mine and Grace memo on Selikoff from T. F. Egan to R. W Starrett.

6. One might expect ... Asbestos: Medical and Legal Aspects, 4th edition, by Barry I. Castleman, Aspen Law and Business: Englewood Cliffs, N.J., 1996.

7. Dr. Michael Harbut ... Interviews by Schneider and Carol Smith of Dr. Michael Harbut.

8. Dr. David Egilman ... Schneider's interviews with David Egilman.

Chapter 8:

1. Almost 600 people ... December 1999. Schneider's interviews and observations of the Libby team at the first public meeting after the *Seattle Post-Intelligencer's* initial Libby stories were published.

2. Gayla stood up ... December 1999. G. Benefield's comments to audience on the contamination that still existed on the mine site.

3. "Alice Priest was left ..." Schneider's interviews with lawyer R. Sullivan.

4. The companies were very savvy ... E. Lovick's comments on Libby's physicians from court transcripts.

5. Richard Irons was ... Schneider's interviews with Dr. Richard Irons about his efforts to get Grace to permit him to test miners for asbestos-related disease and the company's efforts to discredit him.

6. Alan Whitehouse remembers ... Schneider's interviews with Drs. Brad Black and A. Whitehouse about Irons.

7. Soon Alan Whitehouse became ... Schneider's interviews with A. Whitehouse on his history of diagnosing and treating patients from Libby.

Chapter 9:

1. W.R. Grace & Company ... History on Grace from company records and documents, the National Archives and Asbestos: Medical and Legal Aspects, 4th edition, by Barry Castleman, Aspen Law and Business: Englewood Cliffs, N.J., 1996; and Merchant Adventurer: The Story of W.R. Grace, by Marquis James, Scholarly Resources, 1993.

Chapter 10:

1. "This is a case about asbestosis ..." May 13–21, 1997, trial transcript, "Lester and Norita Skramstad vs. W.R. Grace," District Court of the Nineteenth Judicial District for the State of Montana In and For the County of Lincoln.

2. Heberling, in his early 50s, ... Schneider's interviews with Kalispell lawyer Jon Heberling.

Chapter 11:

1. Bill Daniels, ... Schneider's interviews with A. Miller, P. Peronard and C. Weis on the discovery of cases of deaths and illnesses from Zonolite exposure elsewhere in the country.

2. Daniels found a five-year-old article ... Srebro, S. and Roggli, V. "Asbestos-related Disease Associated with Exposure to Asbestiform Tremolite," *American Journal of Industrial Medicine,* 1994.

3. A Minnesota lawyer ... Schneider's interview with Izzi, Justin and Katherine Jorgensen, 2001, 2002, 2003.

4. Arnie Joireman, one of ... Schneider's interview with L. Joireman's brother Arnie.

5. The shipment of lethal ore ... October 2002, tally of Grace Zonolite shipments collected by EPA and the Justice Department. Those who evaluated the data believe it represents only about 70 percent of the total shipments.

6. That year, the health ... October 21, 1964, letter from Dr. H. Siemons, director of Alberta's division of industrial health, questioning whether Grace had reports of illness at other expansion plants.

7. The next year, ... December 8, 1968, letter from N. F. Bushell, Grace's manager in Vancouver, to Grace headquarters about a worker at their Winnipeg plant having asbestosis.

8. Also in 1964, ... April 1, 1964, letter from Dr. W. E. Park of the Minneapolis Health Department writing to Grace vice president C. A. Pratt about the death of a worker renewing his interest in the danger from asbestos in vermiculite.

9. When they exchanged letters ... June 14, 1961, letter from E. Lovick to C. A. Pratt of Western Mineral on the presence of asbestos in Zonolite.

10. That is the recollection ... Schneider's interview with Arland Blanton, former manager of the Zonolite plant in Little Rock, Arkansas.

11. Robert Junker was the treasurer ... Deposition of Robert Junker, October 23, 1991.

12. "It would take two men ... " 1991, trial transcript of Floyd Gebert, general manager of the Robinson Insulation plant in Great Falls, Montana.

13. Edward Moody, ... Schneider's interview with Little Rock lawyer Edward Moody.

14. "It is safe to say ... " November 1, 1971, letter from F. W. Easton, from

Zonolite plant in Weedsport, N.Y., to his superiors about state inspectors finding health violations at a plant processing Zonolite.

15. In August 1971, ... Letter from manager of Zonolite plant in San Francisco area about dust in plant, August 1971.

16. Sunday, September 24, 1995, ... Sept. 24 to Oct. 28, 1995, diary of Lee Joireman of his last weeks before he died.

Chapter 12:

1. Peronard knew one thing for sure ... P. Peronard's recollections on cleaning contamination from Libby and Zonolite Mountain from Schneider's interviews.

2. Owens understood the logic ... Schneider's interview with Mark Owens of Kootenai Development Corporation.

3. EPA's elation ... Discussion on Grace kicking EPA off Zonolite Mountain from Schneider's interviews with P. Peronard and M. Cohn.

4. "The EPA and its representatives, ..." July 18, 2000, letter from Grace lawyer David Cleary to Matt Cohn barring EPA from Zonolite Mountain and other Grace properties.

5. Kelcey Land, EPA's cost-recovery ... July 19, 2000, Consent for Access to Property letter to Grace lawyer D. Cleary from EPA enforcement specialist Kelcey Land.

6. A day later, Grace's ... July 20, 2000, letter from Grace lawyer Kenneth Lund to M. Cohn on paying for access and dumping privileges.

7. Through the summer ... August 3, 2000, letter from U.S. Justice Department attorney James Freeman to Grace requesting the company to permit EPA to return contaminated waste to the mine.

8. On March 9, 2001, ... Ruling by Chief Judge Donald Molloy, U.S. District Court, Missoula, Montana, on March 9, 2001.

9. On May 24, 1977, ... "Confidential" detailed memo from Grace executive Chip Wood to C. N. Graf, chief operating officer for Grace, on May 24, 1977, discussing the company's problems with tremolite.

10. There is no shortage ... November 26, 1980, Grace memo from R. H. Locke on how to thwart NIOSH's proposed study of miners' health at Libby operation.

11. After the demolition, ... Schneider's interviews with P. Peronard, M. Cohn, K. Land, A. Stringer, William Corcoran and others.

12. "A viable use ..." A. Stringer's remarks on government regulations forcing the closing of the mine from Schneider's interviews and stories in *The Western News*.

Chapter 13:

1. *"Don't even joke about it,"* ... Discovery of the existence of earlier EPA reports on dangers at Libby and of vermiculite re-created through Schneider's interviews with P. Peronard, C. Weis and A. Miller.

2. *But the only things* ... "Priority Review Level 1 Report — Asbestos Contaminated Vermiculite," USEPA, June 1980; MRI-82 Report, "Collection, Analysis and Characterization of Vermiculite Samples," USEPA, September 1982; "Exposure Assessment for Asbestos-Contaminated Vermiculite," USEPA, February 1985; "Health Assessment Document for Vermiculite," USEPA, September 1991.

3. *So on May 26, 2000,* ... June 1, 2000, *Bozeman Daily Chronicle,* story of C. Weis's speech to conference of environmental journalists by Scott McMillion.

4. *Weis was oblivious* ... Re-creation of C. Weis being threatened by headquarters for remarks at a conference from Schneider's interviews with C. Weis, P. Peronard and e-mail from headquarters.

5. *Within hours* ... June 1, 2000, e-mail from David Cohen in EPA headquarters to top EPA personnel laying out instructions of how to respond to the findings of the early reports.

6. *In February 1982,* ... President Ronald Reagan naming J. Peter Grace to head what became known as the Grace Commission, Reagan Presidential Papers and White House records at the National Archives.

7. *In January 1984,* ... Speech by J. Peter Grace on the Grace Commission, the National Archives.

8. *The watchdog group* ... August 1985, "Deceiving the Public: The Story Behind J. Peter Grace and His Campaign," a 110-page report by Public Citizen, Washington.

9. *William Ruckelshaus, who was* ... December 2002. Schneider's interviews with William Ruckelshaus, former EPA administrator.

10. *Ruckelshaus questioned the* ... December 2002. Schneider's interviews with W. Ruckelshaus.

11. *On June 27, 2000,* ... Letter to EPA's inspector general, Nikki Tinsley, from Tim Fields, Jr., Susan Wayland and Rebecca Hanmer requesting an IG investigation on whether or not EPA dropped the ball in the earlier Libby studies.

12. *It was signed by* ... April 28, 2000, memo from U.S. Office of Special Counsel about not pursuing Hatch Act violation against Bill Yellowtail in return for the Region 8 administrator accepting a 100-day suspension without pay.

13. Dodson started weekly ... Schneider's interviews with P. Peronard, C. Weis, A. Miller, M. Cohn, Max Dodson and members of EPAs national press staff.

14. The battle continued ... June 2001 series of e-mails between P. Peronard and John Melone.

Chapter 14:

1. Of course, she said no.... Schneider's interviews with R. Sullivan, J. Heberling and G. Benefield about settlement offers from Grace and jury findings.

2. The physician had been ... Schneider's interviews with the Skramstads and Dr. A. Whitehouse on the trip to Spokane to get Norita and the children examined for asbestos-related disease.

Chapter 15:

1. During the 1960s, '70s ... EPA, OSHA, NIOSH and MSHA documents on definitions of asbestos and Public Docket filings on the same issue from the agencies and Congressional Research Service.

2. Contractors for the EPA ... February 2000. Schneider's observations of EPA contractors collecting samples in Libby.

3. As would become his habit, ... March 2000. Schneider's observations of P. Peronard and C. Weis telling Libby group about frustrations with testing and government asbestos regulations.

4. Well past midnight, ... June 7, 1973, memo from Grace scientist Julie Yang about tremolite-analyzing techniques.

5. New USGS technology ... Schneider's interviews with C. Weis, A. Miller and USGS staff in Denver on how new NASA equipment could help in finding asbestos in Libby.

6. "EPA does have methods ... " Comments from Grace's spokesman on EPA using new methods of analysis, July 22, 2000, *The New York Times*.

7. R. J. Lee, ... April 2000 R. J. Lee memo for W.R. Grace to EPA.

8. On January 18, 2001, ... Letter from Grace VP W. Corcoran to Steven Herman, EPA's assistant administrator for enforcement.

9. Michael Beard, ... USGS Meeting, Michael Beard's comments from tape of conference, confirmed to Schneider by Beard.

10. But finally the anger ... "European Communities — Measures Affecting Asbestos and Products Containing Asbestos," May 28, 1999, EPA for the White House.

11. Melone was adamant ... March 29, 2000, e-mail from Arnold Den, EPA

Region 9, to Tom Simons, EPA HQ, on a decade of handling tremolite in California.

12. *In a March 30, 2000, ...* E-mail from J. Melone, EPA HQ, to T. Simons, EPA HQ, on WTO White Paper.

13. *The February 11, 2000, ...* Story in the *Seattle Post-Intelligencer* on asbestos ban, by Schneider and C. Smith, page A-1.

14. *Common sense said ...* March 5, 2001, *The Wall Street Journal,* Page A-1: "Banned in the 1970s by federal regulators, asbestos has spawned more lawsuits than any other product in the history of personal-injury litigation"; and May 28, 2002, *The Wall Street Journal,* page A-4, "Asbestos Makers, Litigants: Uneasy Allies": "The insulation fiber was banned as a carcinogen more than two decades ago, but claims continue to mount."

15. *William Ruckelshaus ...* December 2002, Schneider's interview with W. Ruckelshaus.

16. *When Chuck Elkins ...* Schneider's interview with Chuck Elkins, former head of EPA Office of Toxic Substances.

17. *On February 6, 1992, ...* Letter from EPA's general counsel to the Justice Department requesting them to appeal the overturning of the ban to the U.S. Supreme Court.

18. *"Look back over the decades...."* Schneider's interview with Dr. Richard Lemen, former deputy director of NIOSH, on industry's efforts to block the regulation of asbestos.

19. *"People knew about ..."* Schneider's interview with Neil Pflum, EPA Region 5, who was testing building materials for asbestos.

20. *"Asbestos was not banned," ...* July 31, 2001, testimony by U.S. Senator Patty Murray on "Asbestos Exposure and Workplace Safety."

Chapter 16:

1. *For months after ...* Recollections of conversations between Schneider, McCumber and Smith about calls and e-mail from throughout the country from people whose loved ones died after exposure to vermiculite from Libby.

2. *Two days later, ...* Lab/Cor test results on garden products for the *Seattle Post-Intelligencer.*

3. *Schneider called Grace....* Schneider's interview with W. Corcoran, Grace's vice president of public and regulatory affairs.

4. *"I'm sure it's not ours, ..."* Schneider's interviews with K. McDermott, Bill Dunbar and Chuck Findley, Region 10's deputy administrator, on how they

handled their findings of asbestos in the vermiculite they tested.

5. *"What the hell did you do ..."* Schneider's interviews and e-mail from EPA headquarters reacting to Region 10 news conference on dangers of Zonolite.

6. *McDermott and her team ...* "Exposure Assessment for Asbestos Contaminated Vermiculite," USEPA, February 1985.

7. *"I have some serious concerns ..."* June 14, 2000, e-mail from J. Melone to K. McDermott.

8. *Tom Simons, who worked in ...* June 27, 2000, e-mail from T. Simons to K. McDermott on inspector general's investigation.

9. *The same day, ...* June 27, 2000, e-mail from EPA counsel Richard Mednick to T. Simons.

10. *"Our general benchmark ... "* Schneider's interview with Stephen Johnson, EPA's deputy assistant administrator.

11. *Robert Parks has a ...* Schneider's interviews with Robert Parks as K. McDermott checked his attic for Zonolite.

12. *Sloan issued a warning ...* Schneider's interviews with P. Peronard, A. Miller, C. Weis and U.S. assistant surgeon general Dr. Hugh Sloan on the dangers of asbestos-tainted Zonolite Attic Insulation, and August 1, 2000, letter from Sloan to Dr. Linda Rosenstock, director of NIOSH, regarding the need to warn workers about Zonolite.

13. *Grace lawyers wasted no time ...* September 1, 2000, letter from Grace general counsel David Siegel to DHHS inspector general June Gibbs Brown demanding an investigation of Sloan; letter from Siegel to NIOSH director Rosenstock, stating that facts in Sloan's letter were incorrect. Letter from Siegel to Steven Herman, EPA's assistant administrator for enforcement, complaining that the senior enforcement counsel Mathew Cohn was giving documents to lawyers suing Grace.

14. *In the May 24, 1977, ...* Internal memo to Grace senior officials from Executive Vice President E. S. Wood reported that attic insulation generated the highest levels of asbestos of all the vermiculite products tested.

15. *Christopher Ladera ...* Carol Smith's interview with attic cleaner Christopher Ladera.

16. *According to court records, ...* December 4, 1991, deposition of Edward Harashe, St. Louis plumber, who, the court ruled, died of exposure to tremolite as he installed Zonolite in his attic in the 1950s.

Chapter 17:

1. *They sat at the desk,* ... Recollection of conversations between Schneider and Carol Smith and McCumber on testing cosmetics, medical powders and crayons.

2. *Of course, children eat crayons....* Schneider's and Carol Smith's interviews with Dr. Mike Harbut and Dr. Philip Landrigan.

3. *A Consumer Product Safety* ... Schneider's interview with Ronald Medford, assistant executive director of hazard identification at the Consumer Product Safety Commission.

4. Oglesby didn't blanch .... Schneider and McCumber's discussions with Roger Oglesby, new publisher of the *Seattle Post-Intelligencer, on the heat expected from the asbestos-tainted-crayons story.*

5. *In the Post-Intelligencer's* ... Schneider's interviews with Binney & Smith (Crayola) spokesperson Tracy Muldoon Moran and with Debbie Fanning and Woodhall Stopford of the Arts and Creative Materials Institute; and Dr. Samuel Epstein of the University of Illinois Medical Center and Dr. Michael McCann of the New York Center for Safety in the Arts.

6. *"That's not the case,"* ... Lab/Cor test results on crayons and Schneider's interviews with John Harris.

7. *And then the Post-Intelligencer* ... March 2000 deposition of Richard Lee, with statements that he had testified about 275 times for asbestos industry and his company had been paid about $7 million by asbestos companies.

8. *In 1948, the Gouverneur* ... History of the Gouverneur Talc Company from company documents and publications and library at Syracuse University; and interviews with the St. Lawrence County, N.Y., Historical Society.

9. *By 1974, OSHA was* ... 1972 to 1980, OSHA rulemaking notices, *The Federal Register* and agency files.

10. *Just two weeks before he resigned* ... "Save More, Spend Less, Nixon Urges," United Press International, July 26, 1974.

11. *Nevertheless, on January 2, 1975,* ... Letter from Vanderbilt to GeorgiaPacific in Portland, Oregon, saying the company will continue marketing five grades of talc containing asbestos and the warning label that will be affixed.

12. *John Kelse, manager of Vanderbilt's* ... Schneider's interviews with John Kelse, manager of Vanderbilt's Corporate Risk Management Department.

13. *Schneider found him at home* ... Schneider's interviews with former Vanderbilt miner Herb Conklin and his wife, Margaret, with miners Charlie Minkler and Bill Fuller.

14. "It doesn't bother me ..." Schneider's interviews with Dr. Jerrold Abraham, director of environmental and occupational pathology at Upstate Medical University in Syracuse.

15. Vanderbilt was alarmed, ... 1975 government-funded study by Walter McCrone Associates in Chicago. It found tremolite asbestos in seven talc samples from the Vanderbilt mines.

16. In 1984, Institute records ... Review of NIOSH documents surrounding its investigation of agency epidemiologist John Gamble and Bob Glenn, who headed NIOSH's respiratory disease division and their involvement with Vanderbilt Talc.

17. Dr. John Dement, who ... Schneider's interview with Dr. John Dement.

18. He was eager to start his job ... Schneider's interviews with Dr. George Wineburgh and with Dr. Edward Fitzgerald, assistant director of the New York State Bureau of Environmental and Occupational Epidemiology.

Chapter 18:

1. Schneider's phone rang ... Schneider's interviews with MSHA administrator Davitt McAteer.

2. Some of the miners on the front line ... Schneider's interviews and observations of the late Minnesota senator Paul Wellstone on the lack of action on miners being exposed to asbestos in the taconite they mined.

3. "Our men are dying ... " Schneider's interviews with Dave Trach, president of LTV Steelworkers Local 4108 in Eveleth, Minnesota.

4. About 270 miles east, ... Schneider's interviews with taconite miner George Biekkola in L'Anse, Michigan.

5. Celeste Monforton convinced her boss ... Schneider's interviews with Celeste Monforton, chief of MSHA's health division.

6. MSHA's files do not show ... Schneider's interview with Carol Jones, director of MSHA's Office of Standards.

7. When McAteer took over ... Schneider's interview with former Labor Secretary Robert Reich.

8. He stopped at a convenience ... Schneider's interviews with Louisa, Virginia, lawyer Rae Ely.

9. The Ladies of Green Springs ... History of Green Springs, Virginia, from Virginia Historical Society, Green Springs Historical Society and files of the U.S. Department of the Interior.

10. Boswell's is still serving liquor ... May 1987, "Statement for Management, Green Springs Historic Landmark District," U.S. Department of Interior.

11. By 1972, the company had drilled ... 1972 letter to head of Grace's Zonolite division from company geologist Lewis Hash, who evaluated the vermiculite deposit in Green Springs as the best in the world; August 18, 1992, Preliminary Site Plan for Virginia Vermiculite Ltd.; Correspondence between U.S. Park Service and Interior Department and Commonwealth of Virginia; December 2, 1999, "Virginia Vermiculite v. W.R. Grace and Historic Green Springs," U.S. District Court for the Western District of Virginia, various briefs, motions and facts of the case.

12. But in 1976, ... Letter to Grace from then Interior Secretary Thomas Kleppe urging the company to donate the vermiculite-loaded land as a buffer around the historic homes.

13. Sansom pushed hard ... Schneider's interview with "Cowboy Poet" Steve Lucas.

14. Sansom stunned local residents ... Schneider's interview and correspondence with Robert Sansom, owner of Virginia Vermiculite, Ltd.

15. Finally, they were ready.... Schneider's interview with MSHA's Monforton, McAteer, two mine inspectors and two miners from VVL on the inspection of Sansom's mine.

16. On July 31, 2001, ... July 31, 2001, transcript of hearing of the U. S. Senate Committee on Health, Education, Labor and Pensions, testimony of Virginia vermiculite miner David Pinter.

Chapter 19:

1. It had been two months ... Schneider's interviews with EPA and Labor Department inspectors general and members of their staffs, including Patricia Dalton, acting IG for Labor Department, and Frances Tafer, who headed EPA's IG team.

2. "This is what it's all about...." Schneider's observations of inspectors general staff questioning people in Libby and touring former Grace mine property.

3. Peronard was glad ... Schneider's interviews with P. Peronard, C. Weis, A. Miller and Wendy Thomi about progress of Libby cleanup.

4. On page 24 ... Schneider's interviews with P. Peronard and M. Cohn and the W.R. Grace June 2000 quarterly 10-Q report to the Securities and Exchange Commission.

5. Corcoran, Grace's VP ... Schneider's interview with Grace vice president W. Corcoran.

6. On April 18, 2000, ... Letter from M. Cohn to Grace lawyer Kenneth Lund.

7. He, Miller and Weis ... June 6, 2000, memo from Larry Reed, acting director of EPA's Office of Emergency and Remedial Response, to Superfund National Policy Managers presenting details of how old Grace expansion plants should be examined.

8. He called Tracy ... July 11, 2003. Schneider's interview with Tracy Peronard

9. EPA's inspector general ... March 31, 2001, "EPA's Actions Concerning Asbestos-Contaminated Vermiculite in Libby, Montana," Office of Inspector General, USEPA.

10. The shortcomings ... March 22, 2001, "Evaluation of MSHA's Handling of Inspections at the W.R. Grace & Company Mine in Libby, Montana," Office of Inspector General, Department of Labor.

11. When the report came out ... July 2, 2003, e-mail from MSHA to authors on status of IG recommendations.

Chapter 20:

1. Just as the general public ... Schneider and Carol Smith's interviews of 143 auto repair shop owners, managers and mechanics.

2. Schneider and Smith did ... Test results of brakes and brake shop dust sampling collected by the Seattle Post-Intelligencer and analyzed by Lab/Cor.

3. Bill Rice is 60, ... Schneider and Smith's interviews with Seattle mechanic Bill Rice.

4. In the 1970s and '80s ... Schneider's review of documents from the Public Dockets and EPA, OSHA and the U.S. Public Health Service on early efforts to get automobile manufacturers to remove asbestos from brakes; interview with Steven Johnson, then EPA's deputy assistant administrator, on history of EPA's asbestos-awareness programs for auto mechanics and students and the frustration of having automotive makers back out at the last minute of agreements to end the use of asbestos in their products.

5. "We don't know how many cars ..." Schneider's interview with Peter Infante, then director of OSHA's Office of Standards Review.

6. Schneider contacted six manufacturers.... Schneider's interview with Alan Morrissey, vice president of Brake Products, Inc., of McHenry, Illinois.

7. But the Asbestos Information ... Schneider's interviews with Bob Pigg, chairman of the Asbestos Information Association.

8. *In a 1993 internal* ... EPA memo over concern that scores of mom-and-pop operations are still manufacturing brakes with asbestos.

9. *Patrick Dennis Kine* ... Schneider and photographer Renee Byer's interviews and observations of Kine in the months before the part-time clown and former auto mechanic and teacher died of mesothelioma.

Chapter 21:

1. *The speaker list was impressive* ... Schneider's observations at "Asbestos and Public Health Conference" in Libby from September 21–23, 2000.

2. *It was almost like* ... Schneider's interviews and *The Western News* reporting on beginning of ATSDR screening.

3. *The sparring between ATSDR and EPA* ... Schneider's interviews with Sharon Campolucci, deputy director of ATSDR's Division of Health Studies.

4. *EPA paid for an ad* ... Advertisement in the *Elko Daily Free Press* for the government-run asbestos screening.

5. *"Paul's got to have that money...."* Schneider's interview of P. Peronard, G. Benefield and Senator Max Baucus's staff to re-create his telephone call to EPA's Tim Fields to get more money to pay for additional medical screening.

6. *"Detailed knowledge of their work ..."* Schneider's observations and interviews with P. Peronard, A. Miller and C. Weis about the danger from the tainted vermiculite to the next generation in Libby.

7. *"We are not diagnosing ..."* Schneider's interview with Rick Palagi, head of St. John's Lutheran Hospital in Libby, on impact of screening on the town's medical community.

8. *It wasn't as though there was much doubt* ...   December 12, 2000, "Mortality from Asbestosis in Libby, Montana," ATSDR.

9. *"We see people who may have been exposed ..."* Schneider's interview with Dr. Henry Falk, head of ATSDR, and Kathy Skipper, the agency's chief of communications, on what the largest screening ever undertaken was doing to the agency.

10. *"Grace knew that there ..."* July 8, 1981, Grace memo from R. J. Geiger to W J. McCaig on the results of air sampling on the Libby High School running track.

11. *With her level of exposure,* ... McCumber and Schneider's interviews with G. Benefield and her husband, David, about learning they both have signs of asbestos-related disease.

Chapter 22:

1. Roger Sullivan and ... Schneider's interviews with R. Sullivan about his firm helping EPA document Grace's alleged fraudulent transfer of money to another company it owned.

2. The brief they were preparing ... Schneider's interview with EPA senior enforcement attorney M. Cohn on his dealings with Grace and his knowledge on the actions of his office and Denver's Justice Department team in chasing the transferred funds.

3. EPA wanted money ... 1998, W.R. Grace SEC report list of contaminated sites for which it was responsible.

4. "The list is long...." Schneider's interview with Libby Pharmacist Wendy Dodson on Grace refusing to pay for medication for asbestos victims.

5. American industry has paid out ... March 5, 2003, American Academy of Actuaries testimony before Orrin Hatch's Judiciary Committee on scope of litigation from those harmed by asbestos.

6. In a 1999 case ... June 1999, U.S. Supreme Court, Ortiz v. Fibreboard, "The elephantine mass of asbestos cases ... defies customary judicial administration and calls for national legislation," Justice David H. Souter.

7. In 1977, ... History of actions to push asbestos legislation by former New Jersey representative Millicent Fenwick and former Colorado senator Gary Hart, from Congressional Research Service.

8. The opposition — mostly unions, ... Press releases from Association of American Trial Lawyers on "Asbestos Industry Relief Act."

9. The battle over the proposed ... Schneider's interview with staff on the Senate Commerce Committee and the House Judiciary Committee on issues involving the fairness legislation.

10. On the second day ... Schneider's observations of G. Benefield, L. Skramstad, Alice Priest and R. Sullivan's effort to speak before H. Hyde's committee.

11. The Judiciary Committee ... Congressional Quarterly Report on reaction on the Hill to Post-Intelligencer coverage of Libby and other asbestos efforts.

Chapter 23:

1. In the early 1970s, ... June 9, 1969, "Asbestos Air Pollution in New York City," by Department of Air Resources. A. Holler, commissioner, report on Dr. Irving Selikoff's findings on asbestos fireproofing being sprayed in New York.

2. Among the thousands ... June 20 and November 28, 1969, Grace memos from Tom Egan to R. W. Starrett on Selikoff's warning about spraying fiber containing fireproofing.

3. Other Port Authority papers ... Facts on Selikoff's concern about asbestos fireproofing used in the World Trade Center and other New York buildings came from Selikoff's articles in medical journals, in union newsletters from the period and from Grace documents. April 3, 1969, Grace's monthly report from Jim Cintani to L. P. Hollis discusses the "approximately 100,000 bags" of Monokote that Grace will sell to the World Trade Center; August 6, 1969, Grace memo from Jim Cintani to L. P. Hollis, regarding Grace's fireproofing sales. "We should start supplying the special vermiculite that is going to be used on the spandrel beams and columns on the World Trade Center during August"; November 10, 1970, W.R. Grace & Co. Zonolite invoice 3I-154 for 183 bags of Monokote 3 shipped to the World Trade Center; April 29, 1993, deposition of John Ottinger, a district sales manager for Grace, testifying in the case of the Port Authority of New York and New Jersey v. installers of Grace Monokote in the World Trade Center; November 30, 1995, deposition of Robert Ericson, quality control supervisor for Grace testifying that the Libby mine was the source of the vermiculite used in Grace's New York and New Jersey plants, which produced the Monokote sold to the World Trade Center.

4. The information being shared ... September 13–23, 2001, news releases from EPA's press office on its activity at the World Trade Center, and Administrator Whitman's comments.

5. For his work in Libby, ... Schneider's interviews with Libby team to recreate their reactions to the attacks of September 11 and efforts to rapidly move sophisticated microscopes and qualified lab personnel to New York City to assist in testing the contents of the air and dust and on EPA in New York refusing their offer of help and comments made by Joe Laforara to Peronard.

6. "The agencies ... made it a priority ..." Schneider's interview with Joel Shufro of NYCOSH.

7. A year later, ... Schneider's review of daily government briefings on the WTC cleanup, which stated that "Wall Street must be up and running at all costs." A senior member of EPA administrator Whitman's staff confirmed that the order to not release "any inflammatory or troublesome" statements was made on a repeated basis. E-mail between EPA headquarters and White House office confirm that all statements had to be cleared by a White House representative.

8. The experts Schneider followed ... Schneider's observations of World Trade

Center and lower Manhattan testing and cleanup.

9. "These eminent asbestos researchers ... " Schneider's interview with EPA scientist Cate Jenkins.

10. "It's like all of us ..." Schneider's interview with Steve Swaney, a resident of lower Manhattan whose apartment was covered in dust from the attack.

11. The EPA said ... Schneider's interviews with EPA's New York spokesperson Bonnie Bellows.

12. "They keep calling it ... " Schneider's interview with Dr. Jerrold Abraham, director of Environmental and Occupational Pathology at Upstate Medical University in Syracuse, N.Y.

13. "We didn't see ourselves ..." Transcript of speech given by New York EPA lawyer Walter Mugdan.

14. The USGS scientists, ... September 18, 2001, "Environmental Studies of the World Trade Center area after the September 11, 2001, Attack," USGS, R. Clark, R. Green, G. Swayze, G. Meeker, et al.; Schneider's interviews with C. Weis and USGS scientists in Denver to re-create the flights and testing conducted over Manhattan.

15. On October 16, 2002, ... October 16, 2002. Schneider observed and interviewed the EPA team from New York City finally assigned to clean apartments in Manhattan of asbestos and other dust from the September 11 attack. The group toured Libby and met with P. Peronard and Dr. Brad Black.

16. The leaders of the 19 unions ... September 22, 2003, statement by EPA union leaders.

Chapter 24:

1. "These are the ones that really hurt ..." Schneider reviews G. Benefield's e-mail.

2. At first, Martz was lukewarm ... Schneider's interviews with Montana governor Judy Martz and her staff about her relationship with L. Skramstad; and Schneider's and McCumber's interviews with L. and N. Skramstad and Governor Martz to re-create their first meeting at the governor's office in the statehouse.

3. In December 2001... Transcript of Governor Martz's speech in Libby.

4. Memorial Day 2002... Schneider's observations of and interviews at Libby Memorial Day service 2002.

5. Gayla decided to run ... Schneider's observations of G. Benefield's Senate campaign and election night.

Chapter 25:

1. It looked like the government ... Schneider's numerous interviews, and collection of about 1,800 documents, including "action memos"; e-mail between EPA headquarters and Regions 8 and 10 and various EPA Washington offices; between headquarters and the White House and OMB; and to and from W.R. Grace were the basis of reconstructing the detailed history of the internal and external pressures on EPA to halt the declaration of a public-health emergency and the notification of an estimated 15 million to 35 million home and business owners that they may have asbestos-tainted Zonolite in their attics and walls. These documents were obtained from EPA and the Department of Justice under a Freedom of Information Act request.

2. The Libby team believed ... Schneider's interviews with meeting participants to re-create C. Whitman's reaction to the IG's report and her finding that cleanup in Libby was being stalled by bureaucratic infighting.

3. Before the report ... September 7, 2001, transcript of C. Whitman's speech in Libby.

4. Long threads of e-mail ... Schneider's interviews with A. Whitehouse on the toxicity of tremolite vs. chrysotile based on his study of 800 patients.

5. At Grace's plant ... July 11, 1977, Grace testing results from Weedsport, NY, plant on amount of asbestos released in Zonolite Attic Insulation; April 3, 2002, Grace letter to Whitman insisting that ZAI was safe.

6. In April 1997, ... Report from Canadian Department of National Defense on tremolite released when ZAI was removed from old barracks in Manitoba.

7. The files also contained ... December 20, 2001, "Amphibole Mineral Fibers in Source Material in Residential and Commercial Areas of Libby Pose an Imminent and Substantial Endangerment to Public Health," report by C. Weis, Science Support Coordinator, EPA Region 8.

8. The U.S. Public Health Service ... August 1, 2000, letter from Dr. Hugh Sloan on the dangers of ZAI.

9. No one knows precisely ... Statistics on number and location of Grace plants and customers using Zonolite in U.S. and Canada came from documents collected by EPA and U.S. Department of Justice; June 14, 2000, "Vermiculite Facilities by Region," USEPA/Superfund, including data from USGS.

10. Both OMB and EPA acknowledge ... March 2001, "Safeguards at Risk: John Graham and Corporate America's Back Door to the Bush White House," a 109-page report by Public Citizen, Washington; November and December

2002, Schneider's interviews with John Graham at the White House Office of Management and Budget, and interviews with communications and legal specialists in the department.

11. *William Ruckelshaus says* ... December 2002, Schneider's interviews with William Ruckelshaus, former two-time administrator of EPA.

12. *It was a cold November night* ... Schneider's observations of P. Peronard's last public meeting in Libby.

13. *Three weeks later,* ... Schneider's interviews with participants on refusal to sign the "questionable" action order crafted by EPA headquarters and OMB.

14. *Senator Patty Murray reacted* ... Schneider's interview with Senator Murray and her staffer, Anna Knudson.

15. *In Seattle,* ... Schneider's interviews with K. McDermott on the need for public notification of dangers of ZAI.

16. *"My concern was looking ..."* Schneider's interviews with M. Cohn on the legal battle to get the warning public-health emergency declared.

17. *On May 8, 2003,* ... EPA's announcement on the danger of Zonolite insulation in millions of homes and businesses.

18. *A crisis for asbestos victims* ... Schneider's interviews with G. Benefield, R. Sullivan and P. Murray on Senator Orrin Hatch's new asbestos fairness legislation and on G. Benefield's news conference with Murray.

19. *Then, on June 4,* ... June 4, 2003, testimony from Senator Murray before Senator Hatch's committee; April 21, 2003, "Report of Findings and Recommendations on the Use and Management of Asbestos," Global Environment & Technology Foundation, an EPA-funded report.

20. *The American Thoracic Society* ... Testimony and statements from American Thoracic Society, Drs. M. Harbut and D. Egilman on fairness of proposed medical criteria.

21. *That same week,* ... "Assets Available to Asbestos Victims v. Hatch Bill Payments," July 2003, produced by lawyers opposing the bill.

Chapter 26:

1. *Memorial Day 2003* ... Schneider's interviews with G. Benefield, L. Skramstad and others at the Memorial Day event.

2. *Brad Black says,* ... Schneider's interview with Dr. B. Black on future health needs of people in Libby.

3. *The letter said:* ... August 28, 2003, Health Networks American letter from J. Jay Flynn.

4. The legal skirmishes ... Schneider's interviews with M. Cohn, P. Peronard, K. Land, A. Miller, C. Weis, A. Madigan and members of the Justice Department team to re-create the actions and events of the December 2002 and January 2003 legal battle in federal court in Missoula on the case of U.S. EPA v. W.R. Grace.

5. The big Irishman ... Schneider's interviews of past trial participants to create the description of Judge Molloy.

6. The three days of presentations ... August 26, 2003, final decision in USA v. W.R. Grace & Company and Kootenai Development Corporation, U.S. District Court for the District of Montana, Missoula Division.

7. Les has been married ... Schneider's interviews and observations of L. and N. Skramstad.

8. On a 100-degree day ... July 6, 2003, Schneider's interviews with the Skramstads on their reaction to Sen. Hatch's asbestos legislation.

9. Gayla Benefield looked down ... Schneider's interviews and observations of G. Benefield.

10. By midyear, it became ... EPA memo from Michael Cook to Superfund managers on use of R.J. Lee Group Inc. labs; brief, USA v. W.R. Grace & Company, et al., United States' statement ... to exclude Dr. R.J. Lee's opinion on cleavage fragments, August 2003.

11. Binney & Smith quietly entered ... May and June 2001, Steven F. Schwab, et al., v. Binney & Smith (Crayola), in the Circuit Court of Cook County. Settlement agreement from same court.

Chapter 27:

1. "This is Les, in Montana ..." Schneider's telephone conversation with Les on New Year's Day 2007.

2. In the winter .... Schneider's observations.

3. On the evening of May 10 ... Schneider's interviews with participants.

4. Dressed in denim ... Schneider's observations.

5. David Uhlmann ... Schneider's interviews with team members.

6. When President Bush ... The White House press office.

7. So on Feb. 7, 2005 ... Schneider's observations.

8. According to the Justice Department ... Schneider's interviews, DOJ indictment.

Chapter 28:

1. On Dec. 21, 1995, President Clinton ... DOJ records and Congressional Record.

2. Molloy was called the "greenest judge in the West" ... J. Jensen, Montana

Environmental Information Center.

3. Many in Montana's legal ... Schneider's interviews with Montana lawyers.

4. Mercer and Molloy's long ... Congressional Research Service and *Washington Post.*

5. Before that could happen ... May 17, 2006, Mercer's letter of resignation from DOJ, Tristan Scott, *The Missoulian.*

Chapter 29:

1. Appellate court's definition of asbestos ... "U.S. v. W.R. Grace & Company, opinion," U.S. Court of Appeals for the Ninth Circuit, filed September 20, 2007, http://www.ca9.uscourts.gov/datastore/opinions/2007/09/20/0630472.pdf.

Chapter 30

1. Over the years Whitehouse treated more than 500 patients ... Repeated interviews with Dr. Alan Whitehouse from 1999 to 2015.

2. Their X-rays had dramatically changed ... A.C. Whitehouse, "Asbestos-related pleural disease due to tremolite associated with progressive loss of lung function: Serial observations in 123 miners, family members and residents of Libby, Montana," *American Journal of Industrial Medicine 46* (2004): 219–225.

3. "Whitehouse's numbers were so out of line..." Interviews with Aubrey Miller, 2013.

4. The pair of experienced researchers ... A.C. Whitehouse, C.B. Black, M.S. Heppe, J. Ruckdeschel, S.M. Levin, "Environmental exposure to Libby Asbestos and mesotheliomas," *American Journal of Industrial Medicine 51 (11)* (November 2008): 877-80. doi: 10.1002/ajim.20620.

5. "We examined the deaths of patients at the CARD ..." Schneider interview with Whitehouse, 2015.

6. They found that 2 percent of the workers had documentable asbestos disease ... J.E. Lockey, S.M. Brooks, A.M. Jarabek, P.R. Khoury, R.T. McKay, A. Carson, et al, "Pulmonary changes after exposure to vermiculite contaminated with fibrous tremolite." *The American Review of Respiratory Disease 129 (6)* (1984): 952–8.

7. The results of Lockey's third study on the same Scotts workers ... James E. Lockey, "HRCT/CT and Associated Spirometric Effects of Low Libby Amphibole Asbestos Exposure," *Journal of Occupational and Environmental Medicine (2015): 57 (1).*

8. World Health Organization scientists keep adding to the list of malignancies ... "IARC Monographs on the Evaluation of Carcinogenic Risks to Humans," International Agency for Research on Cancer, last accessed January 11, 2016, http://monographs.iarc.fr/ENG/Monographs/suppl7/Suppl7-20.pdf.

9. *Her interest in studying the people of Libby began soon after ATSDR's ...* Lucy A. Peipins, Michael Lewin, Sharon Campolucci, Jeffrey A. Lybarger, Aubrey Miller, Dan Middleton, Christopher Weis, Michael Spence, Brad Black and Vikas Kapil. "Radiographic abnormalities and exposure to asbestos-contaminated vermiculite in the community of Libby, Montana, USA." *Environmental Health Perspectives,* November 2003, http://www.ncbi.nlm.nih.gov/pmc/articles/PMC1241719/.

10. *The study, published in 2004, ...* Jean C. Pfau, Jami J. Sentissi, Greg Weller, and Elizabeth A. Putnam. "Assessment of Autoimmune Responses Associated with Asbestos Exposure in Libby, Montana, USA."

11. *No significant increase in ANA ...* J.C. Pfau, K. Serve, L. Woods, C.W. Noonan. "Asbestos Exposure and Autoimmune Disease." *Current Topics in Environmental Health and Preventive Medicine:* 2015.

12. *"While physicians and health researchers were investigating an asbestos disease ..."* G. Meeker, A. Bern, I. Brownfield, H. Lowers, S. Sutley, T. Hoefen, et al. "The composition and morphology of amphiboles from the Rainy Creek Complex, near Libby, Montana." Am Mineral (2003) 88:1955–1969.

Chapter 31:

1. *"Pulmonary expert James Lockey ..."* Schneider's interviews and discussions with Dr. James Lockey, 2014 and 2015.

2. *Thousands of Grace invoices ...* Schneider's interviews, EPA testimony, Grace shipping invoices.

3. *It has been about 15 years since the EPA concluded ...* Stephen Nesbitt, assistant EPA inspector general for investigations, in congressional testimony September 25, 2008. http://www2.epa.gov/sites/production/files/2015-07/documents/statement_of_stephen_nesbitt_sep_25_2008.pdf

4. *On June 17, 2009 ...* "EPA Announces Public Health Emergency in Libby," agency news release, http://yosemite.epa.gov/opa/admpress.nsf/d0cf6618525a9e fb85257359003fb69d/0d16234d252c98f9852575d8005e63ac!OpenDocument

5. *As Montana's U.S. Sens. Max Baucus and Jon Tester ...* EPA website, last modified May 22, 2015, https://yosemite.epa.gov/opa/admpress.nsf/d0cf6618525a9efb85 257359003fb69d/0d16234d252c98f9852575d8005e63ac!OpenDocument

6. *Jackson told the seven reporters ...* Speech by EPA administrator Lisa Jackson, announcing assistance for Libby, Montana, June 17, 2009. http://yosemite.epa. gov/opa/admpress.nsf/12a744ff56dbff8585257590004750b6/45259b71259db63 d85257619006ab14e!opendocument

7. *None of the carefully crafted nationwide radio, television ...* Schneider interviews

in 2015 with EPA media office and background discussions with legislative affairs office.

8. But political interference with EPA's efforts to clean up toxic... Schneider interviews in 2014 and 2015 with agency's legislative affairs staff and FEMA personnel.

9. Congressional members from both parties said ... "Justice is distorted and our economy is held back by irresponsible class actions and frivolous asbestos claims. I urge Congress to pass legal reforms this year." George W. Bush in State of the Union address (February 2, 2005), https://www.c-span.org/video/?185324-2/state-union-address.

10. The political component surrounding Libby... Schneider's interviews with Peronard, 2014 and 2015.

11. Many find it absurd and inexplicable that the identical argument made years ago ... A 2015 redacted email between two people in EPA's Office of Enforcement and Compliance Assurance which Schneider was permitted to read.

12. "When it comes to vermiculite, the government ..." Schneider's interviews with Dr. Michael Harbut, 2013-2015.

13. The only government warning for workers in these asbestos ... Patricia Sullivan, "Vermiculite, Respiratory Disease and Asbestos Exposure in Libby, Montana: Update of a Cohort Mortality Study," NIOSH, January 3, 2007. http://www.cdc.gov/niosh/nas/rdrp/Appendices/Chapter3/A3-100s.pdf

14. Almost all the scientists who have studied the effect of Libby asbestos ... Schneider's interviews with Chris Weis and Aubrey Miller, 2014 and 2015.

15. "In order to protect themselves, people must know two things ..." Schneider's interview with Weis, 2011.

Chapter 32:

1. When Miller first got to Libby ... interviews with Schneider, November 1999.

2. "The ability to point to those sickened or killed ..." Interview with Dr. Stephen Levin, spring 2003.

3. Even with his years of experience in documenting the extreme dangers .... Schneider's interview with Dr. James Lockey, 2015.

4. Sometimes knowing the numbers accomplishes nothing ... "Exposure Assessment for Asbestos-Contaminated Vermiculite," prepared for EPA, February 1985. http://nepis.epa.gov/Exe/ZyPDF.cgi/9101LXP5.PDF?Dockey=9101LXP5.PDF

5. It was this group of small-town barristers ... Tristan Scott, "The Firm," Flathead Beacon, April 23, 2014. http://www.flatheadbeacon.com/articles/article/the_firm/38979/

6. *Michelle Boltz is a nurse practitioner who returned home to Libby* ... Schneider's interviews with Boltz, 2013.

7. *"They think they know everything they need to know about it ..."* Schneider's interviews with Lockey, 2014-2015.

8. *There is nothing easy about accurately evaluating a chest film or scan* ... Tom Kimpe, Tom Tuytschaever, "Increasing the Number of Gray Shades in Medical Display Systems – How Much Is Enough?" Journal of Digital Imaging, December 2007. http://www.ncbi.nlm.nih.gov/pmc/articles/PMC3043920/

9. *"There just aren't enough doctors who know what they're doing ..."* Schneider's interviews with Dr. Michael Harbut, 2015.

Chapter 33:

1. *About a third of the 26 attending* ... Executive summary of Human Health Risk Assessment for Libby, December 2014. http://www.epa.gov/sites/production/files/2014-12/documents/libby-asbestos-draft-site-wide-hhra-exec-summ-12-8-2014.pdf

2. *The exposure calculations* ... IRIS toxicological review report of Libby asbestos, December 2014. http://cfpub.epa.gov/ncea/iris/iris_documents/documents/toxreviews/1026tr.pdf

3. *The evaluation documented the relationship...*EPA, last updated December 2015. http://www.epa.gov/iris/basic-information-about-integrated-risk-information-system

4. *The townsfolk "were tired of listening to anything..."* Schneider interview with Gayla Benefield, December 2015.

5. *The industry angst was spawned* ... Statement of Gregory P. Meeker, geologist, February 28, 2008, given before the U.S. House Committee on Energy and Commerce, Subcommittee on Environment and Hazardous Materials.

6. *By the beginning of 2016, EPA reported* ... From material supplied by Jennifer Lane, EPA's community affairs specialist for Libby.

7. *Often, the gatekeepers for detecting abnormalities in the lungs* ... Discussion with NIOSH, 2015. http://www.cdc.gov/niosh/topics/chestradiography/breader.html

8. *When asked after all these years* ... EPA, "Protect your family from asbestos-contaminated vermiculite insulation." http://www.epa.gov/asbestos/protect-your-family-asbestos-contaminated-vermiculite-insulation

9. *The trust was spawned in 2004...*Becky Kramer, "Zonolite deal would offer cash for repairs," The Spokesman-Review, November 26, 2008. http://www.spokesman.

com/stories/2008/nov/26/zonolite-deal-would-offer-cash-for-repairs/

10. It took ten years for Grace's complex, multi-faceted bankruptcy ... Zonolite Attic Insulation Trust notice, 2014. http://static1.squarespace. com/static/538f5fefe4b00b109f128b2d/t/5395e297e4b0d7fc447133cd/ 1402331799624/ImportantNotice.pdf

11. By the end of its 20-year life span ... Zonolite Attic Insulation Trust, last updated January 7, 2016. http://www.zonoliteatticinsulation.com/faqs/

12. The other trust that came from the settlement ... WRG Asbestos PI Trust, last updated January 22, 2016. www.wrgraceasbestostrust.com

13. And even the properly done inspections ... Government Accountability Office report, March 10, 2009. http://www.gao.gov/assets/100/96069.pdf

Acknowledgments

There are scores of people who deserve our deepest thanks for their help in exposing the truth about Libby and the spread of poisonous asbestos throughout the country.

This book would not have been possible without Gayla and David Benefield, Les and Norita Skramstad, Paul Peronard, Chris Weis, Aubrey Miller, Keven McDermott, Matt Cohn, Celeste Monforton, Jim Christiansen, Wendy Thomi and their families. All graciously shared their frustrations, pain, emotions and knowledge while allowing us to disrupt their sleep, their meetings, their dinners and family gatherings, their vacations, their childbirths and the other private moments they squeezed into the few hours when they weren't working.

We are also deeply thankful:

To Joann Byrd for her continued insistence that the revised edition be completed and for the gift of her careful editing to ensure that the complex scientific and medical issues were presented in the most understandable manner. To Kris Higginson, for her great patience and gifted copy-editing, and to Denise Clifton for her great cover and imaginative interactive book design (which you can find in the "Enhanced Edition" of this book designed for Mac and iPad and available on Apple's iBooks Store) and for sticking with the project as Schneider's four-month plan expanded into a four-year ordeal. To Kathleen Best, Schneider's live-in editor, best friend and wife, who wasn't shy about demanding rewrites and pushed hard for the new horrors spawned from Libby to be fully reported. And to Sarah Greene, Dylan and Katy, for putting up with McCumber's long hours and for the joy they bring him.

To Drs. Alan Whitehouse, James Lockey, Brad Black, Michael Harbut, David Egilman, Jerrold Abraham and others like Linda Reinstein who helped us understand the medical plight of those suffering from asbestos-related diseases, and to scientists such as Greg Meeker, Mike Cook, Mike Beard, Barry Castleman, the team at USGS and others who patiently and repeatedly walked us through the maze of asbestos analysis. To lawyers Allan McGarvey, Roger Sullivan and Jon Heberling.

To the staff members of the U.S. House and Senate; the researchers and archivists at the Library of Congress, the Congressional Research Service and eight other government agencies; Sammy Pearson at the Lincoln County Historical Society Heritage Museum; the late Roger Morris, former editor of *The Western News,* and to Kathy Skipper, who persuaded skilled but publicity-shy colleagues at ATSDR to share their stories.

To Carol Smith, my valued reporting colleague on many of the asbestos stories, for her compassion, talent and humor. To J.D. Alexander, former editor and publisher of the defunct *Seattle Post-Intelligencer,* for his enthusiasm for the story, and for giving us the time, resources and encouragement to bring it in. To *St. Louis Post-Dispatch* editor Ellen Soeteber for encouraging Schneider to continue watching what the government was doing with asbestos, particularly after September 11, 2001.

To the unsung heroes at both newspapers – the copy, photo and line editors, page designers, artists, photographers and researchers – whose talent and dedication presented the stories in a way most meaningful to the readers. Thanks to all of our colleagues at the *Post-Intelligencer,* who put out a great newspaper in the face of unbelievable stresses and challenges. To photographers Paul Kitagaki Jr., Renee Byer, Gilbert Arias, and Kevin Manning and their photo editors. Our thanks for their talent as visual journalists.

At International Creative Management, to Robert Lazar, for getting this started and acting as cheerleader along the lengthy path, and to Richard Abate, for selling it; and at Putnam, to then-senior editor David Highfill, for his commitment to the original book and for all he did to make it better.

Lazar is now at The Shuman Company, Abate is literary manager with 3 Arts Entertainment, and Highfill is vice president and executive editor at William Morrow.

And finally, to those we still cannot name at EPA, the Justice and Labor departments, the White House, HHS, other government agencies and at W.R. Grace, who supplied us with insight and documents that helped us report the truth; and to all who "pray for the dead and fight like hell for the living."

About the Authors

ANDREW SCHNEIDER lives in Seattle and continues to do in-depth investigative reporting, mostly on topics of national and international public health. He has worked for a variety of news organizations, including The Associated Press, Scripps Howard News Service, *The Pittsburgh Press, St. Louis Post-Dispatch* and the *Seattle Post-Intelligencer.* He is the winner of numerous prizes, including two Pulitzers, a Society of Professional Journalists public service award, the George Polk Award and the National Headliner Award.

DAVID MCCUMBER is editor of the *Montana Standard* in Butte, Montana. Formerly managing editor of the *Seattle Post-Intelligencer* and Washington bureau chief for Hearst Newspapers, he has worked for several other newspapers, including the San Francisco *Examiner* and the Santa Barbara *News-Press.* A 1984 Pulitzer finalist for special local reporting at the *Arizona Daily Star*, he edited a Pulitzer-winning project there; he is a past winner of the Don Bolles Award for investigative journalism. McCumber's books include *The Cowboy Way: Seasons of a Montana Ranch, Playing off the Rail,* and *X-Rated: The Mitchell Brothers.*

CPSIA information can be obtained
at www.ICGtesting.com
Printed in the USA
BVOW08s2340290117

474740BV00027B/151/P

9 780985 185121